VENTURE CAPITAL AND PRIVATE EQUITY
A Casebook

Volume II

Josh Lerner

Harvard Business School
and
National Bureau of Economic Research

Felda Hardymon

Harvard Business School

John Wiley & Sons, Inc.

Acquisitions Editor	Leslie Kraham
Marketing Manager	Charity Robey
Senior Production Editor	Kelly Tavares
Senior Designer	Kevin Murphy

Cover photo by Romilly Lockyer/The Image Bank.

This book was set in 10/12 New Caledonia by Matrix Publishing, and printed and bound by Hamilton Printing. The cover was printed by Lehigh Press.

This book is printed on acid-free paper. ∞

Library of Congress Cataloging in Publication Data:

Lerner, Joshua.
    Venture capital and private equity : a casebook / Josh Lerner.
       p. cm.
    Includes index.
    ISBN 0-471-07982-0
    1. Venture capital—United States—Case studies.   2. Capital
investments—United States—Case studies.   I. Title.
HG4963.L47   1999
332'.0415'0973—dc21   99-33115
                                   CIP

Printed in the United States of America

10 9 8 7 6 5 4 3 2 1

Acknowledgments

The writing of a case study is an activity that involves many people. From its initial conception to its publication and revision, a case involves practitioners, students, and colleagues at one's own and other schools. Thus, the problem with the acknowledgments section of a casebook is not deciding which individuals to include, but rather worrying about those one has left out!

First it is important to note that a number of case studies in this volume were written jointly with colleagues, students, and practitioners. Beyond these co-authors, many others provided assistance. The partners and managers of the many private equity groups, institutional investors, and companies featured in these cases not only agreed to be the subject of the analyses, but generously set aside time to answer many questions, review drafts, and make numerous helpful suggestions. Ann Leamon provided expert editorial and research support. Chris Allen responded to frequent requests for data, often under severe time constraints. Colleagues at Harvard Business School and many other business schools offered numerous suggestions after reading or teaching these cases. We also thank the many reviewers for their constructive comments and suggestions, which helped us raise the quality of our book: Sharon Brown-Hruska, School of Management, George Mason University; Douglas Cumming, University of Alberta School of Business; Andrew Metrick, University of Pennsylvania, The Wharton School. Marianne D'Amico and Suzanne Plummer managed the many logistical details regarding the casewriting process and provided unflagging administrative support. The Harvard Business School's Division of Research generously funded the considerable cost of developing these case studies. Kelly Tavares provided key assistance on the production of the volume. Finally, the encouragement and assistance of Leslie Kraham at John Wiley & Sons was critical in developing this volume.

Finally, Josh thanks Wendy for putting up with his travels on casewriting trips, and Felda thanks Dena for her unstinting help and long suffering support in managing two careers.

About the Authors

Josh Lerner is a Professor of Business Administration at Harvard Business School, with a joint appointment in the Finance and Entrepreneurial Management Units. He graduated from Yale College with a Special Divisional Major that combined physics with the history of technology, and worked for several years on issues concerning technological innovation and public policy, at the Brookings Institution, for a public-private task force in Chicago, and on Capitol Hill. He then earned a Ph.D. in Harvard's Economics Department. Much of his research, which is collected in *The Venture Capital Cycle* (1999) and *The Money of Invention* (2001), focuses on the structure and role of venture capital organizations. He is a Research Associate in the National Bureau of Economic Research's Corporate Finance and Productivity Programs. In addition, he is an organizer of the Innovation Policy and the Economy Group at the NBER, and serves as co-editor of their publication, *Innovation Policy and the Economy*. In the 1993–94 academic year, he introduced an elective course for second-year MBAs on private equity finance, today one of the five largest elective courses at Harvard Business School. In addition, he chairs and teaches an annual private equity executive education course, teaches several doctoral classes, and performs a variety of administrative roles at the School.

Felda Hardymon is a Senior Lecturer at the Harvard Business School and a career venture capitalist. He joined Bessemer Venture Partners (BVP) in 1981 where he continues as a general partner. BVP is among the oldest venture firms (1911) and is a long-standing specialist in early stage investing. He has led BVP's investments in over 60 companies in the software, communications and retail sectors, including Cascade Communications, Parametric Technology, Staples, and MSI. Previously he was a vice president of BDSI, the original venture subsidiary of General Electric Company, where he led investments in Ungermann-Bass, Stratus Computer, and Western Digital. He has served on the board of the National Venture Capital Association where he was Chairman of the Tax Committee. He received a B.S. from Rose Polytechnic Institute, a Ph.D. (mathematics) from Duke University, and an MBA (Baker Scholar) from Harvard Business School.

Dedication

To Mugsy and Boxy

To Bluesy, ETFF, and Wacker

Table of Contents

1

Private Equity Today and Tomorrow

Over the past two decades, there has been a tremendous boom in the private equity industry. The pool of U.S. private equity funds—partnerships specializing in venture capital, leveraged buyouts, mezzanine investments, build-ups, distressed debt, and related investments—has grown from $5 billion in 1980 to just under $300 billion at the beginning of 2001. Private equity's recent growth has outstripped that of almost every class of financial product.

Despite this growth, many questions about private equity remain unanswered, and many of its features continue to be mysterious. How do venture capital and buyout funds create value? What explains the tremendous growth in these funds? Has the level of fundraising "overshot" the target, and will it decline rapidly in the years to come? To what extent is the model developed and refined over the past several decades likely to be translated into other countries and types of investments? This volume explores these exciting and important questions.

WHAT IS PRIVATE EQUITY?

A natural first question is, what constitutes a private equity fund? Many start-up firms require substantial capital. A firm's founder may not have sufficient funds to finance these projects alone and therefore must seek outside financing. Entrepreneurial firms that are characterized by significant intangible assets, expect years of negative earnings, and have uncertain prospects are unlikely to receive bank loans or other debt financing. Similarly, troubled firms that need to undergo restructurings may find external financing difficult to raise. Private equity organizations finance these high-risk, potentially high-reward projects. They protect the value of their equity stakes by undertaking careful due diligence before making the investments and retaining powerful oversight rights afterward.

Typically, these investors do not primarily invest their own capital but rather raise the bulk of their funds from institutions and individuals. Large institutional investors, such as pension funds and university endowments, are likely to want illiquid long-run investments such as private equity in their portfolio. Often, these groups have neither the staff nor the expertise to make such investments themselves.

In its initial decades, the private equity industry was a predominantly American phenomenon. It had its origins in the family offices that managed the wealth of high net worth individuals in the last decades of the nineteenth century and the first decades

1

of this century. Wealthy families such as the Phippes, Rockefellers, Vanderbilts, and Whitneys invested in and advised a variety of business enterprises, including the predecessor entities to AT&T, Eastern Airlines, and McDonald-Douglas. Gradually, these families began involving outsiders to select and oversee these investments.

The first formal private equity firm, however, was not established until after World War II. American Research and Development (ARD) was formed in 1946 by MIT president Karl Compton, Harvard Business School professor Georges F. Doriot, and local business leaders. A small group of venture capitalists made high-risk investments into emerging companies that were based on technology developed for World War II. The success of the investments ranged widely: almost half of ARD's profits during its 26-year existence as an independent entity came from its $70,000 investment in Digital Equipment Company in 1957, which grew in value to $355 million. Because institutional investors were reluctant to invest, ARD was structured as a publicly traded closed-end fund and marketed mostly to individuals. The few other venture organizations begun in the decade after ARD's formation were also structured as closed-end funds.

The first venture capital limited partnership, Draper, Gaither, and Anderson, was formed in 1958. Imitators soon followed, but limited partnerships accounted for a minority of the venture pool during the 1960s and 1970s. Most venture organizations raised money either through closed-end funds or Small Business Investment Companies (SBICs), federally guaranteed risk-capital pools that proliferated during the 1960s. Although the market for SBICs in the late 1960s and early 1970s was strong, incentive problems ultimately led to the collapse of the sector. The annual flow of money into private equity during its first three decades never exceeded a few hundred million dollars and usually was substantially less. During these years, while a few funds made a considerable number of investments in buyouts and other transactions involving mature firms, private equity organizations were universally referred to as venture capital funds.

The activity in the private equity industry increased dramatically in the late 1970s and early 1980s. Industry observers attributed much of the shift to the U.S. Department of Labor's clarification of the Employee Retirement Income Security Act's "prudent man" rule in 1979. Prior to this year, the legislation limited pension funds from investing substantial amounts of money into venture capital or other high-risk asset classes. The Department of Labor's clarification of the rule explicitly allowed pension managers to invest in high-risk assets, including private equity. Numerous specialized funds—concentrating in areas such as leveraged buyouts, mezzanine transactions, and such hybrids as venture leasing—sprang up during these years. Another important change in the private equity industry during this period was the rise of the limited partnership as the dominant organizational form.

The subsequent years saw both very good and trying times for private equity investors. On the one hand, during the 1980s venture capitalists backed many of the most successful high-technology companies, including Cisco Systems, Genentech, Microsoft, and Sun Microsystems. Numerous successful buyouts—such as Avis, Beatrice, Dr. Pepper, Gibson Greetings, and McCall Pattern—garnered considerable public attention in the 1980s. At the same time, commitments to the private equity industry during this decade were very uneven. The annual flow of money into venture capital funds increased by a factor of ten during the first half of the 1980s but steadily declined from 1987 through 1991. Buyouts underwent an even more dramatic rise through the 1980s, followed by a precipitous fall at the end of the decade.

Much of this pattern was driven by the changing fortunes of private equity investments. Returns on venture capital funds had declined sharply in the mid-1980s after being exceedingly attractive in the 1970s. This fall was apparently triggered by overinvestment in a few industries, such as computer hardware, and the entry of many inexperienced venture capitalists. Buyout returns underwent a similar decline in the late 1980s, due in large part to the increased competition between groups for transactions. As investors became disappointed with returns, they committed less capital to the industry.

By way of contrast, the 1990s have seen dramatic growth and excellent returns in almost every part of the private equity industry. This recovery was triggered by several factors. The exit of many inexperienced investors at the beginning of the decade insured that the remaining groups faced less competition for transactions. The healthy market for the initial public offerings during much of the decade meant that it was easier for all investors to exit private equity transactions. Meanwhile, the extent of technological innovation—particularly in information technology-related industries—created extraordinary opportunities for venture capitalists. New capital commitments to both venture and buyout funds rose in response to these changing circumstances, increasing to record levels by the late 1990s and 2000.

As is often the case, however, the growth of private equity increased at a pace that was too great to be sustainable. Institutional and individual investors—attracted especially by the tremendously high returns being enjoyed by venture funds—flooded money into the industry at unprecedented rates. In many cases, groups staggered under the weight of capital. Too rapid growth led to overstretched partners, inadequate due diligence, and, in many cases, poor investment decisions. The industry will need to address the legacy of this growth in the first years of the twenty-first century.

But the most revolutionary changes in private equity in recent years have not been in the patterns of investment, but rather in the structure of the private equity groups themselves. Private equity organizations, though in the business of funding innovation, had been remarkably steadfast in retaining the limited partnership structure since the mid-1960s. In recent years, however, a flurry of experimentation has taken hold in the industry. Among the changes seen are partnerships between venture capital and buyout organizations, the establishment of affiliate funds in different regions and nations, the launching of physical and "virtual" incubators by venture groups, and the expansion of the funds offered by buyout funds to include real estate, mezzanine, and bond funds.

What explains these sudden changes among the major private equity groups in recent years? We believe that these changes reflect a more fundamental shift in the industry, as private equity groups struggle to address the increasing efficiency of venture investing. Facing increased competition, they are seeking to find new ways to differentiate themselves.

Evidence of the increased efficiency of the venture industry can be seen in many places. Although venture capital for much of its first decades had the flavor of a cottage industry, with a considerable number of relatively small venture groups working alongside one another, today it is much more competitive. The increase in fund size and the decrease in syndication have greatly enhanced the competitive pressures between venture groups.

Given this changed competitive environment, the leading groups are increasingly seeking to differentiate themselves from the mass of other investors. They are employing a variety of tools to build up and distinguish their "brands," which will help distinguish themselves from other investors. These steps include the strategic partnerships, provision of additional services, and aggressive fundraising described earlier, as well as many other initiatives to extend their visibility in the United States and abroad.

To be sure, private equity is not unique in this transformation. For instance, the investment banking industry underwent a similar transformation in the 1950s and 1960s, as the leading "bulge bracket" firms solidified their leadership positions. The gap between the leading banks and the following ones greatly increased during these years, as the leading groups greatly expanded their range of activities and boosted their hiring of personnel. Similarly, the management of the major banks was transformed during these years, as procedures were systematized and management structures formalized.

WHY IS PRIVATE EQUITY NEEDED?

Private equity plays a critical role in the American economy and, increasingly, elsewhere around the globe as well. The types of firms that private equity organizations finance—whether young start-ups hungry for capital or ailing giants that need to restructure—present numerous risks and uncertainties that discourage other investors.

In this section, we will first review the risks that these firms pose. We will then consider briefly how private equity organizations address these problems. Finally, we will discuss why other financiers, such as banks, often cannot address these problems as effectively as private equity groups.

The financing of young and restructuring firms is a risky business. Uncertainty and informational gaps often characterize these firms, particularly in high-technology industries. These information problems make it difficult to assess these firms and permit opportunistic behavior by entrepreneurs after the financing is received.

To briefly review the types of conflicts that can emerge in these settings, conflicts between managers and investors ("agency problems") can affect the willingness of both debt and equity holders to provide capital. If the firm raises equity from outside investors, the manager has an incentive to engage in wasteful expenditures (e.g., lavish offices) because he or she may benefit disproportionately from these expenditures but does not bear their entire cost. Similarly, if the firm raises debt, the manager may increase risk to undesirable levels. Because providers of capital recognize these problems, outside investors demand a higher rate of return than would be the case if the funds were internally generated.[1]

Additional agency problems may appear in the types of entrepreneurial firms in which private equity groups invest. For instance, entrepreneurs might invest in strategies, research, or projects that have high personal returns but low expected monetary payoffs to shareholders. Consider the founder of a biotechnology company who chooses to invest in a type of research that brings him great recognition in the scientific community but provides little return for the venture capitalist. Similarly, entrepreneurs may receive initial results from market trials indicating little demand for a new product but may want to keep the company going because they receive significant private benefits from managing their own firm.

Even if the manager is motivated to maximize shareholder value, information gaps may make raising external capital more expensive or even preclude it entirely. Equity offerings of firms may be associated with a "lemons" problem: if the manager is better informed about the firm's investment opportunities and acts in the interest of current shareholders, then he or she will issue new shares only when the company's stock is overvalued. Indeed, numerous studies have documented that stock prices decline upon the announcement of equity issues, largely because of the negative signal sent to the

---

[1] The classic treatment of these problems is in Michael C. Jensen and William H. Meckling, "Theory of the Firm: Managerial Behavior, Agency Costs, and Ownership Structure," *Journal of Financial Economics* 3 (1976): 305–360.

market. This "lemons" problem leads investors to be less willing to invest in young or restructuring firms or to be unwilling to invest at all. Similar information problems have been shown to exist in debt markets.[2]

More generally, the inability to verify outcomes makes it difficult to write contracts that are contingent upon particular events. This inability makes external financing costly. Many economic models[3] argue that when investors find it difficult to verify that certain actions have been taken or certain outcomes have occurred—even if they strongly suspect the entrepreneur has followed an action that was counter to their original agreement, they cannot prove it in a court of law—external financing may become costly or difficult to obtain.

If the information problems could be eliminated, these barriers to financing would disappear. Financial economists argue that specialized intermediaries, such as private equity organizations, can address these problems. By intensively scrutinizing firms before providing capital and then monitoring them afterward, they can alleviate some of the information gaps and reduce capital constraints. Thus, it is important to understand the tools employed by private equity investors as responses to this difficult environment, which enable firms to ultimately receive the financing that they cannot raise from other sources. It is the nonmonetary aspects of private equity that are critical to its success. It is these tools—the screening of investments, the use of convertible securities, the syndication and staging of investments, and the provision of oversight and informal coaching—that we shall highlight in the second module of the course.

Why cannot other financial intermediaries (e.g., banks) undertake the same sort of monitoring? Although it is easy to see why individual investors may not have the expertise to address these types of agency problems, it might be thought that bank credit officers could undertake this type of oversight. Yet even in countries with exceedingly well-developed banking systems, such as Germany and Japan, policymakers today are seeking to encourage the development of a private equity industry to ensure more adequate financing for risky entrepreneurial firms.

The limitations of banks stem from several of their key institutional features. First, because regulations in the United States limit banks' ability to hold shares, they cannot freely use equity to fund projects. Taking an equity position in the firm allows the private equity group to proportionately share in the upside, guaranteeing that the investor benefits if the firm does well. Second, banks may not have the necessary skills to evaluate projects with few tangible assets and significant uncertainty. In addition, banks in competitive markets may not be able to finance high-risk projects because they are unable to charge borrowers rates that are high enough to compensate for the firm's riskiness. Finally, private equity funds' high-powered compensation schemes give these investors incentives to monitor firms more closely because their individual compensation

---

[2] The "lemons" problem was introduced in George A. Akerlof, "The Market for 'Lemons': Qualitative Uncertainty and the Market Mechanism," *Quarterly Journal of Economics* 84 (1970): 488–500. Discussions of the implications of this problem for financing decisions are in Bruce C. Greenwald, Joseph E. Stiglitz, and Andrew Weiss, "Information Imperfections in the Capital Market and Macroeconomic Fluctuations," *American Economic Review Papers and Proceedings* 74 (1984): 194–199 and in Stewart C. Myers and Nicholas S. Majluf, "Corporate Financing and Investment Decisions When Firms Have Information That Investors Do Not Have," *Journal of Financial Economics* 13 (1984): 187–221.

[3] Important examples include Sanford Grossman and Oliver D. Hart, "The Costs and Benefits of Ownership: A Theory of Vertical and Lateral Integration," *Journal of Political Economy* 94 (1986): 691–719 and Oliver D. Hart and John Moore, "Property Rights and the Nature of the Firm," *Journal of Political Economy* 98 (1990): 1119–1158.

is closely linked to the funds' returns. Banks, corporations, and other institutions that have sponsored venture funds without such high-powered incentives have found it difficult to retain personnel, once the investors have developed a performance record that enables them to raise a fund of their own.[4]

ABOUT THIS VOLUME

This volume is based on a course introduced at Harvard Business School in the 1993–1994 academic year. "Venture Capital and Private Equity" has attracted students interested in careers as private equity investors, as managers of entrepreneurial firms, or as investment bankers or other intermediaries who work with private equity groups and the companies that they fund. These cases have also been used in a variety of other settings, such as executive education courses at Harvard and graduate and undergraduate entrepreneurship courses at many other business schools. This second edition has been extensively revised to reflect the many changes in the industry in recent years.

A natural question for a reader to ask is what he or she will learn from this volume. This casebook has three goals:

- First, the private equity industry is complex. Participants in the private equity industry make it even more complicated by using a highly specialized terminology. These factors lead to the world of venture capital and buyout investing often appearing impenetrable to the uninitiated. Understanding the ways in which private equity groups work—as well as the key distinctions between these organizations—is an important goal.

- Second, private equity investors face the same problems that other financial investors do, but in extreme form. An understanding of the problems faced in private equity—and the ways that these investors solve them—should provide more general insights into the financing process. Thus, a second goal is to review and apply the key ideas of corporate finance in this exciting setting.

- Finally, the process of valuation is critical in private equity. Disputes over valuation—whether between an entrepreneur and a venture capitalist or between a private equity group raising a new fund and a potential investor—are commonplace in this industry. These disputes stem from the fact that valuing early-stage and restructuring firms can be very challenging and highly subjective. This casebook explores a wide variety of valuation approaches, from techniques widely used in practice to methods less frequently seen in practice today but likely to be increasingly important in the future years.

The volume is divided into four modules. Its organization mirrors that of the private equity process, which can be viewed as a cycle. The cycle starts with the raising of a private equity fund; proceeds through the investment in, monitoring of, and adding value to firms; continues as the private equity group exits successful deals and returns capital to their investors; and renews itself with the seeking of additional funds. Each module will begin with an overview that depicts the themes and approaches of the sec-

---

[4] The limitations of bank financing are explored in such theoretical and empirical academic studies as Joseph E. Stiglitz and Andrew Weiss, "Credit Rationing in Markets with Incomplete Information," *American Economic Review* 71 (1981): 393–409 and Mitchell A. Petersen and Raghuram G. Rajan, "The Effect of Credit Market Competition on Lending Relationships," *Quarterly Journal of Economics* 110 (1995): 407–444.

tion. Different classes, however, may choose to use this volume in different ways.[5] Thus, it may be helpful to briefly summarize the organization of the volume at the outset.

The first module of *Venture Capital and Private Equity* examines how private equity funds are raised and structured. These funds often have complex features, and the legal issues involved are frequently arcane. But the structure of private equity funds has a profound effect on the behavior of venture and buyout investors. Consequently, it is as important for an entrepreneur raising private equity to understand these issues as it is for a partner in a fund. The module will seek not only to understand the features of private equity funds and the actors in the fundraising process, but also to analyze them. We will map out which institutions serve to increase the profits from private equity investments as a whole and which seem designed mostly to shift profits *between* the parties.

The second module of the course considers the interactions between private equity investors and the entrepreneurs that they finance. These interactions are at the core of what private equity investors do. We will seek to understand these interactions through two perspectives.

We first consider how the activities undertaken by private equity organizations are a response to the challenges posed by the firms in their portfolio. We highlight how firms in a private equity portfolio typically present three critical problems, which make it difficult for them to meet their financing needs through traditional mechanisms, such as bank loans. This module will illustrate these approaches with examples from a wide variety of industries and private equity transactions.

The second approach emphasizes the influence of the circumstances of the private equity organization itself. There is typically no one "right" investment decision. Rather, the proper response to any given situation will reflect the circumstances of the private equity organization, such as the extent to which successful fundraising in the future can be assured and the experience of the individual investment professionals.

The third module of *Venture Capital and Private Equity* examines the process through which private equity investors exit their investments. Successful exits are critical to ensuring attractive returns for investors and, in turn, to raising additional capital. But private equity investors' concerns about exiting investments—and their behavior during the exiting process itself—can sometimes lead to severe problems for entrepreneurs. We will employ an analytic framework very similar to that used in the first module of the course. We will seek to understand which institutional features associated with exiting private equity investments increase the overall amount of profits from private equity investments and which actions seem to be intended to shift more of the profits to particular parties.

The final module reviews many of the key ideas developed in the volume. Rather than considering traditional private equity organizations, however, the two cases examine organizations with very different goals. Large corporations, government agencies, and nonprofit organizations are increasingly emulating private equity funds. Their goals, however, are quite different: for example, to more effectively commercialize internal research projects or to revitalize distressed areas. Corporate venture funds are also interesting because they represent an alternative way to break into the competitive private equity industry. These cases will allow us not only to understand these exciting and

---

[5] Although some courses may follow closely the order of cases in the volume, others may deviate substantially. For instance, a course concentrating on entrepreneurial finance may focus on cases in the second and third modules in the volume.

challenging initiatives, but also to review the elements that are crucial to the success of traditional venture organizations.

Three cases running through this volume emphasize one more theme: the challenge of managing a career in private equity. We consider the implications of a choice between different private equity organizations and investment opportunities from the perspective of a recent MBA graduate. The final case considers the choices and challenges faced by a venture capitalist almost a decade after graduation, who has had a career that has included corporate development, operating roles in a large corporation, and private equity.

At the same time, it is important to emphasize that there are many opportunities for learning about venture capital and private equity outside of this volume. The four module notes—and many of the topical notes interspersed in the body of the text—suggest further readings. These range from trade journals such as the *Private Equity Analyst* and the *Venture Capital Journal* to handbooks on the legal nuances of the private equity process to academic studies. In addition, a note at the end of this volume provides a systematic overview of many information sources for readers who wish to explore a particular aspect of the private equity industry in more detail.

THE FUTURE OF PRIVATE EQUITY

The cases and notes in this volume are designed to provide an understanding of the history of the private equity industry's development, and the workings of the industry today. Because the case studies must of necessity look at events in the past, they may provide less guidance about the future of the private equity industry. The question of how the venture and buyout industries will evolve over the next decade is a particularly critical one because the recent growth has been so spectacular. It is natural to ask whether the growth of private equity can be sustained. Has too much capital been raised? Is the industry destined to experience disappointing returns and shrink dramatically?

These are fair questions. As will be highlighted throughout this volume, short-run shifts in the supply of or demand for private equity investments can have dramatic effects. For instance, periods with a rapid increase in capital commitments have historically led to fewer restrictions on private equity investors, larger investments in portfolio firms, higher valuations for those investments, and lower returns for investors.

These patterns have led many practitioners to conclude that the industry is inherently cyclical. In short, this view implies that periods of rapid growth generate sufficient problems that periods of retrenchment are sure to follow. These cycles may lead us to be pessimistic about the industry's prospects in the years to come.

It is important, however, to also consider the *long-run* determinants of the level of private equity, not just the short-run effects. In the short run, intense competition between private equity groups may lead to a willingness to pay a premium for certain types of firms (e.g., firms specializing in tools and content for the Internet). This is unlikely to be a sustainable strategy in the long run: firms that persist in such a strategy will earn low returns and eventually be unable to raise follow-on funds.

The types of factors that determine the long-run steady-state supply of private equity in the economy are more fundamental. These are likely to include the pace of technological innovation in the economy, the degree of dynamism in the economy, the presence of liquid and competitive markets for investors to sell their investments (whether markets for stock offerings or acquisitions), and the willingness of highly skilled managers and engineers to work in entrepreneurial environments. However painful the short-run adjustments, these more fundamental factors are likely to be critical in establishing the long-run level.

When one examines these more fundamental factors, there appears to have been quite substantial changes for the better over the past several decades.[6] We will highlight two of the determinants of the long-run supply of private equity in the United States, where these changes have been particularly dramatic: the acceleration of the rate of technological innovation and the decreasing "transaction costs" associated with private equity investments.

Although the increase in innovation can be seen though several measures, probably the clearest indication is in the extent of patenting. Patent applications by U.S. inventors, after hovering between 40,000 and 80,000 annually over the first 85 years of the twentieth century, surged during the 1990s to over 120,000 per year. This does not appear to reflect the impact of changes in domestic patent policy, shifts in the success rate of applications, or a variety of alternative explanations. Rather, it appears to reflect a fundamental shift in the rate of innovation.[7] The breadth of technology appears wider today than it has ever been before. The greater rate of intellectual innovation provides fertile ground for future investments, especially by venture capitalists.

A second change has been the decreasing cost of making new private equity investments. The efficiency of the private equity process has been greatly augmented by the emergence of other intermediaries familiar with its workings. The presence of such expertise among lawyers, accountants, managers, and others—even real estate brokers—has substantially lowered the transaction costs associated with forming and financing new firms or restructuring existing ones. The increasing number of professionals and managers familiar with and accustomed to the employment arrangements offered by private equity-backed firms (such as heavy reliance on stock options) has also been a major shift. In short, the increasing familiarity with the private equity process has made the long-term prospects for such investments more attractive than they have ever been before.

Many of these changes appear to have actually been driven by the activities of private equity-backed firms: for instance, venture capitalists have funded many innovative firms, which have, in turn, created opportunities for new venture investments. It appears that somewhat of a "virtuous circle" is at work. The growth in the activity of pri-

---

[6] It is also worth emphasizing that despite its growth, the private equity pool today remains relatively small. For every one dollar of private equity in the portfolio of U.S. institutional investors, there are about $30 of publicly traded equities. The ratios are even more uneven for overseas institutions. At the same time, the size of the foreign private equity pool remains far below that of the United States. This suggests considerable possibilities for future growth. The disparity can be illustrated by comparing the ratio of the private equity investment to the size of the economy (gross domestic product). In 1998, this ratio was about 17 times higher in the United States than in East and South Asia, and almost three-and-a-half times higher in the United States than in Western Europe. (These statistics are taken from the European Venture Capital Association, *EVCA Yearbook*, Zaventum, Belgium, European Venture Capital Association, 2000; Asian Venture Capital Journal, *Venture Capital in Asia: 2000 Edition*, Hong Kong, Asian Venture Capital Journal, 2000; and World Bank, *World Development Indicators*, Washington, DC, World Bank, 2000.) At least to the casual observer, these ratios seem modest when compared to the economic role of new firms, products, and processes in the developed economies.

[7] These changes are discussed in Samuel Kortum and Josh Lerner, "Stronger Protection or Technological Revolution: What Is Behind the Recent Surge in Patenting?," *Carnegie-Rochester Conference Series on Public Policy* 48 (1998): 247–304.

vate equity industry has enhanced the conditions for new investments, which has in turn led to more capital formation.

As the various cases in this volume highlight, much remains unknown about the private equity industry. The extent to which the U.S. model will spread overseas and the degree to which the American model will—or can—be successfully adapted during this process are particularly interesting questions. It seems clear, however, that this financial intermediary will be an enduring feature on the global economic landscape in the years to come.

2

Martin Smith: January 2000

Martin Smith faced an enviable dilemma but a dilemma nonetheless. A second-year student in the MBA program at Harvard Business School, Martin had been successful in his private equity job hunt: so much so that he had generated three job offers. What was arguably the most attractive offer, from the prestigious Greenlane Group, had just arrived but with the proviso that he accept or reject the offer by the next morning. As he walked in the fading winter twilight to the campus gymnasium, Shad Hall, he wondered what he should do.

During the course of his job search, Martin had come to appreciate the very substantial differences between these funds. The Greenlane Group had an excellent track record, and Martin knew that this was a strong brand name (a "franchise fund" in private equity parlance) in the private equity community. But the organization was in the midst of a transition from the senior to junior partners, which had the potential to disrupt the fund's operations. Martin also worried about the fund's rapid increase in size and approach to compensation. But he had concerns as well about Clifton Investment Partners. Until recently, Clifton had made their money by participating as a syndicate member in other funds' deals, not from transactions that they had actually originated themselves. The funds' partners seemed to be much longer on financial than operating experience. Was it good management or merely good luck that had brought the fund success? Finally, the Terra Nova Venture Fund was an unknown quantity. Several general partners, who individually had strong reputations, had established a venture capital fund with a technological emphasis. Their small first fund was off to a good start, and their fund might represent a ground floor opportunity for Martin. But the partners of Terra Nova had not been together as a group for very long and did not even work in the same city. Martin wondered whether they would stay together as a team long enough for his own track record and reputation to be established.

Another important consideration for Martin was the compensation packages that the different groups offered. The Greenlane offer offered the lowest base pay and made no provision for a share of the carried interest. On the other hand, if he joined Terra Nova, Martin would receive a higher base level of compensation and immediately be-

Professor Josh Lerner prepared this case as the basis for class discussion rather than to illustrate either effective or ineffective handling of an administrative situation. It is partially based on "GMIMCo Venture Capital," HBS case No. 298-052, by Catherine Conneely, Josh Lerner, and Peter Wendell.

gin receiving a share of the fund's profits. The Clifton offer was between these two extremes. While he realized that joining a private equity group as an associate was a long-run investment, Martin was also keenly aware of the impending need to pay off the substantial debt that he had accumulated while attending Harvard Business School.

OPPORTUNITIES IN THE PRIVATE EQUITY INDUSTRY IN 2000

The U.S. private equity industry had been little more than a cottage industry until the late 1970s. While the first funds were established in the 1940s, the industry had largely relied on individual investors for its first three decades. Very little of the very substantial pools of capital associated with pension funds had gone into private equity, due both to their unfamiliarity with the asset class and their fears that such investments violated federal government standards.

The U.S. Department of Labor addressed the concerns in 1979 by clarifying the so-called prudent man rule, unleashing a wave of capital into private equity funds that had continued for two decades. Virtually without exception, each year had seen more money invested into private equity, typically into limited partnerships with a contractually specified 10-year life. (The investors served as limited partners—so-named because their liability was typically limited to the amount they invest—while the private equity group served as the general partners.) Exhibit 2-1 illustrates the growth of commitments to private equity funds over this period. The exhibit also illustrates the growing prominence of funds devoted to making leveraged buyout investments among private equity funds.[1]

Private equity groups were traditionally very "lean" organizations, operating without substantial staffs of analysts or associates. This reluctance to add staff was seen as

---

[1] For an overview of the private equity industry, see Paul Gompers and Josh Lerner, *The Venture Capital Cycle*, Cambridge, MA, MIT Press, 1999.

EXHIBIT 2-1

PATTERN OF PRIVATE EQUITY FUNDRAISING, 1980–1999

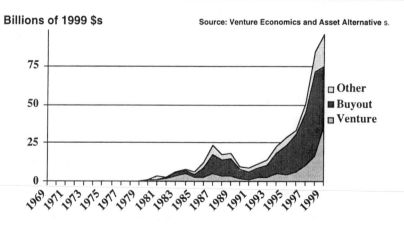

Source: Compiled from the *Private Equity Analyst* and unpublished records of Asset Alternatives.

EXHIBIT 2-2

GROWTH OF PRIVATE EQUITY INDUSTRY, 1982–1999

	National Venture Capital Association Member Organizations (includes many buyout investors)	Harvard Business School Students Accepting Venture Capital or Buyout Positions	Total Venture Capital Principals (includes some but not all buyout and corporate investors)
1982	114	NA	963
1983	130	NA	1134
1984	144	NA	1380
1985	180	9	1495
1986	191	18	1664
1987	207	20	1874
1988	225	11	1954
1989	229	20	2053
1990	223	12	2081
1991	220	11	2136
1992	201	8	2250
1993	193	19	2301
1994	187	16	2347
1995	179	22	2481
1996	194	44	2679
1997	240	70	2883
1998	310	103	3021
1999	370	117	NA

Note: NA = Not available.

Source: Compiled from unpublished National Venture Capital Association, Harvard Business School, and Venture Economics records.

imparting at least two advantages. First, the organizations' small size led to a great deal of flexibility. Private equity, particularly in recent years, was a highly competitive business, where investment opportunities often needed to be acted upon quickly. Small groups could react rapidly with first-hand knowledge. Second, the performance of each partner and associate could be carefully observed and attributed, and compensation and promotion decisions made accordingly. The ability to carefully measure performance limited the internal political activities so common in corporate life.

Despite these concerns, in recent years the number of employees in private equity organizations had climbed. This partially reflected the success of partnerships in raising additional capital and their need to rapidly invest these funds. Exhibit 2-2 illustrates the recent growth of the private equity industry. While many private equity funds shunned recent graduates of MBA programs, preferring to hire people with additional experience in operating firms, recruitment of MBA graduates had also increased. Exhibit 2-2 also indicates the increase of recruitment of Harvard Business School graduates into private equity investing.

The use of compensation in private equity organizations had also undergone a substantial evolution with the recent growth of the private equity industry. Initially, there had been quite distinct schemes employed within traditional independent partnerships and groups affiliated with investment or commercial banks. (These affiliated groups have made up about 25% of the private equity groups active over the past 25 years, though a smaller share of the dollars invested.)[2] Private equity funds would typically pay an annual salary plus a share of the capital gains (or "carried interest") harvested in that year (the latter would be received only by the partners). Affiliated groups, which typically did not employ a partnership structure (they usually simply invested the parent institution's capital rather than that of outside investors), generally provided employees with a salary and bonus. Even with the bonus, however, the compensation level in the affiliated funds was rarely equal to that of independent funds, and many of the leading private equity groups had been established by individuals who had left captive private equity groups such as those of the Bank of Boston, Citibank, the First National Bank of Chicago, and Security Pacific.

During the late 1980s, and especially in the 1990s, the patterns of compensation began subtly changing. In particular, the sharp demarcation between affiliated and independent groups blurred. A number of affiliated groups, anxious to limit the defection of personnel, took two new approaches. Many such organizations adopted "shadow" compensation schemes that more directly tied their employees' rewards to their performance. Other institutions allowed their private equity groups to raise part of their funds from outside investors rather than just from the sponsoring institution. For the

[2] The prevalence and performance of institutionally affiliated private equity groups are summarized in Paul A. Gompers and Josh Lerner, "Conflict of Interest and Reputation in the Issuance of Public Securities: Evidence from Venture Capital," *Journal of Law and Economics* 42 (April 1999): 53–80.

EXHIBIT 2-3

COMPENSATION OF PRIVATE EQUITY INVESTORS ($000s)

	Salary and Bonus		Total Compensation[a]		Carried Interest (%)[b]	
	Median	75th	Median	75th	Median	% Eligible
Managing general partner	$598	$896	$1,150	$3,255	3.7%	100%
Senior partner	539	800	1,035	2,514	2.3	88
Partner (midlevel)	350	532	409	738	1.8	72
Junior partner	198	300	215	304	0.5	59
Senior associate	144	173	144	178	0.3	26
Associate	92	112	92	112	0.2	11
Analyst	68	95	68	95	0.0	0

[a] Total compensation includes carried interest and co-investment distributions, as well as salary and bonus.

[b] Carried interest percentage is for most recent fund. The median is only calculated for those with a positive carried interest.

Source: Compiled from William M. Mercer, *Compensation Survey Performed for Venture Capital and Other Private Equity Firms*, New York, William M. Mercer, 2000. I thank Michael Holt for his asistance.

EXHIBIT 2-4

COMPENSATION OF SENIOR PARTNERS AND SENIOR ASSOCIATES IN PRIVATE EQUITY FUNDS OF DIFFERENT TYPES ($000s)

	Senior Partners		Senior Associates	
	Median Salary and Bonus	Median Total Compensation	Median Salary and Bonus	Median Total Compensation
All Funds:	$530	$1,035	$144	$144
<$200MM in capital	271	293	120	120
$200–$600MM	425	796	143	143
>$600MM	691	1,550	146	146
Private Firms:	613	1,190	150	150
Lower half in size	383	383	135	135
Upper half	691	1,748	153	153
Institutional Funds:	478	933	139	140
Lower half in size	321	662	115	115
Upper half	551	1,400	145	145

Source: Compiled from William M. Mercer, *Compensation Survey Performed for Venture Capital and Other Private Equity Firms*, New York, William M. Mercer, 2000. I thank Michael Holt for his asistance. See footnotes above for definitions.

funds raised from outsiders, there would be a provision for carried interest, at least some of which would be payable to the group's partners.

Meanwhile, intense competition for talented partners and associates had led independent groups to begin awarding bonuses in addition to salaries and carried interest. While precise data was difficult to obtain, survey estimates of compensation levels by the consulting firm William M. Mercer are summarized in Exhibits 2-3 and 2-4.

One factor that these surveys did not fully capture was the presence of co-investment rights. Many private equity groups allowed both partners and associates to invest in their transactions. In some cases there were few restrictions; in other groups, the investors were required to invest an equal amount in each transaction to address the limited partners' concerns about potential incentive and conflict-of-interest problems. In particular, institutional investors were often concerned that large investments by the general partners would reduce their stakes in the most attractive opportunities and that general partners would spend a disproportionate amount of time with the companies in which they had personally invested. In many organizations, associates were extended loans with which to make investments. In many cases, these loans were at a reduced interest level or were only required to be repaid to the extent that the investments yielded any proceeds.

MARTIN SMITH

Martin Smith had a background that made him attractive to many venture capital organizations. After undertaking an undergraduate degree in computer science at Stanford University, he had joined Sun Microsystems as a software engineer in the firm's software development area. After a little more than two years there, he had left to join several friends from college who had begun a start-up geared to developing Internet tools. This company, which had been a "bootstrap" operation funded largely through contract work developing Web sites for major corporations, had been acquired for $9 million two and a half years later. The acquirer, a venture-backed, publicly traded firm whose flagship product was an Internet search engine, was seeking to expand its product line. Martin had left soon after to attend Harvard Business School. While in business school, he had spent a summer internship with a long-established Boston venture capital group. This experience had only reinforced Martin's desire to join the private equity industry after graduation, hopefully in California.

At the same time, he had pursued an effective strategy in identifying private equity opportunities. First, he had focused on the private equity groups that were most likely to be interested in him. Martin had realized that without significant experience in an investment bank or as a financial analyst, it was unlikely that he would be seen as attractive by the many groups specializing in buyout or build-up investments. Consequently, he had targeted groups undertaking venture capital or early-stage investments.

Another important element had been avoiding more marginal private equity organizations. Martin had been contacted by a number of groups that were in the process of raising a first fund and had seen his resume in the Venture Capital and Principal Investment Club's Web site. Rather than seriously pursuing these positions, he had focused on more established groups. Martin believed that if he was unable to obtain an offer from a reputable group, he would probably be better served spending several years in an operating position in the software industry, and then looking once again.

Finally, Martin had extensively researched the private equity industry in order to target organizations that fit his skill set and to understand their situations. He had identified what groups had just raised funds or were likely to be raising funds in the upcoming year (and hence likely to be thinking about adding personnel), researched the key deals that the partnerships had invested in, and sought to ascertain the different groups' investment philosophies. As he had narrowed his job search, he had sought firsthand information about the groups from portfolio companies and an institutional investor. While this was time-consuming, and occasionally raised eyebrows at the private equity groups with whom he was interviewing, he believed it was only prudent. After all, accepting a position with a private equity group could be seen as a decision that required the same degree of due diligence as any other investment. The only difference was that here the investment was not of money—just a substantial amount of Martin's "human capital"!

THE DILEMMA

Martin had received offers from three attractive private equity groups. Two of these groups had established track records, while the other was newer. Exhibit 2-5 summarizes the track records of the two established organizations.

The *Greenlane Group* was a top-tier venture firm. Within the private equity community, it had a strong "brand name" and had historically sponsored very successful partnerships. The group built up a franchise in health care and technology beginning in 1986. In mid-1999, the two senior partners had begun "phasing out" and passing work onto good, proven junior partners.

The group had just begun formally marketing a new fund (Fund V) that was almost twice the same size as the prior fund (Fund IV, raised in 1998). The share of profits going to the private equity investors had been raised in the new fund to 25%, from the 20% that it had been in the previous funds. The justification offered was that this increase was due to performance on Fund III. Nonetheless, the second fund (Fund II)

EXHIBIT 2-5

HISTORICAL PERFORMANCE OF PRIOR FUNDS

TABLE 1: **Greenlane Group**

Fund	Date	Size (millions)	Fund Return (%)[a]	Venture Economics Median (%)	Venture Economics Top ¼ (%)	General Partner (GP) Performance
				—as of 6/30/99—		
Fund I	1986	$ 60	16% (4 times $)	6%	12%	Senior GPs
Fund II	1990	$100	11% (3 times $)	10%	29%	Mixed, with GP turnover
Fund III	1995	$150	59% (2 times $)	21%	55%	Hot public stocks by juniors
Fund IV	1998	$300				
Fund V	2000	$575		(proposed, with 25% carry)		

TABLE 2: **Clifton Investment Partners**

Fund	Date	Size (millions)	Fund Return (%)[a]	Venture Economics Median (%)	Venture Economics Top ¼ (%)	General Partner (GP) Performance
				—as of 6/30/99—		
Fund I	1987	$50	10% (3 times $)	8%	17%	Equal weighted GP performance
Fund II	1992	$100	21% (3 times $)	15%	22%	Equal weighted GP performance
Fund III	1999	$150		(just raised, with attractive terms)		Proposed new deal sourcing strategy

Note: Since the fourth Greenlane and first Terra Nova Venture Fund were less than two years old, no historical data on its performance was yet available. Comparison data is for all venture capital funds but does not include all other private equity organizations.

Source: Compiled from Venture Economics, *VentureXpert Database*, http://www.ventureeconomics.com.

had about the same performance as the median funds formed in the same year (often referred to in private equity industry as funds in the same "vintage year"). Furthermore, there was a potentially disturbing variance within the private equity organization. According to Martin's research, in the technology sector, the group had mixed results. In the health-care area, however, the group was consistently good. Observers attributed this to its extraordinary deal-flow due to the "franchise factor" developed by one of the senior and two of the junior partners.

The initial Greenlane fund (Fund I) was established by two senior partners and generated very good returns. It was the three junior partners, many observers felt, who generated the majority of returns of Fund III. From conversations with a college roommate who now helped manage the private equity portfolio of a major pension fund (who had also provided the performance data reproduced in Exhibit 2-5), Martin had learned that the distribution of the profit participation in the third fund was very uneven: fully 70% of the gains went to the two senior partners. They had received seven points each (a point is defined as one percentage point of the fund's total profits), while the three junior partners had received two points each. While Martin's former roommate was not involved in his organization's decision to invest in the fifth fund, he had heard that the new fund had improved the distribution of the profits, with about 40% of the profits going to the junior partners. Furthermore, the increase in the carried interest to 25% implied that there would be more profits to divide. In any case, they had already "soft circled," or obtained informal commitments, for an amount considerably in excess of its target for the new fund.

Greenlane's offer did not include any provision for a share of the carried interest for Martin. Nonetheless, the question of how much a "founder" should continue to get and the motives for the increase in the carried interest bothered him. Martin was aware that a number of leading private equity groups had broken up because of disputes between generations of partners. Another issue was the uneven returns by subsegment. As a specialist in the computer industry, he wondered what the impact of joining such a group would be. Was there any risk in doing so? Conversely, his experience might help the firm improve results and make him look good.

The partners of the *Clifton Investment Partners* had strong financial backgrounds but no operating experience. The returns for its two funds were in the upper half, but not the upper quartile, of venture capital funds in general. Exhibit 2-5 shows the historical performance of the partnership. In conversations with industry observers, Martin learned that Clifton had a history of participating in other people's deals. Approximately two years ago, the fund had addressed this by hiring "venture partners" with operating experience. Clifton also developed a database along with a cold calling strategy to generate a proprietary deal-flow for the funds. The partnership seemed to be going after market segments being abandoned by other top-tier venture funds that had grown much bigger.

The general partners of the group had reasonable reputations, and the carry was equally distributed. The general partners were regarded as equally good performers but no one was "great." Clifton had just raised its third fund, on terms similar to those of its previous two, though it was 50% larger. His former roommate pointed out that the terms of the fund had been perceived as "friendly" to the limited partners. Nonetheless, Martin was concerned about the general partners' relative lack of operating experience and modest reputation in the industry. Would this be as valuable an experience—either with respect to personal learning or the "stamp of approval" that it would provide to the rest of the venture community—as the Greenlane one?

The *Terra Nova Venture Fund* had just raised a first fund the year before. Only two of the three general partners had worked together before the formation of the fund. The fund was located in offices in San Francisco and Austin, Texas. As a team with an unproven track record, Martin was apprehensive about joining them. On the other hand, the team was developing an interesting deal-flow in a very focused technology niche (Internet infrastructure) that played to Martin's technological training and business experience.

The general partners' backgrounds included a senior analyst from a major investment banking firm, a junior partner at another venture capital fund, and the third from industry. Individually, they had good track records. The banker was successful with his "buy" recommendations, and the industry partner had been chief operating officer at a quality firm. The investment banking and industry partner had worked together, having bought and sold a company that had been very successful.

In early 1999, a $26 million fund had been raised from individual investors. The fund had already invested in 10 companies with what the partners claimed were attractive valuations considering their stage of development. The team had shown an ability to hire key management into portfolio companies, and 3 of the 10 companies had received follow-on financing at higher valuations. The team had one big failure in a syndicated deal. The remaining companies were being carried at cost, but in conversations with several of them, Martin saw indications that they appeared to be ahead of plan. Overall, the portfolio had a great deal of potential, but being new, the group had a much higher risk profile. Martin also wondered about the location of the fund's offices. The management style and decision making could be fragmented due to the geographic spread of the partners. Martin worried that a "lone ranger" general partner could emerge and jeopardize the stability of the organization.

Not only did the situations of the three private equity groups differ considerably, but so did the compensation schemes that they offered. Greenlane's offer had called for a salary of about $100,000, with a projected bonus of about 10% of his base salary in the first year. If his investments proved successful, the partners indicated, Martin might receive a share of the carried interest in his third or fourth year at the firm. When Martin had tried to push for more specifics, the partners had proved unwilling to discuss the matter further. Terra Nova's offer, despite the fund's smaller size and much shorter track record, was considerably more attractive: Martin would receive a base salary of almost $140,000, was guaranteed a bonus of 20% of his base pay, and would receive one point in the 1999 fund. (This stake would "vest" over four years: i.e., if Martin left or was fired before then, he would receive a smaller stake in the profits, according to a set schedule.) Finally, Clifton's offer was midway between the other two offers in terms of salary and bonus. While Martin would not initially receive a share of the fund's capital gains, the partners indicated that this issue would be revisited at the end of 2000.

Martin wondered how to interpret these offers and how much importance to place on compensation in his choice between the three funds.

The first module of *Venture Capital and Private Equity* examines how private equity funds are raised and structured. These funds often have complex features, and the legal issues involved are frequently arcane. But the structure of private equity funds has a profound effect on the behavior of venture and buyout investors. Consequently, it is important to understand these issues, whether one intends to work for, receive money from, or invest in or alongside private equity funds.

The module will seek not only to understand the features of private equity funds and the actors in the fundraising process, but also to analyze them. We will map out which institutions serve primarily to increase the profits from private equity investments as a whole and which seem designed mostly to shift profits *between* the parties. We will seek to understand the functions of and the reasons for each aspect of private equity fundraising.

WHY THIS MODULE?

The structuring of venture and buyout funds may initially appear to be a complex and technical topic, one better left to legal specialists than general managers. Private equity partnership agreements are complex documents, often extending for hundreds of pages. Practitioner discussions of the structure of these firms are rife with obscure terms such as "reverse claw-backs."

But the subject is an important one. For the features of private equity funds—whether management fees, profit sharing rules, or contractual terms—have a profound effect on the behavior of these investors. It is clearly important to understand these influences if one is seeking to work for a private equity fund. But an understanding of these dynamics will also be valuable for the entrepreneur financing his company through these investors, the investment banker underwriting a firm backed by private equity funds, the corporate development officer investing alongside venture capitalists in a young company, and the pension fund manager placing her institution's capital into a fund.

An example may help to illustrate this point. Almost all venture and buyout funds are designed to be "self-liquidating"; that is, to dissolve after 10 or 12 years. The need to terminate each fund imposes a healthy discipline, forcing private equity investors to take the necessary but painful step of terminating underperforming firms in their portfolios. (These firms are sometimes referred to as the "living dead" or "zombies.") But the pressure to raise an additional fund can sometimes have less pleasant consequences. Young private equity organizations frequently rush young firms to the public marketplace in order to demonstrate a successful track record, even if the companies are not ready to go public. This behavior, known as "grandstanding," can have a harmful effect on the long-run prospects of the firms dragged prematurely into the public markets.

A second rationale for an examination of the concerns and perspectives of institutional investors and intermediaries is that they provide an often-neglected avenue into the private equity industry. Many students diligently pursue positions at the traditional private equity organizations but neglect other routes to careers as private equity investors. A position evaluating private equity funds and putting capital to work in these organizations is likely to lead to a network of relationships with private equity investors that may eventually pay handsome dividends.

THE FRAMEWORK

There are a wide array of actors in the private equity fundraising drama. Investors—whether pension funds, individuals, or endowments—each have their own motivations and concerns. These investors frequently hire intermediaries. Sometimes these "gatekeepers" play a consultative role, recommending attractive funds to their clients. In other cases, they organize "funds-of-funds" of their own. Specialized intermediaries concentrate on particular niches of the private equity industry, such as buying and selling interests in limited partnerships from institutional investors. In addition, venture and buyout organizations are increasingly hiring placement agents who facilitate the fundraising process.

This module will examine each of these players. Rather than just describing their roles, however, we will highlight the rationales for and impacts of their behavior. Some institutions and features have evolved to improve the efficiency of the private equity investment process, while others appear to be designed primarily to shift more of the economic benefits to particular parties.

Investing in a private equity fund is in some respects a "leap of faith" for institutional investors. Most pension funds and endowments typically have very small staffs. At the largest organizations, a dozen professionals may be responsible for investing several billion dollars each year. Meanwhile, private equity funds undertake investments that are either in risky new firms pursuing complex new technologies or in troubled mature companies with numerous organizational pathologies and potential legal liabilities.

Many of the features of private equity funds can be understood as responses to this uncertain environment, rife with many information gaps. For instance, the "carried interest"—the substantial share of profits that are allocated to the private equity investors—helps address these information asymmetries by ensuring that all parties gain if the investment does well. Similarly, pension funds hire "gatekeepers" to ensure that only sophisticated private equity funds with well-defined objectives get funded with their capital.

At the same time, other features of private equity funds can be seen as attempts to *transfer* wealth between parties, rather than efforts to increase the size of the overall amount of profits generated by private equity investments. An example was the drive by many venture capital funds in the mid-1980s—a period when the demand for their services was very strong—to change the timing of their compensation. Prior to this point, venture capital funds had typically disbursed all the proceeds from their first few successful investments to their investors, until the investors had received their original invested capital back. The venture capitalists would then begin receiving a share of the subsequent investments that they exited. Consider a fund that had raised capital of $50 million, whose first three successful investments yielded $25 million each. Under the traditional arrangement, the proceeds from the first two offerings would have gone entirely to the institutional investors in their fund. The venture capitalists would have only begun receiving a share of the proceeds at the time that they exited the third investment.

In the mid-1980s, venture capitalists began demanding—and receiving—the right to start sharing in even the first successfully exited investments. The primary effect of this change was that the venture capitalists began receiving more compensation early in their funds' lives. Put another way, the net present value of their compensation package increased considerably. It is not surprising, then, that as the inflow into venture capital weakened in the late 1980s, institutional investors began demanding that venture capitalists return to the previous approach of deferring compensation.

This twin tension—between behavior that increases the size of the "pie" and actions that simply change the relative sizes of the slices—runs through this module. We will attempt to understand both the workings of and the reasons for the key features of these funds using this framework.

THE STRUCTURE OF THE MODULE

The first half of the module introduces the key elements of the private equity fundraising process. Among the actors whose structure and concerns we will examine are institutions, private equity investors, "funds-of-funds," and "gatekeepers." We will put particular emphasis on the agreements that bring these parties together into limited partnerships. Because they play such an important role in shaping behavior, compensation terms will be a special focus.

The second half of the module examines the raising of two funds by private equity organizations. We look at private equity organizations with very different histories and investment targets. The funds that emerged from these circumstances reflected not only the differences between the investments that each fund promised to make, but also each group's ability to persuade—or demand—a better deal from its investors. We will consider a variety of issues, from the role of the key institutions in the fundraising process to how the performance of these funds should be assessed.

FURTHER READING ON PRIVATE EQUITY FUNDRAISING AND PARTNERSHIPS

Legal Works

JOSEPH W. BARTLETT, *Equity Finance: Venture Capital, Buyouts, Restructurings, and Reorganization*, New York, Wiley, 1995, chapters 24 and 29.

CRAIG E. DAUCHY AND MARK T. HARMON, "Structuring Venture Capital Limited Partnerships," *The Computer Lawyer* 3 (November 1986): 1–7.

MICHAEL J. HALLORAN, LEE F. BENTON, ROBERT V. GUNDERSON, JR., KEITH L. KEARNEY, JORGE DEL CALVO, *Venture Capital and Public Offering Negotiation*, Englewood Cliffs, NJ, Aspen Law and Business, 1997 (and updates), volume 1, chapters 1 and 2.

Practitioner and Journalistic Accounts

Asset Alternatives, *Directory of Alternative Investment Programs*, Wellesley, MA, Asset Alternatives, 2000.

Asset Alternatives, *Private Equity Fund of Funds: State of the Market*, Wellesley, MA, Asset Alternatives, 1999.

Asset Alternatives, *Terms and Conditions of Private Equity Partnerships*, Wellesley, MA, Asset Alternatives, 2001.

WILLIAM M. MERCER, INC., *Key Terms and Conditions for Private Equity Investing*, 1997 (available on-line at http://www.assetalt.com/ped/mercer.html).

Venture Economics, *Directory of Limited Partners*, Newark, NJ, Venture Economics, 2000.

Venture Economics, *1992 Terms and Conditions of Venture Capital Partnerships*, Boston, Venture Economics, 1992.

Numerous articles in *Buyouts, Private Equity Analyst*, and *Venture Capital Journal*.

Academic Studies

GEORGE W. FENN, NELLIE LIANG, AND STEPHEN PROWSE, "The Private Equity Market: An Overview," *Financial Markets, Institutions and Instruments* 6, no. 4 (1997): 70–100.

PAUL A. GOMPERS AND JOSH LERNER, "Risk and Reward in Private Equity Investments: The Challenge of Performance Assessment," *Journal of Private Equity* 1 (Winter 1997): 5–12.

PAUL A. GOMPERS AND JOSH LERNER, *The Venture Capital Cycle*, Cambridge, MA, MIT Press, 1999, chapters 2–5.

PAUL A. GOMPERS AND JOSH LERNER, "What Drives Venture Capital Fundraising?," *Brookings Papers on Economic Activity—Microeconomics* (1998): 149–192.

THOMAS HELLMANN, "Venture Capital: A Challenge for Commercial Banks," *Journal of Private Equity*, 1 (Fall 1997): 49–55.

BLAINE HUNTSMAN AND JAMES P. HOBAN, JR., "Investment in New Enterprise: Some Empirical Observations on Risk, Return and Market Structure," *Financial Management* 9 (Summer 1980): 44–51.

LESLIE A. JENG AND PHILIPPE C. WELLS, "The Determinants of Venture Capital Funding: Evidence Across Countries," *Journal of Corporate Finance*, 6 (September 2000): 241–284.

PATRICK R. LILES, *Sustaining the Venture Capital Firm*, Cambridge, MA, Management Analysis Center, 1977.

3

Yale University Investments Office: July 2000

David Swensen leaned back from the antique roll-top desk in his otherwise modest office. Outside, it was a cool and damp day, but as Swensen and his colleague, Dean Takahashi, reviewed the preliminary investment results for the just-ended fiscal year, their spirits were high.

As Yale's chief investment officer, Swensen was responsible for managing the university's Endowment, which totaled approximately $10 billion in July 2000. Under Swensen's leadership, and with the guidance and approval of the Investment Committee, Yale had developed a rather different approach to Endowment management, including substantial investments in less efficient equity markets such as private equity (venture capital and buyouts), real assets (real estate, timber, oil and gas), and "absolute return" investing. This approach had generated successful, indeed enviable, returns. Swensen and his staff were proud of the record that they had compiled and believed that Yale should probably focus even more of its efforts and assets in these less efficient markets. At the same time, the very success of their strategy had generated new questions. How far did they think Yale should or could go in this direction? How should they respond to the growing popularity of the approach they had chosen and the flood of capital pursuing private equity investments?

BACKGROUND[1]

Ten Connecticut clergymen established Yale in 1701. Over its first century, the college relied on the generosity of the Connecticut General Assembly, which provided more than half of its funding. The creation of a formal Endowment for Yale was triggered by

[1] This section is based on Brooks Mather Kelley, *Yale: A History*, New Haven CT, Yale University Press, 1974, David F. Swensen, *Pioneering Portfolio Management: An Unconventional Approach to Investment Management*, New York, Free Press, 2000, and Yale University Investments Office, *The Yale Endowment*, New Haven, Yale University, 1995.

the 1818 disestablishment of Congregationalism as Connecticut's state religion. Students and alumni alike demanded that the school respond by establishing a divinity school to offer theological instruction. To fund this effort, numerous alumni made large gifts, the first of a series of successful fund drives. While Yale used many of these donations to buy land and construct buildings, other funds were invested in corporate and railroad bonds, as well as equities. By the century's end, the Endowment had reached $5 million.

The growth of the Endowment rapidly accelerated during the first three decades of the twentieth century. This was due both to several enormous bequests and to aggressive investments in equities, which comprised well over half the Endowment's portfolio during the "roaring" 1920s. In 1930, equities represented 42% of the Yale Endowment; the average university had only 11%.[2] Yale avoided severe erosion of its Endowment during the Great Depression in the 1930s, however, because many quite recent bequests were kept in cash or Treasuries rather than being invested in equities.

In the late 1930s, Treasurer Laurence Tighe decided that the share of equities in Yale's portfolio should be dramatically reduced. Tighe argued that higher taxes were likely to expropriate any corporate profits that equity holders would otherwise receive even if a recovery were to occur. He argued that bonds would consequently perform better than stocks. His decision, which stipulated that at least two dollars would be held in fixed income instruments for every dollar of equity, set the template for Yale's asset allocation over the next three decades. The Treasurer and Trustees continued to manage the Endowment themselves during this period, selecting individual bonds and high-yield or income-oriented stocks for the portfolio. These policies seemed very prudent in the late 1930s and 1940s. But unfortunately, they were less well suited for the bull market of the 1950s and 1960s. In the mid- and late 1960s, in response, the Endowment's trustees decided on two substantial policy shifts.

First, the trustees decided to substantially increase the University's exposure to equity investments. In this decision, they were influenced by a task force sponsored by McGeorge Bundy, president of the Ford Foundation. This committee—which included Kingman Brewster, president of Yale—argued that most university endowments had taken too conservative an approach:

> It is our conclusion that past thinking by many endowment managers has been overly influenced by fear of another major crash. Although nobody can ever be certain what the future may bring, we do not think that a long-term policy founded on such fear can survive dispassionate analysis.[3]

Second, Yale decided to contract out much of the portfolio management function to an external advisor. The school helped to found a new Boston-based money manager, Endowment Management and Research Corporation (EM&R), whose principals were well-known successful growth stock investors recruited from other Boston money management firms. The plan was that EM&R would function as a quasi-independent external firm and would be free to recruit additional clients. At the same time, Yale would be its largest client and would have priority over other clients.

The high expectations for EM&R were never realized. Like other universities, Yale saw its Endowment's value plummet in the ensuing years because of a "bear" market,

---

[2] General university information is from Institutional Department, Scudder, Stevens & Clark, *Survey of University and College Endowment Funds*, New York, Scudder, Stevens & Clark, 1947.

[3] Advisory Committee on Endowment Management, *Managing Educational Endowments: Report to the Ford Foundation*, New York, Ford Foundation, 1969.

accelerating inflation, and operating deficits. Between 1969 and 1979, the inflation-adjusted value of Yale's Endowment declined by 46%. While the investment performance was not that unusual relative to other endowments, it nonetheless severely strained the financial fabric of the University. Yale terminated its relationship with EM&R in 1979 and embarked on a program to use a variety of external advisors in its evolving asset management framework.

DAVID SWENSEN AND THE INVESTMENTS OFFICE IN 2000

In 1985, David Swensen was hired to head the Investments Office. William Brainard, Yale's provost at the time, and Professor (and Nobel Laureate) James Tobin persuaded their former student—Swensen had earned his Ph.D. in Economics at Yale in 1980—to leave his post at Lehman Brothers. The position offered not only the opportunity to help Yale, but the possibility of some teaching in Yale College as well.

In the succeeding 15 years, Swensen built the capabilities of the Yale Investments Office. Most importantly, he recruited and developed a quite small but very high-quality internal staff. Dean Takahashi, whom Swensen had known as a Yale student, was recruited into the Investments Office and had become Swensen's primary lieutenant. A number of other staff had also been recruited over the years, often recent graduates of Yale College. There were a total of 17 employees (13 professionals) in the office in July 2000. The Investments Office itself filled all three floors of a modest reconstructed Victorian house on the northern edge of Yale's campus. Swensen encouraged his staff to be active members of the larger Yale community, and he had chosen this on-campus location to signal that the Investments Office was an integral part of the University and its financial management function.

Swensen defined the role of the Investments Office broadly. Reporting to the Treasurer and to an Investment Committee (described below), the Investments Office had overall responsibility for Endowment matters. While most of its day-to-day activities involved evaluating, selecting, monitoring, and overseeing external investment advisors, it also played a critical role in the entire policy-making process. For example, it was responsible for recommendations on both the investment policy and the spending policy for the Endowment—that is, in broad terms, how the money should be invested and how much of it could be spent in any given year.

The Investment Committee, to which the Investments Office reported, was composed of influential and knowledgeable Yale alumni, a number of whom were quite active in different segments of the asset management business. The Committee as a whole functioned as an active involved board, meeting quarterly and providing advice, counsel, and ultimately approval of the various investment managers. In addition, David Swensen often consulted with individual members of the Investment Committee on issues within their areas of specific expertise. This helped guide the thinking and recommendations of the Investments Office on various key issues; and it fostered an atmosphere of advice and support within which the Investments Office could take quite different and sometimes unconventional stances if it believed in them and could convince the Investment Committee of their merit.

INVESTMENT PHILOSOPHY

Perhaps the most fundamental difference between Yale and other universities was its investment philosophy. Swensen was fond of quoting John Maynard Keynes' maxim that "worldly wisdom teaches us that it is better for reputation to fail conventionally than to succeed unconventionally." Nonetheless, Swensen was willing to take "the risk of being different" when it seemed appropriate and potentially rewarding. By not following the crowd, Yale could develop its investment philosophy from first principles, which are summarized below.

First, Swensen strongly believed in equities, whether publicly traded or private. He pointed out that equities are a claim on a real stream of income, as opposed to a contractual sequence of nominal cash flows (such as bonds). Since the bulk of a university's outlays are devoted to salaries, inflation can place tremendous pressure on its finances. Not only do bonds have low expected returns relative to more equity-like assets, but they often perform poorly during periods of rising or highly uncertain inflation. To demonstrate convincingly why he believed in the long-run advantages of equity investing, Swensen would often refer to the actual cumulative long-run returns over past decades. An original one dollar investment in December 1925 in large-company U.S. stocks (e.g., the S&P 500) would be worth $2,846 by the end of 1999; a comparable investment in U.S. Treasury bonds would be worth $40; and Treasury bills, $16.[4]

A second principle was to hold a diversified portfolio. In general, Yale believed that risk could be more effectively reduced by limiting aggregate exposure to any single asset class rather than by attempting to time markets. While Swensen and his staff usually had their own informed views of the economy and markets, they believed that most of the time those views were already reflected in market prices. They thus tended to avoid trying to time short-run market fluctuations, and would overweight or underweight an asset class only if a persuasive case could be made that market prices were measurably misvalued for understandable reasons.[5]

A third principle was to seek opportunities in less efficient markets. Swensen noted that over the past decade the difference in performance between U.S. fixed income managers in the 25th and 75th percentiles (of their performance universe) was minimal, and the difference in performance between U.S. common stock portfolio managers in the 25th and 75th percentiles was less than 3% per annum. In contrast, in private equity this same performance difference exceeded 15% per annum. This suggested that there could be far greater incremental returns to selecting superior managers in nonpublic markets characterized by incomplete information and illiquidity, and that is exactly what Swensen and his staff endeavored to do.

Fourth, Swensen believed strongly in utilizing outside managers for all but the most routine or indexed of investments. He thought these external investment advisors should be given considerable autonomy to implement their strategies as they saw fit, with relatively little interference or obstructive monitoring by Yale. These managers were chosen very carefully, however, after a lengthy and probing analysis of their abilities, their comparative advantages, their performance records, and their reputations. The Investments Office staff was responsible for developing close and mutually beneficial relationships with each of these external managers. They prided themselves on knowing their managers very well, on listening carefully to their ongoing advice, and on helping to guide them, if and when appropriate, on various policy matters. From time to time, the Investments Office effectively "put a team in business" by becoming a new man-

---

[4] R.G. Ibbotson Associates, *Stocks, Bonds, Bills and Inflation*, Chicago, R.G. Ibbotson Associates, 2000.

[5] Yale actively rebalanced its portfolio to maintain its target asset allocations, however, and this led to frequent short-term adjustments in its holdings. For instance, as equity values rose in the summer of 1987, Yale sold stocks in order to return to its target allocation level. After the stock market crash later that year, the Endowment repurchased many of the same securities as it sought to raise its asset allocation back to the target level.

ager's first client. And it was not uncommon for managers to consider Yale as one of the most important of their clients.

Finally, the Yale philosophy focused critically on the explicit and implicit incentives facing outside managers. In Swensen's view, most of the asset management business had poorly aligned incentives built into typical client–manager relationships. For instance, managers typically prospered if their assets under management grew very large, not necessarily if they just performed well for their clients. The Investments Office tried to structure innovative relationships and fee structures with various external managers so as to better align the managers' interests with Yale's, insofar as that was possible.

RECENT ASSET ALLOCATION AND PERFORMANCE RESULTS

Yale's Investment Committee annually reviewed its Endowment portfolio to decide upon target allocations to the various asset classes. The actual allocations in recent years are shown in Exhibit 3-1, which illustrates the recent upward trend in the allocation to the private equity, real assets, and absolute return classes, as well as the current (2000) target allocations. The comparable asset allocations for several groups of university endowments are shown in Exhibits 3-2 and 3-3, and for large institutions (including both pension funds and endowments) in Exhibit 3-4.

As a part of the planning process, the Investments Office had completed a "mean-variance analysis" of the expected returns and risks from its current allocation, and had compared them to those of past Yale allocations and the current mean allocation of other universities. These relied on specific assumptions about the expected returns, volatilities, and correlations among asset classes. The results of this comparative mean variance analysis are shown in Exhibit 3-5. In addition, they had examined the long-run implications of their allocation for the "downside risk" to the Endowment. In keeping with a quantitative format for analyzing long-run downside risk that had been used on prior occasions, they examined the probability that the available Endowment spending would fall by more than 25% (adjusted for inflation) over the next five years; they also examined the probability that the inflation-adjusted value of the Endowment would fall by more than one-half over the next 50 years. To undertake this analysis, the Investments Office employed a probabilistic Monte Carlo analysis, which simulated and compiled thousands of possible random outcomes drawn from an assumed distribution of returns and correlations used in the simpler mean-variance analysis. This downside risk analysis suggested that the probability of a 25% spending fall within any five-year period was 4.8% and the probability of a 50% fall in purchasing power over a 50-year horizon was 8.6%.

Yale's allocation philosophy and distinctive approach to investing had paid off handsomely over the past decade. In fiscal year 2000, the fund had returned 41%, exceeding Yale's benchmark by 30%. This performance was above the endowments measured by Cambridge Associates (a mean of 28.9% for the largest schools and 17.8% overall[6]). Perhaps even more impressive had been the fund's long-run performance since Swensen and Takahashi arrived at Yale. Over the 15 years ending in June 2000, Yale's annualized return was 17.4%. This was more than 2% better than its "peers" (other nontaxable endowments with over $1 billion in assets) and about 4% better than the average of all

---

[6] This is based on an unpublished Cambridge Associates tabulation. The return for all schools is equal-weighted; that of the largest schools is value-weighted.

EXHIBIT 3-1

ASSET ALLOCATIONS OF YALE ENDOWMENT, 1985–2000

	1985	1986	1987	1988	1989	1990	1991	1992	1993	1994	1995	1996	1997	1998	1999	2000	Current (2000) Target Allocation
Domestic equity	61.6%	63.5%	61.7%	56.8%	53.2%	48.0%	30.7%	27.5%	23.9%	21.2%	21.8%	22.6%	21.5%	19.2%	15.1%	14.2%	15.0%
Foreign equity	6.3	8.6	10.8	14.0	15.4	15.2	14.8	15.3	16.5	14.6	12.5	12.4	12.8	12.1	11.1	9.0	10.0
Bonds	10.3	12.7	14.6	15.0	16.3	21.2	21.2	22.7	22.5	16.5	12.2	12.3	12.5	10.1	9.6	9.4	10.0
Cash	10.1	5.0	2.1	2.1	0.3	0.9	0.9	0.5	0.1	0.6	1.8	0.9	-0.2	-2.5	1.5	8.1	0.0
Real assets	8.5	7.5	7.2	7.7	8.7	8.0	7.9	7.1	6.0	8.6	13.5	11.2	11.5	13.0	17.9	14.9	17.5
Private equity	3.2	2.7	3.6	4.4	6.1	6.7	8.3	10.4	14.4	18.1	17.2	20.2	18.6	21.0	23.0	25.0	25.0
Absolute return	0.0	0.0	0.0	0.0	0.0	0.0	15.9	16.5	16.6	20.1	21.0	20.7	23.3	27.1	21.8	19.5	22.5

Asset allocations are on June 30th of each year.

Private equity includes venture capital and buyouts (and oil and gas and forestland through 1998).

Absolute return includes hedge funds, high-yield bonds, distressed securities, and event arbitrage.

Real assets includes real estate and (since 1999) oil and gas and forestland.

Source: University documents.

EXHIBIT 3-2

ASSET ALLOCATIONS OF LARGE UNIVERSITY ENDOWMENTS, 1985–2000

	1985	1986	1987	1988	1989	1990	1991	1992	1993	1994	1995	1996	1997	1998	1999	2000
Domestic equity	51.5%	52.1%	53.8%	50.2%	46.1%	45.3%	43.5%	44.4%	43.0%	41.6%	42.8%	41.1%	42.3%	39.9%	36.3%	36.5%
Foreign equity	2.0	2.6	3.0	5.2	6.6	6.6	7.8	8.1	10.2	14.3	15.2	14.0	15.9	14.7	14.5	15.0
Bonds	26.4	28.3	26.0	26.2	27.5	29.2	30.2	30.7	26.9	22.4	17.5	20.1	18.0	15.9	15.0	17.4
Cash	10.8	8.8	8.9	7.7	6.9	6.9	6.1	5.2	4.6	3.2	4.1	3.2	3.1	2.5	3.0	2.8
Real estate	4.8	4.9	5.2	4.3	5.1	4.4	4.2	3.7	3.7	4.2	5.1	5.2	5.2	6.9	6.6	4.7
Private equity	2.7	1.9	2.0	5.8	6.6	6.2	6.2	5.9	6.6	7.7	8.0	8.1	7.2	8.2	11.1	13.9
Absolute return	0.0	0.0	0.0	0.0	0.0	0.1	0.6	0.8	3.3	5.2	6.2	6.7	6.9	10.1	11.3	8.3
Other	1.8	1.4	1.1	0.6	1.2	1.3	1.4	1.2	1.7	1.5	1.1	1.6	1.5	2.0	2.1	1.2

Asset allocations are on June 30th of each year.

Large funds are defined as those with more than $1 billion in assets in 1998 through 2000, as those with more than $400 million in assets in 1988 through 1997, and as those with more than $200 million in assets in 1985 through 1987.

Private equity includes venture capital, buyouts, and oil and gas.

Funds are weighted equally in calculating average allocations in 1985 through 1987.

Absolute return includes hedge funds, high-yield bonds, distressed securities, and event arbitrage.

Funds are weighted by size in calculating average allocations in 1988 through 1994.

1985–1987 classifications may not be completely analogous to those in other years.

2000 data are not fully comparable to those in earlier years.

Source: Compiled from Cambridge Associates, *1999 NACUBO Endowment Study*, Washington, DC, National Association of College and University Business Officers, 2000 (and earlier years) and unpublished Cambridge Associates data.

EXHIBIT 3-3

ASSET ALLOCATIONS OF ALL UNIVERSITY ENDOWMENTS, 1985–2000

	1985	1986	1987	1988	1989	1990	1991	1992	1993	1994	1995	1996	1997	1998	1999	2000
Domestic equity	46.1%	48.7%	51.4%	46.4%	48.5%	48.1%	47.1%	47.1%	48.5%	47.2%	49.2%	51.6%	52.6%	52.4%	53.7%	41.4%
Foreign equity	0.8	1.1	1.6	1.5	1.8	2.4	2.4	3.2	4.2	7.5	9.5	9.5	11.2	11.0	10.6	14.1
Bonds	30.6	30.6	30.8	33.8	32.2	33.9	35.3	35.3	34.4	32.2	28.3	27.3	25.2	24.9	23.1	21.1
Cash	14.5	13.1	12.6	14.2	13.0	10.9	10.1	9.9	7.6	7.1	6.5	5.4	4.8	4.1	4.0	3.5
Real estate	4.2	3.9	2.2	2.5	2.7	2.9	2.9	2.3	2.1	2.1	2.3	2.0	2.0	2.2	2.1	3.0
Private equity	0.7	0.6	0.7	0.9	1.1	1.0	1.1	0.9	1.1	1.2	1.3	1.4	1.4	1.4	2.2	8.7
Absolute return	0.0	0.0	0.0	0.0	0.0	0.0	0.2	0.3	1.1	1.8	2.0	2.2	2.4	3.6	3.8	7.0
Other	3.1	2.0	0.7	0.6	0.7	0.7	0.9	1.0	0.9	0.9	0.9	0.5	0.4	0.4	0.5	1.1

Asset allocations are on June 30th of each year.

Private equity includes venture capital, buyouts, and oil and gas.

Absolute return includes hedge funds, high-yield bonds, distressed securities, and event arbitrage.

All funds are weighted equally in calculating average allocations.

1985 and 1986 classifications may not be completely analogous to those in other years.

2000 data are not fully comparable to those in earlier years.

Source: Compiled from Cambridge Associates, *1999 NACUBO Endowment Study*, Washington, DC, National Association of College and University Business Officers, 2000 (and earlier years) and unpublished Cambridge Associates data.

EXHIBIT 3-4

ASSET ALLOCATIONS OF MAJOR PENSION FUNDS AND ENDOWMENTS, 1992–1999

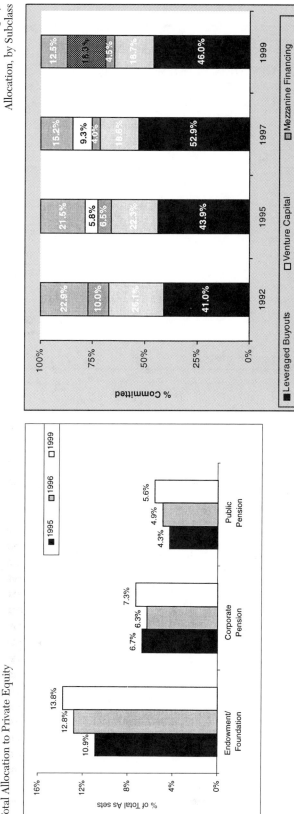

Total Allocation to Private Equity

Private Equity
Allocation, by Subclass

Source: Goldman, Sachs & Co. and Frank Russell Capital Inc., *1999 Report on Alternative Investments by Tax-Exempt Organizations,* November 1999.

EXHIBIT 3-5

YALE'S HISTORICAL RISK AND RETURN PROFILE

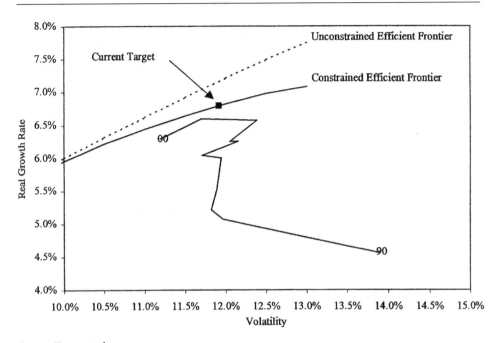

Source: University documents.

such endowments.[7] (The Endowment's performance during recent years is compared to that of other universities in Exhibit 3-6; a more detailed breakdown of Yale's returns by asset class is reported in Exhibit 3-7.) Yale's record placed it in the top 1% in SEI's rankings of large institutional investors.[8]

The primary reason for Yale's superior long-term performance record had been the excess returns generated by the portfolio's active managers. Manager selection accounted for more than half the superior performance by Yale relative to the average endowment over the last five years. As expected, the Endowment's excess returns had been greatest in the least efficient markets. Over the 10 years ending in June 2000, the differences between Yale's asset class returns and related benchmarks were 0.8% in the most efficiently priced asset class, bonds, and 20.8% in what is probably the least efficient market, private equity.

The Investments Office and the Investment Committee had been pleased with these results. As their experience with the distinctive approach grew, and they had become more confident of their ability to produce sustained above-average results, they had adjusted their spending policy upward. In 1992, in response to an Investments Office recommendation, the Yale Corporation adjusted the University's long-term spend-

---

[7] Had the Yale Endowment generated investment performance over the past 15 years at the equal-weighted average of all university endowments, the Endowment in June 2000 would have been $4.4 billion smaller.

[8] Corporate-defined plans with in excess of $100 million in assets.

EXHIBIT 3-6

RETURNS OF ALL UNIVERSITY ENDOWMENTS, YALE ENDOWMENT, AND BENCHMARK INDICES, FISCAL YEARS 1980–2000

	1980	1981	1982	1983	1984	1985	1986	1987	1988	1989	1990	1991	1992	1993	1994	1995	1996	1997	1998	1999	2000	Annualized 1980–2000 Return
Equal-weighted mean	12.6%	14.7%	−0.2%	40.9%	−2.5%	25.4%	26.3%	13.9%	1.4%	13.9%	10.0%	7.3%	13.3%	13.4%	2.9%	15.7%	17.3%	20.5%	18.0%	11.0%	17.8%	13.6%
Dollar-weighted mean	NA	NA	NA	46.0	−2.9	26.1	30.3	16.6	1.1	14.9	10.9	6.2	14.1	14.5	4.4	16.9	20.6	21.7	18.6	11.9	28.9	16.2
Equal-weighted mean, net of fees	NA	NA	NA	40.1	−2.9	25.1	26.3	13.7	1.4	13.9	9.7	7.2	13.3	13.2	2.7	15.6	17.2	20.6	17.8	11.1	NA	14.1
Yale	18.7	22.7	−4.3	50.1	−0.2	25.8	36.0	22.8	−0.2	17.3	13.1	2.0	13.2	17.3	12.0	15.7	25.7	21.8	18.0	12.2	41.0	17.4
S&P 500	17.0	20.4	−11.5	60.9	−4.8	30.7	35.6	25.1	−7.0	20.5	16.5	7.4	13.4	13.6	1.4	22.3	22.7	31.6	30.2	22.8	7.2	16.8
Wilshire 5000	19.2	25.2	−15.0	66.5	−8.7	31.2	35.3	20.1	−5.9	19.5	12.7	7.0	13.9	16.1	1.2	21.7	26.8	7.5	28.9	19.6	7.7	15.5
Long-term bond index	−1.4	−12.3	11.7	32.6	−5.6	40.7	36.4	0.4	5.8	18.2	4.6	9.0	17.0	20.9	−4.6	20.1	3.1	9.0	20.2	−0.2	7.1	10.3
Consumer price index	14.3	9.5	6.9	2.5	3.0	4.1	1.3	3.7	3.8	5.3	4.4	4.6	3.0	2.8	2.4	3.0	2.3	2.9	1.7	2.0	3.7	4.1

Fiscal years end on June 30th of each year.

The first two averages include endowments that report returns either net and gross of fees.

The third average includes only the subset of endowments that report returns net of fees.

No data on dollar-weighted mean or net-of-fee equal-weighted mean returns are available for 1980 through 1982 and 2000 (for net-of-fee returns only). Annualized returns are computed for shorter periods.

Yale's returns are reported net of fees.

Source: Compiled from Cambridge Associates, *1999 NACUBO Endowment Study*, Washington, DC, National Association of College and University Business Officers, 2000 (and earlier years), unpublished Cambridge Associates data, Datastream, and university documents.

EXHIBIT 3-7

RETURNS OF YALE ENDOWMENT, BY ASSET CLASS

Asset Class	Yale 2000 Return	Target Benchmark	Benchmark 2000 Return	Yale vs. Benchmark	Yale 3-Year Annualized	vs. Benchmark	Yale 10-Year Annualized	vs. Benchmark
Domestic equity	28.8	Wilshire 5000	9.5	19.3	20.5	1.5	18.6	1.3
Foreign equity	11.2	Foreign composite	14.9	–3.7	5.2	–1.4	8.6	2.1
Fixed income	4.7	LB government	5.0	–0.3	6.7	0.6	8.6	0.8
Real assets[a]	17.6	HEPI + 6%	9.9	7.7	19.1	5.8	12.6	6.8
Private equity	168.5	HEPI + 10%	14.0	154.5	67.8	53.9	34.5	20.8
Absolute return	15.8	HEPI + 8%	11.9	3.9	8.5	–3.4	11.8	0.1
Total Endowment	41.0	Composite benchmark	11.5	29.5	23.2	10.5	17.3	5.7

[a] This includes only real estate prior to June 30, 1999.

All returns are net of management fees.

Returns are for periods ending June 30, 2000.

The total benchmark return is calculated using Yale's target allocations.

Source: University documents.

ing target upward from 4½% to 4¾% of Endowment assets; and in 1995, it adjusted the rate upward again to 5%.[9] The University was thus benefiting from the strength of its investment program in two ways, both from a larger Endowment and from the justified increase in the target spending rate. The substantial Endowment also played a role in Yale receiving the highest rating to finance capital projects (AAA/Aaa) from the two leading bond rating agencies and in the University's ability to borrow money at extremely favorable interest rates.

THE MANAGEMENT OF MARKETABLE SECURITIES

The investment philosophy outlined above guided Yale's management decisions in all of its asset classes. For example, Swensen and Takahashi approached bonds with skepticism. They viewed the Endowment's current target allocation of 10% in bonds primarily as a disaster reserve, guarding against a severe drop in asset values and/or deflation (such as in the Great Depression). Yale held long-term U.S. government issues (almost exclusively): Swensen was skeptical whether returns from U.S. corporate bonds adequately compensated investors for the added default risk and the callability of corporate issues. He was quite skeptical of foreign fixed income securities as well. Unlike most of the rest of its portfolio, the Investments Office managed its bond portfolio internally. Swensen believed that the government bond market was so efficient, and the spread between the performance of government bond fund managers so small, that it did not make sense to hire an outside manager. The portfolio was managed with no attempt to add value through trading on interest rate movements. The Endowment staff attempted to generate incremental returns only through modest security selection bets, for example, by using mortgage-backed securities issued by the Government National Mortgage Association (GNMA), which were backed by the full faith and credit of the United States.

Yale also owned a substantial amount of U.S. common stocks, though the current target allocation, 15% of assets, was surprisingly small relative to almost all other large institutional investors. Although Yale had been an early adopter of indexing, as the Investments Office staff had become increasingly confident in their ability to find superior managers they eliminated the passive portfolio in favor of a small number of active equity managers. These managers shared several characteristics. First, the majority of Yale's active equity managers tended to emphasize disciplined approaches to investing that could be clearly articulated and differentiated from others. Swensen and Takahashi were convinced that disciplined fundamental-based approaches, when intelligently applied, could generate reliable and superior long-run performance. There were, in addition, several small stock-picking firms among Yale's managers, firms that specialized in a very particular industry or type of investing: for example, a technology specialist fund, one specializing in Canadian oil and gas firms, and another that only held financial stocks. Not surprisingly, none of Yale's managers tended to emphasize market timing, nor did they emphasize fuzzy or intuitive investment approaches that were difficult to articulate. These managers tended to be smaller independent organizations that were owned by their investment professionals. Other things being equal, Yale preferred

---

[9] The amount of the Endowment spent each year was based on a simple formula, namely, the spending rate (currently 5%) times an exponentially weighted average of the value of the Endowment in recent years, with a 30% weight being put on its current value and exponentially smaller weights on the (inflation-adjusted) values of the Endowment in previous years.

managers willing to "co-invest" or be compensated commensurate with their investment performance. Swensen and Takahashi worried that money managers working at many organizations tended to emphasize growth in assets at the expense of performance and that ownership by a large institution reduced organizational stability and dampened incentive to perform.

Foreign equities, another 10% of Endowment assets, were a valuable source of diversification, since their returns tended to be only partially correlated with those of the U.S. equity market. But Yale had encountered some real frustrations in transferring its model for successful domestic equity investing to foreign markets. First, the selection of appropriate active money managers had proven particularly challenging. The relatively slower development of institutional investing in many foreign countries meant there were fewer sophisticated "U.S.-style" money managers abroad, managers with credible audited investment performance records and specialized disciplined investment processes. Perhaps more critically, the best foreign fund managers appeared to work for larger organizations that were in turn owned by large financial institutions, which raised concerns among Swensen and Takahashi about misaligned incentives. Unlike the situation in the United States, there were very few independent investment advisors owned solely by their professionals. As a result of these problems, Yale had initially chosen two independent U.S.-based firms to manage foreign equity portfolios. The university had recently been successful, however, in identifying and hiring investment managers based in London, Singapore, and Hong Kong.

Senior Director Takahashi found the emerging equity markets of Asia, Latin America, and Eastern Europe particularly intriguing because of the widespread opportunities to find undervalued securities in these less efficient markets. At the end of 1999, roughly 26,000 companies were listed on emerging stock market exchanges, amounting to 53% of all listed companies in the world. While the market capitalization of these stocks represented 16% of the non-U.S. market capitalization, the economies of emerging markets amounted to more than 30% of non-U.S. GDP in dollar terms and roughly twice that amount when adjusted for purchasing power. In addition to attractive investment opportunities, emerging markets also provided portfolio diversification since their returns generally had low correlation with those of the United States. Furthermore, emerging markets were growing rapidly, at nearly twice the rate of developed countries. There were concerns, of course, including whether these growth prospects would translate into strong investment returns. Although the linkage between growth and profitability for the corporations of these countries was widely assumed, Takahashi was concerned that the link was by no means guaranteed. Nonetheless, he believed that the rapid rate of change in emerging markets provided opportunities for active management to earn superior returns.

Takahashi believed that Yale's foreign equity portfolio should be heavily weighted toward emerging markets, but he was concerned about the limited universe of acceptable managers conducting research-intensive, fundamentally based analysis. Many of the top, successful global emerging markets funds had grown to have many billions of dollars of assets under management, making it difficult to deploy assets in smaller, less well-followed corporations. On the other hand, small funds often lacked the resources to effectively research and cover the tremendous breadth of global emerging markets. Yale had six emerging markets managers in its portfolio. One was a large U.S.-based value manager who used a blend of judgmental and quantitative analysis to allocate between countries and choose stocks. One was a large, London-based global emerging markets manager who used bottom-up fundamental research to invest in a concentrated portfolio. Four were small, regionally focused managers—one investing in Africa, one in Eastern Europe, and two in Southeast Asia—concentrating on intensively researched value plays.

Yale's emerging market portfolio had generated an annualized 12.9% return since the program's inception in December 1990, 6.1% annually in excess of the International Finance Corporation (IFC) Global Emerging Index. Although Takahashi believed that such excess returns were not sustainable in the long run, he thought that emerging markets generally would continue to be less efficient and provide more opportunities for excess returns than developed markets. While the Investment Committee did not set a distinct target for emerging market equity holdings, it did so indirectly through the definition of a foreign equity benchmark. Currently, foreign equity returns were compared to a benchmark index that comprised one-half of the Morgan Stanley Capital International (MSCI) Europe, Australia, and Far East (EAFE) Index and one-half of the MSCI Emerging Markets Free Index. One issue for Yale was that managers other than those in the publicly traded foreign equity portfolio held positions in emerging market securities. For instance, some of Yale's absolute return managers and private equity funds held substantial positions in companies based in developing nations.

A final, more diffuse category of publicly traded investments was called "absolute return" strategies in which Yale currently allocated 22.5% of its assets. These included a variety of funds specializing in eclectic mixtures of strategies designed to exploit market inefficiencies. Yale divided these into three broad categories: event-driven, value-driven, and opportunistic-value investments. Event-driven strategies generally involved creating hedged positions in mispriced securities and were dependent on a specific corporate event, such as a merger or bankruptcy settlement, to achieve targeted returns. Value-driven strategies also entailed hedged investments in mispriced securities but relied on changing company fundamentals or increasing market awareness to drive prices toward fair value. Opportunistic-value investments were deep value plays with generally unhedgable market exposure. The common denominator of these strategies was that their returns were expected to be equity-like, yet not highly correlated with any particular financial market. It consequently made sense to evaluate their investment performance in terms of the absolute returns achieved rather than relative to any indices of market performance.

Yale's commitment to this asset class was tested in 1998, when many hedge funds suffered in the "flight to liquidity" that followed Russia's August 1998 default on its debt obligations. During this period, many expensive assets rose in price, and cheap assets became cheaper. Even though some of these pricing anomalies were likely to be short-lived—for example, Treasury bonds maturing in 29 years traded at a substantial discount to those maturing in 30 years—a number of investors panicked after the collapse of the Long-Term Capital Management fund and demanded the return of their capital. As a result, some funds were forced to liquidate positions at exceedingly unfavorable prices. While in most cases the university was insulated from the effects of other investors' sales because the fund managers had established separate accounts for Yale's investment, in others, Yale's funds were commingled with those of other investors. In these instances, Yale's returns had suffered: the ill-timed selling decisions depressed the returns of all investors. As a result of this experience, Yale redoubled its efforts to utilize separate accounts that insulated Yale's investments from the poorly timed acts of other investors. The University's use of its market power recalled steps that had been taken in the difficult fundraising environment that real estate funds faced after the early 1990s savings and loan crisis, when Yale obtained more attractive terms on its funds: for instance, insisting that its fund managers only share in the capital gains above a given rate-of-return (a "hurdle rate").

THE MANAGEMENT OF PRIVATE EQUITY

Domestic Venture Capital and Buyout Funds

While Yale had been among the first universities to invest in private equity, entering into its first buyout partnership in 1973 and its first venture capital partnership in 1976, the pace of investing had dramatically increased over time. Exhibit 3-8 summarizes the size of and returns from Yale's private equity portfolio.

Yale's private equity investment strategy was consistent with its overall investment philosophy. First, the Investments Office placed a premium on building long-term relationships with a limited number of premier organizations. Almost 80% of its portfolio was invested in multiple funds sponsored by this limited set of organizations. Yale's prestige, name, and long experience in private equity investing made it a very desirable client and allowed it to invest in some well-regarded funds that might otherwise have been closed.

Second, Yale emphasized private equity organizations that took a "value-added" approach to investing (the hallmark of the venture capital industry). It shied away from any funds that sought to generate the bulk of their returns from simply buying assets at attractive prices, refinancing them, and "flipping" them. Its philosophy was explicated in a discussion of buyout organizations:

> While financial skill is a vital component of LBO investing, we seek firms that build fundamentally better businesses. Financial engineering skill is a commodity, readily available and cheaply priced. Value-added operational experience, however, is rare.[10]

Yale believed that value-added investors could generate incremental returns independent of how the broader markets were performing. In addition, they might also find better deals at cheaper prices, deals away from the auction process that others did not see. For instance, Clayton & Dubilier (where Yale served as limited partner) had purchased Lexmark International from IBM and Allison Engine from General Motors after establishing close relationships with those corporations. As a general rule, however, Yale was willing to give considerable latitude to its firms to sensibly define the types of private equity deals that they wanted to do.

Another key principle was to select organizations where the incentives were properly aligned. For instance, Yale was reluctant to invest in private equity organizations affiliated with larger financial institutions. Such situations, the Investments Office believed, were fertile breeding grounds for conflicts of interest, or lack of incentives for the people actually doing the deals, or both. In addition, Yale preferred an overall structure for each of its funds such that the private equity firm could just cover its ongoing costs from the annual fees, earning essentially all of their economic returns from the "carry" tied directly to investment performance. This policy could at times be problematic: for instance, several of the most successful venture funds had dramatically increased their annual management fee income during the 1990s. Although Yale would have liked to insist that the bulk of the compensation be linked to investment performance, in many cases it had been unable to persuade the venture partners to change the proposed compensation scheme. Some of these venture organizations were sufficiently attractive that the Investments Office decided to participate in their funds anyway. In other cases, because of fundamental changes in the private equity firm's investment strategy or organizational structure, Yale declined to participate.

---

[10] David J. Swensen, Dean J. Takahashi, and Timothy R. Sullivan, "Private Equity—Portfolio Review," Memorandum to Investment Committee, September 29, 1994, p. 5.

EXHIBIT 3-8

RETURNS AND SIZE OF PRIVATE EQUITY INVESTMENTS OF YALE ENDOWMENT, 1978–2000

Fiscal Year	Venture	LBO	Int'l	Total	Portfolio Value	Endowment Value
1978	27.2%	35.3%	NA	33.9%	3.2	545
1979	−2.2	−3.0	NA	−2.8	3.4	578
1980	208.1	231.9	NA	225.5	8.4	669
1981	33.3	−16.6	NA	−0.5	15.6	793
1982	25.6	−47.5	NA	−2.2	19.3	741
1983	123.4	−10.1	NA	91.4	38.6	1,089
1984	3.7	41.6	NA	9.2	37.3	1,061
1985	−10.1	5.6	NA	−5.0	42.0	1,083
1986	2.6	34.0	NA	15.8	46.9	1,739
1987	25.4	23.9	NA	24.3	75.7	2,098
1988	−0.7	7.8	−1.9%	3.3	91.0	2,044
1989	−0.3	38.7	13.4	23.4	120.7	2,336
1990	15.6	7.8	−4.4	11.8	173.7	2,571
1991	11.6	14.7	−10.0	6.1	226.8	2,567
1992	28.3	7.2	4.1	14.6	294.2	2,833
1993	13.6	57.3	−0.2	32.3	464.9	3,219
1994	20.2	18.7	24.0	24.6	640.6	3,529
1995	37.8	26.3	13.1	27.0	684.1	3,390
1996	124.8	30.9	33.7	60.2	846.6	4,860
1997	35.1	22.3	90.2	36.2	1,125.6	5,790
1998	37.4	46.4	1.9	29.0	1,382.8	6,624
1999	132.2	24.8	−15.4	37.8	1,993.6	7,199
2000	444.2	35.1	38.3	168.5	2,513.7	10,085
Three-year	127.1	27.2	6.3	59.1		
Five-year	105.4	26.7	26.1	54.1		
Ten-year	47.9	26.3	20.3	37.9		
Since inception	36.4	32.6	16.7	34.1		
Venture Economics Benchmark Return	19.4	20.4	14.5			
2000 share in Yale Portfolio	38.4	52.4	9.2			

Returns are for year ending June 30th of each year. Value of private equity portfolio and Endowment are as of June 30th and are expressed in millions of dollars.

NA indicates that Yale had no investments in the asset class during that year or that the investments were not classified as private equity.

The Yale fiscal year returns are internal rates of return calculated on a daily basis. Multiyear returns are based on internal rates of return using quarterly data. The 444.2% venture return for fiscal 2000 is an exception and calculated using quarterly data. With daily data, the internal rate of return would be 701.0%. The market value of the venture capital portfolio was approximately $660 million at the beginning of fiscal 2000 and $1,160 at year-end. Net cash flow from the portfolio amounted to $1,200 million with a total return of $1,700 for the year. The large discrepancy in the internal rate of return calculations illustrates the problems that can occur using internal rate of return methodology when there are significant interim cash flows.

All real estate investments were classified in the real estate asset class (and not included in private equity) until 1996 and in the real asset class after 1999. In the interim, certain real estate funds with more "venture-like" characteristics were included in the private equity asset class (and not in the real estate asset class). Similarly, natural resource investments were transferred to the real asset class in 1999. Previously, they were included in the total return for private equity.

"Venture Economics Benchmark Return" is the pooled internal rate of return from inception until March 31, 2000 for all funds of each type in the Venture Economics database. The international compilation only includes European funds and is only through December 31, 1999.

"2000 Share in Yale Portfolio" refers to the share of Yale private equity portfolio devoted to this subclass on June 30, 2000.

Source: Compiled from Venture Economics, *VentureXpert Database,* http://www.ventureeconomics.com, and University documents.

When Yale's private equity portfolio was compared to other universities, three patterns stood out. First, it had considerably greater exposure to this area: Yale's current target allocation to private equity was 25%, considerably more than that of other schools (see Exhibits 3-2 and 3-3). Second, Yale had a larger fraction of its holdings concentrated in the funds of top-flight firms. A third difference related to the composition of the private equity investments. In general, many funds could be categorized as either buyout or venture capital funds, although the distinction between the two had become more and more blurred as buyout funds increasingly purchased technology firms and even invested in start-up firms. The mixture of most major universities' endowments was heavily weighted toward venture capital funds, with the average large endowment (dollar-weighted) holding nearly three-fifths of its investments in this asset class. In contrast, Yale had shifted over time: the proportion of the private equity portfolio in traditional venture capital had declined from 46% in June 1990 to 27% in June 1997 and then risen again to 38% in June 2000. These shifts were the result not of a changing policy objective, but of both factors within Yale's control—for example, "bottom-up" assessments of which individual funds offered the highest returns—and factors outside Yale's control—for example, draw-down schedules of private equity managers.

Swensen and Takahashi believed that Yale should remain committed to private equity for two reasons. First, from its inception in 1973 to June 2000, Yale's private equity portfolio had delivered an annual rate of return of over 34% (with a standard deviation of returns over the past 15 years of 40%). Second, over its nearly 25 years of investing, Yale had developed a deep understanding of the process and strong relationships with key managers, which served as an important competitive advantage. An important aspect of this advantage was the continuity of the team managing the private equity program. Swensen, Takahashi, and Director Timothy Sullivan had worked together on the portfolio for more than a decade.

But Yale faced some significant concerns if it were to further increase its allocation to private equity. First, fundraising by venture and buyout organizations had been soaring in recent years. (Exhibit 3-9 summarizes the inflow into private equity for 1980–2000.) This growth had been fueled by a renewed interest by pension funds and other institutional investors, following a period of few commitments in the early 1990s. Exhibit 3-10 indicates the changing mixture of the organizations investing in private equity since 1980.

These dynamics were all part of the continuing saga of U.S. private equity flows. Venture capital returns had been extremely attractive in the 1970s, often exceeding 25% per annum. This had attracted great interest from institutional investors, causing institutional flows into venture funds to peak in the early 1980s. Similarly, buyout funds produced handsome returns in the early 1980s, leading institutional investors to allocate large sums to LBO partnerships in the 1987–1988 period. Not surprisingly, the returns generated by the many private equity pools raised in these "peak periods" were poor. For instance, Venture Economics estimated that the average venture fund begun in 1982 had realized a return of under 2% through December 1998, and the average buyout fund begun in 1989 had realized a return of 11%.[11] Many institutions, frustrated with these poor returns, had cut back their commitments to private equity in the early 1990s.

The pendulum had begun to swing back again in the mid-1990s. With a soaring stock market and an active IPO window, the returns from private equity funds had again

---

[11] Venture Economics, *1999 Investment Benchmarks: Venture Capital* and *1999 Investment Benchmarks: Buyouts and Other Private Equity*, Boston, Venture Economics, 1999.

EXHIBIT 3-9

PRIVATE EQUITY FUNDRAISING, BY FUND TYPE, 1980–2000

	1980	1981	1982	1983	1984	1985	1986	1987	1988	1989	1990	1991	1992	1993	1994	1995	1996	1997	1998	1999	2000
Venture capital	0.6	0.9	1.3	2.6	3.4	2.1	2.1	3.7	3.1	3.3	1.9	1.4	2.6	2.9	4.2	4.7	6.6	6.1	19.0	35.6	25.2
Buyouts/Corporate finance	0.1	0.1	0.4	0.6	1.5	1.1	4.3	9.6	7.9	8.8	4.6	4.3	6.7	8.2	13.2	19.0	22.8	19.1	57.2	39.0	34.0
Mezzanine	0.0	0.1	0.0	0.8	0.2	0.8	2.4	4.1	1.7	2.6	1.2	1.7	0.8	0.5	1.2	2.4	1.4	2.7	2.8	4.3	3.0
Other	0.0	0.0	0.1	0.2	0.0	0.3	0.2	0.1	0.4	0.2	0.2	0.3	0.6	1.2	0.8	2.2	1.3	3.3	13.1	16.6	6.6
Total	0.7	1.1	1.8	4.2	5.1	4.3	9.0	17.5	13.1	14.9	7.9	7.7	10.7	12.8	19.4	28.3	32.1	31.2	91.1	95.5	68.8

All figures are in billions of dollars.

Other investments include funds-of-funds, secondary purchase funds, and venture leasing funds.

2000 through June only.

Source: Compiled from *The Private Equity Analyst* and the records of Asset Alternatives. I thank Steven Galante for his help.

EXHIBIT 3-10

PRIVATE EQUITY FUNDRAISING, BY INVESTOR TYPE, 1980–1999

	1980	1981	1982	1983	1984	1985	1986	1987	198	1989	1990	1991	1992	1993	1994	1995	1996	1997	1998	1999
Pension funds	29.8%	23.1%	33.3%	31.4%	34.1%	33.0%	50.1%	39.0%	45.9%	36.4%	52.5%	42.2%	47.8%	46.8%	49.1%	49.7%	45.4%	NA	NA	48.6%
Banking/insurance	13.3	15.2	14.0	12.0	13.2	10.9	10.4	15.0	9.4	12.6	9.2	5.4	16.4	15.9	17.0	17.8	19.5	NA	NA	13.5
Endowments/foundations	13.9	11.8	6.8	7.8	5.7	7.7	6.3	10.0	11.6	12.3	12.6	24.1	11.4	13.0	11.7	12.4	12.6	NA	NA	13.0
Individuals/families	15.4	23.1	20.3	20.9	14.7	13.0	11.8	12.0	8.4	6.1	11.4	12.3	10.4	7.1	10.3	8.4	7.5	NA	NA	4.9
Others	27.6	26.8	25.6	27.9	33.4	35.4	21.4	24.0	24.7	32.6	14.3	16.0	14.0	17.3	11.8	11.7	15.1	NA	NA	20.0

Prior to 1992, the tabulations include only investments in venture capital funds; thereafter, all private equity funds.

Others include corporations, foreign investors, and government bodies (excluding pension funds). Commitments by funds-of-funds are not included in the tabulations.

NA = not available.

Source: Compiled from *The Private Equity Analyst* and the records of Venture Economics. I thank Jesse Reyes and Anthony Romanello for their help.

become very attractive. Institutions had begun anew to invest substantial sums in new funds. Sensing a window of real opportunity, many private equity firms had been bringing new funds to the market, perhaps somewhat sooner and perhaps somewhat larger than otherwise might have been the case. Nowhere was the growth more dramatic than in the venture capital industry, where the fundraising in 1999 had exceeded the entire amount raised in the 1980s.

This surge in private equity investing raised several concerns. Some of these concerns were familiar from other "boom" periods in the private equity industry: for instance, the intense competition for transactions and the rising pressure on valuations. But there was also a new set of worries: that the unprecedented inflow of funds was fundamentally reshaping the private equity industry.

In particular, Yale was concerned that the attractive fundraising environment was leading firms to increase the size of the funds that they were raising, altering the incentive structures in an adverse manner. On the buyout side, multibillion dollar funds had become the norm. The Investments Office was concerned that these groups would pursue low-risk, low-return transactions in order to ensure their ability to raise a follow-on fund (with the substantial associated fees), rather than following innovative strategies that had the potential of generating higher returns. As Tim Sullivan noted, "many LBO firms appear to have explicitly lowered their return hurdles in order to compete for transactions, particularly at the larger end of the market, pricing deals to yield returns in the mid-to-high teens."[12] As a consequence, some of these large funds had experienced defections of key personnel who sought to begin new funds of their own. More generally, Yale noted with concern that a number of leading buyout groups were positioning themselves as "asset managers": for instance, raising absolute return, venture capital, mezzanine, and real estate funds in addition to their core buyout funds. Sullivan worried that such moves would profoundly affect the incentives of the private equity organizations. In the most extreme manifestation of this phenomenon, private equity groups such as Thomas H. Lee Co. and Warburg, Pincus had sold stakes in their firms to other asset managers. Yale feared that such transactions, though financially attractive to the private equity groups' founders, would lead to conflicts of interest between the private equity investment activity and the other asset management businesses.

On the venture capital side, the Investments Office was concerned about the plethora of venture organizations raising funds of $1 billion or more. While the Investments Office was aware that many venture investors were convinced that the "minimum efficient scale" of a venture capital organization had increased, they were again concerned about the incentive effects of the increase in fee income. Similarly, they reacted with concern to the tendency of even venture groups with little or no track record to demand 25% or more of the capital gains from their investments, rather than the 20% share that had long been standard for all but the most established groups. Meanwhile, some of the most attractive groups had cut the allocation of Yale and other institutional investors in favor of funds from wealthy technology entrepreneurs and the general partners themselves.

Even if the industry encountered difficulties in future years, Yale hoped that it could continue to realize attractive returns from this asset class, just as it had during the 1980s. First, the Investments Office noted, the deterioration of performance in the 1980s had been far from uniform across firms. While very poor returns characterized some new "spin-off" organizations as well as some established organizations that had grown in an

---

[12] David F. Swensen, Dean J. Takahashi, Timothy R. Sullivan, Alan S. Forman, and Seth D. Alexander, "Private Equity—Portfolio Review," October 7, 1999, p. 15.

undisciplined manner, many of the funds managed by top-tier private equity organizations had continued to generate superior returns. Because Yale had concentrated its portfolio in several of these funds, such as those organized by Bain Capital, Clayton, Dubilier, & Rice, Greylock, and Kleiner, Perkins, Caufield and Byers, the University believed its private equity managers would produce superior performance, even in a difficult environment for private equity.

Second, Yale had a considerable understanding of the private equity process, which allowed it to manage investments in sophisticated ways. One example of Yale's innovative management was the hedging of its positions. Yale carefully tracked the holdings of the private equity firms in which it invested.[13] When it believed that it had too large an exposure to any particular publicly traded firm, it sought to hedge that exposure through short sales and derivatives. Short sales and put options would generate offsetting profits if the share price declined. This effectively helped to reduce the danger of a severe drop in the public market wiping out the gains of a private equity investment. This hedging strategy had allowed Yale to receive a higher return from its investment in Snapple, which declined substantially between its peak 14 months after it was taken public and the liquidation of Thomas H. Lee Equity Partners' position.

Finally being in the private equity market at all times had important benefits. If Yale were to decide not to invest with a top-tier firm merely because the market was "overheated," it might not be able to persuade the organization to accept its money when later market conditions were more favorable. As Tim Sullivan concluded, if Yale were to alter its steady commitment to private equity and seek to time the market, top-tier firms "would not want Yale's unreliable money."[14]

At the same time, Yale realized that the current market conditions might have detrimental effects on private equity. As a consequence, Swensen, Takahashi, and Sullivan had altered their behavior in three ways. First, they examined new funds more skeptically than they might have at other times. Second, they sometimes opted not to push as hard for large allotments in established funds as they might have otherwise. Finally, Yale was increasingly making substantial investments as a lead investor in new buyout funds, which they hoped would become the brand-name funds of the future. At the same time, however, they realized that if Yale invested in too many small funds, the oversight of relationships with private equity groups could become unmanageable.

International Private Equity Funds

An area of continuing interest was international private equity. While Yale's initial strategy had been concentrated on the United Kingdom and France (at the end of 1995 nearly half its foreign investments had been based there), it had also explored developing markets. One noteworthy characteristic was Yale's avoidance of the developing countries of Asia, which represented the largest single share[15] of many large institutions' international private equity portfolios during much of the 1990s.

[13] Private equity organizations typically do not sell the shares of firms in their portfolios at the time they go public. They generally promise the underwriter to continue to hold them for a period of months (often termed the "lock-up" period). Many will continue to hold shares after the lock-up period expires, if they believe the shares will appreciate further.

[14] David F. Swensen, Dean J. Takahashi, and Timothy R. Sullivan, "Private Equity—Venture Capital Strategy," Memorandum to the Investment Committee, March 4, 1992, p. 7.

[15] For instance, Asia represented 35% of all non-U.S. private equity commitments by major institutional investors in 1995. In light of disappointing returns, this share had fallen to 15% by 1999. Goldman, Sachs & Co. and Frank Russell Capital, Inc., *1999 Report on Alternative Investing by Tax-Exempt Organizations,* November 1999.

The Investments Office's move into international private equity had been the consequence of a cautious planning process. As the U.S. market became increasingly competitive, Yale paid more attention to overseas markets where far fewer funds were competing for deals, suggesting the possibility of more attractive valuations. Although many other institutional investors saw international private equity as especially promising,[16] Yale eschewed the typical strategy of investing in large funds devoted to buyouts in Europe and Asia. This reflected several considerations. First, many of the leading foreign private equity investors were subsidiaries or affiliates of large financial institutions. As discussed above, Tim Sullivan was concerned that such situations were rife with compensation and conflict-of-interest problems. Second, the Investments Office often found it quite difficult to evaluate foreign private equity organizations. In most countries, Yale lacked the strong network of relationships that it could rely upon in the United States to assess the quality of potential new partners. A possible alternative was to invest in a number of the new very large "global private equity" funds that were being sponsored by established and well-regarded U.S. firms. Sullivan liked some of these firms and approved of their incentive structures, but he was a little troubled by the U.S. firms' obvious lack of experience and track records in these very different foreign markets. The managers of these global funds suggested that they could and should become the analog of how Yale had managed similar problems in publicly traded equity, namely, by using U.S. firms, but Sullivan was unconvinced.

At the same time, international private equity investing carried real risks, as Yale's experience in Russia illustrated. Yale had made a small initial investment in a Russian "quasi-private equity" fund, which took stakes in both large publicly traded corporations and smaller private firms. As the fund family enjoyed spectacular successes in the mid-1990s, Yale took a significant amount of money off the table but reinvested a considerable share of its gains. This fund family experienced sharply negative returns after the Russian debt crisis of 1998. Overall, the Russian investment yielded Yale an annualized return in the mid-20% range—but in a strikingly uneven manner that was not for the faint of heart!

Private equity funds were also being raised to invest in Latin America and in Southeast and Southern Asia. Yale had been able to identify a number of these emerging market funds that were managed by general partners which seemed attractive by normal standards: small entrepreneurial firms, with operational experience on the ground in these emerging markets, some co-investment and/or incentive fees, and an apparently keen sense of where upside opportunities might lie. It was tempting to participate in some of these funds, as a very long-term contrarian bet if nothing else. But the problems of evaluating and selecting managers were challenging here, perhaps more severe than in almost any other asset class.

THE MANAGEMENT OF REAL ASSETS

Another important class was real assets, which included real estate, oil and gas, and timberland investments. The Investments Office believed that properly managed real estate provided an interesting set of investment opportunities. The returns from real property tended to be uncorrelated with those from marketable common stock, and, in the long run, real property might produce returns protected from inflation. Most importantly, however, real estate was a quite inefficient, cyclical market in which Yale might

---

[16] The Goldman–Russell survey suggested that nearly one-half of large institutional investors saw international private equity as the most attractive subclass of private equity.

well be able to generate very attractive returns if it could find the right managers with the right strategies and the right incentive structures. As in other asset classes, Yale concentrated on pure equity investments, avoiding mortgages and other debt. The Investments Office avoided managers who were just financial advisors who might buy existing buildings with stable rent rolls and apply a little financial engineering. Instead, it sought to establish relationships with real estate operators who had a competitive advantage, either by property type or market, and preferably a focus on an out-of-favor sector.

Historically, Yale's real estate portfolio had consisted primarily of a single Manhattan office building at 717 Fifth Avenue, a direct investment that had been singled out and recommended by a group of alumni in the 1970s. The property, which was located at the corner of 56th Street and for many years had featured the Steuben Glass showroom, performed very well. Yale paid $14 million for a 50% interest in 1978 and $47 million for the remaining 50% in 1994. As of June 30, 2000 the building was valued at $215 million.

In spite of the strong performance, the challenges in managing 717 Fifth Avenue ultimately reinforced Yale's strong preference for external management of Endowment assets. When Steuben Glass announced its intention to vacate its Fifth Avenue retail space to move to a Madison Avenue location, Yale Real Estate Director Alan Forman quickly discovered at first-hand the near impossibility of engaging an agent with an owner's mentality. He subsequently devoted a significant amount of his time to finding suitable replacement tenants—Hugo Boss and Escada—and supervising a major construction project to accommodate their needs.

During the late 1980s, Yale had been substantially underweighted in real estate because it could not identify enough attractive investment opportunities in the market during that period. But beginning around 1990, Yale came to believe that the decline in asset values associated with the savings and loan crisis had created a compelling opportunity. Accordingly, the Investments Office began increasing its real estate investments.

Many institutional investors, having been severely burned, were still wary, if not totally dismissive, of this asset class. Yale's strategy was to focus on deliberately contrarian segments of the real estate market where most other investors feared to tread. They sought out partners who targeted distressed sellers and who possessed the operating expertise to implement value-added strategies that could realize substantial returns over the medium term. For example, Yale engaged managers to buy: downtown and suburban office buildings from insurance companies facing financial pressures or banks that had foreclosed; close-in developable land, a highly illiquid property type, especially in a capital-constrained environment; or strip shopping centers that needed a reconfiguration or a redirected marketing effort.

Perhaps predictably, however, the managers had encountered some interesting challenges in implementing this real estate strategy. First, Yale felt that the institutional real estate industry was dominated by firms that were compensated through transaction fees or fees based on assets under management rather than through sharing in the profits generated for their investors. These firms thus had every incentive to keep their investors' capital tied up over long periods of time, leading to asset accumulation and retention rather than generation of superior investment returns. (During the early 1980s, the Endowment had invested a small amount of money in a number of pools managed by well-known real estate advisors, many of which had performed rather poorly.) Because of these factors, Yale had decided not to deal with the established group of institutional real estate advisors. Luckily, the collapse of the real estate market had provided the Investments Office with an opportunity to find some new firms that might be hungry for funds and might consequently be willing to accept new kinds of incentive structures. From Yale's perspective, the Investments Office wanted to borrow ideas from, and improve upon, the incentive structures typical in private equity funds. In particular, they wanted all the real estate principals' activities to be focused on one pool at a time, they wanted the principals to make a significant cash investment in the pool (sometimes called co-investment), they preferred an intermediate term strategy for the pool (after which they might or might not invest in a later pool), and they wanted most of the principals' compensation to come at the end of the fund and to be linked to investors' returns.

Over time, working their networks, the Investments Office staff had been able to find a number of independent firms with excellent real estate operating skills, which were eager to forge this kind of relationship. But most of these firms were not well known, even by knowledgeable real estate investors. Unlike the case in private equity, where Yale participated in funds considered to be the premier institutional funds, few people knew or even recognized the names of most of their real estate funds. Yale was often the lead investor in these funds, with a sizable percentage of the limited partnership interest. Although it had proven difficult to expand the size of the total real estate portfolio very quickly this way, they had gradually built a portfolio. While it would have been much easier, of course, to use some of the larger, better-known institutional real estate advisors to expand the real estate portfolio quickly, this would surely have meant compromising on Yale's desired strategy and incentive structures—compromises with which the Investments Office was not comfortable.

The other side of the real assets portfolio was the oil-and-gas and timberland partnerships. In some ways, this market remained an attractive one. A substantial supply of energy properties had been on the market in the recent past, as major oil companies downsized and smaller firms consolidated. Although some independent firms had been able to raise capital from the public marketplace, the supply of institutional money for such properties remained relatively limited. Timberland was in an even earlier stage of development, having been added to the portfolios of relatively few institutional investors. Large corporate forest product companies were under considerable pressure to sell forestland to enhance shareholder value.

It was difficult, however, to find well-designed oil-and-gas partnerships led by attractive managers. Much of the partnership-raising business appeared to be in the hands of agents, who were compensated primarily on the basis of arranging deals. In addition, quite a few operators seemed to get rich, even if their clients did not. Furthermore, assessing the skills of the general partners in these funds was often difficult. In many cases, individuals raised funds on the basis of their participation in earlier successful partnerships. But it was generally very difficult for the Investments Office to determine which partner had been responsible for a key discovery or production success.[17] Yale's general impression was that investment opportunities and partnerships with sterling track records, unblemished reputations, and proper deal structures were quite uncommon in the oil-and-gas industry.

As a result, Yale's investments in oil-and-gas tended to emphasize two different investment models. The first focused on partnerships in the business of acquiring existing oil fields and enhancing their operations. In contrast to the high-risk world of ex-

---

[17] This was in contrast to venture or buyout investing, where individual partners' successes and failures could be more or less assessed by examining who represented the partnership as a director on various firms' boards.

ploration, it was somewhat easier to assess performance and responsibility here. Furthermore, the long-term assets provided relatively predictable income and protection from energy-related inflation. The other approach applied a private equity investment model whereby Yale invested in partnerships pursuing equity investments in oil-and-gas and energy service companies. Yale's deliberations were complicated by a recent run-up in oil prices, which had risen 2.5 times from the price level seen as recently as February 1999. Although generally wary of making macro calls, the Investments Office staff knew that attractive oil and gas investments were far more likely to be made in a low-price environment.

Forestland also appeared to be an attractive area for future exploration. Yale had recently invested in two partnerships that focused on sustainable harvesting of naturally regenerative forestland in the United States. Swensen and Takahashi believed that the conventional assessment of natural resource funds did not fully capture the fact that they offered a steady steam of payments in addition to an upside "value-added" exposure, making such investments far more attractive than commodity indices. Recent timberland investments were acquired at substantial discounts to the standing value of the timber and offered projected high single-digit returns assuming that prices remained stable. This appeared to be a ripe area for further expansion in the years to come; however, the opportunity to acquire attractive priced timberland might be fleeting.

By mid-2000, the Endowment had 14.9% of its assets invested in real assets, well below its target allocation of 17.5%. The Investments Office anticipated that the real estate allocation would decline substantially over the next few years after the expected sale of 717 Fifth Avenue. On the one hand, they were pleased because performance had been strong, outpacing substantially the NCREIF Property Index (NPI). Moreover, they were delighted that the incentive structures put in place with their real estate managers a few years earlier were providing a powerful motivation to maximize returns through property sales.

They worried, however, that the decrease in real estate exposure might not serve the needs of the Endowment as a whole. Swensen had gained comfort from Yale's substantial real estate allocation, which might provide protection in the event of a significant downturn in the U.S. stock market. Moreover, 10-year performance of 11.9% indicated that despite the tough times experienced in the early 1990s, Yale's allocation to real estate had served the Endowment well over a long period of time. Swensen and his staff wondered whether they should allow the real estate allocation to drop or whether they should aggressively continue to seek out new opportunities, despite the currently thin real estate market.

FUTURE DIRECTIONS

In July 2000, Swensen and Takahashi believed that they probably wanted to continue with a heavy weighting in what they viewed as less efficient markets. In particular, they wanted to reach the target allocation in real assets. On the other hand, were private investments, which had been so important in contributing to Yale's superior returns over the years, still attractive in a market flooded with capital? How should Yale allocate its new commitments in this overheated environment? In particular, how should the new investments be allocated across venture, buyout, international, real estate, and natural resource funds? What should be the mix between new groups and established organizations? Should Yale expand its international program to include a greater emphasis on Asia and continental Europe?

Looking beyond the short run, Swensen and Takahashi wondered about the risks and challenges that the coming years would pose to the Yale Endowment. Over the past few years, the fraction of traditional publicly traded securities in Yale's Endowment fell below 40% for the first time. This seemed like an important transition. Just how far could such securities—and fixed income in particular—be reduced? At some point, should they begin to worry seriously about issues of decreasing portfolio liquidity and the increasing difficulty in determining precise valuations for the Endowment?[18] Similarly, should they worry about the implications of this evolution for staffing? Should they worry about the fact that an increasing fraction of the portfolio did not really have meaningful benchmarks against which they could reliably measure their managers, themselves, and the success of their strategies? The feedback in these asset classes came only in the very long term, perhaps too long for the decision horizons of most individuals. In the long run, how should they think about the issues of risk? Would it really be true that private markets offered greater returns? In the long run, would it be viable for Yale to adopt an asset allocation that was considerably different from that of its closest peers, such as Harvard, Princeton, and Stanford? More generally, could these few endowments as a group persist with asset allocations that were very different from those of almost every other institutional investor?

---

[18] For example, in terms of the valuation estimates used in the spending rule, which had originally assumed that market prices would be available to value the assets.

4

Acme Investment Trust

In early 1994, officials at Acme Investment Trust were considering investments in the sixth partnership organized by E.M. Warburg, Pincus & Co. The Trust, the employee pension fund of Acme Corporation, a major manufacturer, had recently raised the private equity allocation of its $10 billion pension fund from 3% to 6%.

Warburg intended to raise a $2 billion "mega-fund." This fund, about 15% larger than the organization's 1989 fund (in which Acme had also invested), would be one of the largest funds ever raised by a private equity organization. What concerned Acme's managers the most was not the size of the fund, but the way in which their profits would be split.

Warburg, Pincus proposed that investors would receive 85% of the profits from the fund, with the remaining 15% going to the firm's partners. This differed from the 80%–20% split standard within the industry: a division that the *Private Equity Analyst* termed "sacrosanct."[1] Warburg, Pincus also proposed to raise its annual management fee from 1% of capital, as in its previous fund, to 1.5%. Interpretations of these proposed terms differed. While the *New York Times* termed it a "fat discount to investors,"[2] other observers argued that it was an appropriate response to the changing mixture of Warburg, Pincus's investments. Others wondered how this move would affect the compensation terms in less established venture and buyout partnerships.

E.M. WARBURG, PINCUS & CO.[3]

E.M. Warburg & Co. was established in New York in 1938 by Eric Warburg. Warburg was a member of one of the most illustrious German Jewish families, which had played an integral role in Germany's financial life for several centuries. Eric's father, Max, had

Professor Josh Lerner prepared this case as the basis for class discussion rather than to illustrate either effective or ineffective handling of an administrative situation.

[1] Steven Galante, "Warburg Points the Way to a Lower Carry," *Private Equity Analyst* 4 (July 1994): 7.

[2] Barry Rehfeld, "Even in Hard Times, He's Still the Top Player in Town," *New York Times*, October 23, 1994, 3:9.

[3] This section is based on Ron Chernow, *The Warburgs*, New York, Vintage Books, 1993; "The Mantle of Warburg," *Forbes*, August 12, 1985, 61; Udayan Gupta, "Megafund Chief Pincus Speaks Softly, Carries a $1.17 Billion Venture Stake," *Wall Street Journal*, March 9, 1987, 1:15; and Rehfeld, *op. cit.*

been an advisor to Kaiser Wilhelm, a participant in the Versailles Peace Conference at the end of World War I, and the head of the powerful Hamburg bank, M.M. Warburg & Co. Nonetheless, the Warburg family was forced to flee Germany in 1938 in the face of Nazi persecution.

E.M. Warburg & Co. had initially focused on providing investment services to its German-American clientele. After Eric Warburg returned from service as an intelligence officer in the Army Air Force during World War II, the firm expanded into investment banking activities, participating in underwriting syndicates. Its prominence in the postwar years, however, was eclipsed by that achieved by S.G. Warburg & Co., the London bank founded by Eric's cousin Siegmund.

In 1956, Eric Warburg returned to Germany to reclaim the management of M.M. Warburg & Co. from his father's partners. In the ensuing years, as Eric devoted most of his attention to German affairs, E.M. Warburg & Co. found it difficult to broaden its base of clients and its investment banking activities. In 1966, these concerns led Eric Warburg to sell a half-interest in the New York firm to 34-year-old Lionel Pincus.

Pincus, the grandson of Polish and Russian immigrants, had received an M.B.A. from Columbia University. Instead of entering his family's Philadelphia apparel retailing and real estate business, he had joined the small investment bank Ladenburg, Thalmann & Co. Much of his activity there involved investing wealthy families' money—typically about $1 million in each deal—in small private firms. At age 29, Pincus was made partner and head of the bank's corporate finance activities. In 1964, he left Ladenburg to found Lionel I. Pincus & Co.

Pincus's experiences persuaded him of the opportunities presented by investing in private firms. At the same time, he realized that far greater returns could be realized if the activity was pursued in a more systematic and professional manner. Shortly after joining E.M. Warburg, he recruited John Vogelstein from Lazard Freres, who shared this vision.

These two men—in conjunction with a team of long-standing managing directors—developed a distinctive approach to private equity investing, which they termed "venture banking." The firm made a diverse array of investments, including traditional start-ups, leveraged buyouts, and purchases of major blocks in publicly traded firms. While the firm initially invested only its own money, in 1971 it raised its first formal fund. Like other private equity firms, Warburg organized this and subsequent funds as limited partnerships with a life span of approximately 10 years. (Warburg's funds are summarized in Exhibit 4-1.) The firm served as the general partner of each fund, and the various

---

EXHIBIT 4-1

FUNDS RAISED BY WARBURG, PINCUS & CO.

	Year	Fund Size ($ millions)
EMW Ventures	1971	28
Warburg, Pincus Associates	1980	100
Warburg, Pincus Capital Partners	1983	341
Warburg, Pincus Capital Company	1986	1,175
Warburg, Pincus Investors	1989	1,780

Source: Compiled from public reports.

investors served as limited partners. At about the same time, the firm assumed its current name.

Investors in the five Warburg funds had enjoyed substantial success over the years, earning an average annual return between 1971 and 1990 of over 25%. This was substantially better than the returns of private equity as a whole, summarized in Exhibit 4-2. The funds had enjoyed very attractive returns from quite different classes of investments. These included buyouts, including Mattel, investments to finance industry consolidations (e.g., Waste Management), and start-ups such as U.S. Health Care Systems. (Major investments that had led to initial public offerings by the end of 1992 are summarized in Exhibit 4-3.)

Several distinct themes characterized Warburg, Pincus's approach over these years. The first was a willingness to go against the trends in the industry. During the mid-1980s, for instance, the firm had shunned the computer hardware and software investments then in favor at many venture organizations, focusing instead on buyouts and health care. During the 1990s, when many private equity organizations marketed themselves as having a distinctive specialty, Warburg, Pincus retained its eclectic approach. Second, the firm had been willing to build a core group of managers. Although many venture and buyout funds were run with very lean staffs, Warburg, Pincus had 28 managing directors by 1994, many of whom had been with the firm for a decade or longer. Third, the firm had been aggressive in raising capital. The 1980 and 1989 funds had been the largest ever raised to that date by private equity organizations. The firm had

---

EXHIBIT 4-2

RETURNS OF PRIVATE EQUITY ORGANIZATIONS, AS COMPILED BY VENTURE ECONOMICS. THE TABLE INDICATES THE AVERAGE AND MEDIAN RETURN FOR PRIVATE EQUITY FUNDS BEGUN IN VARIOUS YEARS THROUGH THE END OF 1993.

	Return Through 12/31/93	
Year Fund Began	Mean	Median
1969–1975	23.4	20.6
1976–1979	30.6	24.2
1980	17.4	13.6
1981	6.8	5.0
1982	2.9	2.2
1983	5.5	5.5
1984	4.7	5.1
1985	7.7	9.9
1986	6.6	6.6
1987	5.2	6.2
1988	10.7	8.4
1989	7.4	5.1
1990	3.4	2.1

Source: Compiled from Venture Economics, 1995 *Investment Benchmark Report*, Boston, Venture Economics, 1995.

EXHIBIT 4-3

MAJOR INVESTMENTS BY WARBURG, PINCUS & CO. IN PRIVATE FIRMS THAT WENT PUBLIC BETWEEN 1976 AND 1992

Company	Market Value at Time of IPO ($ millions)	IPO Underwriter[a]	Offering Date	Size of Offering ($ millions)
ADVO-SYSTEMS	N/A	None	9/15/86	N/A
AGRIDYNE TECHNOLOGIES	64.9	Piper, Jaffray & Hopwood	2/14/92	17.5
AI CORP	73.0	Alex. Brown & Sons	6/25/90	21.4
ALLIED CLINICAL LABORATORIES	87.1	Alex. Brown & Sons	7/31/90	22.1
ALLSTAR INNS	145.4	Drexel Burnham Lambert	3/27/87	72.9
ALTA HEALTH STRATEGIES	78.6	Alex. Brown & Sons	1/22/91	14.3
BABBAGE'S	65.3	Alex. Brown & Sons	7/14/88	19.5
BRIDGE COMMUNICATIONS	96.7	Morgan Stanley	4/18/85	24.0
CAMBRIDGE NEUROSCIENCE	82.8	Montgomery Securities	6/06/91	18.0
CENTRA FARM GROUP NV	30.5	L.F. Rothschild Unterberg	1/14/85	6.8
CERTIFIED COLLATERAL	18.3	Blunt	12/08/83	4.0
CHIPSOFT	177.4	Robertson, Stephens & Co.	4/03/92	41.2
FOUR-PHASE SYSTEMS	24.6	Lehman Brothers	6/08/76	14.4
GARTNER GROUP	33.7	Shearson Lehman Brothers	7/17/86	11.6
KOLFF MEDICAL	84.9	L.F. Rothschild Unterberg	7/15/83	18.8
MARINE DRILLING CO.	77.8	Dillon, Read	7/28/89	29.8
STARTEL	19.5	Rooney	11/22/83	4.5
SYNERGEN	86.2	Alex. Brown & Sons	3/07/86	17.6
US HEALTHCARE SYSTEMS	71.3	Merrill Lynch	2/09/83	20.0
VALUE HEALTH	146.3	Alex. Brown & Sons	4/04/91	36.0
VESTAR	42.6	Alex. Brown & Sons	11/05/86	10.6
ZILOG	98.3	Alex. Brown & Sons	2/27/91	22.0

[a] If there were multiple underwriters co-managing the offer, the table reports the one responsible for managing the order book.

Source: Compiled from initial public offering prospectuses.

successfully attracted investments from some of the most sophisticated investors, including pension funds of AT&T, General Electric, IBM, and New York State, as well as the Harvard University Endowment.

By early 1994, the firm had nearly entirely invested its 1989 fund. Its decision to raise a sixth fund had been widely anticipated. It was the proposed terms of the contract that would govern the fund (outlined in the private placement memorandum) that generated widespread discussion within the Acme pension and elsewhere.

Compensation in Private Equity Partnerships[4]

Private equity investors are typically compensated in two ways: a share of the profits and annual fee. These two elements, however, display many variations. For instance, the way in which the fee is calculated and the timing of the profit-sharing often varies tremendously.

The percentage of profits retained by the private equity investors is known as the carried interest. This share, as noted above, is typically about 20%. Exhibit 4-4 presents the percentage of capital gains retained after any provision for the return of invested capital,

---

[4] This section and Exhibits 4-4 through 4-7 are based on Paul Gompers and Josh Lerner, "An Analysis of Compensation in the U.S. Venture Capital Partnership," *Journal of Financial Economics* 51 (1999): 3–44.

EXHIBIT 4-4

THE SHARE OF PROFITS RETAINED BY PRIVATE EQUITY ORGANIZATIONS. THE FIGURE INDICATES THE CARRIED INTEREST (THE SHARE OF CAPITAL GAINS RETAINED BY THE ORGANIZATION AFTER ANY INITIAL RETURN OF INVESTMENT TO THE LIMITED PARTNERS).

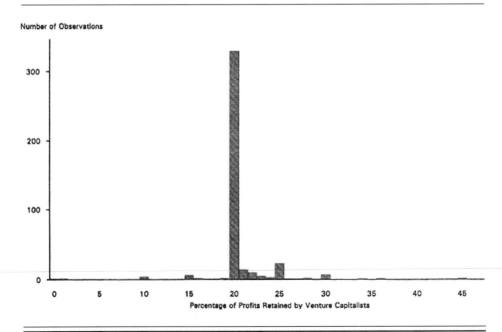

Number of Observations

Percentage of Profits Retained by Venture Capitalists

EXHIBIT 4-5

THE SHARE OF PROFITS RETAINED BY PRIVATE EQUITY ORGANIZATIONS. THE AVERAGE SHARE OF CAPITAL GAINS RETAINED BY THE ORGANIZATION AFTER ANY INITIAL RETURN OF THE ORIGINAL INVESTMENT TO THE LIMITED PARTNERS IS INDICATED. THE SECOND PANEL INDICATES THE CORRELATION COEFFICIENT BETWEEN THE PERCENTAGE AND THE OTHER VARIABLES.

Panel A: Percentage of Profits

	Average	No. of Observations
Date Fund Established		
January 1978–December 1984	20.5	100
January 1985–June 1986	20.9	111
June 1986–December 1988	20.7	120
January 1989–December 1992	20.9	85
Size of Private Equity Organization		
No earlier funds or cannot determine	20.4	170
Between 0.0% and 0.2%	20.9	83
Between 0.2% and 0.7%	20.5	87
Greater than 0.7%	21.6	76
Age of Private Equity Organization		
No earlier funds	20.5	146
Four years or less	20.7	87
Between four and eight years	20.6	93
More than eight years	21.4	90
Objective of Fund		
Focus on high-technology firms	21.2	198
Other industry focus (or no focus)	20.3	218
Focus on early-stage investments	21.1	172
Other stage focus (or no focus)	20.5	244

Panel B: Correlation Coefficients

Variables	Correlation
Date of closing and percentage of profits	0.027
Size of organization and percentage of profits	0.109
Age of organization and percentage of profits	0.104

---

or invested capital plus a premium, for 441 funds established between 1978 and 1993 to make venture or both venture and buyout investments. The carried interest varied from 1.01% to 45%, but the value in 81% of the funds was between 20% and 21%.

Exhibit 4-5 shows how the average carried interest varied over this period. Funds are divided by their date of formation, as well as by two measures of the experience of the private equity organization. The first measures the relative size of the organization's previous funds (their "market share").[5] The second is the time from the establishment

---

[5] The invested capital in all of the organization's funds established in the 10 years previous to the year that this fund closed is totaled. This sum is divided by the total amount raised by independent venture organizations in this period.

of the organization's first partnership to this fund. Older and larger private equity organizations command a slightly larger carried interest, with about a 1% higher share than the less experienced funds.

The second element of compensation is management fees. These fees are typically paid quarterly and finance day-to-day operations. In many funds, the fees change over time. For instance, the fees will often be reduced in later years, reflecting the expectation that the partnership's costs will be lower during the "harvesting period." The fees may also contain provisions for inflation adjustments. As Exhibit 4-6 indicates, the base used to calculate the fee varies. Although most agreements compute the annual fee as a percentage of invested capital, in some cases the value of the partnership's assets is used. Funds that use asset value as the base often will also limit the maximum and/or minimum fee. A number of firms charge fees not only on the funds raised by the partnership, but also on the indebtedness of the companies in which they invest. This fee structure was commonplace during the 1960s, when Small Business Investment Companies (many of which were affiliates of commercial banks) made equity investments in firms and arranged their credit lines.

Exhibit 4-6 also summarizes the level of the fees in the partnerships' fourth year. (As noted above, in some cases the fee will be based on different measures.) The typical fee is 2.5% of fees under management. The table also shows the level of fees for the 15 largest partnerships. Here the percentages are lower, with an average and median fee of about 2.0%.

EXHIBIT 4-6

SUMMARY OF HOW THE ANNUAL MANAGEMENT FEE IS DETERMINED AND THE DISTRIBUTION OF FEE PERCENTAGES, FOR ALL FUNDS AND THE 15 LARGEST FUNDS

Panel A: How Management Fee Is Determined

Percent of capital under management	69.7%
Percent of capital under management, less cost basis of distributions and write-offs	1.3
Percent of net asset value	11.6
Percent of net asset value, but subject to a minimum and/or maximum	7.6
Percent of sometimes capital under management; sometimes capital less distributions	1.9
Percent of sometimes capital under management; sometimes, net asset value	4.6
Percent of debt of portfolio companies, as well as capital or asset value	2.2
Negotiated annually	1.0

Panel B: Fee Percentage

	All Funds	15 Largest
3.5% or higher	4.3%	0.0%
3% to 3.49%	10.1	6.7
2.5% to 2.99%	63.0	13.3
2% to 2.49%	16.2	46.7
1.5% to 1.99%	4.3	20.0
1.49% or lower	2.1	13.3

Fees based on net asset value have virtually disappeared in recent years. While 21% of funds formed between 1978 and 1983 had fees based on asset value, this fell to 2% in the period between 1990 and 1993. Some practitioners attribute this decline to opportunistic behavior on the part of private equity partnerships. As investment manager Harold Bigler relates:

> In the 1970s specific partnerships were referred to as a "West Coast Deal" or an "East Coast Deal." The East Coast deal had its fee generally based on committed capital. . . . The West Coast partnerships had a tradition of management fees related to assets. The general [partner] participated in appreciation both through the management fee and the carried interest, thus having the element of "double-dipping."[6]

More specifically, accounts by Venture Economics[7] suggest that asset value-based fees led private equity partnerships to be very aggressive in valuing firms and to delay exiting investments.

There are also many differences in the timing of compensation. Exhibit 4-7 provides an overview of the restrictions on the receipt of capital gains by general partners. Over 90% of the funds contain some provision that ensures that the private equity investors do not unconditionally receive distributions. This table does not include the exceptions that allow small payments to cover tax obligations.

Most restrictions are of two types. The standard partnership agreement of the 1960s and 1970s called for the private equity investors to receive distributions only after their limited partners had received their invested capital back. Any subsequent distributions were then split according to the carried interest. This arrangement, however, was perceived to have a negative effect on the choice of securities distributed.[8] This is because private equity investors frequently distribute securities of firms that they have taken public, rather than selling the shares and distributing cash.[9] Before the committed capital had been returned, some private equity investors were perceived to distribute overvalued securities. Undervalued securities were retained until after committed capital was returned and the investor was eligible to receive distributions.

During the 1980s, a new contractual form appeared, which allowed private equity investors to receive capital gains as long as the value of the portfolio exceeded 100%, 125%, or some other multiple of the invested capital. (The multiple is referred to as hurdle rate.) Under these arrangements, the cost basis of each investment was first returned to the limited partners. The remainder—the capital gain on this particular investment—was then divided between the limited and general partners according to the agreed-upon formula. Consider the distribution of 1,000 shares of a company that the private equity investors had purchased for $2/share and currently trading at $12/share, under a contract where the proceeds were divided 80%–20%. The limited

[6] Harold E. Bigler, "Am I Really So Bad?: A 'Gatekeeper' Replies to a Recent Challenge," *Venture Capital Journal* 31 (February 1991): 22–39.

[7] See, for example, Venture Economics, "Venture Partnership—Conventions and Customs," *Venture Capital Journal* 20 (July 1980): 9–11.

[8] Venture Economics, *Venture Capital Performance–1989*, Needham, MA, Venture Economics, 1989.

[9] Private equity investors have at least two reasons for distributing securities rather than cash. First, the limited partners usually include both tax-paying and tax-exempt investors, who may have different preferences concerning the timing of security sales. Second, distributions of securities are valued (both in the partnerships' internal accounting and in the records of gatekeepers and other monitors) using the share price prior to the distribution. The actual price that a private equity investor might realize if he sold a large block of a thinly traded security might be considerably lower. See Venture Economics, "A Perspective on Venture Capital Management Fees," *Venture Capital Journal* 27 (December 1987): 10–14.

EXHIBIT 4-7

TIMING OF COMPENSATION FOR PRIVATE EQUITY ORGANIZATIONS. THE TABLE SUMMARIZES THE RESTRICTIONS ON THE RECEIPT OF CAPITAL GAINS.

Restrictions based on return of committed capital	
No distributions until return of 100% of committed capital	43.8%
No distributions until return of 101–25% of committed capital	1.4
No distributions until return of 126–50% of committed capital	0.5
No distributions until return of more than 150% of committed capital	0.2
No distributions until return of 100% of committed capital plus an annual return of 1–10%	0.7
No distributions until return of 100% of committed capital plus an annual return of 11–20%	0.2
No distributions until return of 100% of committed capital plus four times salaries	0.2
No distributions until return of 100% of committed capital plus four times tax distributions	0.5
Restrictions based on return of net asset value	
No distributions until adjusted net asset value exceeds 100% of committed capital	6.2
No distributions until adjusted net asset value exceeds 101–25% of committed capital	15.8
No distributions until adjusted net asset value exceeds 126–50% of committed capital	1.0
No distributions until adjusted net asset value exceeds 150% or more of committed capital	0.5
No distributions until increase in adjusted net asset value exceeds 125% of the S&P 500	0.2
Hybrid restrictions	
No distributions until 100% capital return and adjusted NAV exceeds 100% of capital	0.2
No distributions until 100% capital return and adjusted NAV exceeds 101–25% of capital	1.4
No distributions until 100% capital return and adjusted NAV exceeds 126–50% of capital	1.4
No distributions until 100% capital return and adjusted NAV exceeds 150% or more of capital	0.2
No distributions until 100% capital return or adjusted NAV exceeds 100% of capital	0.5
No distributions until 100% capital return or adjusted NAV exceeds 101–25% of capital	1.2
No distributions until 100% capital return or adjusted NAV exceeds 126–50% of capital	0.2
Requirements to hold distributions in an escrow account	
Distributions held until return of 100% of committed capital	3.4
Distributions held until return of 101–25% of committed capital	1.2
Distributions held until adjusted asset value exceeds 100% of committed capital	0.2
Distributions held until adjusted asset value exceeds 101–26% of committed capital	0.7
Distributions held until 100% capital return and adjusted NAV exceeds 100% of capital	0.2
Distributions held until 100% capital return and adjusted NAV exceeds 126–50% of capital	0.2
Distributions held until 100% capital return or adjusted NAV exceeds 126–50% of capital	0.2
Distributions held set dollar amount reached	0.5
No restriction specified or other restriction	13.9

partners would receive shares with a value of $10,000 [1,000*($2 + .8*($12 − $2))] and the general partners shares worth $2,000 [1,000*(.2*($12 − $2))].[10]

Private equity organizations that have persuaded their investors to allow them to receive accelerated profit sharing are significantly older and larger. Industry observers argue that the ability of larger partnerships to accelerate their compensation through a hurdle rate reflects their market power. For instance, a Venture Economics report noted, "although there are some limited partners which believe they should receive their original capital back before the general [partners] begin to share in the profits, most of the

---

[10] Some recent funds have gone to the other extreme: they do not allow the private equity investors to receive capital gains until *more* than 100% of invested capital has been returned to investors. These tend to have been raised by smaller and younger organizations.

limited [partners] . . . were aware that it was difficult to demand, particularly with more experienced groups."[11]

WARBURG, PINCUS VENTURES, L.P.[12]

The fundraising document that Warburg, Pincus circulated in the spring of 1994 proposed to raise $2 billion for a fund that would last 12 years. Warburg, Pincus would receive an annual management fee of 1.5% on the capital that it had actually drawn down from investors. The fund anticipated drawing down these funds fairly evenly over the fund's first six years. Warburg, Pincus would not begin receiving any profits until it had returned the invested capital to investors.

The offering document attracted considerable attention in the private equity community. The Acme pension's managers discounted the suggestion that the Warburg, Pincus's fee structure was a manifestation of anxiety about reaching the $2 billion fundraising target. The flow of funds into private equity had been accelerating in the past several years, and 1994 was anticipated to be a record year for fundraising. Instead, the reduced carry might reflect the changing mixture of Warburg, Pincus's investments. In particular, a substantial share of its portfolio was publicly traded firms. Public equity managers typically received an annual fee of about 0.5% of assets under management, without any performance-linked compensation. Alternatively, Warburg, Pincus might be anticipating that the recent flow of institutional money into private equity would lead to lower returns and that the lower carried interest represented a way of "in effect sharing the downside of the market."[13]

Another area of discussion within Acme was the implications of the shift for other private equity organizations. One observer noted that "with their action, Warburg, Pincus has given us all an opportunity to reconsider pricing." Others speculated that the move was especially likely to lead to pressure on less established private equity organizations to reduce their share of the profits.[14]

---

[11] Venture Economics, "Stock Distributions—Fact, Opinion and Comment," *Venture Capital Journal* 27 (August 1987): 8–14.

[12] This section is drawn from "Warburg Pincus Preps Huge Fund Launch," *Buyouts* 7, April 4, 1994; Jennifer L. Reed, "Warburg, Pincus Seeks Only 15% Carry," *Venture Capital Journal* 34 (May 1994): 6; and Galante, *op. cit.*

[13] Reed, *op. cit.*

[14] Galante, *op. cit.*

5

A Note on Private Equity Partnership Agreements

Venture capital and leveraged buyouts are by necessity long-run investments. Consequently, the vast majority of U.S. private equity today is raised through private partnerships with a 10-year or longer life span. To govern these investments, complex contracts have sprung up. These contracts provide an insight into the complex challenge of raising and managing a private equity fund.

There are three critical aspects to these contracts: the structure of the funds, the restrictions placed on their activities, and the incentives offered to the private equity investors. This note considers each of these aspects in turn.[1]

HOW THE FUND IS STRUCTURED

Private equity funds typically have limited and general partners. The limited partners are institutional and individual investors who provide capital. These are limited in the sense that their liability only extends to the capital that they contribute. If, for instance, the fund invests in a company that produces a drug which kills some patients, the victims' relatives cannot sue the partnership's investors for damages. The general partners—typically the private equity investors who manage the fund—may, however, be directly liable.[2]

Professor Joshua Lerner, in collaboration with Professor Paul Gompers, prepared this note as the basis for class discussion rather than to illustrate either effective or ineffective handling of an administrative situation.

[1] This section is based on Asset Alternatives, *Private Equity Partnership Terms and Conditions*, Wellesley, MA, Asset Alternatives, 1999; Joseph W. Bartlett, *Equity Finance: Venture Capital, Buyouts, Restructurings, and Reorganization*, New York, Wiley, 1995; Paul A. Gompers and Josh Lerner, "The Use of Covenants: An Empirical Analysis of Venture Partnership Agreements," *Journal of Law and Economics* 39 (October 1996): 566–599; Jack S. Levin, *Structuring Venture Capital, Private Equity and Entrepreneurial Transactions*, Chicago, Commerce Clearing House, 2000; Venture Economics, *Terms and Conditions of Venture Capital Partnerships*, Needham, MA, Venture Economics, 1989; and Venture Economics, *Terms and Conditions of Venture Capital Partnerships—1992*, Needham, MA, Venture Economics, 1992.

[2] Private equity investors protect themselves, at least partially, by not serving directly as the general partners. Rather, they create a corporation that serves as the general partner, which they in turn are shareholders of.

A private equity fund is typically raised in several stages. Initial investors in a private equity fund are often anxious to avoid opportunistic behavior by the general partners as they raise additional funds. As a result, a series of contractual provisions govern the fundraising process.

The first of these provisions is a minimum size of investment. General partners will typically set a minimum size for institutional investors and a smaller minimum for individual investors. Limited partners have at least two reasons to be concerned about the number of partners. Under the Investment Company Act of 1940, funds with more than a few hundred partners (originally 100) must register as investment advisors. This imposes complex regulatory and disclosure requirements. More generally, the costs of administering a private equity fund increase with the number of limited partners.

Most contracts stipulate an explicit minimum and maximum size for the fund. In many cases, limited partners have distinct preferences about fund sizes. If the general partners are unable to attract additional capital from other investors, the initial investors may prefer that the fund be disbanded. The general partners' inability to raise additional funds may imply that other potential limited investors have adverse information that the initial investors do not have.[3] They will in many cases also be concerned that the fund not become too large, lest the management skills of the general partners be strained. In many cases, the private equity investors are allowed to exceed the maximum size stated in the contract by 10% or 20%, as long as they explicitly obtain permission from the existing limited partners. The limited partners who enter late almost always are required to pay the same up-front and organization fees as the original limited partners, and may be restricted from a share of the interest earned on the original limited partner's initial capital commitments.

Prior to the 1986 Tax Reform Act, the contribution of the general partners to the funds was invariably 1%. This was because 1% was the minimum contribution by a general partner required by law. Since this Act, general partners are free to contribute as much or as little as they desire. In most cases, however, 1% is still the general partners' contribution. Deviations are confined to small funds, particularly first funds raised by private equity partnerships. In these cases, a substantial minority of firms contribute either a smaller or larger percentage. A few funds allow firms not to make the contributions in cash, but rather in non–interest-bearing notes.

Contracts uniformly have a "takedown" schedule, which specifies how the funds committed by the limited partners will be paid into the fund. Neither the limited nor the general partners are usually eager for the funds to be paid in immediately. Since the private equity partnership will only invest the funds gradually, if the funds are simply sitting in the fund's bank account, they will depress the partnership's rate of return. Typically, partnership agreements will call for a set amount to be disbursed at closing (most often between 10% and 33%). The dates of subsequent payments may be set in the agreement or else left to the general partner's discretion. Larger funds are more likely to leave the schedule to the discretion of the general partners. Even if they are left to the private equity investors' discretion, usually a minimum and maximum period is set. Typically, all the funds are drawn down by between the second and fourth anniversaries of the fund's formation.

Private equity partnerships almost always have a life of about 10 years. They usually can be extended for at least two more years. In some cases, permission of the limited

---

[3] This is similar to provisions in the riskiest of initial public offerings, the "best efforts" offering. If the underwriter cannot sell a minimum number of shares in a best efforts offering, the offering will be canceled, and the initial investors will be refunded.

partners is required; in other cases, only extensions beyond this point need permission. In general, the decision to extend the life of the partnership is not controversial.

Almost all partnerships allow the limited partners to terminate their investments in the partnership under certain extreme conditions. These include the death or withdrawal of the general partners or the bankruptcy of the fund. Most agreements also allow the limited partners to dissolve the partnership or replace the general partners if between 51% and 100% of the limited partners believe that the general partner is damaging the fund. Often, however, the parties in these cases end up in court.[4]

Most contracts will also have provisions for defaulting limited partners who fail to meet their capital commitments. In many cases, the general partners reserve the right to charge interest for late payments, to seize the limited partner's stake in whole or part, or even to sue the limited partner. In other cases, the terms are less onerous. The general partners may agree to help to market the limited partner's interest, or pay the limited partner an amount that reflects the current fair market value of the partnership interest (or a fraction of this value). In many cases, if a pension fund must withdraw from a private equity fund due to the complex regulations promulgated by the U.S. Department of Labor, these penalties are waived. In addition, limited partners can frequently transfer their shares to other parties, conditional on the approval of the general partners.

WHAT THE PRIVATE EQUITY INVESTORS CAN AND CANNOT DO

An area of protracted negotiation is the discretion with which the general partner can run the private equity fund. In the 1960s and 1970s, partnership agreements contained few such restrictions. These early venture capital organizations were free to invest as they saw fit. As the 1980s progressed, however, institutional investors began viewing themselves as holding a portfolio of private equity funds, each with a distinct focus. They demanded contractual provisions that would limit the ability of general partners to deviate from their area of expertise. A few of the very oldest organizations, however, have managed to maintain simple contracts with few restrictions.[5] These covenants can be divided into three broad classes: those relating to the overall management of the fund, the activities of the general partners, and the permissible types of investments.

Management of the Fund The first of these restrictions relates to the size of investment in any one firm. These provisions are intended to ensure that the general partners do not attempt to salvage an investment in a poorly performing firm by investing significant resources in follow-on funding. The private equity investors typically do not receive a share of profits until the limited partners have received their original investment back. Consequently, the general partners' share of profits can be thought of as a call option. The general partners may gain disproportionately from increasing risk of the portfolio at the expense of diversification. This limitation is frequently expressed as

---

[4] Articles about such disputes include E.S. Ely, "Dr. Silver's Tarnished Prescription," *Venture* 9 (July 1987): 54–58; "Iowa Suits Test LPs' Authority to Abolish Fund," *Private Equity Analyst* 4 (May 1994): 1 and 9; and "Madison L.P.s Oust G.P., Legal Skirmish Ensues," *Buyouts* (October 23, 1995): 4.

[5] It might be wondered why these issues need to be specified within the original partnership agreement. Could not, for instance, the limited partners serve as directors, overseeing the investment decisions of the private equity investors? In actuality, limited partners can only retain their limited liability if they are not involved in the day-to-day operations of the fund. Thus, once the fund is formed, they are limited to a purely consultative role, such as service on the firm's advisory board. This makes the careful delineation of rights in the original partnership agreement critical.

a percentage of capital invested in the fund (typically called committed capital). Alternatively, it may be expressed as a percentage of the current value of the fund's assets. In a few cases, a limit may be placed on the aggregate size of the partnership's two or three largest investments.

The second class of restriction limits the use of debt. As option holders, the general partners may be tempted to increase the variance of their portfolio's returns by leveraging the fund. Partnership agreements often limit the ability of private equity investors to borrow funds themselves or to guarantee the debt of their portfolio companies (which might be seen as equivalent to direct borrowing). Partnership agreements may restrict debt to a set percentage of committed capital or assets, and in some instances also restrict the maturity of the debt, to ensure that all borrowing is short term.[6]

The third restriction relates to co-investments with the private equity organization's earlier and/or later funds. Many private equity organizations manage multiple funds, formed several years apart, which can lead to opportunistic behavior. Consider, for instance, a venture organization whose first fund has made an investment in a troubled firm. The general partners may find it optimal for their second fund to invest in this firm, in the hopes of salvaging the investment.[7] Consequently, partnership agreements for second or later funds frequently contain provisions that the fund's advisory board must review such investments or that a majority (or super-majority) of the limited partners approve these transactions. Another way in which these problems are limited is by the requirement that the earlier fund invest simultaneously at the same valuation. Alternatively, the investment may only be allowed if one or more unaffiliated private equity organizations simultaneously invest at the same price.

A fourth class of covenant relates to reinvestment of profits. Private equity investors may have several reasons to reinvest funds rather than distribute profits to the limited partners. First, many partnerships receive fees on the basis of either the value of assets under management or adjusted committed capital (capital less any distributions). Distributing profits will reduce these fees. Second, reinvested capital gains may yield further profits for the general (as well as the limited) partners.[8] The reinvestment of profits may require approval of the advisory board or the limited partners. Alternatively, such reinvestment may be prohibited after a certain date or after a certain percentage of the committed capital is invested.

Activities of the Private Equity Investors   Five frequently encountered classes of restrictions limit the activities of the general partners. The first of these restricts the ability of the general partners to invest personal funds in firms. If general partners in-

---

[6] A related provision—found in virtually all partnership agreements—is that the limited partners will avoid unrelated business taxable income. Tax-exempt institutions must pay taxes on UBTI, which is defined as the gross income from any unrelated business that the institution regularly carries out. If the venture partnership is generating significant income from debt-financed property, the limited partners may have tax liabilities.

[7] Distortions may also be introduced by the need for the private equity investors to report an attractive return for their first fund as they seek capital for a third fund. Many venture funds will write up the valuation of firms in their portfolios to the price paid in the last venture round. By having the second fund invest in one of the first fund's firms at an inflated valuation, they can (temporarily) inflate the reported performance of their first fund.

[8] Another reason why private equity investors may wish to reinvest profits is that such investments are unlikely to be mature at the end of the fund's stated life. The presence of investments that are too immature to liquidate is a frequently invoked reason for extending the partnership's life beyond the typical contractual limit of 10 years. In these cases, the private equity investors will continue to generate fees from the limited partners (though often on a reduced basis).

vest in selected firms, they may devote excessive time to these firms and may not terminate funding if the firms encounter difficulties. To address this problem, general partners are often limited in the size of the investment that they can make in any of their fund's portfolio firms. This limit may be expressed as a percentage of the total investment by the fund, or (less frequently) of the net worth of the private equity investor. In addition, the private equity investors may be required to seek permission from the advisory board or limited partners. An alternative approach employed in some partnership agreements is to require the private equity investors to invest a set dollar amount or percentage in every investment made by the fund.[9]

A second restriction addresses the reverse problem: the sale of partnership interests by general partners. Rather than seeking to increase their personal exposure to selected investments, general partners may sell their share of the fund's profits to other investors. While the general partnership interests are not totally comparable with the limited partners' stakes (for instance, the general partners will typically only receive a share of the capital gains after the return of the limited partners' capital), these may still be attractive investments. The limited partners are likely to be concerned that such a sale would reduce the general partners' incentives to monitor their investments. Partnership agreements may prohibit the sale of general partnership interests outright, or else require that these sales be approved by a majority (or super-majority) of the limited partners.

A third area for restrictions on the general partners is future fundraising. The raising of an additional fund will raise the management fees that the general partners receive and may reduce the attention that the private equity investors pay to existing funds. Partnership agreements may prohibit fundraising by the general partners until a set percentage of the portfolio has been invested or until a given date. Alternatively, fundraising may be restricted to a fund of certain size or focus (e.g., a venture organization may be allowed to raise a buyout fund, whose management would presumably be by other general partners).

In a similar vein, some partnership agreements restrict other actions by general partners. Because outside activities are likely to reduce the attention paid to investments, private equity investors may be restricted to spending "substantially all" (or some other fraction) of their time managing the investments of the partnership. Alternatively, the general partners' ability to be involved in businesses other than the companies in which the private equity fund has invested may be restricted. These limitations are often confined to the first years of the partnership, or until a set percent of the fund's capital is invested, when the need for attention by the general partners is presumed to be the largest.

A fifth class of covenant relates to the addition of new general partners. By hiring less experienced general partners, private equity investors may reduce the burden on themselves. The quality of the oversight provided, however, is likely to be lower. As a result, many funds require that the addition of new general partners be approved by either the advisory board or a set percentage of the limited partners.

It should be noted that while many issues involving the behavior of the general partners are addressed through partnership agreements, several others typically are not. One area that is almost never discussed is the vesting schedule of general partnership inter-

---

[9] Another issue relating to co-investment is the timing of the investments by the general partners. In some cases, venture capitalists involved in the establishment of a firm will purchase shares at the same time as the other founders at a very low valuation, then immediately invest their partnership's funds at a much higher valuation. Some partnership agreements address this problem by requiring venture capitalists to invest at the same time and price as their funds.

ests. If a general partner leaves a private equity organization early in the life of the fund, he may forfeit all or some of his share of the profits. If the private equity investors do not receive their entire partnership interest immediately, they are less likely to leave the fund soon after it is formed. A second issue is the division of the profits between the general partners. In the case of some funds, most of the profits accrue to the older general partners, even if the younger private equity investors are providing the bulk of the day-to-day management. These issues are addressed in agreements between the general partners, but they are rarely discussed in the contracts between the general and limited partners.

Types of Investments The third family of covenants limits the types of assets in which the fund will invest. These restrictions are typically structured in similar ways: the private equity fund is allowed to invest no more than a set percentage of capital or asset value in a given investment class. An exception may be made if the advisory board or a set percentage of the limited partners approve. Occasionally, more complex restrictions will be encountered, such as the requirement that the sum of two asset classes not exceed a certain percentage of capital.

Two fears appear to motivate these restrictions on investments. First, the general partners may be receiving compensation that is inappropriately large. For instance, the average money manager who specializes in investing in public securities receives an annual fee of about 0.5% of assets, while private equity investors receive 20% of profits in addition to an annual fee of about 2.5% of capital. Consequently, limited partners seek to limit the ability of private equity investors to invest in public securities. Similarly, the typical investment manager receives a one-time fee of 1% of capital for investing an institution's money in a private equity fund. Partnership agreements often also include covenants that restrict the ability of the general partners to invest capital in other private equity funds.

A second concern is that the general partners will invest in classes of investments in which they have little expertise, in the hopes of gaining experience. For instance, during the 1980s, many venture capital funds began investing in leveraged buyouts. Those that developed a successful track record proceeded to raise funds specializing in buyouts; many more, however, lost considerable sums on these investments.[10] Similarly, many firms explored investing in foreign countries during the 1980s. Only a relative handful proved sufficiently successful to raise funds specializing in these investments.

HOW ARE PRIVATE EQUITY INVESTORS COMPENSATED?[11]

Even with these covenants, the key limited partners in private equity funds—for instance, pension fund trustees and university overseers—find it challenging to monitor the funds in their portfolio or to select the funds most likely to do well in the future. This reflects the difficult environment in which general partners operate. The typical firms backed by general partners have severe information problems, very important strategic and operational decisions to make, and substantial capital needs.

In order to ensure the success of their investments, general partners must carefully work with and oversee entrepreneurs and portfolio companies. These activities help the

[10] The poor performance of venture-backed LBOs such as Prime Computer has been much discussed in the popular press; quantitative support of these claims is found in analyses of the returns of funds with different investment objectives by Venture Economics.

[11] This section and Exhibits 5-1 through 5-5 are based on Paul A. Gompers and Josh Lerner, "An Analysis of Compensation in the U.S. Venture Capital Partnership," *Journal of Financial Economics* 51 (January 1999): 3–44, and subsequent updates by the authors.

general partners assess the activities of their portfolio companies. But given the difficulty of observing the interactions between general partners and company managers, and the long gestation period from the time that investments are made until they are exited, it is difficult for limited partners to ensure optimal behavior after they commit to the fund.

The structure of private equity partnerships, in which a large share of the compensation is dependent on the fund's performance, helps solve the limited partners' difficulties in evaluating potential investment opportunities. The design of an appropriate incentive scheme for the general partners can play a critical role in alleviating these problems.

In particular, the carried interest may be important for two reasons. First, it provides an incentive for the private equity manager to work hard, even if his effort cannot be observed. It may be that in the initial funds, a private equity manager will work diligently even without explicit pay-for-performance incentives because if he can establish a good investment track record, he will gain additional compensation in later funds because of the increased ease of fundraising. Once a reputation has been established, explicit incentive compensation is needed to induce the proper effort levels. A second possibility is the signal that accepting a large portion of compensation in the form of carried interest may provide. If the institutional investors see that a new private equity manager is willing to take a cut in his base fee in the hopes of making a substantial amount of carried interest, they may be more willing to invest in that fund: the move signals that the venture capitalist is confident of his ability to create value.

The management fee also plays an important role. Traditionally, private equity groups were exceedingly "lean" organizations: aside from some spending on support staff, travel, and office space, there was little overhead. Thus, most of the management fees flowed to investment professionals.

Over the past few years, however, a flurry of experimentation has characterized the private equity industry. Among the changes seen are partnerships between venture capital and buyout organizations, sometimes in conjunction with corporations, the establishment of affiliate funds in different regions and nations, and the launching of physical and "virtual" incubators by private equity groups. Each of these efforts requires a greater investment in people and infrastructure, which places far great demands on management fees than traditional efforts.

Our research has examined the evolution of compensation in private equity partnerships over the past two decades. This information has been gathered from a broad cross-section of institutional investors and intermediaries. Because investors often focus on the level of carried interest, we first consider the level that the carry has taken across various private equity types, for example, U.S. venture capital, U.S. buyout, and non-U.S. funds.

One particularly interesting pattern is the effect of the private equity firm's reputation on the level of carried interest charged by the fund. Reputation is, of course, a difficult thing to measure. Instead, one has to examine the characteristics of private equity groups that we suspect are related to reputation. In this analysis, we focus on the size of the private equity fund being raised. Fund size is a useful measure of the investment's track record: investors will provide larger sums to investors with proven success, even if they have not raised any earlier funds. Fund size, however, may also capture differences in industry or geographic focus.[12] The patterns of carried interest for

---

[12] Ideally, we would have a measure of the cumulative experience of the general partners associated with the fund. While we try to address this problem by considering buyout, non-U.S., and venture funds separately, we realize that this measure is inexact.

EXHIBIT 5-1

CARRIED INTEREST, BY FUND TYPE AND SIZE, 1995–2000

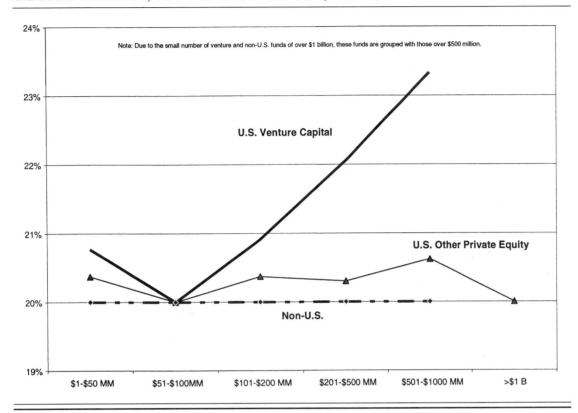

various types and sizes of private equity funds are presented in Exhibit 5-1. We tabulate the carried interest for the more than 650 funds in our sample raised between 1995 and 2000. We show the average carried interest for U.S. venture capital funds, other U.S. private equity funds, and non-U.S. private equity funds across various size categories from under $50 million in committed capital to more than $1 billion. For both U.S. nonventure private equity funds and non-U.S. funds, the carried interest deviates little from 20%.

The pattern within U.S. venture capital funds, however, is strikingly different. Carried interest in all groups (except those funds between $50 and $100 million in committed capital) are significantly higher than 20%. The carried interest rises steadily for funds above $100 million, reaching an average of nearly 24% for the largest venture capital funds.

These depictions of the average level of carried interest are somewhat misleading, for they disguise the fact that these measures are very concentrated. This point is illustrated in Exhibit 5-2, which shows the distribution of the carried interest for U.S. venture capital and buyout and other private equity firms. The vast majority of funds have carried interest of 20%, 25%, or 30%.

Because the organized venture capital funds have a longer history in the United States, we next explore the changes in the mean level of carried interest for venture capital funds raised between 1978 and 2000. These results are shown in Exhibit 5-3.

EXHIBIT 5-2

DISTRIBUTION OF CARRIED INTEREST, BY FUND TYPE

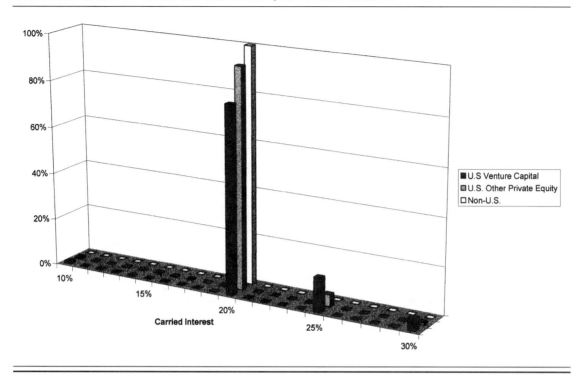

Surprisingly, despite the widespread belief that carried interest on venture capital funds has been steadily rising in recent years, the trend is highly volatile. There appears to be little upward trend in carried interest when all funds are considered.[13]

How do we reconcile the results of Exhibits 5-1 and 5-3? The increased visibility of the large, successful venture capital groups has generated substantial press. In the accounts of these successful venture capital funds, journalists often focus on the rising carried interest they have received. As an industry, however, carried interest has not risen appreciably.

We next examine management fees. It is surprising that relatively little attention has been paid to the pattern that these fees have taken. These fees represent a significant fraction of the venture capitalist's compensation. They are calculated in myriad ways, however. Fixed fees may be specified as a percentage of the committed capital (the amount of money investors have committed to provide over the life of the fund), the value of fund's assets, or some combination or modification of these two measures. Both the base used to compute the fees and the percentage paid as fees may vary over the life of the fund. These differences make it difficult to do a straightforward comparison among the various funds.

---

[13] Both 1978 and 1992 are extreme cases. Both were poor markets, where relatively few funds were raised. Thus, these measures are considerably "noisier" that the others.

EXHIBIT 5-3

AVERAGE CARRIED INTEREST OF VENTURE CAPITAL FUNDS, BY YEAR

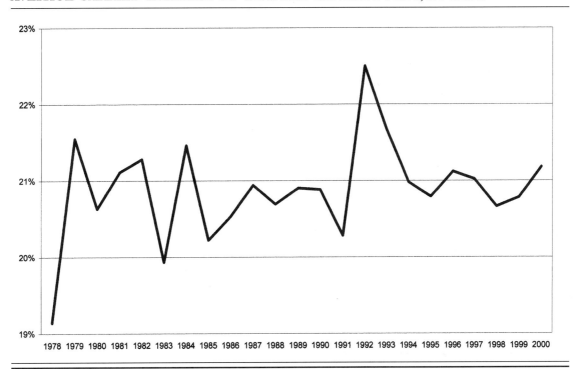

Thus, we use two measures of fixed fees to gauge their importance for general partners. The first measure of fees that we examine is the level of fees in the third year of the fund. The choice of the third year reflects several important features of fees in private equity partnerships. First, fees in the early years are often lower than they are in later years. For most of the funds in our sample, fees reach their maximum percentage by the third anniversary of the fund. A second pattern also makes the third anniversary appropriate. Many funds reduce their fees after a certain number of years or when a new fund is raised (typically after the third anniversary of the fund's closing).

The level of fees in year 3 for U.S. venture capital, U.S. nonventure private equity, and non-U.S. private equity are presented in Exhibit 5-4.[14] The funds are once again those that were raised between 1995 and 2000. For non-U.S. funds and U.S. nonventure private equity funds, fees decline with fund size. Fees for the smallest funds average nearly 2.4%. For non-U.S. private equity funds, fees decline to 1.9% while for U.S. nonventure private equity, fees decline even further, to 1.6%. Once again, U.S. venture capital funds have a very different fee pattern. Fees increase across all fund size groups with the highest fees, as a percentage of committed capital, being paid to the largest funds.

[14] In this calculation, as well as the one below, we make a series of assumptions about fund draw-downs, investment rate, and performance, which are spelled out in detail in the article cited in footnote 11.

EXHIBIT 5-4

MANAGEMENT FEE IN YEAR 3, BY FUND TYPE AND SIZE, 1995–2000

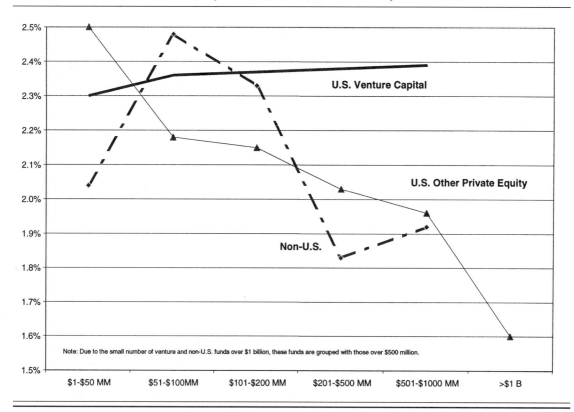

Note: Due to the small number of venture and non-U.S. funds over $1 billion, these funds are grouped with those over $500 million.

This measure, however, actually understates the changes. In particular, many of the changes in fees have been in the rates charged during the initial and final years of the funds. An alternative to simply looking at the level of management fees is to examine the net present value implications of various compensation terms.

A net present value analysis requires assumptions about the drawdowns of capital, the rate of return on investments, and the timing of the distribution of returns to general and limited partners. In our analysis of compensation, we project out the returns to limited and general partners under various return scenarios. We discount relatively certain compensation (e.g., fees based on committed capital) at 10%, while applying a 20% discount rate to more uncertain compensation (such as carried interest paid, returns to the limited partners, or fees based on net asset value). These calculations take into account the entire stream of fees that limited partners agree to pay out over the lifetime of the private equity fund. In other words, calculating the net present value of fees and the net present value of carried interest is a better measure of the burden that they place on the fund's potential return to the limited partners. We express the net present value of *all* management fees that are specified in the partnership agreement as a percentage of the committed capital.

Exhibit 5-5 reports the mean net present value of the base compensation as a percentage of committed capital for the industry segment that has seen the most dramatic

EXHIBIT 5-5

VENTURE CAPITAL FEES OVER FUND LIFE (AS % OF COMMITTED CAPITAL)

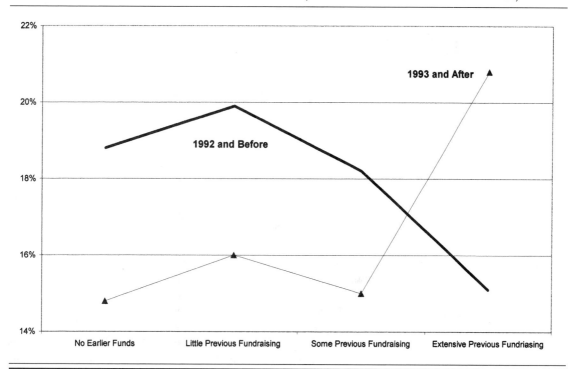

changes, venture capital. The basic pattern has been one of declining fees; that is, the average level of fees for all funds is lower for funds raised after 1993 than for those raised earlier. The changing pattern across groups with different experience levels, however, is quite striking. For funds raised prior to 1992, the level of fees declined with prior fundraising experience; that is, experienced venture capitalists actually charged lower fees. (Because these groups raised larger funds, the actual fees received were actually larger for these groups.) After 1993, however, the pattern reversed. The most experienced venture capital organizations now charge substantially higher fees than inexperienced firms. The fees of these experienced groups have increased substantially from the level of fees that these funds charged prior to the recent fundraising boom.

6

University Technology Ventures: October 2000

Tommy Vardell walked across the Stanford campus. It was a mild and cloudless day, the type of weather that makes fall the best season in northern California. As he approached the engineering complex, his thoughts drifted back a decade. While on Saturdays he had been the toast of the campus as "Touchdown Tommy," much of the rest of the week had been spent in these same buildings, working late into the night on grueling problem sets.

Today, he and two colleagues who had played together for the San Francisco Forty-Niners—Brent Jones and Mark Harris—were on campus in a competitive endeavor but on a very different playing field. Along with chief financial officer Mark Williams and former teammate Steve Young, they had launched University Technology Ventures. This fund-of-funds sought to bring together university professors and academics in a way that would benefit both parties, as well as the academic institutions themselves.

A great deal of thought had gone into the design of the fund, and the interest it had stirred was substantial. At the same time, the partners were finding that the fundraising process was proving more challenging than they had initially anticipated. Should they shift their strategy? For instance, did it make sense to involve investors outside of academia? Should the group aggressively seek media coverage? As they strode into Terman Hall, they wondered about these issues.

INDIVIDUALS AS PRIVATE EQUITY INVESTORS[1]

Individuals played a critical role in the history of the U.S. private equity industry. Many of the earliest venture capital organizations were established as part of family offices (which invested the wealth of a single family). For instance, the Whitney

Professor Josh Lerner prepared this case as the basis for class discussion rather than to illustrate either effective or ineffective handling of an administrative situation.

[1] This section is largely based on Josh Lerner, "FOX Venture Partners: Enriching the Private Equity Investor Pool," Harvard Business School Case no. 296-041, 1995, and Michael J. Halloran, *Venture Capital and Public Offering Negotiation*, 3rd edition, Gaithersburg, MD, Aspen Law and Business, 1997.

family established the J.H. Whitney venture organization; the Rockefeller family, Venrock Associates; and the Phipps family, Bessemer Venture Partners. Even in the cases where the venture groups eventually opened up to accept funds from outside investors, the founding family typically remained the primary source of capital for many years thereafter.

Even as venture partnerships with multiple investors proliferated, individuals continued to be an important source of capital. For instance, the first funds of Greylock, Mayfield, Patricof & Co., and TA Associates (all of which were raised between 1965 and 1969) were entirely capitalized by individuals. As late as 1978, individual investors accounted for 32% of the funds flowing into the private equity industry.

The dramatic reduction in the importance of individual investors was largely caused by the "institutionalization" of private equity in the 1980s. Pension funds had been essentially barred from investing in venture funds by U.S. Department of Labor guidelines until 1979. When these guidelines were relaxed, pension funds flowed into the industry. In 1978, pensions invested $64 million in private equity; eight years later, they invested $4.4 billion. One consequence was that the average size of funds increased. For instance, the average venture fund raised in 1978 was $17 million; in 1986, the average size was $50 million; in 1999, $217 million. Among established private equity organizations, the increase was even more pronounced.

These size increases were important—and problematic—due to U.S. securities regulations. Private equity funds were typically exempt from the Investment Advisors Act of 1940. This exemption was important, because the 1940 Act required mutual funds to make extensive and time-consuming filings about their holdings and organization; it also imposed exhaustive regulations concerning the management of such funds. The Act provided several ways in which groups could attain this exempt status. Most private equity groups relied on Section 3 (c) (1), also known as the "Rule of 99." Essentially, this provision exempted from the Act those funds that had less than 100 "accredited" investors.[2,3]

In order not to be troubled by these regulations, private equity groups began establishing substantial minimums for investments. For instance, a private equity group seeking to raise a $100 million fund might set a $2 or $3 million dollar minimum for each investment. An investor in private equity would typically seek to diversify along several dimensions: ideally, one would select funds with different geographic, industry,

---

[2] An accredited investor had to satisfy one of several tests. If the investor was an individual, they were defined as accredited if their net worth (alone or with their spouse) exceeded $1 million. Alternatively, they satisfied the test if their net income in the past two years exceeded $200,000 (or over $300,000 when their spouse's income was included). Trusts, retirement plans, and partnerships were also regarded as accredited investors, as long as their assets exceeded $5 million. Finally, a number of financial institutions, such as banks and business development companies, met these criteria as well. This exemption was one of several ways in which groups could avoid coming under the purview of the 1940 Act. For a discussion of other ways in which funds could avoid coming under the coverage of the Act, see "CMGI: Organizational and Market Innovation," in this volume.

[3] The National Securities Market Improvement Act of 1996 created a second class, the "qualified" investor. (This category included individuals with investable assets of over $5 million and institutions with over $25 million.) Private equity organizations were allowed to establish parallel funds: one that had up to 99 "accredited" investors and the other that had up to 499 "qualified" investors. The 1996 Act also helped funds-of-funds by eliminating the danger that an investment by a fund-of-funds into a private equity fund would count as more than one investment. Previously, if any single limited partner had contributed more than 10% of a fund-of-funds' capital, then an investment by a fund-of-funds into a private equity fund would not be considered to be a single investment. Rather, each individual limited partner in the fund-of-funds would count against the 99 investors that the private equity fund was allowed.

and stage focuses, as well as funds begun in different years. (Returns for private equity as a whole have varied dramatically from year to year.) The growth in the size of private equity funds meant that the construction of a diversified portfolio moved beyond the reach of all but the wealthiest individuals: that is, those with over $100 million in assets.

Meanwhile, many of the individual investors who did begin private equity investment programs in these years encountered difficulties. Many of the best funds—seeking to prevent too rapid growth and the organizational disruption that ensued—did not accept funds from new investors. Among those funds that did accept funds from new investors, discerning those who had demonstrated sustained superior performance was often difficult, and identifying those where the success was likely to persist even harder. As a result, individuals beginning private equity investment programs frequently had to settle for second- or third-tier funds. These funds enjoyed mediocre returns for much of the 1980s and 1990s. In addition, many of the families that initiated private equity programs found that the administrative, legal, and tax costs generated by these investments were not inconsiderable. Consequently, both the absolute amount and the share of the total investment by individuals fell sharply during these decades.

This decline was unfortunate, for there were at least two reasons why this asset class was particularly appropriate for individual investors. First, individuals stood to benefit from the preferred tax treatment of long-term investments in private firms. (These benefits were unimportant to many institutional investors, such as pension funds, university endowments, and foundations, whose investment gains were not taxed.) More specifically, the 1993 tax reform had created a substantial gap between the tax rates on capital gains and ordinary income. Although the marginal tax rate for the highest income brackets was 39%, long-term capital gains were taxed at 28%. In addition, a special provision in the 1993 tax reform act set a 14% rate on capital gains from certain small business equities held for five years or longer.[4]

Second, private equity could have important benefits for estate planning purposes. A major concern of wealthy individuals was the avoidance of inheritance taxes, which could be substantial. (In 2000, a substantial share of any estate worth more than $675,000 was due to the federal government: the tax rate began at 37% rate and reached as high as 60%.) In addition, bequests to grandchildren of over $1 million were subject to an additional "generation skipping" tax. Furthermore, taxpayers' annual gifts to each child or grandchild could not exceed $10,000 without being subject to a gift tax, which was calculated according to the same schedule as estate taxes. Because interests in private equity funds were frequently valued very conservatively in the funds' initial years, they made a particularly attractive way to transfer wealth across the generations. In all likelihood, the value of the expected cash flows would be greater than the valuation assigned to the fund. In addition, U.S. tax law allowed the value assigned to such a gift to be reduced (often by as much as 30%) since the securities being transferred were illiquid and represented a minority interest in the fund.

---

[4] Eligible businesses were required to have under $50 million in assets at the time the securities were issued. Investments in certain service providers, such as law and consulting firms, were not eligible. An additional complication was introduced by the Alternative Minimum Tax, which attempted to prevent taxpayers from taking advantage of excessive deductions. Investors subject to the Alternative Minimum Tax could only employ one-half of this special credit, and consequently had to pay a 21% [28% − (14%/2)] tax on these capital gains.

EXHIBIT 6-1

RAISING OF FUNDS-OF-FUNDS AND NEW FUND SPONSORS, BY YEAR

Year	Number of Closings	New Funds-of-Funds Sponsors
1979	0	Brinson Partners
1980	0	
1981	0	
1982	1	Chancellor, Crossroads, Horsley Keogh, John Hancock
1983	2	
1984	2	
1985	2	
1986	5	Larimer Venture Advisors, MC Techinvest Inc.
1987	3	
1988	5	CommonFund Capital
1989	6	Knightsbridge Advisers
1990	3	
1991	1	
1992	6	Pantheon Ventures
1993	6	
1994	12	Auda Advisor Associates, Fairview Capital Partners, Venture Investment Associates
1995	15	Abbott Capital, Bessemer Trust, FLAG Venture Partners
1996	16	Progress Investment Management, Wood, Struthers & Winthrop (now DLJ Management)
1997	30	Castle Private Equity, Goldman Sachs Asset Mgt., Investment Fund for Foundations, Merrill Lynch & Company, Sovereign Financial Services, Wilshire Associates
1998	55	Banc Boston Capital, Bankers Trust, Bank J. Vontobel, Bear Stearns, Capital Z Partners, Carson Private Capital, Chase Alternative Asset Mgt., CS First Boston, Fleet Equity Partners, Frye-Louis Capital, Hamilton Lane Advisors, Pacific Corporate Group, Pomona Capiital, Tucker Anthony
1999	66	AXA Investment Managers, CIBC Oppenheimer, Forstmann Leff Int'l., Grove Street Advisors, Independence Mgt. Co., Indosuez Capital, J.P. Morgan, Meritage Advisors, Mesirow Private Equity, Salomon Smith Barney, Scudder Kemper

Note: A number of groups announced their intention to begin private equity fund-of-funds programs a number of years prior to the closing of their initial funds.

Source: Compiled from Robert Pease, *Private Equity Funds-of-Funds: State of the Market*, Wellesley, MA, Asset Alternatives, 2000.

THE FUNDS-OF-FUNDS INDUSTRY[5]

A fund-of-fund can be defined as a financial instrument that aggregates funds from a number of investors (limited partners) for investment into a number of private equity partnerships. The growth of the funds-of-funds industry is summarized in Exhibits 6-1

[5] This section is based in large part on "Investment Managers—A Force in the Venture Capital Industry," *Venture Capital Journal* 29 (September 1989): 10–17; Robert Pease, *Private Equity Funds-of-Funds: State of the Market*, Wellesley, MA, Asset Alternatives, 2000; and David Toll, "Funds of Funds Begin to Specialize as the Field Grows More Crowded," *Private Equity Analyst* 8 (August 1998): 1, 32–39.

EXHIBIT 6-2

GROWTH IN COMMITMENTS TO FUNDS-OF-FUNDS (TOTAL DOLLARS AND SHARE OF TOTAL FUNDRAISING)

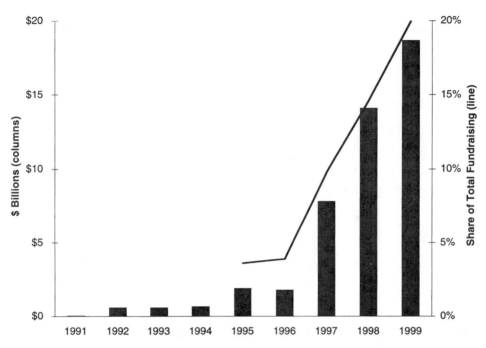

Source: Compiled from Robert Pease, *Private Equity Funds-of-Funds: State of the Market*, Wellesley, MA, Asset Alternatives, 2000.

and 6-2. The charts highlight the growing number of funds raised as well as their increasing share of the capital raised in the private equity industry.

In the earliest funds, the limited partners tended to be institutional investors. In many cases, these organizations were just beginning private equity investment programs and found a fund-of-funds an attractive way to get exposure to the industry. In many cases, the fund-of-funds could also access higher quality private equity groups than they could reach by themselves. Over time, many of the institutions "graduated" to investing themselves in private equity funds. But because many smaller pension funds began private equity investment programs in the 1990s, there was steady demand of institutions for these funds. In addition, some larger institutions continued to use funds-of-funds to invest in specialized niches where they had less expertise (for instance, in non-U.S. private equity funds or in small venture groups).

Funds-of-funds geared toward individual investors became increasingly common at the end of the 1990s. This popularity reflected a growing recognition of the barriers to investing in private equity partnerships that were discussed above. In addition, it reflected a rising demand for private equity as a result of the attractive returns many funds had enjoyed, as well as the publicity given to the success of private equity funds in the popular and business press. Asset Alternatives estimates that, while virtually all the capital raised by funds-of-funds in the years 1987 through 1990 were from institutions, in the years 1995 through 1998 fully 24% of the capital they raised was from individuals.

Like the private equity funds in which they invest, a fund-of-funds is typically an illiquid investment. The fund managers usually begin identifying private equity funds in which to invest while still raising funds from limited partners. (Some funds will inform potential limited partners of some or all of the partnerships selected while raising the fund.) Thus, capital commitments almost always begin soon after the fund closes. Even so, the capital usually takes several years to be drawn down from the limited partners: it is very rare for private equity partnerships to ask for all of their capital up-front. Rather, they will seek to have capital drawdowns coincide as closely as possible with the arrival of investment opportunities in order that they not have substantial unused capital under management. (Such unused funds—which the groups deposit in a money market account until invested—depress the rate of return reported for the fund.[6]) The private equity groups will then invest these funds and several years later will return the proceeds (either in the form of cash or stock) to the fund-of-funds. The proceeds—less any share taken by the managers of the fund-of-funds—will then be sent to the limited partners.

Most fund-of-funds managers focus exclusively on investments into new partnerships (sometimes referred to as "primary" investments). A significant minority of funds, however, also makes two other types of investments. The most frequent of these additional investments are "secondary" purchases: the acquisition of stakes in already-active private equity partnerships from other investors. (Many of the sellers of partnership interests are corporations. For instance, a corporate chief financial officer may feel that the pension plan of a recently acquired firm has too great an exposure to private equity, or a new CEO may decide that his predecessor's program of investing corporate funds in venture funds is not yielding any strategic benefits. Rather than waiting until the funds gradually liquidate themselves, the executives may seek to reduce their exposure by selling off the portfolio.) Funds-of-funds making such purchases argue that their existing portfolio allows them to better evaluate such transactions. Furthermore, the purchase of a stake in a mature fund allows them to begin returning capital sooner than if they needed to wait until their primary investments began bearing fruit.

The other class of investments that many fund-of-funds managers make are "direct" transactions: the purchase of a direct equity stake in a private firm. In many cases, these investments are made alongside private equity groups: many funds will allow their limited partners to co-invest, particularly in the latter financing rounds just before going public. (These financing rounds are, of course, also at higher valuations than earlier rounds.) Fund-of-funds managers that make such investments argue that they give them a better sense of market conditions. Other fund-of-fund managers shun such transactions, expressing concerns about the potential conflicts-of-interest that can emerge in such settings.

Funds-of-funds also differ in the types of private equity groups that they select for investments. Some of these funds seek to offer a diversified array of private equity investments, commingling U.S. buyout and venture capital funds with international funds.

---

[6] Consulting firms such as Cambridge Associates and Venture Economics compute the rate of return from the perspective of the limited partner, examining the date and size of capital draw-downs and distributions. They typically do not consider the fact that limited partners must set funds aside in order to fund capital calls from these funds, which may impact their returns.

Others specialize in specific categories (e.g., early-stage venture capital or European buyout funds). Finally, some groups offer a family of funds, each specializing in a particular area.

A final set of differences relates to the sponsors of these funds. In some cases, such as Grove Street Advisors or HarbourVest Partners, the raising and management of funds-of-funds is the primary (or even sole) focus of the organization. These groups typically argue that their single focus helps limit the conflict-of-interest problems that might emerge elsewhere. In other cases, private equity funds are just one of a series of asset management offerings. For instance, Brinson Partners markets to its clients a wide variety of public equity, fixed income, and private equity products. Taking this one step further, commercial and investment banks offer funds-of-funds to their clients, as well as to outside investors. In many cases, these funds may invest in affiliated private equity groups as well as independent funds with which the bank has a close working relationship (e.g., ones for which it also serves as a placement agent). Reflecting the depth of their client bases, these bank-affiliated funds have tended to be the largest in size.

Exhibits 6-3 and 6-4 provide some information about the costs associated with investing in funds-of-funds. Historically, funds-of-funds charged a management fee of about 1%. (These fees are, of course, in addition to those charged by the private equity funds in which they invest.) With the extensive entry into the industry in recent years, fees have become much more varied. In addition, these groups are increasingly

EXHIBIT 6-3

DISTRIBUTION OF MANAGEMENT FEES IN 41 REPRESENTATIVE FUNDS-OF-FUNDS

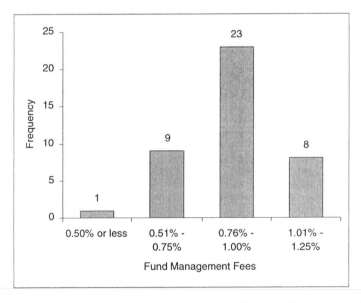

Source: Compiled from Robert Pease, *Private Equity Funds-of-Funds: State of the Market*, Wellesley, MA, Asset Alternatives, 2000.

EXHIBIT 6-4

DISTRIBUTION OF CARRIED INTEREST ON PRIMARY INVESTMENTS IN 41 REPRESENTATIVE FUNDS-OF-FUNDS

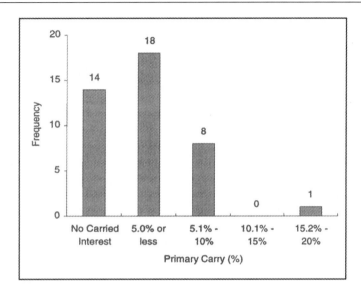

Source: Compiled from Robert Pease, *Private Equity Funds-of-Funds: State of the Market*, Wellesley, MA, Asset Alternatives, 2000.

taking a share of the capital gains.[7] These general comparisons obscure some of the differences between various types of funds-of-funds. For instance, fees are higher in funds that are geared to individual investors than those aimed at institutional investors. Many funds also take a greater carried interest on the returns from secondary purchases and direct investments than they do for primary investments.

One consequence of the growth of funds-of-funds has been a changing attitude among the general partners of private equity funds. During much of the 1980s and early 1990s, it was commonplace to hear general partners express their unhappiness about accepting capital from funds-of-funds and other intermediaries.[8] These organizations were perceived as adding little value while mercurially jumping between funds in search of the highest returns. Furthermore, some intermediaries were seen as insisting on restrictive terms-and-conditions, even if they hindered the flexibility of general partners

---

[7] One reason why early funds-of-funds did not take any carried interest was that the investors were primarily pension funds. The Employment Retirement Investment Security Act severely limits the ability of funds that receive at least 25% of their capital from pension funds to receive incentive-based compensation. While an exception for "venture capital operating companies" allows private equity organizations to receive carried interest, funds-of-funds do not meet this criterion because they do not primarily make direct investments.

[8] For illustrations of such discussions, see Renee Deger, "Barbarians behind the Gate: Gatekeepers Guard Wary Investors from Would-be Venture Predators," *Venture Capital Journal* 35 (November 1995): 45–48 and Edwin A. Goodman, "Gatekeepers' 'Reforms' Reap Negative Consequences," *Venture Capital Journal* 30 (December 1990): 25–28.

while giving investors few added protections. (General partners claimed that because the performance of the funds recommended by intermediaries took so long to evaluate, these organizations instead sought to impress investors by negotiating "tough" agreements, even when not needed.) As the bargaining power in partnership negotiations have swung increasingly to the general partners, these complaints have become less common.

THE ORIGINS OF UNIVERSITY TECHNOLOGY VENTURES

The genesis of University Technology Ventures can be traced back to 1996. In that year, Mark Harris was signed by the San Francisco Forty-Niners upon graduating from Stanford University, and veteran Tommy Vardell joined the team from the Cleveland Browns.

Upon joining his new team, Vardell soon gravitated to Brent Jones, a Forty-Niners veteran. They soon realized that they shared an interest in getting a better understanding of the financial world, particularly venture capital. Jones, an economics major in college, had been since 1990 an active investor in publicly traded technology stocks. His interest had initially been triggered after experiencing early successes with investments in companies such as Cisco and Microsoft. While his initial investments may have been selected because they were building major facilities near the Forty-Niners training camp, over time Jones gained considerable experience in public equity investing and built relationships with a number of local fund managers. He had been interested since 1994 in complementing his public equity investments with venture capital. While he soon identified the groups with which he wanted to invest, he also learned that getting access to top-tier funds could be daunting.

After discussing these issues, the two men set out to schedule a series of meetings with local venture firms. Although they were able to get appointments to see a number of groups, establishing credibility with the general partners proved challenging. In particular, a meeting with a partner at an old-line Silicon Valley venture group brought this reality home to the two. Almost immediately after sitting down, the partner brought up the fact that innumerable institutional and institutional investors had been attempting to get access to their fund for years. What precisely, he asked, could Jones and Vardell do for the partnership to justify them getting preferred access? The men raised the possibilities of 50-yard line seats and training camp passes. The partner abruptly informed them that he and his colleagues already had access to these, and brought the meeting to a close.

Over the next years, however, Jones and Vardell began establishing a relationship with this and other groups. When the partners came to training camp, for instance, the players made a point to come over and greet them—much to the delight of the partners, but even more so of their children! Similarly, they were able to obtain sideline passes for a number of partners for a Monday Night Football game. In turn, they began being asked to participate in angel financings of firms and to invest in companion funds that many venture organizations raise for the entrepreneurs they have backed and other close associates.

Meanwhile, Mark Harris had been undertaking his own explorations of venture investing. He had been interested in venture capital since his enrollment as an undergraduate in a course at Stanford Business School taught by Larry Mohr, founding partner of Mohr Davidow Ventures. Harris had undertaken a series of angel investments while a member of the Forty-Niners and had resolved to deepen his knowledge of the industry.

A second spur for the creation of the fund was Champion Ventures, a fund-of-funds established by and for athletes that was launched in June 1999. Jones and Vardell provided important assistance to former teammates Ronnie Lott and Harris Barton, who had established the fund inspired by accounts of sport stars who had lost much of their wealth through investments in ill-considered businesses and outright scams.[9] Jones and Vardell presented the concept to a number of their colleagues (who ultimately accounted for about 40% of the total capital raised) and introduced Barton to his first venture capitalist contacts. When Champion's first fund closed in November 1999 (Barry Bonds, Dan Marino, Jerry Rice, and Steve Young were among the investors in the $40 million fund), Jones and Vardell were asked to serve as advisors to Champion Ventures.

In late 1999, Harris and Vardell retired from the National Football League and began seriously contemplating their futures. In long talks with Jones, the men realized that they had a strong desire to work in the venture capital arena. For instance, Harris, seeking to deepen his knowledge, had undertaken a four-month internship at New Enterprise Associates shortly after retiring.

At the same time, the three men shared a real desire to make a broader contribution to society: just using their access to invest in venture capital transactions was not what they had in mind. In mulling over this challenge, they soon came up with a brainstorm: they should use their access to the venture funds to enable access by others to venture capital. And what better group than those affiliated with academic institutions? Indeed, many of the ideas behind the venture capital explosion had originated in university laboratories and seminars. But while the university endowments had invested heavily in venture capital, few faculty members had the chance to benefit from these activities. Meanwhile, there was also a serious information gap. Harris recalled the dilemma of one of his father-in-law's colleagues at Stanford. An expert on wireless communications, the faculty member was approached on almost a daily basis by venture groups seeking advice and involvement. Without a clear understanding of which callers were credible and which were not, the calls went largely unanswered.

As their thinking evolved, they expanded their conversations to include two others. Steve Young, the legendary quarterback, had also joined, expressing a particular interest in working on the charitable side of the fund's activities. They had also recruited Mark Williams, who had extensive accounting experience in start-up and venture capital environments, as the fund's chief financial officer. The biographies of the principals of the fund are reproduced in Exhibit 6-5.

The challenge, the founders realized, was to structure the fund in such a way that everyone would benefit. In particular, the partners needed to figure out how three sets of parties—the academics, the venture funds, and the universities—could benefit from this new effort. While the financial benefits to the academics were clear—the opportunity to invest with top-tier groups that they would otherwise not have a chance to access—there were also other possible advantages. Informal contacts with entrepreneurs and venture capitalists might stimulate research ideas, as well as being personally

---

[9] At the same time, they realized that the high-profile athletes might be of assistance to companies in the venture capitalists' portfolios, many of which were struggling to stand out among a sea of competitors. By serving as celebrity endorsers or even just showing up at a launch party, the athletes might significantly enhance the firms' prospects. The information on Champion Ventures is drawn from Laura M. Holson, "What Shatner Hath Wrought; The Intersection of the Internet and Celebrity," *New York Times*, June 6, 2000, C1 *ff*.; Roy S. Johnson, "Playing for Big Money," *Fortune* 141 (May 15, 2000): 328–338; "Champion Ventures Closes Its First Fund-of-Funds," PR Newswire, November 30, 1999; and http://www.championventures.com.

EXHIBIT 6-5

THE FUND MANAGERS

Brent Jones Co-founder and general partner of UTV, graduated with a BS degree in Economics from the University of Santa Clara. He subsequently played 12 years in the National Football League, 11 of those years with the San Francisco Forty-Niners. A four-time All-Pro performer and three-time Super Bowl champion, Brent received the Forty-Niners' NFL Man of the Year award in 1997. He was also the NFL's Bart Starr Award recipient in 1998, given annually to the player that most exemplifies outstanding character in the home, on the field, and in the community. Brent has been a technology investor for over 10 years and is a limited partner at several of the world's top venture capital funds. He has direct investment experience in VA Linux, Assured Access, Nvidia, Netro, Rightworks, and in several new start-ups.

Tommy Vardell Co-founder and general partner of UTV, he recently retired from the NFL after eight seasons with the Cleveland Browns, the Detroit Lions, and the San Francisco Forty-Niners. He graduated with a BS degree in Industrial Engineering from Stanford University, where he was honored as the top student-athlete in the nation, garnering the GTE Academic All-American of the Year award. Tommy was a first-round pick (ninth overall) of the Cleveland Browns in 1992 and holds the all-time best marks for rushing and scoring at Stanford. Vardell has been involved in venture capital projects as a limited partner of several top-tier funds, an angel investor, and an advisory board member. He currently endows a scholarship at Stanford for character, athletic and academic excellence.

Mark Harris Co-founder and general partner of UTV, he retired from the NFL in 1999 after a four-year career with the San Francisco Forty-Niners. Mark graduated from Stanford University with a degree in Psychology. At Stanford, Harris excelled athletically and academically, receiving All-Pac 10 athletic and academic honors as a senior. In addition, he was voted as a team captain for his senior season. Mark has experienced venture capitalism at various levels: he has seen the inner workings of a venture capital firm as an intern for New Enterprise Associates, and he has also participated in private company funding as a limited partner and angel investor. Mark has traveled extensively and is fluent in Spanish.

Steve Young General partner of UTV, he joined UTV after 15 years in the NFL, primarily with the San Francisco Forty-Niners, where he received numerous accolades, including Most Valuable Player of Super Bowl XXIX, *Sports Illustrated* and *Sporting News'* Player of the Year from 1992 to 1994, and the NFL's Most Valuable Player for 1992 and 1994. Steve is a graduate of Brigham Young University where he earned a *Juris Doctorate* degree from the College of Law in 1994, along with a BS degree in 1983. In 1993, he established the Forever Young Foundation, an international, nonprofit, public charity that focuses on the development, security, strength and education of children. Steve has had extensive experience in venture capital investments and in entrepreneurial projects as a limited partner, angel investor, and board member. He currently serves as chairman of Found, Inc, an Accel Partners investment.

Mark Williams Chief Financial Officer, he brings over 15 years of Silicon Valley business experience to UTV. From 1982 to 1990, Mark worked at Price Waterhouse, primarily in its tax division, in San Jose, CA. At Price Waterhouse, Mark worked with private and multinational public companies. In 1990, Mark joined Ruzzo, Scholl & Murphy, he worked with many start-ups providing accounting and business consulting services. Mark also served as CFO to Redleaf Venture I, a venture capital fund with investments in Internet start-ups, from 1996 to 1999. Mark has served on the boards of several nonprofit organizations, including the Boy Scouts of America (Santa Clara County Council) and Child Advocates of Santa Clara & San Mateo Counties.

Source: Corporate document.

rewarding. Contacts with the young companies might also lead to consulting opportunities for the faculty members as well.

It was also important to articulate the benefits to the other parties. The founders also believed that the network of academics could be of real benefit to the venture capitalists in generating deal-flow and undertaking due diligence. Although some of the largest venture capital groups had academic advisory boards, in many cases they consisted of senior scientists who were far from the "cutting edge" of research. Many other groups relied on informal ties with scientists for assistance in due diligence, but these had a "hit or miss" quality: the fit between the expertise of the academic and the situation being evaluated was often far from exact. Venture capitalists and academics had a great deal to gain from each other, but neither set of individuals had the time to seek out contacts with each other.

Another potential benefit for the venture capitalists was the anticipated development of an on-line job exchange. The founders realized that faculty members often were in the situation of advising students making career choices. In many cases, students at top-tier schools had a bewildering array of choices and little information to help them choose between firms. By allowing faculty members to better direct students to firms associated with top-tier venture groups, the site could ease these firms' recruiting woes.

If the fund could create a network of academicians that the venture capitalists could readily draw upon, it would add real value. It would allow the venture capitalists to expand their network of contacts without exhausting their already overtaxed "bandwidth." The founders were confident that they could add value to portfolio companies: in fact, they had already helped place a chief technical officer at a portfolio firm of one of the venture funds in which they had invested as individuals.

Finally, ensuring real benefits to the academic institution was important. In initial conversations with university officials, they learned that the attrition of faculty to entrepreneurial ventures was a real concern, particularly at universities in the Bay Area. In many cases, junior faculty in engineering and the physical sciences, skeptical that their ideas would ever be commercialized by the school's technology transfer office, were opting to leave their teaching positions to pursue these ideas.[10] The academic officials, concerned about holding on to these young stars, suggested that such investment opportunities could offer faculty an important avenue to build their wealth while remaining inside the academy. More directly, the partners hoped to include an explicitly philanthropic component to the fund.

STRUCTURING THE PARTNERSHIP

Over the past decade, many funds-of-funds had been raised. In formulating University Technology Ventures, the partners sought to draw on this experience. At the same time, they wanted to ensure that the terms of the fund-of-funds would be fair to investors.

---

[10] Because faculty members are employees of the university, they typically must disclose and assign all ideas to their employer. The responsibility for determining how to commercialize the idea is usually assigned to the school's technology transfer office. While the size of and revenues generated by university technology transfer offices had increased sharply during the 1980s and 1990s, in most cases they still remained quite modest in size. Furthermore, they remained largely focused on the commercialization of biomedical (as opposed to information technology) innovations. For a detailed discussion, see David C. Mowery and Arvids A. Ziedonis, "Numbers, Quality, and Entry: How Has the Bayh-Dole Act Affected U.S. University Patenting and Licensing?," *Innovation Policy and the Economy* 1 (2000):187–220.

EXHIBIT 6-6

SUMMARY OF FUND TERMS

Structure	University Technology Ventures, L.P. (the "Fund") will be a Delaware limited partnership. The general partner of the Fund will be UTV, L.L.C. (the "General Partner,") a Delaware limited liability company. All investors must qualify as "accredited investors" within the meaning of the United States Securities Act of 1933.
Purpose	To acquire and hold limited partnership interests in leading venture capital funds. The Fund will invest idle cash in high-quality "money market" securities on a short-term basis pending making investments.
Fund Management	The Fund will be managed by its General Partner. The managing members ("Managing Members") of the General Partner will be Mark Harris, Brent Jones, Tommy Vardell, and Steve Young (the "Fund Managers").
Fund Term and Management Fee	The Fund will have a 12-year term. The General Partner (or an entity affiliated with the General Partner) will receive an annual management fee of up to 1.0% of the Fund's committed capital. The annual management fee shall be payable quarterly in advance.
Capital Contributions	The Limited Partners will contribute capital to the Fund in installments, upon 15 days' notice. The General Partner will contribute 1% of committed capital. The Fund may admit additional Limited Partners or accept increased committed capital from existing Limited Partners at one or more additional closings held within nine months after the initial closing.
Investment Scholarships	The General Partner will grant Investment Scholarships to distinguished university professors. Each Investment Scholarship will consist of an interest in the General Partner representing an indirect investment of up to $20,000 in the Fund. With respect to each Investment Scholarship that is granted, the General Partner will increase its capital commitment to the Fund (i.e., if the General Partner grants a $20,000 Investment Scholarship, then the General Partner will increase its capital commitment to the Fund by an additional $20,000). The principal contributions for the scholarships will be made in the form of a full recourse promissory note.
Allocation of Income, Gains, and Losses	Net recognized capital gains and losses will be allocated 95% to the partners (General and Limited) in proportion to capital contributions; the remaining 5% will be allocated to the General Partner. Operating income (loss) will be allocated to the partners (General and Limited) in proportion to their capital contributions.
Distributions	A portion of net recognized capital gains and net ordinary income sufficient to pay income taxes resulting from such gains and income will be distributed to the Fund's partners annually in the proportions that such income is allocated to the partners. In addition, the General Partner may, in its discretion but subject to the satisfaction of certain conditions, make additional distributions in cash and distributions in kind of portfolio securities, with such distributions being made 5% to the General Partner and 95% to the Partners (General and Limited). Twenty percent of the distributions made to the General Partner will be donated to charitable organizations and university fellowships.
Lookback	If at the time the Fund is liquidated the General Partner's cumulative distributions of profits exceed 5% of the Fund's net recognized profits from portfolio investments, the General Partner will refund such excess distributions—provided that the General Partner shall not be required to refund an amount in excess of the cumulative carried interest distributions received by the General Partner less the amount thereof that the General Partner has donated to charities and fellowships, and less taxes paid or deemed paid by the General Partner in respect of its carried interest. Each member of the General Partner will guarantee his or its pro rata portion of the obligations of the General Partner under this lookback.

(Continued)

EXHIBIT 6-6   *(Continued)*

General Partner Advisory Board	The General Partner will have an Advisory Board experienced in the university community and venture capital investments. The seven initial members are: Jehoshua Bruck from California Institute of Technology; Tom Byers from Stanford University; Joe Goodman from Stanford University; Dave Hodges from U.C. Berkeley; Randy Katz from U.C. Berkeley; Raman Khana from Diamondhead Ventures; and John Kohler from Redleaf Ventures. The Advisory board will be available to consult with the Fund Managers on university issues, technologies, and vehicles for university benefits, but generally will have no other power to participate in the Fund's management.
Investment Restrictions	Except with the approval of a majority in interest of the Limited Partners, the Fund shall not invest (i) in securities the issuer of which is not an existing portfolio investment after the fourth year of the Fund's operations, (ii) in entities other than investment funds or (iii) in any options or futures contracts, or any other security, the value of which is based upon, or derived from, any underlying index, reference rate (e.g., interest rate or currency exchange rate), other security, commodity or other asset; provided, however, that this restriction shall not be deemed to prohibit the General partner from hedging against currency exchange rate risk.
Formation of New Fund	The Fund Managers will not form or manage any new investment fund with similar objectives and operations until such time as at least 70% of the Fund's capital commitments have been invested in portfolio investments, used to pay expenses or reserved for follow-on investments or additional capital calls in portfolio investments. Until such time, the Fund Managers shall devote substantially all of their business time to the affairs of the General Partner and the Fund and entities formed to manage the Fund.
Partnership Expenses	All "overhead" expenses (i.e., salaries, rent, equipment, and utilities) in connection with activities related to the Fund shall be paid out of the management fee. The Fund will, however, bear all expenses incident to the organization of the Fund, the General Partner, and entities formed to manage the Fund, and all legal, administrative, audit, registration, financial fees and any extraordinary expense of the Fund.
Attorneys	Legal counsel will be Gunderson, Dettmer, Stough, Villeneuve, Franklin & Hachigian, LLP, Menlo Park, California.
Auditors	Auditors for the Partnership will be PriceWaterhouseCoopers or any other nationally recognized independent accounting firm as the General Partner may so decide.

Source: Corporate document.

In particular, as a starting point they used the structure of Connecticut-based FLAG Venture Partners (a pioneer in funds-of-funds designed for individuals). They anticipated charging an annual management fee of 1% as well as a 5% share of the capital gains. The lawyers advising them suggested that many funds in the market were more aggressive in their terms, such as receiving 10% of all capital gains above a 10% rate-of-return. The partners resisted adding such a feature.

Many other provisions were also standard in partnership agreements. For instance, the partners were restricted from investing directly in entrepreneurial transactions or funds other than those specializing in private equity. Similarly, they were not allowed to form a new fund until this one had been 70% invested or committed. (See Exhibit 6-6 for the partnership's term sheet.)

Other features were more unusual. The partners realized that many of the most dynamic thinkers—young researchers early in their careers who were most likely be at the "cutting edge" of science—were likely to be precluded from investing in the fund. Many of these young scientists, who were likely to be starting families and purchasing homes, might not have enough disposable income to meet the $25,000 minimum investment requirement. Even if they did, they were unlikely to meet the net worth criteria that determined whether or not an investor was "sophisticated."

To include this group, they developed a novel concept of an "investment scholarship." The general partners would set aside $1 million to fund a number of these scholarships. Essentially, each scholarship recipient would receive a $20,000 interest in the fund as a (nonrecourse[11]) loan. They would be listed in a directory of limited partners which the partners planned to distribute to the venture capitalists, and they could be contacted by the venture investors just as the other limited partners. The proceeds from their investments would first go to repaying the loan and then flow to the scholarship recipients as if they had invested their own capital.

The final element of the fund was also unusual: the explicit earmarking of a portion of the general partners' incentive compensation for charity. In particular, 20% of the carried interest (or 1% of the overall capital gains) would be devoted to charities and to fellowships at the universities of the participating faculty members.

THE FUNDRAISING CHALLENGE

As the partners began to explore the raising of the fund in the fall of 2000, they soon encountered a variety of challenges. Although in some cases these were pleasant ones, others posed challenges to their initial business model.

One pleasant surprise was the degree of interest exhibited by the venture capital community. Their initial thought was to invest in no more than 10 funds. They intended to ask for an investment slot of $10 million in each fund, expecting in many cases to be allocated a smaller amount. (In many cases, rather than shutting out chosen investors, venture capitalists will limit the fund size by trimming the allocation to each investor.) Instead, a number of groups had been so enthusiastic about the concept that they had given them the entire allocation requested, and one had indicated that they could invest as much as $15 million. In addition to the size of the commitments, the quality of the funds that had agreed to accept funds was excellent as well. The funds included Accel Venture Partners, Greylock, Highland Capital, Kleiner, Perkins, Caufield & Byers, Mohr Davidow, New Enterprise Associates, Redpoint Ventures, Sequoia Capital, and U.S. Venture Partners.

Another surprise was the concern shown about conflict of interest, particularly at the state-run universities that they visited. In many conversations, the question surfaced whether the university sponsored the fund. If so, offering the opportunity to some but not all faculty members might violate university employment policies. The partners had to repeatedly make clear that while they hoped the activity would benefit the university, the fund was strictly independent of the academic institution, and that the fund managers were solely responsible for selecting those who were offered the investment opportunity.[12]

---

[11] That is, the individuals would not be liable for repayment of the loan in the unlikely event that the fund was unsuccessful and did not generate any returns. Originally, the partners had considered the possibility that these loans would come from the fund itself, but they decided not to include any provisions that might depress the returns of the limited partners.

[12] Other issues also surfaced. For instance, in some cases, the size of the commitment to venture capital that potential investors desired had declined after the April 2000 market correction and the subsequent volatility in technology stocks.

But the most fundamental challenge was the need to balance the relatively small investments that many academic investors wished to make with the need to raise a significant-sized fund with 99 or fewer investors. Although they had obtained commitments from almost three dozen investors and had received over $30 million in capital commitments, the fundraising challenge had been larger than initially anticipated. The pressure imposed by the "Rule of 99" was substantial. If they were to raise a $75 million fund, for instance, the fund needed an average capital commitment of over $750,000. If they were to target dramatically smaller investments, this would sharply increase the number of potential investors. Such a step would also be likely to substantially reduce the final fund size and the viability of their investment strategy.

The partners realized that in future funds they might be able to ameliorate this problem by raising two funds at a time. One could be for accredited investors, and the other for qualified ones that met the higher net worth test. The number of qualified investors in the fund could be substantial, though they would still only be able to raise money from 99 accredited investors. Such a step would have a real cost, however: they would need to ask the venture capitalists for two slots rather than just one.

One way to address these problems, they realized, would be to open the fund to other types of investors. Many wealthy individuals, from scions of "old money" families to newly liquid entrepreneurs, were clamoring to access venture capital funds. The partners could expand their investor target and allow such individuals to invest as well. Similarly, a number of institutions, particularly smaller university and foundation endowments, were interested in investing in the fund. Such a step posed a real danger however. The fund might lose its focus as a result, producing an offering that had less appeal to both academics and venture capitalists. How serious was this problem? How far could the partners go in accepting such money without jeopardizing the fund's appeal?

Another way to accelerate the fundraising process would be to generate publicity for the effort. A number of major business periodicals had expressed interest in writing feature stories about the new fund. Such coverage could alert potential investors about the opportunity to invest in University Technology Ventures.

The partners were reluctant to do so, however, for several reasons. First, they worried that the articles would focus more on who they were than on what they hoped to accomplish. More importantly, they were also concerned that the publicity might displease both the academics and venture capitalists. Even though many scientists had substantial commercial involvement, in many institutions such activities were still somewhat denigrated. Thus, publicity about their investment activities might not be welcome. Similarly, many venture capital funds that had agreed to accommodate their funds had been turning away institutional investors for a number of years. These investors might be antagonized if they learned that a new group had been able to get access to the fund while they had not.

7

A Note on the Private Equity Fundraising Process

The process by which private equity groups raise funds is often shrouded in obscurity. While established groups can often raise their new funds in a matter of weeks, if not days, the process is very different for less established private equity organizations. For these groups, the fundraising process can prove to be a painfully slow one.

This note seeks to remove some of the mystery from the fundraising process. It highlights three aspects. First, the key actors in the fundraising drama are considered. We then consider the special case of first-time funds and the challenges that these organizations face. Finally, we consider the broader question of what determines the overall level of private equity fundraising.

THE ACTORS

The general partners are the venture capitalists or private equity investors who are responsible for the day-to-day management of the fund. Although they receive a substantial share of the capital gains from the fund, the general partners typically only contribute a modest amount of its capital. U.S. tax law formerly stipulated that the general partners needed to invest at least 1% of the capital in a limited partnership. While this requirement has been relaxed, 1% remains the typical share to invest. Particularly in first-time funds and in very large buyout funds, much of this investment may be in the form of notes rather than cash. This reflects the fact that the general partners may not have the liquid resources in order to place this much capital into the fund up-front.

In two circumstances, however, it is common to see general partners making larger investments. The first is first-time funds, when establishing the credibility with potential limited partners may be very difficult. The general partners may consequently supply a larger share of the capital. Not only does this contribution allow the fund to achieve a "critical mass" in some cases, but it signals the commitment of the general partners

---

Professor Josh Lerner prepared this note as the basis for class discussion rather than to illustrate either effective or ineffective handling of an administrative situation.

to the success of the fund. (Some limited partners, however, find such large commitments worrisome, believing that the venture capitalists may become unwilling to make risky but attractive investments.) The other circumstance is becoming increasingly common: established funds whose partners have amassed significant amounts of wealth. In these instances, the partners may desire to put more and more of the capital into the fund, even if it "crowds out" other investors.

The limited partners include a wide array of individual and institutional investors, from families to pension funds to corporations. They often vary widely in their experience and sophistication. Although established university endowments and old-line families may have long-standing relationships with well-established venture and buyout funds, many investors find themselves "on the outside looking in." Without established relationships, they are likely to find it hard to invest in top-tier organizations. In many cases, these investors also lack the experience (or the confidence) to identify which first-time private equity groups are attractive, and consequently refuse to invest in funds organized by less established organizations as a rule.

There are also several distinct kinds of limited partners. One of these, the special limited partner, will be discussed in detail in the next section. Another is the "friend" of the fund. These friends include successful entrepreneurs who had been backed by the venture fund and former general partners who have retired from the fund. These friends typically invest in a special companion fund, which often has more favorable terms than the main fund.

Also on the stage are a variety of intermediaries. Some of these are hired by the limited partners, others by the general partners.

Investment advisors, or "gatekeepers," have been a fixture in the private equity world since the early 1970s.[1] The first such organization was established in 1972, when the First National Bank of Chicago established an advisory group as part of its trust department. (This operation was ultimately purchased in a management buyout in 1989 and took on the name Brinson Partners. Among the other pioneers of the advisory business were Bigler Investment Management and Horsley Bridge Partners, formerly known as Horsley Keough.) These organizations typically provide advisory services to some clients (who still make the ultimate decision where to invest) while exercising discretionary control over other clients' assets. Typically, these advisors will set up separate accounts for the larger investors but commingle the assets of smaller investors into one or more "funds-of-funds."

The 1990s saw a dramatic growth in and increasing specialization of funds-of-funds. Many new entrants organized these funds, most notably the major investment banks, which raised multibillion funds from their high net worth clients. The new funds included some geared toward certain classes of investors, such as the Common Fund (university and other educational endowments) and FLAG Venture Partners (high net worth families). Others targeted certain investment niches: for instance, international private equity funds, minority-managed funds, and those based in a particular state. In the late 1990s, some funds-of-funds were even established to invest in a single fund.[2] The fund organizers typically charge an annual fee based on capital under management, typically around 1%. Some funds-of-funds, however, also receive a share of the carried interest in addition to management fees.

---

[1] For a more detailed discussion of the role of investment advisors, see "University Technology Ventures," Chapter 6 in this volume.

[2] Many buyout groups welcomed investments by new investors but had high minimum investment amounts due to federal securities regulations. By investing through a fund, a number of individuals who could not otherwise reach the minimum investment size could obtain access to the private equity fund.

A related set of intermediaries are the consulting firms. These groups, such as Venture Economics and Cambridge Associates, help limited partners make investment decisions but do not actually manage funds themselves. Rather, they monitor the performance of the private equity groups and the industry as a whole. These organizations provide institutional and individual investors with a view of the relative performance of the groups already in their portfolio and investments that they are considering. In some cases, they may even make recommendations to limited partners as to whether or not to invest in particular funds.

Placement agents play a similar role for the general partners. Although the typical private equity group only raises a fund every two or three years, these groups continually represent groups that are raising funds. Thus, they maintain close ties to the leading investors and have a keen sense of the market. Placement agents range from the major investment banks (e.g., Merrill Lynch) to specialist boutiques (for instance, the Monument Group) to a myriad of one-person shops. Traditionally, established placement agents only worked for buyout groups. In recent years, however, as venture organizations have begun raising considerably larger funds from a more diverse base of investors, more of these groups have retained placement agents as well.

The fees charged by these groups for their services are highly variable. For the very largest buyout funds, the fee may be as low as one-half of 1% of the capital actually raised by the placement agent. For a first-time fund, on the other hand, the fee may be as high as 3% of the fund's total capital. In these instances, some of the fee may be demanded up-front (on a non-refundable basis, even if the fundraising is unsuccessful), and the placement agent may even ask for some of the general partners' carried interest as well.

THE SPECIAL CHALLENGE OF FIRST-TIME FUNDS

Nowhere is the inefficiency of the private equity fundraising process more apparent than in the raising of first-time funds. Many investors are reluctant to invest in an unproven team. Even if the partners have successful individual track records, their failure to have worked together before as a team may deter investors. Horror stories abound of groups who spent more than two years on the road fundraising, in some cases visiting a single investment advisor a dozen times before being told that they did not invest in first-time funds as a matter of principle.

How does one raise a fund without a track record, when to obtain a track record one needs a fund? New private equity organizations have addressed this conundrum in several ways.

The first is to identify investors who are not purely motivated by financial returns but instead seek some strategic benefit from the fund. For instance, a state pension fund may reserve a certain portion of its venture capital allocation for funds based in the state, in the hopes of stimulating local economic development. Similarly, a corporation with extensive activity in an industry not well served by existing venture funds (e.g., advanced ceramics) may find it attractive to invest in a new fund specializing in this area. In these cases, the investors are willing to accept a lower expected financial return in return for the indirect benefits that the investment will provide.[3]

---

[3] Along similar lines, many first-time funds have found individual investors (particularly those with a background in hedge funds or investment banking) to have a greater appetite for risk than institutional investors and willing to accept the higher variance of returns that come with first-time funds.

A second strategy is to establish an alliance with an existing institution. In some cases, first-time funds have established ties with investment banks or existing private equity groups. These arrangements typically entail the joint ownership of the management company that runs the private equity group. In many instances, the strategic partner has an important role in the governance of the fund, even to the point of having the right to review and approve all investment decisions.

Although such an alliance may impart credibility to a fledgling private equity group, it also comes with some real costs. Other investors may fear that the institutional partner will distort the investment decisions (e.g., blocking otherwise promising investments that potentially compete with its longstanding clients). Alternatively, they may fear that having much of the profits flow to the institution will lead to the private equity investors not having sufficiently strong incentives. Even if the fund can be successfully raised and invested, problems may ensue. Many private equity groups with such ties have gone on to establish stellar track records and realized that the institutional ties were no longer needed to raise funds. In a number of cases, the investors have found their partnership ties time-consuming and costly to unwind.

The final strategy is to recruit what is termed a lead investor (often termed a special limited partner). Such an investor typically contributes a significant percentage of the capital of the fund. It may also provide some "seed funding" to the general partners before the fund closes, in order to cover the often-substantial costs associated with marketing a new fund.

In exchange, the special limited partner typically benefits in at least two ways. For instance, if a special limited partner contributes $25 million to a first-time fund with a total of $100 million in capital commitments, it will receive 25% of the payouts to the limited partners. Since the limited partners typically receive 80% of the capital gains of a first-time fund, this translates into 20% of the overall profits from the fund. In addition, the special limited partner is likely to receive a share of the fund's carried interest. In this example, the special limited partner may receive in addition one-quarter of the carried interest, or 5% of the overall profits of the fund. (This is frequently referred to as five "points.") Finally, the special limited partner may pay lower management fees than other limited partners.

Involving a special limited partner, however, may prove costly to the general partners. First, these payments directly reduce the returns of the private equity investors. Second, the investors may need to make important concessions regarding the governance of the fund, such as allowing the special limited partner to control a powerful advisory board that monitors the fund's activities. Finally, these concessions can alienate other potential investors in the fund. These investors may demand similar concessions for themselves, even if they are not making the "leap of faith" of investing first in the fund that the special limited partner did.

THE DETERMINANTS OF FUNDRAISING ACTIVITY

In the last section of this note, we consider a broader question: what determines the overall level of private equity fundraising? This question can be best answered from a vantage point of 30,000 feet rather than the 300-foot altitude that has characterized most of the discussion in the note.

At the same time, however, this is a very practical question. As the cases in this module have repeatedly emphasized, the ebb and flow of private equity fundraising can have a profound effect on private equity groups. An understanding of fundraising dynamics can thus provide an important competitive advantage to private equity investors.

Various factors may affect the level of commitments to private equity organizations. These factors may be divided into those that affect either the supply of or the demand for private equity.[4] By the *supply* of private equity, we mean the relative desire of institutional investors to commit capital to the sector.

The number of entrepreneurs with good ideas who want financing determines the *demand* for private equity. It is very likely that decreases in capital gains tax rates might increase commitments to the funds, even though the bulk of the funds come from tax-exempt investors. Even a modest drop in the capital gains tax rate may have a substantial effect on the willingness of corporate employees to become entrepreneurs, thereby increasing the need for private equity. This increase in demand due to greater entrepreneurial activity may lead to more fundraising.

Both the supply of and demand for private equity may be stimulated by a robust public equity markets. A vibrant public market permits new firms to issue shares, allowing entrepreneurs and investors to ultimately achieve liquidity and unlock the value in their firms. Furthermore, it has been suggested that only when such a public market exists can private equity investors make a credible commitment to entrepreneurs that they will ultimately relinquish control of the firms in which they invest.[5]

The preceding paragraphs have emphasized rational explanations for the variability in private equity fundraising. But some critics[6] attributed the apparent cyclicality in the amount of venture funds raised to irrational forces. They have argued that institutional investors are prone to either over- or underinvest in speculative markets such as venture capital and private equity. They suggest that this apparently irrational pattern of investing can explain the extreme swings in fundraising. Furthermore, these works argue that such dramatic swings may hinder entrepreneurship and innovation in the American economy.

Empirical research has explored these various claims in the context of U.S. venture capital funds.[7] (Buyout fundraising remains to be explored.) Strong evidence supports the claims regarding capital gains tax rates: lower capital gains taxes seem to have a particularly strong effect on the amount of venture capital supplied by tax-exempt investors. This suggests that the primary mechanism by which capital gains tax cuts affect venture fundraising is by increasing the demand of entrepreneurs for capital. If the effect were on the supply of funds, changes in tax rates should have affected the contribution by taxable entities more dramatically.

A number of other factors influence venture capital fundraising. Not surprisingly, regulatory changes such as the Department of Labor's shift in 1979 in the "prudent

---

[4] The ideas in this paragraph are from James M. Poterba, "How Burdensome Are Capital Gains Taxes? Evidence from the United States," *Journal of Public Economics* 33 (1987): 157–172, and James M. Poterba, "Venture Capital and Capital Gains Taxation," in Lawrence Summers, ed., *Tax Policy and the Economy*, Cambridge, MA: MIT Press, 1989.

[5] See the discussion, for instance, in Bernard S. Black and Ronald J. Gilson, "Venture Capital and the Structure of Capital Markets: Banks versus Stock Markets," *Journal of Financial Economics* 47 (1998): 243–277, and Philippe Aghion, Patrick Bolton, and Jean Tirole, "Exit Options in Corporate Finance: Liquidity versus Incentives," Unpublished working paper, Harvard University, 2000.

[6] Examples include Michael C. Jensen, "Corporate Control and the Politics of Finance," *Journal of Applied Corporate Finance* 4 (Summer 1991): 13–33, and William A. Sahlman and Howard Stevenson, "Capital Market Myopia," *Journal of Business Venturing* 1 (1986): 7–30.

[7] Paul A. Gompers and Josh Lerner, "What Drives Venture Capital Fundraising?," Brookings Papers on Economic Activity: *Microeconomics* (1998): 149–192.

man" rule had an important impact on commitments to private equity funds. In addition, performance influences fundraising. Higher returns—which are typically associated with periods with large number of initial public offerings—lead to greater capital commitments to new funds.

A related study examines the factors that influence venture capital fundraising in 21 countries.[8] It finds that the strength of the IPO market is an important factor in the determinant of venture capital commitments, echoing the conclusions of Black and Gilson. The strength of the IPO market does not, however, seem to influence commitments to early-stage funds as much as later-stage ones. While this work represents an important initial step, much more remains to be explored.

One provocative finding from this analysis is that government policy can have a dramatic impact on the current and long-term viability of the venture capital sector. In many countries, policymakers face a dilemma. The relatively few entrepreneurs active in these markets must deal with numerous daunting regulatory restrictions, a paucity of venture funds focusing on investing in high-growth firms, and illiquid markets where investors do not welcome IPOs by young firms without long histories of positive earnings. It is often unclear where to begin the process of duplicating the United States' success. In these settings, well-targeted government efforts can well play an important and positive role.

---

[8] Leslie A. Jeng and Philippe C. Wells, "The Determinants of Venture Capital Funding: An Empirical Analysis," *Journal of Corporate Finance* 6(2000):241–284.

8

Columbia Capital Corporation: Summer 1998

In August of 1998, the equity owners of Columbia Capital Corporation gathered in the meeting room at the West Chop Club on Martha's Vineyard. The primary question in front of them: should Columbia, a venture capital firm and an investment bank, raise a fund of outside money? Or should they continue, as they had for the firm's 10-year history, making private equity investments with capital supplied entirely by Columbia's own partners?

Based in Alexandria, Virginia, Columbia Capital was founded in 1988 as a boutique investment bank focused on the telecommunications industry, but soon afterward began to shift its focus toward direct private equity investments. Now, 10 years later, even as it maintained its investment banking activity, the firm had come to look a lot like a traditional venture capital firm, placing over $100 million in private equity investments since January of 1994. The main difference was that Columbia had no outside fund—it relied on the personal wealth of its partners to place these venture investments.

As the partners and other Columbia employees drank beer and watched the sun set over the ocean, they contemplated the benefits that an outside fund would afford. A fund would mean a management fee, which would allow them to fund the firm's overhead by means other than the investment banking business—allowing them, as they had wanted to for a number of years, to wind down that side of the business and focus exclusively on venture investing. Moreover, the deep pockets of a $400 million fund would allow them to make larger investments in individual deals, enabling them to own more of attractive companies and, in some cases, to participate in deals that they had been forced to forgo in the past. An outside fund would also ease the succession of a new generation of partners, for whom partnership in the firm did not necessarily imply having adequate personal resources to invest equally with the more senior partners.

But raising outside capital could have disadvantages as well—for the partners' own pocketbooks, first and foremost. After all, since the partners were acting as their own

Bill Wasik prepared this case under the supervision of Senior Lecturer G. Felda Hardymon as the basis for class discussion rather than to illustrate either effective or ineffective handling of an administrative situation.

limiteds, they alone reaped the rewards of their investments' success. With an outside fund, outside investors would snare the lion's share of the profits, although a larger fund would hopefully create a larger pie for everyone. The partners also wondered whether raising a fund might change Columbia's culture and discourage them from making the more opportunistic or speculative investments that had been so rewarding for them in the past.

As the sun crept below the horizon, Columbia's owners realized they had a decision to make. Should they continue, as they always had, as a "quasi-venture capital firm," making venture investments out of their own pockets at their own discretion? Or should they bring in outside funds—with the outside voices and outside responsibilities that came with them?

TELEPHONY AND THE WIRELESS INDUSTRY

Before the 1980s, there were only a handful of telephone companies, and one of them—AT&T—held monopolies over almost all long-distance service and most local service nationwide. By 1998 there were thousands of telephone companies. How did this happen?

1. Divestiture (1984). A heavily regulated monopoly, AT&T was, for most Americans, the single source for both local and long-distance telephone service. By court order, on January 1, 1984, AT&T was broken up into eight separate entities. The first, which retained the name AT&T, was a long-distance arm that retained the facilities used to switch calls between local service areas. Local service was allocated to seven Regional Bell Operating Companies (RBOCs, or "Baby Bells"), each of which was granted a monopoly over local phone service in a distinct region, along with all of AT&T's facilities for switching calls within that region. The divestiture allowed competitive long-distance carriers (called *inter-exchange carriers*, or IXCs) such as MCI and Sprint equal footing with AT&T in offering long-distance services to the RBOCs' customers.

(As a side note, by 1998, as further deregulation of the telecommunications industry had taken root and both AT&T *and* the "Baby Bells" began to face competition, some of the RBOCs were allowed to merge with one another, and AT&T was allowed, via its purchase of Teleport Communications Group, to get back into the local phone market.)

2. Wireless (1982–present). In 1982, the FCC began to award licenses to companies intending to offer wireless telephone services. For each geographic area, the FCC awarded two licenses: the first to the incumbent local telephone company (after 1984, the local RBOC), and the second to the winner of a lottery. The license allowed the holder to offer wireless phone and paging services in the specified frequency band. By 1987, there were over 1 million wireless subscribers; by 1992, over 10 million. Later the FCC would enable the creation of even more wireless carriers through its auctions of more spectrum: most notably, the spectrum using a new technology called "PCS," which was auctioned to three companies in each market for purposes of digital wireless phone services.

3. Deregulation of local markets (mid-1980s–present). While not allowing full competition with the RBOCs, the provisions of early-1980s telecom deregulation did allow competitive local carriers (called *competitive access providers*, or CAPs) to compete for certain special services, such as dedicated leased lines for corporations. Through the 1990s, as states began to deregulate local telecom markets on a state-by-state basis, CAPs were allowed to offer more and more services, reaching out directly to consumers

EXHIBIT 8-1

COLUMBIA CAPITAL PORTFOLIO INVESTMENT SUMMARY— AUGUST 31, 1998

Initial Investment	Portfolio Company	Columbia Investment to Date ($000)	Initial Distribution Date	Distributions to Date ($000)
12/89	Company A	$588	11/94	$4,057
9/91	Company B	16,368	11/95	162,921
5/92	Company C	5,670	1/94	88,705
6/93	Company D	132	12/94	157
8/93	Company E	4,190		
1/94	Company F	19,146		
2/94	Company G	4,456	6/96	3,000
6/94	Company H	6,746		
7/94	Company I	920	12/95	18,176
5/95	Company J	392	6/96	143
6/95	Company K	1,343	2/98	44,976
10/95	Company L	393		
2/96	Company M	27,350	4/98	76,517
8/96	Company N	6,949		
12/96	Company O	1,030	4/98	2,121
4/97	Company P	1,532		
10/97	Company Q	1,080		
12/97	Company R	1,090		
1/98	Company S	4,400		
2/98	Company T	1,970		
2/98	Company U	1,275		
4/98	Company V	2,570		
8/98	Company W	2,400		
	Subtotal	$111,990		$400,773

Source: Corporate document.

and, in some states, actually building their own local facilities. These companies are now typically referred to as *competitive local exchange carriers*, or CLECs, a semantic shift designed to indicate parity with the RBOCs in their fight for local customers.

4. Convergence of voice, data, and video networks (1997–present). Even as corporations adopted local area networks (LANs) and wide area networks (WANs) to share data among their various users and campuses, these data networks were always entirely separate—that is, based on different technologies and run over different physical lines—from their voice networks. During the Internet explosion of the late 1990s, however, new networking technologies (together with deregulation) allowed companies to rethink this separation. New would-be "telephone companies" sprang up, hoping to offer tele-

phone services to businesses and consumers via existing networks not designed for voice at all: the Internet, for example, or cable television systems.

By 1998, a major portion of the deal-flow of venture capitalists and technology investment bankers was transactions involving start-up carriers—a term that two decades ago would have seemed an oxymoron. Telephony, once so monolithic, looked forward to a wide-open future.

"A QUASI-VENTURE CAPITAL FIRM"

In 1983, the FCC's process of awarding cellular licenses was still in relative infancy; initially, it used a process called a "cooperative hearing," and later it moved to a lottery system. Both methods often wound up allocating licenses to parties—partnerships of doctors or lawyers, for example—who had neither the ability nor the inclination to actually run a cellular phone company. Two of Columbia Capital's four eventual founders, Mark Warner and Robert Blow, were at that time both acting as brokers on behalf of these lottery winners, representing them in their negotiations to sell their licenses to the corporations hoping to build cellular networks to compete with the Bells. David Mixer and James Murray, Columbia's other founders, were at that time involved in the burgeoning industry on the "buy" side: Mixer as president of Providence Journal Cellular, which was purchasing and developing cellular properties across the country, and Murray as an independent investor, broker, and advisor for various cellular and paging partnerships.

In 1988, the four men incorporated under the name Columbia Cellular, forming what was in essence an investment bank focused on the cellular and paging industries. "We wanted to form a partnership to do M&A on a more professional and structured basis, but we didn't know where it would go," recalls Murray. "We knew that we each had the right resources and skill sets to be successful, but we knew we had a better chance of doing it together than individually."

The group was entirely focused on M&A work until the end of 1989, when they saw some valuable opportunities to consolidate cellular properties in rural markets. In founding and spinning out Sterling Cellular in December 1989, Columbia Capital made its first foray into direct investment. Capital for the venture ($588,000) was provided by the four partners themselves. Over the next four years, Columbia began to focus more on direct investment, making four additional investments in 1990–1993:

- September 1991: Saville Systems, which designs billing software for telecommunications providers. Columbia's initial investment in Saville was approximately $1.5 million.
- May 1992: Telular Corporation, which builds wireless network interface equipment. Columbia invested $5.6 million in Telular.
- June 1993: CCT/Boatphone, a cellular operator in the British Virgin Islands. Columbia invested $132,000.
- August 1993: Skywire, a developer of end-to-end solutions for wireless data applications. Columbia's initial investment was approximately $3.5 million.

Like the Sterling investment, these four investments were made with the personal capital of the partners (who now numbered five, with the addition of Mark Kington, who had been a commercial banker focusing on wireless). In the meantime, the company also continued its M&A activities in telecommunications, continuing to put together small to midsize ($5–150 million) deals in primarily the cellular and paging industries.

Columbia's direct investment business took a dramatic upturn in January 1994 with the initial public offering of Telular Corporation, in which they had invested only 20 months prior. With the gains from Telular, which at the time of its IPO had a total market capitalization of over $450 million, Columbia was able to greatly increase the number and size of its direct investments over 1994 and 1995. In less than two years, from January 1994 to October 1995, Columbia made seven new direct investments, which included Columbia Spectrum Management, a wireless services company that Columbia itself founded; and Advanced Radio Telecom, which was operating wireless data networks in the broadband 38 Ghz spectrum. They also made substantial follow-on investments in two of their earlier investments, including Saville Systems, where they took their initial $1.5 million investment up to over $16 million.

By November 1995, when Saville Systems went public, Columbia (now Columbia Capital) had blossomed into a full-fledged venture capital firm. In the period between January 1994 and August 1998, Columbia invested over $100 million in 20 different companies. A cascading chain of successes—begun by the IPOs of Telular and Saville and continued with the June 1996 sale of Columbia Spectrum Management to P-COM and the November 1996 IPO of Advanced Radio Telecom—allowed Columbia's principals to invest this formidable total out of their own pockets (see Exhibit 8-1).

"We were not classic venture capitalists by any means," says Warner of the firm's early years. "We were simply guys with a little bit of money in our pockets doing deals in the wireless space. We then started to add infrastructure around this and we became a quasi-venture capital firm."

LIFE WITHOUT LIMITEDS

Venture firms usually raise a fund in advance and then draw down capital from the fund over a predetermined period of time. For example, a typical early-stage venture fund might raise $300 million to be invested over some fixed period of time, perhaps six years. Typically, 2% of the total committed capital (i.e., 2% of $300 million, or $6 million) is paid to the firm annually by the limited partners as a "management fee" to pay employee salaries and assorted overhead. As deals achieve liquidity—in the form of cash or public stock—the firm distributes the proceeds to its limited partners according to a predetermined formula. Typically, that formula involves first, returning invested capital to each limited partner; second (in some firms, notably LBO firms) awarding a "preferred return" of 8–10% to each limited; and third, splitting the remaining profits (if any) 80–20 between the limiteds and the firm, respectively. The firm's 20% would typically then be divided among the firm's partners according to its partnership agreement.

In Columbia's case, no funds were raised ahead of time. After a deal was approved, each partner of the firm would write a personal check for his share. Although each partner was free not to take his full share in a deal, there was, for obvious reasons, "an enormous social pressure" to step up in full. In reality, only on a few occasions did a partner not take his full share of a deal, and even then that partner would not opt out entirely.

After a deal became liquid, Columbia stuck to the formula fairly closely, treating each partner like a typical firm might treat a limited. Capital, a preferred return, and 80% of remaining profits were returned to each partner in the proportion of his initial investment; the remaining 20% of profits was distributed among the firm's partners according to their partnership split. (The distinction between these proportions—the percentage each partner invests in each deal and the percentage each partner "owns" of the firm as a whole—became more important as time went on. For more on this, see below.) Typically, a sizable portion of the 20% "firm" carry was awarded to those professionals who had spearheaded the deal—a share the principals dubbed the "worker-bee split."

Since there was no fund, there was also no management fee. The partners relied on the firm's M&A activity to fund salaries and overhead for the direct investment practice.

As compared to other venture firms, how did Columbia's lack of limiteds impact their investment performance? There are three distinguishing features of Columbia's direct investment pattern, all of which can be traced (at least in part) to their lack of reliance on outside money.

1. No restrictions on investments   Venture capital funds vary as to the strictness of requirements placed on investments. By and large, however, limited partners require firms to meet certain guidelines: not to invest more than a given dollar amount in any single company, for example, or to invest only in companies in a certain industry or stage of development. "With limited partners, you lose a little bit of the flexibility to do speculative-type stuff," says Mixer. "Sometime I see deals and I say, 'I'd do that—but would I do that with *your* money?'"

Although the majority of Columbia's investments have fallen within the typical parameters of early-stage venture investments, with total fund exposures in individual deals running from $1 to $7 million, there have been notable exceptions at both the low and high ends. One such exception was a $27 million investment in Digital Television Services, a reseller of satellite TV service provider DIRECTV—a gamble that paid off big in April 1996, when DTS merged with a public competitor, Pegasus Communications Corporation.

2. Conceiving and spinning out deals   While venture capitalists often incubate entrepreneurs in "entrepreneur-in-residence" programs, providing them an office and a salary while they develop a business plan, Columbia is uncommon in its penchant for creating companies out of whole cloth. Of the 23 investments that Columbia made from its inception through August 1998, seven were founded—from the initial concept and writing of a business plan to recruitment of the management and investors—by the principals of Columbia themselves. "We would sit around the table and say, here's the niche—let's build a company to fill it," says Murray. "Only then we would go out and recruit management."

Why has Columbia taken this path when others have not? One reason is, no doubt, the backgrounds of the principals themselves. Each of Columbia's managing directors has a deep base of experience in the wireless industry—either as a dealmaker or, in many cases, an operator—and this makes them as a group more predisposed than their generalist colleagues at other firms to see unfilled niches in the wireless sector. But the partners at Columbia felt their lack of limiteds plays into it as well. When playing with one's own money—and *only* one's own money—the principals have both the time and the incentive to start their own companies, a move that involves more work than a typical venture investment but that is better controlled and affords an opportunity for greater ownership.

3. Hands-on investing   Columbia, unlike most early-stage venture firms, makes a point of having new employees work for a time in one of their portfolio companies. Phil Herget, for example, was hired by Columbia in 1992 and almost immediately placed full-time in Telular Corporation. Herget served as Telular's CFO through the company's IPO in early 1994, after which he returned to Columbia as a managing director. Again, Columbia's limited-less structure encourages such individual attention to deals: while

EXHIBIT 8-2

BIOGRAPHIES OF COLUMBIA CAPITAL'S PROFESSIONALS

Robert B. Blow, Managing Director   Bob Blow co-founded Columbia Capital in 1988. He has been actively involved in Skywire, Inc. (Director) and Telular Corporation (Director). Prior to joining Columbia Capital, Mr. Blow was active in the broadcasting, cellular, and paging industries. He was a co-founder of Dynatel Communications Corporation and Capital Cellular Corporation and the Managing General Partner of Celltellco Nationwide Paging. In addition, he was a management consultant for broadcast radio stations and an application provider for applicants of early-round MSA cellular licenses. Mr. Blow attended Memphis State University.

James B. Fleming, Managing Director   Jim Fleming joined Columbia Capital in 1994. He has been actively involved in Phoenix Wireless Group, Advanced Radio Telecom, Digital Television Services, Veninfotel, Xemod (Director), WNP Communications (Director), Taqua Systems, Inc. (Director), and Global Connect Partners (Director). Prior to joining Columbia Capital, Mr. Fleming served as President of Prime Cellular, Inc., an entity involved in the operation of rural cellular markets. He is a former member of the audit department of Price Waterhouse. Mr. Fleming received his B.A. from Stanford University.

R. Philip Herget III, Managing Director   Phil Herget joined Columbia Capital in 1992. He has been actively involved in Telular, Saville Systems, Columbia Spectrum Management, Phoenix Wireless Group (Director), SpaceWorks (Director), Torrent Networking Technologies (Director), Call Technologies, Altiga Networks (Director), and NMP, Inc. (Director). Prior to joining Columbia Capital, Mr. Herget served in various financial management positions for Energy Service Company, Inc., Energy Insurance International, Inc., Marsh & McLennan, Inc, and Lloyd's of London broker C.T. Bowring & Co. in London, England. In 1993, he joined Telular Corporation as its Chief Financial Officer where he led the company through an initial public offering, returning to Columbia in 1994. Mr. Herget received his B.A. from the University of Virginia and his M.B.A. from Kenan-Flager Business School at the University of North Carolina-Chapel Hill.

Harry F. Hopper III, Managing Director   Harry Hopper joined Columbia Capital in 1994. He has been actively involved in Digital Television Services (Director) and Columbia Spectrum Management (Director). In addition, from January 1995 through August 1998, Mr. Hopper served as Managing Director in charge of The Columbia Group, Inc., Columbia's affiliate investment banking arm. Under his leadership, The Columbia Group completed over 60 telecommunications transactions valued in excess of $3 billion. Prior to joining Columbia Capital, Mr. Hopper served as Executive Vice President of Bachtel Cellular Liquidity, LP, a $41 million cellular investment fund. Prior to Bachtel, he was a founder of Sky Broadcasting Corporation, a founder of AFSC Corporation, and a corporate finance and transaction lawyer for Cummings & Lockwood and Union Carbide. He is also a Director of Pegasus Communications Corporation. Mr. Hopper received his B.A. degree (Phi Beta Kappa) from the University of California at Berkeley and a J.D. degree from Berkeley's Boalt Hall School of Law.

Mark J. Kington, Managing Director   Mark Kington joined Columbia Capital in 1990. He has been actively involved in Phoenix Wireless Group (Director), Columbia Spectrum Management (Director), and Spaceworks (Director). Prior to joining Columbia Capital, Mr. Kington served as Vice President of Communications Lending at First Union National Bank in Charlotte, North Carolina, and Vice President of Investments of Malarkey-Taylor Associates in Washington, D.C. He is also a Director of Boston Communications Group, Inc. Mr. Kington received his B.S. from the University of Tennessee and his M.B.A. from the Colgate Darden School of Business at the University of Virginia.

David P. Mixer, Managing Director   David Mixer co-founded Columbia Capital in 1988. He has been actively involved in Sterling Cellular (Director), Saville Systems (Director), Spaceworks (Director), Digital Television Services (Director), and Taqua Systems, Inc. (Director). Prior to joining Columbia Capital, Mr. Mixer served as President of Providence Journal Cellular where he led the company in the acquisition of U.S. cellular properties. In addition, he held various management positions within corporate planning for AT&T. Mr. Mixer received his B.A. from Union College and his M.B.A. from the Harvard Business School.

James B. Murray, Jr., Managing Director   Jim Murray co-founded Columbia Capital in 1988. He has been actively involved in Advanced Radio Telecom (Director), Saville Systems (Director), Columbia Spectrum Management (Director), Torrent Networking Technologies (Director), and CCT/Boatphone (Director). Prior to joining Columbia Capital, Mr. Murray was active in the cellular and paging industries, including license negotiation, venture capital, system construction and operation, and general management. He is also a Director of Merrick Tower Corporation, Community Wireless Structures, LLC and Contact Paging of Albuquerque, N.M., the largest independent paging carrier in the SouthWest. From 1991 through 1996 by appointment of the Governor of Virginia, Mr. Murray served on the Board of Visitors of the College of William and Mary and was elected Rector (Chairman) of that Board. Mr. Murray received his B.A. from the University of Virginia and a J.D. from the Marshall-Wythe School of Law at the College of William and Mary.

(Continued)

EXHIBIT 8-2 (Continued)

Mark R. Warner, Managing Director   Mark Warner co-founded Columbia Capital in 1988. He has been actively involved in Telular (Director), Spaceworks (Director), and NMP, Inc. (Director). Prior to joining Columbia Capital, Mr. Warner was active in the cellular and wireless communications industries. He was a co-founder of Nextel (formerly Fleet Call) and Capital Cellular Corporation. He is also a Director of George Washington University, Virginia Union University, Virginia Health Care Foundation, and the Metropolitan Washington Y.M.C.A. Mr. Warner is a former Chairman of the Democratic Party in Virginia and a former candidate for the United States Senate. Mr. Warner received his B.A. from George Washington University and J.D. from Harvard Law School.

Jane A. Dietze, Principal   Jane Dietze joined Columbia Capital in 1998. She has been actively involved in Spaceworks. Prior to joining Columbia Capital, Ms. Dietze was the Director of International Business Development at Wayfarer Communications. She was the President, Chief Executive Officer, and co-founder of TORSO, a developer of middleware tools for emerging technologies. In addition, she served as an investment officer at the International Finance Corporation (IFC) in Albania, Macedonia, and Turkey and served as a mergers and acquisitions analyst with Goldman, Sachs & Co. in New York. Ms. Dietze received her B.A. from Princeton University and her M.A. from John Hopkins University.

Karl N. Khoury, Principal   Karl Khoury joined Columbia Capital in 1996. He has been actively involved in Digital Television Services, CCT/Boatphone and NMP, Inc. In addition, he has been involved in the origination and execution of mergers and acquisitions, private equity and debt financings, and financial advisory services for The Columbia Group, Inc., Columbia's affiliate investment banking arm. Prior to joining Columbia Capital, Mr. Khoury served as an Associate in the Leading Technologies Group at J.P. Morgan & Co. in New York. Mr. Khoury received his B.S. from Lehigh University.

Jay D. Markley, Principal   Jay Markley joined Columbia Capital in 1996. He has been actively involved in Torrent Networking Technologies, Xemod, Altiga Networks, and WNP Communications. Prior to joining Columbia Capital, Mr. Markley served at the Federal Communications Commission where he developed U.S. government wireless communications and spectrum auction policy, and assisted in the implementation of the Telecommunications Act of 1996. In addition, he held positions in real estate and corporate finance for Kidder, Peabody & Co. Incorporated in both New York City and Hong Kong. Mr. Markley received his B.A. from Washington & Lee University and his M.B.A. from Harvard Business School.

Jeffrey H. Patterson, Principal   Jeff Patterson joined Columbia Capital in 1996. He has been actively involved in Digital Television Services, Phoenix Wireless Group (Director), Call Technologies, Veninfotel, Taqua Systems, Inc., and Global Connect Partners. Prior to joining Columbia Capital, Mr. Patterson served as Assistant Vice President of Bank of Boston in the Media & Communications Finance Group in Boston and in the European Cable & Telephony Finance Group in London. Mr. Patterson received his B.A. degree from Bowdoin College and his M.B.A. from the J.L. Kellogg Graduate School of Management at Northwestern University.

Corey V. Holloran, Associate   Corey Holloran joined Columbia Capital in 1995. She has been actively involved in Torrent Networking Technologies, Phoenix Wireless Group, CCT/Boatphone, and SpaceWorks. Ms. Holloran received her B.S. in Business Adminstration from Georgetown University.

Matthew C. Newton, Associate   Matt Newton joined Columbia Capital in 1996. He has been actively involved in WNP Communications, Taqua Systems, Inc., NMP, Inc., Altiga Networks, Inc., and Global Connect Partners. Prior to joining Columbia Capital, Mr. Newton served as an analyst in the Corporate Finance Department of Dean Witter Reynolds Inc. in New York where he specialized in structuring and executing public and private equity financings. Mr. Newton received his B.S. in Business Administration from Washington and Lee University.

George Stelljes, III, Venture Partner   Chip Stelljes joined Columbia Capital in 1997. Prior to that he served as Executive Vice President and Principal of Allied Capital Corporation, a publicly traded investment company. At Allied, he also served as the portfolio manager of Allied Venture Partnership and Allied Technology Partnership, two private investment funds with $45 million in committed capital. In addition, he held positions with a venture capital subsidiary of NationsBank and Sun Trust Banks. He is a Director of Virginia Telecom Towers and the Advisory Board of Virginia Capital. He received his B.A. in Economics from Vanderbilt University and his M.B.A. from the Colgate Darden School of Business Administration at the University of Virginia.

Source: Corporate document.

investing only $25 million per year, the firm has employed 12 to 15 professionals, comparable to venture firms that annually invest twice that dollar amount or more.

But Columbia's reliance on internal capital hindered them in two crucial respects. The first was that, in certain deals, the financial capacity around the table was simply too small to invest as much as was appropriate. For example, one of Columbia's managing directors, Jim Fleming, spearheaded the creation of and fundraising for WNP Communications, the largest purchaser of licenses in the FCC's auction of LMDS spectrum in 1998. Fleming helped raise an astonishing $198 million for WNP, but only $8.2 million of that figure came from Columbia—because the capacity just wasn't there. "It was the biggest deal of all time," says Jim Murray, "and we didn't just incubate it—we invented it."

"[WNP] was a classic case where we were at a disadvantage not having a fund," says Warner. "We did much more than our share of the heavy lifting, in terms of putting the whole group together and organizing it. We probably should have put more like $20 million in it. If you have a $250M or $300M fund, you can *put* $20M in it."

This capacity constraint was especially difficult for Columbia because of its focus on carrier investments, that is, investments in companies providing telephone or data services directly to home or business customers. Though potentially quite lucrative, such investments require tremendous up-front capital, since they involve either huge capital expenditures (in starting a company from scratch) or rapid acquisition (in the case of a consolidation, or "roll-up" strategy). When such deals come together, then, management will often raise upward of $50 million in equity in the first round and look for each venture participant to invest to the tune of $10 million. These investors will also be expected to participate in later financings of the company, often increasing their exposure two- or threefold.

Although Columbia's experience base—almost every principal has substantial experience working with carriers, particularly those driven by acquisition—and "carrier-driven" investment strategy both pointed toward these carrier investments, the high price of entry was sometimes prohibitive. The firm found that, in some instances, they were forced to pass on carrier deals (especially in the CLEC sector) that they would have otherwise pursued because the required commitment of funds was simply too large.

The sheer lack of capacity would sometimes keep Columbia out of attractive deals, but the *relative* lack of capacity among the various Columbia partners began to pose problems as well. By 1998, the group of partners (or "managing directors," as they were called) had expanded to eight, one of whom joined the firm in 1992 and two of whom joined in 1994 (see Exhibit 8-2). None of these three participated in the firm's original investments in Saville Systems and Telular, the two investments whose proceeds sustained the firm's growth from 1994 to 1997. None, certainly, had the personal wealth of any of the four original partners, each of whom had found success as a broker or operator in the wireless industry prior to his association with Columbia.

As the three younger partners—Phil Herget, Jim Fleming, and Harry Hopper—began to take the leadership reins of the firm, a disconnect began to develop between their partnership stake and the proportion that they were able to invest in deals.

"They were getting squeezed," says Warner. "While on the one hand they were having a larger and larger share of Columbia Capital, their ability to keep pace with their growing share in terms of writing checks wasn't realized. It was as if we were saying, 'You're getting your additional share, but you can't enjoy the benefit of it because you may not have the equivalent of $2–4 million a year to put in deals.'"

The way they got around this problem was simple leverage: the newer managing directors (or principal- and associate-level professionals, who also had the ability to invest) would borrow from the older managing directors to invest in deals. But this solution was awkward and unsustainable. The fundamental problem was that the expansion of the firm, combined with the rise of a new generation of leaders, made it less tenable to expect the senior managing directors to shoulder such a great financial burden.

OPTIONS

Given Columbia's annualized return of 194% over the life of the firm (1989–1998), it was difficult to argue that the firm was in any peril. But looking down the road, the managing directors hoped to avoid what Warner ironically terms "the classic venture capital model": namely, "the first-generation partners want to keep hold of the reins too long and get too greedy, and the younger guys splinter off and start their own fund." Says Mixer: "We knew that unless we created a situation where Phil and Jim and Harry felt justly rewarded, the company would self-destruct. We needed to have these guys feel that they're in control, and create a culture where they know that their turn will come. We were not going to blow up the firm by greeding out."

(For whatever reason, the history of venture capital firms is certainly littered with examples of younger partners leaving an established firm to start their own. High-profile examples include Highland Capital Partners, which spun out of Charles River Ventures; Sigma Partners and Technology Venture Investors (TVI), whose founding partners each came from Institutional Venture Associates (IVA); and Alta Partners, whose founder spun out of Burr, Egan and Deleage.)

By the beginning of 1998, the firm began to investigate plans to raise outside capital. The time was right from a market prospective because there was a phenomenal boom in venture fundraising activities. In fact, venture funds raised in 1997 amounted to $10 billion, three times the amount raised just four years earlier in 1993.

As the values of public technology stocks exploded and returns of venture funds grew, money poured into venture funds in record levels. Existing limited partners desired to increase their exposure in venture investments, and nontraditional sources of venture funding—hedge funds, corporate investors, foreign funds—entered the venture market in hopes of getting into high-growth technology equities earlier in their life cycle.

One option, which Columbia had considered on and off since 1992, was simply to raise a large fund of $250 million or more, effectively ending the firm's reliance on inside capital. Such a move would give Columbia a structure similar to the structures of other early-stage venture firms. Under this plan, they would also wind down their investment banking practice which, despite being a consistent revenue producer (revenues had grown to $7 million by 1997), did not begin to match the value created by the direct investment arm. Columbia's partners felt that they could raise such a fund on terms similar to those funds raised by established early-stage venture firms of comparable size.

A second option arose after a few of Columbia's portfolio companies had alerted the firm to some opportunities for making communications investments internationally—particularly in Russia, where they had seen attractive investments in the wireless and long-distance markets. Columbia believed that these investments could provide phenomenal returns to investors, but the firm was wary about taking on such investments from thousands of miles away. Says Herget: "We had always said that if we were going to do international deals, we needed strong local partners where we did those deals."

During late 1997, the firm began to examine the possibility of putting together a fund for communications investments in Russia. Besides the exciting growth apparent in Russia's infant economy, there were a few other particular positives to creating a fund in Russia at that time. The first was the formidable aid, from quasi-governmental organizations like OPIC (the Overseas Private Investment Corporation) or multilateral financial institutions like IFC (the International Finance Corporation), which was becoming available to private equity investment funds in developing nations like Russia. This aid would typically take the form of a guaranteed return of invested capital (or some significant portion thereof); or, alternately, low-interest leverage at some ratio to the fund's equity, sometimes as high as 2:1. The second was the interest of the United Financial Group, a Russian investment bank founded and run by Boris Fedorov. Fedorov, one of the architects of Yeltsin's economic reforms, was interested in partnering with Columbia on the fund, giving on-the-ground assistance to the fund's managers while also acting as a limited partner.

By the fall of 1997, Columbia began to explore the idea of the Russia fund more seriously. Under the plan, managing director Jim Fleming would devote half his time to running the new fund, while still being based in the United States. Jay Markley, a principal at Columbia, would move to Moscow and run the fund's day-to-day operations. The fund would total $70–75 million, with terms similar to a domestic venture fund—2% management fee, 80-20 split of profits between limited and general partners after return of capital—but with the 20% carried interest itself split among Columbia, Fedorov's UFG, and one or two other value-added limiteds.

If the firm decided to raise a Russia fund, what then? The logical extension of such a plan, the Columbia directors realized, was to turn Columbia into a family of equal funds, each of which would place private equity investments into specific countries or types of company.

As Herget describes it, the idea was to "split Columbia Capital into three separate groups. One would be a fund management company, that would start with Russia fund; the second would continue with early-stage private equity as we had done before." The third component would be the investment banking operation, for which Columbia could bring in new management to run day to day. The first piece—the fund management company—would eventually include funds in South America and Africa. The domestic private equity practice would expand as well, augmented by a later-stage fund, allowing Columbia an entry into the kinds of carrier deals and later-stage equipment deals from which their limited internal capacity had sometimes barred them. The partners would continue to fund the early-stage equity investing out of their own pockets.

Such a plan presented several risks. One was simply the organizational risk of managing a family of funds. When investing $25 million each year, a team of 15 professionals is more than adequate; when investing $50 to $75 million per year, out of four different funds, in divergent markets across the globe, 15 professionals doesn't begin to cover it. From an infrastructure point of view, Columbia would have to complete a transition from a loose confederation of dealmakers to a multinational investment corporation. A second risk was the foreign market risk. Compared to the U.S. economy, the economies of Russia and South America were unstable. Even factoring in the risk of private equity investment in start-up technology companies, investments in Russian and South American companies (particularly the former) were arguably much riskier.

The third risk involved the logistical problems associated with having two domestic technology "funds" under the same management. For example: Where would the early-stage "fund" end and the later-stage fund begin? "One of the things that we tried to do was define stage based on the round of the investment," Herget said, but acknowledged the difficulty of doing so. As an example, he gives a typical CLEC, who, like the hypothetical "carrier investment" described above, raises $50 million in capital in the first round. Was such an investment "early-stage" or "late-stage"?

Another example: given that Columbia's entire track record was in early-stage investments, would limiteds be confident investing in their late-stage fund? The fact that Columbia's partners would also be pursuing, at their own enrichment, early-stage deals—deals that they would later look for the later-stage fund to invest in, at a higher cost basis—would likely only exacerbate these concerns among potential limiteds.

Despite these potential headaches, the family of funds concept had obvious appeal. First and foremost, it was ambitious and would extend the Columbia brand internationally. It would allow Columbia to make communications investments in developing economies, where, it was easy to imagine, tomorrow's telephone giants were taking root today. Also, perhaps most importantly, while leveraging their personnel and brand to its full potential, it would also allow the principals of Columbia to continue to fund the early-stage investing out of their own pockets, reaping all of the profits on their investments where other firms saw only carried interest.

In fact, Columbia had a third option: the firm could scrap its plans for raising outside capital entirely. As Warner noted, "the model clearly wasn't broken."

9

Francisco Partners

Dave Stanton didn't notice that it was already 10 P.M. on a chilly evening in late December 1999, as he peered out the window of Sequoia Capital's incubator offices to reflect on the events of the last six months. In August, Stanton had resigned from Texas Pacific Group (TPG), one of the world's largest leveraged buyout firms, where he was a senior partner. He took with him another TPG principal and joined forces with Sandy Robertson, the founder of the investment banking firm Robertson Stephens, to form Francisco Partners.

Francisco Partners, Stanton hoped, would become the leading buyout firm focused exclusively on companies in the technology sector. The firm would target businesses with values ranging from $50 million to over $2 billion and would aim to invest in leveraged buyouts, divisional spinouts, fallen angels, recapitalizations, management turnarounds, strategic restructurings, and growth equity situations. Before the firm could invest in anything, Stanton would need to raise a large buyout fund, and this would be no easy task. Stanton was confident, however, that he had done everything in his power to put his firm in the best position possible. He felt that the team he had assembled was second to none: they had an outstanding technology investment track record, they had an extremely deep understanding of technology investing, and their exclusive relationship with Sequoia Capital, one of Silicon Valley's best known venture capital firms, had the potential to reap large dividends going forward.

Stanton also felt that there was never a better time to be investing in the technology sector. This view, however, was not shared by everybody: conventional wisdom held that a "technology leveraged buyout" was an oxymoron and such a transaction was simply not possible. Traditional buyouts were typically done on lower growth, undervalued businesses with steady cash flows; technology companies were viewed to be too volatile, richly priced, and rapidly changing to support any meaningful amount of leverage. How would Stanton address this issue with potential investors? Was there enough evidence that technology buyouts were not only feasible but also highly lucrative? If he were able to convince investors that technology buyouts were indeed a worthwhile endeavor, would he then be able to persuade them that Francisco Partners was the horse they should

David Gallo (MBA 2000) prepared this case under the supervision of Professor Josh Lerner as the basis for class discussion rather than to illustrate either effective or ineffective handling of an administrative situation.

bet on? Had his firm established enough of a competitive advantage to be successful in the tech investing space? On the fundraising front, Stanton needed to finalize the terms of his fund before the offering memorandum went to print. How much money should Francisco Partners raise? How should the investment returns be divided? How large of a management fee should his firm charge? These and other items would need to be largely resolved before Francisco Partners could begin raising money.

As part of his departure terms with TPG, Stanton agreed not to commence fundraising until January 1, 2000, which was now merely days away. Stanton looked up at the clock: 10:30 P.M. It looked like this was going to be the fourth late night this week.

THE FORMATION OF FRANCISCO PARTNERS

Dave Stanton, 37, was born and raised in northern California. A self-proclaimed "math and science geek," Stanton majored in chemical engineering at Stanford University and immediately continued on to Northwestern University to pursue a Ph.D. After about eight months, he decided that he didn't want to be an academician and returned to the Bay Area to work for Bain Consulting. Three years later Stanton returned to Stanford to pursue an MBA.

In business school, Dave was struck by two insights: first, he discovered that his true passion and interests lay in technology. Second, he found that being a principal, or equity owner, of a business had much more appeal to him than being an agent (such as a consultant, banker, or straight salaried employee of an operating company). Over the summer between his first and second years, Stanton thus secured a job at High Voltage Engineering, an industrial technology company run by an ex-Bain consultant that had recently undergone a leveraged buyout (LBO). At High Voltage, Stanton witnessed the convergence of finance, technology, and operations, and he left convinced that he wanted to become a technology-focused investor.

After graduating from Stanford Business School in 1991, Stanton took a job with the venture capital firm, Trinity Ventures, then based in San Mateo, California. As Stanton put it,

> I knew nothing about computer science or information technology. Working at Trinity was a huge crash course in both. I basically ended up teaching myself C++ and a slew of other programming languages, thinking it would make me this great venture capitalist. Boy, was that a dumb mistake. So my next move was to do a big top-down analysis of the technology space and figure out where I can make a difference as an investor. That fared a little better—I decided to focus on database technology and application development tools. We did a bunch of deals in those two sectors and did quite well—we achieved over 70+% IRRs.

Through his work and analysis at Trinity, Stanton was struck by another insight: technology wasn't just about the cutting edge of Silicon Valley. In fact, the *majority* of the money being made in the technology space was being made by older, stodgier companies—like the IBMs of the world. By investing in these larger companies through leveraged buyouts, Stanton thought that he could put much more capital to work, yet still achieve very attractive rates of return due to the underlying growth of the technology sector. Although conventional wisdom at the time held that one cannot perform an LBO on a technology company, Stanton "never bought into that idea because I had worked at an LBO technology company—High Voltage Engineering—and thus didn't have a legacy of thinking that it couldn't be done."

In early 1993, Stanton received a phone call from Bill Price, a former partner at Bain Consulting with whom Stanton had worked. Price had recently teamed up with David Bonderman and Jim Coulter, two of investor Robert Bass's key investment advisors, to form Texas Pacific Group, a leveraged buyout firm. After a one-year wooing process, Price finally convinced Stanton to join TPG, where he would work as a generalist (i.e., no specific industry focus).

Shortly after joining TPG, Stanton put together a large study on telecommunications and technology investing and identified several specific subsectors in which he thought TPG could marry technology and leveraged buyouts. These sectors typically comprised much more mature, high cash flow businesses with embedded technologies that were difficult to displace. The other partners at TPG were intrigued by Stanton's ideas and thus made him the de facto leader of TPG's technology investing efforts, where he would concentrate all of his time.

Over the next four years, Stanton invested $537.3 million of equity capital into five technology companies with a combined enterprise value of $2.5 billion. These companies included a rural telecom services provider, two communications products companies, a designer and manufacturer of application-specific standard products semiconductors, and the largest independent supplier of semiconductor components in the world. In the process of executing these transactions, Stanton was responsible for placing over $1.4 billion of bank debt and over $900 million of high-yield and mezzanine debt. As of December 31, 1999, these investments were valued at $3.5 billion—a multiple of 6.5x invested capital, implying an IRR of 166.0%. (See Exhibit 9-1 for a summary of Stanton's investment performance.) TPG's technology deals ended up comprising a disproportionately large share of the firm's profits, especially relative to the amount of the firm's equity that was invested in such transactions.[1]

Through early 1999, TPG's technology investments were made through its $2.5 billion generalist fund, TPG Partners II. In June 1999, however, TPG was on track to raise a completely separate technology fund. This would give Stanton the freedom to run the technology practice the way he saw fit. It would enable him to recruit his own people, compensate his people primarily on their technology investment performance (and not the performance of TPG's other investments), partner with other firms, and attract a technology-focused investor base. Perhaps most importantly, it would allow Stanton to make swifter investment decisions. As Stanton described it,

> Being a specialist at a generalist firm was becoming increasingly difficult. The technology team would spend 100% of our time trying to keep up with current tech trends, and we still barely kept our heads above water. The other TPG guys were generalists, who by definition spent the bulk of their time looking at investments in non-tech areas. As smart as these guys were, it simply took longer for them to get comfortable with putting TPG's money into any given tech company, because they weren't as familiar with the space. I eventually realized that you couldn't be a dilettante in technology investing—you needed to be a full-time specialist.

Despite TPG's earlier intentions, in late June the firm decided to raise TPG Partners III and keep the technology effort as part-and-parcel of TPG proper.[2]

---

[1] David Snow, "TPG and Stanton Split, Plan Technology Funds," *Buyouts* 12, no. 17 (August 30, 1999): 26.

[2] TPG also decided to raise a "stapled" fund, T3 Partners, that would invest side by side with TPG Partners III only in technology deals. While this allowed investors to have exposure only to TPG's technology transactions, it did not change the internal operating structure of TPG's technology effort.

EXHIBIT 9-1

SUMMARY OF INVESTMENT PERFORMANCE

Summary of Investment Performance
April 1996 through December 31, 1999
($ in thousands)

Company Name	Date of Initial Investment	Total Enterprise Value	Total Capital Invested	Total Realized Proceeds	Total Realized Proceeds and Unrealized Value	Multiple of Cost	Gross IRR[1]
Realized or Publicly Traded Investments							
GT Com[2]	April 1996	$117,463	$29,400	$129,469	$129,469	4.4×	49.8%
Paradyne Networks, Inc.[3]	August 1996	179,000	51,746	200,485	490,288	9.5	110.6
GlobeSpan, Inc.[3]	August 1996	6,000	4,754	27,600	526,737	110.8	311.4
Total Realized or Publicly Traded Investments		$302,463	$85,900	$357,554	$1,146,494	13.3×	118.9%
Unrealized Investments							
Zilog, Inc.[4]	February 1998	$405,000	$113,900	$0	$325,000	2.9×	77.2%
ON Semiconductor[5,6]	August 1999	1,780,000	337,500	0	2,000,000	5.9	492.6
Total Unrealized Investments		$2,185,000	$451,400	$0	$2,325,000	5.2×	346.5%
TOTAL INVESTMENTS		$2,487,463	$537,300	$357,554	$3,471,494	6.5×	166.0%
Other Investments[7]							
Messrs. Ball and Garfinkel (14 companies)[8]		$1,030,000	$298,100				

[1] The IRRs are based on the actual timing of the investment inflows and outflows, aggregated monthly, and the return is annualized. IRRs are before management fees, expenses and carried interest.

[2] GT Com has entered into a definitive sale agreement, subject to limited closing conditions. The transaction is expected to be completed in the second quarter of 2000.

[3] Public unrealized investments are valued based on their trailing 10-day average closing share price as of December 31, 1999, less a 15% liquidity discount.

[4] The unrealized value of Zilog, Inc. is based on a third-party valuation. The valuation implies an enterprise value equal to 2.5× forward revenue. Its closest public comparable is trading at 5.5× forward revenue.

[5] The unrealized value of ON Semiconductor is based on a Morgan Stanley IPO analysis.

[6] The IRR calculation shown for ON Semiconductor assumes a 12-month holding period.

[7] Mr. Stanton led two oil and gas investments at TPG, with an aggregate enterprise value of $770 million and $260 million of capital invested. These investments are currently valued at cost.

[8] Messrs. Ball and Garfinkel were senior investment professionals on deal teams that invested $298.1 million in 14 portfolio companies representing a combined enterprise value in excess of $1.0 billion.

Source: Francisco Partners, L.P. Offering Memorandum.

The very next day Stanton called Donaldson, Lufkin & Jenrette (DLJ)'s Private Fund Group to explore his options. Given Dave Stanton's reputation and track record, the attractive fundraising environment, and DLJ's fundraising capabilities, DLJ advised Stanton that he would potentially be able to raise $1 to $2 billion should he strike out on his own.

Sandy Robertson's Role and the Decision to Leave TPG   Sandy Robertson was the founder and Chairman of Robertson Stephens, a leading technology investment bank based in San Francisco. Sandy sold Robertson Stephens to BankBoston in 1998 but remained active in advising several former technology company clients. Right around the time of the sale, Dipanjan "D.J." Deb, one of Sandy's top protégés and head of semiconductor banking at Robertson Stephens, left the investment bank to join Stanton at TPG.

From time to time, Sandy's old clients would call him to complain about their undervalued stock price and solicit his advice on what they could do to correct their company's valuation. Increasingly, Sandy would advise them to consider undergoing a leveraged buyout and would direct them to TPG, given his strong relationship with D.J. As a result, Sandy began to spend a significant amount of time working with Stanton and TPG's technology team.

Throughout July 1999, Stanton continued discussions with DLJ about fundraising, while still trying to persuade TPG to raise a separate technology fund. Stanton also came clean with D.J., informing him that he was seriously considering leaving TPG, and asked D.J. to join him. D.J. agreed. Stanton then informed Sandy Robertson of his situation and asked Sandy to join him as well. Sandy also agreed, turning down an offer to join TPG as a senior partner. As Stanton and Sandy discussed their plans, they code-named their project "Francisco Partners," named after the street they had both lived on in San Francisco.

Finally, on August 12, 1999, Dave Stanton and D.J. resigned from TPG. Because the two were leaving TPG to form a rival buyout firm, Stanton, D.J., and TPG negotiated a departure agreement that addressed several important economic and strategic issues among the parties.[3]

And thus Francisco Partners was formed.

RECENT TRENDS IN FUNDRAISING

As of mid-1999, both the dollar commitments to U.S. private equity funds and the actual number of U.S. private equity firms had increased dramatically over the prior 10 years (see Exhibit 9-2). According to DLJ, these trends had been driven primarily by four factors. First, more institutions (such as corporate and public pension funds, banks, and insurance companies) were investing in the private equity space. Second, the 1990s bull market had greatly increased the size of such institutional funds. Third, such institutions were allocating an increasing percentage of their total assets to private equity investments (which compounded the bull market effect). Finally, many of these institutions needed to re-deploy the capital gains they had realized from prior private equity investments. As a result, the top 20 buyout funds controlled close to $60 billion in equity capital (see Exhibit 9-3). Assuming a conservative 3:1 debt-to-equity ratio in a typical buyout, this represented close to $240 billion in purchasing power.

---

[3] For example, Stanton agreed not to begin raising his fund until January 1, 2000.

EXHIBIT 9-2

COMMITMENTS TO U.S. PRIVATE EQUITY

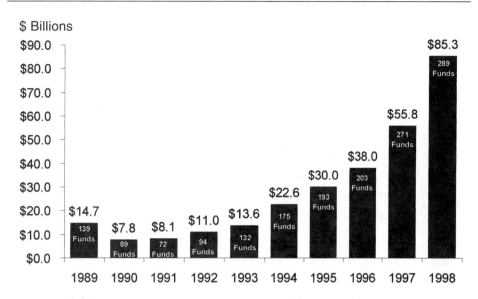

Source: Compiled from DLJ Presentation to Francisco Partners, July 30, 1999; *The Private Equity Analyst*; Asset Alternatives, Inc.

These trends had several implications for the leveraged buyout business. First, it appeared that the demand for deals was outstripping the supply, resulting in increased purchase prices. For example, the average company purchase price as a multiple of EBITDA had increased from 5.4x in 1993 to 8.3x in 1998 (see Exhibit 9-4), and the total dollar volume of LBOs nearly quadrupled over the same period (see Exhibit 9-5). Second, given the increased purchase prices and the fixed amount of leverage that a given business can support, equity capital as a percentage of total purchase price had been steadily increasing, from a low of 7% in 1987 to a high of 32% in 1998 (see Exhibit 9-6). Industry observers felt that the combination of the above two forces would have a substantial negative impact on buyout fund returns going forward. LBO firms attempted to combat this in a variety of ways, including partnering together to buy companies instead of competing for deals, expanding into other geographic regions that were perceived to be less competitive, and specializing in one or two industries instead of remaining generalists.

OVERVIEW OF THE INFORMATION TECHNOLOGY INDUSTRY

As of December 1999, information technology (IT) companies comprised approximately $6 trillion in total equity market capitalization. Nearly 30% of the S&P 500's market capitalization was derived from technology companies, up from 5.5% in 1992 (see Exhibit 9-7).

EXHIBIT 9-3

TOP PRIVATE LBO/CORPORATE FINANCE FUNDS— 1998 ($ IN MILLIONS)

Firm	Size of Fund
Kohlberg Kravis Roberts & Co.	$ 6,000
E.M. Warburg, Pincus & Co., L.L.C.	5,000
Blackstone Group, L.P.	3,780
Hicks, Muse, Tate & Furst Inc.	3,710
Apollo Advisors, L.P.	3,600
Thomas H. Lee Company	3,500
Carlyle Group L.P.	3,500
Forstmann Little & Co.	3,200
DLJ Merchant Banking	3,000
Welsh, Carson, Anderson & Stowe	3,000
Goldman, Sachs Capital	2,775
Texas Pacific Group	2,500
Credit Suisse First Boston	2,500
Doughty Hanson & Co.	2,500
Cinven	2,500
Lehman Brothers Merchant Banking	2,000
Morgan Stanley Capital Partners	1,875
Capital Z Partners	1,600
Bain Capital	1,500
Total	**$58,040**

Source: Compiled from DLJ Presentation: "Recent Developments in the Private Equity Industry," October 27, 1999.

Growth in the information technology sector had exceeded 10% per year for the prior 15 years and was projected to continue at similar rates for the next decade. From 1988 through 1999, the rate of growth for the IT industry had been nearly four times that of the overall U.S. economy (see Exhibit 9-8). As a result, IT growth had accounted for over 35% of the total growth in the domestic economy in recent years, and technology as a percentage of total U.S. gross domestic product had almost doubled in the prior 20 years from 4.2% to 8.2% (see Exhibit 9-9).

The rapid growth in the IT sector was fueled primarily by business investment, with technology capital expenditures accounting for over 50% of all durable equipment purchases in 1999. As a result of this investment, IT capacity had been expanding at a rate of 40% per year, compared with less than 2% for the rest of the business sector. Technology investment was seen as a major contributor to the low inflation rates experienced in the United States in the 1990s, where overall prices had risen 3% per year, while IT prices had actually declined 5% per year.

EXHIBIT 9-4

COMPANY PURCHASE PRICE AS A MULTIPLE OF EBITDA

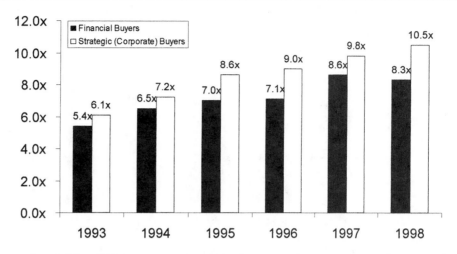

Source: Compiled from DLJ Presentation: "Recent Developments in the Private Equity Industry," October 27, 1999; *Buyouts*.

EXHIBIT 9-5

TOTAL TRANSACTION VALUE OF LBOS, 1991–1998

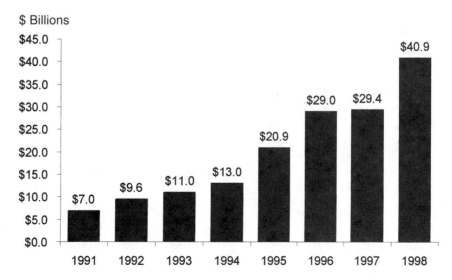

Source: Compiled from DLJ Presentation: "Recent Developments in the Private Equity Industry," October 27, 1999; Asset Alternatives, Inc.

EXHIBIT 9-6

AVERAGE EQUITY CONTRIBUTION TO LEVERAGED BUYOUTS

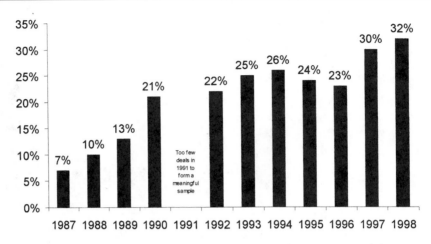

Source: Compiled from DLJ Presentation: "Recent Developments in the Private Equity Industry," October 27, 1999; Portfolio Management Data.

EXHIBIT 9-7

TECHNOLOGY AS A PERCENTAGE OF S&P 500 MARKET CAPITALIZATION

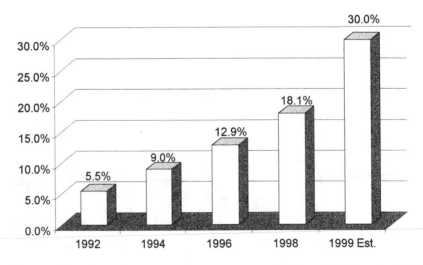

Source: Compiled from Silver Lake Partners' Presentation to Harvard Business School, October 11, 1999; Standard & Poors.

EXHIBIT 9-8

TECHNOLOGY GROWTH VERSUS THE REST OF THE ECONOMY

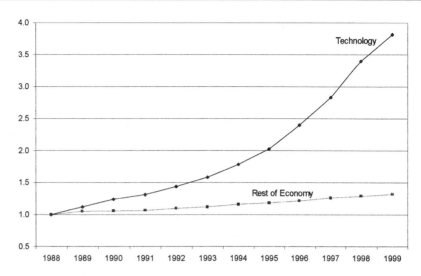

Sources: Compiled from Department of Commerce; Bureau of Economic Analysis: Economics and Statistics Administration; Francisco Partners Analysis.

EXHIBIT 9-9

TECHNOLOGY AS A PERCENTAGE OF TOTAL
U.S. GROSS DOMESTIC PRODUCT

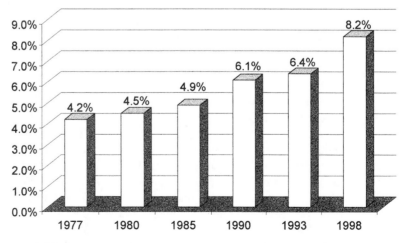

Source: Compiled from Silver Lake Partners' Presentation to Harvard Business School, October 11, 1999; U.S. Department of Commerce.

Industry Structure

Francisco Partners broke down the IT industry along three dimensions: sector, lifestage, and strategic position.

Sector   The IT industry could be divided into four main sectors—hardware, software, communications, and services—each with its own unique economic models and competitive dynamics. *Hardware* represented over $470 billion in annual revenue and included semiconductors, semiconductor capital equipment, computer systems, storage, peripherals, and contract manufacturing. *Software* represented over $135 billion in annual revenue and included packaged applications such as Enterprise Resource Planning and Customer Relationship Management software, vertical market applications, middleware and Enterprise Application Integration products, tools, database and other system software, and the emerging category of Application Service Providers. *Communications* represented over $1.1 trillion in annual revenue and included data networking and telecom equipment, wireless equipment, optical components, data service providers (such as ISPs), CLECs, and other network service providers. Finally, *services* represented over $290 billion in annual revenue and included staffing, consulting, systems integration, outsourcing, and transaction processing.

Lifestage   Francisco Partners segmented technology companies into three lifestages: start-up, emerging growth, and mature. Similar businesses at different lifestages confronted very different issues. For example, a start-up company would typically compete on technology, be focused on developing its market, and have a high failure rate. On the other hand, a mature company would typically compete on brand and customer franchise, be focused on maintaining innovation, and have a very low failure rate. Emerging growth companies would lie in the middle of these two extremes.

Strategic Position   Francisco Partners believed that even for companies within the same subsector and at the same point in their lifestage, significant differences could exist in the strategic position of a firm. These strategic "inflection points" could result from business issues, including product transitioning, merger integration, management change, cultural change, strategic rationalization, and technological paradigm shifts (see Exhibit 9-10 for examples of inflection points). Francisco Partners believed that the future prospects for a company could become unclear at such inflection points, thus creating the opportunity for differential investment insight and for outside resources to bring to bear a favorable resolution to those strategic issues.

Myths vs. Realities

Conventional wisdom within the leveraged buyout community typically held that buyouts of technology companies were neither practical nor attractive. Critics would often point to Prime Computer, one of the first technology buyouts, as proof that such transactions could not be done. Prime, a manufacturer of minicomputers and developer of computer-aided-design software, was bought by J.H. Whitney & Co. through an LBO in 1989. Whitney saddled the company with some $1.3 billion of very high cost debt. Although many felt that the underlying business of Prime was solid, the company eventually had to undergo massive layoffs and restructurings as a result of the heavy debt load. Whitney ultimately lost its entire equity investment in the deal. Stanton commented that the Prime Computer failure "set the tech buyout market back for years. Paradoxically, it was the best thing to happen to our careers because it froze the market for tech buyouts for five years until we got active in 1994 at TPG."

EXHIBIT 9-10

EXAMPLES OF STRATEGIC INFLECTION POINTS

Inflection Points	Example
Product transition	*Apple Computer, Inc.*—iMac product line rejuvenation
Merger integration	*NCR Corporation*—Poor fit with AT&T; subsequent spin
Management change	*IBM Corporation*—Lou Gerstner and team as catalyst
Strategic rationalization	*Intel Corporation*—Microprocessor focus; exit memory business
High-growth/low-growth	*Unisys Corporation*—Systems integration vs. mainframes
Earnings vs. cash flow	*Applied Materials, Inc.*—Downcycle losses yet with high cash flow
Cultural change	*Lucent Technologies Inc.*—Prospers when separated from AT&T
Innovator's dilemma	*DEC*—Overreliance on minicomputer market leadership
Platform shifts	*SAP AG*—Packaged applications going to the Web
Capital constraint	*Micron Technology, Inc.*—DRAM cycle deters investment
Paradigm shift	*Netscape Communications*—PC-based to Internet-based computing

Source: Francisco Partners, L.P. Offering Memorandum.

Critics often cited several specific reasons as to the unattractiveness of tech buyouts. These reasons included IT company dynamics such as highly volatile cash flows; unpredictable product obsolescence risk; unproven or unstable business models; rich valuations; inability to use financial leverage; and complexities in analyzing technology companies.

Volatility   The IT industry was commonly perceived as having highly volatile cash flows. Upon closer inspection, however, the technology sector was not measurably more volatile than the rest of the economy. Specifically, when one looked at the absolute growth rates of the IT industry versus that of the overall economy, it *did* appear that IT growth exhibited significantly more fluctuation (see Exhibit 9-11a). But when one considered the rate of change of these growth rates around their respective growth baselines, technology was no more volatile than the overall economy (see Exhibit 9-11b). In other words, because the IT industry had averaged over 10% compounded growth versus 2.4% for the overall economy, apparently large *absolute* changes in IT growth were actually quite moderate from a *relative* perspective, that is, when compared to IT's high level of baseline growth. In addition, according to CS First Boston, the average EBITDA volatility for technology firms from 1994 through 1999 had not been substantially different from that of other sectors of the economy.

Product Obsolescence   Another common misperception was that all technology companies were characterized by rapid product life cycles and large product obsolescence risk. In reality, for both whole industry segments as well as for specific companies, information technology development had proceeded more through long-waved trends of recreation, reformulation, and adaptation than by sudden shocks of technological displacement. Typically, once technology companies had passed proof of the technical

EXHIBIT 9-11

INFORMATION TECHNOLOGY INDUSTRY VOLATILITY

(a) **(b)**

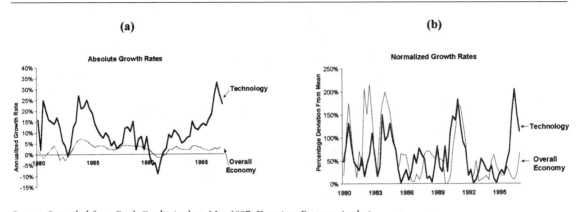

Source: Compiled from Bank Credit Analyst, May 1997; Francisco Partners Analysis.

and commercial feasibility of their products, they had been surprisingly resilient and adaptable.

Failure Rates The common perception was that technology companies had high failure rates. Although this was true for very early-stage companies, more mature technology firms were generally very stable. According to Morgan Stanley, of the over 1,300 technology companies that had gone public since 1985, less than 8% had gone bankrupt or were out of business, while the balance had either remained public or been acquired.

Valuations Conventional wisdom held that technology companies traded at very lofty equity valuations. In reality, relatively few IT companies traded at high valuations, although such companies received a disproportionate amount of public attention. Indeed, the market tended to reward success and punish any indication of failure, such that technology stock valuations tended to bifurcate into "Haves" and "Have-Nots." Market leaders, or "Haves," with a track record of success and clear prospects for growth often enjoyed valuation multiples several times that of market laggards, or "Have-Nots." For example, the average sales multiple for the market leader and follower in data networking was 22x and 3x; in PC hardware, it was 5x and 1x; in microprocessors, it was 9x and 2x; and in database software, it was 17x and 2x (see Exhibit 9-12). In fact, when ranking technology companies on a market price-to-sales basis, the top 25% traded at a 9.6x price-to-sale ratio, while the bottom 75% traded at a 1.4x price-to-sales ratio (see Exhibit 9-13).

While some "Have-Nots" deserved their depressed market valuations, Francisco Partners believed that many did not. Capital markets had historically exhibited little patience for earnings disappointment from technology companies, almost regardless of cause. Furthermore, Wall Street typically did not welcome difficult-to-explain transitions or complicated stories that required several quarters for a company to prove out.

EXHIBIT 9-12

PUBLIC TECHNOLOGY LEADER VERSUS FOLLOWER ANALYSIS

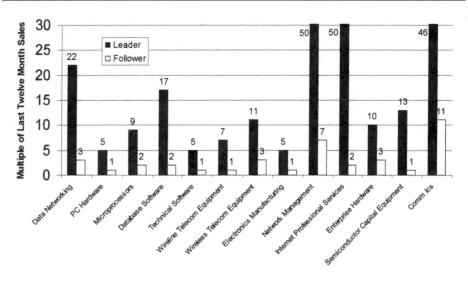

Source: Compiled from Morgan Stanley Dean Witter, 2/2/00; Francisco Partners Analysis.

Other Myths and Realities   Other common perceptions of technology companies were that all technology was "high tech"; that technology companies could not be leveraged; and that technology companies had to continually reinvent themselves to survive. In reality, all of these perceptions were unfounded. First, many "low-tech" sectors existed within the IT industry, such as contract manufacturing, discrete semiconductors, enterprise software, and IT services. These sectors piggybacked on the growth of the broader technology market while retaining much lower exposure to the rapid technological changes in other IT sectors. Second, many technology companies could support a prudent amount of leverage. This was primarily because many technology companies had large installed bases of customers and products, which in turn resulted in strong recurring cash flows. In addition, IT companies typically had highly flexible operating expenses and capital expenditure requirements should they face temporary sales downturns. Finally, although it was true that technology companies needed to continually reinvent themselves in order to survive, most reinvention was evolutionary and incremental rather than revolutionary. As Dave Stanton described it,

> The technology industry's history is one of ongoing change. On the surface, the change appears chaotic and incomprehensible, with new inventions and technologies appearing on the scene apparently out of nowhere. In actuality, the industry is like a pond with pebbles sporadically being thrown into it—forecasting actual technological events may be extremely difficult, like guessing when a pebble will be thrown into a pond, but the ripple effects of each impact, and the subsequent wave interaction with other ripple patterns, can be understood with rigorous analysis.

EXHIBIT 9-13

PRICE/SALES MULTIPLES FOR TECHNOLOGY COMPANIES

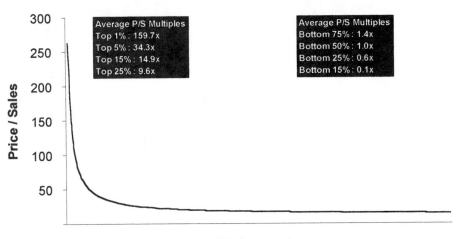

Source: Compiled from Silver Lake Partners' Presentation to Harvard Business School, October 11, 1999; Standard and Poors, Compustat, Merrill Lynch.

COMPETITIVE LANDSCAPE

Despite the dramatic growth and importance of technology in the modern economy, the sector had been widely viewed as unsuitable for buyout investors as a result of the disastrous Prime Computer transaction and the misperceptions discussed above. As a consequence, the sector remained relatively underserved by private equity capital: only approximately 5% of all buyouts in 1998 and 1999 involved technology companies, and fewer than 1% of all private equity firms were dedicated solely to technology buyout investing.

However, the growth and magnitude of the technology sector had made it increasingly difficult for buyout firms to ignore this space. As a result, technology buyout competition had begun to arise from various sources. First, several new technology-focused buyout firms had been formed in 1999. Second, many traditional LBO firms had begun to formally explore the IT sector. Finally, there was the possibility that existing middle-market technology-focused investment firms, as well as venture capitalists, would begin to explore larger scale technology buyouts.

New Tech-Focused Buyout Firms Several newly formed technology-focused buyout firms raised large funds in 1999, the largest of which were raised by Silver Lake Partners and Thomas Weisel Capital Partners.

Silver Lake Partners was formed by four individuals: Jim Davidson, the former head of technology investment banking at Hambrecht & Quist; Glenn Hutchins, a former partner of the Blackstone Group (a large leveraged buyout firm); David Roux, a former

Executive Vice President of Oracle Corporation (one of the world's largest software companies); and Roger McNamee, the current head of Integral Capital, a technology-focused hedge fund. Prior to the formation of Silver Lake, both Davidson and Roux were actually in discussions with Dave Stanton and TPG about potentially joining TPG's technology effort should the firm raise a separate technology fund. Integral Capital, which was funded by the venture capital firm Kleiner Perkins Caufield & Byers, was a direct investor in Silver Lake, which in turn made Kleiner Perkins an indirect investor in Silver Lake. Although Silver Lake did not have an exclusive relationship with Kleiner Perkins, industry observers felt that this association added to Silver Lake's cachet. In September 1999, Silver Lake closed on a $2.3 billion fund, making it the largest first-time buyout fund in history.

Thomas Weisel Capital Partners (TWCP) was the private equity arm of Thomas Weisel Partners, a rapidly growing technology-focused investment banking firm. Thomas Weisel was the former founder and CEO of Montgomery Securities, a technology-focused investment bank he sold to NationsBank Corporation in late 1997. TWCP was staffed by former partners and principals of Hicks, Muse, Tate & Furst (a leading lever-aged buyout firm) and by former partners of Montgomery Securities. Through its af-filiation with Thomas Weisel Partners, TWCP would have access to proprietary deal-flow, research, and financing capabilities. By December 1999, TWCP had raised just over $1 billion, with a final closing expected in January or February of 2000. TWCP planned to invest primarily in "growth" companies, which included technology firms.

Existing Buyout Firms' Tech Efforts   Several traditional leveraged buyout firms were exploring the technology space to varying degrees by investing money from their existing "generalist" funds into technology companies, by forming dedicated technology efforts, or by raising separate dedicated technology funds.

Kohlberg Kravis Roberts (KKR) was an example of the first extreme. KKR man-aged nearly $9 billion of capital in both the United States and Europe. Although the firm did not have a dedicated technology team, it had recently made several invest-ments in "lower-tech" technology companies such as a manufacturer of electronic con-nectors, a start-up telecomm equipment manufacturer, and a broadband Internet ac-cess company. Other prominent buyout firms that had recently invested in technology companies through their generalist funds included the Blackstone Group, Hicks, Muse, Tate & Furst, and Forstmann Little (see Exhibit 9-3 for fund sizes).

TPG was an example of the other extreme. In December 1999, the firm was out raising two new funds: a $3 billion generalist fund, and a $1 billion fund that would in-vest specifically in TPG's telecommunications and technology deals. In addition to TPG, Hicks Muse and Blackstone, among others, were rumored to be potentially raising tech-nology-focused funds.

Middle-Market Tech Investors and Venture Capitalists   Summit Partners, TA As-sociates, and General Atlantic Partners were examples of middle-market technology-focused private investment firms. Generally, each of these firms targeted equity in-vestments in the $5–$100 million range in private companies in exchange for minority positions. Often these firms shied away from transactional complexity by focusing on straight equity investments rather than more complex deal structures such as leveraged buyouts. In November 1999, however, one of KKR's top partners left the firm to join General Atlantic Partners.

In addition to middle-market investment firms, there existed the possibility that venture capitalists might migrate into larger-scale and later-stage investing. Venture cap-ital firms tended to have substantial industry knowledge and deep personal connections throughout the technology world. Such firms, however, typically had little experience in buyout transactions, particularly those that were highly structured and complex.

ESTABLISHING COMPETITIVE ADVANTAGE

Despite the increasing competitive intensity within the technology buyout space, Dave Stanton felt that Francisco Partners would have significant and sustainable competitive advantages vis-à-vis its rivals. These advantages derived from the team Stanton had assembled, their track record, their domain expertise, and the firm's relationship with Sequoia Capital, among other factors.

The Team   Stanton believed that he had assembled one of the world's most experienced teams of professionals focused on structured private equity investments in technology companies. In addition to Sandy and D.J., Dave recruited Ben Ball and Neil Garfinkel to become founding partners of the firm. Both had significant experience in analyzing and executing high-technology buyouts. (See Exhibit 9-14 for full bios of the five founding partners of Francisco Partners.) In aggregate, the team had over 50 years of technology buyout and investment banking experience. Furthermore, all of the founding partners had worked with each other in various capacities throughout their professional careers, thus mitigating any potential cultural issues.

Stanton felt that Sandy Robertson's initial involvement in the firm would be particularly important. Sandy was the founder of two highly successful technology investment banks, and in his 30 years of banking experience he had been involved in more technology public offerings and mergers than any other individual in the world. Stanton felt that Sandy had an unparalleled network of relationships within the technology space which would significantly boost Francisco Partners' deal origination, due diligence, and fundraising capabilities.

Track Record   Stanton believed that his team had amassed a proven and exceptional track record in technology investing, spanning a variety of industry sectors, investment sizes, growth profiles, capital structures, and structuring complexities. In addition to the highly successful investment performance Stanton and D.J. enjoyed at TPG (see Exhibit 9-1), Ball and Garfinkel were senior executives on deal teams that had invested over $298 million in 14 portfolio companies representing a combined enterprise value in excess of $1 billion. Collectively, the founding partners had evaluated over 250 additional technology investment opportunities representing over $15 billion in aggregate enterprise value. Furthermore, in addition to the $2.3 billion in debt financing that the team had raised in prior completed transactions, they had received commitments for over $5 billion in additional financing for unconsummated deals, all in the technology sector. Finally, Stanton and Deb's $1.8 billion LBO of ON Semiconductor was the largest technology buyout ever completed.

In addition to greatly facilitating fundraising, Francisco Partner's track record would help the firm in several other ways. First, because the founders had built a proven reputation for consummating complex technology transactions, Stanton felt that sellers would show a greater desire and confidence in working with his team than with other private equity firms. Related to this, Stanton believed that Francisco Partners would have an execution advantage in financing technology companies. Because the market for technology debt issues was relatively thin and required more expertise than for plain-vanilla issues, Francisco Partners' track record would be instrumental in enabling the firm to raise the financing necessary to consummate transactions.

EXHIBIT 9-14

BIOS OF FRANCISCO PARTNERS' FOUNDING PARTNERS

David M. Stanton   Prior to founding Francisco Partners, Mr. Stanton led TPG's technology investing activities from 1994 until August 1999. Mr. Stanton led TPG's investments in GlobeSpan, Inc., ON Semiconductor, Paradyne Networks, Inc., GT Com, and Zilog, Inc. as well as two oil & gas investments, Denbury Resources Inc. and Belden & Blake Corporation. Mr. Stanton is a board member of each company, as well as of MVX.com. Prior to joining TPG in 1994, Mr. Stanton was a venture capitalist with Trinity Ventures specializing in information technology, software, and telecommunications investing. Earlier in his career, Mr. Stanton was a strategy consultant with Bain & Company. Mr. Stanton received a B.S. in Chemical Engineering with Distinction from Stanford University and an M.B.A. from the Stanford Graduate School of Business. Mr. Stanton also pursued Ph.D. studies in Materials Science at Northwestern University where he was a Cabell Fellow.

Sanford R. Robertson   Prior to founding Francisco Partners, Mr. Robertson was the founder and Chairman of Robertson Stephens, Inc., a leading technology investment bank that was formed in 1978 and sold to BankBoston in 1998. Since the sale, Mr. Robertson has been an active technology investor and advisor to several technology companies. Mr. Robertson was also the founder of Robertson, Colman, Siebel & Weisel, later renamed Montgomery Securities, another prominent technology investment bank. Mr. Robertson was one of the pioneers in the creation of West Coast technology banking as an industry in the late 1960s and has remained one of the industry's most renowned participants to this date. He has had a significant financing involvement in over 500 growth technology companies throughout his career, including 3Com Corporation, America Online, Inc., Applied Materials, Inc., Ascend Communications Inc., Dell Computer Corporation, E*Trade Securities, Inc., Siebel Systems, Inc. and Sun Microsystems, Inc. Mr. Robertson received both a B.A. and an M.B.A. with Distinction from the University of Michigan.

Benjamin H. Ball   Prior to founding Francisco Partners, Mr. Ball was a Vice President with TA Associates where he led or co-led private equity investments in the software, semiconductor, and communications segments. At TA Associates, Mr. Ball played a key role in investing over $90 million in six portfolio companies. Prior to TA Associates, Mr. Ball worked for Genstar Capital LLC, a middle-market LBO firm, where he focused on investments in the semiconductor capital equipment and communications industries. Earlier in his career, Mr. Ball worked for AEA Investors Inc., a New York-based private equity firm and also for the consulting firm of Bain & Company. Mr. Ball formerly served on the boards of several privately held companies. Mr. Ball received his A.B. from Harvard College and an M.B.A. from the Stanford Graduate School of Business.

Dipanjan Deb   Prior to founding Francisco Partners, Mr. Deb was a Principal with TPG involved in its technology investment activities with Mr. Stanton. Mr. Deb is on the board of GlobeSpan, Inc. and Blackstar.com, and was formerly a director of ON Semiconductor. Prior to joining TPG, Mr. Deb was the head of semiconductor banking for Robertson Stephens, Inc. Earlier in his career, Mr. Deb was employed by Netro Corporation, a wireless broadband communications company. Mr. Deb received a B.S. in Electrical Engineering and Computer Science from the University of California, Berkeley, where he was a Regents Scholar, and an M.B.A. from the Stanford Graduate School of Business.

Neil M. Garfinkel   Prior to founding Francisco Partners, Mr. Garfinkel was a Managing Director of Friedman Fleischer & Lowe, a leading San Francisco private equity firm where he co-led the firm's information technology investing. Previously, Mr. Garfinkel was a Vice President with Summit Partners, where he was responsible for private equity transactions in the software and IT services sectors. At Summit Partners, Mr. Garfinkel played a key role in investing approximately $180 million in seven portfolio companies. Mr. Garfinkel is a former director of HMT Technology Corporation and seven privately held companies. Earlier in his career, Mr. Garfinkel was an attorney with Wilson Sonsini Goodrich and Rosati in Palo Alto and with Cravath Swaine & Moore in New York. Mr. Garfinkel received his A.B. from Harvard College and a J.D. from Columbia Law School, where he was a Harlan Fiske Stone Scholar.

Source: Francisco Partners, L.P. Offering Memorandum.

Domain Expertise Stanton believed that the technology sector was indeed very complicated and difficult to understand. He felt, however, that the competitive dynamics that resulted from technological innovation were ultimately comprehensible when rigorously researched and analyzed. Stanton believed that when an investor had sufficient experience and domain expertise to evaluate a technology company, IT investing was not dissimilar from investing in more traditional buyout candidates.

Stanton hoped to leverage Francisco Partners' technology domain expertise into a three-pronged investment approach. First, the firm would employ research-intensive, top-down industry analysis in order to identify and exploit trends in targeted subsectors of the technology industry. Second, the firm would leverage its knowledge base to identify companies at strategic or operational inflection points. Stanton felt that at such points of inflection, a company's future potential could be difficult to calibrate, and, as a result, substantial value could be created and realized if the proper strategic decisions were made. Furthermore, firms at such inflection points tended to be priced more attractively than other firms. Third, the firm would leverage its substantial expertise in crafting complex structural solutions to technology transaction problems. This would enable Francisco Partners to facilitate the execution of investment opportunities where complicated structures were required to consummate a transaction or to create value by virtue of the transaction structure itself.

Given that the learning curve in technology investing was very steep, Stanton believed that generalist leveraged buyout firms would find it extremely difficult to keep pace with the changing technology industry. Thus, Francisco Partners would establish a strong lead over these firms by focusing exclusively on the technology space. In addition, Stanton believed that Francisco Partners' domain expertise would provide inherent speed advantages in making investment decisions and consummating transactions, which was often highly desired by sellers.

Sequoia Capital In September 1999, Francisco Partners entered into an exclusive, long-term relationship with Sequoia Capital, one of Silicon Valley's oldest and most successful venture capital firms. Established in 1972, Sequoia Capital had provided early-stage capital to over 350 technology companies, including 3Com, Apple Computer, Cisco Systems, Electronic Arts, Linear Technology, LSI Logic, Oracle, Scient, WebVan, VA LiNUX Systems, and Yahoo! As of December 1999, Sequoia's portfolio investments had an aggregate market capitalization in excess of $700 billion, nearly 15% of the NASDAQ's entire market capitalization. Industry experts typically considered Sequoia Capital and Kleiner Perkins to be the top two venture capital firms in Silicon Valley.

Stanton expected Francisco Partners to derive significant benefits from its relationship with Sequoia. First, Sequoia would serve as an exclusive and proprietary source of deal-flow for companies that fall outside the scope of its venture capital operations. Second, Sequoia's network of executives, entrepreneurs, consultants, and limited partners would be available for Francisco Partners' due diligence efforts and thus would enhance Francisco Partners' strategic investing insight and speed in analyzing investments. Finally, by leveraging Sequoia's extended presence and knowledge in technology markets through the relationships the firm had built over the last 28 years, Francisco Partners would be able to continue to develop its own intellectual property base in technology investing.

To further cement its relationship with Sequoia, Francisco Partners was planning to co-locate with Sequoia, giving the firm instant access to Sequoia's resources. Furthermore, Sequoia Capital's partners personally committed to invest $100 million in Francisco Partners' first fund on a no-fee, no-carry basis. In addition, Sequoia received a small ownership piece of Francisco Partners, roughly equivalent to that of a junior partner.

Executive Council   Stanton planned to form an Executive Council, which would consist of a group of prominent industry executives who have agreed to invest in Francisco Partners and to act as strategic advisors to the firm. Stanton expected Executive Council members to provide strategic investment insight, operating advice, market intelligence, due diligence assistance, and management reference checks, as well as to contribute to deal-flow.

Strategic Investor Base   Stanton aimed to persuade 50 to 100 prominent Silicon Valley CEOs and executives to invest in Francisco Partners' fund. Stanton hoped he would be able to call on these strategic investors to provide all of the resources that Executive Council members would provide.

Executive-in-Residence Program   Stanton also intended to rotate two or three senior executives through the Francisco Partners offices at three- to six-month intervals. He hoped that these executives would participate in active, full-time due diligence on deals pursued by the firm, as well as provide a source of idea generation and deal-flow. Furthermore, these executives would also represent a source of potential operating executives for Francisco Partners' portfolio companies. The founding partners had successfully employed programs similar to this in the past.

FUNDRAISING ISSUES

Dave Stanton had been in almost daily dialogue with DLJ's Private Fund Group since he left TPG in August. Stanton agreed that DLJ would be the exclusive placement agent for Francisco Partners' first fund. DLJ's Private Fund group consisted of some 30 professionals located in five offices throughout the United States and Europe. In the past, DLJ's team had collectively raised over $50 billion in commitments to private equity funds, more than any other placement agent.

In exchange for a placement fee, a placement agent served several purposes in a buyout firm's fundraising effort. For example, DLJ would help draft Francisco Partners' offering memorandum and investor presentations, coordinate the firm's marketing strategy, advise the firm on the best set of fund terms, help with the firm's regulatory filings, plan and schedule the investor roadshows, help negotiate the final limited partnership agreement with prospective investors, and perhaps most importantly, give Francisco Partners access to a much larger investor network than it would have been able to tap otherwise.

From September through December, Stanton and the other partners worked assiduously to draft their offering memorandum. This would be the formal marketing document sent out to all prospective investors. It included a summary of the key terms of the fund, information on the founders' prior investment performance, an overview of the firm's investment strategy, background information on the technology industry, employee bios, summaries of the founders' prior transactions, and a list of risks, legal considerations, and tax implications involved with investing in the fund.

Before the offering memo went to press, Francisco Partners would need to finalize most of the key economic terms of the fund, for these factors would play a large role in whether potential investors committed money to the fund. Stanton debated almost all of these terms with his partners and with DLJ on a daily basis.

Committed Capital How much money should Francisco Partners set out to raise for its first fund? On the one hand, the fundraising market was very robust. On the other hand, Stanton did not want to bite off more than his firm could appropriately invest. A related issue was the amount Francisco Partners should put on the cover of its offering memorandum. Often, funds would put one number "on the cover" but subsequently raise significantly more money. By having the fund "oversubscribed," Francisco Partners might be able to have more leverage in negotiating final fund terms. In addition, oversubscription can make a fund appear "hot." If the cover number were too large, however, it might be hard to reach, thus potentially casting a negative shadow on the firm. On the other hand, if the number were too small, it might be hard for the firm to raise significantly more than the cover amount (as limited partners might object to this), thus limiting the potential size of the fund.

General Partners' Commitment Although Sequoia Capital would be contributing $100 million to Francisco Partners' fund, how much should Stanton and the other general partners commit to the fund? Limited partner (LP) investors liked to see the general partners (GPs) commit a significant amount of money to a fund to keep the GPs' interests aligned with those of the LPs. At the same time, however, Stanton and his partners were investing a lot of their "human capital" in the firm.

Return Formula How should Francisco Partners allocate the profits from its investments? LBO funds typically offered their LPs a preferred return in the 8–10% range, then had a GP "catch-up" and split the remaining profits on an 80/20 basis with their LPs. This meant that the LPs would receive their original capital contribution plus an 8–10% return before the LBO firm received anything. After the LPs received this distribution, the LBO firm "caught up" at some rate (e.g., 80% to the GP and 20% to the LPs) until the GP had received 20% of aggregate profits, and the LPs had received 80%. Thereafter, profits were split 80% to the LPs and 20% to the GPs. Some firms offered no preferred return, and other firms kept more than 20% of the total profits after the catch-up.

A related issue to the return formula was the claw-back provision. If a fund did not have a claw-back provision and made a lot of profit on one deal but lost all of its money on another, the GP could keep the profits from the first deal. If the fund had a claw-back provision, however, the LPs could "claw back" the money the GP made on the first deal to compensate for the losses the LPs suffered on the second deal. This claw-back was typically settled at the end of the fund term (usually 10–12 years) so that total fund profits after accounting for all profits and losses from individual deals were split 80% to the LPs and 20% to the GPs. Although claw-back provisions were not common in very early LBO funds, they had become a standard feature in most funds raised in the 1990s.

Management Fee The management fee was the annual fee paid by the limited partners to the general partners to cover the GP's operating expenses as well as to compensate the GPs for investing the LPs' money. These fees were generally in the range of 1–2% of total fund size per annum. How large should Francisco Partners' management fee be? A related issue was whether Francisco Partners would have to "give back" the management fee. If this were indeed the case, then the GPs would have to return the management fees to the LPs before the GPs would see any profit; thus, the management fee was in reality an interest-free loan from the LPs against future GP profits. If, however, Francisco Partners could have "first dollar carry," the firm would "keep" the management fees—that is, never pay them back to the LPs.

Transaction, Break-Up, and Other Fees   In the course of executing investments, buyout firms typically earned various types of fees. These fees included transaction and investment banking fees, which were fees paid by the target company to the buyout firm upon consummation of a transaction; advisory, director, and monitoring fees, which were fees paid by portfolio companies to a buyout firm as compensation for the ongoing advice the companies received from the buyout firm; and break-up fees, which were fees paid by a target company to the buyout firm if after signing a deal to be acquired by the buyout firm, the target company was ultimately purchased by another acquiror. Should Francisco Partners keep all of these fees, or give some or all of these fees to the limited partners by crediting such income against future management fees? Buyout firms varied widely on how they treated this. Many LPs, however, believed that buyout groups should earn the bulk of their return from carried interest rather than from fee income.

Investment Restrictions   LBO funds typically were restricted as to the percentage of the fund that could be invested in any single portfolio company. Buyout funds were also often restricted as to the percentage of the fund that could be deployed internationally. These restrictions could sometimes be relaxed upon the approval of a number of the fund's LPs. Should Francisco Partners have any of these types of restrictions? If so, how should they be structured?

Organizational Expenses   Who should bear the offering and organizational expenses (such as legal, accounting, and regulatory fees) associated with setting up Francisco Partners' first fund? If the LPs were to pay this expense, up to how much should they bear? Should they be "given back" to the LPs like management fees may be?

Placement Agent Fee   How much should DLJ be compensated for helping Francisco Partners raise its fund? These fees were typically in the range 0.5–2.0% of total fund size, payable over several years by the general partners of the fund. Should DLJ have a formula that ratchets up (i.e., 1.0% for the first $500 million raised, 1.5% for the next $500 million, and 2.0% thereafter), or should the formula be a straight percentage of fund size? Should DLJ get credit for the entire amount Francisco Partners raises, or just the amount that can be clearly attributable to DLJ?

See Exhibit 9-15 for a comparison of the terms and conditions of several different buyout funds.

CONCLUSION

It was just after 1 A.M. as Dave Stanton settled into his car to make the 45-minute drive from Sand Hill Road back to his home in San Francisco. As he drove along Highway 280, his mind could not stop racing. As he thought about his presentation to investors, he wondered whether he had built a convincing enough case for the feasibility of technology buyouts. He also wondered whether the competitive advantages he believed that he built into his firm were sustainable. Next, he thought about the fund terms he was going to propose to DLJ the following day.

Stanton also thought about hiring issues. What mix of skills should he look for in new junior people—significant buyout experience or deep technology knowledge? Where would he find these people? Would the Francisco Partners opportunity be attractive enough to recruit top job candidates? What kind of culture would he promote in his firm? How could he foster teamwork, open communication, and the sharing of ideas?

EXHIBIT 9-15

COMPARISON OF TERMS AND CONDITIONS OF SELECTED BUYOUT FUNDS

Fund	Blackstone Capital Partners III	Hicks Muse Tate & Furst Equity Fund IV	Kohlberg Kravis Roberts 1996 Fund
Strategy	Equity and equity-related investments in a broad range of businesses	Equity investments in a diversified portfolio of businesses	Equity and equity-related investments in a broad range of businesses
Final Closing	1997	1999	1996
Cover Amount	$2.5 billion	$3.5 billion	None
Actual Commited Capital	$3.8 billion	$4.1 billion	$6.0 billion
GPs' Commitment	$180 million	$180 million	$125 million
Return Formula	(i) Return of organizational expenses and management fees; (ii) 10% preferred return; (iii) 80/20 GP/LP catch-up; (iv) 80/20 LP/GP thereafter	(i) 8% preferred return; (ii) return of organizational expenses and management fees; (iii) 80/20 GP/LP catch-up; (iv) 80/20 LP/GP thereafter	(i) Return of 20% of management fees; (ii) 80/20 LP/GP thereafter
Claw-back	Yes	Yes	Yes
Management Fee	(i) Up to $2 billion: 1.5%; (ii) Over $2 billion: 1.0%	1.5%	(i) Up to $3 billion: 1.5%; (ii) From $3-$4 billion: 0.75%; (iii) 0.5% thereafter
Transaction Fees	80% credited against management fees	50% credited against management fees	First $6 million kept by GP. 80% credited against management fees thereafter.
Break-up Fees	80% credit	50% credit	80% credit
Director/Monitoring Fees	50% credit	Kept by GP	Same as transaction fees.
Investment Restrictions	Max 25% in any single portfolio company. Max 25% outside the U.S.	Max 25% in any single portfolio company	Max 25% in any single portfolio company. Max 20% outside the U.S.
Organizational Expenses	Unlimited, charged to LPs	Max of $1.5 million, charged to LPs	Paid by GP
Placement Agent Fee	N/A	N/A	N/A

(Continued)

EXHIBIT 9-15 (*Continued*)

Fund	Silver Lake Partners	Thomas Weisel Capital Partners	TPG Partners II
Strategy	Equity buyout and recapitalization investments in technology and related growth businesses	Equity and equity-related investments in a broad range of growth and technology businesses	Equity investments in operating companies through acquisitions and restructurings
Final Closing	1999	Expected early 2000	1997
Cover Amount	$1.0 billion	None	$1.5 billion
Actual Commited Capital	$2.3 billion	Expected $1+ billion	$2.5 billion
GPs' Commitment	$50 million	5% of total commitments	5% of total commitments
Return Formula	(i) Return of organizational expenses and management fees; (ii) 8% preferred return; (iii) 100% GP catch-up; (iv) 80/20 LP/GP thereafter	(i) Return of organizational expenses and management fees; (ii) 8% preferred return; (iii) 100% GP catch-up; (iv) 80/20 LP/GP thereafter	(i) Return of organizational expenses and management fees; (ii) 8% preferred return; (iii) 65/35 GP/LP catch-up; (iv) 80/20 LP/GP thereafter
Claw-back	Yes	Yes	Yes (through escrow account)
Management Fee	(i) Up to $1 billion: 1.75%; (ii) Over $1 billion: 1.5%	2.0%	1.5%
Transaction Fees	50% credited against management fees	50% credited against management fees	50% credited against management fees
Break-up Fees	50% credit	50% credit	50% credit
Director/Monitoring Fees	50% credit	50% credit	50% credit
Investment Restrictions	Max 20% in any single portfolio company. Max 25% outside the U.S.	Max 25% in any single portfolio company. Max 20% outside the U.S.	Max 25% in any single portfolio company. Max 25% outside the U.S.
Organizational Expenses	Max of $1 million, charged to LPs	Max of $1 million, charged to LPs	Max of $1.25 million, charged to LPs
Placement Agent Fee	Paid by GP	Paid by GP	Paid by GP

Source: Compiled from DLJ Presentation to Francisco Partners, July 30, 1999; Individual Fund Offering Memoranda.

Finally, he thought about longer-term issues. How would Stanton manage the transition of Sandy Robertson's network to the rest of the firm? How would the firm establish an e-commerce strategy? Surely such companies would become attractive buyout candidates in the future. Finally, Stanton expected that Europe would present Francisco Partners with an abundance of opportunities, given the opening up of cross-border markets and the reorganization of many European companies. How could he pursue investment opportunities over 5,000 miles away?

Although Stanton had accomplished a tremendous amount since leaving TPG in August, he knew the hard part was about to begin.

The second module of the course considers the interactions between private equity investors and the entrepreneurs that they finance. These interactions are at the core of what private equity investors do.

We will approach these interactions through a framework that seeks to understand the actions of private equity investors along two dimensions. First, we will explore the particular challenges that young and restructuring firms pose to private equity investors. Second, we will understand how the competitive situation facing the private equity firm itself determines its interactions with the firms in its portfolio.

WHY THIS MODULE?

It is easy to build a case that the financing and guidance of dynamic private businesses lie at the heart of the private equity process. The frequently complex interactions between investors and the firms in their portfolios could fill several courses! In order to help organize this complex material, we will approach the cases in this module through two frameworks.

First, we categorize the reasons why the types of firms backed by private equity investors find it difficult to meet their financing needs through traditional mechanisms, such as bank loans. These difficulties can be sorted into four critical factors: uncertainty, asymmetric information, intangible firm assets, and varying market conditions. At any one point in time, these factors determine the choices that a firm faces. As a firm evolves over time, however, these factors can change in rapid and unanticipated ways.

We also highlight the manner in which the circumstances of the private equity group can affect the investment decision. In some cases, the need to soon return to limited partners for capital—or an approaching decision as to whether an investment professional is to be promoted to partner—may lead to the rejection of an otherwise attractive transaction. In other cases, concerns about competition from within and outside the private equity industry are leading groups to undertake substantial investments in the services they provide entrepreneurs. These company- and private equity organization-level issues will help organize our analyses of the complex interactions between private equity investors and the firms in their portfolios.

Professor Joshua Lerner prepared this note as the basis for class discussion.

THE FRAMEWORK (1): THE FINANCING CHALLENGE

Entrepreneurs rarely have the capital to see their ideas to fruition and must rely on outside financiers. Meanwhile, those who control capital—for instance, pension fund trustees and university overseers—are unlikely to have the time or expertise to invest directly in young or restructuring firms. It might be thought that the entrepreneurs would turn to traditional financing sources, such as bank loans and the issuance of public stock, to meet their needs. But a variety of factors are likely to lead to some of the most potentially profitable and exciting firms not being able to access these financing sources.

Private equity investors are almost invariably attracted to firms that find traditional financing difficult to arrange. Why are these firms difficult to finance? Whether managing a $10 million seed investment pool or a $5 billion leveraged buyout fund, private equity investors are looking for companies that have the potential to evolve in ways that create value. This evolution may take several forms. Early-stage entrepreneurial ventures are likely to grow rapidly and respond swiftly to the changing competitive environment. Alternatively, the managers of buyout and build-up firms may create value by improving operations and acquiring other rivals. In each case, the firm's ability to change dynamically is a key source of competitive advantage, but also a major problem to those who provide the financing.

As mentioned above, the characteristics of these dynamic firms will be analyzed using a four-factor framework. The first of these, uncertainty, is a measure of the array of potential outcomes for a company or project. The wider the dispersion of potential outcomes, the greater the uncertainty. By their very nature, young and restructuring companies are associated with significant levels of uncertainty. Uncertainty surrounds whether the research program or new product will succeed. The response of a firm's rivals may also be uncertain. High uncertainty means that investors and entrepreneurs cannot confidently predict what the company will look like in the future.

Uncertainty affects the willingness of investors to contribute capital, the desire of suppliers to extend credit, and the decisions of firms' managers. If managers are averse to taking risks, it may be difficult to induce them to make the right decisions. Conversely, if entrepreneurs are overoptimistic, then investors want to curtail various actions. Uncertainty also affects the timing of investment. Should an investor contribute all the capital at the beginning, or should he stage the investment through time? Investors need to know how information-gathering activities can address these concerns and when they should be undertaken.

The second factor, asymmetric information, is distinct from uncertainty. Because of his day-to-day involvement with the firm, an entrepreneur knows more about his company's prospects than investors, suppliers, or strategic partners. Various problems develop in settings where asymmetric information is prevalent. For instance, the entrepreneur may take detrimental actions that investors cannot observe: perhaps undertaking a riskier strategy than initially suggested or not working as hard as the investor expects. The entrepreneur might also invest in projects that build up his reputation at the investors' expense.

Asymmetric information can also lead to selection problems. The entrepreneur may exploit the fact that he knows more about the project or his abilities than investors do. Investors may find it difficult to distinguish between competent entrepreneurs and incompetent ones. Without the ability to screen out unacceptable projects and entrepreneurs, investors are unable to make efficient and appropriate decisions.

The third factor affecting a firm's corporate and financial strategy is the intangible nature of many firms' assets. Firms that have tangible assets—for example, machines, buildings, land, or physical inventory—may find financing easier to obtain or may be able to obtain more favorable terms. The ability to abscond with the firm's source of value is more difficult when it relies on physical assets. When the most important assets are intangible, such as trade secrets, raising outside financing from traditional sources may be more challenging.

Market conditions also play a key role in determining the difficulty of financing firms. Both the capital and product markets may be subject to substantial variations. The supply of capital from public investors and the price at which this capital is available may vary dramatically. These changes may be a response to regulatory edicts or shifts in investors' perceptions of future profitability. Similarly, the nature of product markets may vary dramatically, whether due to shifts in the intensity of competition with rivals or in the nature of the customers. If there is exceedingly intense competition or a great deal of uncertainty about the size of the potential market, firms may find it very difficult to raise capital from traditional sources.

THE FRAMEWORK (2): THE IMPACT OF THE PRIVATE EQUITY ORGANIZATION'S SITUATION

Although the circumstances of the firm are important, so too are those of the private equity group itself. Three classes of circumstances are among the most influential in shaping the strategies of private equity organizations.

In some cases, actions taken in previous fundraising cycles can profoundly shape private equity investments. For instance, a private equity group may commit to investing in certain types of industries or stages at the time that the fund is raised, and consequently may be hesitant to deviate from the stated plan. In a similar manner, the allocation of responsibility and compensation at the time that a fund closes may have a substantial impact on the investment decisions made, even if in hindsight the private equity organization would have been far better off with another arrangement.

In other instances, it is the concerns about the raising of subsequent funds that are critical. For instance, the fact that the venture capital organization will soon be in the market with a new fund may drive it to refinance a troubled portfolio company, in order to avoid a write-off that might lead potential investors to question their performance. Similarly, groups may worry about a series of large failures endangering a private equity organization's "franchise" with limited partners. As a result, they may seek to balance the portfolio between highly risky investments offering the potential for large returns and a number of more modest but safer investments (for instance, syndicated investments in the latter financing rounds of transactions originated by other private equity groups). These concerns are at work not only at the organization level, but also among individuals: worries about promotion and relative compensation can also have a profound effect on the decisions of private equity professionals.

Finally, concerns about the group's success in persuading top-flight entrepreneurs to choose their capital are important as well. During the early days of the industry, established private equity organizations had the upper hand in bargaining with entrepreneurs: there were relatively few alternatives to venture financing. The pool of private equity was also quite small. As a consequence, when groups found themselves interested in the same transaction, they often chose to share (or "syndicate") the transaction rather than to compete with each other. Today, the situation has changed dramatically. Not only has the amount of private equity expanded sharply, but groups are facing increasing competition from sophisticated angel investors and groups of high-net worth investors organized by investment banks and other intermediaries. As a result, leading private equity groups today are increasingly engaging in what might be termed "branding": seeking to dramatically expand the range of services provided to, and their visibility among, entrepreneurs. Through such steps, the organizations seek to differentiate themselves from competitors within and outside the private equity industry.

THE STRUCTURE OF THE MODULE

This module will illustrate these two frameworks with examples from a wide variety of private equity funds and industries. We will carefully identify the types of problems that emerge in transactions involving different industries, countries, types of transactions, and private equity fund circumstances. We will then see how private equity groups respond to these changing settings by, for instance, altering deal structures.

A second important aspect of this module will be to explore the institutional and legal aspects of each type of private equity transaction. Among the specific issues raised in private equity transactions that we will consider are:

- The investment criteria, deal terms, and post-transaction tactics of venture capital investors.
- The alternative criteria and approaches employed by latter-stage investors, as well as the associated providers of debt financing to these firms.
- The nature of transactions that incorporate elements both of venture capital and buyouts, such as technology buyouts.
- The extent to which deal structures can be translated into overseas markets, such as developing nations.
- The various ways in which valuation issues are addressed, including many of the methodologies specific to the private equity industry and the opportunities for the application of new valuation techniques.
- The relationship between financing choices and firm strategy.
- The structure and implementation of relationships with strategic co-investors.
- The restructuring of entrepreneurial ventures in distress.

FURTHER READING ON PRIVATE EQUITY INVESTING

Legal Works

JOSEPH W. BARTLETT, *Equity Finance: Venture Capital, Buyouts, Restructurings, and Reorganization*, New York, Wiley, 1995, chapters 5–10 and 16–27.

MICHAEL J. HALLORAN, LEE F. BENTON, ROBERT V. GUNDERSON, JR., KEITH L. KEARNEY, and JORGE DEL CALVO, *Venture Capital and Public Offering Negotiation*, Englewood Cliffs, NJ, Aspen Law and Business, 1997 (and updates), volume 1, chapters 5 through 9.

JACK S. LEVIN, *Structuring Venture Capital, Private Equity, and Entrepreneurial Transactions*, Boston, MA, Little, Brown, 2000, chapters 2 through 8.

Practicing Law Institute, *Venture Capital* (Commercial Law and Practice Course Handbook Series), New York, Practicing Law Institute, various years, various chapters.

Practitioner and Journalistic Accounts

JEFF ANAPOLSKY, "How to Structure and Manage Leveraged Build-Ups," *Journal of Private Equity* 1 (Summer 1998): 33–50.

Asset Alternatives, *Venture Capital and Health Care* [periodical and annual overview], Wellesley, MA, Asset Alternatives, 2000 (and earlier years).

Asset Alternatives, *Venture Capital and Information Technology* [periodical], Wellesley, MA, Asset Alternatives, 2000 (and earlier years).

LEONARD A. BATTERSON, *Raising Venture Capital and the Entrepreneur*, Englewood Cliffs, NJ, Prentice-Hall, 1986.

COOPERS & LYBRAND, *Three Keys to Obtaining Venture Capital*, New York, Coopers & Lybrand, 1993.

COOPERS & LYBRAND, *The Economic Impact of Venture Capital in Europe*, Paris, Coopers & Lybrand, 2000.

STEVE HARMON, *Zero Gravity: Riding Venture Capital from High-Tech Start-Up to Breakout IPO*, Princeton, NJ, Bloomberg Press, 1999.

HAROLD M. HOFFMAN and JAMES BLAKEY, "You *Can* Negotiate with Venture Capitalists," *Harvard Business Review* 65 (March–April 1987): 16–24.

JAMES L. PLUMMER, *QED Report on Venture Capital Financial Analysis*, Palo Alto, CA, QED Research, 1987.

RUTHANN QUINDLEN, *Confessions of a Venture Capitalist: Inside the High-Stakes World of Start-Up Financing*, New York, Warner Books, 2000.

Many accounts in *Buyouts*, *Private Equity Analyst*, and *Venture Capital Journal*

Academic Studies

GEORGE P. BAKER and KAREN H. WRUCK, "Organizational Changes and Value Creation in Leveraged Buyouts: The Case of O.M. Scott & Sons Company," *Journal of Financial Economics*, 25 (December 1989): 163–190.

GEORGE W. FENN, NELLIE LIANG, and STEPHEN PROWSE, "The Private Equity Market: An Overview," *Financial Markets, Institutions, and Instruments* 6, no. 4 (1997): 27–69.

PAUL A. GOMPERS and JOSH LERNER, *The Money of Invention*, Boston, MA: Harvard Business School Press, 2001, chapters 2–4.

PAUL A. GOMPERS and JOSH LERNER, *The Venture Capital Cycle*, Cambridge, MA: MIT Press, 1999, chapters 6–9.

PAUL A. GOMPERS and JOSH LERNER, "Money Chasing Deals? The Impact of Fund Inflows on Private Equity Valuations," *Journal of Financial Economics* 55 (February 2000): 281–325.

PAUL HALPERN, ROBERT KIESCHNICK, and WENDY ROTENBERG, "On the Heterogeneity of Leveraged Going Private Transactions," *Review of Financial Studies* 12 (Summer 1999): 281–309.

THOMAS F. HELLMANN and MANJU PURI, "The Interaction Between Product Market and Financing Strategy: The Role of Venture Capital," *Review of Financial Studies*, 13 (Winter 2000): 459–484.

STEVEN N. KAPLAN and RICHARD S. RUBACK, "The Valuation of Cash Flow Forecasts: An Empirical Analysis," *Journal of Finance* 50 (September 1995): 1059–1093.

STEVEN N. KAPLAN and JEREMY STEIN, "The Evolution of Buyout Pricing and Financial Structure in the 1980s," *Quarterly Journal of Economics* 108 (May 1993): 313–358.

STEVEN N. KAPLAN and PER STROMBERG, "Financial Contracting Theory Meets the Real World: An Empirical Analysis of Venture Capital Contracts," Center for Economic Policy Research Working Paper No. 2421, 2000.

SAMUEL KORTUM and JOSH LERNER, "Assessing the Impact of Venture Capital on Innovation," *Rand Journal of Economics*, 31 (Winter 2000): 674–692.

KRISHNA G. PALEPU, "Consequences of Leveraged Buyouts," *Journal of Financial Economics* 27 (September 1990): 247–262.

CHRISTINE C. PENCE, *How Venture Capitalists Make Investment Decisions*, Ann Arbor, MI, UMI Research Press, 1982.

WILLIAM A. SAHLMAN, "The Structure and Governance of Venture Capital Organizations," *Journal of Financial Economics* 27 (October 1990): 473–521.

TYZOON T. TYEBJEE and ALBERT V. BRUNO, "A Model of Venture Capitalist Investment Activity," *Management Science* 30 (September 1984): 1051–1066.

10

Adams Capital Management: March 1999

On February 24, 1999, the advisory board of Adams Capital Management convened for its quarterly meeting at the firm's headquarters in Sewickley, Pennsylvania, a suburb of Pittsburgh. One point on the agenda: whether or not to proceed with due diligence on an investment in Three Points, a maker of Internet-based team management software for softball teams.

That such a topic would ever be raised at a meeting of a venture capital firm's advisory board is highly unusual. But, then again, Adams Capital was somewhat of an unusual venture capital firm. It had developed and raised its fund on the basis of a strict set of guidelines for conducting the business of early-stage venture capital. Adams Capital invested only in applied technology companies that sold to businesses, not consumers, and that exploited fundamental sea changes (or *discontinuities*) in large established markets it hoped to penetrate. Adams Capital managed these investments according to a strict system called *structured navigation*, a set of five benchmarks that the firm's partners believed were crucial to the success of early-stage applied technology companies.

Joel Adams and Bill Hulley, Adams Capital's founding partners, had spearheaded the formulation of this investment strategy in part to differentiate their fund to potential limited partners. But they also believed that the loose structures of most venture firms—where each investor is often given wide leeway in determining which, and how many, markets and business models to invest in—can sometimes cause them to lose sight of the portfolio as a whole. Without a "markets first" strategy, where a firm as a whole agrees on which markets to target *before* considering particular companies in those markets, Adams felt that firms tend to invest more on the basis of "street buzz" than on business fundamentals or market analysis.

But now, with Three Points, Adams Capital was confronted by a seemingly attractive investment that fell far outside its stated focus. Even though the Internet element of Three Points' product placed it in a large and attractive market, the company sold

Bill Wasik prepared this case under the guidance of Senior Lecturer Felda Hardymon as the basis for class discussion rather than to illustrate either effective or ineffective handling of an administrative situation.

its software to consumers, not businesses. Nevertheless, Joel Adams saw in Three Points the germ of a tremendous business and, in its founder, Tom Anderson, the makings of a successful entrepreneur.

Although Adams Capital had raised its $55 million fund in 1997 on the basis of its strict processes of discontinuity-based investing and structured navigation, nothing in its limited partnership agreement required it to adhere to these rules on every investment. Surely, come next fundraising time, the firm's limited partners would welcome one or two examples of opportunistic investments like Three Points, assuming they were successful; but if such an investment failed, Adams worried about his credibility.

More importantly, however, he worried about the implications of short-circuiting the very process that he and Bill had created. Would they be guilty of the same sin that they had so long ascribed to other venture investors—placing investments based more on personalities (his own and the entrepreneur's) than on rigorous research in predetermined markets? They hoped their advisory board[1] would give them a reality check.

ADAMS CAPITAL MANAGEMENT

Joel Adams was raised in Phelps, New York, a small dairy community between Rochester and Syracuse. "My dad owned a dairy farm," recalled Adams, "and his program was the following: you turned six, you start getting up at 4:45 in the morning and do chores." Adams was 15 when his mother passed away, during the recession of the early 1970s. His father had no choice but to delegate most of his wife's responsibilities to the three kids. Looking back on those days, Adams said: "At the time the confluence of events was a hell of a wake up call for a teenager, but I learned invaluable lessons about money and time management."

After graduating from the University of Buffalo in 1979, Adams went to work for nuclear submarine manufacturer General Dynamics. He quickly rose to the position of test engineer—the lead engineer responsible for starting and testing the nuclear reactor and representing General Dynamics during the Navy's sea trials of new subs. "After numerous trials on about nine subs, I got bored," he said. "I saw that I wanted to do something else with my career." So in 1984 he moved to Pittsburgh to attend Carnegie Mellon's business school, lured by its strong program in Entrepreneurship.

During Adams' second year at CMU he began working part-time for Fostin Capital, a small venture capital firm that invested on behalf of the Fosters, a wealthy family in Pittsburgh. By the time of his graduation, Fostin had closed a $14 million fund—of which the Fosters were only one of several limited partners—and Joel was offered a position as a junior partner. In 1985, the state of Pennsylvania passed legislation allowing 1% of the state's pension funds to go into venture capital investments. By 1986, the state was planning to create a $40 million fund for this purpose, and there would be "best efforts" to put half into Pennsylvania deals. To manage this fund, the state wanted a national venture capital player that had offices in Pennsylvania. There was one problem: "About a hundred funds threw their name in the hat," recalled Adams, "but nobody met those criteria." Certainly, New York-based Patricof & Co. Ventures didn't meet the criteria, but its then-president Bob Faris had an idea: create a joint venture with a Pittsburgh fund, with whom Patricof could bid jointly on the business. He contacted

---

[1] The Adams Capital advisory board was made up of several limited partners who convened quarterly primarily to approve the quarterly valuation report, but also acted as a sounding board on broad partnership issues such as the rate of investment, reserves, and timing on raising new funds.

Bill Woods, Fostin's managing partner, and the two bid on the fund and won. The resulting $40 million fund, the APA Fostin Pennsylvania Venture Capital Fund, would typically (but not exclusively) make investments alongside one of its two parent firms, and each investment from the joint fund required the approval of both firms.

In 1989, Fostin raised Fostin Capital Associates II ($18.8 million), and Bill Hulley, another engineer and CMU MBA, joined Fostin; and in 1992, Patricof and Fostin closed on APA Fostin II, a $60 million fund. At the insistence of the State Employees Retirement System (SERS), one of the fund's limited partners, Fostin reorganized its internal compensation structure concurrent with the closing of APA Fostin II, increasing the carried interest received by the partners but cutting their salaries dramatically. By 1993, most of Fostin's partners were unhappy with the arrangement and were threatening to disband.

Adams and Hulley sensed opportunity. The pair approached the Foster family (who controlled the fund) and offered to take over the Fostin piece of APA Fostin II and they agreed. Along with CFO Andrea Joseph and longtime secretary Lynn Patterson, the two partners left Fostin, and Adams Capital Management was born.

DISCONTINUITY-BASED INVESTING

Joel Adams had always been dissatisfied with what he considered a lack of focus and discipline in Fostin's investing. "Here's a nuclear engineer, walking into this industry, with a very small fund in Pittsburgh whose strategy was to be diversified by stage, by industry, *and* by geography," Adams recalled. "After about a year, I said, 'This isn't a strategy at all.' You could do anything." He was especially chagrined by their methods for developing deal-flow. Rather than becoming knowledgeable about markets and then targeting specific deals in those markets, he said, "the approach at Fostin was to open the mail in the morning" and see what business plans were there.

Two experiences Adams had at Fostin opened his eyes to the power of targeted investing. The first was his involvement with Sherpa Corporation, which made a software application for engineering product data management. "I knew engineering data management from my days at General Dynamics, and I understood the issues," Adams said. "And I was a much smarter investor looking at an industry that I knew." Not only did it make him a better investment manager and board member, he realized, but it also made him more savvy as a negotiator. "Entrepreneurs are passionate and biased about their businesses," he said. "If the first time I hear about a market is from the entrepreneur, I'm at a big disadvantage."

His second revelation was even more psychologically powerful. "I went to buy a computer in 1987," recalled Adams, "so I went to BusinessLand [then a top computer retailer] in downtown Pittsburgh. The sales guy was clueless—he didn't know what I was talking about or what I was trying to buy." When relating this story to a friend, the friend told Adams about his experience with a start-up in Texas called PCs Limited, where they had made his computer to spec for cheaper than going to the store.

Adams called the start-up's CEO and asked him to send him a computer, but also asked him about his business. "Ultimately," Adams recalled, "Dell called back and we ended up doing a deal." Fostin's $750,000 investment in the first outside venture round of what would become Dell Computer was valued at $80 million. Had Fostin's limited partners held their stock, that $750,000 position in 1999 would be worth over $500 million.

How had Michael Dell managed to create such an explosion of value, Adams wondered? The answer was, he had exploited a *discontinuity*—a dramatic and sudden change in a large and established market. In this instance, the discontinuity was one of distribution. The rise of direct distribution snuck up on the large PC manufacturers, who had highly entrenched networks of retail dealers. These networks, Adams noted, "couldn't be unwound overnight." Dell could build a multibillion dollar business from scratch because his large and sleepy competitors couldn't respond to this distribution discontinuity in time.

As Adams and Hulley prepared to raise their own $55 million fund in 1996, they looked back over their own investing track record. They came to the conclusion that their most successful investments to date—deals like Dell (IPO in 1988), InSoft (acquired by Netscape), Cytyc (IPO in 1996), and Scaleable (acquired by Fore Systems)—had been made in markets that they had *already* known well and *already* identified as attractive. Their new fund, they resolved, would continue to invest in *markets first*. Moreover, like the two of them, any new partners in Adams Capital would be engineers, who would bring their technical training to bear during thorough examinations of a few promising markets. But how would they decide on which markets to focus?

There were a few initial prerequisites. The first was that the companies they invested in would sell to businesses, not consumers, and their value propositions would be ROI-driven. ("That's ROI for the customers, not us," joked Adams. "Our first question is, 'If somebody is going to buy this company's product, what does the CFO recommendation look like?'") The second prerequisite was that the businesses be "first-generation applied technology," or one of the first crop of companies to leverage a specific technology for a specific application.

But these two criteria still did not define targeted markets for investing. The most important criterion was that, as in the case of Dell, Adams Capital's portfolio companies would be exploiting discontinuities in existing markets, discontinuities that would create openings for start-up companies to create huge businesses.

They identified four primary types of discontinuities (see Exhibit 10-1).

1. Standards. Despite the emergence of a technology standard in some fields, existing manufacturers with proprietary technologies often try to hold onto those technologies and, by extension, their captive customer base. Even as customers cry out for the standard, the existing manufacturers perceive the standard to be a threat to their oligopolistic market positions and are hence too slow to adopt it.

Adams cites the example of FORE Systems, which built communications devices that conformed to the ATM (asynchronous transfer mode) standard for communications in wide area networks. The big players at the time, AT&T/Lucent and Northern Telecom, among others, each had proprietary protocols for those communications. These manufacturers clearly had the technical prowess and market muscle to exploit ATM as well, but they were slow to do so, out of fear of cannibalizing their own market shares. In April 1999, FORE was acquired by General Electric Co. PLC for $4.5 billion.

2. Regulation. In a regulation-based discontinuity, unexpected regulatory change forces market players to adapt quickly to new challenges and opportunities. Adams offers the example of the U.S. cellular market, where the government's creation of the PCS spectrum suddenly created a host of new opportunities for would-be cellular service providers and a race to build out new networks. From a technology point of view, it provided an opening for GSM, the cheaper and more easily deployed base station technology which had become popular in Europe and the rest of the world, to gain ground on AMPS, the proprietary and more unwieldy technology which had become dominant in the United States. GSM equipment manufacturers and the upstart carriers who

---

EXHIBIT 10-1

EXCERPTED FROM THE ADAMS CAPITAL MANAGEMENT, INC. BROCHURE

Discontinuity: The Mother of Opportunity

Our strategic focus is built upon the concept of a discontinuity—a circumstance or event that disrupts the equilibrium in a particular industry and creates new entry opportunities. Discontinuities are rapid and permanent structural changes in established markets that incumbents, hindered by economics or aging infrastructure, are not able to respond to in a timely fashion.

Examples of specific discontinuities that create new entry points into large established markets include:

- The development of software technology allowing protection of content without proprietary hardware;
- The de-monopolization of the utility industry to permit customer choice among power producers, leaving incumbent utilities burdened with uneconomical infrastructures;
- The changes in the FDA approval processes affecting the introduction of advanced, technology-driven diagnostic devices supporting the convergence of new technologies into tightly integrated, software-based lifesaving systems;
- The emergence of communications protocols that support efficient transaction clearing over public networks, allowing digital content owners to greatly lower distribution costs and improve customer service;
- The move to a property-based spectrum management regime via FCC spectrum auctions, vastly increasing the amount of spectrum available for the introduction of innovative narrow-band and broad-band wireless technologies.

Compelling market opportunities that can be exploited by breakthrough innovation are created by discontinuities such as **industry standards**, **regulations**, **technology convergence** and **distribution**. And because even the best product or service will not stimulate great returns in a small or mediocre market, we focus on established markets approaching a billion dollars in size. We constantly watch these markets for discontinuities and the emerging companies that are positioned to take advantage of them. This is where we concentrate our investments.

Executing the Model

Currently, our strategy is focused on penetrating the **information technology**, **telecommunications** and **medical equipment** industries that have experienced or are now experiencing significant discontinuities.

1. **Information Technology**—Emphasis on the global virtual enterprise represents a fundamental shift in how information technology and application software are selected, deployed, and managed. Information systems organizations can no longer create highly intertwined applications that constrain enterprises from continually changing to meet new pressures. As enterprises go through the transition to adopt a global virtual enterprise model, the essential areas of market opportunity to invest in are Electronic Commerce Management (E-Commerce) and Supply Chain Management. The combination of E-Commerce, the Internet and the need for new types of solutions has created excellent opportunities for entrepreneurs.

(Continued)

EXHIBIT 10-1   (Continued)

2. **Telecommunications**—Thanks to the regulatory changes introduced by the Telecommunications Act of 1996, there has never been a better time to invest in wide-area telecommunications start-ups or the vendors clamoring to supply them. Spectrum auctions by the FCC continue to create diverse market entry opportunities that do not depend on access to incumbent carriers' facilities. Entrepreneurs who skillfully leverage new technologies to satisfy burgeoning user demand can reap tremendous rewards.

3. **Medical Equipment**—Important lifesaving and cost-saving technological advances combined with recent changes in FDA regulations have created a fertile environment for software-based medical diagnostic equipment. A dramatic transformation from fluid-based manual diagnostic techniques to highly accurate, non-invasive real-time systems applying signal processing and mathematical algorithms utilized in other industries, is rapidly unfolding. We see many opportunities to introduce better medicine through new technology.

Navigation: Sailing to Liquidity

We have developed a disciplined, five-step approach toward navigating companies to liquidity:

1. Round out the management team
2. Obtain a corporate partner or endorsement
3. Gain early exposure to investment bankers
4. Expand the product line
5. Eliminate non-execution business risks

This navigation system is a proven approach to building value for investors and building companies for the future.

Source: Corporate documents.

---

leveraged them were able to challenge the giants because they were more nimble in the face of regulatory change.

3. Technology.   A technology-based discontinuity can take two forms. In one form, it can simply be the development of a whizbang technology that takes big competitors months or years to duplicate, such as Apple's Macintosh operating system or Ciena's wavelength-division-multiplexing technology for optical networks. In another form, it involves the *convergence* of technologies that had hitherto been separate, necessitating devices or software that allow these once-disparate technologies to interact. An example here would be the rise of corporate remote access, which forced companies to buy products (like those made by Ascend Communications and others) to "bridge" connections between the public carrier telephone networks and corporations' internal local area networks.

4. Distribution.   As noted above, Dell Computer is the ultimate example of a distribution-based discontinuity. The rise of mail-order took existing PC manufacturers by surprise, to the great enrichment of Dell and its shareholders.

This top-down approach to identifying markets was, in Adams' view, crucial in having control over and consensus about where its partners would place investments. "Market due diligence is the only due diligence you can do independent of a transaction," he said. "If you present the partners with the industry and market dynamics ahead of time, then we can all talk about each other's prospective deals, and leverage each other's knowledge base and contacts, before we make an investment."

Adams Capital's approach to identifying discontinuities centered on their *Discontinuities Roundtable*, a group of advisors to the fund who met several times a year with the Adams Capital partners to identify and discuss market discontinuities that could lead to fruitful investment thesis. The Roundtable was composed of industry experts and observers and had grown to a pool of over 20 people who rotated through meetings. They included such people as Clayton Christensen of the Harvard Business School, known for his research on how innovation affects markets, George Kozmetsky, inveterate entrepreneur and founder and backer of over 200 companies, Atiq Raza, former CEO of AMD, and K.C. Murphy, former COO of Cadence. The process required partners to write discontinuity white papers that advanced investment thesis and to present these papers to a Roundtable of appropriate experts drawn from the pool of Adams Capital advisors. The group would engage in spirited discussion over the merits of the thesis being advanced, usually coming to consensus to pursue two or three of the 8 to 10 papers presented in a meeting. The meetings would also identify other areas for the partners to work on for future meetings.

Once an investment thesis was thoroughly vetted by the Discontinuities Roundtable, the Adams partners would systematically search for deal opportunities in those areas. Sometimes this took the form of identifying pockets of excellence in the appropriate technology and seeking out entrepreneurs to seed in forming a company. Sometimes the deal process was a matter of identifying and sorting through several existing potential investment companies. The process the partners used made them deeply knowledgeable of these companies' opportunities and therefore made them more attractive investment partners when it came to convincing the companies to accept an investment from Adams Capital.

STRUCTURED NAVIGATION

In addition to a systematized approach for identifying markets, Adams Capital also developed a system for managing its investments, called "structured navigation." The system was born out of the observation that early-stage technology companies share many of the same benchmarks and need many of the same elements to succeed. "Our investments typically have high development costs coupled with direct sales forces characteristic of companies at these stages," Adams said. "The majority of our investments—90%—are software based, so resource planning and allocations are well understood by all of our general partners. We feel that our structured navigation strategy applies to all companies within the model."

1. Round out the management team. Like most other venture capital firms, Adams Capital spends a lot of effort helping its entrepreneurs complete their management teams. "70 to 80% of the time we're the first money in, so that means that the entrepreneur is trying to build a management team without capital," Adams said. "People are going to join a company that's got some capital behind it, so we fundamentally believe that if you've got a great opportunity that's well-funded, you're going to attract a lot of talent."

2. Obtain a corporate partner or endorsement. It seems contradictory: an early-stage company, hoping to exploit a sea change in a large existing market, would be able to forge a partnership (an endorsement, a distribution deal, an equity investment, etc.) with one of the very players from whom they hoped to steal market share. But in reality, Adams and his partners believed, you should almost *always* be able to strike such a partnership. "If you're in an oligopoly, with, say four players, and the market is impacted by a discontinuity, then my bet is that one of the four players isn't quite ready for that change," Adams said. "If you've got something interesting, then you ought to be able to cut a deal with them." Furthermore, he observes, forging these relationships early will often create other exit opportunities while on a path to a public offering.

3. Gain early exposure to investment bankers. Investment bankers are the gatekeepers to liquidity for most private companies, and Adams' strategy was to make sure they meet early. "First of all, the good analysts really do understand the businesses of these little companies," Adams said. "But the second thing is, [bankers are] in the fee business, and they need to go put marriages together. [Introducing them early] is a tactic that will set you up for deals later on."

4. Expand the product line. A first-generation applied technology company will be confronted by high development costs and high sales costs. In such a case, Adams said, "the marginal cost of the development for subsequent products or the next sale is much lower." That is, once a new technology product has been developed and a base of customers has been secured, the costs of leveraging that technology into another, similar product—and selling it into a base of existing accounts—is comparably small. But "sometimes the entrepreneur hasn't thought that out yet," Adams explained. "Our approach ensures that the companies are adequately focused on this value creation opportunity."

5. Eliminate the nonexecution business risks. Adams felt that his entrepreneurs should focus their energies on developing their products and selling them to customers, not on structuring stock option or compensation plans. He reasoned that venture capitalists, after working tens or hundred of companies with similar structures, should be able to supply their companies with boilerplate versions of plans that work. "Anything other than executing the business, wipe that risk out," he said. "We'll provide that stuff to you."

Adams Capital used these five "steps" (in no particular order) as a method for managing its investments, keeping track of which steps each company had "finished" and which it still needed to achieve. The process, they felt, not only made their investments more successful, but also provided them with an internal barometer of how an investment was progressing. "If 10 months into a deal you can't attract talented people, corporations don't care, and you can't get the bankers interested—you're learning something," Adams said. "And maybe you ought to punt."

Was it really necessary to formulate such a rigorous strategy for investing in early-stage venture capital? Adams admitted that, to a certain extent, the strategy was motivated by the practical necessities of trying to raise a $55 million fund in 1996 for a small firm based in Pittsburgh. "We had to get ourselves above the muck, and the way you do that is with a well-defined, market-centric strategy that you execute in a disciplined manner," he said.

But Adams also balked at the conventional wisdom about venture capital and venture capitalists—namely, that venture capital is a personality-driven business and that successful venture capitalists are all genius dealmakers whose vision turns everything they touch into Amazon.com stock. "I just don't buy the 'rock star' model that many venture firms promote," Adams said.

Instead, Adams wanted to build a venture firm in the same way that most businesses are built—with a structure in which any of its employees were, in principle, replaceable. "We wanted to develop a system where you could throw anybody out of here and the thing would still cook along," he said. "We wanted to build a system for

EXHIBIT 10-2

BIOGRAPHIES OF ADAMS CAPITAL MANAGEMENT'S PARTNERS

Joel P. Adams   Before establishing Adams Capital Management in 1994, Joel served for eight years as Vice President and General Partner of Fostin Capital Corp. At Fostin, he made investments and supported businesses in the medical technology and telecommunications industries. Prior to Fostin, Joel served for seven years as a nuclear test engineer for General Dynamics, where he managed chemical, electrical, and mechanical engineering teams and directed nuclear power plant sea trials.

Joel graduated with distinction from Carnegie Mellon University, earning a Master of Science degree in Industrial Administration. His Bachelor's degree in Nuclear Engineering is from the State University of New York at Buffalo. Joel is a director of several private companies and a member of several charitable organizations. Joel is a frequently requested speaker on the topic of venture capital.

William C. Hulley   Bill co-founded Adams Capital Management after a five-year career at Fostin Capital Corp., where he specialized in investing in biomedical and information technology companies. He joined Fostin in 1989 and was named a general partner in 1993. Prior to his tenure at Fostin, he spent eight years managing marketing and engineering teams for three venture-backed technology companies.

Bill has a Master of Science degree in Industrial Administration from Carnegie Mellon University and a Bachelor's degree in Electrical Engineering from Pennsylvania State University. He is a director of several public and private companies and nonprofit organizations. Bill is also a frequent speaker on new business creation and business technology.

William A. Frezza   Before joining Adams Capital Management, Bill was President of Wireless Computing Associates, providing technology strategy consulting to major vendors in the telecommunications industry. Prior to founding Wireless Computing, Bill was Director of Marketing and Business Development at Ericsson, Inc. Bill has held engineering and product management positions at General Instrument Corp. and Bell Laboratories and has been involved in several start-up ventures.

Bill obtained his Bachelor and Master of Science degrees in Electrical Engineering and a Bachelor's degree in Biology, from the Massachusetts Institute of Technology. He holds seven patents, serves on several private company boards, and is a regular op-ed columnist for Internet-Week.

Jerry S. Sullivan   Prior to joining Adams Capital Management, Jerry was the President of Design Technologies, Inc., a company specializing in the evaluation and assessment of design and manufacturing processes utilized in electronic product creation. Before Design Technologies, Jerry was Vice President of the Microelectronics and Computer Technology Corporation (MCC). Prior to joining MCC, Jerry spent several years at Tektronix and 10 years with N.V. Philips. In addition, Jerry spent five years in Europe in the field of international management.

Jerry completed the Advanced Management Program at Harvard Business School and received a Ph.D. in Physics and a B.S. in Engineering from the University of Colorado. Jerry has served on the boards of a number of companies and is currently a director of several private companies.

Source: Corporate documents.

EXHIBIT 10-3

EXCERPTED FROM THE ADAMS CAPITAL MANAGEMENT, L.P. PARTNERSHIP INVESTMENT SUMMARY—DECEMBER 31, 1998

Contributed capital	$22,935,000
Capital due from partners	32,065,000
Committed capital	$55,000,000
Realized gains or (losses)	$ 0
Unrealized gains or (losses)	1,691,324
Income from investments	0
Net operating loss from inception	(1,517,764)
Gross value of partnership	$55,173,560
Less distributions	$ 0

Net Partnership Capital (includes capital due from partners)	$55,173,560
Percentage increase from inception	0.32%

Represented by:	
Value of current portfolio investments	$20,065,449
Cash and temporary investments	2,925,163
Capital due from partners	32,065,000
Other net current assets	(7,843)
Organization costs (net of amortization)	125,791
Partnership Capital	55,173,560
Less capital due from partners	(32,065,000)
Current Net Partnership Capital	$23,108,560

Source: Corporate documents.

---

executing this business. All of us are engineers, we think that way. We're not rock stars. We've got a system for finding areas that are of interest, getting deals and making them valuable. That's what we do" (see Exhibits 10-2 through 10-6).

"If a prospective general partner walks in here tomorrow and says, 'I'm the smartest guy around'—I'd say, 'For God's sake, go run for President,'" Adams said. "We don't need him. We look for team players who look at an entire portfolio of investments, not just their own deals, in order to create value for our entrepreneurs and our limited partners. The single-purpose approach to investing is not how it's done."

THREE POINTS SOFTWARE

Three Points was founded in 1995 by three ex-Microsoft employees: Tom Anderson, Marianne Reid Anderson, and Bob Taniguchi (Exhibit 10-6). Tom Anderson had worked as a Program Manager for a number of Microsoft's software packages, including Windows 95 and their Multimedia HOME Series. His wife Marianne developed Microsoft training materials—co-authoring numerous manuals on Microsoft Excel—and later worked as

EXHIBIT 10-4

EXCERPTED FROM THE ADAMS CAPITAL MANAGEMENT, L.P. PORTFOLIO INVESTMENT SUMMARY—FEBRUARY 24, 1999

Initial Investment	Portfolio Company	Investment Cost at 12/31/98	Investment Purchases/ (Disposables) 1/1–2/24/99	Investment Cost at 2/24/99	Estimated Reserves
9/97	Company A	$1,300,000		$1,300,000	$ 0
10/97	Company B	2,750,000		2,750,000	1,750,000
11/97	Company C	4,001,000		4,001,000	500,000
11/97	Company D	1,080,000	$222,943	1,302,943	0
2/98	Company E	2,000,000		2,000,000	2,667,000
2/98	Company F	1,800,000		1,800,000	1,250,000
3/98	Company G	1,500,000		1,500,000	100,000
6/98	Company H	1,718,750		1,718,750	2,000,000
10/98	Company I	2,224,375		2,224,375	1,500,000
1/99	Company J	0	2,500,000	2,500,000	2,000,000
	Subtotal	$18,374,125	$2,722,943	$21,097,068	$11,767,000
	Total reserves as of 2/24/99			11,767,000	
	Total completed investments and reserves			$32,864,068	
	% of committed capital			59.8%	

Source: Corporate documents.

an account manager in a group that managed Microsoft's OEM relationships in the U.S. and abroad. Taniguchi was a senior product manager for Windows 95.

While working for Microsoft in Seattle, the three had often spoken about one day starting their own business. By the spring of 1995, the Andersons had both left Microsoft and moved to Pittsburgh (where Marianne had grown up). The three formed Three Points Consulting in August of 1995 as an "electronic information consulting firm," with the Andersons working out of Pittsburgh and Taniguchi working remotely from Redmond, Washington. The group mostly did one-off projects for corporations in Pittsburgh, including building the Pittsburgh Pirates' on-line catalog and designing the on-line annual report for the Heinz Corporation.

In the spring of 1996, however, Tom Anderson had the idea that would eventually turn Three Points Consulting into a software company. What happened that spring was that Anderson joined a local softball team. "I played softball at Microsoft—I was on several softball teams there—and when I came here to Pittsburgh I kind of missed it," he recalled. At the same time, "there was some new technology coming out of Microsoft that I wanted to play around with and test, and I don't like to test on customers. So I said, 'Let's play around with something for the softball team.'"

Tom spent a few weeks designing an application to allow communication among

EXHIBIT 10-5

FROM BUSINESS PLAN FOR THREE POINTS CONSULTING

THREE POINTS CONSULTING, INC. is an Internet development firm that participates in and sponsors a local Pittsburgh softball team. One day, the manager of the team was complaining to our CEO about the communication headaches of informing team members regarding rainouts, rescheduled games, directions to the fields, finding out whether or not he had enough players for the game, etc. Our CEO decided to develop a Web site for the team to access and make it interactive so it was easy for the manager to update all of the team information, including sortable statistics (stats) to stop any arguments of best hitter, most RBIs, and so forth.

Based on its success and warm reception from our team and others, this first version became our proof of concept. Realizing our communication problem was universal and across all teams and clubs, we then began designing a full software product for the public that could be adapted to a full product line. This second version of the product was not released until June 1998, and it was only then released as a minor marketing test to gather feedback prior to a major launch. The timing of the 1998 release also coincided with the closure of the noncompete agreements of the principals and Microsoft Corporation.

Three Points was founded in 1995 by three Microsoft alumni led by Tom Anderson (nine-year Microsoft veteran, program manager of several Windows product releases including Window 95 and Internet Explorer, key presenter with Bill Gates, and creator of the Resource kit series).

A major launch of *Softball Manager* is being planned for the spring 1999. According to the Sporting Goods Manufacturers Association (SGMA), approximately 30.8 million people per year participate in softball in the United States alone. Three Points is seeking to raise a minimum of $3 million in capital for stock to market the product both nationally and internationally and to expedite the expansion of the product into other markets. These markets include other sports, schools, clubs, organizations, and other languages. Three Points plans to release another product version into at least one other market segment by fall 1999.

Although there are stand-alone team software packages, none currently dominates the market and most are statistical data only. The main complaint with stand-alone packages is the lack of accessibility to the information for the whole team. Three Points' technology uses the Internet to solve team management problems by enabling team members to interact with the software. Team members can post messages, directions, statistical data, and images enabling them to automatically create a customized, up-to-date, multi-page Web site.

Three Points' Internet software has the following important benefits:

- **Communication**—Both public and private areas for messaging, e-mail, and information for efficient team coordination via the Internet. Also includes statistics, charting, roster, schedule, Expedia maps, and individual player pages.

- **Accessibility**—Fans, players, coaches, etc., can all access team information anywhere and at anytime. Coaches can update their team site anywhere and anytime without the need of HTML coding or FTP software.

- **Recurring Revenue Stream**—Pricing is based on an annual subscription rate rather than a one-time fixed cost and without the expense of a packaged product. This plan does not currently examine any additional income via Web advertising; however, Three Points does anticipate advertising revenue.

(Continued)

the team members. Besides providing an on-line home for schedules, directions, and game results, the application provided messaging, so that the captain could auto-send e-mail to players in the event of rainouts, location changes, and so on. Tom didn't think much of his little program at first, but as the season went on, he noticed a curious phenomenon developing.

"Our softball team was made up of about 15 guys," Tom remembered, "and of the 15 guys I would estimate that maybe 4 of them had access to the Internet. [This was spring 1996.] We found out that basically the team members that didn't have access to the Internet would start finding ways to have access to the Internet just to look at this site. They would go to their buddies at work that had it. Some of them would even go

EXHIBIT 10-5 *(Continued)*

Softball Domestic Subscription Sales			
Assuming 5% Growth:	Year 1	Year 2	Year 3
Base-year sales/renewals	$9,998,000.00	$9,998,000.00	$9,998,000.00
Projected Yr. 2 growth at 5%	0.00	4,499,100.00	4,499,100.00
Projected Yr. 3 growth at 5%	0.00	0.00	4,249,150.00
Total revenues	$9,998,000.00	$14,497,100.00	$18,746,250.00

Assuming 10% Growth:	Year 1	Year 2	Year 3
Base-year sales/renewals	$9,998,000.00	$9,998,000.00	$9,998,000.00
Projected Yr. 2 growth at 10%	0.00	8,998,200.00	8,998,200.00
Projected Yr. 3 growth at 5%	0.00	0.00	8,098,380.00
Total revenues	$9,998,000.00	$18,996,200.00	$27,094,580.00

- Base-year sales computed as 10% of the number of U.S. teams (based on number of participants).

- 30.8 million participants, assuming an average 15-person roster, is approximately 2,000,000 teams.

Assuming annual subscription rate: $49.99

Three Points and its products are advantageous due to:

- **Fully Developed Existing Product**—With a strong marketing campaign, the company can begin generating revenues immediately from subscriptions to the Softball Manager edition. In 1999, these revenues are estimated at $10–$30 million, domestically.

- **Easy Transfer to Other Markets**—The main core of the product stays relatively similar with minor customizations (e.g., new statistics module for each sport), allowing fast release to additional markets.

- **Innovation Technology**—The technology is patent-pending and several generations beyond any technology currently available on the Web or being attempted by other Internet developers. Also, the strong favorable feedback received from industry relationships will continue to foster release strategies with additional features and product types. (Members of the American Softball Association have requested league and tournament versions in addition to the currently available team version.)

- **Volume of Participants and Growth Potential**—According to the SGMA, more than 153 million youth and adults in the United States participated in the top six sports of softball, baseball, football, soccer, basketball, and hockey in the past year.

- **18–24 Month Investor Strategy**—Three Points' research realistically predicts the technology and the technology expansion plans of Three Points to achieve more than a quarter-billion dollar status with worldwide sales over the next three to five years. The financing will fund operations through to the goal of either the sale of Three Points or its technology or when it has its IPO in late 2000. A comparison to like Internet development companies shows clearly that these companies have commanded a premium over other software development firms. Three Points plans to commission a study of the potential timing of sale or IPO and expects to receive the report by first quarter 1999.

Three Points, currently an S-corporation, is actively investigating, changing its corporate status to a C-corporation, and will provide shares of company stock to the investors. To finalize this financing promptly, Three Points intends to raise the minimum of $3 million by the start of second quarter 1999 in time to fully capture the spring selling season.

Three Points Sports, Summary of Income Statement

Case 1 Year 1999 sales represents base-year sales of softball manager computed at 5% of total teams.

Year 2000 sales represents 100,000 renewals of softball manager with a growth of 5% of the remaining teams plus base-year sales of baseball manager computed at 5% of total teams.

(Continued)

EXHIBIT 10-5 (Continued)

	Actual	Estimates	
	1998	1999	2000
Total sales	$ 99,210	$4,999,000	$11,514,347
Cost of sales	67,526	1,327,200	1,733,286
Gross profit	31,684	3,671,800	9,781,061
Operating expenses	452,589	3,352,980	6,103,166
Taxes on income	S-Corp	178,733	1,507,936
Net income (loss)	$(420,905)	$ 140,087	$2,169,959

Case 2 Year 1999 sales represents base-year sales of softball manager computed at 10% of total teams.

Year 2000 sales represents 200,000 renewals of softball manager with a growth of 5% of the remaining teams plus base-year sales of baseball manager computed at 10% of total teams.

	Actual	Estimates	
	1998	1999	2000
Total sales	$ 99,210	$9,998,000	$18,029,743
Cost of sales	67,526	1,387,186	1,821,603
Gross profit	31,684	8,610,814	16,208,140
Operating expenses	452,589	4,303,111	7,524,221
Taxes on income	S-Corp	1,181,413	3,560,407
Net income (loss)	$(420,905)	$3,126,290	$5,123,513

Business Description   Three Points manufactures and sells innovative Web-based software to the amateur sports market. Our premier, released product, *Softball-Manager*™ team management software, providing communication, tracking, and statistical analysis, is currently being adapted for other team sports and is the focus of marketing and sales efforts.

Strategies   The overall business strategy of Three Points is to increase public awareness, branch current product into other sports and associations, and to create innovative technology in all products.

To increase public awareness, Three Points is planning expensive marketing and advertising campaigns. The product has been well received by the public amateur athletes and sport associations. The more people who see the benefits of the software and the value provided, the more sales result. The current key to this strategy is through a revenue-sharing plan with representatives of the main softball association, both nationally and internationally. Revenue sharing provides an incentive for the associations and their commissioners to sell the product for a fee while also providing them with the information and data necessary for choosing their hall of fame candidates and all-star players. However, advertising is also to be a key factor regarding public awareness in order to reach the teams that are not members of any association.

As long-time employees of Microsoft, the principals understand the importance of continued innovation within a product and product line. Although Three Points is first in both Web-based software and its adaptation in team management, we fully realize that we will not be alone in this market for any extended period of time. Therefore, innovation in speed, ease-of-use, and extended feature set remains critical to maintain our dominance in the market. The plans include a new release every year to inspire renewal subscriptions. This focus, coupled with the previous strategies of awareness and adaptation, will emphasize brand and promote the cross-selling of products.

Source: Corporate documents.

EXHIBIT 10-6

BIOGRAPHIES OF THREE POINTS MANAGEMENT

Tom Anderson, CEO, Three Points Consulting   For nine years prior to the founding of Three Points Consulting, Mr. Anderson was program manager for Microsoft Corporation working on its premier packages including Microsoft Windows and Microsoft Multimedia HOME Series.

Tom was also the inventor of the Resource Kit series and creator of the original Resource Kit, which, from its first Windows release, immediately became Microsoft's third highest selling application and top-selling Windows companion piece. The Resource Kit also saved Microsoft substantial product support costs as it detailed every nuance about Microsoft Windows.

Through Tom's vast technical knowledge of Windows and its interaction with hardware, memory, peripherals, and other software packages, he became the key presenter at the Windows Technical Workshops, trade shows, and various user groups with Bill Gates, CEO of Microsoft.

In addition, Tom's stunning presentation skills made him a frequent presenter to groups internal to Microsoft such as the national sales meeting. Tom was also the creator of the acclaimed SuperDemo for Steve Balmer, president of Microsoft.

His high-exposure position at Microsoft also made Tom frequently quoted in trade journals and magazines including *PC Week* and *Esquire*, to name only a few.

Tom's management skills and driving force led to many successful projects for Microsoft, including the Ohare project (later to become Microsoft Internet Explorer), the Windows 95 10K program, Windows 3.11, and Windows for Workgroups 3.11 projects, Resource Kit series, the Windows Technical Workshops, and the award-winning architectural CD-ROM HOME title "Frank Lloyd Wright."

Among Microsoftees, however, one of Tom's most notable achievements was the simultaneous shipment of product through both retail and OEM channels in eight languages concurrently—a feat never before achieved in the existence of Microsoft.

Having basically achieved everything there was to achieve at Microsoft, Tom retired in 1995 to start his own company of Three Points Consulting, which has already become a highly successful venture. In addition to CEO of Three Points Consulting, Tom sits on the boards of two other companies: J&M Group and Transplant Network Services (TNS).

Technology is not only Tom's profession but his main hobby as well. Tom's other interests include woodworking, brewing his own microbrews, and softball.

Marianne Reid Anderson, President of Business Development, Three Points Consulting   After graduating magna cum laude with a B.S. degree in Business Computer Systems Analysis from Saint Vincent College in Latrobe, Pennsylvania, Marianne Anderson accepted a position as Corporate Trainer for the Forhan & Wakefield Group located in Westport, Connecticut. The Forhan & Wakefield Group was a training and documentation house where Marianne traveled around the country teaching software to various corporations, including Exxon, Pitney Bowes, and Uniroyal Goodrich. Marianne quickly moved into technical writing and instructional design and became a training mentor. Besides coaching new trainers, Marianne also wrote various courses for Forhan & Wakefield, Exxon Research and Development, and Ashton Tate, most notably "An Introduction to dBASE IV" and "dBASE IV: Marketing Overview." Shortly thereafter, Marianne was named Forhan & Wakefield's "ROOKIE OF THE YEAR."

Marianne's final project for Forhan & Wakefield was as assistant project manager on "IBM AS-400 Office Implementation Assist," a localization project between IBM-Germany and IBM-White Plains. The Implementation Assist was a set of 12 books aimed at helping IBM and the IBM Business Partners install, administer, address connectivity, and create e-mail accounts over the IBM AS400.

(*Continued*)

EXHIBIT 10-6   (Continued)

After the IBM AS400 project, Marianne was offered a position with Microsoft Corp. as a technical writer and instructional designer. Her first project was Windows 3.0 Class-in-a-Box, a set of training materials that won the Society of Technical Communicators' "Award for Excellence in Training Materials." The Class-in-a-Box design eventually led to the Microsoft Press Step-by-Step Series for which Marianne co-authored "Microsoft Excel 4.0 Step-by-Step." Carried by most of the major bookstores throughout the United States and the world, "Microsoft Excel 4.0 Step-by-Step" was translated into 27 languages and was on the Microsoft Press Best-Seller list for more than a year.

Marianne also authored or co-authored various Microsoft manuals based on software specifications and alpha versions, including "Microsoft Excel (versions 3.0 and 4.0) User's Guide," "Microsoft Graph (version 3.0 and 4.0) User's Guide," "Microsoft Excel (versions 3.0 and 4.0) help topics", and "Switching to Microsoft Excel from Lotus 1-2-3" (also both versions 3.0 and 4.0).

After two versions of Microsoft Excel and with her business background, Marianne was offered a position as account manager in a newly formed Microsoft Group dealing with OEMs and their third-party manufacturing firms. Marianne managed accounts and corporate contracts in the United States, Canada, and Asia, including Phoenix Technologies, Kao Industries, and Jung Moon Publishing. Aimed at eliminating software piracy through the third-party channel, Marianne worked closely with Microsoft Legal and served on the original committee for the Certification of Authenticity. A highly successful program, the certificate and the third-party reporting requirements became some of the most important tools to date for tracking and finding pirated copies of Microsoft software.

Marianne retired from Microsoft in May 1993. Since retiring, Marianne has continued to broaden her education through Dale Carnegie Management Training for which she won two awards in human relations, as well as courses through Seattle's bon Vivant School of Cooking, the Bartending Academy, and CCAC courses in creative writing. After relocating to the Pittsburgh area, together with her husband, Tom, they founded Three Points Consulting, Est. 1995.

Robert Taniguchi, President of Software Development, Three Points Consulting   With over 15 years of computer software industry experience, Mr. Taniguchi has been involved with all stages of software development, from programming to marketing and business development. For the nine years prior to founding J&M Group with Tom Anderson, Mr. Taniguchi was senior product manager for Windows 95 for Microsoft Corporation. In this role he was responsible for marketing Windows 95 networking, communication and Internet components, and PR.

Bob was also one of the original "evangelists" for Microsoft, one of the founders of the now famous Microsoft Developer Relations Group. In this role, Bob developed relationships, licensing programs, and technical workshops for the computer industry to develop more high-quality products for Windows. Bob developed the Microsoft Porting Lab, the Open Tools Licensing Program, was the lead evangelist on Windows NT, and aided its specification and design. Bob also was responsible for leading the computer industry to Windows 95 "Plug and Play" and was Microsoft's pointman establishing a series of industry standards to make computer hardware configuration easy to manage.

In his various roles, Bob was also a featured public speaker, leading the Professional Developer Conferences and speaking at industry conferences too numerous to list. He has been a featured presenter on Microsoft Educational Television cable and satellite broadcasts as well as numerous corporate briefings with audiences ranging from MIS staffers to CEOs from major corporations.

Prior to Microsoft, Bob worked as a software engineer at Telecalc, a telephony system startup where he developed a graphical user interface environment, John Fluke Manufacturing where he developed custom C compilers and assemblers, and maintained the Fluke version of the Unix operating system, and Boeing Aerospace where he developed a 2D and 3D multimedia authoring environment for the development of training and simulation courseware development.

After retiring from Microsoft in 1995, Bob founded Akira Ltd., a computer consulting firm, and a joint venture, the J&M Group, with Tom Anderson. Both Akira Ltd. and J&M Group target Internet and Internet software development. Bob also sits on the board of Transplant Network Services, a medical software company.

Source: Corporate documents.

as far as to go to the local library to log on to look at it. So once we heard that these guys were doing it, we said, 'Hmm. If our guys are interested in doing it, then maybe other teams are too.'" Tom and his partners realized that they had an interesting product idea on their hands. Through late 1996 and 1997, they worked at developing the product and expanding its functionality.

By June 1998, Three Points had a product that was "ready for prime time": Softball-Manager 2.0, an Internet-based application for managing softball teams. Softball-Manager's features included up-to-the-minute team news, schedules and cancellations, roster with personalized player pages, detailed maps to game locations, and in-depth statistical tracking of both team and individual performance. Like most Internet-based applications, Softball-Manager would be sold as a service, priced at $49.99 per team per year, where Three Points would operate the servers.

According to the Sporting Goods Manufacturers Association, there were roughly 2 million softball teams in the United States, so, by Tom's reckoning, the available market for the product was large—nearly $100 million per year. The product technology was also applicable to baseball, hockey, soccer, and other group activities. He believed that, properly capitalized, Three Points could hope to capture 2½–5% of that market in the first year. The trick, of course, would be to get the softball-playing public aware of their product, through Web and print advertising campaigns and co-marketing agreements with sports organizations. Tom also realized that much of the intellectual property (both the software itself and the processes that it codified) that Three Points had developed for Softball-Manager would be easily applicable to other kinds of teams and other team-like organizations. If softball teams would pay for it, he thought, then why not baseball teams? If Three Points could parlay success with softball teams into success with similar Internet groupware for other kinds of teams and clubs, then Anderson believed that he could conceivably build a tremendous business.

Tom had been introduced to Joel Adams by an old friend of Joel's, Tom Farrell, in the spring of 1997, while still in the thick of development of Softball-Manager 2.0. "We were very premature" in discussions with Adams, Anderson admitted. "We hadn't thought out the marketing strategies, we hadn't thought out the market size, we hadn't thought out anything. But we felt that we had a product, we felt that there was a market out there for it on our small little trials, and we knew that if anybody could develop a product around it, we could." Despite the embryonic nature of Three Points' business, Adams was intrigued. Farrell helped the company write a business plan and establish partnerships with some of the major softball organizations—true to point #2 of Adams Capital's program of structured navigation, obtaining corporate endorsements.

"I really stuck them into the model," said Adams. "I said, 'You've got to go get some distribution, you need some management team building. But you guys own the company and you need to think about it—what do you want to be when you grow up?"

After a strong showing at the Amateur Softball Association convention in 1998, Three Points was able to strike co-marketing agreements with a number of the major softball organizations in the United States and Canada. In the meantime, over the course of the year, Adams was doing his own "due diligence" of sorts—as the coach of his son's baseball, soccer, and basketball teams. "I'd also gone out and talked to friends of mine who have teams, and all of us had the same issue," Adams said. "We have parents coming up to us looking for the date of the game, or the statistics, or asking for the map to the next game." He intuitively saw the need for the Three Points product and recognized how applicable its technology and workflow could be to other sports teams and even other kinds of clubs.

For Adams, the Three Points product also had a strong personal resonance. "If you have kids, you don't ever realize how pressed you are for time to do stuff for them that's memorable," he said. "They grow so fast, and you're constantly trying to capture vignettes of their life. I've got a 16-year-old and a 12-year-old, and they're blowing through my life like you can't believe."

The next time he met with the company, Adams hammered the company on refining their business model. He recalled: "I said, 'You've got to get this business model down to where, at around 10,000 to 15,000 teams, you break even. Then you've got something that's fundable." Regardless of product revenue, Adams realized that a softball "portal" site with 20,000 teams—200,000 users or more—would be extremely valuable to someone. On this advice, Three Points came back with a plan that would have them reach operating breakeven at 14,000 teams (see Exhibit 10-5).

Throughout his conversations with Anderson and Three Points, Adams knew that their business fell well outside the purview of Adams Capital's targeted strategy for venture investing. It was, in fact, all wrong—the company sold to consumers and didn't especially take advantage of some fundamental discontinuity in a huge existing marketplace. It also wasn't especially engineering-focused. In fact, Adams was prepared to give up on Three Points entirely, until Bill Frezza, a partner at Adams who had sat in on an early meeting with the company, intervened.

Frezza, it seems, had begun managing a bowling team for both of his young sons and had come to appreciate personally and keenly the potential value of the Three Points product. Adams recalled: "[Frezza] came up to me and said, 'If you want to do this, I will absolutely support you. The partnership agreement gives us the flexibility to go outside the bounds of our model, and that flexibility is meant for just this occasion." Besides, Frezza argued, an investment in Three Points would conform to the spirit of the Adams Capital model because it really was still "markets first:" after all, Adams knew the coaching market as well as he knew any of the markets he invested in. "This just happens to be the consumer thing that you know," Frezza told him.

Bill Hulley had a different perspective. He felt strongly that Adams Capital's strict strategy—its "relentless focus," as he termed it—gave the firm a distinct competitive advantage in the venture industry. While he saw the potential in Three Points' core technology, he was very reluctant to enter any deal that could threaten that position. In that light, he felt at the time that "this investment was at best, a lose/tie proposition. Our limited partners could rightly ask us why we did a deal that was so clearly out of our sweet spot." Furthermore, he was concerned that even if Adams Capital made an attractive return on Three Points, it would be perceived as having purchased a lottery ticket rather than having made an investment that fit its profile. "We could spend the rest of our lives explaining it in either case," Hulley said. "We don't lack for good deal opportunities that make sense given our model, and why take a risk on this one given the downside?"

It was an interesting question and one that the three decided to bring up at the next meeting of the firm's advisory board. Here was an attractive investment opportunity, in a market that both Adams and Frezza knew intimately—but an opportunity that nevertheless fell far outside Adams Capital's stated mission. Adams could imagine the advisory board's response, throwing his own logic back at him: "You've got a model that's working. You've figured it out. Don't screw it up by doing this outlying deal. If you couldn't get deal-flow, if you couldn't find discontinuities, if something was broken in the model, and you were still trying to work your way through it, maybe that would be one thing. But it isn't broken."

Was Adams Capital's system imprisoning it or protecting it? Had they come to the point where they would categorically forsake attractive investments, just for the sake of their self-imposed structure? Or, if Adams pursued it, would he be proclaiming himself to be above the system and structure that he himself created? Would such a deal make Joel Adams, in a sense, just another VC rock star?

11

Martin Smith: May 2000

Martin Smith gazed out on the scrub pines of 3000 Sand Hill Road and sighed. Had things gone according to plan, he mused, he would now be looking at magnificent palm trees while lying on a beach in the South Seas. Instead, he was working, or rather delaying work by considering the uninspiring plantings that surrounded the northern California office park. Apparently, he was not the only one laboring on this Sunday morning: outside he could hear the dull roar of traffic from the nearby superhighway.

After weighing the three different job offers from venture capital firms as a second-year student at the Harvard Business School, Martin had decided to accept a position at the Greenlane Group. He had a background that made him attractive to many venture capital organizations. After undertaking an undergraduate degree in computer science at Stanford University, he had joined Sun Microsystems as a software engineer in the firm's software development area. After a little more than two years there, he had left to join several friends from college who had begun a start-up geared to developing Internet tools. This company, which had been a "bootstrap" operation funded largely through contract work developing Web sites for major corporations, had been acquired for $9 million two-and-a-half years later. The acquirer, a venture-backed, publicly traded firm whose flagship product was an Internet search engine, was seeking to expand its product line. Martin had left soon after to attend Harvard Business School.

In assessing job offers, Martin ultimately put a great deal of weight on the certification—or "stamp of approval"—that working at an "old-line" group such as Greenlane would provide. The Greenlane Group was a top-tier venture firm: within the private equity community, it had a strong "brand name" and had historically sponsored very successful partnerships. The group built up a franchise in early-stage investments in health care and technology beginning in 1986. The group consisted of two senior partners who had founded the firm, three proven junior partners, and half-a-dozen principals, associates, and analysts. What Martin had not anticipated was the tremendous workflow that the group was currently buried under. Besieged by entrepreneurs seeking venture funding and awash with cash after the closing of their fifth fund (which

Senior Lecturer Felda Hardymon and Professor Josh Lerner prepared this case from general industry knowledge as the basis for class discussion rather than to illustrate either effective or ineffective handling of an administrative situation.

raised $600 million, twice the original target), Greenlane was evaluating more business plans than ever before.

Martin had received an urgent call three weeks before from Courtney "Crusty" Weatherstorm III, Greenlane's legendary senior partner. Weatherstorm had indicated in no uncertain terms that Martin should begin work as soon as possible. As a result, Martin's long-awaited (and much deserved!) pregraduation trip to Polynesia had been canceled. Instead, he had flown to California immediately after finishing his last final examination at the Harvard Business School and had begun work the next day.

If there was a silver lining to these events, Martin mused, it was that he was getting much earlier exposure to challenging investment decisions than he had anticipated. His current assignment was a case in point. On Friday afternoon, Weatherstorm had forwarded him three presentations for data communications companies. In the e-mail, he had asked Martin to make a presentation about the merits of the three proposals at the partners' meeting on Monday morning. The potential investments were in many respects similar, but each appeared to have its own strengths and weaknesses. A brief conversation with Weatherstorm on Saturday, who had called between rounds at a "pro-am" golf event at Pebble Beach in which he was participating, had suggested a number of other considerations.

Martin looked back to his blank computer screen and wondered which investment to recommend.

THE EVOLUTION OF THE COMMUNICATIONS INDUSTRY

The communications industry emerged as one of the most fruitful areas for venture capital investment over the past decade. Between 1988 and 1998, the venture investment in communications had increased from $92 million (1.6% of all venture investments) to $1.8 billion (11%).[1]

On a fundamental level, much of this growth had been fueled by the confluence of three major trends, each feeding on the others in a "virtuous cycle" of value creation:

New Applications   Beginning with the introduction of local area networks (LANs) in the late 1970s, the basic underlying organization (or "architecture") of computing had evolved. Centralized computers where all computing and storage functions took place had been replaced by distributed networks of computers. The personal computer revolution of the early 1980s accelerated the trend toward distributed architectures ("client/server computing") in which the networked elements both computed and communicated. Suddenly, new applications (such as automatic teller machines and e-mail) were not only possible but in high demand by consumers. As companies organized their business processes around the new applications, computing architectures changed again. Computer networks extended outside single company buildings to encompass wide area networks (WANs). Someone in a branch office across the country could carry out a business process, say an order entry, exactly as someone in the headquarters office. This change in business practices created an explosion in demand for communications services. Moreover, the demand was for *data-oriented services* as opposed to *voice-oriented services*. Thus, the new applications fed the need for newer, more data-oriented communications technologies.

---

[1] Venture Economics, *1999 National Venture Capital Association Yearbook*, Newark, Venture Economics, 1999.

New Technologies and Standards   For nearly 100 years, the basic communications infrastructure was the telephone system. The supporting technology was *circuit-based*, which is most appropriate for voice communications. The endpoints of a phone call are people, not computers, and verbal communication requires a constant connection—or circuit—to be established between the parties. Once established, there is no real need to vary the quality or capacity of the circuit.[2]

Consequently, the architecture of public phone systems was designed to handle occasional short (measured in minutes, not hours) voice phone calls. With the demand for data communications capacity, the requirements on the networks changed. Computers do not require "constant conversation" with one another. Instead, they can break up information into pieces, called *packets* or *frames,* send the pieces in noncontiguous time slices—and even over different paths in the network—and reassemble the information at the receiving end. This *packet-based* architecture required new standards as to how to break up and reassemble the packets,[3] which evolved rapidly through the 1980s. Moreover, packet-based networks allowed for dynamic reallocation of bandwidth, so when an endpoint required bandwidth to send a burst of data, the network could accommodate it easily. Finally, computers are connected for longer periods of time than traditional phone calls; in fact, some are permanently connected to the network. This fact alone rendered many legacy networks obsolete.

Most importantly, the rise of packet-based networks meant that the devices that ran them were more closely related to personal computers and workstations than to communications switches. Due to the high volumes of the computer industry, the components to build the devices that ran the networks were several orders of magnitude cheaper and much more modular than the components used to build circuit-based switches. Therefore, new technology networks were cheaper and faster to build.

Finally, the need for massive bandwidth, especially in the backbones of large networks, was satisfied by the rise of optical technology, which reduced packets to bits of data and in turn to modulated laser light. With optical technology, backbones routinely carry the information equivalent of millions of phone calls. Even more exciting, technologies have emerged that allow service providers to upgrade the capacity of existing fiber optic cables in the field, further fueling the availability of bandwidth and therefore the rise of new applications (such as video streaming), which in turn fuel the technology cycle.

Deregulation of the Telephone Industry[4]   Concomitant with the two forces discussed above, the telephone monopolies around the world were deregulated, allowing for the rise of new communications service providers. These new service providers took advantage of the cheaper technology to build brand-new lower-cost networks that were often dedicated to one or two new applications. Their business strategies often involved addressing the needs of the biggest and best business customers, leaving the old monopolies struggling to upgrade technology and offer new services while still satisfying legacy customers.

---

[2] Communications capacity is most often measured as bandwidth, the amount of information one can get from point to point in a unit of time. Typically, this is measured in radio frequency units (hertz, megahertz, etc.) or in bits of data (bits per second). There are conversions between the two that depend on the actual form and organization of information being transmitted.

[3] Industry associations have evolved to be global, as are the standards that they set. Some of these packet-based standards include Asynchronous Transfer Mode (ATM), Frame Relay, and Internet Protocol (IP).

[4] For a more complete discussion of the effects of deregulation, see Chapter 8 in this volume.

THE ROLE OF VENTURE CAPITAL

Venture capital emerged as the driving force in the rapidly converging[5] voice and data communications industry. Venture-backed companies led the development of many of the new applications. For instance, Ungermann-Bass (founded in 1978) and 3COM (founded in 1979) introduced the first LANs. Several venture-backed companies also led the development of the software to exploit these opportunities. For instance, Microsoft and Lotus (among others) developed commercial e-mail, and Real Networks, VideoServer, and a host of other venture-backed companies developed video applications. Cisco, Cascade Communications, Stratacom, Omnia, Ascend, Sycamore, and Aptis are just a few of the venture-backed network equipment vendors that participated in the network market. Finally, many of the new service providers were funded by venture capital. Northpoint, Rythms, Teleport, PSINet, and Telocity are examples of such providers funded by venture capital. Not since the early days of the biotechnology industry had venture capital been so important in developing an industry.

As the volume of venture investments grew, the pattern of starting packet-based communications vendors became well established:

- A new application or service provider created the need for a new device. Often the venture capitalist gained this insight from direct involvement with the application company or service provider.

- A venture capitalist funded a start-up (often around an entrepreneur he/she previously backed) that began early product development. These efforts generally required between $10 and $50 million, and 12 to 24 months of time.

- The company entered trials with several service providers, often associated with the venture investors. This phase usually required $10 to $25 million to develop a sales force and contract for manufacturing (nearly always outsourced).

- The company began sales to one or two "charter" customers. If the firm was successful, it was not uncommon for the first full-year revenues to approach or exceed $100 million.

- The firm was acquired by a larger vendor such as Cisco,[6] 3Com, Lucent, or Nortel, who needed the new capability in their product line. These firms justified high acquisition prices by incorporating the acquired companies' products into their manufacturing, support, and sales systems. Integrating product lines was made easy by the standards that vendors adhered to, allowing products from different vendors—or from acquired vendors—to be connected and managed together effectively.

---

[5] In another example of the virtuous value creation circle, packet-based equipment became so cheap and so fast that it became possible to break up voice calls into packets, send them over the network, and reassemble them without the user sensing any degradation in quality. Thus, Voice over Internet protocol (VoIP) became a new application for the new networks providing the demand for a new round in technology development.

[6] Cisco is the premier example of this industry. Founded in late 1984, it shipped its first products in 1986. With the help of financing from Sequoia (and later the public markets), it experienced rapid sales growth. By 1999, its revenues had grown to over $12 billion, which it accomplished while remaining profitable and enjoying nearly 70% gross product margins. Cisco made a specialty of growing by acquisition, often using Sequoia as a partner in funding the most promising start-ups.

THE INVESTMENT CHOICES

The three presentations that Martin had before him (see Appendices) were a study in parallels and contrasts. On the one hand, they shared many elements. Some of the slides from the different presentations were almost identical to each other! On the other hand, each had distinct strengths. One seemed to have the best management team, the second appeared to have a very clear vision of the market and its evolution, and the third had the lead in cutting-edge technology.

The first of these, Electra Networks, sought to deliver telephone services over the Internet[7] (also known as Voice over Internet protocol, or VoIP). The company was intending to introduce a number of product lines that would allow telephone companies to migrate users from the traditional circuit-based approach to a packet-based technology. The market projections for this segment were exceedingly large. But so was the number of firms targeting this opportunity.

This investment seemed in many respects the least risky of the three. Unlike the other investments, it had already raised an extensive amount of financing ($23 million) in three financing rounds from top-tier venture groups. (Indeed, the transaction had originally been referred by one of Greenlane's peers.) Now it sought another $35 million, which would allow it to accelerate the development of its product line prior to an anticipated initial public offering (IPO) at the end of the year. Looking over the background of the management team, he could understand why the firm had already attracted the attention of investment bankers and technology journalists. The team was an "all-star" assemblage of experienced entrepreneurs from a wide variety of successful start-ups. Moreover, the management team had leveraged their relationships to form a number of strategic alliances with leading corporations in the industry.

At the same time, Martin saw several reasons for worry with the proposal. The foremost of these was the lack of specifics about the company's plans. When Martin had originally received the presentation, he had thought it was incomplete, as it contained no details about the underlying technology, the nature or timing of the new products it was developing, or the financial evolution of the firm. Even the valuation of the new proposed financing round was left unstated (though he knew that the previous round, in which customers and corporate investors had participated with the venture groups, had a post-money valuation[8] of $125 million). Weatherstorm had assured him that this was indeed the complete package. While his senior colleague did not seem very concerned about the company's lack of specifics, Martin wondered what it implied about the firm. Martin also wondered about the evolution of VoIP technology more generally. He wondered whether it would prove to be like "videotex" services in the 1980s or interactive television in mid-1990s: an interesting technology that nonetheless ultimately failed, perhaps because it was ahead of its time.

The second proposal, Uptal Communications, was quite different. Unlike Electra, the firm seemed to have a very clear vision of the market opportunity. It was pursuing the high-speed access market, which enabled families to connect more quickly to the

---

[7] The Internet is perhaps the "killer application" resulting from these forces of change. It is essentially a public, packet-based WAN that is minimally regulated and nontoll based (i.e., the cost of using it is based on access rather than on amount of usage, like the old local phone system in the United States).

[8] Pre-money valuation is defined as the number of shares outstanding prior to the financing times the price per share in the new financing round. Post-money valuation is defined as the number of shares outstanding after the financing times the price per share in the new financing round.

Internet, employees to tap into remote office networks, and corporations to link remote offices. It was clear that there was an immense demand in this market and that the company had a clear vision as to how this demand could translate into new product opportunities. Finally, the financial risk that the company represented appeared small. The company projected that it would consume only about $5 million before breaking even. The management team projected that this financing round and a small mezzanine or debt round early in 2001 would be all the financing required before it went public.

At the same time, Martin saw reasons for concern here. First, he understood from Weatherstorm that this was likely to be a hotly contested transaction. Thus, Uptal was likely to command a high valuation in the market. Second, he wondered whether the firm could execute on its vision. In particular, he worried whether Uptal would be able to fulfill its ambitious plan for shipping new products for a wide variety of markets within the time and budget that the management team had allowed. Martin wondered whether these ambitious plans realistically reflected the nature of the technology under development, or rather the relative inexperience of the management team.

The final choice, Cordent Systems, was somewhat different in its nature. Rather than being a finished proposal, it was a preliminary document that was being shown to Greenlane on a confidential basis. The firm had received one financing round of $5 million six months earlier from the Mayfield Fund. While Cordent still had several million dollars in its bank account, Greenlane was being shown the proposal at the special request of Mayfield's senior partners. (Greenlane and Mayfield frequently brought each other into transactions. One transaction in which Greenlane had involved Mayfield as a co-lead investor, an Internet portal for pet owners, had recently gone public with a market capitalization of over $1.2 billion at the end of the first trading day.)

Martin found this proposal in many respects to be the most interesting. First, the company—which was focusing on optical switching technologies—clearly had an interesting technical niche. The engineering team was an exceedingly strong one, and Cordent was at the cutting edge of new product design. The recent IPO of Sycamore Networks, which commanded a $29 billion market capitalization soon after going public, underscored that the market understood the promise of these technologies as well. Furthermore, the proprietary nature of the transaction was appealing. In particular, Weatherstorm had intimated that this might be seen more as an "A-1" financing round rather than a "B" round: in other words, that the valuation would not be significantly higher than the $19 million post-money valuation in the last financing round.

At the same time, Martin found the proposal to be quite frustrating. Reflecting the circumstances around the proposed transaction, it was not surprising that it was not as finished as the others. But many ambiguities remained. In particular, it was clear that bringing the technology to the market would be an expensive proposition. The company anticipated raising $22 million to do so, but Martin wondered whether the real number might be much larger. Compounding this worry was the background of the management team, which was much less seasoned than that of the engineering staff.

EVALUATING THE CHOICES

As he looked again out the window, Martin wondered which investment to recommend. Ideally, Martin mused, he would have several weeks to sort through these issues and determine which investment to recommend. But this was not to be!

He also wondered how Weatherstorm would receive his presentation. In the two weeks that he had been at Greenlane, he had already noticed that the two of them had very different approaches to looking at transactions. While Martin began by seeking to understand the underlying technology and market dynamics, Weatherstorm's approach seemed to be surprisingly unsystematic. Martin wondered how much of this was due to their differing backgrounds. While Martin had a strong engineering background, Weatherstorm had been a graduate of Rhode Island School of Design. After a brief and unsuccessful effort at a painting career in New York City, he had joined his father at his boutique investment bank of Hornblower, Weatherstorm, & Weekes. Weatherstorm's entry into venture capital had been almost accidental: upon graduating from Stanford Business School (which his father had also attended), he had joined the venture capital affiliate of a California commercial bank after failing to obtain a corporate finance position with one of the leading New York investment banks. To Martin, it seemed surprising that a venture capitalist could have succeeded while employing such an intuitive, even seemingly scattershot, approach.

Martin was sometimes frustrated by Weatherstorm's approach. At the same time, he had to admit that at least a few of the points that the senior partner had raised in their conversation yesterday were very valid. In particular, he had highlighted the issue of "portfolio risk," an issue Martin had not considered. Weatherstorm noted that in the past few months, Greenlane had initiated a number of high-risk investments, each of which would consume several tens of millions of dollars before shipping any products. Weatherstorm raised the consideration that it might be unwise for the fund to undertake another investment of this type, lest the portfolio become too unbalanced.

Finally, there was "The Resource Problem." When Martin had first heard this term, which seemed to be dropped into every partner-to-partner conversation, he had fleeting concern that Greenlane's fabled fundraising prowess was a myth. How could such a famous firm be concerned about resources? During his first week, Julia Romana, a 1997 graduate of Harvard Business School and a principal in the firm, clued Martin in:

> Look, I know it seems crazy with all of the people trying to get into venture capital, much less a firm like this, but the truth is our biggest problem is scarcity of *partner time.* Everyone wants us in their deal, but they also want us *working* their deal. For example, Crusty is on 11 boards and is essentially maxxed out. Principals and associates do what we can to extend the partners, but in the end the good deals want a Greenlane partner actively involved if not on the board. If there is anything influencing decisions around here, it's this problem—we call it The Resource Problem and it's serious. We had to pass on what we knew was an interesting east coast Internet infrastructure deal because Hank Serial [Greenlane's Internet guru] just couldn't spare the time for an east coast deal. It turned out to be Akamai [which went public in October 1999 with a market capitalization of approximately $15 billion at the end of its first trading day]. We not only missed a big payday, but we allowed Battery [Akamai's lead investor] to move up a notch in the competitive food chain. Now they are competing with us on every Internet deal.

Julia's description of Greenlane "passing" on Akamai had been particularly poignant since the day before Martin had heard that Akamai had actually turned down a Greenlane term sheet that had Julia as their designated board member. Julia was a smart if inexperienced investor, and Martin was keenly aware of what the Akamai situation had cost her in stature within the firm. He thought about that as he turned back to his computer screen to review the presentations one more time.

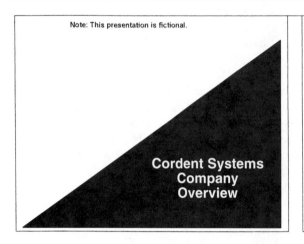

Note: This presentation is fictional.

**Cordent Systems
Company
Overview**

Company Background

- Founded in January 2000 by team from Stratacom, Cisco, 3Com
- Initial financing from Mayfield:
  - $5 million provided.
  - $14 million pre-money valuation.
  - $19 million post-money valuation.
- Located in San Jose, CA

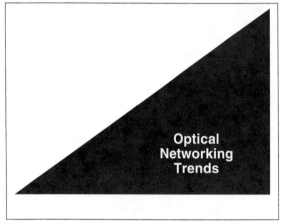

**Optical
Networking
Trends**

Data Bits Will Overtake Voice Bits Within 2 Years

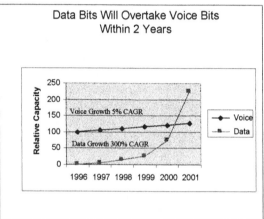

Optical Multiplexing Changes Everything

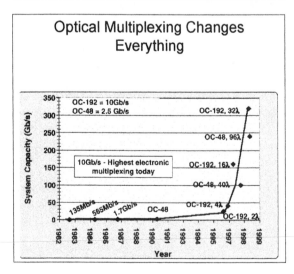

DWDM is Re-shaping Network Architecture

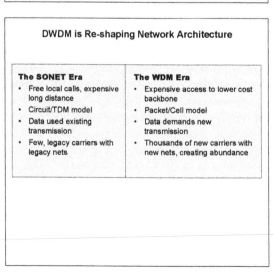

The SONET Era	The WDM Era
• Free local calls, expensive long distance	• Expensive access to lower cost backbone
• Circuit/TDM model	• Packet/Cell model
• Data used existing transmission	• Data demands new transmission
• Few, legacy carriers with legacy nets	• Thousands of new carriers with new nets, creating abundance

(*Continued*)

Optical Network Trends

- Rings will continue to play a role but meshed architectures will become increasingly common
- Optical cores will evolve from basic transport to architectures formed by cross connects
- There will be a growing need for platforms which can derive more than just raw bandwidth from the optical core

Optical Networking Market

Core Edge	Metro	Service Access	Long Haul
Hybrid Electronic and Optical	Primarily Optical	Hybrid Electronic and Optical	Primarily Optical
Service Centric	Bandwidth Centric	Service Centric	Bandwidth Centric
Ring and Mesh Topologies	Ring and Simple Bus Topologies	Ring and Mesh Topologies	Point to Point Topologies

Cordent Believes A New Class of Product Is Required

A Contemporary Core

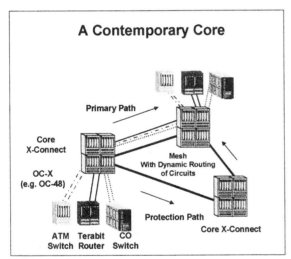

Next Generation Network

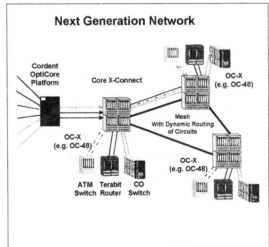

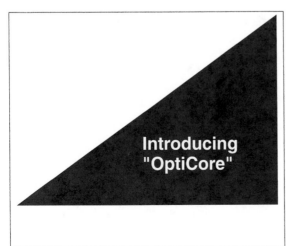

Introducing "OptiCore"

Technology Convergence

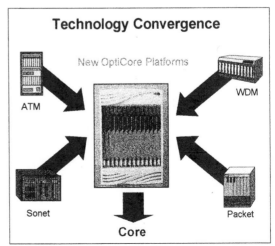

(Continued)

Key Technologies

- Cordent Is Applying a Combination of Optical and High Speed Switching Technology to New Networking Applications
- High Speed Electronic Switch Fabrics
- Multi-wavelength Optical Fabrics and Backplane
- Protocol Agile Trunk Interfaces
- Single Product Functionally Replaces:
  - DWDM Multiplexers & ADMs
  - High End ATM Access Multiplexers
  - Edge Router & Multi-service Edge Devices

Cordent Family of OptiCore Products

- Hybrid Optical / Electronic Platform
- Product Combines DWDM, IP, MPLS & ATM Technology
- Carrier Class, Sophisticated Fault Tolerance - 99.999% Availability
- Cost Effective / Scalable Architecture

OpCr90

OpCr40

OpCr20

CAPACITY

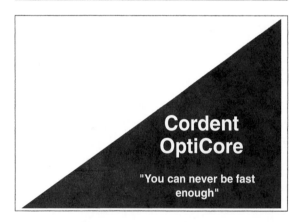

Cordent
OptiCore

"You can never be fast enough"

Note: This presentation is fictional.

Central Office IP Telephony

Electra Networks:
The Future of Telephony

Mission

- The Mission
- Deliver carrier-class, carrier scale IP telephony network equipment that lets carriers:
    - achieve major operational savings by migration from circuit to packet networks
    - build new revenue streams through the delivery of competitive new features and services

Company Information

- **Founded 1998**

- **90 employees**

- **$ 23 million in venture funding to da**
    - Kleiner Perkins
    - Accel Partners
    - Mohr Davidow

- **$35 million financing sought.**

- **IPO projected November 2000.**

Electra Networks Executive Staff

- **Harry Wellstone, Chairman**
    - 3Com/Synopsis, Summa Four, IBM
- **John DiMota, President and CEO**
    - Sun Microsystems, Novell
- **George Chang, VP & CTO**
    - Ridgeway, Compression Labs, Intel, AT&T Bell Laboratories
- **John Jones, VP Sales and Marketing**
    - Cisco, Stratacom, Tandem, Ungermann-Bass
- **Harry Wong, VP Engineering**
    - Novell, Tandem, Ungermann-Bass
- **John Harriston, VP Carrier Relations**
    - Lucent, Ascend, Cascade
- **Don Harvey, VP Manufacturing**
    - 3Com, Polycom, Compression Labs

The Electra Networks Team

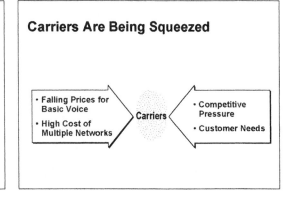

- **Unique background**
- **Experienced management**
    - Successful startups
    - Implementation of large networks

Carriers Are Being Squeezed

- Falling Prices for Basic Voice
- High Cost of Multiple Networks

Carriers

- Competitive Pressure
- Customer Needs

(Continued)

Toll/Tandem Replacement

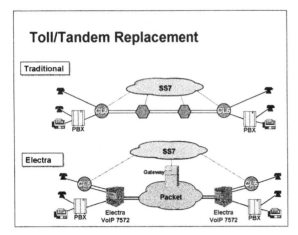

Integrated Access

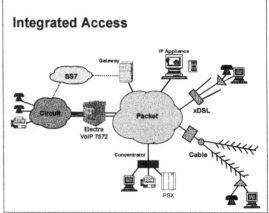

NEBS-Compliant Hardware

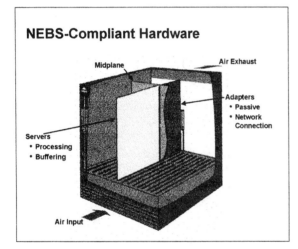

True Central Office Class Products

- Designed for the Central Office environment
- Toll-quality voice
- High reliability
- Comprehensive manageability
- Scalable for large networks
- Powerful enhanced services

Central Office IP Telephony

- **Unparalleled scalability (100,000+ calls)**
- **700,000 BHCA/shelf**
- **Carrier-grade hardware**
  - NEBS Level 3
  - 99.999% Reliability
    - Redundancy, Hot-swap
  - T1/E1/J1, T3/E3, 100BaseT, OC3c, OC12c, STM-1, STM-4

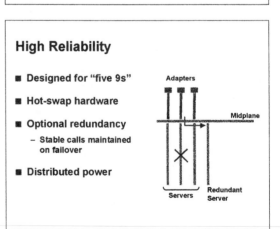

High Reliability

- Designed for "five 9s"
- Hot-swap hardware
- Optional redundancy
  - Stable calls maintained on failover
- Distributed power

(Continued)

Scalable to Large Networks

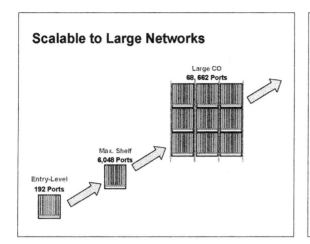

Large CO
68,662 Ports

Max. Shelf
6,048 Ports

Entry-Level
192 Ports

Seamless OSS Integration

Integrate With Existing Service and Support Systems

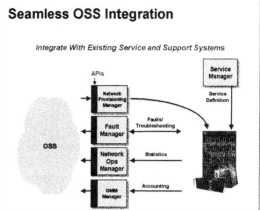

Open Architecture

Carrier-Class Packet Telephony

Open Services Partner Alliance

- Fully leverages the new converged voice network

- Pre-tested "Best-in-Class" applications

- Shorter deployment cycles

- Differentiated services to drive competitiveness

Open Services Partner Alliance

- **Enhanced Services**
  - Accord - conferencing
  - Aspect - call centers
  - eFusion - click-to-talk, Internet call waiting
  - Iperia - voice and messaging services
  - NetCentric - fax
  - Priority Call Mgt. - prepaid, one number, voice dialing
  - Ridgeway - audio/video collaboration
  - VideoServer - conferencing

ACCORD
ASPECT
eFusion
iperia
NETCENTRIC
VIDEOSERVER

Electra Delivers

Most Comprehensive IP Telephony Solution

- Central Office telephony
- Full integration with OSS
- Graceful evolution from legacy PSTN

Note: This presentation is fictional.

Uptal Communications

Agenda

- ➤ Status and Timeline
- ➤ Target Market
- ➤ Product Plans
- ➤ Sales/Marketing Plans
- ➤ Staffing Plans
- ➤ Financial Plans

Status

- ➤ Incorporated
- ➤ 5 Employees
- ➤ Mountain View-based
- ➤ Market/Product Planning
  - ➤ Market feedback/validation trip
- ➤ Timing
  - ➤ First round financing sought by end of June

Uptal Communications

- ➤ Uptal Communications designs, manufactures, markets and supports high performance multiservice WAN access systems. The systems are designed to be sold to public Network and Service providers who are able to offer high value services to their business and consumer customers. The systems are designed to support high speed access technologies, including xDSL and Frame Relay, as well as Frame Relay, ATM and LAN Network interfaces.

Key Points to Emphasize

- ➤ Large untapped market -- mkt projections
- ➤ Team -- proven
- ➤ Target positioning -- business focus
- ➤ Why better than others -- specific
- ➤ Product details -- roadmap, phases
- ➤ Financial plan -- target model
- ➤ Staffing plan -- key hires
- ➤ Funding plan -- $, rounds, dilution

Target Market

- ➤ High-speed access market is forming, but not ready yet
  - ➤ Cost and infrastructure
- ➤ Projected to be between 1M and 2M lines installed by end of 2000
- ➤ Vendors fragmented between
  - ➤ Current xDSL vendors
  - ➤ Current access vendors
  - ➤ Startups

(Continued)

High-Speed Access Market Projections

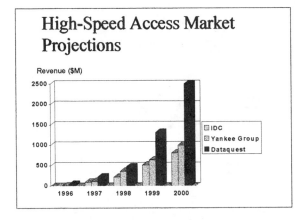

Revenue ($M)

IDC
Yankee Group
Dataquest

1996 1997 1998 1999 2000

Business Applications

➤ Telecommuting & Day Extenders
➤ Branch Office Connectivity

Telecommuting Is Increasing in Popularity Worldwide

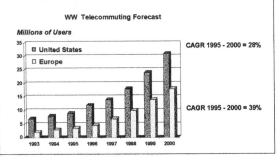

WW Telecommuting Forecast

Millions of Users

United States
Europe

CAGR 1995 - 2000 = 28%

CAGR 1995 - 2000 = 39%

1993 1994 1995 1996 1997 1998 1999 2000

New Applications Will Contribute to Continued Growth

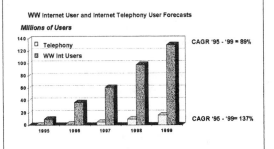

WW Internet User and Internet Telephony User Forecasts

Millions of Users

Telephony
WW Int Users

CAGR '95 - '99 = 89%

CAGR '95 - '99= 137%

1995 1996 1997 1998 1999

Multimedia Applications

➤ Microsoft, Netscape and Intel are investing heavily
  ➤ MS NetMeeting (H.323) video and data conferencing
  ➤ Intel ProShare (H.324, H.323) video and data conferencing
➤ Voice over IP
➤ Require high bandwidth and low latency
  ➤ Plumbing being installed -- RSVP, RTP, QoS, RTSP

Internet Access

➤ High bandwidth consumer Internet access
  ➤ Multimedia applications become usable
    ➤ Telephony; video
  ➤ Multiplayer gaming
➤ Power users demand and will pay for higher bandwidth
  ➤ World Wide Wait.

(Continued)

Product Plans

High Speed Access to Corporation and Internet

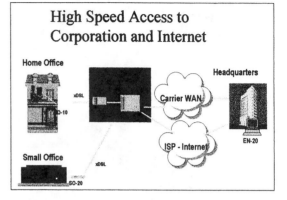

Product Roadmap

- Home Office-10
  - Prototype 5/00; beta/trials 6/00; FCS 9/00
- Small Office-100
  - Prototype 45/00; beta/trials 7/00; FCS 2/01
- Central Office-1000
  - Prototype 10/00; beta/trials 12/00; FCS 2/01

Product Roadmap (cont.)

- Next Generation Products:
  - Home Office-20
    - Prototype 9/00; beta/trials 12/00; FCS 2/01
  - Central Office-2000
    - Prototype 1Q01
  - Enterprise Network-10
    - Prototype 9/00; beta/trials 12/00; FCS 2/01

Competitive Landscape

Competitive Positioning

- Strong, proven team that knows how to build and market BOTH ends of the connection
  - Must have end-to-end
  - Proven ability to lead in both ends...
- Existing xDSL vendors -- weak on data
- Existing Access vendors -- weak platforms
- Startups -- lack of "both ends" expertise

(Continued)

Competitive Differentiators

➤ Built for DSL -- price/performance

➤ Muxing -- price per subscriber

➤ PBX extensions -- additional services

➤ Voice support -- additional services

➤ Plug and play remote -- cost of deployment

➤ Remote LAN access via VPN -- additional services

Lucent [Ascend] TNT

➤ Designed with 64 Kbps in mind (TDM)

➤ TNT has 4 x 155 Mbps backplane (620 Mbps) -- Uptal CO products have 4 Gbps backplane
  - ➤ TNT max config = 50 ADSL ports (6 Mbps down)
  - ➤ CO-1600 max conf = 128 ADSL ports (6 Mbps down); designed to handle up to 676 ports

➤ TNT copies data 4 times to move through box --- Uptal moves data 1 time

➤ Price -- TNT base is $20,000

Lucent [Cascade] AX

➤ Performance -- 1 Gbps backplane
  - ➤ Uptal CO products have 4 Gbps backplane
    - ➤ AX-1600 max initial config = 128 ADSL ports (6 Mbps down); designed to handle up to 169 ports
    - ➤ CO-1600 max initialconf = 128 ADSL ports (6 Mbps down); designed to handle up to 676 ports

➤ Density AX-1600 -- 16U vs. CO-1600 -- 10U
  - ➤ Uptal provides higher density (12.8 ports per U vs. 8 ports per U)

➤ Price -- AX-1600 base is $32,500

Copper Mountain

➤ Focused on cost
  - ➤ Using muxing -- will sell muxes with or without access concentrators

➤ Not a lot of access expertise
  - ➤ Certainly not SOHO products

➤ Not focused on multiservice applications

➤ Initial focus is on consumer Internet market

➤ Strong management team

NetSpeed

➤ Again focused on cost
  - ➤ Using mux'ing and purport to have filed for patents

➤ Not strong on internetworking
  - ➤ Background in LAN hubs

➤ Not focused on multiservice applications

Diamond Lane

➤ End-to-end ATM focused

➤ Lots of local loop experience
  - ➤ DLCs, etc.

➤ No data networking

➤ Have spent a lot of $$ ... no products yet

(Continued)

Sales & Marketing Plans

- Market to ISPs, CLECs, CAPs
  - Offer full service offering (dry pair rental and installation)
- Market to Telcos
  - ILECs, IXCs
    - Direct presence
    - Initial focus on North America
- OEM targets include Nortel, Lucent, Ericsson, Siemens

Management & Organization

Founding Team

- John Uptal, CEO
  - 5 years at Shiva
    - For last 2 years Sr. Dir. Bus. Dev. (direct report to CEO; member Operating Committee)
    - First 3 years Dir. Product Mgmt (launched and managed LanRover line)
  - 3 years at Raychem; 5 years at Apple
    - Product marketing and development

Founding Team

- George Packer, VP Development
  - 6 years at Shiva
    - Currently Dir. Platform Development (hardware and firmware) -- manages 12 reports
    - Employee # 12; first HW developer hired
    - Architected and developed LanRover, LanRover PLUS, NetModem, Access Switch
  - 2 years at Sun
  - BSEE, MSEE Emory University

Founding Team

- Dan George, Director SW Development
  - 9 years at Shiva
    - Dir. SW Development
      - Responsible for all ShivOS development (LanRover family code base)
    - Employee #3 -- first non-founder
    - Lead developer on NetModem, LanRover family
  - BSEE MIT

Staffing Plans -- Key Hires

- Software/firmware developers
  - Have identified four for kickoff
- Hardware developers/techs
  - Paul Skinner, Sr. HW developer from Shiva hired
- Market/business development
  - Shuang Deng,, ADSL service architect from GTE hired
- VP Sales -- telco hitter
- VP Manufacturing

(Continued)

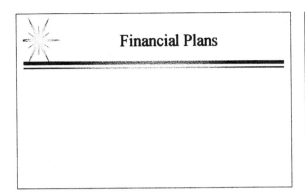

Financial Plans

P&L ($Ms)

	2000	2001	2002
Revenues	0.0	18.0	68.5
COGS	0.0	6.1	14.6
SG&A	4.5	12.2	42.9
Net Inc.	(4.5)	(0.3)	11.0

Funding Plans

- Goals
  - "A" Player Investors
  - Minimize Process Time
  - Reasonable Valuation and Terms
- Process
  - Business plan and pitch to 5-10 firms
  - Additional information/follow-up
  - Close on investors/terms

Funding Requirements

- Development Round (May '00)
  - Used for staffing, capital equipment, HW prototypes/alpha units, lease, etc.
- Beta/Production Round (Jan '01)
  - Used for beta, production, sales/marketing launch
  - May be structured as debt or mezzanine financing

12

Apax Partners and Dialog Semiconductor: March 1998

Michael Risman, an assistant director of Apax Partners, an international private equity firm, stared out of his London office window in disbelief. The Union Bank of Scotland had failed to meet the 11 A.M. deadline for international cash transfers. It was 4:30 P.M. on Friday, March 20, 1998. On Monday morning the board of directors of Ericsson, the Swedish mobile telephony giant, was meeting to approve the sale of Dialog Semiconductor to a group of investors lead by Apax. Without the cash transfer from Apax to Ericsson, the entire deal was likely to fall apart at the last minute. Risman reflected on the events over the last month that had led to this moment.

Apax had been brought into the Dialog deal only four weeks before. Michael Glover, a nonexecutive director[1] of another Apax portfolio company and a board member of Dialog, had called Apax to offer the opportunity to lead a buyout of Dialog Semiconductor, a mixed-signal ASIC chip supplier to the mobile phone industry. A senior Ericsson executive and long-term Dialog board member, Jan Tufvesson, together with Dialog's CEO Roland Pudelko, were considering organizing a two-stage management buyout of the business. Ericsson would acquire Dialog from Daimler-Benz after exercising its preemptive right to do so when Daimler decided to divest the company. Thereafter, as Ericsson's long-standing corporate policy prevented it from owning controlling stakes in its suppliers, Ericsson would resell the majority of Dialog to another "friendly" investor. Having discussed the idea provisionally with the Ericsson board, Tufvesson had been told that both transactions had to occur before its next board meeting on March 23.

As a result of this sudden opportunity, the last four weeks had been a demanding time for the Apax team, to say the least. In this short period of time, Risman had had to construct a semi-binding acquisition agreement and monitor Ericsson's acquisition of Dialog. Then he had to conduct the due-diligence, valuation, and structuring of Apax's

Antonio Alvarez-Cano (MBA 2000) and Borja Martinez (MBA 2000) prepared this case under the supervision of Senior Lecturer Felda Hardymon and Professor Josh Lerner as the basis for class discussion rather than to illustrate either effective or ineffective handling of an administrative situation. The authors wish to thank Ann Leamon, manager of the Center for Case Studies at Harvard Business School, for her many valuable comments.

[1] That is, a director who was not an officer of the firm.

buyout of Dialog. He had sought and obtained internal approval at Apax to close the deal.

But at the last minute, everything seemed to be going wrong. Perhaps it was for the better, Risman thought. Four weeks was a very short time to analyze, negotiate, and close a deal like this. Risman had been very impressed by Dialog's senior management, but he would still have liked to conduct additional technical diligence before making a firm purchase offer. The noise from nearby Oxford Street distracted him for a moment. People down there seemed to be having more fun than he was on this Friday afternoon.

APAX PARTNERS[2]

Apax Partners & Co. was one of the world's leading private equity groups, managing $3.5 billion on behalf of institutional investors. Apax was an international firm, with offices in London, Leeds, New York, Palo Alto, Philadelphia, Paris, Munich, Madrid, Zurich, Dublin, Tel Aviv, and Tokyo. In contrast to other firms that specialized in industries or stages of development, the group diversified its investments across industries and invested in buyouts as well as early-stage deals. This investment strategy was intended to reduce the company's exposure to specific market niches and provide flexibility in the allocation of funds into the most attractive segments at each point in the market and industry cycle.

Apax Partners[3] was formed by uniting two firms from both sides of the Atlantic. Alan Patricof had launched Alan Patricof Associates in the United States in 1969. Separately, the London, Paris and Chicago operations of MMG were co-founded in 1972 by Ronald Cohen (HBS '69) and Maurice Tchénio (HBS '70) to provide international corporate finance advice to and to invest in high-growth businesses. Five years later, in 1977, the three men joined forces. Together with the partners who had joined over the years, Apax took a pioneering role in venture capital, first in the United States, then in the United Kingdom and in Continental Europe, and most recently in Israel and Japan.

Many members of the firm had become leading figures in the international private equity industry. President Clinton appointed Alan Patricof chairman of the White House Conference on Small Business. Ronald Cohen was a former chairman of the British Venture Capital Association and a founding director of that organization as well as the European Venture Capital Association and City Group for Smaller Companies. Maurice Tchénio was a founder and vice-chairman of France's Venture Capital Association (AFIC) and a director of the European Venture Capital Association.

In an increasingly competitive market, Apax tried to differentiate itself by preserving an entrepreneurial spirit and culture, and by having a "hands-on" investment philosophy. This strategy required Apax teams to add value to the companies in which they invested through active management and supplying industry expertise. To support the strategy of active diversification across industries, the firm divided its 85 investment professionals into six industry teams: telecommunications, information technology (IT), media, health care, financial services, and specialty retailing. In addition, there was a

---

[2] This section is based on Chad Ellis, Walter Kuemmerle, and M. Frederic Paul, "Infox System Gmbh," Harvard Business School Case no, 899-061, www.apax.com, Nigel Holloway, "Globetrotter," *Forbes* 165 (April 17, 2000), 128ff., and conversations with Apax managers.

[3] "Apax" in classical Greek means something that occurs once and only once. The name was supposed to symbolize, first, the unique nature of the role that the group played and, second, the full integration of that role across activities and frontiers.

EXHIBIT 12-1

APAX PARTNERS' EARLIER FUNDS AND OBJECTIVES

Fund	Year Raised	Size
Apax Venture Capital Fund	1981	£10 million
Apax Ventures II	1984	£30 million
Apax Ventures III	1987	£75 million
Apax Ventures IV	1990	£110 million
Apax German European Ventures	1990	DM96 million
Israel Growth Fund	1994	$40 million
Apax UK V	1995	£164 million
Apax UK VI	1997	£313 million
Apax Germany II	1997	DM260 million
Funds Planned for 1999:		
Apax Israel II	1999	$100 million
Apax Europe IV	1999	∈1.8 billion euros

Apax Partners Ventures follows a strategy different from that of most European private equity firms. This strategy can be summarized as follows:

- To create a balanced portfolio by stage and industry in order to achieve consistently superior returns over the economic cycle
- To be the leading European private equity investor in the information technology, telecommunications, media, biotechnology/health-care, financial services, and specialty retailing sectors
- To deploy a large multinational team comprising many specialists in each sector
- To originate investment opportunities and to be the sole or lead investor
- To hold substantial stakes and to play an active role in portfolio companies
- To take advantage of its international reach and size to perform due diligence and support the growth of its companies

Source: Corporate documents.

seventh group that specialized in leveraged transactions. This structure enabled the specialists in each group to develop the expertise in their respective fields. Each group brought together people recruited from within the industry itself (the head of the telecom group, for example, was John McMonigall, a former management board member of British Telecom), as well as finance specialists and strategic consultants.

This strategy had enabled Apax Partners' European funds to provide returns in the top quartile of the industry for the last 10 years. Among the most successful recent investments were the British Internet company Autonomy which was expected to be listed by mid-1998[4]; Baltimore Technology, an information security software company; and

---

[4] By the end of 2000, Autonomy was trading at a $7 billion valuation, around 400 times the value at the time of the original investment.

TelDaFax, an ISDN network operator. Before this period, Apax had made its name with investments such as America Online, Computacenter, Dr. Solomon, Esprit Telecom and PPL Therapeutics (of "Dolly the Sheep" fame). Exhibit 12-1 contains background information on Apax.

DIALOG SEMICONDUCTOR

Dialog Semiconductor developed and marketed "chips" or semiconductors: more specifically, ASICs (Application Specific Integrated Circuits) primarily for customers in the mobile communications industry. ASICs were semiconductors designed for specific applications. Dialog specialized in mixed-signal ASICs that combined both digital and analog functions on a single semiconductor. The company enjoyed a leadership role in two segments of the mobile telephony market, power management and Audio Codec.[5] The wireless communications sector presented attractive prospects both due to overall market growth and the phone's increasing functionality (which increased the demand for semiconductors). In addition, Dialog also had relationships with suppliers of automotive electronic components, where mixed-signal expertise was also highly applicable.

Origins and Evolution

The origins of Dialog Semiconductor were in the European activities of International Microelectric Products (IMP), a semiconductor company based in California. In 1985 IMP (Europe) was formed with capital from IMP and a consortium of venture capital investors (Citicorp, CinVen, Grosvenor, and Prudential, among others). In April 1989, IMP (Europe) expanded its operations in Germany through a joint venture with Deutsche Aerospace AG. Deutsche Aerospace was Germany's largest aerospace company and a subsidiary of Daimler Benz (now Daimler-Chrysler). Pursuant to this agreement, IMP (Europe) sold 50% of its interest in its IMP Deutschland subsidiary to Deutsche Aerospace. The joint venture was to develop analog and digital applications for the defense and aerospace industries. It was at this point that IMP (Europe) developed its first Audio Codec.

In 1990, IMP (Europe) encountered several business problems that led to a significant increase in leverage and eventually to a complete corporate restructuring. As part of the reorganization, IMP (Europe) changed its name to Dialog Semiconductor. Both Deutsche Aerospace and Ericsson invested in Dialog to secure supply of key components for their operations. Simultaneously, some of the venture capital investors exited the business, while others obtained put options on their shares from the corporate investors. Two years later, Dialog was merged into Temic, a Daimler subsidiary that manufactured automobile parts and semiconductor components. In 1996, along with the rest of the ASIC industry, Dialog had a difficult year and posted operating losses of £2.6 million. One year later, however, the market turned and Dialog experienced 150% revenue growth and returned to profitability. Exhibit 12-2 provides a timeline for Dialog's evolution.

---

[5] A Codec (coding/decoding) device converts, or encodes, analog signals into a form for transmission on a digital circuit. The digital signal is then decoded back into an analog signal at the receiving end of the transmission link. Codecs allow voice and video transmission over digital links and may also support signal compression.

EXHIBIT 12-2

DIALOG SEMICONDUCTOR HISTORY

Date	Event
1981	International Microelectric Products (IMP) is founded in California.
1985	IMP (Europe) is formed with capital from IMP and a consortium of venture capital investors.
1989	German operation is established as a 50/50 joint venture with Deutsche Aerospace (Daimler group).
1990	Financial difficulties are encountered, and so group reorganization takes place. Ericsson and Deutsche Aerospace invest in IMP (Europe). Name is changed to Dialog Semiconductor.
1992	Dialog is integrated into Temic MBB Microelektronik, a Daimler subsidiary that manufactures automobile parts and electronic components.
1994	Temic begins to reorganize the Dialog board. Ericsson objects, and the integration process stops.
1996	Dialog has a difficult year along with the rest of the ASIC industry. Losses of £2.6 million accrue.
1998	Ericsson decides to exercise the preemptive right to buy Dialog from Daimler in order to preserve its independence from Atmel, a U.S. semiconductor company.

Source: Dialog Semiconductor offering circular and corporate documents.

The ASIC Market

Semiconductors were essential components of electronic products, appearing in everything from mobile phones to domestic appliances. Integrated circuits (ICs) were complex semiconductor devices that consisted of a piece of silicon on which an electronic circuit is printed. Traditionally, complex applications were designed by combining several ICs to create a system. This was expensive, however, and soon application-specific integrated circuits (ASICs) were introduced to save costs and improve functionality. An ASIC was therefore a group of integrated ICs capable of processing both analog and digital data. Analog circuits provide the interface between electronic systems and real-world phenomena such as sound or temperature. Digital devices use a series of on/off (1/0) states to perform arithmetic functions that are used to process data. Successfully combining analog and digital circuits on a single chip was technically challenging due to the high risk of interference, although it could represent substantial cost savings.[6]

The global ASIC market was large, with 1997 revenues of $18.5 billion. It was also growing very fast, at 16% annually through 2001. The narrower mixed-signal ASIC market, in which Dialog competed, represented a $1.4 billion market in 1997 and was expected to grow even faster than the overall ASIC market, at 26% per year until 2001. ASICs' main uses were in telecommunications, which represented 82% of ASIC revenues in the European market. Other sectors that required ASIC chips were industrial applications, automotive, military, consumer, and data processing (see Exhibit 12-3 for

---

[6] This paragraph and those that follow draw in part from the Dialog Semiconductor Offering Circular (October 11, 1999), pp. 35, 38–41.

EXHIBIT 12-3

ASIC MARKET INFORMATION

World ASIC Market

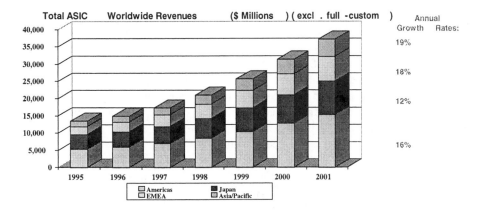

European ASIC Market

Europe	1995	1996	1997	1998	1999	2000	2001	CAGR 95-01
Revenues ($b)	2.7	3.4	4.2	5.1	6.2	7.5	8.8	22%
Revenue Growth		26%	24%	21%	22%	21%	17%	

World Mixed-Signal ASIC and World Digital ASIC Markets

World	1995	1996	1997	1998	1999	2000	2001	CAGR 95-01
Mixed-Signal ASIC $b	0.9	1.1	1.4	1.8	2.3	3.0	3.6	26%
Digital ASIC $b	14.6	15.5	17.2	20.2	24.0	28.9	33.8	15%

Breakdown of European ASIC Market by Industry

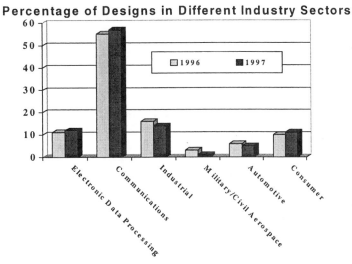

Source: Compiled from corporate documents.

a breakdown of designs in different industry sectors and other market information). Within telecommunications, the mobile market represented 33% of total sales, while public switching and transmission provided equipment another 33%, and data networking 21%.

In order to reduce manufacturing costs, power consumption, and size, the semiconductor market was in constant search of smaller "geometries" (the minimum distance used in the semiconductor design). In 1998, the digital market was dominated by 0.5 and 0.8 micron geometries, although smaller geometries such as 0.35 micron were gaining importance.[7] In addition, experts believed that the move toward System Level Integration (SLI, or systems on a chip) would play a major role in shaping the future of the ASIC market. This trend would enable ASIC designers to place larger amounts of content on a single chip. Industry specialists believed that this trend could polarize the semiconductor market into large content integrators (with or without in-house manufacturing capabilities) and a new breed of content suppliers (so-called Chipless Chip suppliers). As the mobile phone chipsets consolidated into large integrated systems, Apax believed that Dialog would need either to license additional technology to create a more complete system or, alternatively, to position itself as a chipless intellectual property supplier. Both Apax and Dialog believed that existing chip partitioning was not under threat for three to five years, particularly in the mixed-signal area.

Dialog's Product Offerings

Dialog focused its activities on three main segments: the communications market (wireless handsets), the automotive market, and other industrial applications (see Table A).

Wireless Communications ASICS   The wireless market was experiencing rapid growth. In 1998, wireless services reached 309 million subscribers. This figure was expected to grow at a compound annual growth rate of 23% to over 754 million by 2002. Over 171 million handsets were shipped worldwide in 1998, and 369 million were expected to be sold in 2002.[8] This phenomenal growth came from two main sources. In less developed markets, the introduction of wireless networks was expected to occur in areas with little or no landline infrastructure. In areas where wireless services were already present, market growth was expected to be driven by technological improvements. Among the most important one was the development of so-called third-generation

---

[7] A micron is 0.00004 of an inch.

[8] 1999 Dataquest forecast as mentioned in the Dialog Semiconductor Offering Circular (October 11, 1999), p. 35.

TABLE A   Dialog Semiconductor Business Segments

	Communications	Automotive	Industrial
% of Revenues	71%	14%	15%
Technologies	Audio/Radio Interface Power management ISDN/HDS/DDS	Sensor conditioning Timer/Counters Motor control	Lighting management Sensor conditioning Motor control
Segment Characteristics	Very high volume Low average selling price Short product life	Medium volume High average selling price Long product life	High volume (slow ramp up) Low average sell price Aggressive buyers

Source: Apax Partners.

systems, which were being designed to support broadband data applications, such as wireless Internet access, videoconferencing, and remote local area network applications. Mixed-signal ASICs were well suited to support the development of these new applications, for they could combine analog and digital signals. Moreover, the expertise required to manufacture these ASICs had motivated the handset manufacturers to increasingly rely on outsourcing the production of mixed-signal ASICs to companies like Dialog, while remaining focused on their core wireless communications competencies.

Within the communications segment, Dialog focused on two main types of ASICS, Audio Codecs and Power Management chips. Audio Codecs served as the interface between the human voice and the digital processing inside the mobile phone. They converted the digital signal received from the subsystem into an analog signal that is sent to the loudspeaker and vice versa. Audio Codecs were therefore critical for the voice quality performance of a wireless device. The power management chip was responsible for the supply of power from the battery to the other subsystems within the mobile phone. It was instrumental in extending the life of the battery by allowing certain parts of the phone to "sleep" when not in use, while preserving other functions constantly. As handset performance increased, the tradeoff of power (i.e., battery life) versus functionality became more important, making efficient power management chips a critical component of the mobile phone.

Automotive ASICS Automobiles use semiconductors in areas such as safety (airbag and braking systems), dashboard control, comfort and body (seat control, airconditioning), and power-train (engine management, transmission). The automotive semiconductor market was $8.2 billion in 1998 and was expected to grow by 10% annually to $12.9 billion in 2002.

Although Dialog's main focus was on wireless applications, the company had identified the automotive market as an attractive one to leverage its technological know-how into new applications. Apart from the applicability of its previous knowledge in wireless ASICs, the main attraction of the automotive market was its long product life cycle (up to seven years per product). This meant that once a chip had been designed for a particular application in a new car model, it would most likely be used for the next few years without any modifications. The company concentrated its efforts in the areas of safety and dashboard products. Safety chips were the main intelligent component in the airbag system, telling the airbag when to deploy and regulating the inflation of the bag to adjust for external conditions such as the speed of the vehicle. Dashboard control chips were used to deliver information to the driver from various sensors such as oil pressure and speed.

Industrial ASICS Industrial applications represented approximately 14% of the total number of designs of the European ASIC market. This segment was growing at a much slower pace than the other two markets. Dialog had also developed a small product range oriented toward certain industrial applications such as motor control, dimming, and lighting systems. Like the automotive chips, some of these systems had long life cycles.

Organization

Dialog operated from three locations in the United Kingdom, Germany, and the United States. Its main office was located in Swindon (Wiltshire, U.K.), where the company carried out all of its development activities for Ericsson and other communications customers. Swindon also served as the marketing center for the United Kingdom and the rest of the world, excluding Germany and Central Europe. A total of 50 people worked in Swindon. The German facility was located in Nabern, near Stuttgart, and employed 45 people. From this location Dialog served Germany and Central Europe and performed development activities for nontelecommunications applications. Finally, the office in Baskin Ridge (New Jersey) was a marketing branch for the United States, employing five people.

Dialog did not have its own sales force. Instead, it relied on the sales organization of Temic and Daimler Benz, its parent companies, to whom it paid a 7% sales commission. This allowed the company to access the vast resources and network of the Daimler group to market its ASIC chips. A disadvantage of this system, however, was that much of the Temic sales organization was geared toward fast-moving, high-volume products and not toward long-term, complex products such as mixed-signal ASICs.

A "Fabless" Company

Dialog outsourced all manufacturing and assembly of its products to third parties while concentrating on designing and testing the chips in-house. Chip manufacturing was a highly capital-intensive business that presented several technical and financial challenges. The Dialog model, however, was unique. Unlike Dialog, the majority of ASIC producers owned and operated their own foundries ("f9bs"), given the importance of close cooperation between design and production when innovation and short time to market were key competitive variables. Other companies, known as Application Specific Standard Product manufacturers, could afford to outsource manufacturing because the rate of product redesign was substantially slower and the production runs longer. They could then effectively auction off their business to several different manufacturers without becoming too dependent on any one.

Dialog had reached a compromise between the two models. It outsourced most of its manufacturing activities but relied on one main specialist supplier for each critical component. To keep up with the fast rate of design changes, a close partnership had to be established with the supplier to maximize production yields and product performance. For example, Dialog outsourced approximately 90% of its wafer production to ESM Ltd. in Newport, Wales. In the past, Dialog had protected itself by obtaining agreements from its main suppliers that guaranteed a minimum level of production capacity for the company for a specified period of time (typically three years). In addition, Dialog was actively grooming other potential suppliers in order to spread its production between at least two partners for each critical component. Switching between suppliers was challenging, however, since designs were process-dependent and production yields typically took considerable time to ramp up to economic levels.

Customers and Competition

Over the last two previous years, Dialog had adopted a policy geared toward key accounts. Each potential customer was evaluated against several criteria to determine the potential size of the account and the potential for the acquisition of new technical skills. This policy had resulted in sales being very heavily concentrated on a few large customers. The most important of those was Ericsson, which represented almost 40% of total sales, Siemens (approximately 20%), Temic-Daimler, and Bosch. Other important customers included Adtran, Sagem, Motorola, and Telital.

Dialog was a small player in the overall ASIC market, with a market share of around 1.8% of total sales. However, Dialog's position in the mobile communications mixed-

TABLE B   **Competitive Landscape in the Mobile Communications Market**

Transceiver/Power Amplifier	Flash Memory	Digital Signal Processors	Power Management	Audio CODEC
ST Microelectronics	Atmel	Analog Devices	**Dialog**	NEC
Anadigics	Intel	DSP	Analog Devices	**Dialog**
Fujitsu	Sharp	Conexant	NEC	ST Microelectronics
Infineon	Fujitsu	Infineon	ST Microelectronics	Texas Instruments
Philips	ST Microelectronics	ST Microelectronics	Texas Instruments	
RF Micro		Texas Instruments		
TriQuint		Philips Semiconductors		

Source: Compiled from Charles Elliott, "Dialog Semiconductor: bASIC Growth," *Goldman Sachs Investment Research* (February 22, 2000).

signal ASICs market was much stronger. The company was the leader in power management and second in the Audio Codec segments. Dialog competed with giants such as NEC, ST Microelectronics, Texas Instruments, Infineon (previously Siemens Semiconductor), and Philips Semiconductor (see Table B).

Two main factors protected Dialog from intense competition. First, these large companies used BiCMOS (comprising Bipolar plus Complementary Metal Oxide Semiconductors (CMOS)) or BCD (Bipolar and CMOS Dielectric), while Dialog used CMOS, which was up to 30% cheaper as it required a lower number of production processes. CMOS also offered other technical advantages such as lower output noise and maximum use of the energy in the battery. Although these big players could develop CMOS skills, it would take them about two to three years to catch up with the design expertise and intellectual property developed by Dialog.

The second barrier that prevented the large companies from competing directly with Dialog was their need to produce high-volume, long life-cycle chips to keep their internal foundries busy, and to provide the large-scale economies that generated healthy margins. This strategy did not suit the rapid life cycle of the mid- and high-end handset market where Dialog competed.

Despite being protected from most of its largest competitors, three large companies were well positioned to compete with Dialog Semiconductor within both Power Management and Audio Codec: Texas Instruments, NEC, and ST Microelectronics.[9] See Exhibit 12-4 for more information on Dialog's main competitors.

Management

Dialog's top management team was led by Roland Pudelko, who had been with the company since 1989 and had 21 years of experience in the industry. He was supported by Gary Duncan, VP of Marketing, Hervé Labouré, VP of Financial Control, Richard Schmitz, VP of Engineering, and Peter Hall, VP of Operations and Quality. Except for Labouré, who joined Dialog in 1996, the rest of the executive team had been with the company for at least eight years. Dialog's management had been instrumental in establishing the relationships with Ericsson and other major customers that allowed Di-

[9] Charles Elliott, "Dialog Semiconductor: Absolutely Fabless," *Goldman Sachs Investment Research* (November 26, 1999), 4.

EXHIBIT 12-4

DIALOG SEMICONDUCTOR'S COMPETITION IN 1998

Texas Instruments.   With over $1 billion in annual sales in the wireless equipment sector, Texas Instruments used CMOS processes. However, it focused in standard, not embedded products, and rather than competing on price, it emphasized growth outside the handset sector and in new applications.

NEC.   This company had been focused mainly on Asian companies, Panasonic and Samsung, which required a high-volume and low-price strategy, and differed from the needs of the customers served at that moment by Dialog.

ST Microelectronics.   As part of its strategic alliance with Nokia, ST provided a large number of passive and standardized components. Nokia used these simpler components to support their particularly rapid model change strategy, which favored the use of standardized and readily available parts over specially designed ones, which needed a longer product cycle.

Other Smaller Companies.   An additional threat was posed by several smaller companies that had the flexibility to challenge Dialog in its own market niches. For instance, Linear Technology and Austria Micro Systems (AMS) were considered potential threats in the future.

Source: Compiled from Charles Elliott, "Dialog Semiconductor: Absolutely Fabless," *Goldman Sachs Investment Research* (November 26, 1999).

---

alog to become one of their key suppliers. Pudelko's team was also responsible for establishing the alliances with foundries that had led to the "fabless" strategy.

THE DEAL

Origination

At the beginning of 1998, Daimler decided to divest certain noncore assets. The Temic division (which included Dialog) was earmarked for sale and eventually sold to Vishay Intertechnology, an electronic component manufacturer. The integrated circuit business of Temic was, however, to be acquired by Atmel, a U.S. manufacturer of integrated circuits. This last development worried Ericsson because Atmel was already one of its main IC suppliers. Atmel's purchase of Dialog would lead to further supplier concentration, which Ericsson wanted to avoid. Ericsson was also concerned that Texas Instruments, its largest supplier, would ultimately acquire either Dialog or Atmel. Ericsson therefore preferred to preserve Dialog's independence from other large semiconductor companies.

Consequently, Ericsson decided to prevent the sale to Atmel by exercising its preemptive right to buy Dialog from Daimler. This right of first refusal allowed Ericsson to match any offer for Dialog by February 28, 1998. Ericsson then had to immediately sell the firm, since long-standing internal policy prohibited the corporation from holding controlling stakes in its suppliers. It was therefore imperative that the majority of

Dialog acquired by Ericsson be rapidly sold to another "friendly" investor group before the March board meeting.

Michael Glover, a former private equity professional who was also a nonexecutive director of another Apax portfolio company and a board member of Dialog, had invited Apax Partners into the deal in late February. By that time, Risman had less than four weeks to complete both transactions before the Ericsson board meeting.

Due Diligence

The Apax deal team was led by John McMonigall, who was assisted by Michael Risman, an assistant director with substantial experience in the technology sector. While McMonigall oversaw the transaction and managed relationships, Risman conducted the assessment of the opportunity, structuring of the transaction and management of the deal process. Risman was assisted by Richard Wilson (another assistant director) and by an analyst, Jamie Hutchinson. Two members of the Munich office, Martin Halusa and Peter Blumenwitz, who helped build relationships in Germany, completed the team (see Exhibit 12-5 for information on Apax team members). As was customary, Apax used external advisors to help with due diligence, although there was insufficient time to write fully informed briefs and conduct thorough analysis. The Gartner Group provided a quick overview of the market and its growth prospects. Accounting help was provided by a top-five accounting firm. The law firm of Rowe and Mawe was also retained to look at legal issues.

Risman and the team spent most of their time calling on customers, performing additional research on the industry, and building the financial model. Apax executives paid only two one-day visits to Swindon (United Kingdom) and Nabern (Germany), while the accountants and lawyers spent most of their time performing accounting and legal due diligence on Dialog's premises. In Risman's words:

> We made one one-day visit to Swindon and Nabern. Jim Tully [The Gartner Group] spent two days in Swindon (United Kingdom) and the accountants and lawyers were in for two weeks. The rest was telephoning customers, desk research, modeling, and discussions with management.

Opportunities

As the due diligence was still progressing, the Apax team realized that the Dialog investment opportunity presented several attractive features. First, mixed-signal ASIC expertise seemed to be in short supply, while the demand for the chips, particularly power management for handsets, kept increasing. As the technology became more complex and the requirement for accumulated experience increased, barriers to entry became more relevant.

Second, the ASIC market was expected to experience very significant growth, in excess of 20%, and Dialog was well positioned to take advantage of it. The company's internal projections showed revenues from the main customers doubling over the next three years, excluding new products currently under development.

Third, the reference interviews conducted by Apax had shown that the company's main customers were very pleased with Dialog. Ericsson and Adtran had even indicated that they might be willing to take a minority position in the company. Finally, Dialog's management team was very well regarded by Dialog's customers and seemed to be very knowledgeable about the mixed-signal ASIC market (see Exhibit 12-6).

EXHIBIT 12-5

THE APAX PARTNERS' TEAM IN THE DIALOG TRANSACTION

Apax London

John McMonigall (Director).   Joined Apax Partners in 1990 from British Telecommunications Plc, where he was Divisional Managing Director and a member of the management board. Prior to this, his experience included a variety of industrial companies in the fields of software, electronics, and telecommunications. At Apax Partners, John focuses on Telecommunications and Electronics.

Michael Risman (Assistant Director).   Joined Apax Partners in 1995. He previously worked for Gemini Consulting as a strategy consultant and at Jaguar Cars as an engineer. Michael specializes in IT investments, including IT-related MBOs and LBOs. Michael has an MBA from Harvard Business School and an MA (Hons) degree in Electrical Engineering and Management from Cambridge University.

Richard Wilson (Assistant Director).   Joined Apax Partners in 1995 and specializes in network-related businesses, in both technology and services. Previously, he worked as a consultant for four years with Scientific Generics, a business and technical consulting company. He has also worked for Marconi Space Systems in computer simulation. Richard obtained a MBA with distinction from INSEAD and graduated with a first-class degree (BA) from Cambridge University, where he studied Engineering. He is a Chartered Engineer.

Jamie Hutchinson (Analyst).   Joined Apax Partners in 1997, after working as a strategy consultant at the LEK Partnership. He focuses on IT and Internet infrastructure. Jamie graduated with a Master's degree in Chemistry from Oxford University.

Apax Munich

Dr. Martin Halusa (Director).   A graduate of Georgetown University, received his MBA from the Harvard Business School and his Ph.D. in Economics from the Leopold-Franzens University in Innsbruck. He began his career at The Boston Consulting Group (BCG) in Germany and left as a Partner and Vice President of BCG worldwide in 1986. He joined Daniel Swarovski Corporation, Austria's largest private industrial company, first as President of Swarovski Inc (USA) and later as Director of International Holding in Zurich. In 1990, he joined Apax Partners in Germany as Managing Director. His investment experience has been primarily in telecommunications and service industries.

Peter Blumenwitz (Assistant Director).   Joined Apax Partners Private Equity in August 1997, continuing his focus on early-stage venture capital companies in IT and software. He followed a period as credit analyst for Allgemeine Kredit and four years as Investment Manager at Technologieholding, where he specialized in leading-edge IT investments. Peter is a graduate in Business Administration from Munich University.

Source: Compiled from corporate documents.

EXHIBIT 12-6

DIALOG SEMICONDUCTOR'S MANAGEMENT, 1998

CEO & President
Roland Pudelko

Marketing	Engineering	Operations & Quality	Finance & Control
Gary Duncan	Richard Schmitz	Peter Hall	Hervé Labouré
(VP)	(VP)	(VP)	(VP)

Roland Pudelko (45). Joined Dialog Semiconductor in 1989 as a Managing Director. He has 21 years of experience in electronics and microelectronics, primarily in management positions within the Daimler-Benz Group. During that time, he was a board member of a joint venture with the Taiwanese company ACER, and in the TEMIC Group he was responsible for the co-ordination of worldwide design and engineering. Mr. Pudelko has a diploma in Communication Technologies from the vocational college (Fachhochschule) of Esslingen.

Gary Duncan (42). Joined Dialog Semiconductor in October 1987. Prior to joining Dialog, Mr. Duncan held various marketing and engineering positions at GEC Plessey, Texas Instruments, and European Silicon Systems. During his time at Dialog he has been responsible for all aspects of marketing and business development. He obtained a Higher National Certificate in Electronics and Mathematics in 1978 from Plymouth Polytechnic. Mr. Duncan is also a Technical Engineer of the Chartered Engineering Institute.

Hervé Labouré (34). Joined Dialog Semiconductor in October 1996 as Vice-President of Finance and Control. Mr. Labouré was Financial Controller of the UK subsidiary of Matra MHS Ltd., with responsibilities for the Scandinavian and Asian subsidiaries. At Dialog, Mr. Labouré is responsible for all aspects of financial controlling, including consolidation for Dialog worldwide. He has a Degree in Business Administration (with a Finance elective) from the University of Lyon.

Richard Schmitz (41). The Vice-President of Engineering. He joined Dialog Semiconductor in 1989. Prior to joining Dialog Semiconductor, he held various design-related positions at Hewlett-Packard's instruments division in Böblingen and the Institute for Microelectronics, Stuttgart. Mr. Schmitz received a Diploma in Engineering for Communications Electronics in 1983 from vocational college (Fachhochschule) in Trier.

Peter Hall (46). The Vice-President of Operations and Quality. Mr. Hall is responsible for all production-related issues within the company. He joined Dialog Semiconductor in July 1987. Before joining the company, he held various management and engineering positions at STC Semiconductors and MEM in Switzerland. He obtained his BSc (Honors) in Electrical and Electronic engineering in 1974 from the University of Newcastle upon Tyne and his MSc in Digital Techniques in 1977 from the University of Edinburgh.

Source: Compiled from corporate documents.

Risks

The due diligence also unearthed some areas for concern. Chief among those was the company's dependence on a few accounts. Ericsson and Siemens together represented approximately 60% of the total revenues. Although both companies seemed very enthusiastic about Dialog, they were only willing to provide letters of support and soft commitments for future orders. As a result, Dialog's fortunes were very closely tied to those of its main customers. In 1996 Dialog had failed to meet Ericsson's specification for an ASIC chip and hence missed out on an entire generation of mobile phones, losing close to £2.2 million in revenues. Also in 1996, Motorola released its surplus stock of handsets that it had failed to sell during the 1995 Christmas season. Ericsson's sales were affected, and orders for Dialog's ASICs dropped sharply.

Selling constituted another risk. Once Dialog was divested from Daimler, it would lose its entire sales organization. The company would have to build a sales department from scratch in the midst of a fast-growing and highly dynamic market. The impact that the loss of its sales force might have on Dialog's revenues was uncertain. Risman knew the company could not afford to lose momentum.

Moreover, Dialog was in the middle of a SAP R/3 implementation. If successfully installed, an enterprise resource planning system could become a very important competitive tool in the semiconductor market. Risman knew, however, that every SAP installation was risky. According to a Harvard Business School survey,[10] only 33% of companies that implemented SAP considered its implementation a success; 77% of companies experienced benefits below the planned levels; 84% of the projects went over budget; and 62% experienced delays in their implementation. Some companies, such as Foxmeyer Drug, had even filed for bankruptcy, claiming that the primary cause of its difficulties was the failed ERP (enterprise resource planning) implementation that had crippled the business.[11] This was already a very delicate period for the company, and the SAP implementation simply added another layer of risk.

In addition, Dialog had recently started to move toward a new Cadence computer design tool that would allow the company to move from its traditional 0.7 and 1.2 micron scale to a smaller 0.35-micron scale. This was seen as a positive development that would help to defend the technological lead of the company. However, in the short term it represented more risk. It was impossible to predict what problems Dialog's engineers might encounter when moving to Cadence. Furthermore, the deal with Cadence ($5–10 million) had not been finalized yet, and it was difficult to project what the overall incremental cost would be for the company. Risman commented:

> We did not know if the engineers would adapt from Mentor to Cadence or what problems we would have migrating designs from one environment to the other. The new deal with Cadence ($5 to $10 million) was also not nailed down, and we did not know quite what the incremental cost was going to be for the P&L. In the end we had to take a guess at what we thought it would be.

The "fabless" strategy was also risky. While the technology to build and operate a foundry was already well established, semiconductors were very sensitive to the pro-

---

[10] Robert P. Austin, Mark J. Cotteleer, and Cedric X. Escalle, "Enterprise Resource Planning (ERP): Technology Note," Harvard Business School Case no. 699-020. This survey was conducted among 83 companies with representatives attending executive programs at the Harvard Business School.

[11] Bankruptcy trustees filed suit against Andersen Consulting and SAP seeking to recover damages of $500 million from each. See the previous footnote.

duction process. It was very challenging to move the production of a chip from one foundry to another. The level of changes necessary to fit a semiconductor to a different foundry entailed a minor "redesign" of the chip and requalification of the new chips by the customer. This was especially true for mixed-signal products. Dialog was therefore very dependent on the health and efficiency of its suppliers. In Risman's words:

> Whilst the concept of subcontracted foundry was very much established (TSMC, UMC, Chartered, etc), semiconductors were not easily portable from one foundry to another. These had to be recharacterized, even redesigned, to fit a particular process. This is especially true for analog and mixed signal products. Very few mixed signal companies outsourced production for these reasons.

To make matters worse, the accounting firm failed to provide Apax with reliable accounting information. Risman commented:

> The accounting firm failed to deliver any form of useful accounting report—the manager went on holiday to recover from exhaustion two days before the closing deadline. He could not be replaced. We therefore had to use their working papers to take a punt on unaudited numbers including most of the associated P&L and balance sheet issues.

In addition to all these uncertainties, the team was being forced to make a decision in less than four weeks. At Apax, the typical investment process lasted at least eight weeks (see Exhibit 12-7 for a depiction of the Apax investment process). In fact, the legal due diligence and negotiation alone often took over four weeks. This made Risman uneasy. He wished the team had more time to conduct a more thorough technical analysis of the business. Under these circumstances, he was being forced to make more judgment calls than he was accustomed to.

> The legal (due diligence) alone could take two weeks. Part of Dialog's value proposition was to take warranty for the product, and we uncovered some minor product liability issues. We had to just pick off the key points and make a judgment call. We would have liked to spend more time with all aspects of the due diligence—in particular technical.

Finally, a clause in the sale agreement drafted by Ericsson particularly concerned Risman. Under the terms set out by Ericsson, once Apax bought Dialog it was precluded from selling it at a private sale until 2002, unless the business was performing at less than 50% of plan. This clause essentially meant that Apax would have to rely on the public markets to sell Dialog in an initial public offering. Although the number of IPOs had soared in 1998, Risman was worried that a public market downturn could seriously compromise the possibility of reaching liquidity for Apax in the next two to three years.

Valuation

The process of estimating Dialog's value was not straightforward. Very few companies were directly comparable to Dialog; most of them were larger and competed in broader markets than Dialog's niche. In addition, despite Apax's due diligence efforts, management's financial projections were highly uncertain. Growth in the market was extremely high, but Dialog's sales were very undiversified and concentrated with a small number of customers. Thus, Dialog revenue projections were highly dependent on the commercial success of its major customers and the company's ability to maintain its relationships with these customers.

EXHIBIT 12-7

APAX PARTNERS INVESTMENT PROCESS

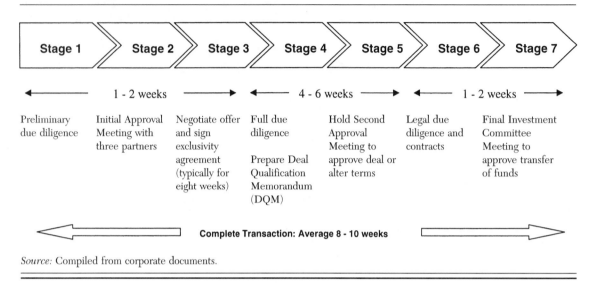

Source: Compiled from corporate documents.

Comparable Companies   Risman and his team had found a group of companies that they thought were comparable to Dialog. The group included large semiconductor companies with mixed-signal expertise, a few mixed-signal specialists, small telecom ASICs companies, and fabless ASSP companies (see Exhibits 12-8 and 12-9). The team, however, was somewhat cautious, as there was no perfect comparable. These companies were larger and had a more diversified customer base. Therefore, they had a lower risk profile but less exposure to the high-growth telecom sector. Overall, the comparable analysis suggested a range of multiples of between 1.2 and 3.0 times historic revenues and of between 14 and 20 times historic EBIT. Risman understood that these comparable firms had lower growth rates than Dialog was projecting, but it was difficult to estimate the incremental valuation that Dialog would be awarded.

Financial Projections   Dialog's management had prepared detailed financial projections for 1998 to 2000. They had used a bottom-up approach to forecast revenue growth, with detailed revenue and gross margin projections for each component to be manufactured for every client (60 components in total). The due diligence process had shown that these projections were conservative, so the Apax team decided to build a best case scenario to account for probable improvements in performance. Moreover, the Apax team thought the 57% tax rate used by management, assuming all revenues were booked in Germany, was too pessimistic. Risman considered a hybrid between the United Kingdom and the German tax rate, of about 40%, to be more likely. Exhibit 12-10 summarizes Dialog's historical financial statements and management projections.

Deal Structure

In addition to evaluating the offer price, Risman had to decide how much debt Apax should use in this deal. Although the deal was a buyout and debt could improve the

EXHIBIT 12-8

TRADING COMPARABLES ANALYSIS

Small Comparable Companies

Company	Currency	LTM Y/E	Revenues	EBIT	Net Income	Enterprise Value	EV/ Revenue	EV/ EBIT	Equity/Net Income
AMS	Aus Sch	12/96	1,794	−75.1	52	2,123	1.2×	−28.3×	−48.2×
Mitel	US$	12/97	568	61.1	47.2	866	1.5×	14.2×	19.5×
Lattice	US$	12/97	242	74	55.6	1,222	5.0×	16.5×	23.1×
Cypress	US$	09/97	523	23.4	19.6	1,803	3.4×	77.0×	81.2×
Sierra	US$	12/97	127	48.9	34.3	818	6.4×	16.7×	24.9×
						Mean	**3.5×**	**19.2×**	**39.4×**
						Median	**3.4×**	**16.5×**	**24.9×**

Large Comparable Companies

Company	Currency	LTM Y/E	Revenues	EBIT	Net Income	Enterprise Value	EV/ Revenue	EV/ EBIT	Equity/Net Income
Atmel	US$	09/97	999	238	150	4,123	4.1×	17.3×	24.6×
Texas Instruments	US$	12/97	9,750	616	302	19,038	2.0×	30.9×	61.9×
SGS Thomson	US$	12/97	4,019	520	407	9,809	2.4×	18.9×	23.9×
Lucent Technologies	US$	12/97	26,360	1,631	541	54,221	2.1×	33.2×	95.0×
						Mean	**2.7×**	**25.1×**	**51.4×**
						Median	**2.3×**	**24.9×**	**43.2×**

Details on Closest Comparable Companies

Company	Large Comparables			Small Comparables		
	Atmel	Texas Instruments	Lucent Technologies	Mitel	Lattice	Cypress
Ticker	ATML	TXN	LU	MLT	LSCC	CY
Market Capitalization ($MMs)	3,450	18,284	51,374	941	1,282	1,780
Net Debt ($MMs)	673	754	2,847	(75)	(60)	23
Equity Beta	2.26	1.41	1.64	0.76	1.56	1.05
Firm Value ($MMs)	4,123	19,038	54,221	866	1,222	1,803

Note: 20-Year U.K. Gilt Yield as of March 1998 was 6.01%.

Source: Compiled from corporate documents and Bloomberg, Gartner Group, and Yahoo! Finance databases.

EXHIBIT 12-9

BRIEF DESCRIPTIONS OF CLOSEST COMPARABLE FIRMS

Atmel Corporation.   A global semiconductor company that designs, manufactures and sells a wide range of semiconductor integrated circuit products. The company has been instrumental in developing and commercializing non-volatile memory, or memory that continues to store information after power is turned off. Atmel offers complex system-on-a-chip solutions for a broad array of markets by combining its leading-edge semiconductor process technologies with system-level building blocks such as microcontrollers, digital signal processors, and analog and nonvolatile memory. The company manufactures more than 90% of its products in its own wafer fabrication facilities.

Texas Instruments, Inc. (TI).   A global semiconductor company and the world's leading designer and supplier of digital signal processors and analog integrated circuits. These two types of semiconductor products work together in digital electronic devices such as digital cellular phones. TI also is a world leader in the design and manufacturing of other semiconductor products. These products include standard logic, application-specific integrated circuits, reduced instruction-set computing microprocessors, microcontrollers, and digital imaging devices. TI's Materials & Controls business sells electrical and electronic controls, electronic connectors, sensors, radio-frequency identification systems, and clad metals into commercial and industrial markets. The company is also a leading supplier of educational and graphing calculators. TI has manufacturing, design, or sales operations in 27 countries.

Lucent Technologies.   Designs, develops, and manufactures communications systems, software, and products. Lucent is engaged in the sale of public and private communications systems, supplying systems and software to most of the world's largest communications network operators and service providers. Lucent is also engaged in the sale of business communications systems and of microelectronic components for communications applications to manufacturers of communications systems and computers. Lucent Technologies was formed from the systems and technology units that were formerly a part of AT&T Corp., including the R&D capabilities of Bell Laboratories.

Mitel Corporation.   A global designer, manufacturer, and marketer of networked systems and specialty semiconductors for the communications industry. Mitel Communications Systems' products are primarily customer premises-based communications systems that are used in networks that enable businesses to communicate within and between locations to support the needs of branch offices and mobile workers. Mitel Semiconductor manufactures and sells semiconductor products in the following categories: communications; telephony; ASICs; home gateway; wireless access; WAN internetworking; optical; and medical. The company also provides foundry services to third parties on a contract basis.

Lattice Semiconductor Corporation.   Designs, develops, and markets high-performance programmable logic devices (PLDs) and related development system software. The company is the inventor and world's leading supplier of in-system programmable (ISP) PLDs. The company introduced ISP devices to the industry in 1992. PLDs are standard semiconductor components that can be configured by the end customer as specific logic functions, enabling shorter design cycle times and reduced development costs. Lattice products are sold worldwide, primarily to manufacturers of communication, computing, industrial, and military systems. Lattice offers seven distinct families of ISP products, all of which are supported by the company's third-generation software development tool suite.

Cypress Semiconductor Corporation.   Designs, develops, manufactures, and markets a broad line of high-performance digital and mixed-signal integrated circuits for a range of markets, including data communications, telecommunications, computers, and instrumentation systems. The company offers over 425 products. Cypress' memory products division offers static random access memories (RAMs) and multi-chip modules. Non-Memory Products include programmable logic products and programming software, programmable-skew clocking, data communication products, computer products, and nonvolatile memory products.

Source: Compiled from corporate documents and Bloomberg, Gartner Group, and Yahoo! Finance databases.

EXHIBIT 12-10

HISTORICAL FINANCIAL STATEMENTS AND MANAGEMENT PROJECTIONS

Income Statement

Figures in £m	1995	1996	1997	1998F	1999F	2000F
Revenue	13.8	10.8	26.5	29.0	39.6	48.9
Growth (%)		−21.7%	145.4%	9.4%	36.6%	23.5%
Direct costs	−12.0	−9.8	−17.0	−17.4	−24.5	−30.8
Gross margin	1.8	1.0	9.5	11.6	15.1	18.1
% of sales	13.0%	9.3%	35.8%	40.0%	38.1%	37.0%
Overhead	−1.0	−3.6	−8.1	−8.9	−10.8	−12.2
EBIT	0.8	−2.6	1.4	2.7	4.3	5.9
EBIT margin %	5.8%	−24.1%	5.3%	9.3%	10.9%	12.1%
Interest expense	0.0	0.0	0.0	−0.1	−0.1	−0.1
Taxes				−0.7	−2.5	−3.3
Net income				1.9	1.7	2.5

Balance Sheet

Figures in £m	1995	1996	1997	1998F	1999F	2000F
Fixed assets[a]			1.6	2.6	3.5	3.3
Current assets			8.6	8.7	11.1	13.4
Cash			0.2	0.4	1.0	1.6
Total assets			**10.4**	**11.7**	**15.6**	**18.3**
Current liabilities			6.1	5.5	7.8	8.0
Unsecured loan			2.0	2.0	2.0	2.0
Debt			0.0	0.0	0.0	0.0
Equity			2.3	4.2	5.8	8.3
Total liabilities			**10.4**	**11.7**	**15.6**	**18.3**

[a]Excludes Acquisition Goodwill.

Cash Flow

Figures in £m	1995	1996	1997	1998F	1999F	2000F
Net income				1.9	1.7	2.5
Depreciation				0.8	1.1	1.2
Net working capital				−0.7	−0.1	−2.0
Capital expenditure				−1.8	−2.0	−1.1
Cash increment				0.2	0.6	0.6
Ending cash balance			0.2	0.4	1.0	1.0

Note: Management projected a tax rate of 57%. (The calculation of the projected taxes for 1998 was complicated by the fact that the firm would be spun out in midyear.) The Apax team believed, however, that Dialog could reduce its tax rate to 40% (a blend of U.K. and Germany tax rates).

Source: Compiled from corporate documents.

returns of the investment, Dialog was expected to grow very quickly, so that cash flows might not be sufficient to repay the interest and principal on a large amount of debt. The projections were also highly uncertain, and an unexpected decrease in revenues or an increase in costs could force Dialog to default.

In terms of equity structure, Apax was interested in getting both ordinary shares and cumulative redeemable preference shares.[12] The latter would protect Apax from an eventual liquidation of the company or a sale below the valuation at which Apax would invest in this round. The team also wanted to set aside 10% of the equity and a further 10% in options to compensate management and align their incentives with shareholder value creation.

Risman considered the merits of bringing other strategic partners into the deal as had been proposed by Ericsson and the management team. Currently, having Ericsson as shareholder had helped Dialog to benefit from higher sales, improved design capabilities, and a better industry network. Bringing another key customer into the deal might make Dialog more attractive and less dependent on a single customer.

THE DECISION

Now that the bank had failed to make the cash transfer, Apax had the opportunity to stop the deal and still save face. What should Risman propose?

As he contemplated this question, Risman wondered how this transaction would affect his own career at Apax. After three years in the firm since graduating from business school, things seemed to be going well. To date, Risman had been involved in several successful investments. He was gaining good experience working with four portfolio company boards. If the deal went well, it could significantly enhance his prospects of becoming a partner. On the other hand, if the transaction was unsuccessful, it could cut short his career. Several assistant directors and associates had departed the firm for supporting excessively risky transactions that had lost the firm money. Perhaps he should be more cautious with the Dialog opportunity.

He stepped out of his office to take a break and read the Apax mission statement that hung on the wall of the Portland Place offices in London:

> We are entrepreneurs: both the corporate clients we advise and the companies in which we invest are entrepreneurial businesses. We have grown because we understand the entrepreneurial spirit and culture. As a finance house for businesses which need that understanding, we are committed to working as close corporate partners in creating new and profitable enterprises and in realizing the full potential of well-established businesses.

Should Apax invest in Dialog? Was the investment simply too risky, or was the opportunity too good to pass up? Under the circumstances, what was the right price for Dialog? And, was Dialog the right investment at this stage in Risman's career? He walked back into his office where the deal documentation was already taking up all the available space. As he looked at his crowded desk, he wondered what to do next.

---

[12] Cumulative redeemable preference shares, sometimes called straight preferred, are preferred stock that has no convertibility into equity. Its intrinsic value is therefore its face value plus any dividend rights or coupon it carries. Redeemable preferred stock always carries a negotiated term specifying when it must be redeemed by the company—typically the sooner of a public offering, sale, or five to eight years. In most ways, it behaves in a capital structure like deeply subordinated debt. It is used in private equity transactions in combination with common stock or warrants. For a further discussion, see Chapter 17 in this volume.

13

A Note on Valuation in Private Equity Settings

The valuation of private companies, especially those in the earlier stages of their life cycle, is a difficult and often subjective process. Early-stage companies typically forecast a period of negative cash flows with highly uncertain—but tantalizing—future rewards. This cash flow profile is very sensitive to the valuation assumptions made.

This note will discuss a variety of valuation techniques that can be used in private equity settings. The intention is to provide a practical toolkit to be used when tackling cases in the second and third modules of *Venture Capital and Private Equity*. Much of the background theory will be glossed over: the focus will be on the essential underlying mechanics of each method and a discussion of strengths and weaknesses. The references at the end of this note provide more detailed information on the various valuation techniques discussed.

This note addresses the Comparables, Net Present Value, Adjusted Present Value, Venture Capital, and Options valuation methods. It also discusses the use of Monte Carlo simulation employing the software package Crystal Ball® to enhance these valuations. Each of the following five sections is dedicated to one valuation method. Each section has a corresponding appendix with a detailed example of the method.

COMPARABLES

The use of comparables often provides a quick and easy way to obtain a "ballpark" valuation for a firm. When searching for comparables, we seek other firms that display similar "value characteristics" to the company we are interested in. These value characteristics include risk, growth rate, capital structure, and the size and timing of cash flows. Often, these value characteristics are driven by other underlying attributes of the company which can be incorporated in a multiple. For example, the anticipated cash flows for a new Health Maintenance Organization (HMO) might be accurately predicted by the number of members it has enrolled (see the example in Appendix 1).

John Willinge, MBA '96, prepared this note under the supervision of Professor Josh Lerner as the basis for class discussion. It supersedes an earlier note, "A Note on Valuation in Venture Settings," No. 295-064.

The use of comparables for private companies presents many potential problems, however. (The strengths and weaknesses of each method are summarized in Exhibit 13-1.) First, it is often difficult to ascertain what valuations have been assigned to other privately held firms. Consequently, it may be impossible to compare our firm to the companies that are the most similar. Second, because accounting and other performance information on private firms is often unavailable, key ratios may not be calculable, or other important impacts on valuation may be missed. Finally, the valuations assigned to comparable firms may be misguided. Periodically, whole classes of firms have been

EXHIBIT 13-1

STRENGTHS AND WEAKNESSES OF VARIOUS VALUATION METHODS IN PRIVATE EQUITY SETTINGS

Method	Strengths	Weaknesses
1. Comparables	• Quick to use • Simple to understand • Commonly used in industry • Market based	• Private company comparables may be difficult to find and evaluate. • If public company comparables are used, the resulting valuation needs to be adjusted to take into account the private company's illiquidity.
2. Net Present Value	• Theoretically sound	• Cash flows may be difficult to estimate. • Private company comparables (β and capital structure) can be difficult to find and evaluate. • WACC assumes a constant capital structure. • WACC assumes a constant effective tax rate. • Typical cash flow profile of outflows followed by distant, uncertain inflows is very sensitive to discount and terminal growth rate assumptions.
3. Adjusted Present Value	• Theoretically sound • Suitable (and simple to use) in situations where the capital structure is changing (e.g., highly leveraged transactions such as leveraged buyouts) • Suitable in situations where the effective tax rate is changing (e.g., when there are NOLs)	• It is more complicated to calculate than the NPV method. • It has the same disadvantages as the NPV Method except it overcomes the shortfalls of WACC assumption (i.e., constant capital structure and tax rate).
4. Venture Capital	• Simple to understand • Quick to use • Commonly used	• It relies on terminal values derived from other methods. • It is oversimplified (large discount rate "fudge factor").
5. Asset Options	• Theoretically sound • Overcomes drawbacks of NPV and APV techniques in situations where managers have flexibility	• Methodology is not commonly used in industry and may not be understood. • Real-world situations may be difficult to reduce to solvable option problems. • Black-Scholes model makes strict assumptions which may not be realistic.

valued at prices that seem unjustifiable on a cash flow basis, as the recent Internet frenzy illustrates.

Sound judgment should consequently drive the use of comparables. One must search for potential measures of value that can be sensibly applied from one company to the next. In public markets, common ratios are *(1)* the share price divided by the earnings per share (the P-E ratio), *(2)* the market value of the firm's equity divided by total revenue, and *(3)* the market value of the firm's equity divided by the shareholder's equity on the balance sheet (market-to-book ratio). These ratios, however, may be misleading. Consider the price-earnings ratio. The earnings (profit after tax) reflect the capital structure of the company, since earnings are after interest expenses and taxes. Common sense would therefore tell us that when comparing two companies with similar characteristics except for substantially different capital structures, it would be more appropriate to use a multiple based on earnings before interest and taxes (EBIT). By using this latter comparable, we compensate for the differing capital structures of the two entities. This is because EBIT ignores the different levels of interest expense incurred by the two companies. (Of course, the use of EBIT ignores the interest tax shields associated with these capital structures, which we may wish to factor into the comparisons.)

Accounting-based comparables, such as those mentioned above, are clearly less suitable in a private equity setting where companies are often unprofitable and experiencing rapid growth. One must therefore look for other sensible measures of value. For example, in an Internet business a good indicator of value may be the number of subscribers enrolled by a company. A valid proxy for the value of a biotechnology firm may be the number of patents awarded. In a gold exploration company, a typical measure of value is the number of ounces of gold indicated by initial drilling results. These are just a few examples of nonfinancial, industry-specific measures that can be used to estimate the value of a firm.

Interestingly, a recent study suggests that industry-specific multiples have strong explanatory power for the offering prices of IPOs. In contrast, accounting-based multiples, such as the price-earnings ratio and the ratio of the market to book value of equity, were found to have little predictive ability. The reason is that among young, publicly traded firms in the same industry, accounting-based multiples vary substantially.[1]

Another issue related to the use of public market comparables to value private companies is the marketability of the equity. Because shares in private firms are typically less marketable than those of publicly traded firms, it may be appropriate to apply a discount for illiquidity. The size of the proper discount will depend on the particular circumstances. Surveys suggest, however, that discounts for lack of marketability used in practice fall within a very narrow band, often between 25% and 30%.[2] Whether such large discounts are justified, though, is still an open question.

THE NET PRESENT VALUE METHOD

The Net Present Value (NPV) method is one of the most common methods of cash flow valuation. (Others include the Equity Cash Flow and Capital Cash Flow methods. The Adjusted Present Value method discussed in the next section is a variation on the Capital Cash Flow method.) This section briefly visits the basics of the NPV method.

---

[1] M. Kim and J. Ritter, "Valuing IPOs," *Journal of Financial Economics* 53(1999):404–437.

[2] S. Pratt, *Valuing a Business: The Analysis and Appraisal of Closely Held Companies*, Homewood, IL, Dow Jones-Irwin, 2000.

The NPV method incorporates the benefit of tax shields from tax-deductible interest payments in the discount rate (i.e., the Weighted Average Cost of Capital, or WACC). To avoid double-counting these tax shields, interest payments must not be deducted from cash flows. Equation (1) shows how to calculate cash flows (subscripts denote time periods):

$$CF_t = EBIT_t * (1 - \tau) + DEPR_t - CAPEX_t - \Delta NWC_t + other_t \qquad (1)$$

where:

CF = cash flow

$EBIT$ = earnings before interest and tax

τ = corporate tax rate

$DEPR$ = depreciation

$CAPEX$ = capital expenditures

ΔNWC = increase in net working capital

other = increases in taxes payable, wages payable, etc.

Next, the terminal value should be calculated. This estimate is very important as the majority of the value of a company, especially one in an early-stage setting, may be in the terminal value. A common method for estimating the terminal value of an enterprise is the perpetuity method.

Equation (2) gives the formula for calculating a terminal value (TV) at time T using the perpetuity method, assuming a growth rate in perpetuity of g and a discount rate equal to r. The cash flows and discount rates used in the NPV method are typically nominal values (i.e., they are not adjusted for inflation). If forecasts indicate that the cash flow will be constant in inflation-adjusted dollars, a terminal growth rate equal to the rate of inflation should be used:

$$TV_T = [CF_T * (1 + g)]/(r - g) \qquad (2)$$

Other common methods of terminal value calculation used in practice include price-earnings ratios and market-to-book value multiples, but these shortcuts are not encouraged!

The net present value of the firm is then calculated as shown in Equation (3):

$$NPV = [CF_1/(1 + r)] + [CF_2/(1 + r)^2] + [CF_3/(1 + r)^3]$$
$$+ \cdots + [(CF_T + TV_T) / (1 + r)^T] \qquad (3)$$

The discount rate is calculated using Equation (4):

$$r = (D/V) * r_d * (1 - \tau) + (E/V) * r_e \qquad (4)$$

where:

r_d = discount rate for debt

r_e = discount rate for equity

τ = corporate tax rate

D = market value of debt

E = market value of equity

$V = D + E$

If the firm is not at its target capital structure, however, the target values should be used for D/V and E/V.

The cost of equity, r_e, is calculated using the familiar Capital Asset Pricing Model shown in Equation (5):

$$r_e = r_f + \beta * (r_m - r_f) \tag{5}$$

where:

r_e = discount rate for equity

r_f = risk-free rate

β = beta, or degree of correlation with the market

r_m = market rate of return on common stock

$(r_m - r_f)$ = market risk premium

When determining the appropriate risk-free rate (r_f), one should attempt to match the maturity of the investment project with that of the risk-free rate. Typically, we use the 10-year rate. Estimates of the market risk premium can vary widely: for the sake of the course, 7.3% can be assumed.

For private companies, or spin-offs from public companies, betas can be estimated by looking at comparable public firms. The beta for public companies can be found in a beta book or on the Bloomberg machine. If the firm is not at its target capital structure, it is necessary to "unlever" and "relever" the beta. This is accomplished using Equation (6):

$$\beta_u = \beta_l * (E / V) = \beta_l * [E / (E + D)] \tag{6}$$

where:

β_u = unlevered beta

β_l = levered beta

E = market value of equity

D = market value of debt

An issue arises in which there are no comparable companies. This often occurs in entrepreneurial settings. Common sense is the best guide in this situation. Think about the cyclical nature of the particular firm and whether the risk is systematic or can be diversified away. If accounting data are available, another way is to calculate "earnings betas," which have some correlation with equity betas. An earnings beta is calculated by comparing a private company's net income to a stock market index such as the S&P 500. Using least squares regression techniques, we can calculate the slope of the line of best fit (the beta).

Strengths and Weaknesses of the Net Present Value Method

Estimating firm values by discounting relevant cash flows is widely regarded as technically sound. The values should be less subject than comparables to distortions that can occur in public and, more commonly, private markets.

Given the many assumptions and estimates that have been made during the valuation process, however, it is unrealistic to arrive at a single, or "point," value for the firm. Different cash flows should be estimated under "best," "most likely," and "worst" case assumptions. These should then be discounted using a range of values for WACC and the terminal growth rate (g) to give a likely range of values. If you can assign probabilities to each scenario, a weighted average will determine the expected value of the firm.

Even with these steps, the NPV method still has some drawbacks. First, we need betas to calculate the discount rate. A valid comparable company should have similar financial performance, growth prospects, and operating characteristics to the company being valued. A public company with these characteristics may not exist. On a similar note, the target capital structure is often estimated using comparables. Using comparable companies to estimate a target capital structure has much the same drawbacks as finding comparable betas. Third, the typical start-up company cash flow profile of large initial expenditures followed by distant inflows leads to much (or even all) of the value being in the terminal value. Terminal values are very sensitive to assumptions about both discount and terminal growth rates. Finally, recent finance research has raised questions as to whether beta is the proper measure of firm risk. Numerous studies suggest that firm size or the ratio of book-to-market equity values may be more appropriate.[3] Few have tried to implement these suggestions, however, in a practical valuation context.

Another drawback of the NPV method is in the valuation of companies with changing capital structures or effective tax rates. Changing capital structures are often associated with highly leveraged transactions, such as leveraged buyouts. Changing effective tax rates can be due to the consumption of tax credits, such as net operating losses, or the expiration of tax subsidies sometimes granted to fledgling firms. Under the NPV method, the capital structure and effective tax rate are both incorporated in the discount rate (WACC) and assumed to be constant. For this reason the Adjusted Present Value method is recommended in these cases.

Monte Carlo Simulation

When calculating values using spreadsheets, we arrive at a single, or "point," estimate of value. Even when undertaking sensitivity analysis, we simply alter variables one at a time and determine the change in the valuations. Monte Carlo simulation is an improvement over simple sensitivity analysis because it considers all possible combinations of input variables. The user defines probability distributions for each input variable, and the program generates a probability distribution describing the possible outcomes.

One such package is Crystal Ball®.[4] The first step is to set up the base case spreadsheet. We then define the assumption and forecast variables: we will determine the effect of changes in the assumption cells on the value contained in the forecast cell. Assumption cells contain variables such as the discount rate, terminal growth rate, and cash flows, and must contain numerical values, not formulas or text. Probability distributions are used to define the way in which the values in the assumption cells vary. Crystal Ball® has a suite of probability distributions to choose from in describing the behavior of each variable. The user needs to select an appropriate distribution and estimate the key parameters (e.g., mean and standard deviation).

---

[3] For an overview, see Eugene F. Fama and Kenneth R. French, "The Cross-Section of Expected Stock Returns," *Journal of Finance* 47 (1992): 427–465.

[4] Crystal Ball® is a personal computer simulation package produced by Decisioneering, Inc., which is located at 1515 Arapahoe Street, Suite 1311, Denver, CO 80202. Its phone is 800-289-2550 or 303-534-1515; its fax, 303-534-4818; and its address on the World Wide Web, http://www.decisioneering.com.

Assumptions can be defined by highlighting one variable at a time and using the command *Cell Define Assumption*. Similarly, the forecast is defined by highlighting the cell with the valuation calculation and using the command *Cell Define Forecast*. A simulation is then generated using the command *Run Run*. To create a report, use the command *Run Create Report*. A summary of the report for the NPV valuation performed in Appendix 2 is shown in Exhibit 13-2. It shows the probability distribution for the value of the subsidiary, Hi-Tech. The report also indicates that the assumptions were defined as normal distributions with means equal to the values initially contained in the cells and standard deviations set at +10% of the mean.

The availability and simplicity of simulation packages make them a useful tool. Simulation allows a more thorough analysis of the possible outcomes than does regular sensitivity analysis. An additional benefit is that simulation packages allow the user to consider the interrelationships between the different input variables: as the Crystal Ball manual describes, it is easy to define correlations between the various explanatory variables. One must remember, however, that in reality the shapes of distributions, and interrelationships between variables, can be very hard to discover. As sophisticated as the output reports look, the old adage about a model being only as good as the assumptions behind it still applies.

THE ADJUSTED PRESENT VALUE METHOD

The Adjusted Present Value (APV) method is a variation of the NPV method. APV is preferred over the NPV method where a firm's capital structure is changing or it has net operating losses (NOLs) that can be used to offset taxable income. (An example demonstrating the APV method can be found in Appendix 3.)

The NPV method assumes that the capital structure of the firm remains constant at a prespecified target level. This is inappropriate in situations such as leveraged buyouts, where initially the capital structure is highly leveraged, but the level of debt is reduced as repayments are made. In this case, the "target" capital structure changes over time. A way of illustrating this issue is by considering a LBO firm with an ultimate target capital structure of zero: i.e., after a certain period it aims to have paid off all its debt. Under the NPV method, the discount rate (WACC) would be calculated using an all-equity capital structure. This ignores the fact the firm has been levered up. APV overcomes this drawback by considering the cash flows generated by the assets of a company, ignoring its capital structure. The savings from tax-deductible interest payments are then valued separately.

The NPV method also assumes that the firm's effective tax rate, incorporated in the WACC, remains constant. This is inappropriate where a firm's effective tax rate changes over time. For example, it is typical for a start-up company to have incurred NOLs before it attains profitability. Under certain circumstances, these NOLs can be carried forward for tax purposes and netted against taxable income. APV accounts for the effect of the firm's changing tax status by valuing the NOLs separately.

Under APV, the valuation task is divided into three steps. First, the cash flows are valued, ignoring the capital structure. The cash flows of the firm are discounted in the same manner as under the NPV method, except that a different discount rate is used. We essentially assume that the company is financed totally by equity. This implies that the discount rate should be calculated using an unlevered beta, rather than the levered beta used to compute the WACC used in the NPV analysis. The discount rate is calculated using the Capital Asset Pricing Model shown in Equations (5) and (6).

EXHIBIT 13-2

SIMULATION REPORT PRODUCED BY CRYSTAL BALL USING DATA FROM APPENDIX 2

Statistics:	Value
Trials	500
Mean	562
Median	535
Mode	---
Standard Deviation	194
Variance	37485
Skewness	0.89
Kurtosis	4.05
Coeff. of Variability	0.34
Range Minimum	162
Range Maximum	1296
Range Width	1134
Mean Std. Error	8.66

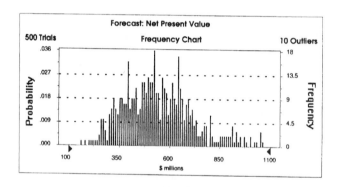

Assumptions

Assumption: WACC

Normal distribution with parameters:
Mean   15.0%
Standard Dev.   1.5%

Assumption: Terminal Growth Rate

Normal distribution with parameters:
Mean   3.0%
Standard Dev.   0.3%

Assumption: Free Cash Flow (Year 1)

Normal distribution with parameters:
Mean   -140
Standard Dev.   14

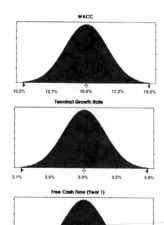
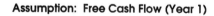

The tax benefits associated with the capital structure are then estimated. The net present value of the tax savings from tax-deductible interest payments have value to a company and must be quantified. The interest payments will change over time as debt levels are increased or reduced. By convention, the discount rate often used to calculate the net present value of the tax benefits is the pre-tax rate of return on debt. This will be lower than the cost of equity. Conceptually this is sensible as the claims of debt holders rank higher than those of ordinary shareholders and therefore are a safer stream of cash flows.

Finally, NOLs available to the company also have value which must be quantified. NOLs can be offset against pre-tax income and often provide a useful source of cash to a company in its initial profitable years of operation. For instance, if a company has $10 million of NOLs and the prevailing tax rate is 40%, the company will have tax savings of $4 million. (Note, however, that this ignores the time value of money. The net present value of the NOLs will only be $4 million if the firm has taxable income of $10 million in its first year. If the NOLs are utilized over more than one year, then discounting will reduce their value to some amount less than $4 million.)

The discount rate used to value NOLs is often the pre-tax rate on debt. If you believe that the realization of tax benefits from the NOLs is certain, (i.e., the firm will definitely generate sufficient profits to consume them), then use the risk-free rate. If, however, there is some risk that the firm will not generate enough profits to use up the NOLs, then discounting them by the pre-tax rate of corporate debt makes sense.

THE VENTURE CAPITAL METHOD

The Venture Capital method is a valuation tool commonly applied in the private equity industry. As discussed, private equity investments are often characterized by negative cash flows and earnings, and highly uncertain but potentially substantial future rewards. The Venture Capital method accounts for this cash flow profile by valuing the company, typically using a multiple, at a time in the future when it is projected to have achieved positive cash flows and/or earnings. This "terminal value" is then discounted back to the present using a high discount rate, typically between 40% and 75%. (The rationales for these very high target rates are discussed below.)

The venture capitalist uses this discounted terminal value and the size of the proposed investment to calculate her desired ownership interest in the company. For example, if the company's discounted terminal value is $10 million, and the venture capitalist intends to make a $5 million investment, she will want 50% of the company in exchange for her investment. This assumes, however, that there will be no dilution of the venture capitalist's interest through future rounds of financing. This is an unrealistic assumption, given that most successful venture-backed companies sell shares to the public through an IPO.

The underlying mechanics of the Venture Capital method are demonstrated by the following four steps. (An example demonstrating the Venture Capital method can be found in Appendix 4.) The method starts by estimating the company's value in some future year of interest, typically shortly after the venture capitalist foresees taking the firm public. The "terminal value" is usually calculated using a multiple: for example, a price-earnings ratio may be multiplied by the projected net income in the exit year. (See the discussion of comparables in Section 1.) The Terminal Value can of course be calculated using other techniques, including discounted cash flow methods.

The Discounted Terminal Value of the company is determined by, not surprisingly, discounting the Terminal Value calculated in the first step. Instead of using a traditional cost of capital as the discount rate, however, venture capitalists typically use a Target Rate of Return. The Target Rate of Return is the yield the venture capitalist feels is required to justify the risk and effort of the particular investment. The formula for calculating the Discounted Terminal Value is shown in Equation (7):

$$\text{Discounted Terminal Value} = \text{Terminal Value}/(1 + \text{Target})^{\text{years}} \tag{7}$$

Third, the venture capitalist calculates the Required Final Percent Ownership. The amount of the proposed investment is divided by the Discounted Terminal Value to determine the ownership necessary for the venture capitalist to earn her desired return (assuming that there is no subsequent dilution of her investment):

$$\text{Required Final Percent Ownership} = \text{Investment}/\text{Discounted Terminal Value} \tag{8}$$

Finally, she estimates future dilution and calculates the required current percent ownership. Equation (8) would be the correct answer if there were to be no subsequent "rounds" of financing to dilute the venture capitalist's interest in the company. As we have seen in the course, venture-backed companies commonly receive multiple rounds of financing, followed by an IPO. Hence, this assumption is usually unrealistic. To compensate for the effect of dilution from future rounds of financing, she needs to calculate the Retention Ratio. The Retention Ratio quantifies the expected dilutive effect of future rounds of financing on the venture capitalist's ownership. Consider a firm that intends to undertake one more financing round, in which shares representing an additional 25% of the firm's equity will be sold, and then to sell shares representing an additional 30% of the firm at the time of the IPO. If the venture capitalist owns 10% today, after these financings her stake will be $10\%/(1+.25)/(1+.3) = 6.15\%$. Her retention ratio is $6.15\%/10\% = 61.5\%$.

The Required Current Percent Ownership necessary for the venture capitalist to realize her Target Rate of Return is then calculated using Equation (9):

$$\text{Required Current Percent Ownership} = \text{Required Final Percent Ownership} / \text{Retention Ratio} \tag{9}$$

Strengths and Weaknesses of the Venture Capital Method

A major criticism of the Venture Capital method is the use of very large discount rates, typically between 40% and 75%. Venture capitalists justify the use of these high target returns on a number of grounds. First, they argue that large discount rates are used to compensate for the illiquidity of private firms. As discussed in Section 1, equity of private companies is usually less marketable than public stock, and investors demand a higher return in exchange for this lack of marketability. Second, venture capitalists view their services as valuable and consider the large discount rate as providing compensation for their efforts. For example, they provide strategic advice, credibility, and access to specialized intermediaries such as lawyers and investment bankers. Finally, venture capitalists believe that projections presented by entrepreneurs tend to be overly optimistic. They submit that the large discount rate compensates for these inflated projections.

Financial economists suggest that although the issues raised by venture capitalists may be valid, they should not be addressed through a high discount rate. They propose that each of the "justifications" should be valued separately using more objective techniques. First, they argue that the discount for lack of marketability makes sense, but that the estimated premium is far too large: there are numerous investors with long-run time horizons, including endowments, foundations, and individuals. Second, financial economists contend that the services provided by the venture capitalist should be valued by determining what that would have to be paid to acquire equivalent professional services on a contract basis. Once the fair market value of the services provided was determined, shares equal to this value could be given to the venture capitalist. Finally, financial economists submit that discount rates should not be inflated to compensate for the entrepreneurs' overly optimistic projections. They argue that judgment should be applied to determine the likely values of various scenarios and the probability that they will occur. This will result in unbiased estimates of the cash flow of the firm.

The use of high discount rates suggests an element of arbitrariness in the venture capitalist's approach to valuing a company. A better process is to scrutinize the projections and perform reality checks. This involves asking a number of questions. What has been the performance of comparable companies? What share of the market does the company need to meet its projections? How long will it take? What are the key risks? Are contingency plans in place? What are the key success factors? This type of analysis is far more meaningful than just taking the entrepreneur's pro formas and discounting them at a very large rate.

OPTIONS ANALYSIS

In some cases, it is appropriate and desirable to use option pricing techniques to value investment opportunities. Discounted cash flow methods such as NPV and APV can be deficient in situations where a manager or investor has "flexibility." Flexibility can take many forms, including the ability to increase or decrease the rate of production, defer development, or abandon a project. These changes all affect the value of the firm in ways that are not accurately measured using discounted cash flow techniques. One form of flexibility that is of particular interest to the venture capitalist is the ability to make "follow-on" investments.

Private equity-backed companies are often characterized by multiple rounds of financing. Venture capitalists use this multi-stage investment approach to motivate the entrepreneur to "earn" future rounds of financing and also to limit the fund's exposure to a particular portfolio company. Often, the first right of refusal for a later stage of financing is written into the investment contract.

The right to make a follow-on investment has many of the same characteristics as a call option on a company's stock. Both comprise the right, but not the obligation, to acquire an asset by paying a sum of money on or before a certain date. As we shall see, this flexibility is not readily accounted for by discounted cash flow techniques. By way of contrast, option pricing theory accounts for the manager's ability to "wait and then decide whether to invest" in the project at a later date.

To illustrate the drawback of using NPV flow methods when pricing options, consider the following simplified example. A project requiring an investment of $150 today is equally likely to generate revenues next year, that—discounted to today's dollars—total $200, $160, or $120. Consequently, the project will have a net present value of $50, $10, or −$30. The expected return is $10 $[= (\frac{1}{3}) * (50 + 10 - 30)]$.

EXHIBIT 13-3   Financial and Firm Option Variables

Variable	Financial Option	Firm Option
X	Exercise price	Present value of the expenditures required to undertake the project
S	Stock price	Present value of the expected cash flows generated by the project
t	Time to expiration	Length of time that the investment decision can be deferred
σ	Standard deviation of returns on the stock	Riskiness of the underlying assets
r_f	Time value of money	Risk-free rate of return

Now consider an investor who has the ability to delay his investment until period 1.[5] By delaying investing until he obtains further information, he can avoid investing when revenues will only be $120. Essentially, by waiting and gathering more information, the investor modifies the expected return profile from [$50, $10, −$30] to [$50, $10, $0]. The option to delay investing is worth $10, the difference between the new expected NPV of $20 [= (1/3) * (50 + 10 + 0)] and the earlier $10 expected value.

This section introduces a developing area in finance. For the purposes of brevity a basic knowledge of option pricing theory (at the level, for instance, of Brealey and Myers) is assumed. Readers are referred to the references at the end of this note for further literature on option pricing techniques.

Valuing Firms as Options

The Black-Scholes model values European options using five variables as inputs. For an option on a stock, these comprise the exercise price (X), the stock price (S), the time to expiration (t), the standard deviation (or volatility) of returns on the stock (σ), and the risk free rate (r_f). Using these variables, we can value the right to buy a share a stock at some future point. We can evaluate a firm's decision to invest in a project using a similar framework. The equivalents are shown in Exhibit 13-3.

Once the input variables have been estimated, the value of the option can be calculated using a Black-Scholes computer model or a call option valuation table.

Reducing Complex Problems to Options Analyses

Real-world decisions can be difficult to reduce to mathematically solvable problems. There is often great value, however, in attempting to simplify these types of problems. For example, the right to abandon the development of a gold mine is similar to a put option. A finance lease gives the lease holder both the right to cancel the lease by paying a fee (a put option), and the right to purchase the asset for a fixed price at the end of the lease (a call option). This note will consider only the solution of call options using the Black-Scholes formula for European options (which can only be exercised at the end of the period).

---

[5] We assume the net present value of the investment in today's dollars is still $150, whether the investment is made in Period 0 or Period 1.

Exhibite 13-3 describes the five inputs necessary to value an investment option by a firm. The approximation of four of the variables (X, S, t, r_f) is fairly intuitive and is illustrated in the example in Appendix 5. The process of estimating the fifth variable, the standard deviation (σ), merits further discussion. One way to estimate the standard deviation is to look at the stock price volatility for businesses with assets comparable to the project or company under consideration. These are, for instance, available on the Bloomberg machine. An important point is that volatilities estimated using this method will require adjustment to take into account the leverage of the comparable company. Remember that leverage amplifies risk, and hence comparable companies with higher leverage than the project under consideration will have higher risk. As a guide, volatilities of 20% to 30% are not unusually high for single companies, and many small technology companies have volatilities of between 40% and 50%.

Strengths and Weaknesses of Using Option Pricing to Value Investment Opportunities

Option pricing theory is useful in situations where there is the "flexibility" to wait, learn more about the prospects of the proposed investment, and then decide whether to invest. As discussed, opportunities that incorporate flexibility will consistently be undervalued using discounted cash flow techniques.

At least three concerns are associated with the use of option pricing methodology. First, it is not well known to many businesspeople, particularly in the private equity community. As with most "new technologies," it may be difficult to convince associates and counterparties that its use is valid. A second drawback of the option pricing methodology is the difficulty of reducing real-world opportunities to simple problems that can be valued. While the models can accommodate cases where the firm pays dividends or where the option can be exercised early, the calculations may be more complex. Option pricing used inappropriately can inflate values achieved using other methods, thereby falsely justifying projects that would otherwise be rejected. Finally, some situations may not be appropriate for the Black-Scholes formula. For instance, the exact pricing of a series of call options that are nested (i.e., where one cannot be exercised before the other one) has a difficult problem. In these cases, it may be best to use simulation techniques.

FOR FURTHER READING

R. BREALEY and S. MYERS, *Principles of Corporate Finance*, New York, McGraw-Hill, 2000.

T. COPELAND and A. ANTIKAROV, *Real Option: A Practitioner's Guide*, New York, Texere, 2001.

T. COPELAND, T. KOLLER, and J. MURRIN, *Valuation: Measuring and Managing the Value of Companies*, New York, John Wiley & Sons, 2000.

European Venture Capital Association, "The EVCA Performance Measurement Guidelines," Zaventum, Belgium, EVCA Venture Capital Special Paper, 1994.

E. FAMA and K. FRENCH, "The Cross-Section of Expected Stock Returns," *Journal of Finance* 47 (1992): 427–465.

S. FENSTER and S. GILSON, "The Adjusted Present Value Method for Capital Assets," Note 9-294-047, Harvard Business School, 1994.

R. HIGGINS, *Analysis for Financial Management*, New York, Irwin, 2000.

S. KAPLAN and R. RUBACK, "The Valuation of Cash Flow Forecasts: An Empirical Analysis," *Journal of Finance*, 51 (1995), 1059–1093.

M. KIM and J. RITTER, "Valuing IPOs," *Journal of Financial Economics* 53(1999): 409–437.

T. LUEHRMAN, "Capital Projects as Real Options: An Introduction," Note 9-295-074, Harvard Business School, 1995.

S. PRATT, *Valuing a Business: The Analysis and Appraisal of Closely Held Companies,* Homewood, IL, Dow Jones-Irwin, 2000.

R. RUBACK, "An Introduction to Capital Cash Flow Methods," Note 9-295-155, Harvard Business School, 1995.

D. SIEGAL, J. SMITH, and J. PADDOCK, "Valuing Offshore Oil Properties with Option Pricing Models," *Quarterly Journal of Economics,* 103 (1988): 473–508.

SAMPLE VALUATION USING COMPARABLES

The 50-year-old chairman and major shareholder of Private Health, a private regional Health Maintenance Organization (HMO), is considering selling his stake in the company and retiring. He has asked Private Health's chief financial officer (CFO) to calculate the value of the firm by the following morning. The two main options that he is entertaining are the sale of his interest to an Employee Share Ownership Plan (ESOP) and to one of the firm's publicly traded competitors. The CFO regularly receives research reports from investment bankers eager to take the company public. From these reports she is able to compare the following information for Private Health and two public HMOs operating in the same region. Data are for the 1995 financial year (amounts in millions of dollars unless indicated):

	Private Health	Happy Healthcare	Community Health
Balance Sheet			
Assets	160	300	380
Long-Term Debt	5	100	0
Net Worth	80	120	175
Income Statement			
Revenues	350	420	850
EBITDA	45	55	130
Net Income	30	20.0	75.0
Market Data			
Earnings per Share ($/share)	3.00	0.67	2.14
Price-Earnings Ratio (times)	n/a	21.0	14.5
Shares Outstanding (m)	10	30	35
Number of Members	500,000	600,000	1,100,000

From the above information, the CFO was able to calculate the following multiples and implied valuations for Private Health:

	Happy Healthcare	Community Health	Average	Private Health Implied Value ($m)
Price-Earnings Ratio	21.0	14.5	17.7	533
Market Value/EBITDA	7.64	8.37	8.00	360
Market Value/Sales	1.00	1.28	1.14	399
Market Value/Book Value of Equity	3.52	6.21	4.86	389
Market Value/Member	700	989	844	422

The CFO felt that on an overall basis the multiples gave a good indication of the value of Private Health but that it was overvalued on a P/E multiple basis. She believed this was because Happy Healthcare (long-term debt to total assets of 33%) was substantially more leveraged than Private Health (3%). Valuing Private Health using Community Health's P/E ratio of 14.5 gave an implied valuation of $435 million. Based on her analysis, she was confident that the value of Private Health was in the range of $360–435 million if sold to a public company. If the shares were sold to an ESOP, she believed that, because of the company's private status, it would be appropriate to assume a discount of 15–20%, or a valuation of $290–360 million.

SAMPLE VALUATION USING THE NET PRESENT VALUE METHOD

Lo-Tech's shareholders have voted to cease its diversification strategy and refocus on its core businesses. As a part of this process, the company is seeking to divest Hi-Tech, its start-up high-technology subsidiary. George, a venture capitalist, has been approached by the management of Hi-Tech, which wants to purchase the company. He decides to value Hi-Tech using the NPV method. George and Hi-Tech management have agreed on the following projections (all data are in millions of dollars):

	Year 1	Year 2	Year 3	Year 4	Year 5	Year 6	Year 7	Year 8	Year 9
Revenues	100	140	210	250	290	380	500	650	900
Costs	230	240	260	275	290	310	350	400	470
EBIT	−130	−100	−50	−25	0	70	150	250	430

The company has $100 million of NOLs that can be carried forward and offset against future income. In addition, Hi-Tech is projected to generate further losses in its early years of operation that it will also be able to carry forward. The tax rate is 40%. The average unlevered beta of five comparable high-technology companies is 1.2. Hi-Tech has no long-term debt. Treasury yields for 10-year bonds are 6.0%. Capital expenditure requirements are assumed to be equal to depreciation. The market risk premium is assumed to be 7.5%. Net working capital requirements are forecast as 10% of sales. EBIT is projected to grow at 3% per year in perpetuity after Year 9.

George first calculated the Weighted Average Cost of Capital (WACC):

$$\text{WACC} = (D/V) * r_d * (1 - \tau) + (E/V) * r_e = 0 + 100\% * [6.0 + 1.2 * (7.5)] = 15\%$$

He then valued the cash flows, which showed the company had a net present value of $525 million. As suspected, all the value of the company was accounted for in the terminal value. (The present value of the cash flows was $(44) million and the present value of the terminal value $569 million, giving a net present value of $525 million.)

The terminal value was calculated as follows:

$$\text{TV}_T = [\text{CF}_T * (1 + g)]/(r - g) = [233 * (1 + 3\%)]/(15\% - 3\%) = \$2,000$$

George also performed a scenario analysis to determine the sensitivity of the value of Hi-Tech to changes in the discount rate and the terminal growth rate. He developed a scenario table[6] shown in the attached spreadsheet.

George's scenario analysis gave a series of values ranging from $323 million to $876 million. Clearly, this large range did not provide precise guidance as to Hi-Tech's actual value. He noted that the cash flow profile of negative early cash flows followed by distant positive cash flows made the valuation very sensitive to both the discount rate and the terminal growth rate. George considered the NPV method a first step in the valuation process and planned to use other methods to narrow the range of possible values for Hi-Tech.

[6]Sensitivity analyses can be easily undertaken using the Microsoft Excel command *Data Table*.

(Continued)

WACC Calculation	
Tax Rate	40%
Rm–Rf	7.5%
EN	100%
Bu	1.2
10 Year Treasury Bond	6.0%
WACC	15.0%

Cash Flows	
Terminal Growth Rate	3.0%

Year	0	1	2	3	4	5	6	7	8	9
Revenues		100	140	210	250	290	380	500	650	900
Less: Costs		230	240	260	275	290	310	350	400	470
EBIT		−130	−100	−50	−25	0	70	150	250	430
Less: Tax		0	0	0	0	0	0	0	26	172
EBIAT		−130	−100	−50	−25	0	70	150	224	258
Less: Ch. NWC		10	4	7	4	4	9	12	15	25
Free Cash Flow		−140	−104	−57	−29	−4	61	138	209	233
Discount Factor		0.870	0.756	0.658	0.572	0.497	0.432	0.376	0.327	0.284
PV (Cash Flow)		−122	−79	−37	−17	−2	26	52	68	66

PV (Cash Flows)   (44)

Terminal Value   2000

PV (Terminal Value)   569

Net Present Value and
Sensitivity Analysis

PV (Cash Flows)	(44)
PV (Terminal Value)	569
Net Present Value	525

		WACC		
		13%	15%	17%
Terminal	2%	699	476	323
Growth	3%	778	525	355
Rate	4%	876	583	391

Tax Calculation									
EBIT	−130	−100	−50	−25	0	70	150	250	430
NOLs Used	0	0	0	0	0	70	150	185	0
NOLs Added	130	100	50	25	0	0	0	0	0
Tax	0	0	0	0	0	0	0	26	172
Beginning NOLs	100	230	330	380	405	405	335	185	0
Ending NOLs	230	330	380	405	405	335	185	0	0

Net Working Capital (10% sales)									
Beg NWC		10	14	21	25	29	38	50	65
End NWC	10	14	21	25	29	38	50	65	90
Ch. NWC	10	4	7	4	4	9	12	15	25

SAMPLE VALUATION USING THE ADJUSTED PRESENT VALUE METHOD

Vulture Partners, a private equity organization specializing in distressed company investing, was interested in purchasing Turnaround. Mr. Fang, a general partner at Vulture, used the following projections to value Turnaround (all data are in millions of dollars):

	Year 1	Year 2	Year 3	Year 4	Year 5
Revenues	200	210	220	230	240
Costs	100	105	110	115	120
EBIT	100	105	110	115	120
ΔNWC	3	3	4	4	5

Turnaround had $220 million of NOLs which were available to be offset against future income. At the beginning of Year 1, the company had $75 million of 8% debt, which was expected to be repaid in three $25 million installments beginning at the end of Year 1. The tax rate was 40%. Mr. Fang believed an appropriate unlevered beta for Turnaround was 0.8. The 10-year Treasury Bond yield was 7.0%, and the market risk premium 7.5%. Net cash flows were forecast to grow at 3% per year in perpetuity after Year 5. Mr. Fang performed the following steps.

Mr. Fang employed the APV method to value Turnaround and, as such, used the cost of equity as the discount rate:

$$\text{Cost of Equity} = r_f + b_u * (r_m - r_f) = 7.0 + 0.8 * (7.5) = 13.0\%$$

Cash flows and the terminal value were both calculated in the same manner as under the NPV method. Mr. Fang arrived at a terminal value of $690 million using the perpetuity method (assuming a growth rate of 3% per annum).

Mr. Fang then calculated the interest tax shields by multiplying the interest expense for each period by the tax rate of 40%. The interest expense was calculated using the debt repayment schedule. The present value of the interest tax shields, equal to $4.2 million, was determined by discounting each year's interest tax shield at the pretax cost of debt.

To value the tax shields from the NOLs, Mr. Fang first determined the taxable earnings for each period and hence the rate at which the NOLs would be utilized. By subtracting the interest expense on debt from taxable earnings (EBIT), he determined the amount of NOLs that would be used each period. The NOL tax shields were then calculated by multiplying the NOLs consumed each period by the tax rate. Mr. Fang discounted the NOL tax shields at the pretax cost of debt. The present value of the NOLs was equal to $77 million.

The sensitivity analysis showed the likely valuation range for Turnaround to be on the order of $650 to $750 million. The range of values indicated that the valuation was reasonably sensitive to both the discount and terminal growth rate assumptions.

(Continued)

Discount Rate Calculation			
Tax Rate	40%	Rm–Rf	7.5%
10-Year Treasury Bond	7.0%	Bu	0.8
Discount Rate (Unlevered)	13.00%		

Step 1: Value Cash Flows

Terminal Growth Rate 3.00%

Year	0	1	2	3	4	5
Revenues		200	210	220	230	240
Less: Costs		100	105	110	115	120
EBIT		100	105	110	115	120
Less: Tax		40	42	44	46	48
EBIAT		60	63	66	69	72
Less: Ch. NWC		3	3	4	4	5
Net Cash Flow		57	60	62	65	67
Discount Factor		0.885	0.783	0.693	0.613	0.543
PV (Cash Flow)		50	47	43	40	36
PV (Cash Flows)	217					
Terminal Value						690
PV (Terminal Value)						375

Step 2: Value Interest Tax Shields

		1	2	3	4	5
Beginning Debt		75	50	25	0	0
Repayment (End of Year)		25	25	25	0	0
Ending Debt		50	25	0	0	0
Interest Expense		6.0	4.0	2.0	0.0	0.0
Interest Tax Shield		2.4	1.6	0.8	0.0	0.0
Discount Factor	8.00%	0.926	0.857	0.794	0.735	0.681
Present Value		2.2	1.4	0.6	0.0	0.0
Net Present Value	4.2					

Step 3: Value NOLs

		1	2	3	4	5
EBIT		100	105	110	115	120
Interest Expense		6.0	4.0	2.0	0.0	0.0
EBIT less Interest Expense		94	101	108	115	120
NOLs Used		94	101	25	0	0
Beginning NOLs		220	126	25	0	0
Ending NOLs		126	25	0	0	0
NOLs Used		94	101	25	0	0
NOL Tax Shield		38	40	10	0	0
Discount Factor	8.00%	0.926	0.857	0.794	0.735	0.681
Present Value (NOL)		35	35	8	0	0
Net Present Value (NOLs)	77					

Step 4: NPV and Sensitivity Analysis

PV (Cash Flows)	217
PV (Terminal Value)	375
PV (Tax Shields)	4
PV (NOLs)	77
Net Present Value	673

		WACC		
		12.0%	13.0%	14.0%
Terminal	2%	692	635	589
Growth	3%	739	673	619
Rate	4%	798	718	655

SAMPLE VALUATION USING THE VENTURE CAPITAL METHOD

James is a partner in a very successful Boston-based venture capital firm. He plans to invest $5 million in a start-up biotechnology venture and must decide what share of the company he should demand for his investment. Projections he developed with company management show net income in year 7 of $20 million. The few profitable biotechnology companies are trading at an average price-earnings ratio of 15. The company currently has 500,000 shares outstanding. James believes that a target rate of return of 50% is required for a venture of this risk. He performs the following calculations:

$$\text{Discounted Terminal Value} = \text{Terminal Value}/(1 + \text{Target})^{\text{years}} = (20 * 15)/(1 + 50\%)^7 = \$17.5 \text{ million}$$

$$\text{Required Percent Ownership} = \text{Investment/Discounted Terminal Value} = 5/17.5 = 28.5\%$$

$$\text{Number of New Shares} = 500{,}000/(1 - 28.5\%) - 500{,}000 = 200{,}000$$

$$\text{Price per New Share} = \$5 \text{ million}/200{,}000 \text{ shares} = \$25 \text{ per share}$$

$$\text{Implied Pre-money Valuation} = 500{,}000 \text{ shares} * \$25 \text{ per share} = \$12.5 \text{ million}$$

$$\text{Implied Post-money Valuation} = 700{,}000 \text{ shares} * \$25 \text{ per share} = \$17.5 \text{ million}$$

James and his partners believe that three more senior staff will need to be hired. In James's experience, this number of top caliber recruits would require options amounting to 10% of the common stock outstanding. In addition, he believes that, at the time the firm goes public, additional shares equivalent to 30% of the common stock will be sold to the public. He amends his calculations as follows:

$$\text{Retention Ratio} = [1/(1 + .1)]/(1 + .3) = 70\%$$

$$\text{Required Current Percent Ownership} = \text{Required Final Percent Ownership/Retention Ratio} = 28.5\%/70\% = 40.7\%$$

$$\text{Number of New Shares} = 500{,}000/(1 - 40.7\%) - 500{,}000 = 343{,}373$$

$$\text{Price per New Share} = \$5 \text{ million}/343{,}373 \text{ shares} = \$14.56 \text{ per share}$$

SAMPLE VALUATION USING OPTION PRICING

Sharon Rock, a famous venture capitalist, was considering whether to invest in Think-Tank, Inc., a company owned and managed by Mr. Brain. ThinkTank had developed a new product that was ready to be manufactured and marketed. An expenditure of $120 million was required for the construction of research and manufacturing facilities. Rock was of the opinion that the following projections developed by Mr. Brain and his associates were justifiable (all data are in millions of dollars):

	Year 0	Year 1	Year 2	Year 3	Year 4	Year 5
Cash Flow except CapEx	0.0	0.0	0.0	10.0	25.0	50.0
Capital Expenditures	−120.0	0.0	0.0	0.0	0.0	0.0
Total Cash Flow	−120.0	0.0	0.0	10.0	25.0	50.0

Rock performed a NPV valuation using a discount rate (WACC) of 25% and a terminal growth rate of 3%. She was unimpressed with the resulting valuation of −$11.55 million.

After thinking more carefully, Rock realized that the investment could be divided into two stages. The initial investment, which would need to be made immediately, would be $20 million for R&D equipment and personnel. The $100 million expenditure on the plant could be undertaken any time in the first two years. (Whenever the project would be undertaken, the present value of the plant construction expenditures would total $100 million in today's dollars.) Rock decided that the option to expand should not be valued using discounted cash flow methods, for she would only pursue the opportunity if the first stage of the project were successful. The expansion opportunity could more validly be considered as an initial $20 investment bundled with a two-year European call option and priced using the Black-Scholes model.

The easiest variables to estimate were the time to expiration (t) and the risk-free rate (r_f), being 2 years and 7%, respectively. The "exercise price" (X) was equal to the present value of the investment to build the plant, or $100 million. The "stock price" (S) was estimated by discounting the expected cash flows to be generated by the underlying assets associated with the expansion opportunity. Using a discount rate of 25% and a terminal growth rate of 3% per year, S was calculated as worth $108.45 million in Year 0. The only Black-Scholes input variable remaining to be calculated was the standard deviation (σ). Rock found this difficult to estimate but proceeded to look at some comparable companies. She estimated that the value of σ, was likely to lie in the range of 0.5 to 0.6.

Using this data, Rock then calculated the Black-Scholes European call option to be worth between $38.8 and $43.7 million. The total net present value of the project, equal to the cost of the first-stage investment and the value of the call option (the stage 2 opportunity), was therefore between $18.8 and $23.7 million [= −$20 million + $38.8 to $43.7 million].

Based on this analysis, Sharon Rock decided to invest in ThinkTank on the provision that she would be granted first right of refusal on any subsequent rounds of financing.

14

A Note on European Private Equity

INTRODUCTION

About 35 billion Euros[1] were invested by European private equity funds in companies during 2000, making Europe the second most developed private equity market after the United States (see Exhibit 14-1). But important differences remain between the various European nations. The largest and most developed private equity market in Europe is the United Kingdom, followed by fast-growing Germany and then France (Exhibit 14-2).

Until very recently, over 90% of European private equity funds were devoted to buyouts or other later-stage investments. Although the term *venture capital* in Europe is synonymous with private equity, true venture capital (i.e., early-stage investments) did not come into its own until the late 1990s. While the venture capital industry seems to have substantial opportunities for growth, some observers argue that the buyout market may in fact be *too* developed in some European countries and that a dramatic fall in fundraising and investments is likely.

This note will discuss the trends in European private equity through mid-2000, comparing private equity in Europe with the U.S. industry wherever possible.[2] It will also highlight differences among the European countries. It focuses entirely on West-

This note was prepared by Reynir Indahl (MBA '98) and Eric Zinterhofer (MBA '98), under the supervision of Professor Josh Lerner as the basis for class discussion rather than to illustrate either effective or ineffective handling of an administrative situation.

[1] This case presents all tabulations in Euros (and its predecessor, the ECU, or European Currency Unit). During 1999, one Euro equaled on average U.S. $1.06. The tabulations do not include investments in Europe by American private equity funds, which the European Venture Capital Association (EVCA) estimates totaled approximately 1.5 billion Euros in 1999.

[2] Unless otherwise noted, the analysis is based on numerous interviews with European and American private equity professionals, as well as an analysis of the database of the Centre for Management Buyout Research (CMBOR) at the University of Nottingham and the publications of the European Venture Capital Association and Initiative Europe.

EXHIBIT 14-1

TOTAL PRIVATE EQUITY INVESTMENT (BILLIONS OF ECUS OR EUROS)

	Venture Capital	Buyouts and Other Private Equity	Total
1984	0.15	0.36	0.51
1985	0.35	1.02	1.37
1986	0.33	1.07	1.40
1987	0.34	2.50	2.84
1988	0.43	3.02	3.45
1989	0.42	3.85	4.27
1990	0.35	3.77	4.12
1991	0.32	4.31	4.63
1992	0.28	4.42	4.70
1993	0.20	3.92	4.12
1994	0.31	5.13	5.44
1995	0.32	5.23	5.55
1996	0.44	6.35	6.79
1997	0.71	8.94	9.65
1998	1.62	12.84	14.46
1999	3.24	21.87	25.11
2000	6.64	28.33	34.47

Source: European Venture Capital Association, *EVCA Yearbook*, Zaventum, Belgium, EVCA, 2000 and earlier years, and http://www.evca.com.

ern Europe and does not consider the emerging private equity industries in such nations as Poland and Russia.[3]

PRIVATE EQUITY FUNDS IN EUROPE

European private equity has gone through cycles similar to those in the United States. A boom in the late 1980s was followed by a bust in the early 1990s. The late 1990s saw an extraordinary recovery. Fundraising—fueled by the increasing interest in Europe by U.S. institutional investors—far surpassed earlier levels (Exhibit 14-3). This increase in fundraising was due largely to the strong returns that the European funds have delivered to investors—the returns from all European private equity funds have averaged 24.9% over the past few years—as well as concerns about the degree of competition in the U.S. market.[4] The late 1990s were years of strong growth in the volume of deals as well, with the activity in many markets exceeding the levels of the late 1980s.

---

[3] These countries, among others, are discussed in Chapter 27 in this volume.

[4] Venture Economics, *Investment Benchmark Reports: International Private Equity*, Newark, NJ, Venture Economics, 2000.

EXHIBIT 14-2

**PRIVATE EQUITY INVESTMENT BY COUNTRY
(MILLIONS OF ECUS OR EUROS)**

	Venture Capital	Buyouts and Other Private Equity	Total
1995			
Austria	0	1	1
Belgium	6	105	111
Denmark	3	27	31
Finland	8	26	34
France	27	824	851
Germany	89	577	666
Greece	3	5	8
Ireland	1	18	19
Italy	45	209	253
Netherlands	76	391	467
Norway	5	115	120
Portugal	4	51	55
Spain	18	145	163
Sweden	6	79	86
Switzerland	1	48	48
United Kingdom	28	2,605	2,633
Total[a]	320	5,226	5,546
1999			
Austria	14	75	89
Belgium	211	462	673
Denmark	31	85	116
Finland	68	181	249
France	519	2,298	2,817
Germany	1,001	2,158	3,159
Greece	20	51	71
Ireland	41	64	105
Italy	147	1,632	1,779
Netherlands	342	1,368	1,710
Norway	30	235	265
Portugal	8	111	119
Spain	93	630	723
Sweden	241	1,036	1,277
Switzerland	203	237	440
United Kingdom	255	11,246	11,501
Total[a]	3,214	21,869	26,083

[a] Total may not equal sum of items due to rounding, or because very small countries are included in the total but not tabulated separately.

Source: European Venture Capital Association, *EVCA Yearbook*, Zaventum, Belgium, EVCA, 2000 and earlier years.

We will first consider the patterns in buyouts. Although the aggregate trends may be similar to those in the United States, many striking differences exist between the individual European countries and the United States. The United Kingdom had almost the same level of investment in 1999 than the United States, compared on a per capita basis, while most Continental European markets had far less (Exhibit 14-4). (Similar

---

EXHIBIT 14-3

TOTAL PRIVATE EQUITY FUNDRAISING (BILLIONS OF ECUS OR EUROS)

1986	1.88
1987	2.95
1988	3.48
1989	5.11
1990	4.58
1991	4.19
1992	4.21
1993	3.43
1994	6.69
1995	4.40
1996	7.96
1997	20.00
1998	20.34
1999	25.40
2000	48.02

Source: European Venture Capital Association, *EVCA Yearbook*, Zaventum, Belgium, EVCA, 2000 and earlier years, http://www.evca.com.

---

patterns appear in the size of the public market relative to GDP.) These differences, however, may be declining with time. In particular, Germany has experienced rapid growth. Furthermore, the level of private equity in the United Kingdom may be above a sustainable level and may fall in coming years: the dramatic increase of capital under management and the emergence of high-yield debt issues have led to a setting where there is highly competitive bidding for deals.

Historically, European buyout funds grew out of financial institutions, although many of these have lately gone through management buyouts themselves and become independent. Some of the largest and most prestigious independent European funds are offshoots from financial institutions, including Doughty Hanson (Charterhouse and Westdeutsche Landesbank), BC Partners (Barings), Industri Kapital (Skandinaviska Enskilda Banken), and Cinven (the Government Coal Board Pension Fund). Other top-tier funds are still operated as subsidiaries, including Charterhouse and DMG Capital. The United Kingdom was the cradle of European private equity, and most of the top-tier players are of British origin. The industry's capital is increasingly concentrated among a few organizations: the top 15 firms increased their share of the funds raised from 43% in 1995 to 83% in 1996–1997.

Germany surpassed France as the largest Continental private equity market in 1996. The driver behind this growth has been the new focus on shareholder value that has forced companies to spin-off companies as a part of their restructuring and refocusing efforts. Another reason for the German growth has been the increasing frequency of

EXHIBIT 14-4

PRIVATE EQUITY INVESTMENT PER CAPITA, 1999 (ECUS OR EUROS)

	Venture Capital	Buyouts and Other Private Equity
Austria	1.71	9.17
Belgium	20.79	45.52
Denmark	5.83	15.98
Finland	13.15	35.01
France	8.78	38.88
Germany	12.19	26.29
Greece	1.88	4.80
Ireland	10.93	17.07
Italy	2.56	28.46
Netherlands	21.63	86.53
Norway	6.77	53.05
Portugal	0.80	11.14
Spain	2.36	15.98
Sweden	27.20	116.93
Switzerland	28.47	33.24
United Kingdom	4.34	191.45
All Europe	8.39	56.64
United States[a]	120.51	204.17

[a] The U.S. calculation uses fundraising data rather than investment figures. In some cases, the capital may have been invested in another country.

Source: European Venture Capital Association, *EVCA Yearbook*, Zaventum, Belgium, EVCA, 2000; and International Monetary Fund, *International Financial Statistics*, Washington, DC, International Monetary Fund, 2000).

succession issues among the Mittelstand companies. (The Mittelstand companies are small- to medium-sized family business, many of which were started after the Second World War.) These perceived opportunities have led to widespread optimism among German buyout organizations and to the entry of numerous new groups.

France and Italy have been more erratic markets. The uneven nature of these markets has been attributed to the lackluster performance of some high-profile deals in the 1990s, as well as the difficult regulatory environment of these countries, especially in France. Probably the most developed buyout industries outside the United Kingdom are the Dutch and Swiss markets. In both cases, the presence of a strong private pension system has facilitated the raising of funds from local sources. Among the Nordic countries, Sweden has been the only country with a steady transaction flow, although lately Finland has experienced a surge in activity. Denmark and Norway have been more erratic with a limited stream of deals, which is attributed to the many small- to medium-sized family companies and difficult ownership rules of these countries.

A majority of the new entrants on the Continent are United Kingdom-based private equity organizations, along with some American firms. It remains unclear how successful these new entrants will be. Deals are more challenging on the Continent than in the United Kingdom or the United States. Accounting standards, government regulations, and union contracts inhibit due diligence and limit the ability to turn around underperforming businesses. Management culture has been another obstacle. While financial incentives commonly work well in the United Kingdom and the United States, these are less emphasized on the Continent, especially in Germany: numerous observers suggest that German managers put a higher priority on community standing and cooperation at the workplace. Hence, some buyout firms have found it challenging to identify managerial talent who can lead their new acquisitions and make the difficult operational improvements needed. This reluctance, however, appears to be rapidly easing.

On the venture capital side, similar changes have occurred on a much more accelerated time frame. As Exhibit 14-1 makes clear, in its earliest years, the European private equity industry had a significant representation of venture capital investments. Over time, however, the venture capital portion dwindled dramatically. The shrinking representation of venture capital investments reflected their poor performance. Between 1980 and 1994, for instance, the average mature large buyout fund in Great Britain boasted a net return of 23.1%, and the average mid-sized buyout fund had a return of 14.7%. Meanwhile, the typical venture fund had a net return of 4.0% over the same period.[5] As a result, most venture capital specialists were unable to raise new funds, and generalist investors (such as Apax and 3i) shifted to an emphasis on buyouts.

This situation began reversing itself around 1997. The shifting attitudes were in part triggered by American venture groups, particularly East Coast-based organizations such as General Atlantic and Warburg Pincus. Attracted by the modest valuations of European technology and biotechnology start-ups relative to their European counterparts, general partners began increasingly traveling to Europe to invest in portfolio companies. This trend accelerated at the end of the decade, as American groups such as Benchmark and Draper Fisher Jurvetson began targeting large amounts of capital (sometimes in dedicated funds) for European venture investments. The trend was also helped by the superior performance of venture investments in the last years of the decade. In fact, by the end of 1999, the 10-year performance of venture capital funds (17.2%) was almost indistinguishable from that of buyout ones (17.5%).[6] (Generalist funds performed significantly more poorly, with 9.5% rate of return over this period.)

Meanwhile, European-based funds also became more active. The increase in activity was manifested in three ways. First, groups that had been active for a number of years, such as Atlas Ventures, were able to raise significantly larger amounts of funds. Second, new entrants—in many cases modeled after American groups—became increasingly active. (Examples include Amadeus in the United Kingdom and Early Bird in Germany.) Finally, generalist funds increased their allocation to venture capital again: for instance, over the late 1990s, 3i moved from a 15% allocation to technology investments to a 40% share.

---

[5] See "European Performance Surveyed—A Tentative First Step," *European Venture Capital Journal* (December 1996): 3–6.

[6] Venture Economics, *Investment Benchmark Reports: International Private Equity*, Newark, NJ, Venture Economics, 2000.

THE EUROPEAN PRIVATE EQUITY CYCLE

Fundraising

The key sources for European private equity funds have traditionally been segmented by national boundaries. Private equity groups would raise funds from banks, insurance companies, and government bodies in their own country, with little involvement of other investors. The one exception was the United Kingdom, where fundraising has had a strong international flavor—with a heavy involvement of U.S. institutional investors—since the earliest days of the industry.

These barriers are now breaking down, as Exhibit 14-5 reports. The changes are being driven by two factors. First, institutional investors—particularly in the United States—are becoming increasingly interested in European funds. Second, many international private equity firms are becoming much more active in Europe. American firms such as Chase Capital Partners, Kohlberg, Kravis, and Roberts (KKR), and Texas Pacific Group (on the buyout side), Benchmark, Draper Fisher Jurvetson, and General Atlantic (on the venture side), and Carlyle (on both the venture and buyout fronts) have entered Europe in one way or another in recent years.

A consequence of these changes is the increasing presence of investment advisors, sometimes called gatekeepers. (These are firms that advise investors, primarily large institutions, about their private equity investments or directly manage their holdings.) In the United States, this is a very well-developed market: firms such as Abbott Capital, Brinson Partners, and Cambridge Associates have built strong franchises assisting pen-

---

EXHIBIT 14-5

GEOGRAPHIC SOURCES OF NEW PRIVATE EQUITY

	Same Country	Other European Country	Outside Europe
1985	92.0%	2.7%	5.3%
1986	91.9	3.8	4.3
1987	77.1	9.0	13.9
1988	79.8	11.1	9.1
1989	67.6	8.0	24.4
1990	71.0	14.0	15.0
1991	77.0	13.0	10.0
1992	83.5	7.7	8.8
1993	81.1	7.2	11.7
1994	73.1	7.0	19.9
1995	77.2	11.6	11.2
1996	71.8	11.4	16.8
1997	49.2	17.3	33.5
1998	52.1	16.8	31.1
1999	57.1	21.3	21.6

Source: European Venture Capital Association, *EVCA Yearbook*, Zaventum, Belgium, EVCA, 2000 and earlier years.

sion funds and endowments with private equity investments. Gatekeepers and advisors in Europe have been few, reflecting both the immature nature of the private equity market and the lack of large institutional investors with an appetite for private equity. Several of the large U.S. private equity advisors and gatekeepers are currently entering Europe, attracted by pension reforms in Europe as well as an increasing allocation to European private equity by European and American institutional investors. Local advisors are also gaining an increasing following.

One challenge to institutional investors in selecting investments is that there appears to be less strategic differentiation between European private equity firms than between those in the United States. In the United States, private equity players have increasingly focused on developing a niche or a specialty, while in Europe the niches are just emerging. For instance, Doughty Hanson, dubbed the KKR of Europe, has achieved considerable success by undertaking large transactions with a heavy reliance on financial engineering and little operating involvement.

Investing

Competition for buyout transactions is intense in Europe, especially in the United Kingdom. According to the Centre for Management Buyout Research at the University of Nottingham, private equity firms in recent years have been involved in nearly 60% of all mergers and acquisition activity in the United Kingdom, far above the 15% to 20% range seen in the United States. Most of the deals in the United Kingdom are initiated through auctions. Investment banks have made the United Kingdom auction process very efficient: there is little opportunity to buy firms for below their market value. On the Continent, the process is less efficient. For instance, in Germany and France, personal relationships with lawyers and accountants are important sources of deals for private equity investors. But increasingly, large Continental firms are being sold to private equity groups through auctions as well.

The companies that are purchased by European private equity funds are primarily subsidiaries of conglomerates or family businesses. Unlike the United States, buyouts of public companies are rare. One reason for this is the stringent corporate control rules in some countries: for instance, in France, interest expense of debt can only be deducted if 95% or more of the equity is acquired, which is difficult to accomplish in the case of a public firm with widely scattered holdings.

In the early years of the European private equity industry, a management buyout (MBO) transaction was typical. A typical buyout was initiated by the existing management team. The managers would negotiate with the parent, hire an intermediary to represent them, and find a buyout firm that would provide the equity. Accounting firms were until recently the intermediary of choice to either auction or "shop around" a firm. During the 1990s, the leading investment banks entered the auction market, and the role of the accountants was reduced to due diligence work. (They continue to play a role in the auctioning of smaller deals.) On the Continent, lawyers and accounting firms appear to continue to manage more deals than investment banks.

Although many American private equity groups seek to initiate and control transactions themselves, U.K. buyout firms have often been described as "process integrators." For example, buyout firms involve investment banks, accounting firms, and lawyers to support them in preparing the bid, assembling the capital structure, and undertaking the due diligence. A management consulting firm is then involved to improve firm operations post-acquisition. A strong tie to intermediaries may be an important competitive advantage in Europe: Doughty Hanson is reported to have gotten a significant part of their deal-flow through PriceWaterhouseCoopers in Germany.

As a result of this environment, buyout firms often find it difficult to identify proprietary deal-flow, that is, transactions that are reviewed by only one private equity group. Until recently, this was not too troubling for the major private equity groups, for most investments were syndicated by a number of these groups. (The lead investor would collect a fee from the other participants and could be confident that the other investors would reciprocate in subsequent transactions.) As the size of private equity funds has increased, relationships have become less collegial, and syndication has grown less frequent.[7]

These changes have had three consequences. First, private equity organizations have become much more aggressive in initiating transactions. There has been an increase in management buy-ins (MBI) and investor buyouts (IBOs), where an outside management team or a private equity firm initiates the deal, and the existing management team may or may not play a role. Second, the reliance on intermediaries for the identification and management of transactions appears to be declining. Alchemy, Industri Kapital, and CVC, among others, are reported to rely more on internal resources than on outsourcing. Finally, larger buyouts have become more common. It is increasingly common to see pan-European deals, which are often financed at least in part with high-yield debt.

Substantial differences also appear between the way venture capital investment is undertaken in the United States and Europe, though these are gradually diminishing. Many European venture capitalists have traditionally had financial or consulting backgrounds rather than operating experience. Perhaps as a result, the relationships between venture capitalists and portfolio companies have tended to be much more distant, with a greater emphasis on an assessment of financial performance than on "hands-on" scrutiny.[8]

Another difference relates to the geographic distribution of investments. As in buyout investing, there has been a strong tendency to invest in the same country as the fund is located. The reluctance to co-invest reflects both the legacy of legal and regulatory barriers to such transnational investments (now greatly reduced) and the very distinct business cultures that characterize many European nations. As Exhibit 14-6 reports, although this pattern is gradually changing, localization of investment remains an important part of the landscape.

A third difference is the size of transactions. Although the past few years have seen a dramatic increase in the size of a typical venture capital transaction in the United States, European investors have not followed suit. For instance, in 1999, the typical seed or early-stage transaction in Europe was only about one-tenth the size of the average venture capital financing in the United States.[9] The result, some observers claim, is that European start-ups find it challenging to compete in the many "winner-take-all" competitions that characterize many segments of high technology.

---

[7] Similar behavior is seen in many other economic settings. For an overview, see Jean Tirole, *The Theory of Industrial Organization*, Cambridge, MA, MIT Press, 1989, chapter 6.

[8] See, for instance, the case studies presented in Gavin Reid, *Venture Capital Investment: An Agency Analysis of Practice*, London, Routledge, 1998.

[9] This comparison is based on European Venture Capital Association, *EVCA Yearbook*, Zaventum, Belgium, European Venture Capital Association, 2000, and National Venture Capital Association, *National Venture Capital Association Yearbook*, Newark, NJ, Venture Economics, 2000. The U.S. tabulation excluded buyouts funded by venture capital organizations.

EXHIBIT 14-6

GEOGRAPHIC DISTRIBUTION OF PRIVATE EQUITY INVESTMENT

	Same Country	Other European Country	Outside Europe
1987	89.7%	3.0%	7.3%
1988	92.3	4.3	3.4
1989	87.9	8.9	3.2
1990	86.6	10.8	2.6
1991	90.6	6.5	2.9
1992	89.0	7.9	3.1
1993	89.4	7.3	3.3
1994	86.5	11.3	2.2
1995	87.9	9.3	2.8
1996	83.7	12.5	3.8
1997	80.5	17.0	2.5
1998	76.8	16.8	6.4
1999	77.3	17.7	5.0

Source: European Venture Capital Association, *EVCA Yearbook*, Zaventum, Belgium, EVCA, 2000 and earlier years.

Exiting

A sale to a corporate acquirer—also known as a trade sale—is the most common form of exit, both in the United Kingdom and on the Continent. The United Kingdom has an advantage over the other European countries in terms of exit, since it has a well-developed capital market. Even when a private equity group sells a company to a corporate acquirer, having the option to take the firm public helps ensure an attractive sale price.

The lack of a developed capital market on the Continent has been a particular challenge to smaller, venture-backed companies. Over the past two decades, a variety of efforts have been made to create liquid markets for venture-backed firms in Europe. In the early 1980s, many European nations pushed to develop secondary markets. These markets were designed to be more hospitable to smaller firms than the primary exchanges in these countries, which often had rigorous listing requirements (e.g., high levels of capitalization or extended records of profitability were required). At the same time, they sought to retain many of the regulatory safeguards for investors that were found in the major exchanges. (In addition, a number of countries had lightly regulated third-tier markets.) The secondary markets allowed venture capitalists to successfully unwind their positions. Their success, in turn, generated new investments in venture capital.

After the October 1987 decline in world equity prices, IPO activity in Europe dried up, as it did in the United States.[10] But unlike the United States, which recovered with

---

[10] This paragraph is drawn from Graham Bannock and Partners, *European Second-Tier Markets for NTBFs*, London, Graham Bannock and Partners, 1994.

a "hot" IPO market in 1991, in Europe there was not a rapid recovery. In 1992–1993, there were 432 IPOs on the NASDAQ; on European secondary markets (with 30% of the number of listed firms), there were only 31. In some countries, the decline in IPO activity was even more extreme: only five companies listed in Germany's two secondary stock markets in 1992–1993; none listed in Denmark's between 1989 and 1993. Consequently, European private equity investors found IPOs of firms in their portfolios to be much more difficult to arrange and were more likely to exit firms through the sale of firms to third parties. Trading volume in European markets for small-capitalization firms had also lagged. The ratio of total transaction volume to end-of-year market capitalization was 21% in European secondary markets in 1992; for the NASDAQ, the corresponding ratio was 138%.

One response to these problems was the EASDAQ market. The European Venture Capital Association developed the concept of a new pan-European public market for growing companies with international operations after observing the difficulties in other exchanges. EASDAQ had been designed after the liquid and generally efficient NASDAQ market in the United States, and began operations in 1996. EASDAQ hoped to become an effective financing route for those companies that could not afford or simply wanted to avoid their nation's primary markets.

The success of EASDAQ, however, was relatively limited. Only a modest number of firms had listed on the new exchange. In many of these cases, the firms cross-listed on NASDAQ or another established exchange. In almost all cases, the bulk of the trading took place elsewhere, where transaction costs were considerably lower. In addition, EASDAQ soon attracted competition for a variety of sources. Many national exchanges reestablished or upgraded their second-tier markets. In March 2001, NASDAQ acquired EASDAQ and renamed it NASDAQ Europe.

The most successful of these challengers was EuroNM, a coalition of five new equity markets. In 1999, the number of technology firms listed on that exchange doubled, and their capitalization grew to 35 billion Euros. The most successful of these new markets was the Neuer Markt, the German small-capitalization exchange. One aspect of this exchange that many believe contributed to its success was its strict disclosure and listing standards, which equaled or exceeded those seen in the NASDAQ market. This contrasted sharply with the British small-capitalization Alternative Investment Market and many other European second-tier markets, which have had modest disclosure standards.

ISSUES FACING EUROPEAN PRIVATE EQUITY INDUSTRY

Many challenges face the European private equity industry today. This final section highlights two of these concerns. These are likely to continue to be important issues in the years to come.

First, as the market becomes more competitive—particularly in the United Kingdom—the majority of private equity players will need to focus on adding value to their holdings beyond financial engineering. Numerous European private equity firms in Europe today are grappling with the need to build their competence in helping portfolio firms with their operations. Developing such skills is unlikely to be easy for many groups, whose partners have a primarily financial orientation.

Second, many of the British and American private equity organizations are currently expanding into other European countries. This is driven by the maturity of the British and American markets, the seemingly attractive opportunities on the Continent, and the pressure to deploy the increasingly large equity funds that they are raising. But numerous challenges are associated with growing from a one-office small fund to a larger multinational one. Among the issues are how to provide incentives across countries and offices, how to govern each office's decision processes, and how to implement the expansion. For instance, how should the carried interest be split if the French deal team wants the German deal team to help a French portfolio firm enter Germany? If the German team is highly productive, but the French office does not do any deals for a year, who should get compensated and in what way? How can a team used to working in the United Kingdom break into the German buyout market, given both their lack of business relationships and the different business practices?

15

Securicor Wireless Networks: February 1996

On Valentine's Day, 1996, the board of Securicor Wireless Networks (SWN) convened for dinner at the Yarrow Bay Grill in Kirkland, Washington, an upscale Asia-fusion restaurant perched on the shores of beautiful Lake Washington. From the restaurant's deck, the board members could make out cranes in the distance, presiding over one of the nation's largest private construction sites: the future home of Microsoft CEO Bill Gates, seven years and $60 million in the making, encompassing some 20 rooms and 20,000 square feet.

The date notwithstanding, the board had come to the restaurant that evening for a decidedly unromantic purpose. They had convened to decide whether or not to merge SWN, which sold software products to wireless telephone carriers, with its largest shareholder, Securicor Telesciences, Inc. (STI), itself a wholly owned subsidiary of the large British security company Securicor PLC.

On the one hand, thought Wireless Networks CEO John Hansen, sales for his year-old company had come far slower than expected. A merger with Securicor Telesciences would ease his concerns about financing his fledgling business. Moreover, Telesciences would help him sell into some important accounts: since they also sold software to telephone carriers, they already had contacts at many of the large wireless telephone companies that Hansen was targeting as customers. Finally, the Securicor name, synonymous worldwide with security, had already proved useful in assuaging the fears of prospective buyers about the risks of purchasing mission-critical software from a start-up.

On the other hand, Hansen thought, as part of a merged Securicor Telesciences, a majority owned subsidiary of Securicor PLC, his business might not be able to achieve the explosive growth he had hoped for. After all, he had seen first-hand the way Securicor operated. While he liked and respected the Securicor executives with whom he most closely worked, as a 40% owner in Wireless Networks, the corporation had proved

Bill Wasik prepared this case under the supervision of Senior Lecturer G. Felda Hardymon as the basis for class discussion rather than to illustrate either effective or ineffective handling of an administrative situation.

far too conservative for Hansen's tastes—too reluctant to pay up for strong management, too cautious to invest equity in the business, too skittish to allow short-term losses that might impact corporate earnings.

As he dined in the shadow of Gates's palace—destined, no doubt, to serve as a visible monument to the phenomenal wealth created by the American high-technology industry in the 1990s—Hansen pondered how he could best build his *own* business and his *own* wealth. Within Securicor, he wondered, would he be able to build a $100 million software company? And even if he were successful, would he ever personally see much financial gain?

NETWORKS NORTHWEST, INC.

John Hansen seemed to have entrepreneurship in his bones. After leaving Brigham Young University in 1981, he went to work as a programmer for a small Seattle-based telecommunications software company called Telematic Products. During his tenure at Telematic, Hansen on two separate occasions took leaves of absence to join start-up ventures—the first, in 1984, to join his father at a company developing process control software for the forest products industry, and the second, in 1987, to found a company that was trying to run high-speed data over ordinary phone lines. In each instance, the venture failed and Hansen returned to Telematic, where he eventually became Director of Engineering.

Telematic Products built software products for telephone carriers that did "data mediation," meaning the collection of telephone call information and the aggregation of that data in a central location. In order to bill customers correctly for telephone calls, carriers like Pacific Bell and AT&T need to capture records from the complex switches that rout calls through their networks. In the early 1980s, when Hansen first started working for Telematic, this data was written out to magnetic tapes every day. The tapes were shipped to a processing center, where records of individual phone calls were reconstructed.

Telematic was the first company to build a system that used computers—called Automated Message Accounting Transmitters, or AMATs—to interface with the large telephone switches. These computers extracted the data from the switches and sent it via modem to a mainframe computer in the processing center, eliminating the magnetic tapes and significantly reducing the time required to create billable records. This technology proved quite popular with the large carriers: by 1989, all seven Regional Bell Operating Companies (RBOCs), the major local telephone service providers in the United States, had standardized on Telematic's system or systems like it.

When Telematic was acquired by New Jersey-based competitor Telesciences (later to become Securicor Telesciences) in 1989, Hansen was faced with a choice: lose his job, or relocate his family three thousand miles away. "My wife's grandfather pulled me aside," Hansen recalls, "and he said, 'You've made people money for the last 10 years—isn't it about time you made money for yourself?'" Heeding this advice, Hansen in March of 1990 incorporated his own consulting company, called Networks Northwest, Inc. (NNI), of which he was the sole employee.

Hansen's first big consulting project came from a predictable source. Since he had spearheaded the group that built Telematic's data mediation product, Telesciences contracted with NNI to provide long-term maintenance and support of the Telematic product. The relationship between the two companies deepened throughout 1991: NNI began doing substantial design work on Telesciences' next-generation data mediation product, a system that would give carriers their data instantaneously and allow them to view in "real time" what calls were on their networks.

As Telesciences and NNI talked to potential customers about the next-generation system, they encountered especially strong interest among cellular (wireless) carriers, much more so than among the traditional "wireline" (nonwireless) carriers. Unlike the traditional telephone market, where the RBOCs still had monopolies on local service and long-distance competition was still relatively tame, the wireless market was undergoing a period of fierce competition, as a host of new entrants in the marketplace began to turn on their expensive cellular networks. These new carriers hoped that a real-time information system would help them maximize their returns on investment, not just by automating their billing but also by controlling fraud (a constant scourge of the cellular industry), by helping them provide better customer service (for example, allowing them to immediately reimburse a customer's account for a dropped call) and, in general, by helping them better understand their customers' calling patterns. By the end of 1991, Telesciences and NNI had decided to narrow the project's focus exclusively to wireless carriers.

Their labors paid off in January 1993, when U.S. West New Vector Group (the cellular arm of U.S. West, a large RBOC) awarded Telesciences a five-year, $2.5 million contract to design and implement this next-generation system for their network. Telesciences in turn signed a $1.5 million subcontract with NNI for most of the software development. By this time NNI had grown to over 20 employees, roughly half of whom were working on the Telesciences project, and the other half of whom were developing an unrelated communications product called BReeze—a "dial-up bridge router" that corporations could use to connect their local area networks over standard telephone circuits.

By the end of 1993, however, Telesciences was going through dire financial straits and had placed the company for sale through an investment banker. It had also stopped paying NNI for its subcontract. Hansen approached Telesciences in January 1994 about purchasing the U.S. West project and the associated technology which, though largely developed by NNI, belonged to Telesciences by the terms of the subcontract. He was rebuffed in his offer and informed that if he wanted the product and technology he would need to buy the entire company.

So Hansen set out to buy the entire company. In March 1994, Hansen flew to London and met with Trevor Sokell, the head of Securicor 3Net, a wholly owned subsidiary of British security giant Securicor PLC (see below for a detailed discussion of Securicor). The two men had met some months earlier to discuss a potential distribution relationship between NNI and 3Net, whereby 3Net might distribute BReeze into the European market. Now Hansen was meeting Sokell for a different purpose entirely: to introduce the floundering Telesciences as a potential acquisition for Securicor. Before Hansen made the introduction, the two agreed upon (and put in writing) a noncircumvention agreement which stipulated, in effect, that after Hansen revealed Telesciences' name to Sokell, Securicor could only acquire Telesciences with Hansen's permission.

Sokell flew to New Jersey and visited Telesciences in April 1994. He liked what he saw—most of it, that is: "Telesciences was really two companies, not one," says Sokell.

It was a company which was focused heavily in the wireline side of industry, but for the last several years it had been trying to get into the wireless world by inventing a brand-new billing system. In [the wireless market], they were struggling—they were spending lots of money, but getting nowhere very quickly. Right in the middle of this billing software capability was the technology that John Hansen was talking about, which he and Networks Northwest understood, but nobody within Telesciences understood, because it had been engineered outside the company.

In June, Sokell and Hansen reached a tentative agreement concerning Telesciences. Securicor would purchase Telesciences and split off the U.S. West New Vector Group project and the associated intellectual property into a joint venture, called Securicor Wireless Networks. Securicor would contribute the intellectual property (and the account receivable) from the U.S. West project, along with $1 million of start-up capital. NNI would contribute any unpaid subcontract work to date, the management and technical team, and $100,000. Each company would have an equal ownership stake in the resulting venture.

There was only one catch: tiny NNI didn't have the cash to stay in business much longer, let alone $100,000 to contribute to the joint venture. It was clear that it would need additional funding to carry out its end of the project. Accordingly, that fall Trevor introduced NNI to Hardy Smith, a partner at Bessemer Venture Partners in Massachusetts.

Smith was interested in Securicor Wireless Networks as a business but not in the joint venture structure. As an investor in NNI, he would own stock only in NNI but not in the partnership, the place where he felt the real value was being created. Also, the path to liquidity for such a joint venture was murky at best. Instead, Smith proposed to Sokell and Hansen that the project be spun out into a separate company, in which Networks Northwest, Securicor (via Telesciences), and Bessemer would each have an interest.

Smith made the case to both sides. To Hansen, he argued that the presence of a large investment firm like Bessemer would provide NNI with some protection from their large and powerful corporate partner, and help ensure a path to liquidity for NNI's existing investors. To Sokell, he argued that Bessemer's U.S. presence and experience with start-ups would help them supervise the new company's inexperienced U.S.-based management team.

"This structure gives STS [Securicor Telesciences] a control mechanism, namely BVP [Bessemer], for the care and feeding of this far-away entrepreneurial outpost," Smith wrote in a memo to Sokell. "One of the best ways to be effective in keeping dollars spent efficiently at SW [Securicor Wireless] . . . is to have someone with aligned interest and with experience in the area looking after the investment. We offer skills in this area—particularly building infrastructure—and our interest in efficiency is aligned with yours."

Smith got his way. On January 20, 1995, Securicor Wireless Networks was incorporated in Delaware as a separate entity. Securicor Telesciences contributed $500K, plus the U.S. West project and the associated intellectual property rights, and in return were allocated 40% ownership (on a fully diluted basis) of the new company. The shareholders of Networks Northwest contributed $100,000 (and the new company's management) and owned 31% of the entity. Bessemer invested $1 million for 19% of the company, and the remaining 10% was left as a management option pool.[1] Sitting on the company's board were Sokell, the new company's chairman; Hansen, the CEO; Smith; Andrew Maunder, the CEO of Securicor Telesciences; and Michael Tennican, an early angel investor in Networks Northwest.

EXHIBIT 15-1

SUMMARY OF WIRELESS NETWORK'S EQUITY FINANCING HISTORY TO DATE

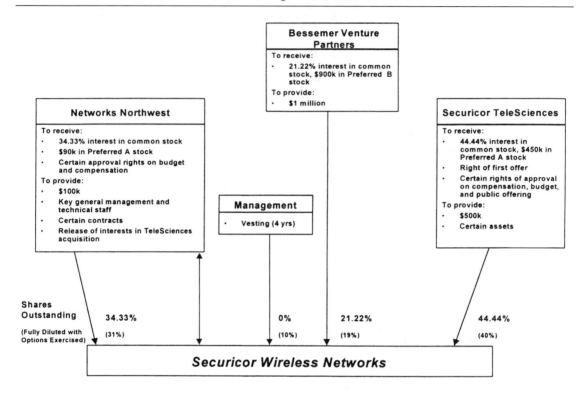

	Pfd A	Pfd B	Pfd C
Date	January 20, 1995[1]	January 20, 1995[1]	September 30, 1995[2]
Amount	$600,025.00	$999,975.00	$1,000,002.00
Participants	Securicor Telesciences	Bessemer Venture Partners	Bessemer Venture Partners
Price/common share	$1.05[3]	$1.05[3]	$1.05
In event of liquidation or sale	Paid out after Series C, pro rata with Series B	Paid out after Series C, pro rata with Series A	If not converted, paid out first
In event of IPO	Gets redeemed	Gets redeemed	Converts to common
Voluntary conversion to common	Not convertible	Not convertible	Convertible with $> 66\frac{2}{3}\%$ vote of round
Dividend	Immediate quarterly payments of LIBOR + 1%	After January 1, 2000, annual payments of 8% face value	After January 1, 2000, annual payments of 8% face value
Mandatory redemption?	Yes: 3 equal annual increments beginning January 17, 2000	Yes: 3 equal annual increments beginning January 17, 2000	No

(Continued)

EXHIBIT 15-1   (Continued)

	Pfd A	Pfd B	Pfd C
Anti-dilution	Yes	Yes	Yes
Demand registration rights	Demand rights granted upon request of >50% of Series A-C	Demand rights granted upon request of >50% of Series A-C	Demand rights granted at the earliest of (a) July 31, 1999; (b) six months after IPO; or (c) the request of >50% of Series A-C

[1] Note that A and B are the same round (January 20, 1995) wherein the company sold Non-Convertible Redeemable Preferred stock packaged with common stock. The only difference between A and B is the dividend policy: the stock owned by Securicor Telesciences paid a current dividend and the stock owned by Bessemer did not. This was the result of the original three-way negotiations between the founders, Securicor Telesciences, and Bessemer that originally capitalized the company. In all other respects, the stock from the original capitalization held by Bessemer and Securicor Telesciences was identical.

[2] At the time of the Preferred C round, Securicor extended a $1.5 mm line of credit to SWN and sold back some of its common equity position from the first round in return for warrants which, when exercised, would restore its original equity position.

[3] The price per share of a round composed of packaged securities, in this case a Non-Convertible Redeemable Preferred packaged with common stock, is calculated by the total amount invested divided by the number of common shares received. Usually, some low value is assigned to the common shares; in this case, for every $1 of face value of Preferred Stock the investor bought, he also bought a common share for 5¢; hence the "price per common share" is $1.05.

Note that this is inconsistent with the chart above that was lifted directly from Smith's investment memorandum to his partners. In that chart, it was contemplated that each unit would cost $1.00 and consist of 90¢ of preferred face value and 10¢ ascribed to the purchase of each share of common stock. The unit was changed in the final papers to lower the amount assigned to the common stock and make the units of face value for the preferred an even $100. Such a change was immaterial to the fundamental ownership agreement.

SECURICOR WIRELESS NETWORKS

Founded in 1935, Securicor PLC is best known in Britain for its ubiquitous armored cars, the British equivalent of America's Brinks trucks. Every night, Securicor's guards and trucks worldwide handle over £1 billion, including over 60% of the United Kingdom's currency. The company also operates Europe's largest privately owned distribution and delivery network.

Securicor also has a communications division, which was begun in a somewhat roundabout fashion. When Great Britain awarded cellular licenses in 1983, the regulatory authorities required British Telecom to bring on a partner as a prerequisite for their receiving a license. BT chose Securicor because Securicor was already operating a wireless network in Great Britain whose sole purpose was to track their security trucks at all times. (This was a result of Great Britain's law that forbade Securicor agents from carrying weapons.) The resulting partnership, CellNet, became the first cellular network in Britain, and Securicor's 40% stake in CellNet quickly grew to be worth nearly £2 billion—a windfall that prompted Securicor's board to make more telecommunications investments. As part of that strategy, Securicor had bought Trevor Sokell's company 3Net and had in turn given Sokell the mandate to continue to build a communications division by acquisition.

One of Britain's most trusted corporations, Securicor is a name synonymous with safety, stability, and reliability. This suited John Hansen just fine. "Down to the fiber of my body," he says today, "I knew I needed a Securicor."

The reason for this need had everything to do with the nature of Hansen's product. The software that Securicor Wireless Networks hoped to sell to wireless carriers was what those in high-tech business call *mission-critical*. The term is used to refer to a piece of technology that is (or becomes) absolutely vital to the customer's day-to-day operations. In this case, SWN was trying to sell a product to wireless carriers that handled every single piece of data about a customer's call, including its billing records.

Large corporations are wary of buying a mission-critical piece of business software from an unproven start-up. After all, how can they be sure that the start-up will be around in a year, or five years, if the software breaks or needs to be upgraded? "This is one of the barriers to entry into this marketplace," says Hansen. "With a mission-critical system, you have to have the credibility to say that no matter what, you're going to be there long-term."

Hansen and the Wireless Networks sales force played up the Securicor connection when trying to get into accounts. They would hand copies of Securicor corporate annual reports to prospective buyers, hammering home the point that the buyers were dealing with a £1B company. To further drive the point home, the Wireless Networks sales brochures featured a full-color photo of an armed Securicor guard, clad in an intimidating protective facemask. For especially important meetings, Sokell would fly over from London and serve as a visible representative of Mother Securicor.

"When I was out pitching to [wireless carriers] PrimeCo, or Sprint, or BellSouth, I would have Trevor fly over and say, 'We're Securicor. We take 60% of the cash of the U.K. every night.'" says Hansen. "Which is, in a sense, what [Wireless Networks] did: we transfer the equivalent of money for the carriers. The underlying theme of Securicor resonated with a lot of them."

But while Securicor's sponsorship helped Wireless Networks with their sales process, their involvement with the operations of the company created a fair amount of friction. "Philosophically, Securicor is not a venture capital or equity capital organization," says Sokell today. "The only time it was in the business of starting a company was when they started the company."

In the case of Wireless Networks, this fact was apparent right from the beginning. Rather than placing their $500,000 investment in a standard venture capital equity instrument, Securicor insisted on an investment that looked a lot more like debt: a non-convertible preferred stock with mandatory redemption and a dividend of LIBOR + 1%, plus common stock. This structure was consistent with the way Securicor funded its wholly owned subsidiaries, that is, with working capital, subject to strict corporate oversight.

Indeed, even as a 40%-owned subsidiary, Wireless Networks was bound to abide by the corporation's operating policies and procedures. After the closing, Hansen recalls, "policy books were shipped over. One was on how to use the name and colors of the company. Another was on authorization and approvals. Another was on budgetary control. Another was on financial reporting." Hansen felt that the procedures amounted to "micromanagement."

Any public document—press releases, brochures, business cards—that used the Securicor name had to be approved by the Securicor group in London. Capital expenditures over $50,000, salaries over $70,000 or contracts over $200,000 had to be approved as well. These policies were designed to minimize discrepancies of discretion, budgetary or otherwise, that the group feared might develop among their many and far-flung subsidiaries. "Even though it's difficult to compare the way a U.S. company gets established versus the way a U.K. company is established," says Sokell,

nevertheless, there's always a concern at the group level about creating a situation where there are enormous disparities between what's happening in, say, Hong Kong, or Jakarta, or the United States, as compared to the United Kingdom.

One particularly difficult fight—which Securicor Wireless Networks won—was over the granting of stock options, which Securicor had never before issued to any employees, including its most senior executives.

Complicating things further was Securicor's financial profile. As a predominantly service-oriented business, Securicor operated on razor-thin margins: in FY94 and FY95, the company reported operating income of £25.7 million and £28.6 million on revenues of £800.2 million and £1.03 billion, respectively. As a 40% owner of Securicor Wireless Networks, publicly traded Securicor was required to take on 40% of any losses incurred by the start-up. "If Securicor Wireless Networks had come across with $5 million worth of loss, of which Securicor would have to collect a large share, that would actually have had a important impact on the Securicor overall group profit," notes Sokell.

Accordingly, Hansen felt pressure for the company to break even as quickly as possible. He put together a breakeven budget (see Exhibit 15-2) for the first year—an unlikely outcome for a venture-backed start-up of their stage—and promptly overran it, a result that didn't surprise his venture capital backer but seemed like gross underperformance to Securicor senior management in Great Britain. "Hardy [Smith] and myself, we're like, 'Go, go, go. Build, build, build. Seize the market opportunity,'" says Hansen. "But Securicor would call and say, 'I think you're hiring too fast.'"

In the end, perhaps the most important tension between Securicor Wireless Networks' management and its corporate investors was a cultural one. Sokell recalls a famous quote by Churchill, who once joked that America and Britain are two peoples "separated by a common language":

> The United States is, in general, a much more commercially centered nation than Britain. Tied in with the notion of free enterprise and entrepreneurialism is also the mighty dollar and its importance. That is much, much less emphatic in the U.K. culture. The notion of everything being subservient to commercial demands is not something that the typical Briton would accept.

As an example, he points to the reticence of Securicor managing director Roger Wiggs to award stock options to Wireless Networks' employees. "The biggest thing that Roger Wiggs was worried about was not whether John Hansen had 10, 20 or a million shares," says Sokell, but whether it was fair that Hansen have options at all when no other Securicor employees did. "That was very important to him. It wasn't a negotiating ploy. It was just a real concern. . . . That is a moral dilemma that the American wouldn't even countenance—he'd just do it."

For his part, Hansen was frustrated by what he perceived as the lethargic style of the Securicor group CEOs—of which Hansen, at 35, was by far the youngest. "I'm flying over quarterly to London for ops reviews, and sitting in rooms where there's nothing but gray hair, and they're all British," recalls Hansen. "They behave a certain way. I'm saying things like, you guys have got to help me get into CellNet, and you over in Hong Kong, help me get some leverage there. They're going, 'we'll put it into the plan and we'll try to get to it next year.'"

By anyone's measure, revenue progress at Wireless Networks had been disappointing (see Exhibits 15-3 through 15-5). The company had an impressive pipeline of prospects: during 1995, it moved fairly far into the sales process with Sprint (potentially a $19 million contract), AllTel Mobile ($2–$3 million), U.S. Cellular ($1.5 million) and PCS PrimeCo ($1 million), and was also pitching a $2.5 million expansion to its existing customer, U.S. West. By October 1995, however, only PCS PrimeCo had signed, the result being that Wireless Networks was performing considerably below budget and was nearly out of money.

EXHIBIT 15-2

SECURICOR WIRELESS NETWORKS, FY95 BUDGET, PRESENTED JANUARY 5, 1995 BY CEO JOHN HANSEN

	Actual			Estimated									FY95
	Oct-94	Nov-94	Dec-94	Jan-95	Feb-95	Mar-95	Apr-95	May-95	Jun-95	Jul-95	Aug-95	Sep-95	FY95
RECEIPTS													
Systems	—	—	—	—	—	—	100,000	—	150,000	1,000,000	—	2,000,000	3,250,000
Maintenance	—	—	—	—	—	—	—	—	—	—	—	100,000	100,000
Services	—	—	—	—	50,000	—	100,000	50,000	50,000	50,000	50,000	50,000	400,000
Total receipts	—	—	—	—	50,000	—	200,000	50,000	200,000	1,050,000	50,000	2,150,000	3,750,000
PRODUCT PURCHASES	—	—	—	—	—	—	40,000	7,500	45,000	257,500	7,500	522,500	880,000
NET RECEIPTS	—	—	—	—	50,000	—	160,000	42,500	155,000	792,500	42,500	1,627,500	2,870,000
OPERATING BUDGET													
Personnel													
Salaries and wages	26,600	42,350	58,059	114,058	112,875	114,958	138,458	124,708	135,958	173,208	151,541	204,041	1,396,814
Payroll taxes and benefits	3,474	4,856	5,874	9,888	12,406	12,881	15,046	15,046	16,068	18,015	18,490	18,490	150,534
Total personnel	30,074	47,206	63,933	123,946	125,281	127,839	153,504	139,754	152,026	191,223	170,031	222,531	1,547,348
Facilities	2,400	9,600	10,100	10,600	10,600	10,600	18,200	11,200	11,200	11,200	11,200	11,200	128,100
Engineering and development costs	—	7,100	38,600	21,250	21,550	21,700	22,650	22,650	22,800	23,100	23,250	23,250	247,900
Office equipment and supplies	—	—	2,650	2,550	2,700	2,700	2,700	2,700	2,850	3,000	3,000	3,000	27,850
Sales and marketing costs	4,500	4,500	17,500	34,500	38,500	37,000	16,500	16,500	29,500	16,500	16,500	26,500	258,500
Professional services (legal, accounting, payroll)	—	—	300	55,300	10,300	3,800	300	300	3,800	300	300	3,800	78,500
Taxes—state, city, county, local	—	—	—	—	1,225	—	3,200	1,225	2,350	8,725	1,225	20,675	38,625
Business insurance	—	—	—	6,500	250	250	6,500	250	250	6,500	250	6,500	27,250
Meetings, seminars, meals	—	—	2,750	—	—	1,750	—	—	1,750	—	1,000	1,750	9,000
Interest expense	—	—	—	—	3,333	3,333	3,333	3,333	3,333	3,333	3,333	3,333	26,664
Fixed asset purchases (software and engineering tools)	—	—	20,000	33,600	33,600	13,600	12,400	11,200	10,000	1,200	—	—	135,600
TOTAL OPERATING BUDGET	36,974	68,406	155,833	288,246	247,339	222,572	239,287	209,112	239,859	265,081	230,089	322,539	2,525,337
NET PROFIT (without capitalizing)	(36,974)	(68,406)	(155,833)	(288,246)	(197,339)	(222,572)	(79,287)	(166,612)	(84,859)	527,419	(187,589)	1,304,961	344,663

EXHIBIT 15-3

SECURICOR WIRELESS NETWORKS, ACTUAL STATEMENTS OF OPERATION, FINANCIAL STATEMENT BY MONTH, OCTOBER 1994 THROUGH JANUARY 1996

	Oct-94	Nov-94	Dec-94	Jan-95	Feb-95	Mar-95	Apr-95	May-95	Jun-95
STATEMENT OF OPERATIONS									
Revenue									
System sales	—	—	—	—	—	—	—	86,650	—
Services	—	—	—	—	—	3,194	—	100	—
Total revenue	—	—	—	—	—	3,194	—	86,750	—
Costs and expenses									
Cost of system sales	—	—	—	—	—	—	—	70,626	—
Service and implementation	—	—	—	—	—	—	—	—	—
Product development	3,099	27,702	22,126	88,531	55,031	79,837	82,862	111,540	138,297
Sales	—	—	1,362	57,857	10,918	26,540	11,089	26,590	16,830
Marketing	—	19,875	6,336	16,832	26,757	22,698	7,797	16,189	23,012
General and administrative	14,231	—	22,121	90,405	35,411	5,453	49,043	53,903	80,907
Total costs and expenses	17,331	47,577	51,945	253,625	128,117	134,528	150,791	278,848	259,046
Operating income (loss)	(17,331)	(47,577)	(51,945)	(253,625)	(128,117)	(131,334)	(150,791)	(192,098)	(259,046)
Other									
Interest income	—	—	—	—	—	69	1,672	1,115	590
Interest expense	—	—	—	—	—	—	(10,623)	(3,536)	(7,428)
Other, net	—	—	—	—	—	69	(8,952)	(2,421)	(6,838)
Income before taxes	(17,331)	(47,577)	(51,945)	(253,625)	(128,117)	(131,265)	(159,742)	(194,520)	(265,883)
Income tax expense	—	—	—	—	—	—	—	—	—
Net earnings (loss)	(17,331)	(47,577)	(51,945)	(253,625)	(128,117)	(131,265)	(159,742)	(194,520)	(265,883)

(Continued)

239

EXHIBIT 15-3 (Continued)

	Oct-94	Nov-94	Dec-94	Jan-95	Feb-95	Mar-95	Apr-95	May-95	Jun-95
BALANCE SHEET									
Assets									
Current assets:									
Cash	—	—	—	1,293,727	1,139,587	918,834	656,333	384,220	226,964
Accounts receivable	—	—	—	2,886	2,886	13,036	9,842	94,462	6,960
Unbilled revenue	—	—	—	—	—	—	—	—	—
Inventory	—	—	—	60,000	60,000	174,645	288,594	218,533	240,919
Prepaid expenses	—	—	—	4,400	4,400	12,042	11,960	41,332	54,440
Total current assets	—	—	—	1,361,013	1,206,874	1,118,558	966,728	738,547	529,283
Furniture and fixtures	—	—	—	—	—	—	—	—	23,213
Engineering equipment	77,000			84,616	84,616	85,523	88,803	98,232	99,832
Computer equipment		77,000	77,000	—	—	64,718	70,499	72,225	72,225
Office equipment	—	—	—	—	—	—	—	9,974	31,491
Software	—	—	—	—	—	5,520	5,520	7,316	28,425
Accumulated depreciation	—	—	—	(9,279)	(43)	(1,863)	(4,624)	(7,554)	(13,738)
Fixed assets, net	77,000	77,000	77,000	75,337	84,572	153,898	160,198	180,193	241,448
Deposits	—	—	—	660	660	660	660	13,788	12,847
Total assets	77,000	77,000	77,000	1,437,010	1,292,106	1,273,116	1,127,586	932,527	783,578

(Continued)

EXHIBIT 15-3 (*Continued*)

	Oct-94	Nov-94	Dec-94	Jan-95	Feb-95	Mar-95	Apr-95	May-95	Jun-95
Liabilities and Shareholders' Equity									
Current liabilities									
Accounts payable	77,000	77,000	77,000	85,000	86,317	232,787	230,733	206,043	286,598
Accrued liabilities	17,331	64,907	116,852	122,487	104,383	30,170	46,436	60,733	58,179
Deferred revenue	—	—	—	—	—	—	—	500	450
Shareholder loan	—	—	—	—	—	—	—	—	—
Short-term notes	—	—	—	—	—	—	—	—	—
C/P notes payable	—	—	—	—	—	—	—	—	—
C/P of capital leases	—	—	—	—	—	27,674	27,674	29,136	42,325
Total current liabilities	94,331	141,907	193,852	207,487	190,700	290,630	304,842	296,413	387,552
Long-term debt									
Capital lease obligations	—	—	—	—	—	73,120	73,120	81,012	106,755
Total long-term liabilities	—	—	—	—	—	73,120	73,120	81,012	106,755
Preferred stock—class A	—	—	—	511,400	511,400	51	51	51	51
Preferred stock—class B	—	—	—	976,100	976,100	98	98	98	98
Total mandatorily redeemable preferred stock	—	—	—	1,487,500	1,487,500	149	149	149	149
Shareholders' equity									
Common stock	—	—	—	111,250	111,250	11,250	11,250	11,250	11,250
Preferred stock—class C	—	—	—	—	—	—	—	—	—
Preferred stock—class D	—	—	—	—	—	—	—	—	—
Additional paid-in capital	—	—	—	1,250	1,250	1,527,825	1,527,825	1,527,825	1,527,825
Accumulated loss	(17,331)	(64,907)	(116,852)	(370,477)	(498,594)	(629,859)	(789,601)	(984,121)	(1,249,955)
Total shareholders' equity	(17,331)	(64,907)	(116,852)	(257,977)	(386,094)	909,217	749,474	554,954	289,121
Total liabilities and shareholders' equity	77,000	77,000	77,000	1,437,010	1,292,106	1,273,116	1,127,585	932,527	783,577

(*Continued*)

EXHIBIT 15-3 *(Continued)*

	Jul-95	Aug-95	Sep-95	FY95	Oct-95	Nov-95	Dec-95	Jan-96
STATEMENT OF OPERATIONS								
Revenue								
System sales	—	25,000	96,000	207,650	—	75,000	21,615	—
Services	16,650	50,050	8,690	78,684	7,990	690	56,190	690
Total revenue	16,650	75,050	104,690	286,334	7,990	75,690	77,805	690
Costs and expenses								
Cost of system sales	—	1,522	38,672	109,298	—	—	807	—
Service and implementation	1,740	118,054	223,094	226,356	40,643	38,509	39,782	34,428
Product development	155,115	24,922	(106,396)	775,798	119,721	115,972	128,231	108,137
Sales	28,790	13,637	12,984	217,881	32,160	27,834	38,546	51,037
Marketing	20,694	77,097	31,844	185,798	12,449	9,812	16,939	24,971
General and administrative	84,908	235,233	90,016	623,370	68,221	71,906	63,991	76,160
Total costs and expenses	291,246	235,233	290,214	2,138,500	273,193	264,032	288,297	294,733
Operating income (loss)	(274,596)	(160,183)	(185,524)	(1,852,166)	(265,203)	(188,342)	(210,492)	(294,043)
Other								
Interest income	181	26	7	3,659	208	566	404	329
Interest expense	(6,134)	(13,236)	(6,364)	(47,320)	(8,869)	(4,075)	(6,904)	(6,793)
Other, net	(5,953)	(13,210)	(6,357)	(43,661)	(8,661)	(3,508)	(6,500)	(6,464)
Income before taxes	(280,549)	(173,392)	(191,881)	(1,895,827)	(273,864)	(191,850)	(216,993)	(300,507)
Income tax expense	—	—	—	—	—	—	—	—
Net earnings (loss)	(280,549)	(173,392)	(191,881)	(1,895,827)	(273,864)	(191,850)	(216,993)	(300,507)

(Continued)

EXHIBIT 15-3 (*Continued*)

	Jul-95	Aug-95	Sep-95	FY95	Oct-95	Nov-95	Dec-95	Jan-96
BALANCE SHEET								
Assets								
Current assets:								
Cash	18,853	293,530	601,813	601,813	329,885	162,386	291,827	124,227
Accounts receivable	17,961	75,232	195,945	195,945	601,190	480,244	152,995	54,395
Unbilled revenue	—	—	—	—	—	75,000	50,000	—
Inventory	180,919	302,218	282,083	282,083	293,088	293,088	293,333	293,333
Prepaid expenses	60,227	43,391	40,997	40,997	49,711	83,422	78,182	67,863
Total current assets	277,960	714,372	1,120,839	1,120,839	1,273,873	1,094,140	866,338	539,819
Furniture and fixtures	24,208	24,208	24,208	24,208	24,208	24,208	24,208	24,208
Engineering equipment	100,564	96,916	93,635	93,635	93,635	93,635	94,288	94,288
Computer equipment	118,912	118,912	118,912	118,912	118,912	118,912	127,812	134,317
Office equipment	31,491	32,032	32,032	32,032	32,032	32,032	32,032	34,736
Software	110,611	111,211	111,211	111,211	111,211	111,211	111,211	113,731
Accumulated depreciation	(33,715)	(43,250)	(52,896)	(52,896)	(62,780)	(72,663)	(82,863)	(93,398)
Fixed assets, net	352,071	340,028	327,102	327,102	317,218	307,335	306,689	307,883
Deposits	14,775	14,115	14,115	14,115	14,115	14,115	14,115	14,115
Total assets	644,806	1,068,515	1,462,056	1,462,056	1,605,206	1,415,590	1,187,141	861,816

(*Continued*)

EXHIBIT 15-3 *(Continued)*

	Jul-95	Aug-95	Sep-95	FY95	Oct-95	Nov-95	Dec-95	Jan-96
Liabilities and shareholders' equity								
Current liabilities								
Accounts payable	351,099	425,443	223,741	223,741	257,453	118,147	120,425	196,300
Accrued liabilities	91,631	97,722	201,214	201,214	219,547	215,862	200,869	123,845
Deferred revenue	400	321,350	328,980	328,980	699,210	698,520	697,830	697,140
Shareholder loan	—	200,000	—	—	—	146,038	147,226	157,616
Short-term notes	—	—	—	—	—	—	—	—
C/P notes payable	—	—	—	—	—	—	—	—
C/P of capital leases	56,227	57,135	57,135	57,135	58,978	58,996	59,950	60,918
Total current liabilities	499,357	1,101,650	811,070	811,070	1,235,188	1,237,564	1,226,299	1,235,819
Long-term debt								
Capital lease obligations	136,729	131,537	131,537	131,537	121,042	120,900	115,452	109,916
Total long-term liabilities	136,729	131,537	131,537	131,537	121,042	120,900	115,452	109,916
Preferred stock—class A	51	51	51	51	51	51	51	51
Preferred stock—class B	98	98	98	98	98	98	98	98
Total mandatorily redeemable preferred stock	149	149	149	149	149	149	149	149
Shareholders' equity								
Common stock	11,250	11,250	8,200	8,200	8,200	8,200	8,200	8,200
Preferred stock—class C	—	—	1,592	1,592	1,592	1,592	1,592	1,592
Preferred stock—class D	—	—	—	—	—	—	—	—
Additional paid-in capital	1,527,825	1,527,825	2,405,285	2,405,285	2,405,285	2,405,285	2,410,542	2,408,902
Accumulated loss	(1,530,504)	(1,703,896)	(1,895,778)	(1,895,778)	(2,166,250)	(2,358,100)	(2,575,093)	(2,902,762)
Total shareholders' equity	8,571	(164,821)	519,300	519,300	248,828	56,977	(154,758)	(484,068)
Total liabilities and shareholders' equity	644,806	1,068,515	1,462,056	1,462,056	1,605,206	1,415,590	1,187,141	861,815

EXHIBIT 15-4

SECURICOR TELESCIENCES, QUARTERLY STATEMENT OF OPERATIONS

	Quarter Ended				
	Dec-94	Mar-95	Jun-95	Sep-95	Dec-95
Revenues					
Unrelated third parties	6,746	3,316	5,868	7,836	3,767
Related parties	—	921	431	450	1,145
Total revenues	6,746	4,237	6,299	8,286	4,912
Cost of revenues					
Unrelated third parties	3,573	2,203	2,898	3,529	2,699
Related parties	—	695	297	282	902
Total cost of revenues	3,573	2,898	3,195	3,811	3,601
Gross profit	3,173	1,339	3,104	4,475	1,311
Operating expenses					
Research, development, and engineering	1,287	1,469	1,562	1,630	1,522
Selling, general and administrative	1,148	1,309	1,357	1,392	1,549
Parent charges	93	93	93	107	97
Total operating expenses	2,528	2,871	3,012	3,129	3,168
Operating income (Loss)	645	(1,532)	92	1,346	(1,857)
Interest expense, net	36	17	53	6	107
Other income (expense)	—	—	7	141	397
Equity in loss of investee	—	177	268	49	18
Income (loss) before income taxes	609	(1,726)	(222)	1,432	(1,585)
Income tax (expense) benefit	(229)	649	83	(538)	605
Net profit (loss)	380	(1,077)	(139)	894	(980)

On September 30, 1995, Bessemer invested $1 million in a new round of convertible preferred stock, and Securicor Telesciences extended a $1.5 million line of credit. Concerned about taking on its share of Wireless Networks' loss, Securicor also converted just over half its position into a warrant at the new share price. This brought Securicor's ownership in the company down to 19.9%, just below the 20% hurdle for profit/loss consolidation, but it preserved the option to regain its position when SWN became profitable.

MERGER DISCUSSIONS

Despite some of the friction created by differences in company cultures, Hansen, Sokell, and Maunder liked one another and worked well together on a personal level. Throughout most of Wireless Networks' short history, Hansen and Telesciences CEO Maunder had been discussing the possibility of merging the two companies together. Wireless Networks stood to benefit from the financial stability of the established Telesciences business, plus its already developed sales and service infrastructure. Telesciences, in turn, stood to benefit from bringing Wireless Networks' cutting-edge real-time technology in house and incorporating it into its next-generation offering for wireline car-

EXHIBIT 15-5

SECURICOR TELESCIENCES, STATEMENT OF OPERATIONS

	Predecessor Business (Wireline Division of Securicor Telesciences)			Period from July 1, 1994 to September 30, 1994	Year Ended September 30, 1995
	Year Ended June 30,				
	1992	1993	1994		
Revenues					
Unrelated third parties					
Equipment	15,701	14,799	13,963	4,242	18,000
Services	8,484	6,899	6,266	1,364	5,766
	24,185	21,698	20,229	5,606	23,766
Related parties	—	—	—	—	1,802
Total revenues	24,185	21,698	20,229	5,606	25,568
Cost of revenues					
Unrelated third parties					
Equipment	7,564	6,315	8,785	2,271	9,110
Services	3,417	4,586	4,018	1,086	3,093
	10,981	10,901	12,803	3,357	12,203
Related parties	—	—	—	—	1,274
Total cost of revenues	10,981	10,901	12,803	3,357	13,477
Gross profit	13,204	10,797	7,426	2,249	12,091
Operating expenses					
Research, development, and engineering	4,106	4,913	5,450	1,348	5,948
Selling, general and administrative	6,313	4,986	4,985	1,072	5,206
Parent charges	—	—	—	—	386
Charge for purchased R&D	—	—	—	6,700	—
Total operating expenses	10,419	9,899	10,435	9,120	11,540
Operating income (Loss)	2,785	898	(3,009)	(6,871)	551
Interest expense, net	—	—	—	9	112
Other income (expense)	—	—	—	66	148
Equity in loss of investee	—	—	—	—	494
Income (loss) before income taxes	2,785	898	(3,009)	(6,814)	93
Income tax (expense) benefit	—	—	—	2,716	(35)
Net profit (loss)	2,785	898	(3,009)	(4,098)	58
Balance sheet					

riers (see Exhibit 15-6). On November 17, 1995, the two presented a formal proposal to the board, of which excerpts follow:

> Both companies have seen success, STI in an increasing customer list, SWN in the level of interest from customers in what they are preaching as well as from the financial markets. . . .

> The markets of both companies are converging. Wireline, Wireless, ATM [Asynchronous Transfer Mode] and Cable companies will all have the same requirements—to provide unique and revenue-driven services to their customers. . . .

EXHIBIT 15-6

SECURICOR TELESCIENCES AND SECURICOR WIRELESS NETWORKS, PROJECTED FY96 AND FY97 STATEMENT OF OPERATIONS AND BALANCE SHEET, POST-MERGER, PRESENTED NOVEMBER 17, 1995 BY ANDREW MAUNDER AND JOHN HANSEN

					Quarter Ending					
	Dec-95	Mar-96	Jun-96	Sep-96	FY96	Dec-96	Mar-97	Jun-97	Sep-97	FY97
Sales										
Equipment	6,276	7,605	9,213	11,439	34,533	12,920	18,442	19,960	22,100	73,422
Contractual	1,888	1,265	1,419	1,409	5,981	2,597	2,452	2,916	3,354	11,319
Total sales	8,164	8,870	10,632	12,848	40,514	15,517	20,894	22,876	25,454	84,741
Cost of goods sold										
Materials	2,566	1,568	1,894	2,515	8,543	4,332	5,922	6,567	7,541	24,362
Subcontract—H/W maintenance	69	75	75	75	294	150	150	150	150	600
Other COGS	444	408	392	558	1,802	620	730	645	585	2,580
Total COGS	3,079	2,051	2,361	3,148	10,639	5,102	6,802	7,362	8,276	27,542
Gross profit	5,085	6,819	8,271	9,700	29,875	10,415	14,092	15,514	17,178	57,199
Gross profit %	62%	77%	78%	75%	74%	67%	67%	68%	67%	67%
Overheads										
Operations	1,028	1,293	1,280	1,211	4,812	1,283	1,353	1,416	1,458	5,510
Support services	798	835	924	920	3,477	1,438	1,700	1,800	1,943	6,881
Engineering	1,863	2,136	2,033	2,055	8,087	2,908	2,989	3,126	3,301	12,324
Marketing	475	492	681	547	2,195	613	657	832	690	2,792
Sales	883	1,081	1,195	1,202	4,361	2,073	2,172	2,237	2,860	9,342
Program management	134	120	180	166	600	276	294	330	348	1,248
General and administrative	738	692	695	1,022	3,147	1,222	1,321	1,378	1,456	5,377
Total overheads	5,919	6,649	6,988	7,123	26,679	9,813	10,486	11,119	12,056	43,474
Balance sheet adjustments	—	—				—				—
Incentive plan payments		—	42	308	350		—			—
Operating profit (loss)	(834)	170	1,241	2,269	2,846	602	3,606	4,395	5,122	13,725
Interest and other expense	(217)	292	285	294	654	295	269	231	188	983
Profit (loss) before taxes	(617)	(122)	956	1,975	2,192	307	3,337	4,164	4,934	12,742
Tax provision	—	—	—	635	635	—	—	—	2,215	2,215
Net profit (loss)	(617)	(122)	956	1,340	1,557	307	3,337	4,164	2,719	10,527

(*Continued*)

EXHIBIT 15-6 (Continued)

					Quarter Ending					
	Dec-95	Mar-96	Jun-96	Sep-96	FY96	Dec-96	Mar-97	Jun-97	Sep-97	FY97
Balance Sheet										
Assets										
Cash	400	268	400	1,185	1,185	1,279	1,568	1,801	1,846	1,846
Accounts receivable	10,751	11,255	12,272	8,867	8,867	12,115	12,001	12,826	13,921	13,921
Inventory	3,323	3,554	4,100	4,609	4,609	5,692	5,719	6,493	7,127	7,127
Fixed assets	2,689	3,214	3,413	3,782	3,782	4,161	4,550	4,954	5,326	5,326
Other assets	647	408	374	380	380	460	362	386	445	445
Intangible asset	1,336	1,336	1,336	1,336	1,336	1,336	1,336	1,336	1,336	1,336
Investment—SWN	481	481	481	481	481	481	481	481	481	481
Goodwill	9,127	9,127	9,127	9,127	9,127	9,127	9,127	9,127	9,127	9,127
Total assets	28,754	29,643	31,503	29,767	29,767	34,651	35,144	37,404	39,609	39,609
Liabilities and Equity										
Liabilities										
Accounts payable	2,191	2,584	2,666	2,806	2,806	3,697	3,753	3,810	4,024	4,024
Accrued expenses	3,109	3,220	3,349	4,136	4,136	3,453	3,813	4,155	6,875	6,875
Deferred revenue	3,287	2,709	2,431	2,137	2,137	4,146	3,838	3,349	2,649	2,649
I/C Payable (Rec)	78	83	88	83	83	109	93	87	77	77
Capitalized leases	217	531	546	603	603	728	722	669	624	624
Borrowings	7,710	8,488	9,457	5,714	5,714	7,463	4,534	2,779	89	89
Total liabilities	16,592	17,615	18,537	15,479	15,479	19,596	16,753	14,849	14,338	14,338
Equity										
Beginning equity	12,788	12,162	12,028	12,966	12,788	14,288	15,055	18,391	22,555	14,288
Net income	(626)	(134)	938	1,322	1,500	767	3,336	4,164	2,716	10,983
Ending equity	12,162	12,028	12,966	14,288	14,288	15,055	18,391	22,555	25,271	25,271
Total liabilities and equity	28,754	29,643	31,503	29,767	29,767	34,651	35,144	37,404	39,609	39,609

For our two companies to continue alone will mean competing head-to-head within six to twelve months. To merge means to gain critical mass and strengthen vision, infrastructure, customer base, and . . . the story. . . .

Reasons for a merger:

- There is very little overlap in operations.
- A combination of the wireline and wireless stories adds a lot of weight.
- Senior management has an excellent working relationship.
- Competing will cause a waste of effort on both sides.
- Provides a strong story for the financial markets.
- Both companies will be duplicating many resources.
- Gives critical mass.

Disadvantages:

- Location—the two companies are on different sides of the continent. While this provides a management issue, the need for offices covering the U.S. domestic market is understood by all companies.
- Diversion of senior management focused on merging may cause business to suffer—but not if it is done quickly.
- A merging of company cultures is always difficult.

The two CEOs convinced the board that the merger was worth pursuing. Sokell and Smith were charged with negotiating the deal, which would be approved the morning of February 15 at Wireless Networks' next board meeting in Seattle. Negotiations began in mid-December and continued right up until the February deadline.

There were five major points of negotiation, and Sokell and Smith were able to make substantial progress on each of them before the February meetings.

1. Valuation

The two sides began worlds apart on valuation. SWN's first two financings had valued it at $4.7 million and $8.7 million post-financing, respectively. Because all of management's efforts had been in making the merger happen, very little thought had been given to how SWN would fare in a third-party financing in the venture market. Smith thought it could bring a post-financing valuation between $10 million and $15 million, but it would not be an easy sale with STI not participating and with the lack of sales momentum.

In any event, the SWN shareholders felt that the technology that SWN was developing represented the real growth opportunity for the combined company. Telesciences, they believed, was a stagnant business that was worth little more than the $11 million Securicor had paid for it. Accordingly, they wanted their company (after a $4 million private placement, which would be placed in Wireless Networks just prior to the merger) to represent 40% of the combined company's ownership.

Sokell, on the other hand, valued Telesciences at $25 million. His argument: Securicor had paid $11 million for the company in 1995 and supplied another $8M in working capital, plus the prospects for the company had improved considerably. "STI was profitable last year and has succeeded in achieving important new contracts," Sokell wrote in a memo to Smith on January 3. "The prospects for further new wins over the next few months are as good if not better than for SWN. This year STI should grow well with profitability pretty well assured."

Wireless Networks, on the other hand, Sokell valued post-private placement at $10 million. "[I]f we look at things empirically, we see SWN currently as being worth about $5M, pre-investment," Sokell wrote. "The rationale is that it was established with capital of $1.6 million plus technology and a major contract transferred from STI. To this has been added a further $1 million. . . . If we then add $4 million of new money and a new $1 million contract is closed this month then, generously, we can accept a valuation of some $10M overall." This split implied a 28.5% stake for the Wireless Networks shareholders.

By the February meetings, the sides had agreed that, fully diluted, Wireless Networks shareholders would own 38.4% of the combined company.

2. Risk of Securicor Having to Consolidate a Loss

Wireless Networks had a number of interesting sales prospects, but still only two customers—U.S. West New Vector Group and PCS PrimeCo. In the meantime, Wireless Networks was losing considerable amounts of money. Securicor initially wanted the merger to be contingent on Wireless Networks' booking a new order, to minimize the risk that, as majority owner of the combined company, it might be forced to consolidate a loss. Going into the February meetings, however, Wireless Networks had not yet closed a third customer.

Securicor agreed to drop the requirement, agreeing instead on a plan that, in the event of a substantial projected loss, would convert some of its position into warrants to bring its ownership below 50%. As a minority shareholder, while still required take on its percentage of any losses, Securicor would not be required under U.K. reporting laws to consolidate the full loss on its financial statements.

3. Employee Stock Options

Bessemer and the Wireless Networks management wanted the combined company to have a real stock option plan, with 10% of the combined company set aside for management options. As mentioned above, however, stock options ran counter to the Securicor culture. Even senior management at the corporation had never been awarded stock options.

By the time of the February meetings, the two sides had agreed on a smaller percentage—6%—going into a "phantom" plan, where management would be given "stock appreciation rights" that vested and appreciated like options but were paid out as compensation. This agreement made some of the participants uneasy, however. Maunder noted that, since payouts under such a phantom plan were expensed as compensation, the impact on the company's P&L statement would be "dire." Also, for the recipients of these phantom options, payouts would be taxed immediately as ordinary income—in contrast to standard stock options, which are taxed at capital gains rates upon the sale of the underlying stock.

4. Operating Loans from Securicor

As with most of its operating companies, Securicor had funded both Wireless Networks and Telesciences with interest-bearing corporate debt—nearly $8 million in the two companies together. Securicor wanted at the time of merger to be repaid $1.5M in cash, representing the line of credit extended to Wireless Networks at the time of the second round of financing. Securicor expected that the balance of the loans would continue to pay interest.

On the other side, Smith in particular felt that the $1.5M should convert to equity (since the loan was originally extended in lieu of equity) and that whatever Securicor loans remained on the books of the combined company should be interest-free. "Assuming around $8 million in debt at U.S. Prime (say, 7%), the carrying cost per quarter is around $140,000," Smith noted in a memo. "That's five engineers. More importantly, at a conservative 20 times earnings, the interest drag costs at least $2mm to the market value of STI [after IPO]. Since the Securicor interest is protected on the downside at the expense of the SWN interest, this is unfair."

As a compromise, Smith proposed that the entire outstanding loan be converted to a straight redeemable preferred stock that bore no dividend until January 1, 1997, and paid out 5% thereafter. Going into the meetings, however, the issue remained unresolved.

5. Registration Rights

Bessemer and the Wireless Networks management wanted absolute registration rights, which would allow the minority shareholders to force the combined company to go public at some predetermined point in time. This was unacceptable to Securicor, who wanted control over any IPO.

At the meetings, the Wireless Networks shareholders agreed to drop the requirement in favor of language which expressed, in effect, that it was in the best interest of all parties that the combined company be taken public.

In the end, the Wireless Networks shareholders were left with a difficult decision. Should they agree to become 38% of a subsidiary of a U.K.-based company, with an unclear path to liquidity and an uphill battle of cultures? Or should they continue independently and brave the venture financing market again, where investors might balk at their lackluster sales—not to mention the 40% ownership stake held by an increasingly reluctant corporate partner?

They needed to decide soon. Wireless Networks lacked the cash to cover payroll on the 19th—four business days away.

16

Metapath Software: September 1997

On September 29, 1997, John Hansen called together his board to debate an interesting choice that his company had to make. Hansen—the CEO of Metapath Software Corp., a Seattle-based provider of software and services to wireless carriers—had two offers to describe to his board.

The first was an offer to be acquired by CellTech Communications, a wireless products company that had only recently gone public. Under the terms of the deal, Metapath's shareholders would at closing receive common stock in CellTech valued at $115 million. CellTech at that time had a market capitalization of approximately $260 million. The second offer was from a consortium of investors led by Robertson & Stephens Omega Fund (RSC) and Technology Crossover Ventures (TCV) to buy $11.75 million of stock at a $76 million pre-money valuation. Although the price seemed generous for a private company of Metapath's stage, the terms of the preferred stock the funds were proposing to buy were much stricter than the terms of the stock owned by existing shareholders.

For Metapath's shareholders, CellTech's offer had much to commend it: near-term liquidity at an attractive price, without the dilution of further financings and an IPO. And the terms on the financing proposed by RSC could make a sale of the company extremely dilutive to the founders in the event of a sale further down the road. However, Hansen and his board believed Metapath had great potential as an independent public company—probably greater than CellTech—and wondered whether the two businesses made sense together.

HISTORY OF METAPATH

Metapath (formerly called Securicor Wireless Networks) was formed in January 1995 out of a joint venture with Securicor Telesciences Inc. (STI) and a consulting company,

Senior Lecturer Felda Hardymon and Bill Wasik prepared this case as the basis for class discussion rather than to illustrate either effective or ineffective handling of an administrative situation.

Networks Northwest, operated by Hansen himself. The mission of SWN was to build a software product that allowed wireless carriers—that is, operators of wireless telephone networks—to see exactly what calls were on their networks at any point in time. The company began with a single contract, with US West New Vector Group, the cellular arm of the large telephone company, US West. Despite sluggish sales early on, SWN rebuffed an offer by Securicor Telesciences to purchase the company in February 1996, opting to go it alone. In addition to taking new capital from their existing investor, Bessemer Venture Partners, SWN brought in two new firms, Norwest Capital and U.S. Venture Partners, and bought out STI's position (see Exhibit 16-1).

The company had continued to make good progress in developing its business. Soon after the Norwest/USVP financing, the company closed a mammoth $19 million order with Sprint and also beefed up its product offering. By the time of the CellTech offer in September 1997, Metapath's revenue had grown to $6.4 million in the preceding quarter, representing three large customers.

Hansen felt that Metapath was emerging as the premier company in its market space and would have an excellent chance of going public within the next two years. Recent public offerings for vendors to wireless service operators had gone well, and the market was paying three to five times the revenue for such companies.

In his discussions with analysts at major investment banks that underwrite technology IPOs, Hansen had come away with two requirements for Metapath to be salable as a public company. One was that Metapath needed to attract more customers. As it stood, its revenue was all concentrated in four accounts, and the analysts feared that Metapath's dependence on these few key customer relationships would make it seem too risky an investment. The other requirement was that Metapath smooth out its quarter-to-quarter revenues, which had been choppy. Hansen's plan assumed that both of these problems would be worked out in a year.

With that in mind, Hansen and his board embarked on raising enough money to see them through to cash breakeven and, ultimately, an initial public offering.

RSC'S OFFER

Hansen and his CFO, Paul Bialek, contacted several late-stage and mezzanine funds to solicit their interest in a Metapath financing. Over time, two funds emerged as candidates to lead the round—Robertson Stephens Omega Fund and Technology Crossover Ventures. In the subsequent discussions, RSC emerged as quicker to provide specific term sheets, and so most of the negotiations took place with the partners at RSC. Subsequent to a term sheet being settled, the company invited TCV to join with RSC and the existing insiders to form a $11.75 million round. Originally, the company wanted to limit the round to $10.75 million, but the appetite around the table was such that to include everyone it was agreed to expand the round by $1 million. The term sheet is presented in Exhibit 16-2.

Unlike investors in public stocks, venture capital investors usually purchase *preferred stock* in the private companies they fund. The chief attribute of such stock is its *liquidation preference*—in the event of a sale or liquidation of the company, the holder of the preferred stock has a right to receive consideration equal to the face value of the stock (that is, equal to the cost basis of the stock) in preference to all other shareholders. Venture capitalists insist on such stock for a simple reason: since the management of a private start-up company typically owns "founder's stock" with little or no paid principal,

EXHIBIT 16-1

SUMMARY OF METAPATH'S FINANCING HISTORY TO DATE

	A	B	C	D
Date	January 20, 1995[1]	January 20, 1995[1]	September 30, 1995	April 30, 1996
Amount	$600,025.00	$999,975.00	$1,000,002.00	$7,000,00.00
Participants	Securicor Telesciences	Bessemer Venture Partners	Bessemer Venture Partners	Bessemer, U.S. Venture Partners, Norwest Venture Partners
Price/common share	$1.05[2]	$1.05[2]	$1.05	$1.62
In event of liquidation or sale	Paid out after Series C and D, pro rata with Series B	Paid out after Series C and D, pro rata with Series A	If not converted, paid out after Series D	If not converted, paid out first
In event of IPO	Gets redeemed	Gets redeemed	Converts to common	Converts to common
Voluntary conversion to common	Not convertible	Not convertible	Convertible with >66⅔% vote of round	Convertible with >80% vote of round
Dividend	Immediate quarterly payments of LIBOR +1%	After January 1, 2000, annual payments of 8% face value	After January 1, 2000, annual payments of 8% face value	After January 1, 2000, annual payments of 8% face value
Mandatory redemption?	Yes: 3 equal annual increments beginning January 17, 2000	Yes: 3 equal annual increments beginning January 17, 2000	No	No
Antidilution	Yes	Yes	Yes	Yes
Demand registration rights	Demand rights granted upon request of >50% of Series A–D	Demand rights granted upon request of >50% of Series A–D	Demand rights granted at the earliest of (a) July 31, 1999; (b) six months after IPO; or (c) the request of >50% of Series A–D	Demand rights granted at the earliest of (a) July 31, 1999; (b) six months after IPO; or (c) the request of >50% of Series A–D

[1] Note that A and B are the same round (January 20, 1995) wherein the Company sold Non-Convertible Redeemable Preferred stock packaged with common stock. The only difference between A and B is the dividend policy: the stock owned by Securicor Telesciences paid a current dividend, and the stock owned by Bessemer did not. This was the result of the original three-way negotiations between the founders, Securicor Telesciences, and Bessemer that originally capitalized the company. In all other respects, the stock from the original capitalization held by Bessemer and Securicor Telesciences was identical.

[2] The price per share of a round composed of packaged securities, in this case a Non-Convertible Redeemable Preferred packaged with common stock, is calculated by the total amount invested divided by the number of common shares received. Usually, some low value is assigned to the common shares; in this case, for every $1 of face value of Preferred Stock the investor bought, he also bought a common share for 5¢; hence, the "price per common share" is $1.05.

EXHIBIT 16-2

TERM SHEET PRESENTED TO JOHN HANSEN BY ROBERTSON, STEPHENS ON SEPTEMBER 22, 1997

Issuer:	Metapath Software Corporation (the "Company")
Amount:	$10,750,000
Security:	Series E Convertible Preferred Stock ("Series E Preferred").
Price per Share:	$6.00 (the "Original Purchase Price"). The Original Purchase price represents a fully diluted share count (12,497,928) for an approximate pre-money equity valuation of $75 million.
Investors:	New investors led by Omega Ventures II, Crossover II, and other funds managed by Robertson, Stephens & Company (together "Omega") will invest $5.0 million. Existing investors (Bessemer, Norwest, and USVP) will invest $4.5 million. Partners of Wessels, Arnold & Henderson will invest $250,000. Integral Capital partners will invest $1.0 million. If Integral does not invest, both Omega and existing investors will each invest another $500,000.
Board Representation:	The size of the Board of Directors will be increased to six to accommodate an experienced industry executive who is acceptable to the Company and holders of Series E Preferred.
Board Observation Rights:	A representative from Omega shall have the right to attend all meetings of the Board of Directors in a nonvoting advisory capacity and shall be entitled to receive all information given to board members, consult with and advise management of the Company on significant business issues, and shall have the right to examine Company records. Such rights will terminate upon the closing of the Company's IPO.
Dividend:	Holders of Series E Preferred receive an accruing 8% dividend to be paid only in the event that either Series A, B, C, or D dividends are paid.
Liquidation:	Upon any liquidation of the Company, the holders of Series E Preferred shall be paid out of the assets of the Company an amount equal to the purchase price plus any accrued but unpaid dividends. The remaining proceeds will be used to pay the holders of all other Preferred shareholders an amount equal to their purchase price plus any accrued but unpaid dividends. After all obligations to preferred shareholders are met, the remaining assets of the Company shall be distributed on a pro rata basis to all common and Series E preferred shareholders on an as-converted basis.
Redemption Rights:	Same as Series D. However, the Company will not have the option to redeem the Series E Preferred.
Registration Rights	The holders of Series E Preferred will be entitled to one demand registration and will have full piggy-back rights on all public offerings.
Other Terms:	Similar to Series D Preferred except where changes are necessary to accommodate specific circumstances of Series E Preferred.
Closing:	The closing will be subject to usual closing conditions including satisfactory completion of Omega's due diligence. Anticipated closing is October 6, 1997.
Exclusivity:	From the date of the acceptance of this term sheet, until 30 days thereafter, the Company shall not solicit, nor engage to solicit, offers related to the financing of the Company from other parties and shall not "shop" the term sheet.
Expenses:	Company will reimburse Omega its reasonable legal and due diligence expenses. The current maximum estimate is $15,000

nearly *any* sale of the company—even one at a price below that paid by their venture investors—will provide the management with an attractive return on their investment.

Accordingly, venture capitalists typically insist on convertible preferred stock, where in the event of a liquidation the shareholder has the option of *either* converting to common stock at a predetermined ratio *or* invoking her liquidation preference and receiving her entire principal up front. This protects venture investors in the event of a "cheap sale" by management: if you're going to get rich, the argument goes, at least give me my money back first.

All in all, Metapath had raised $9 million to date in four rounds of financing, summarized in Exhibit 16-1. The first two "rounds" occurred simultaneously, at the founding of the company in January 1995, when STI and Bessemer supplied the initial funds for the venture. In addition to common stock, the two entities were each awarded *redeemable preferred* stock that could not be converted into common. In fact, the stock looked a lot like debt: it paid a dividend, and the principal—essentially all of the funds STI and Bessemer contributed, the common having been purchased at a nominal amount—had to be repaid starting in five years, after which it had to be returned in three annual payments. STI insisted on such a structure (often called a "straight redeemable, cheap common" structure) because it was uncomfortable with investing nonredeemable equity—even equity with a liquidation preference—in a start-up company. The third and fourth rounds, which together constituted $8 million of the $9.6 million invested in the company, were both standard convertible preferred stock instruments.

What worried Bialek and Hansen was that Robertson Stephens' proposed instrument was a *participating convertible preferred stock (PCPT)*. Like a convertible preferred stock, a PCPT has a conversion rate at which the holder can convert from the preferred into common equity. This conversion rate sets the "price" of the offering. Moreover, in the event of a qualified public offering, the stock automatically converts into common stock. And like a standard convertible preferred stock, a PCPT carries a liquidation preference.

But a PCPT differs from a convertible preferred in that in the event of a sale, even though the holder has received the face value in consideration, he still has a right to "participate" in further consideration *as if he had converted* into common stock. Therefore, unlike a convertible preferred, where the holder has to choose between taking his consideration based on his liquidation preference or taking his consideration based on his percentage of ownership after conversion to common equity, the holder of a PCPT does not have to choose. He gets both his liquidation preference *and* his equity participation.

As an example, let's assume that two firms (A and B) each buy 10% of a company (WidgetCo) for $1,000,000, but A is issued convertible preferred stock and B is issued participating preferred (PCPT) stock. Some time later, WidgetCo is sold to Consolidated Widget for $20,000,000 in cash. At the time of the sale, A has the option of either converting to common stock or invoking its liquidation preference, that is, demanding the return of its $1,000,000 and forgoing its "participation" in the cash distribution to the common shareholders. In this case, clearly A will convert to common stock; after conversion, A's position is worth 10% of $20,000,000, or $2,000,000, a healthy step-up from its initial investment.

But B does not have to make any such choice. Under the terms of its stock, B receives its $1,000,000 as a liquidation preference and then also participates in the cash distribution, that is, receives its share of common stock as well. So B receives $1,000,000, plus 10% of $19,000,000 (the remaining cash proffered for the company), for a total of $2,900,000. (A's stake, one will note, is in fact only $1,900,000—10% of the value has been paid out in B's liquidation preference.)

(Note that, if Consolidated Widget had gone public in a qualified offering, both A and B would have been forced to convert to common stock and each would own an equal amount of the company. In that case, the difference between their preferences is erased.)

Hansen had tried to negotiate the participating feature away. He offered to lower the price from $6 to $5.50 per share if RSC agreed to drop the participating feature. RSC countered that the participating feature was necessary to protect them in the event of a sale of the company at a small step-up from the current round. Such a sale would provide quite attractive returns to management and the earlier shareholders—who enjoyed a significantly lower cost basis—but leave RSC with little more than they put in. Besides, they pointed out, the company's plans were to go public at a significant step-up from this round, in which case the PCPT would be forced to convert to common stock with no additional payout.

THE CELLTECH OFFER

In the midst of soliciting the round of financing, Metapath had received an unsolicited offer to be acquired by CellTech for $115 million in common stock (see Exhibit 16-3). This had been a surprise to the management, who knew CellTech as a vendor of wireless technology that was largely hardware-based. The two companies had some contact because Metapath's newest product had integrated with one of CellTech's products.

A report written by an investment banking analyst and released in the summer of 1997 assessed CellTech's market opportunity as follows:

> The key growth driver for CellTech's services is the increasingly competitive nature of the telecommunications industry. Increasing competition will force wireless service providers to demand value-added solutions that provide a competitive advantage and that differentiate their service offerings from others. Now solutions will enable wireless service providers to compete on new features and total service offerings instead of price alone.

> CellTech is uniquely positioned to fulfill these needs by providing open access to its platform and leveraging its [technical] expertise. . . . Access to the CellTech platform will provide other [application providers] with a physical connection to wireless service providers and access to real-time data.

> CellTech's long-term strategy is to be the leading provider of value-added solutions to wireless telecommunications carriers. As part of its strategy, management plans to: 1) maintain the Company's leadership in its current product market; 2) expand its market share in domestic markets; 3) pursue international market opportunities; 4) leverage the CellTech platform to provide new low-cost, value-added solutions; and 5) provide superior customer support.

A merger with CellTech would provide some distinct operating benefits to Metapath. Metapath's sales and marketing infrastructure was still embryonic; CellTech, which was selling solutions to the same customers, already had a fully formed marketing and domestic sales organization. (Like Metapath, CellTech was just beginning the process of building an international presence.) Also, despite the fact that CellTech's and Metapath's respective technologies were quite different—Metapath's products largely

EXHIBIT 16-3

TERM SHEET PRESENTED TO JOHN HANSEN BY CELLTECH COMMUNICATIONS ON SEPTEMBER 25, 1997

This draft term sheet outlines some of the principal terms of Alpha's potential acquisition of all of the capital stock of Zenith by means of a merger of a wholly owned subsidiary of Alpha ("Alpha Sub") with and into Zenith. This draft term sheet is for discussion purposes only and is not binding. In addition, this draft term sheet does not address all of the material terms of the potential transaction, which will only be addressed after all due diligence has been completed and a definitive agreement between Zenith, Alpha, and Alpha Sub has been executed.

Structure of Acquisition: Merger of Alpha Sub with and into Zenith, with Zenith being the surviving entity.

Merger Consideration: Pursuant to the merger, Alpha would issue or reserve for issuance shares of and options on Alpha Common Stock in exchange for all of the shares, options, and warrants of Zenith. The aggregate number of shares issued or reserved for issuance by Alpha ("Merger Consideration") would be equal to $115,000,000.00 divided by the average closing stock price of Alpha's common stock over the five trading day period ending two trading days prior to closing; provided that a collar would exist such that in no event would the average closing stock price used in such calculation vary by more than 5% relative to the average closing stock price as of the day immediately preceding execution of definitive agreements. For purposes of calculating the number of shares of Alpha Common Stock to which Zenith shareholders, option holders, and warrant holders would be entitled, the exchange ratio ("Exchange Ratio") would equal the Merger Consideration divided by the "Total Zenith Shares," subject to any adjustments required on account of any applicable liquidation preferences. The "Total Zenith Shares" would be equal to the sum of the Zenith common shares outstanding plus all the Zenith common shares that would be issued upon the conversion or exercise of Zenith securities convertible into or exercisable for common stock (including but not limited to, all vested and unvested employee stock options, warrants, and convertible preferred stock).

Treatment of Zenith Employee Stock Options: Zenith's outstanding stock options would not be accelerated by virtue of this transaction (beyond mandatory, nondiscretionary acceleration provisions, if any, currently described in Zenith's option plans) and will be rolled over into Alpha stock options (with identical vesting) such that each Zenith stock option would be converted into an Alpha stock option exercisable for a number of shares equal to the existing number of shares multiplied by the Exchange Ratio (subject to the effect of any liquidation preference). The new exercise price would be equal to the existing exercise price divided by the Exchange Ratio (subject to the effect of any liquidation preference).

Marketability of Shares: Subject to compliance with securities laws and pooling and tax requirements. Alpha would provide shares of Alpha common stock to Zenith initially through exemption from registration, and would amend the Investors' Rights Agreement with certain of Alpha's investors (originally executed with Alpha's venture capital investors) such that existing holders of Zenith registration rights would become parties to the Investors' Rights Agreement.

Lock-up of Alpha Stock: All shares of Alpha Common Stock received by Zenith shareholders in the merger will be subject to a lockup for a period of up to 90 days as required by underwriters in connection with any public offerings by Alpha.

Employee Issues: Key employees of Zenith as may be identified during the due diligence process (collectively the "Key Employees") will enter into a three-year noncompete/nonsolicitation agreement with Alpha.

(Continued)

EXHIBIT 16-3 *(Continued)*

Closing Conditions:	Conditions to Closing, (or, in particular cases, execution of definitive agreements) would include, among other things:

- Completion of due diligence to the satisfaction of Zenith.
- The transaction being accounted for as a pooling of interests business combination.
- The transaction being a tax-free reorganization.
- No material adverse change in Zenith between execution of a Merger Agreement and closing.
- Receipt by Alpha of a satisfactory legal opinion, dated as of the closing.
- Execution of employment and noncompete and nonsolicitation agreements by Zenith Key Employees.

Survival of Representations and Escrow Provision: Representation and warranties would survive closing by 1 year. An escrow of 10% of the shares issued in the transaction would be established to support the representations and warranties.

Fees and Expenses: All legal, broker or finder fees incurred by Zenith or its shareholders in connection with the transaction would be deemed to be expenses of the shareholders, and would be borne by the shareholders of Zenith and would not become obligations of Alpha or Zenith.

Timing: Alpha and its legal and financial advisors would begin their due diligence review of Zenith as well as negotiation of definitive agreements promptly. The parties would seek to execute definitive agreements as soon as practical.

Board Representation: Alpha agrees to use good faith efforts to obtain the approval of its Board of Directors to nominate an individual designated by a majority of the Zenith stockholders (which person must be acceptable to Alpha's Chairman and must have prior relevant experience) to serve one three-year term on the Alpha board of Directors.

Voting Rights/Proxy: Selected insiders and other shareholders of Zenith would agree to vote for this transaction and would grant Alpha an irrevocable proxy to vote the shares owned by such shareholders with respect to any matter requiring a Zenith shareholder vote.

No Other Negotiations: Zenith would immediately enter into an agreement under which, for a period ending six weeks from the date of such agreement (the "Expiration Date"), Zenith would not, directly or indirectly, through any officer, director, affiliate, or agent of Zenith, or otherwise, take any action to solicit, initiate, seek, entertain, encourage, or support any inquiry, proposal, or offer form, furnish any information to, or participate in any negotiations with, any third party regarding any acquisition of Zenith, any merger of consolidation with or involving Zenith, or any acquisition of any material portion of the stock or assets of Zenith.

Confidentiality: This Term Sheet and related discussion would not be disclosed by Zenith or any of its representatives.

EXHIBIT 16-4

METAPATH SOFTWARE CORPORATION—QUARTERLY INCOME STATEMENTS ($ 000'S), PREPARED AS OF SEPTEMBER 30, 1997

	Quarter Ended				
	3/31/97 Actual	6/30/97 Actual	9/30/97 Actual	12/31/97 Forecast	Total Forecast
Revenue					
System sales	3,412	4,598	4,738	3,072	15,820
Service	792	1,560	1,697	2,405	6,453
Total revenue	4,204	6,158	6,435	5,476	22,273
Cost and Expenses					
Cost of systems sales	1,134	1,243	1,189	807	4,373
Service & implementation	1,231	1,331	1,398	1,456	5,416
Product development	1,191	1,392	1,573	1,571	5,727
Sales	530	774	718	906	2,928
Marketing	343	502	519	627	1,990
General & administrative	892	966	805	889	3,551
Total costs & expenses	5,321	6,208	6,201	6,256	23,985
Operating income (loss)	(1,117)	(49)	234	(780)	(1,712)
Other					
Interest income	18	20	10	71	120
Interest expense	(45)	(91)	(996)	(98)	(330)
Other, net	0	0	0	0	0
Income before taxes	(1,144)	(120)	149	(806)	(1,921)
Income tax expense	0	0	0	0	0
Net earnings (loss)	(1,144)	(120)	149	(806)	(1,921)

consisted of software running on standard server platforms in the wireless switching office, while CellTech's products were mostly hardware-based and installed in the field with the cellular base stations—Hansen felt that some of CellTech's engineers could potentially be useful to Metapath's development group.

Just by the numbers, the CellTech deal had other immediate merits. A valuation of $115 million was certainly attractive for a company with a revenue run-rate of $25.6 million (see Exhibits 16-4 and 16-5). Moreover, the transaction would give the existing shareholders liquidity in the near future (after a 90-day lockup, plus whatever restrictions regular securities rules might place on the stock). This was quite tempting for Metapath's investors given that, even with stellar execution, the company was over a year away from its own IPO. Also, unlike in an IPO, a stock sale like the CellTech deal would not dilute the ownership of the existing shareholders.

In the end, Metapath's board members were left asking themselves how CellTech's stock would perform over the next 12 to 18 months (see Exhibits 16-6 and 16-7). This was a difficult question to answer, for the company had gone public only a few months prior and thus had little history as a public stock. One of Metapath's board members had been an investor in CellTech and had a mixed opinion of the company. But in the three months leading up to their offer for Metapath, the stock had traded up from its IPO price of $15/share to the $19–$22 range.

EXHIBIT 16-5

**METAPATH SOFTWARE CORPORATION—BALANCE SHEET
($ 000s), CURRENT MONTH AND PREVIOUS MONTH,
PREPARED SEPTEMBER 30, 1997**

	As of 9/30/97	As of 8/31/97
Assets		
Current assets:		
Cash	557	950
Accounts receivable	846	635
Inventory		
WIP	807	905
Spare parts	920	944
Prepaid expenses	415	424
Total current assets	3,545	3,857
Property & equipment	5,376	5,033
Accumulated depreciation	(1,288)	(1,162)
Property & equipment, net	4,088	3,871
Total assets	7,633	7,728
Liabilities & shareholders' equity		
Current liabilities:		
Accounts payable	1,754	1,385
Accrued liabilities	429	365
Deferred revenue		
System revenue	3,365	3,736
Maintenance revenue	1,465	1,753
C/P of long-term obligations	2,576	1,446
Total current liabilities	9,590	8,685
Long-term obligations	2,247	2,366
Total liabilities	11,837	11,051
Preferred stock—class A	61	61
Preferred stock—class B	976	976
Stockholders' equity:		
Preferred stock—class C	2	2
Preferred stock—class D	7	7
Common stock	6	6
Additional paid-in capital	6,363	6,357
Accumulated loss	(11,619)	(10,733)
Total shareholders' equity	(5,241)	(4,361)
Total liabilities & equity	7,633	7,728

EXHIBIT 16-6

CELLTECH COMMUNICATIONS—QUARTERLY RESULTS OF OPERATIONS (1000s)

	Quarter ended					
	31-Mar-96	30-Jun-96	30-Sep-96	31-Dec-96	31-Mar-97	30-Jun-97
Revenues						
System revenue	0	4,825	6,038	8,906	8,882	11,022
Service revenue	159	336	405	654	1,010	1,184
Total revenues	159	5,161	6,442	9,559	9,892	12,206
Cost of revenues						
Cost of system revenues	46	5,035	5,617	8,045	8,135	8,142
Cost of service revenues	232	607	596	699	902	769
Total cost of revenues	277	5,642	6,213	8,745	9,036	8,911
Gross profit (deficit)	(119)	(481)	229	815	856	3,295
Operating expenses						
Research and development	1,034	1,295	1,369	1,720	1,503	1,753
Sales and marketing	905	1,304	1,494	2,141	1,683	1,939
General and administrative	617	695	632	874	1,078	1,062
Total operating expenses	2,556	3,294	3,495	4,736	4,264	4,755
Operating loss	(2,674)	(3,775)	(3,266)	(3,922)	(3,408)	(1,459)
Interest income (expense), net	79	(20)	(163)	(136)	(3)	50
Loss before income taxes	(2,595)	(3,794)	(3,429)	(4,057)	(3,411)	(1,409)
Income taxes	1	0	1	3	2	2
Net loss	(2,596)	(3,794)	(3,430)	(4,060)	(3,413)	(1,411)

EXHIBIT 16-7

CELLTECH COMMUNICATIONS—BALANCE SHEETS (IN THOUSANDS)

	As Of		
	31-Dec-95	31-Dec-96	30-Jun-97
ASSETS			
Current assets:			
Cash and cash equivalents	7,691	18,544	11,419
Short-term investments	2,128	2,667	10,642
Accounts receivable	894	3,592	3,396
Inventories	2,406	10,112	12,308
Prepaid expenses	123	90	747
Total current assets	13,241	35,004	38,513
Property & equipment, net	1,973	2,636	3,061
Other assets	181	325	397
Total assets	15,395	37,966	41,971
LIABILITIES AND STOCKHOLDERS' EQUITY			
Current liabilities			
Accounts payable	368	3,728	1,381
Accrued expenses	785	2,721	3,524
Notes payable (current portion)	241	1,961	2,072
Capital lease obligations (current portions)	48	311	412
Deferred revenue	1,178	4,880	12,072
Total current liabilities	2,620	13,600	19,461
Notes payable	1,138	4,111	3,142
Capital lease obligations, noncurrent portion	119	668	653
Total liabilities	3,876	18,379	23,255
Stockholders' equity			
Convertible preferred stock, $0.001 par value	5	10	11
Common stock, $0.001 par value	0	1	1
Additional paid-in capital	27,238	49,178	53,130
Accumulated deficit	−15,724	−29,602	−34,427
Total stockholders' equity	11,519	19,587	18,715
Total liabilities and shareholders' equity	15,395	37,966	41,971

Also, financial analysts seemed to be bullish on the stock. Another analyst report on CellTech from the summer of 1997 ended as follows:

> Due to the Company's large addressable market opportunity, rapid forecasted growth in EPS, technology leadership and conservative financial policies, we believe the shares could trade between 40×–45× forward earnings. This suggests a near-term price target between $21–$24 per share. Longer-term, we believe the Company will be able to maintain its rate of earnings growth by internally developing new products and extending its expertise and product offerings through acquisition. Based on preliminary 1999 EPS estimates of $0.80 per share, we believe a 12–18 month price target above $30 is appropriate.

Although Hansen was not sure how much weight to give to the valuation estimates in the analyst report, he was struck by the positive consensus of observers in the financial community about the prospects for CellTech's stock.

17

A Note on Private Equity Securities

IN THE BEGINNING, THERE WAS COMMON STOCK . . .

Common stock is the basic unit of ownership. It does not carry any special rights outside of those described in the company charter and bylaws. It gives the holder ownership, but that ownership is subordinated to (1) all government claims (read "taxes"), (2) all regulated employee claims (e.g., pension obligations), (3) all trade debt (accounts receivable), (4) all bank debt, and (5) all forms of preferred stock. Specifically, were the company liquidated—or sold in an asset sale—the common shareholder stands behind all of those other stakeholders before getting the residual value, that is, what's left after all other obligations are satisfied.

Typically, venture capitalists do not buy common stock. The fundamental reason is illustrated by the following example:

Joe Flash has a great idea for a new Internet company and goes to his local venture capitalist, Rex Finance. Joe and Rex agree that $1.5 million will fund the project to the next big value accretion point, and they further agree to a 50.05/49.95 split, with Joe holding the majority stake. But contrary to standard venture practice, perhaps because the competition to finance Joe's deal is so great, Rex agrees to an all common stock structure. Therefore, immediately after the closing, the company has an implied enterprise value of $3 million (since the market price that Rex paid was $1.5 million for 49.95%), one employee (Joe), one class of tangible assets (cash), and some intangible assets (Joe's Power Point slides and a business plan).

On the day of the closing as they walk out of the lawyers' office, Joe bumps into his old friend, John Terrific, who is Vice President for Business Development of WooWee!, a public Internet company valued in the market at just over $12 billion. WooWee! needs ideas and talent to maintain the promise of its "full" market valuation, so John pulls Joe aside and offers him $2 million for Joe's new company. Seeing a quick

Senior Lecturer Felda Hardymon and Professor Josh Lerner prepared this note as the basis for class discussion.

return on the hours he put in writing his business plan and realizing WooWee! will use its considerable resources and market clout to enter the market ahead of him should he decline its offer, Joe accepts the offer.

How is the pie divided? Joe and Rex each get $1 million from WooWee! So in a matter of minutes, Joe's investment goes from $0 (sweat equity) to $1 million, while Rex's investment goes from $1.5 million (cash) to $1 million. Rex was powerless through the whole process; and WooWee! was able to recruit Joe and own his idea for a mere $500,000 since it ends up with the $1.5 million (less the legal fees) that was in Joe's company. How could Rex have avoided this disaster?

Most venture securities have three features, any one of which would have saved Rex from having to explain to his partners how he lost $500,000 in an afternoon:

1. Preferred stock.
2. Vesting of founder, management, and key employee shares.
3. Covenants and super-majority provisions.

This note will briefly discuss each feature and the major variations commonly used in practice.

Key to all of these structural features is the concept of the entrepreneur earning his equity through value creation. In our example, Rex was valuing Joe's company based on its potential value, not on its current tangible value. In a perfect, frictionless world, Rex's money might be metered into Joe's company precisely in proportion to value being created and to the expenses incurred; but in the real world entrepreneurs need to finance ahead of their expenses. Moreover, value is created in lumps coincident with important events like first proof of product feasibility, first customer shipment, and major successes in the marketplace. Venture capital exists as a bridge between such value accretion events; at the same time, the entrepreneur's stake should not be perfected until he or she has delivered on the promised value. This is the basis of most deviations of typically used venture securities from common stock. In the above example, Joe had not *earned* his equity interest at the time of the WooWee! buyout, and that violated the principle of reward for performance.

PREFERRED STOCK

Preferred stock has a *liquidation preference* over common stock: that is, in the event of sale or liquidation of the company, the preferred stock gets paid ahead of the common stock. There must be a face value to preferred stock, which is the amount that gets paid to the preferred stock before moving on to paying the common stock. Generally, the face value of a preferred stock in a private equity transaction is the cost basis the venture capitalist pays for the stock. If in the original example Rex had invested his money in Joe's company in the form of preferred stock, then when WooWee! purchased Joe's company, Rex's $1.5 million would have been returned to him through a redemption of the preferred stock. But how would the remainder $500,000 been divided? That leads to the variations of preferred stock used in private equity transactions.

Redeemable Preferred Redeemable preferred, sometimes called "straight preferred," is preferred stock that has no convertibility into equity. Its intrinsic value is therefore its face value plus any dividend rights it carries.[1] In most ways it behaves in a capital structure like deeply subordinated debt. Redeemable preferred stock always carries a negotiated term specifying when it *must* be redeemed by the company—typically, the sooner of a public offering or five to eight years. It is used in private equity transactions in combination with common stock or warrants. For example, had Rex agreed with Joe to the same 50.05/49.95 split, but had specified that his investment would be in the form of a redeemable preferred stock with $1.5 million face value plus 49.95% of the common stock, then the WooWee! transaction would have first redeemed out the straight preferred stock ($1.5 million to Rex) and the remaining $500,000 would have been split proportionally to the ownership of common stock ($250,000 each to Rex and to Joe).

Had the company gone on to a successful public offering, Rex could have expected his initial $1.5 million investment to be returned through a redemption of the redeemable preferred without affecting his basic ownership position held in common stock. He would, in effect, be getting his money back *and* keeping his investment. This aspect of "double-dipping" is sometimes troubling to entrepreneurs. Moreover, when a material portion of the proceeds of a public offering is used to redeem out a venture capitalist's preferred stock, the public market value of the company can be adversely affected. These negatives of the redeemable preferred[2] led to the use of convertible preferred stock in private equity transactions.

Convertible Preferred Stock   Convertible preferred stock is preferred stock that can be converted *at the shareholder's option* into common stock. This forces the shareholder to choose whether he will take his returns through the liquidation feature or through the underlying common equity position. Clearly, if the value being offered for the company exceeds the implied total enterprise value at the time of the investment, then the shareholder will convert the preferred stock to common stock in order to realize his portion of the gain in value.

---

[1] Generally, venture securities carry no dividends, or defer dividends considerably out into the future because venture capitalists are capital gains oriented. In fact, many venture partnerships do not grant a carried interest to the general partners on dividends received. Moreover, dividends can limit the ability of a growth company to raise capital since it raises the question: "Why are you returning cash to your shareholders when you need it to grow?" Finally, dividends create an asymmetry of rewards between the preferred shareholders (typically the investors) and the common shareholders (typically the founders, management, and key employees), which in turn leads to a misalignment of incentives between investor and company. Large public companies often issue preferred stock with high dividends, which are themselves preferential to common stock dividends, in order to attract certain classes of investors who desire high-income streams. The use of preferred stock in venture securities is based on the preference value and the "earn out" principle and should not be confused with this common use of preferred stock in large public companies.

[2] One might suggest a solution to this problem of assigning more of the value of the unit to the common stock. However, it is accepted practice to assign as much value as possible to the preferred. There are three reasons for this practice: 1. Tax deferral—Since redemption of preferred stock is simply a return of capital with no associated gain, there is no tax on redemption. Moreover, since the preferred is much more likely to be redeemed before the common is sold, then putting more value in the preferred portion of the unit defers tax. 2. Security—The preference is protection from the common receiving value before it is earned, and so it makes sense to put as much in that instrument as possible. 3. Pricing employee incentive shares—In declaring a fair market value for incentive stock option exercise prices or for employee purchase plans, a board of directors wants as low a share price as possible in order to embed as much value as possible in the incentive shares. Since these incentive plans use common stock as their underlying equity, the board can use the "cheap common" part of the transaction as the basis of a low share price.

In our example, if Rex had proposed a convertible preferred stock, then he would have received his original $1.5 million investment back from redemption of the un-converted preferred and Joe would have gotten the residual $500,000. Rex would have left his preferred stock unconverted since converting the preferred to common would have left him with 49.95% of the proceeds ($1 million) and in a loss position. Clearly, if WooWee! had chosen to pay more than $3 million for Joe's company, Rex would have had an incentive to convert to common stock in order to enjoy his portion (49.95%) of whatever premium over the $3 million implied enterprise value that WooWee! was offering.

Conceptually, convertible preferred allows the entrepreneur to "catch up" to the investor after the investor's initial investment is secured. Therefore, convertible preferred stock differs from the redeemable preferred plus cheap common as follows:

Portion of Proceeds Received by Investor

Amount of Proceeds	Redeemable Preferred	Convertible Preferred
Up to face value of preferred (FV)	All to Investor	All to Investor
From FV to implied enterprise value at time of investment (IEV)	FV plus common equity proportion of increment over FV to Investor	FV only to Investor
Above IEV	FV plus common equity proportion of increment over FV to Investor	Common equity proportion to Investor

In general, the public markets expect companies to have simple capital structure using only common stock and debt. Therefore, underwriters nearly always insist that all preferred stock be converted coincident with an initial public offering. To avoid a round of negotiations wherein investors demand to be compensated for their conversion to common, convertible preferred stock routinely contains a *mandatory conversion term* which specifies that the company can force conversion as part of an underwritten IPO of a certain (negotiated) size and price. The size is usually large enough to ensure a liquid market (recently these terms have tended to specify a $30 million or larger offering), and the price is negotiated to be high enough to ensure that it is in the venture capitalist's clear interest to convert (recently, these terms have tended to specify at least a factor of three increase in share price from that at the time the investment).

Convertible preferred stock naturally led to the idea that the conversion ratio need not be fixed. Many convertible preferred stocks contain *antidilution provisions* that automatically adjust the conversion price down[3] if the company sells stock below the share price that the investor has paid. The rationale for these provisions is that the company is presumably selling at a lower price (a "down round") because of underperformance. By having an automatic adjustment, the investor is less likely to oppose or forestall a

---

[3] The adjustment mechanism is a negotiated term and can range from complete adjustment ("full ratchet") to one based on the size of the round and the size of the price decrease ("weighted average formula"). Some antidilution provisions only apply below a certain negotiated price level, and some except smaller financings.

dilutive financing to take on much needed capital when the company needs it most or when the private equity markets are difficult.[4]

Anecdotally, private equity deals in the 1970s tended to be of redeemable preferred structure reflecting the paucity of capital available and the need to get it back as soon as possible to do more deals. As venture capital became more institutionalized during the 1980s, the market became more competitive and convertible preferred became the standard security. As the pattern of multiple private venture capital rounds became prevalent, later round players who were paying significantly higher prices than early round players insisted on having preferred stock with liquidation preferences over *both* common stock and lower-priced preferred stock.[5] This trend accelerated in the 1990s as later round investors paid higher and higher prices. These investors insisted on structures that gave them more participation in the returns reaped from the early sale of private companies at prices that gave astonishing returns to the early-stage investor, but gave considerably less returns to the later stage investor who had paid a high price expecting an exit in the hot public markets. The structure that satisfies this need is participating convertible preferred stock.

Participating Convertible Preferred Stock Participating convertible preferred stock is convertible preferred stock with the additional feature that in the event of a sale or liquidation of the company, the holder has a right to receive the face value *and* the equity participation as if the stock were converted. Like a convertible preferred, these instruments carry a mandatory conversion term triggered on a public offering. The net result is an instrument that acts like the redeemable preferred structure while the company is private, and converts to common on a public offering.

A key companion term to a participating convertible preferred is the specification of when the participation term is in effect. Usually, the term reads "in the event of sale or liquidation" and often goes on to define liquidation as being any merger or transaction that constitutes a change of control. As a result, in a merger transaction between two private firms where the private surviving merged company issues new preferred stock in exchange for the preexisting preferred stock, these clauses may be triggered. This may set off a demand from the holders of the participating convertible preferred for both new preferred stock equal in face value to the old preferred stock plus a participation in the common equity of the new company. All of this can occur without any true liquidity event.

The driver behind the recent acceptance of participating convertible preferred is the willingness of later stage investors to pay very high prices if the terms include a participation feature. If the company goes public, the highly dilutive participating feature

---

[4] While antidilution provisions became prevalent based on adjusting the conversion ratio of convertible preferred stock, venture capitalists have applied the concept to the redeemable preferred structure by having the company issue free common shares in a down round according to similar formulas. Other antidilution structures include the use of payable-in-kind dividends should the company miss its targets.

[5] In the case of sharply increasing share prices in multiple private rounds, the later round players hold the same relationship to early round players that early round players hold to the founders in the initial financing. If the first financing is at $1/share (that is, $1 per *common equivalent share*—the price of the convertible preferred divided by the number of share into which it converts), and the later financing is at $5/share, then the early round investors as well as management would be delighted with an offer to purchase the company for $4/share. Unless the later round investor had a liquidation preference, he would lose money in such a transaction just as Rex lost money in our starting example.

goes away.[6] Therefore, companies and their current shareholders feel confident issuing such instruments when the public market is "hot," and a public offering appears feasible if the company has any business success at all.

To summarize the various preferred structures:

Portion of Proceeds Received by Investor			
Amount of Proceeds	Redeemable Preferred	Convertible Preferred	Participating Convertible Preferred
Up to face value of preferred (FV)	All to Investor	All to Investor	All to Investor
From FV to implied enterprise value at time of investment (IEV)	FV plus common equity proportion of increment over FV to Investor	FV only to Investor	FV plus common equity proportion of increment over FV to Investor
From IEV to public offering	FV plus common equity proportion of increment over FV to Investor	Common equity proportion to Investor	FV plus common equity proportion of increment over FV to Investor
Above public offering	FV plus common equity proportion of increment over FV to Investor	Common equity proportion to Investor	Common equity proportion to Investor

VESTING

The concept of vesting is simple. It holds that an entrepreneur's stock does not become his or her own until he or she has been with the company for a period of time, or until some value accretion event occurs (e.g., the sale of the company). Typically, vesting is implemented over a time period (currently four years on the East Coast, three years on the West Coast), and the stock "vests" (i.e., the entrepreneur obtains unqualified ownership of the shares) proportionately over that time period. For administrative purposes, stock vesting usually occurs quarterly, occasionally annually, and maybe even monthly.

In our example, suppose Rex had eschewed preferred stock entirely but had insisted that Joe's shares vest proportionately over four years (1/16th per quarter). Then when the WooWee! transaction occurred, Rex could have insisted the company buy back Joe's stock at cost (probably a nominal 1¢ per share) and theoretically received the entire $2 million of proceeds. Of course, since Joe likely would have objected to receiving no proceeds from the sale to WooWee! and since WooWee! wanted to acquire Joe's talents and wished to see that Joe was a happy WooWee! employee, the transaction may have been called off under those conditions. Having foreseen this situation, Rex may have agreed to a partial acceleration of Joe's vesting in the event of acquisi-

---

[6] Later stage, high-priced financings are almost always large, so the participating feature can be quite dilutive to management and existing shareholders.

tion.[7] If that agreement called for 25% acceleration, then the proceeds would be split 12.5% to Joe (25% of 50.05%) and the remainder to Rex.

In general, preferred stock structures do a better job of implementing the "reward for performance" principle since they rely on the investment's terminal value. Furthermore, vesting is contractual: potential events and situations must be anticipated and written down if vesting is to do the same job as preferred stock. However, vesting does perform the very important function of preventing an employee from leaving and taking with him value disproportionate to the time he was employed at the company. Vesting creates the "golden handcuffs" that motivates an employee to stay when other opportunities call. If a company is doing well and a key employee holds valuable options or stock that would be lost if the employee left before a certain date or event, then the possibility of an early departure is greatly diminished.

Vesting also performs the function of returning shares to the incentive stock pool from employees who in some sense "haven't finished the job," thereby providing incentive stock for their replacements. This allows companies to budget their incentive stock by position or task with some assurance that they are somewhat protected from turnover. Similarly, vesting protects morale by assuring employees that those who leave will not benefit as much as those who stay behind and create value.

COVENANTS

Maybe the most basic way venture capitalists protect their investments is by covenant provisions. Covenants are contractual agreements between the investor and the company and fall into two broad categories: positive covenants and negative covenants. Positive covenants are the list of things the company agrees to do. They include such things as producing audited reports, holding regular board meetings, and paying taxes on time.

In addition to the positive commitments, the preferred equity agreements also contain numerous covenants and restrictions that serve to limit detrimental behavior by the entrepreneur. Certain actions are expressly forbidden or require the approval of a super-majority of investors. For instance, sales of assets are often restricted. Any disposal of assets above a certain dollar value or above a certain percentage of the firm's book value may be limited without the approval of private equity investors. This prevents the entrepreneur from increasing the risk profile of the company and changing the firm's activities from its intended focus. It also prevents the entrepreneur from making "sweet heart" deals with friends.

The private equity investors are also often concerned about changes in control. The contracts may state that the founders cannot sell any of their common stock without approval of the private equity investors or offering the securities to the private equity

---

[7] Often venture terms allow for a 25% to 50% acceleration of vesting for certain managers on acquisition based on the theory that (1) many managers lose their job in an acquisition, and it is not fair for those who have created the value to lose a big portion of it by the very act of perfecting that value for the shareholders, and (2) it is better to have the cooperation of management and key employees in the event of a potential acquisition, and acceleration acts as an incentive to get the deal done. Of course, acceleration acts *against* the interest of the acquiring company who may have to spend stock option shares to re-motivate the acquired employees who have had the benefits of acceleration. It also acts against the interest of the nonmanagement shareholders by effectively adding shares to the pool of shares to be bought. The fixed negotiated share price is therefore divided among more shares. For these reasons, acceleration usually is restricted to a few employees and often is only partial.

investors. Similarly, restrictions may prevent a merger or sale of the company without approval of the investors. Transfer-of-control restrictions are important because venture capitalists invest in people. If the management team decides to remove its human capital from the deal, venture capitalists will want to approve the terms of the transfer. Control transfers may hurt the position of the private equity investor if they are done on terms that are unfavorable to earlier investors.

The purchase of major assets above a certain size threshold may also be forbidden without the approval of private equity investors. This restriction may be written in absolute dollar terms or may be written as a percentage of book value. The wording is usually broad enough to cover purchases of assets or merger of the firm. Restrictions on purchases may help prevent radical changes in strategy or wasteful expenditure by the entrepreneur. Many such strategy changes could have detrimental effects on the value of the private equity investors' stake.

Finally, the contracts usually contain some provision for restricting the issuance of new securities. Almost all documents contain a provision that restricts the issuance of senior securities without the approval of previous investors. Many documents alter the restriction to include securities on the preferred equity level or any security issuance. Usually, a majority of preferred shares must vote in favor of such an issue. Restricting security issuance prevents the transfer of value from current shareholders to new security holders.

Often negative covenants are coupled with super-majority voting provisions wherein the company agrees not to do certain things unless a greater than 50% majority of shareholders (or in some cases, the board) agrees. So, for example, if Rex had insisted in the original deal that the company could only be sold if two-thirds of common shares agreed in a shareholder vote, then he would have had a veto over the WooWee! transaction, and presumably he would have had the negotiating leverage to insist on an acceptable deal.

A few frequently encountered covenants are somewhat different from the positive and negative ones considered above. Many contracts also contain mandatory redemption rights. These are rights of the private equity investors that allow them to "put," or sell at a predetermined price, the preferred stock back to the company. Essentially, the venture capitalists can force the firm to repay the face value of the investment at any time. This mechanism can often be used to force liquidation or merger of the firm. The mandatory redemption provisions are often included for two reasons: (1) most venture partnerships have a limited life so they must have some mechanism to force a liquidity event before the partnership expires, and (2) mandatory redemption clauses help prevent "lifestyle companies," that is, companies that exist only to provide a good living to the management but do not accrete value to the investors. By demanding redemption, the investors can get their money back, or in the event there isn't enough money available in the company, force a negotiation to create a liquidity event.

Usually, a contract explicitly states the number of board seats that venture capital investors can elect. Typically, in companies that are venture backed from the beginning, private equity investors control the board or the board has a majority of outside (i.e., nonmanagement) directors where the investors at least have approval rights over those seats not held by them or the management. Even if the private equity investors do not own greater than 50% of the equity, the contracts may allocate control of the board to venture capitalists. The board control serves as an important check on management that may try to exploit minority shareholders. Similarly, in any future initial public offering, an outsider-dominated board lends credibility to the firm.

All in all, the most frequent use of covenants is to effectively disconnect control on important issues from owning a majority of the equity. Price and control then become separate items for negotiation. Control issues implemented through covenants and super-majority voting provisions can be settled quite specifically and therefore appropriately to each side's concerns. For example, management often has stronger concerns about operational matters than financing ones, while investors' concerns are typically the reverse. A negotiated set of covenants can leave investors minimally involved in determining operating policy but heavily consulted and involved in financial strategy.

18

Venture Capital Case Vignettes

ATLANTIC NETWORKS

Hardy Smith glanced over the term sheet for Atlantic Networks. He and the founders had easily come to an agreement to split the equity 53% for $4.4 million from the investors and 47% for the founders and an unallocated option pool to attract the initial employees. They had further agreed that of the 47%, 20% would be put into the option pool and 27% would go to the three founders.

The last issue to be addressed was that of the founders' split among themselves. From the beginning, the three founders had presented their arrangement as being an equal three-way split (see table below). But Hardy viewed each of the founders very differently as to their potential contribution to the deal as well as who was most important to attracting Hardy and his partners to invest. He had put off addressing the issue until now.

Ron Jasper was the CEO and technical founder. A general manager of the communications division at XYZ Corp., Jasper had practically invented the first new-style communications switch long before better known venture-backed start-ups such as Cascade even ventured into central office-based equipment. Jasper, 37 years old and a well-trained engineer, exuded the confidence and charisma of a technical visionary. It was Jasper who had really attracted Hardy and his partners.

Karl Timmons, age 36, most recently had been a regional sales manager for a competitor of XYZ but had served with Jasper at XYZ several years before. Timmons was aggressive, known to the customer base, and a bit crass in his style; he was the one responsible for badgering Ron Jasper into leaving XYZ and forming Atlantic Networks. He was to be Vice President of Sales. He had started out as Vice President of Sales and Marketing, but Smith had convinced the founders to split the Sales from the Marketing job, partly on his belief that Timmons couldn't handle the bigger job.

Steve Thomas was 41 years old and more mature in demeanor than the other two founders. Thomas had held a series of nontechnical jobs at XYZ, including a stint in the XYZ marketing department. His most recent job was director of investor relations. Be-

Senior Lecturer G. Felda Hardymon prepared these case vignettes as the basis for class discussion rather than to illustrate either effective or ineffective handling of an administrative situation. The companies, events, and people described are fictitious.

ing a Harvard graduate (liberal arts degree) and having held many jobs, Thomas had an air of maturity that made Jasper feel comfortable. In fact, it was clear that although Thomas's role in the new enterprise was somewhat undefined other than specifying he had "financial and other administrative duties," Jasper would not have left XYZ to start the venture had Thomas not agreed to go along.

As Hardy thought about how he should address the issue with the founders, the phone rang. Ron Jasper was on the line.

Shareholder	Ownership
Investors	53%
Option Pool	20
Ron Jasper	9
Karl Timmons	9
Steve Thomas	9
Total	100%

PONDERANT TECHNOLOGY: BUILDING A BOARD OF DIRECTORS

Text of e-mail to Hardy Smith from Dan Singer, CEO of Ponderant Technology sent May 19, 1999

Hardy,

We got the termsheet from Denzal Capital. It's everything we wanted and XYZ and ABC *[two passive private equity funds who indicated they wanted in the round but wanted another outside lead to set price and terms]* have said they are in on Denzal's terms, so we have the whole $15 million. The only problem is they want a board seat. I like Craig, but while he would be marginally better than Jennifer, and certainly better than Mark, I don't think we need a fourth VC on the board. I'm happy to do some swapping around, especially if I can get someone better than Mark in the outsider's seat. Craig sees this as important to both Denzal and to his own career so he's hanging tough on having a board seat. He won't listen to the idea of observer rights. The betas are going well and we have about eight weeks of cash, but we've got to turn our attention to ramping this thing up. You introduced me to Craig. Help! Give me a call this afternoon when you get a chance.

Dan

Facts about Ponderant

Product

Ponderant makes a software product that enables disparate groups within companies and even groups from different companies to work together. The product is very complex, and its potential has benefited enormously with the ubiquitous spread of the Internet. The company is about to launch its Internet-based product which has been warmly received by existing customers who have been trialing the product.

Current Board

1. Dan Singer, CEO
2. Hardy Smith, partner at Bessemer Venture Partners and co-lead investor
3. Don Fentripp, partner at Charles River Ventures and co-lead investor

4. Jennifer Loden, partner at Caffen Capital Partners, a solid $80 million fund which just launched a fundraising effort for a $150 million fund

5. Mark Segras, former EVP of Rockwell Intl., now retired, on the board because original technology of Ponderant Tech came from a Rockwell project

6. Open Seat: designated as an "unaffiliated" seat, it has been open since the Series B round. Everyone agrees this should be a "marquis" director, but there have been other priorities and the position has remained open.

TITANIC TECHNOLOGY: PUTTING OUT A FIRE

Background

Titanic is a very high-profile vendor of expensive communications equipment. It has raised over $50 million and is within a few weeks of delivering its first product. Jason Banter, a partner of Greenlane Partners, is the chairman of the company. Greenlane has over $7 million in the deal, but there are two other investors with even more. Jason was recruited as chairman before joining Greenlane and has had a role as an active participant in management. Jason meets with the senior management several times a month and actively manages the board meetings. The other investors look to him for leadership. Jason relies on Courtney "Crusty" Weatherstorm III, Greenlane's legendary senior partner, for "venture advice" when the situation warrants.

Transcription of Voicemail from Jason Banter to Courtney Weatherstorm on January 14, 1999

The sales VP at Titanic, Steve Dunnigan, is somebody who when we hired him was slightly scarred and had battled management at his previous company and was kind of political and there were money battles. Unfortunately he was the best guy we could find and he came with a whole team. We decided to go for him.

The issue isn't that he is bad; it's just that the combination of Steve and Bill *[the CEO of Titanic]* is tough. Bill is still doing an OK job. The thing that has come up here is that we gave Kerry Veritte, the CFO, acceleration on change of control of his options, which is appropriate for a CFO. We didn't give that to anyone else and I was very comfortable not giving it to anyone else. Along the way somehow Kerry got confused and thought that the other executives were getting the same thing and someone mentioned it to Steve. Steve claims that Bill said that he was getting acceleration. This is probably not true. From what I have seen of Bill he generally doesn't say things differently, it's just that he might say one thing and someone might interpret something else.

I have a million different issues with this guy and he is making an issue over this. My initial reaction was to tell him to go stuff it. Practically speaking, all Titanic has is a lead, and there's no chance of replacing the sales team and not losing the lead. Steve and all five guys that work for him all worked together at Nortel and kind of came as a package. Steve is not threatening to leave but this is an issue. At CellTech *[a company that Jason was previously associated with]* we gave the sales guy some protection and acceleration. It seems what I ought to do for Steve is give him acceleration in the event of termination after a change of control. Frankly this is in my interest.

The buyer would probably get no acceleration, but it does seem to me that when we go down to the point of trying to sell this company it would be useful to have Steve on board. If he's sitting around nervous that he's going to get popped out of the deal after the deal is consummated, he probably wouldn't be supportive of selling, which is really my goal. I think to be pragmatic I should give the guy acceleration in the event of termination after a change of control. Maybe I will give him one-year acceleration in the event of termination after change of control. Basically I want him on board, and I won't be able to make these adjustments later.

At the same time, the downside is of course he gets what he wants when he whines and plays politics. The guy is a good sales guy and has a good team, but he is a high maintenance guy. He sent Bill a nasty email saying that Bill had lied to him and Bill didn't respond. I would like to have something in my pocket that I can hand to him. I think what I should give him is acceleration if he is terminated after change of control or some partial acceleration.

Of course no one knows that we are planning on replacing Bill. If we give in and they find out, then there's blood on the water and we'll never get a new CEO in here.

I'm on the way to the airport now and will be in Texas tonight. I'm supposed to have dinner with Bill and meet Steve for breakfast tomorrow. If you have any words of wisdom, I'll check voicemail on my way from the airport.

19

New Business Investment Company: October 1997

Takeshi Nakabayashi, the manager of the New Business Investment (NBI) Company's second department, sat at his desk in central Tokyo. It was already 6:30 P.M., but around him the office still buzzed with activity. In front of him lay business plans from prospective entrepreneurs and drafts of a memorandum that summarized the progress of the year-old venture capital fund with which he was affiliated.

Nakabayashi thought about his day, which had included a visit with one of his analysts to one of his two portfolio companies, as well as a presentation by the management team of a firm in which he was considering investing. The NBI fund, it was clear, was making progress. At the same time, sometimes it seemed that the obstacles associated with being a public entity were great and limited the fund's potential impact in addressing the immense problem of creating an entrepreneurial culture in Japan. To what extent could a public policy initiative make progress against such challenges? Were there ways in which his fund could be more effectively implemented? Across the room, he saw one of his colleagues beckoning. It was time for dinner with some officials at the Japan Development Bank, one of his fund's primary sponsors. These worries would have to wait until tomorrow morning.

THE CHALLENGES FACING JAPANESE ENTREPRENEURS

Japan's venture capital industry cannot be discussed without considering the environment for entrepreneurial companies in Japan more generally. Several of the most vexing of these challenges are as follows:

- Professional training in Japanese universities is at a relatively early stage of development. Japan has few equivalents to Stanford University's graduate program in electrical engineering, to say nothing of its Graduate School of Business. Because

Professor Josh Lerner, Professor Lee Branstetter of the University of California at Davis, and Takeshi Nakabayashi, Kennedy School of Government (MPP '87) prepared this case as the basis for class discussion rather than to illustrate either effective or ineffective handling of an administrative situation.

of the limited capabilities of the Japanese universities, much of the training of research and administrative personnel takes place through company-run programs. This training is difficult for outsiders to assess, and much of it is firm-specific. This limits the liquidity of the market for researchers and managers, particularly in technology-intensive industries.

- Explicit and implicit contracts between manufacturers, suppliers, and retailers create a substantial barrier to entry for new firms, especially for industrial goods and intermediate products. Practices that would have been scrutinized by U.S. antitrust authorities (had they occurred domestically) have been allowed to persist in Japan for many decades. As a result, new firms find it difficult to compete directly with established firms, and many entrants are left to pursue marginal markets with few prospects for growth. Nor do strategic alliances with established corporations usually represent an attractive opportunity: aware of the weak position of most start-ups, many corporations are able to negotiate very one-sided transactions.

- The compensation and promotion systems serve to reinforce these trends. (Whether this is a cause or an effect is not clear.) Typically, major corporate and government agencies only hire professionals at the time of their graduation from college, with the most prestigious firms confining their offers to graduates of Japan's elite universities. Thus, potential entrepreneurs have a very low probability of being rehired by a major corporation if their new venture is unsuccessful: even if the entrepreneur is seeking a new position because the venture failed for reasons beyond his control, he is likely to be stigmatized. Leaving a corporate position entails forsaking not only one's salary, but also the subsidized housing, low-interest loans, and many other tax-exempt fringe benefits that the Japanese "salaryman" enjoys. This makes the cost of beginning a new business substantially higher than in the United States. Historically, entrepreneurs in Japan have disproportionately consisted of those who could not get managerial positions within major corporations, such as those with only a high school education.[1]

- Many new industries are governed by extensive regulations. The delays in authorizing new products and services can be particularly harmful to smaller firms, which rely on getting to the market quickly as a critical source of competitive advantage. These also translate into substantial costs to access existing services: for example, the installation of a new phone line can cost upwards of $1,000 and involve an extensive wait. This can have a detrimental effect on, for instance, Internet-related businesses. Another facet of regulations has been restrictions on the compensation offered employees, in particular, the limitations that have until very recently prohibited firms from offering stock options to employees.

- Accessing technology from universities has been very difficult. Until recently, national universities, which comprise the bulk of the Japanese research-performing institutions, have operated under strict guidelines. In particular, professors and researchers—as government employees—have been subject to strict regulations that essentially prohibit their involvement with any commercial enterprise, including the establishment of a new business. Even if such an involvement were permitted, all financial rewards would flow to the university. Many private universities have emulated these rules. Furthermore, few universities have invested in developing technology licensing offices that might facilitate technology transfer transactions.

---

[1] For statistical evidence, see Shuichi Matsuda, *Japan's Independent Entrepreneurs: A Survey Report*, Tokyo, System Science Institute, Waseda University, 1995.

- Reflecting the central role of banks in the Japanese economy, much of the financing available has been in the form of debt. Small businesses with intangible assets such as trade secrets and patents and without positive cash flows may find it difficult to obtain or repay debt financing. Even government programs designed to aid these businesses have often been in the form of loan programs. One consequence is that entrepreneurs are unfamiliar with and highly suspicious of equity financing.

Although these barriers were indeed vexing ones, they appeared to be lowering slowly. Certainly, there had been a dramatic surge in interest in entrepreneurship, particularly among students and young professionals. Exhibit 19-1 provides some summary data on these trends and on the Japanese economy more generally.

THE HISTORY OF THE JAPANESE VENTURE CAPITAL INDUSTRY[2]

The origins of the Japanese venture capital industry date back to 1963, when the Japanese government introduced the Small Business Investment Company program. This was modeled after a 1958 initiative of the same name in the United States, which provided loan guarantees to federally sponsored venture capital funds. But while many of the American SBIC participants soon opted out of the program (which had numerous regulatory restrictions) and established independent venture capital funds, the path to development of a private venture capital sector in Japan was slower. Not until 1972 was the first true venture capital organization formed. In that year and in 1973, eight venture capital firms were formed, seven of which were affiliates of major commercial banks or securities firms.

This group of firms rapidly developed a style of investing that was very different from that seen in the U.S. venture capital industry:

- First, the mixture of companies receiving funds differed considerably. Rather than investing in start-ups, Japanese venture capitalists concentrated on firms that were close to completing an IPO. Many of these firms tended to be older, family-run businesses that needed to gain liquidity in order to address the succession and inheritance tax issues.

- Second, the venture capitalist's involvement with the companies in their portfolios was much more limited. Typically, a Japanese venture capitalist purchases common stock, with no stock purchase agreement that provides special privileges. Due to concerns about the restrictions in the Anti-Monopoly Law (established after World War II by the American Occupational Forces to prevent the revival of *zaibatsu*-style industrial groupings), the venture investors did not take a board seat or retain any active involvement with the firm after the investment was finalized. Post-deal involvement with portfolio firms was typically confined to a quarterly review of the published financial statements. If the venture organization did retain any post-investment involvement, it was likely to be through a separate division of the organization that specialized in consulting—on a fee-for-service basis—with portfolio firms. In many cases, the consultants had little experience with entrepreneurial firms, or the entrepreneur resisted the advice offered. In most cases, the primary

---

[2] This section is based in part on Rodney Clark, *Venture Capital in Britain, America, and Japan*, New York, St. Martin's Press, 1987, and Zen Ishibashi and Pitch Johnson, "Schroder PTV Partners K.K.," Stanford Business School Case #SB-116, 1990, as well as a large number of news stories.

EXHIBIT 19-1

ECONOMIC CONDITIONS AND ENTREPRENEURIAL ACTIVITIES IN JAPAN, 1988–1997

General Economic Conditions in Japan

	1988	1989	1990	1991	1992	1993	1994	1995	1996	1997
Real GDP growth rate	6.2%	4.8%	5.1%	3.8%	1.0%	0.3%	0.6%	1.5%	3.9%	−0.7%
Unemployment rate	2.5%	2.3%	2.1%	2.1%	2.2%	2.5%	2.9%	3.2%	3.4%	3.5%
Active job openings ratio[a]	1.01	1.25	1.40	1.40	1.08	0.76	0.64	0.63	0.70	0.72[b]
Stock price index	2,357.03	2,881.37	1,733.83	1,714.68	1,307.66	1,439.31	1,559.09	1,577.70	1,470.94	1,388.32[b]
Yen/$1 at year end	125.85	143.45	134.40	125.20	124.75	111.85	99.74	102.83	116.00	121.00[b]

[a] The job openings ratio is constructed from taking the ratio of the number of job openings and active job seekers. (Both are determined through regular surveys by the Ministry of Labor.) Numbers around 0.6 and 0.7 indicate that there are many applicants for each position—that there is weak demand for labor.
[b] Indicates figures as of third quarter, 1997.

Sources: Compiled from various articles in Japanese Economic Planning Agency, *Nihon Keizai no Genkyou*, Tokyo, Japanese Economic Planning Agency, various years, and International Monetary Fund, *International Financial Statistics*, Washington, DC, International Monetary Fund, various years.

Indicators of Entrepreneurial Activities in Japan, 1966–1994

	1966–1969	1969–1972	1972–1975	1975–1978	1978–1981	1981–1986	1986–1989	1989–1991	1991–1994
Business starts	6.5%	7.0%	6.1%	6.2%	6.1%	4.7%	4.2%	4.1%	4.6%
Business closures	3.2%	3.7%	4.3%	3.4%	3.7%	4.0%	4.0%	4.7%	4.7%

Note: The business start numbers represents an estimate of the average annual number of new businesses begun in each period, expressed as a percentage of the businesses in existence in the first year of the period. The business closures ratio is constructed similarly.

Source: Compiled from various exhibits in Masato Ono, *Bencha Kigyou to Toushi no Jissai Chishiki: Bencha Economy no Kaisetsu*, Tokyo, Toyo Keizai Shimpo Sha, 1997. The original data was from a number of reports by the Jigyousho Toukei Chousa, the General Management and Coordination Agency.

concern of the securities company-affiliated funds was instead that the parent firm would have the right to underwrite the eventual IPO, if any resulted.

- Third, the portfolios looked very different. The portfolios of a major U.S. venture firm often consist of several dozen firms, clustered by geography or industry. This clustering is driven in large part by the need for venture investors to provide intensive and knowledgeable oversight. In Japan, where historically there has been much less oversight, investments were widely scattered across industries and locations.[3] A major fund might have several hundred investments, often with holdings of just a small percentage of the firm's equity. In many cases, an equity investment was paired with a loan administered by an affiliated commercial bank.

- Fourth, the mix of investors in venture funds was quite different. Restricted initially from adopting a limited partnership structure, venture funds relied primarily on the funds of their corporate affiliates: for example, the largest Japanese fund—the Japan Affiliated Finance Company (JAFCO)—relied on the capital resources of the Nomura Group. Because the corporate parents invested in these funds for a variety of reasons, the returns that the venture units generated were often of secondary importance.

- Finally, the reward and personnel practices of these funds were dramatically different. Although U.S. private equity groups typically were thinly staffed with a few highly motivated partners, the Japanese groups adopted the practices of their corporate parents. Each of the key functions at a major Japanese venture firm—whether responsible for initiating transactions, performing due diligence, structuring the transaction, or consulting with the firm after the investment—was assigned to a different department. Each department might consist of several dozen, or even more than 100, employees. In venture capital organizations affiliated with banks or insurance companies, these employees were typically rotated into these responsibilities for a two- to three-year period, then shifted elsewhere in the parent corporation.[4] These employees typically worked for a straight salary, just as other corporate employees did. Few venture capitalists were likely to have started a corporation themselves or even to have the inclination to do so.

These pioneering firms faced very trying initial years. Both the world economy and Japan in particular were in the grips of a major recession during much of the 1970s, triggered by the oil shocks of 1973 and 1979. Exiting investments was particularly problematic. Not only did regulatory barriers limit the firms that could be taken public to those with a sustained level of profitability but also Japanese markets had little appetite for new offerings. (This problem was compounded by regulatory restrictions on the ability of securities firms to solicit investments in stocks traded on the over-the-counter (OTC) market.) During the first 10 years of the industry's existence (1973 to 1982), a total of 16 firms were taken public. By 1982, two of the eight pioneers were inactive.

The Japanese venture capital industry experienced a revival in the 1980s. A major step was the relaxation of regulatory barriers to the listing of new firms in 1982, which

---

[3] Many of the transactions were identified by "cold calling" firms seeking employees in newspaper ads or whose expansion decisions were announced in trade journals, or else identified through the screening of public databases for firms that met certain criteria. In many cases, investments officers had quotas as to how many investments must be made on a quarterly or annual basis, which created tremendous pressures to complete transactions.

[4] Such short rotations were not characteristic of venture capital organizations affiliated with securities firms.

lifted almost all restrictions. (See background information on the Japanese OTC market and listing requirements in Exhibits 19-2 and 19-3.)[5] The rapid growth of the Japanese economy also created many new opportunities. The improved conditions attracted many entrants into the industry, typically affiliates of the smaller banks and securities houses that did not have earlier funds. The number of venture-backed firms' IPOs climbed, reaching 31 in 1988.

A second important change was the introduction of a new structure of venture funds, known as an Investment Enterprise Partnership (IEP), or investment cooperative. The innovation was initiated by JAFCO after its chairman visited the United States and was impressed by the prevalence of the limited partnership structure in the U.S. market. The organizational form—based on an interpretation of Japanese common law rather than an explicit legislative mandate—resembled a limited partnership, with the important exception that the investors did not have limited liability. As a result, most institutions, such as pension funds and endowments, were reluctant to invest in these partnerships. (In addition, a variety of regulatory barriers limited these institutions from investing in private equity funds.) These partnerships were quite successful, however, in attracting capital from Japanese corporations, who often hoped that their investments would lead to strategic benefits. One consequence was that there were few financially motivated investors with long experience and a sophisticated understanding of private equity markets, as is encountered, for instance, among the larger U.S. endowments and corporate pension funds.

During the 1980s and 1990s, most venture funds continued to be affiliates of commercial and investment banks, rather than freestanding firms. Of the 40 largest venture firms in 1989, for instance, fully 84% were associated with commercial and investment banks. (JAFCO alone accounted for 57% of the capital.) Only 4 of these—accounting for a mere 3% of the capital—were independent firms of the type that dominated the U.S. industry. These independent funds, though few in number, were among the most successful in the Japanese industry. Independent organizations such as Schroders PTV Partners placed much greater emphasis on obtaining strong control rights and working closely with portfolio firms.

One of the most visible changes in the Japanese venture capital industry during the 1980s was an increased emphasis on investing in the United States. Between 1986 and 1990, Japanese funds and corporations invested over $1 billion in U.S. high-technology corporations.[6] Not only were these investments frequently controversial—U.S. politicians and pundits alike expressed anxiety that myopic short-run American investors were allowing valuable technologies to be acquired[7]—but they were also remarkably unsuccessful. In many cases, the Japanese investors invested in companies that could not attract any American venture funds at all or in struggling concerns into which the existing venture investors had decided not to invest any more of their own capital. To cite

---

[5] The significance of this policy shift has been debated. In particular, the volume of IPOs after the policy shift remained relatively modest when compared to that of the U.S., suggesting that informal barriers may still be important limitations. In particular, few IPOs appear to have occurred where the firm has been earning less than 300 million yen ($2.5 million) annually. In 1995, the Ministry of Finance and Japan Securities Dealers Association announced that there was no unofficial standard for IPOs.

[6] William M. Bulkeley and Udayan Gupta, "Japanese Find U.S. High Tech a Risky Venture," *Wall Street Journal*, November 8, 1991, B1–B2.

[7] See, for instance, Charles H. Ferguson, "America's High-Tech Decline," *Foreign Affairs* (Spring 1989): 123–145, and Michael E. Porter, *Capital Choices: Changing the Way America Invests in Industry*, Washington, DC, Council on Competitiveness, 1992.

EXHIBIT 19-2

THE OTC MARKET IN JAPAN, 1988–1996

Overall Market Activity

Year	1988	1989	1990	1991	1992	1993	1994	1995	1996
Number of new listings	53	73	86	95	15	55	107	138	115
Initial public offerings	53	73	86	94	14	54	106	137	112

Industry of Newly Listed Firms

Industry	1995	1996	Industry	1995	1996
Construction	8	3	Precision instruments	2	2
Food products	2	3	Other manufacturing	6	2
Textiles	2	1	Land transportation	4	3
Pulp/paper	1	1	Sea transportation	4	3
Chemicals	11	4	Telecommunication	0	1
Pharmaceuticals	3	1	Wholesale	26	18
Oil, coal	1	0	Retail	17	14
Glass/stoneware	6	3	Security	3	4
Iron/steel	1	0	Other financial services	3	3
Nonferrous metals	0	2	Real estate	1	3
Metal products	3	4	Other services	24	23
Machinery	3	4		138	115
Electrical machinery	6	9			
Transport equipment	1	4			

Distribution of Newly Listed Firms by Years in Operation Prior to
Listing on the OTC Market, 1996

Less than 10 years	7
10–20 years	24
20–30 years	28
30–40 years	25
40–50 years	22
50–60 years	5
60–70 years	1
Average 29.5 years	112

Distribution of Newly Listed Firms by Sales, 1996

Less than 5 billion yen	17
5–10 billion yen	35
10–20 billion yen	31
20–30 billion yen	14
30–50 billion yen	10
50–100 billion yen	3
Over 100 billion yen	2
Average 20 billion yen	112

Source: Compiled from Masato Ono, *Bencha Kigyou to Toushi no Jissai Chishiki: Bencha Economy no Kaisetsu*, Tokyo, Toyo Keizai Shimpo Sha, 1997, Figures 1–5.

EXHIBIT 19-3

LISTING REQUIREMENTS FOR JAPAN OTC, JAPAN SECOND OTC AND NASDAQ

	Japan OTC	Japan Second OTC	NASDAQ
Application companies	No restriction	1. Limited to companies unable to meet profit and asset requirements for OTC market. 2. Must be a new area of business and one with high growth potential 3. R&D must be greater than 3% of sales	No restriction
Number of shares issued	Over two million shares as of date of listing and over one million average in the immediately preceding fiscal year	None	N/A
Number of stockholders (on day of listing)	• Over 200 for companies with under 20 million shares issued • Over 400 for companies with over 20 million shares issued	Over 50	400
Profits	Over ¥10 per share in pretax profits in the immediately preceding fiscal year	None	$750,000[a]
Net assets	Over ¥200 million in immediately preceding fiscal year	Over ¥200 million on day of offering	Over $4 million in total assets
Audit by independent auditor prior to IPO	Minimum two years immediately prior	Minimum two years immediately prior	N/A
Number of shares offered	Minimum greater of ((112.5% × existing shares) + 250,000) or 500,000	Minimum 500,000	Minimum 500,000
Reporting	Twice a year	Every quarter—must include progress of development in detail. Disclosure must also include reports on R&D activity, new technologies, and projections.	Every quarter

[a] This requirement was waived if the firm's assets or market capitalization were large enough.

Source: Compiled from assorted press accounts.

just one spectacular failure, Stardent Computer attracted $215 million in venture financing, primarily from Japanese funds, before being written off in late 1991.

The early 1990s saw a decline in the activity of the Japanese venture capital industry. Much of this withdrawal was due to the severe recession that plagued Japan in the 1990s, which in turn was a consequence of the dramatic fall in real estate and equity market valuations. The poor experiences with the U.S. market were also detrimental.

Despite the changes, the essential characteristics of the Japanese market remained unchanged. For instance, the share of venture capital-backed firms that were less than five years old at the time of financing remained under 15% in the years 1994–1996. In the same period, by contrast, the *average* venture-backed firm has been under five years of age in the United States.[8] This reflected the extreme difficulty in taking young companies public: in Hamao, Packer, and Ritter's sample of 456 IPOs on the Japanese OTC market between 1989 and 1995, the average age of the venture-backed IPOs was just over 32 years, and those of the nonventure firms, just under 37 years.[9] The other primary avenue to exit successful venture investments in the United States, the mergers and acquisition market, also remained underdeveloped in Japan. Venture capitalists continued to hold very modest stakes. Of the 210 venture-backed IPOs in the Hamao–Packer–Ritter sample, for instance, the mean stake for the lead venture capitalist prior to the IPO was 5.92%. For the securities firm-affiliated and bank-affiliated funds, the stake was only 4.97%.[10]

But at the same time, a series of policy reforms were fundamentally changing the landscape of the Japanese venture capital industry:

- In August 1994, the ability of venture capitalists to work with portfolio firms was greatly enhanced by a fundamental reinterpretation of the Anti-Monopoly Law by the Japanese Fair Trade Commission. This reinterpretation effectively freed venture capital firms from the requirement that venture groups could hold only minority stakes in firms.

- There was a gradual expansion of exit options. In July 1995, the Second OTC Market was established, which was intended to be a more hospitable environment for small IPOs than the primary OTC market. Within the first two years of operations, however, only two firms listed on the exchange. The primary U.S. exchange for small high-technology firms, the NASDAQ, had also begun aggressively seeking listings from Japanese firms.

- A gradual process led to the relaxation of restrictions on stock option holdings. In November 1995, new legislation enabled private R&D-intensive companies to offer stock options, conditional on registration with the government and satisfying certain criteria. By early 1997, only 14 such firms had secured permission. After coming under pressure from larger firms that also wished to offer stock options plans, however, the commercial code was revised in June 1997 to permit the issuance of stock options with few restrictions and favorable tax treatment.

---

[8] VentureOne Corporation, *Venture Capital Investment Report—1997*, San Francisco, VentureOne, 1998.

[9] Yasushi Hamao, Frank Packer, and Jay R. Ritter, "Institutional Affiliation and the Role of Venture Capital: Evidence from Initial Public Offerings in Japan," *Pacific-Basin Finance Journal* 8(2000): 529–558, Table 3.

[10] Ibid., Table 3. A comparable figure for a sample of U.S. offerings is 13.6%. (See Christopher B. Barry, Chris J. Muscarella, John W. Peavy III, and Michael R. Vetsuypens, "The Role of Venture Capital in the Creation of Public Companies: Evidence from the Going Public Process," *Journal of Financial Economics* 27 (1990): 447–471, Table 7.)

- A series of reforms in 1997 removed legal impediments against pension funds investing in privately held companies (or funds that invest in private companies). The capital under management by Japanese pensions, about $250 billion in 1997, had essentially been prohibited from venture capital until that point. Just as the 1979 reforms by the U.S. Department of Labor had a dramatic impact on fundraising in the U.S. venture market, so too this shift might be an important catalyst to Japanese fundraising.[11]

- The Ministry of Trade and Industry had proposed in 1997 a new Investment Partnership Law, which would closely mirror the regulatory regime in the United States. In particular, under the proposed legislation, investors would be granted limited liability from their investments in venture capital partnerships.

- In 1997, the Japanese government introduced the "Angel Tax System," which offered modest benefits for investors in small R&D-intensive firms. In particular, it allowed capital losses (which in Japan, unlike the United States and United Kingdom, cannot be applied against ordinary income) to be carried forward for up to three years if the investor does not have enough capital gains to offset them. Previously, the credits would expire at the end of the year in which the losses were realized. No provisions were made, however, for reduced tax rates for capital gains from investments in small firms, or the deferral of taxes on these gains (as characterized the British and American systems).

- Perhaps most important, a more general relaxation of restrictions on individual and institutional investors was planned for April 1998. This "big bang" was anticipated to lead to a widespread restructuring of how and where investment capital was allocated in the country. Investment practices and performance levels that had been little questioned in previous decades were likely to attract much greater scrutiny.

An additional change was the birth of a large number of public efforts to stimulate venture financing directly (including the New Business Investment Co.). In addition, numerous corporations and banks established venture capital units, seeking to invest in promising start-ups either in the United States or Japan. By late 1997, there were approximately 270 venture capital organizations in Japan, about one-half of whom had active investment programs.

Interestingly, one policy avenue employed by many countries was not emphasized in Japan: the involvement of overseas venture capitalists. The Israeli Yozma program, for instance, offered matching funds to venture funds that were willing to commit about $10 million to $12 million for an Israeli fund. This return that the government could enjoy from these funds was capped, with the remainder flowing to the venture group. At least partially as a result of this program, Israel experienced not only an increase in venture capital under management (from $29 million in 1991 to over $550 million in 1997), but also a burst of investment by foreign high-technology companies in Israeli R&D and manufacturing facilities. This program structure was also the model for Germany, which in 1995 introduced the BioRegio program to stimulate the creation of a number of regional centers of biotechnology activity.[12] Perhaps the reluctance to un-

---

[11] As of October 1997, however, there had been little movement of pension funds into the financing of venture capital funds.

[12] For background information on the Israeli venture capital industry, see VentureOne Corporation, "Investing in Israel," *VentureEdge* 1 (Third Quarter 1997). In light of the discussions above, it is interesting to note that observers suggest that the willingness both to begin new firms and to sell equity to outside investors has increased dramatically in Israel in a few years' time. For background on the German initiative, see Daniel Green, "Number of European Biotech Companies Rises," *Financial Times*, April 28, 1998, p. 2.

dertake such a program in Japan was due to Japan's experiences in the mid-1980s when a number of Silicon Valley groups made a series of unsuccessful and poorly managed investments in Japanese start-ups.[13]

One unforeseen consequence of the recent initiatives was that at least some observers believed that there was a surfeit of venture capital in late 1997. Although the overall level of activity might be modest when compared to that in the United States or Israel, the relatively small number of qualified entrepreneurs was intensely courted by venture groups. Promising companies could attract funds with few restrictions and at relatively attractive valuations. The history and key characteristics of the Japanese venture capital industry are summarized in Exhibits 19-4 and 19-5.

NEW BUSINESS INVESTMENT CO., INC.

The Japan Development Bank (JDB) was established in the aftermath of the economic devastation of World War II. Its initial focus was on "policy-based lending": for example, the redevelopment of basic industries.[14] As a government financial institution, it could issue bonds at lower rates than could the many Japanese commercial banks or corporations. Even more important, it could draw on the trust funds that were established to invest Japan's postal savings and national pension plans.[15] This low-cost financing enabled the JDB to make loans to firms in targeted industries at attractive rates.

Gradually, the Bank broadened its focus to include petrochemical, machinery, and electronics manufacturers. In the 1970s, the Bank largely shifted its focus: many of the major manufacturing firms that were its initial targets could now directly access global capital markets on attractive terms. Instead, the JDB shifted to encouraging economic development and, later, the development of environmental and energy conservation technologies. At the close of the fiscal year that ended in March 1997, the Bank had total loans outstanding of 15.8 trillion yen ($127 billion).[16] At the same time, the JDB was under increasing pressure to demonstrate that it was still relevant in the Japanese economy.

The decision to undertake a venture fund was triggered by both external and internal pressures. The Bank had been criticized by the chairman of the Keidanren, the powerful Japanese business roundtable, as having outlived its usefulness. This created a strong incentive to demonstrate that the Bank could deliver new and relevant products and services. Second, the Bank was becoming increasingly aware of the limitations of the financial products that it offered to small technology-intensive firms. In fact, capital-constrained small high-technology firms in Japan were actively requesting this kind of assistance. In 1995, the Bank established the Entrepreneurial Development

---

[13] For instance, Robert Kunze of Hambrecht and Quist describes flying to Japan to check on an investment he had made a few weeks before, only to discover that all the funds had been transferred to creditors and the business was now liquidated! (Robert J. Kunze, *Nothing Ventured: The Perils and Payoffs of the Great American Venture Capital Game*, New York, HarperBusiness, 1990.)

[14] For instance, in fiscal year 1955, 45% of new loans went to electric power generators, 32% to shipbuilding concerns, and 8% to coal mines. Japan Development Bank, *Annual Report–1995*, Tokyo, Japan Development Bank, 1995.

[15] Postal savings accounts were one of the few options available to Japanese individuals for most of the postwar period. These accounts, which still accounted for 60% of household savings in 1997, paid very low interest rates: in October 1997, these accounts earned an interest rate of one-quarter of 1%. After the proposed "big bang" of 1998, however, it was unclear whether consumers would settle for such modest rates.

[16] For detailed financial data, see http://www.jdb.go.jp/english/guide/financial.html.

EXHIBIT 19-4

MILESTONES IN THE HISTORICAL DEVELOPMENT OF THE JAPANESE VENTURE CAPITAL INDUSTRY, 1949–1997

Date	Activity	Explanation	Era
May 1949	Stock Exchange reopens		
February 1963	Japan Securities and Exchange Association reestablishes Over-the-Counter Brand Registration System		
November 1963	Small Investment Promotion Companies are established in Tokyo, Osaka, and Nagoya	The semigovernmental organizations were patterned after the SBICs in the United States.	
1965	A serious stock market decline is halted by massive Ministry of Finance intervention and a bailout of Yamaichi Securities		
1971	Japan Venture Business Association is established		The first Japanese venture capital boom, 1971–1973
November 1972	Kyoto Enterprise Development, the first Japanese private sector venture capital firm, is established	This triggers a rush of entry into the venture capital market.	
1973	Japan Joint Finance (JAFCO) established	JAFCO will survive the end of Japan's first venture capital boom, growing to become the predominant firm in the domestic venture capital industry.	
1974–1975	First Oil Shock occurs	This triggers Japan's worst economic downturn of the postwar era and brings to an end the first wave of venture capital investment in Japan.	
July 1975	The Center for the Promotion of R&D Intensive Businesses, forerunner of the current Venture Enterprise Center, is established	This semigovernmental organization, run by MITI, represents a departure from the technology promotion policies of MITI, which tended to focus on larger, more established firms.	

(Continued)

EXHIBIT 19-4 (*Continued*)

Date	Activity	Explanation	Era
April 1982	JAFCO establishes Japan's first "Investment Enterprise Association"	This bore some resemblance to U.S.-style venture capital limited partnerships but lacked the liability limitations. This marked the beginning of the second venture capital boom.	The second capital boom, 1982–1986
December 1982	Kanagawa Science Park is established	This is the first experiment in the development of an "incubator" for high-tech businesses.	
November 1983	The over-the-counter market is substantially reformed	There is a considerable relaxation of standards for registration and for public offerings of stock. This accelerates the second venture financing boom.	
1986	The "Endaka" (Yen Appreciation) recession occurs	The sharp appreciation of the yen following the Plaza Accord agreement triggers a brief economic slowdown in Japan, which leads to the bankruptcies of many venture businesses and brings the second boom to a close.	
1987	The recovery takes place	The Japanese economy recovers quickly from the recession, partially thanks to easy monetary policy conducted by the Bank of Japan. Over the next three years, Japanese equity and land prices will climb to unprecedented heights.	The "Bubble Years," 1987–1990. Easy monetary policy contributes to an asset price bubble. Stock prices peak in 1989. The ensuing fall in asset prices triggers the onset of Japan's worst postwar recession.
1988	The "Recruit" Scandal breaks	The involvement of several leading politicians in a stock scandal leads to stricter regulation of stock trading prior to IPOs.	
June 1989	The New Business Act passes	This act directs the Industrial Structure Improvement Fund (ISIF) to screen guarantees for new business loans.	
June 1990	The New Business Investment Company is established	This semigovernmental venture capital investment corporation was set up to provide early-stage equity financing to entrepreneurial businesses.	

(*Continued*)

EXHIBIT 19-4 (Continued)

Date	Activity	Explanation	Era
1991	Operation JASDAQ begins	As the name implies, JASDAQ is modeled after the NASDAQ system in the United States. However, an OTC market had been active in Japan for some time.	
December 1991–May 1992	MOF begins its PKO (price-keeping operations)	The Ministry of Finance intervenes heavily in Japanese financial markets to arrest the free-fall in stock prices. IPOs are informally, but completely, prohibited. MOF relaxes this informal ban substantially in 1994, after a substantial upswing in stock prices.	
July 1994	MITI establishes a New Business Promotion Division within the Industrial Policy Bureau	This marks a major shift in MITI's policy focus from the promotion of investment and research by established firms to the encouragement of venture businesses. The promotion of venture businesses, particularly in high technology, is increasingly seen as the key to restoring dynamism and growth to the moribund Japanese economy.	The third venture, capital boom begins, 1994–1997
July 1994	The Center for Promotion of Research-Intensive Enterprises, is reorganized, renamed Venture Enterprise Center (VEC)	This semigovernmental body provides loan guarantees to venture businesses, with a focus on high-technology businesses.	
April 1995	Passage of the Small Business Creation Activity Promotion Act	This act encourages local governments to establish public "venture foundations."	
July 1995	The "Second" over-the-counter market is established	This offers a relaxation of standards for R&D-intensive new businesses (sales/R&D ratio of more than 3%). These firms are allowed to undertake initial public offerings even when operating at a loss.	
November 1995	Amendment to the New Business Act passes	Designated venture businesses are allowed to offer stock options to employees.	

(Continued)

EXHIBIT 19-4 (Continued)

Date	Activity	Explanation	Era
1996	A "boom" in the establishment of venture capital firms takes place		
1996–1997	Investor enthusiasm for venture capital grows	By mid-1997, the financial press begins to speculate that the stock prices of venture businesses have been bid up higher than is justified by the fundamentals.	
May 1997	The Commerce Law is amended to allow all corporations to issue stock options		
1997	Debate over legislation to create Investment Business Association	This legislation would create U.S.-style limited investment partnerships.	
Late 1997	A series of high-profile bankruptcies of Japanese corporations and financial institutions (including Yamaichi Securities and Hokkaido Takushoku Bank) sends the Nikkei stock price average and the yen down.	Worries about the viability of the Japanese financial system intensify in the wake of the East Asian financial crisis. Credit tightens as banks attempt to meet their capital adequacy requirements. Investor sentiment toward venture businesses cool, and the "bailout" of Japanese banks takes center stage in policy circles, crowding out venture business promotion.	

Source: Compiled from Masato Ono, *Bencha Kigyou to Toushi no Jissai Chishiki: Bencha Economy no Kaisetsu,* Tokyo, Toyo Keizai Shimpo Sha, 1997, Figure 1–2, Shuichi Matsuda, *Kigyou Ron: Entrepreneur No Shishitsu, Chishiki, Senryaku,* Tokyo, Nihon Keizai Shinbum Sha, 1997, Figures 1–2 and 1–9, and assorted press accounts.

EXHIBIT 19-5

STATISTICS ON THE JAPANESE VENTURE CAPITAL INDUSTRY

Annual Statistics (all figures in millions of yen unless otherwise noted)

	1988	1989	1990	1991	1992	1993	1994	1995	1996
Venture capital organizations (number)	90	94	107	115	116	120	275	276	270
Pool of venture capital (includes investments, loans, and cash)[1]	952,999	1,102,569	1,755,631	2,022,610	1,999,565	1,981,081	1,528,935	1,528,935	1,295,405
New funds raised (excluding loans)		37,021	120,913	102,980	108,568	67,570	168,079	168,079	182,013
New funds invested (excluding loans)					50,602	35,991	151,076	151,076	164,449
Total unexited investments (includes loans)			526,940	698,958	749,560	694,056	834,460	853,069	825,782

Distribution of Entire Venture Capital Pool as of 1996

Institutional Sources of Venture Capital Pool	Amount
Corporations	45.9%
Banks	27.5%
Insurance companies	9.4%
Pension funds	4.4%
Individuals	2.9%
Government agencies	0.3%
Other	9.6%

Geographic Sources of Venture Capital Pool	
Japan	91.8%
Other Asian countries	1.5%
Non-Asian countries	6.7%

Distribution of Unexited Investments by Financing Stage	
Seed	3.2%
Start-up	13.8%
Expansion	45.0%
Mezzanine	37.8%
Turnaround	0.2%

Distribution of Unexite Investments by Region	
Japan	82.2%
Other Asian countries	11.4%
Non-Asian countries	6.4%

Distribution of Unexited Investments by Industry	Amount	Number
Consumer	16.1%	19.3%
Computer or software	4.0%	5.7%
Electronics	6.2%	9.2%
Industrial products	12.3%	12.4%
Medical/biotechnology	0.7%	0.5%
Communications	1.3%	0.9%
Energy	3.4%	3.0%
Transportation	1.6%	1.3%
Construction	5.0%	7.7%
Financial services	16.5%	9.4%
Other services	16.1%	14.6%
Other manufacturing	16.9%	16.0%

Note: All 1996 figures are at end of third quarter.

Source: Asian Venture Capital Journal, *Guide to Venture Capital in Asia*, Hong Kong, Asian Venture Capital Journal, 1998 and earlier years.

Financing Center, which sought to stimulate the development of small, high-technology firms. The primary mechanism to do so was through loans for research and development expenditures, which could be secured by patents or other intellectual property. Although a number of firms did take advantage of this option, increasingly the JDB officials had become aware of the need for equity financing.

Other agencies had already come together to create a public equity investment firm. In June 1990 the New Business Investment Company (NBI) had been established under the Law on Temporary Measures to Facilitate Specific New Businesses. The fund was capitalized with two billion yen (about $20 million). The funds had been raised primarily from the Industrial Structure Improvement Fund (ISIF) and about 100 industrial corporations.

Like any new public institution, NBI faced a number of challenges. In filling its management positions, NBI relied primarily on officials seconded from the ISIF, who, in turn, were often seconded from the major policy agencies such as the Ministry of Finance or the Ministry of International Trade and Industry. Analyst positions were often staffed with persons seconded from commercial banks, securities firms, and government-affiliated financial agencies. In attempting to carry out their mission, the staff immediately encountered a number of challenges. Many of the staff assigned to screen loan guarantees and investment applications had little previous experience with private equity investments or the special financial challenges faced by young entrepreneurial firms. The applications were, therefore, quite difficult to evaluate. Initial attempts to negotiate equity investments encountered resistance, often from the entrepreneurs themselves. Finally, NBI's initial investment guidelines directed it to invest only in enterprises at the par value of their share price.[17] As NBI's operations progressed, it became obvious that there were attractive opportunities to invest in firms at a later stage of development, when their stock value had risen above par. Such investments were ruled out by these guidelines. Finally, investments were subject to review by the other government agencies that had contributed to the fund. Doing this review properly took time. When the reviewing agency felt that an NBI investment conflicted with or duplicated the agency's own efforts to promote venture businesses in that sector, the reviewing agency might request that investment not be undertaken.

Increasingly aware of these problems, the JDB sought to raise a new fund that would not be encumbered by these difficulties. It was necessary to coordinate the activities of this new fund with those of the other public efforts to finance small high-technology firms, a number of which were under the supervision of MITI.[18] After extensive discussions with MITI officials, it was agreed that JDB would be allowed to raise a new fund for a restructured NBI. In November 1996, NBI raised a second, more substantial fund in conjunction with JDB and 100 private companies. The fund raised a total of six billion yen (about $48 million) and was established as the second department of NBI. This time the funds came from JDB and the aforementioned industrial firms, many of whom had also participated in the first NBI fund.

---

[17] This was dictated by the objective of investing only in enterprises at the start-up stage. According to current commercial law in Japan, the minimum par price of shares at the time of establishment is 50,000 yen.

[18] The NBI fund was only one of a series of contemporaneous public efforts to finance small high-technology firms. MITI had devoted at least some effort to this topic since the creation of the Venture Enterprise Center (VEC) in 1975. While its focus had initially been on overseeing the Japanese SBICs, these were largely privatized in the mid-1980s. It then shifted its focus to providing loan guarantees to small technology-intensive firms. In the mid-1990s, it also began aggressively making equity investments on an *ad hoc* basis.

At the same time, there was a substantial rethinking of the fund's objectives. Following the insights of Takeshi Nakabayashi, who transferred from the JDB at the time of the new fund and served as the manager of the fund, the approach it took was somewhat different from traditional Japanese venture funds or other government efforts. Nakabayashi, a graduate of Harvard's Kennedy School of Government, had spent the past five years as deputy director of the Entrepreneurial Development Financing Center at the JDB. Consequently, he was well aware of the limitations of the traditional venture capital model as practiced in Japan. He had argued for a structure that differed in at least three respects from many of its peers, as well as from the earlier JDB effort.

First, an aggressive emphasis was placed on identifying transactions not through "cold calling," but rather through referrals from a wide variety of outside shareholders and business intermediaries with whom the staff had relationships. Unlike the earlier NBI fund, the investments did not need to undergo a lengthy review by a variety of agencies: rather, they simply needed to be approved by NBI's investment committee. In its first year of operation, the fund had screened over 170 proposals and had funded two of these. While this was well below the 13 transactions in the first year projected in the original business plan, Nakabayashi felt that a deliberate pace was essential if the quality of transactions was to be maintained.

Second, the goal of the fund was to *combine* financing with management assistance for portfolio companies. It was foreseen that these investments would have several advantages in addition to the capital and management assistance provided. A particular goal was the certification of the firm to strategic partners and other inventors. As the organization stated,

> One of the biggest problems when initiating a new business is that the business or the product/service is often undervalued due to the lack of a track record. Investments by NBI as a governmental entity impart credibility to a venture and raise their standing in the eyes of other investors and their business partners.[19]

Another important place where the certification might play an important role was when firms sought to recruit researchers. In addition, the fund's managers hoped to catalyze informal interactions between its investors and portfolio firms.

Third, in order to facilitate its working with portfolio firms, NBI insisted that firms sign a four-page contract. This required the firm, among other provisions, to *(1)* let NBI research and inquire about its business conditions, *(2)* report major changes in its balance sheet, agree to periodic audits, and provide clear disclosure of important developments, *(3)* make the best efforts for its IPO, *(4)* accept NBI's pricing if the firm was sold to a third party, and *(5)* agree to penalty clauses for breach of contract. Whether for formal reviews or informal consultations, NBI found itself interacting with its two portfolio companies on at least a weekly basis and frequently more often.

At the same time, the second department had important restrictions on its flexibility. First, NBI officials were not allowed to take a board seat in portfolio companies, due to JDB's concerns about liability. Second, the types of firms financed were limited. The fund was restricted to companies under 10 years of age, which had been actively marketing a product for less than 5 years. Third, the size and mixture of the investment were restricted. The size for expansion-stage investments by NBI was limited to 100 million yen. Firms needed to raise matching funds. For instance, for a 100 million yen

---

[19] *A Guide to the ISIF (Industrial Structure Improvement Fund) and NBI (New Business Investment Co., Ltd.)*, Tokyo, Japan Development Bank, 1996.

investment, the NBI could contribute up to 25% of the funds. For a total investment of 200 million, NBI can contribute in aggregate no more than 40 million yen, or 20%.[20] Fourth, the fund had agreed that it would not "compete" with independent venture organizations. Finally, in the recruitment of its own staff, NBI had to rely largely on staff that were "seconded," or lent, from the JDB, large commercial banks, and other institutions. (The previous employer also bore the cost of the employee's salary while they worked for NBI.) Often this staff had little previous exposure to the financing of entrepreneurial firms and consequently required extensive training. It was likely that many of these seconded employees would be recalled to their former employers after a few years at NBI.[21] The fund's structure is summarized in Exhibits 19-7 and 19-8.

CURRENT INVESTMENTS AND FUTURE CHOICES

To date, the fund had made two investments. The first of these, Mazeran, was a designer of computer software, while the other, the Brighton Corporation, designed specialized electronic equipment (e.g., handheld devices that hotels could provide blind guests with in order to allow them to readily access services). The successes and challenges of each of these investments illustrated both the valuable role that NBI could potentially play, and the challenges that the fund would face in future years.

Mazeran had been founded by Mutsuhiro Hayashi in 1989 (see the summary of the firm in Exhibit 19-9). Hayashi had worked for seven years after college at Recruit, a highly successful "start-up" firm specializing in corporate recruiting publications. Recruit was unusual among Japanese firms in having a very entrepreneurial culture and a tendency to encourage employees to leave after no more than a decade at the firm. (Many of Japan's recent successful entrepreneurs are Recruit "graduates.") After a brief stint with a stress management firm, Hayashi was asked by Gakusei Engo Kai, Recruit's main competitor, to start a business producing a variety of magazines for the corporation. This "corporate venture" was jointly owned by Gakusei Engo Kai (70%), Hayashi (15%, partially owned under a corporate shell), and Keisuisha (15%), Mazeran's business partner.

With the collapse of the bubble economy, however, Gakusei Engo Kai's recruiting business began declining dramatically. Mazeran encountered increasing difficulties in 1994 and 1995, as business from Gakusei Engo Kai fell, and replacement orders were increasingly difficult to identify.

As a result, Hayashi shifted from desktop publishing to CD-ROM design, lining up Sony as an initial client with a contract to produce an electronic book. Gradually, the firm also shifted into on-line and Internet content development, developing Japanese content for America On-line and Microsoft Network. Reflecting the changed business model, Mazeran sought in negotiations beginning in 1996 to buy back the shares of his two external investors. To do so, however, required additional financial resources. As the balance sheet reproduced in Exhibit 19-9 indicates, by the end of the 1996 fiscal year (July 31, 1996), the firm was highly leveraged and had negative net worth.

---

[20] New Business Investment Co., Ltd., *Toushi Dai Ni Bu Gyoumu no Go-annai*, Tokyo, New Business Investment Co., 1997. These limits are summarized in more detail in Exhibit 19-6.

[21] One dimension of these personnel issues was the selection of a head for JDB. While Nakabayashi and his supervisor at JDB, Takashi Watanabe, had pushed for the selection of a venture capitalist, the JDB's General Coordination Department had decided that a corporate client should make the decision. Dr. Shoichiro Toyada, the chairman of Toyota Motor and the Keindanren, was asked to "second" an employee. Tadao Suzuki, former general manager of Toyota Motor's Oceania division, was selected for the position.

EXHIBIT 19-6

GUIDELINES ON INVESTMENT LIMITS

	Equity Ratio	
	Investment Department I	Investment Department II
1st 100 million yen	30%	25%
2nd 200 million yen	20%	15%
Any additional capital	10%	5%
Total investment limit	200 million	100 million

For example, for a 400 million yen company, Investment Department II could invest an amount up to 25% of the first 100 million yen of the company's capital (25 million yen) plus 15% of the next 200 million yen of the company's capital (30 million yen) plus 5% of the next 100 million, for a total of 60 million yen. The total amount Investment Department II can invest at any one company cannot exceed 100 million yen.

Source: The sources of Exhibits 6 through 9 are internal NBI documents.

EXHIBIT 19-7

NBI "NETWORK"

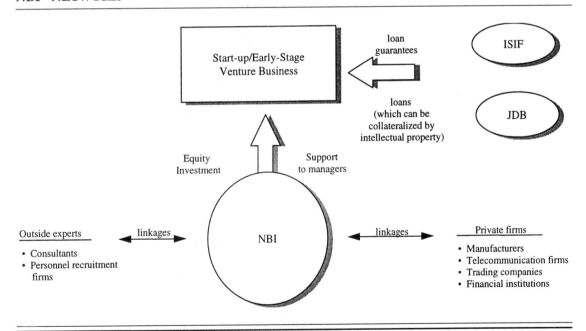

EXHIBIT 19-8

BACKGROUND OF STAFF AND THE ORGANIZATIONAL CHART IN INVESTMENT DEPARTMENT II

Tadao Suzuki, Managing Director (Torishimariyaku)	BA Education, Tokyo University, 1964 General manager of the Oceania Region of Toyota Motors, 1995
Nitta, General Manager (Bucho):	Served as general manager of Sapporo Branch of JDB until he came to NBI
Senior Manager (Jicho):	Audited small to medium firms for loans at Industrial Bank of Japan
Takeshi Nakabayashi, Manager (Kacho):	Graduated the J.F.K. School of Government at Harvard Did loans to venture businesses at JDB
Analysts (Tanto):	
A:	Was an analyst and auditor at Nippon Investment and Finance before coming to NBI
B:	Worked on venture business loans for three years at JDB
C:	Loaned to automobile industries and small firms for six years at JDB
D:	Worked at JDB for three years before coming to NBI

THE ORGANIZATIONAL CHART OF INVESTMENT DEPARTMENT II

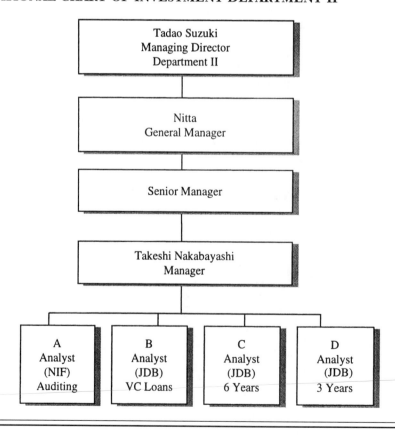

EXHIBIT 19-9

NBI STATUS REPORT ON MAZERAN INVESTMENT, SEPTEMBER 1997

I. Basic Information

Company name: Mazeran Publishing, Inc.
President: Mutsuhiro Hayashi
Address: Chiyoda-ku, Tokyo
Established: February, Heisi 2 (1990)
Capital: 40 million yen (800 shares)
Shareholders: Hayashi (500), New Business Investment (200), Ozawa Investment (100)
Employment 19 full-time employees, 21 contract and part-time employees
Business focus:
1. Edit electronic publications
2. Edit general publication
3. Create "Network Contents"

II. Main Business Goal ("Corporate Mission Statement")

Provide comprehensive digital editing services and supply network contents.

III. Outline of the Business

A. Editing electronic publications in the past   Recently, there has been increased movement toward electronic publication of general publications, such as dictionaries and encyclopedias. In the past, the publication companies wrote texts that were edited for general publication in electronic format on the CD-ROM. However, since the publication companies did not possess digital editing know-how, and it was usually systems engineers who actually placed the text onto the CD-ROM, the final product was quite dull. Also, it is possible to add pictures, illustration, animation (including movies), and sounds to the original texts in this format. However, in the past, the addition of multimedia was done as an afterthought.

B. Providing comprehensive digital editing services   Our company adds the element of specialized digital editing services to the dull electronic publications of the past. The development of this editorial factor comes from combining our five years of experience as an editing company of general publications with new technology developed jointly with Microsoft and Sony. We have developed a user interface that is based on the human engineering and cognitive psychological research. Also we supply and modify multimedia components to add to electronic publications.

C. Providing network content   Through experiences from editing electronic publications and utilizing computer technology, we are seeking to develop a new line of business: shifting from the editing of CD-ROM-based publications to becoming a provider of computer network "contents."

IV. Performance and Profit Forecast

Corporate Performance (millions of yen) (1997 fiscal year runs through July 31, 1997, etc.)

Fiscal Year	1994	1995	1996	1997
Sales	546	241	218	342
Earnings	119	72	74	106
Operating income	49	3	13	26
Ordinary income	46	2	10	20
Net income	46	2	3	20

(Continued)

EXHIBIT 19-9 *(Continued)*

Earnings Forecasts (millions of yen)

Fiscal Year	1997	1998	1999	2000
Sales	300	480	730	1,030
Earnings	110	140	245	325
Operating income	30	45	104	185
Ordinary income	20	35	130	175
Net income	20	17	65	87

A. Performance   Our total sales showed a downward trend from the fiscal years ending in July 1994 to that ending in July 1996. This is because of the substantial decline following the slow-down and eventual cessation of orders from a single customer, Gakusei Engo Kai (Student Support Organization). Our sales declined from 473 million yen to 93 million yen to 6 million yen. Facing this decline in sales to Gakusei Engo Kai, we have shifted our emphasis from editing employment (recruitment) magazines to electronic publications. In the fiscal year ending in July 1997 period, fully 70% of our sales are electronic publications produced for Shogakukan and Microsoft. This shows a 56.9% increase in sales over the previous fiscal year.

Fiscal Year	1994		1995		1996		1997	
Total Sales	546	100%	241	100%	218	100%	342	100%
Gakusei Engo Kan	473	86.6%	93	38.6%	6	2.8%	3	0.9%
Other Customers:	73	13.4%	149	61.8%	212	97.2%	339	99.1%
Shogakukan	23	4.2%	83	34.4%	106	48.6%	163	47.7%
Microsoft	0	0.0%	0	0.0%	17	7.8%	74	21.6%

Units in million of yen. 1997 Fiscal year runs through July 31, 1997, etc.

Concerning profitability, gross return on sales (ROS) in July 1994 was 21.8%. Compared to that figure, profitability has improved 10 percentage points (from 29.9% to 33.9% to 31.%). This is due to the successful shift from general publication orders from "Gakusei Engo Kai" to the more profitable production of electronic publications for Shogakukan. Despite the fact that the return on sales increased, operating income has dropped substantially from 8.9% in 1994 to 1.3% in 1995. This is due to the increase in selling and general administrative expenses (SG&A) resulting from decline in orders from Gakusei Engo Kai. On the other hand, operating income has improved to 6.0% and 7.6% due to the decline in sales cost in 1996 fiscal year and the increase in sales in 1997 fiscal year.

B. Profit plan   We have increased sales excluding the orders of Gakusei Engo Kai from 73 to 339 million yen. Most of these sales in the above figures are from orders of electronic publications. Compared to this, we are expecting an increase in sales to 480, 730, and 1,030 million yen in the fiscal years 1998–2000, increases of 180, 250, and 300 million yen, respectively. To achieve this goal, we need to increase sales through an increase in our customer base, with an increase in employment to handle the increased workload.

(Continued)

EXHIBIT 19-9   (Continued)

Even though we can expect continued orders from Shogakukan for its periodical, the Nippon Dai Hyakka Zensho (Japan Encyclopedia) worth approximately 60 million yen, it seems that we can expect no new orders for big dictionaries (nonperiodicals) and other such publications. We anticipate that new orders will shift to smaller publications such as general education and cultural publications. Therefore, orders from Shogakukan will be stable or declining from their current level. On the other hand, we are in negotiations with Microsoft to provide contents for the Microsoft Network (MSN) and "localization" of Microsoft games, in addition to the orders for MS Bookshelf (approximately 80 million yen). Microsoft has decided to increase their orders from us based on our performance on the Microsoft Bookshelf project. We are also negotiating with Kadokawa Shoten, Media Works, Megasoft and others. Kadokawa Shoten aims to strengthen its weak electronic publications division before "spinning out" this division via a public stock offering. In light of this goal, we are negotiating with Kadokawa Shoten to digitalize their "contents." Thus, even though we do not expect to see increase in orders from Shogakukan, we do expect increases in sales from Microsoft and other companies.

We have increased our employment from 15 to 20 to 27 from FY 1995 to FY 1997 due to the increase in sales from 149 to 212 to 339 million yen, excluding Gakusei Engo Kai. During this period, sales per employee have increased to 12,556 thousand yen. The sales figures and employment have increased in lock-step. Therefore, for us to expand sales from 480 to 1,030 million yen from 1998 to 2000, we need to hire 11, 20, and 24 more employees respectively in the 1998, 1999, and 2000 fiscal years (this figure is based on the sales-per-employee figure of 12,556 thousand yen). The question is whether we can hire this many qualified personnel in the future. The policy we are currently following is to increase the number of contract workers and part-time workers, rather than increasing full-time employees.

Balance Sheet—Assets (thousands of yen)

Variable	FY 1994	FY 1995	FY 1996	FY 1997
Cash deposits	30,409	4,626	8,390	26,364
Accounts receivable	13,917	21,181	20,363	65,867
Products (inventory)	6,295	6,789	0	0
Reimbursable advance payments	462	440	294	487
Advance payments	0	0	275	1,853
Deposit for merchandise	0	192	0	0
Short-term loans receivable	0	0	0	3,435
Liquid assets	51,083	33,228	29,322	98,006
Buildings/facilities	0	0	0	250
Machinery/tools	2,659	2,957	2,957	8,504
Less cumulative depreciation	−2,183	−2,318	−2,437	−3,428
Tangible assets	476	639	520	5,326
Fixed assets	1,341	1,504	5,375	12,928
Deposit for phone use	750	750	750	992
Contributed capital	100	100	100	110
Investment guarantee	15	15	4,005	6,500
Investments, etc.	115	115	4,105	6,610
Premium	542	589	0	0
Corporate bond issuing discount	0	0	0	781
Deferred assets	542	589	0	781
Less payee discounted bills	−5,098	−7,138	−9,074	−8,653
Total assets	49,209	29,687	31,008	115,990

Note: The 1997 fiscal year for Mazeran runs through July 31, 1997, etc.

(Continued)

EXHIBIT 19-9   (Continued)

Balance Sheet—Liabilities and Equities (thousands of yen)

Variable	FY 1994	FY 1995	FY 1996	FY 1997
Accounts payable	46,838	18,178	6,238	17,613
Short-term loans	5,000	8,000	12,245	5,274
Amount in arrears	31,807	32,472	31,099	20,938
Deposits received	2,385	1,090	4,883	2,298
Right to receive newly issued stocks	0	0	0	800
Taxes payable	0	0	0	180
Current liabilities	86,030	59,740	54,465	47,103
Long-term loans	16,736	23,572	25,197	39,331
Corporate bonds (3iBJ/Nissei)	0	0	0	40,000
Long-term liabilities	16,736	23,572	25,197	79,331
Contributed capital	30,000	30,000	30,000	30,000
Proceeds from newly issued stock (NBI)	0	0	0	10,000
Retained earnings	−79,801	−77,991	−74,967	−54,720
Total (equity) capital	−49,801	−47,991	−44,967	−14,720
Liabilities and equity capital	52,965	35,321	34,695	111,714

Note: The 1997 fiscal year for Mazeran runs through July 31, 1997, etc.

Profit and Loss Statement (thousands of yen)

Variable	FY 1994	FY 1995	FY 1996	FY 1997
Sales	546,273	241,371	218,111	341,553
Cost of goods sold	427,087	169,614	144,119	235,274
Inventory write-offs	6,295	6,789	0	0
Total direct costs	433,382	176,403	114,119	235,274
Gross margin	119,186	71,757	73,992	106,279
Sales, General, and Administrative expenses (SG&A)	70,354	68,617	61,333	80,114
Operating income	48,832	3,140	12,659	26,165
Interest received	19	34	5	29
Dividends received	39	42	25	5
Miscellaneous income	1,066	376	338	0
Total nonoperating income	1,124	452	368	34
Interest accrued/discounts	3,607	1,022	1,873	3,417
Interest on corporate bonds	0	0	0	145
Nonperforming loans	0	0	0	1,326
Depreciation	432	330	589	19
Miscellaneous losses	0	431	752	866
Total nonoperating expenses	4,039	1,783	3,214	5,773
Ordinary income	45,917	1,809	9,813	20,426
Loss on sale of fixed assets	0	0	6,789	0
Income before taxes	45,917	1,809	3,024	20,426
Corporate tax	0	0	0	180
Net income	45,917	1,809	3,024	20,246

Note: The 1997 fiscal year for Mazeran runs through July 31, 1997, etc.

The transaction proceeded in three parts in 1996 and 1997. First, Hayashi repurchased the firm's shares from Gakusei Engo Kai and Keisuisha for a total of 25.5 million yen. In between the first and second repurchase, Ozawa Investment made a 5 million yen investment in the company in April 1997.[22] This left the company with 600 shares outstanding, of which Hayashi held 500 shares and Ozawa Investment, 100.

The firm then raised 80 million yen in "warrant bonds"—bonds with attached warrants—from two venture groups, Hokusai Ventures and 3VCC (a venture firm that was jointly owned by a European venture group and a large Japanese commercial bank). These would convert into 1,600 shares. In a side agreement, however, the parties concurred that Mazeran would be allowed to reacquire half the bonds for their face value.[23] Forty million yen worth of the bonds were redeemed within one month, along with the associated warrants. While the remaining 40 million yen in bonds remained outstanding, 600 of the 800 attached warrants were sold to Mazeran shortly thereafter, leaving the two venture investors with 200 warrants.

Finally, NBI had made an equity investment in Mazeran. Nakabayashi had met Hayashi through an acquaintance, an insurance broker who had formerly worked at a venture capital organization affiliated with the Long-Term Credit Bank of Japan. She attracted small-business clients by helping them with their business plans, and had thought that there might be a good match between NBI's investment objectives and Mazeran. While some of Mazeran's existing investors were concerned that NBI, as a government entity, might seek to control the firm, Nakabayashi and his associates were able to allay their concerns. In exchange for 10 million yen, the company issued NBI 200 shares of common stock, or 25% of the outstanding equity (without effect to the dilution that would result from the issuance of the venture groups' warrants). Prior to this investment, NBI negotiated an investment contract that included provisions for NBI to exert management oversight over Mazeran.

A major focus of NBI's efforts with Mazeran has been to provide introductions to the fund's corporate investors in the hopes that Mazeran could establish some additional strategic relationships. Hayashi also hoped that the certification provided by an NBI investment might make recruitment easier: while Mazeran had been increasingly successful in hiring young programmers attracted by its entrepreneurial culture, finding experienced middle managers to oversee projects was a substantial challenge.

As Nakabayashi contemplated his progress to date, there were several challenges ahead. Clearly, the implementation of NBI's vision would be a major challenge. The limited financial and human resources, as well as the complex environment in which the fund operated, would be major, and perhaps insurmountable, barriers.

The changing environment in the Japanese venture capital industry also posed threats to the fund's success. One change was the increasing interest by traditional Japanese venture firms in early-stage transactions. Nakabayashi doubted that the "hands-off" approach that many funds employed would be very successful in their early-stage investments. But the effort could have several detrimental effects on NBI in any case. First, the competition might lead to higher valuations for early-stage firms. Second, because NBI was prohibited from directly competing with private firms, this interest might translate into more restrictions on its investment focus. Finally, as traditional Japanese venture firms struggled to move into the financing of start-up firms, his team of ana-

---

[22] The names of the venture firms investing in Mazeran have been disguised to protect corporate confidentiality.

[23] The objective here was to provide Hayashi with the opportunity to maintain a high degree of ownership if the firm did well.

lysts might be attractive recruitment targets: the retention of his team might become an increasing challenge.

At the same time, Nakabayashi's concerns about his group were tempered by a broader understanding of the evolution of the public venture capital initiatives in other countries. These public efforts tended to have limited lives, even if successful, as the recent efforts to privatize the Yozma program in Israel illustrated. The very success of a public effort, he mused, makes it ultimately become redundant, as the private sector develops its own experience and resources. Even if relatively short-lived, however, such a public effort could still play an important catalytic role in stimulating the growth of an independent venture capital sector.

The third module of *Venture Capital and Private Equity* examines the process through which private equity investors exit their investments. Successful exits are critical to ensuring attractive returns for investors and, in turn, to raising additional capital. But private equity investors' concerns about exiting investments—and their behavior during the exiting process itself—can sometimes lead to severe problems for entrepreneurs.

We will employ an analytic framework very similar to that used in the first module of the course. We will not only seek to understand the institutional features associated with exiting private equity investments in the United States and overseas, but also to analyze them. We will map out which features are designed primarily to increase the overall amount of profits from private equity investments, and which actions seem to be intended to shift more of the profits to particular parties.

WHY THIS MODULE?

At first glance, the exiting of private equity investments may appear outside the scope of *Venture Capital and Private Equity*. It might seem that such issues are more appropriate for courses that focus on public markets. But since the need to ultimately exit investments shapes every aspect of the private equity cycle, this is a very important issue for both private equity investors and entrepreneurs.

Perhaps the clearest illustration of the relationship between the private and public markets was seen during the 1980s and early 1990s. In the early 1980s, many European nations developed secondary markets. These sought to combine a hospitable environment for small firms (e.g., they allowed firms to be listed even if they did not have an extended record of profitability) with tight regulatory safeguards. These enabled the pioneering European private equity funds to exit their investments. A wave of fundraising by these and other private equity organizations followed in the mid-1980s. After the 1987 market crash, initial public offering activity in Europe and the United States dried up. While the U.S. market recovered in the early 1990s, the European market remained depressed. Consequently, European private equity investors were unable to exit investments by going public. They were required either to continue to hold the firms or to sell them to larger corporations at often unattractive val-

Professor Josh Lerner prepared this note as the basis for class discussion.

uations. While U.S. private equity investors—pointing to their successful exits—were able to raise substantial amounts of new capital, European private equity fundraising during this period remained depressed. The influence of exits on the rest of the private equity cycle suggests that this is a critical issue for funds and their investors.

The exiting of private equity investments also has important implications for entrepreneurs. As discussed in the first module, the typical private equity fund is liquidated after one decade (though extensions of a few years may be possible). Thus, if a private equity investor cannot foresee how a company will be mature enough to take public or to sell at the end of a decade, he is unlikely to invest in the firm. If it was equally easy to exit investments of all types at all times, this might not be a problem. But interest in certain technologies by public investors seems to be subject to wide swings. For instance, in recent years "hot issue markets" have appeared and disappeared for computer hardware, biotechnology, multimedia, and Internet companies. Concerns about the ability to exit investments may have led to too many private equity transactions being undertaken in these "hot" industries. At the same time, insufficient capital may have been devoted to industries not in the public limelight.

Concerns about exiting may also adversely affect firms once private equity investors finance them. Less scrupulous investors may occasionally encourage companies in their portfolio to undertake actions that boost the probability of a successful initial public offering, even if they jeopardize the firm's long-run health: for example, increasing earnings by cutting back on vital research spending. In addition, many private equity investors appear to exploit their inside knowledge when dissolving their stakes in investments. Although this may be in the best interests of the limited and general partners of the fund, it may have harmful effects on the firm and the other shareholders.

THE FRAMEWORK OF THE ANALYSIS

The exiting of private equity investments involves a diverse range of actors. Private equity investors exit most successful investments through taking them public.[1] A wide variety of actors are involved in the initial public offering. In addition to the private equity investors, these include the investment bank that underwrites the offering, the institutional and individual investors who are allotted the shares (and frequently sell them immediately after the offering), and the parties who end up holding the shares.

Few private equity investments are liquidated at the time of the initial public offering. Instead, private equity investors typically dissolve their positions by distributing the shares to the investors in their funds. These distributions usually take place one to two years after the offering. A variety of other intermediaries are involved in these transactions, such as distribution managers who evaluate and liquidate distributed securities for institutional investors.

This module will examine each of these players. Rather than just describing their roles, however, we will highlight the rationales for and impacts of their behavior. We

---

[1] A Venture Economics study finds that a $1 investment in a firm that goes public provides an average cash return of $1.95 in excess of the initial investment, with an average holding period of 4.2 years. The next best alternative, an investment in an acquired firm, yields a cash return of only 40 cents over a 3.7 year mean holding period. See Venture Economics, *Exiting Venture Capital Investments*, Wellesley, MA, Venture Economics, 1988.

will again employ the framework of the first module. We will seek to assess which institutions and features have evolved to improve the efficiency of the private equity investment process, and which have sprung up primarily to shift more of the economic benefits to particular parties.

Many features of the exiting of private equity investments can be understood as responses to many uncertainties in this environment. For example, the "lock-up" provisions prohibit corporate insiders and private equity investors from selling at the time of the offering. This helps avoid situations where the officers and directors exploit their inside knowledge that a newly listed company is overvalued by rapidly liquidating their positions.

At the same time, other features of the exiting process can be seen as attempts to transfer wealth between parties. An example may be the instances where private equity funds distribute shares to their investors that drop in price immediately after the distribution. Even if the price at which the investors ultimately sell the shares is far less, the private equity investors use the share price *before* the distribution to calculate their fund's rate of return and to determine when they can begin profit sharing.

THE STRUCTURE OF THE MODULE

This module begins by exploring the need for avenues to exit private equity investments, examining Europe's private equity markets. As described earlier, the inability to exit investments has been a major stumbling block to the development of its private equity industry.

We then examine the exiting of private equity investments in the United States. We explore the perspectives of and implications for private equity investors, entrepreneurs, limited partners, and the specialized distribution managers that they hire. Once again, we will seek to assess which behavior increases the size of the "pie" and which actions simply change the relative sizes of the slices.

FURTHER READING ON EXITING PRIVATE EQUITY INVESTMENTS

Legal Works

JOSEPH W. BARTLETT, *Equity Finance: Venture Capital, Buyouts, Restructurings, and Reorganization*, New York, Wiley, 1995, chapter 14.

MICHAEL J. HALLORAN, LEE F. BENTON, ROBERT V. GUNDERSON, JR., KEITH L. KEARNEY, and JORGE DEL CALVO, *Venture Capital and Public Offering Negotiation*, Englewood Cliffs, NJ, Aspen Law and Business, 1997 (and updates), volume 2.

JACK S. LEVIN, *Structuring Venture Capital, Private Equity, and Entrepreneurial Transactions*, Boston, MA, Little, Brown, 2000, chapter 9.

Practitioner and Journalistic Accounts

PAUL F. DENNING and ROBIN A. PAINTER, *Stock Distributions: A Guide for Venture Capitalists*, Boston, MA, Robertson, Stephens & Co. and Testa, Hurwitz & Thibeault, 1994.

European Venture Capital Association, *Venture Capital Special Paper: Capital Markets for Entrepreneurial Companies*, Zaventum, Belgium, European Venture Capital Association, 1994.

Venture Economics, *Exiting Venture Capital Investments*, Wellesley, MA, Venture Economics, 1988.

Numerous articles in *Buyouts, Private Equity Analyst,* and *Venture Capital Journal.*

Academic Studies

CHRISTOPHER B. BARRY, CHRIS J. MUSCARELLA, JOHN W. PEAVY III, and MICHAEL R. VETSUYPENS, "The Role of Venture Capital in the Creation of Public Companies: Evidence from the Going Public Process," *Journal of Financial Economics* 27 (October 1990): 447–471.

BERNARD S. BLACK and RONALD J. GILSON, "Venture Capital and the Structure of Capital Markets: Banks versus Stock Markets," *Journal of Financial Economics* 47 (March 1998): 243–277.

GEORGE W. FENN, NELLIE LIANG, and STEPHEN PROWSE, "The Private Equity Market: An Overview," *Financial Markets, Institutions, and Instruments* 6, no. 4 (1997): 1–26.

PAUL A. GOMPERS and JOSH LERNER, "Conflict of Interest and Reputation in the Issuance of Public Securities: Evidence from Venture Capital," *Journal of Law and Economics* 42 (April 1999): 53–80.

PAUL A. GOMPERS and JOSH LERNER, "Venture Capital and the Creation of Public Companies: Do Venture Capitalists Really Bring More Than Money?," *Journal of Private Equity* 1 (Fall 1997): 15–32.

PAUL A. GOMPERS and JOSH LERNER, *The Venture Capital Cycle*, Cambridge, MA, MIT Press, 1999, chapters 10–14.

STEVEN N. KAPLAN, "The Staying Power of Leveraged Buyouts," *Journal of Financial Economics* 29 (October 1991): 287–313.

TIM LOUGHRAN and JAY R. RITTER, "The New Issues Puzzle," *Journal of Finance* 50 (March 1995): 23–51.

WILLIAM C. MEGGINSON and KATHLEEN A. WEISS, "Venture Capital Certification in Initial Public Offerings," *Journal of Finance* 46 (July 1991): 879–893.

20

Investitori Associati: Exiting the Savio LBO (A)

It was a foggy morning in February 1996, as Franco Cattaneo was driving on La Serenissima, the highway that links Milan to Venice. Despite the heavy traffic and his family's recommendations to drive carefully, his mind was elsewhere. As the CEO and a co-investor in Savio Macchine Tessili SpA (Savio), a company that had been acquired in a leveraged buyout by the investment group Investitori Associati, he knew that it was almost time to make a decision on how and when to exit the investment. If executed well, the transaction could generate great wealth for all parties concerned. At the same time, he feared that the risks were also substantial.

Sitting next to Cattaneo was Gianfilippo Cuneo, one of the pioneers of strategy consulting in Italy and a director who had been appointed to Savio's board by Investitori Associati. The two had decided to ride together and take advantage of the three-hour drive to discuss some of the issues that would arise in the next day's meeting of the board of directors. As the clutter of the Milan suburbs receded behind them, the two men began considering their many options.

THE PRIVATE EQUITY INDUSTRY IN ITALY[1]

Significant differences existed in 1996 not only between the American and European private equity industries, but also within Europe. In spite of the trend towards European integration, each country in Europe retained a distinct culture, and, to a large (though diminishing) extent, different financial and regulatory environments.

It could be generalized, however, that the development of European private equity in 1996 was far behind that of the United States. Italy was no exception. Private equity

Dino Cattaneo (MBA '96) and and Giampiero Mazza (MBA '96), prepared this case under the supervision of Professor Josh Lerner as the basis for class discussion rather than to illustrate either effective or ineffective handling of an administrative situation.

[1] This section is based on Associazione Italiana degli Investitori Instituzionali nel Capitale di Rischio, *Capitale per lo Sviluppo, Quinto Rapporto Biennale 1995–1996*, Guerini e Associati, 1996, a wide variety of publications of the European Venture Capital Association, http://www.borsaitalia.it, and numerous press accounts.

activity in Italy had started in the 1980s, first through isolated transactions sponsored by financial institutions, and later with the formation of a professional sector of specialized operators. While small and medium-sized companies have traditionally been the backbone of Italy's economic growth, they did not appear to have benefited much from the private equity industry: with the exception of government funds, most of the transactions had been restructurings and later-stage financings.

Size and Trends The total pool of private equity investments (available funds and portfolio investments) at the end of 1995 was Lit. (short for Italian lira) 6.5 trillion, or about US$4 billion. This was up from Lit. 5.3 trillion in 1993 and about six times the size of the pool eight years earlier. About 600 portfolio companies were financed by private equity groups at the end of 1995. Funds averaged approximately Lit. 75 billion in size, with median portfolio investments in the range of Lit. 5 billion and with little industry-specific focus.

In spite of the growing importance of independent private equity funds and merchant banks, a large part of Italy's funds for young businesses was provided by the public sector. In recent years, nearly three-quarters of the total private equity had been supplied by the state and local governments. Government programs focused their investments on companies in sectors strategically important for the country's economic development and macroeconomic stability, especially seeking to foster employment. For instance, a substantial government-sponsored program sought to foster entrepreneurial activity by young people. This new law allocated Lit. 2.2 trillion (Lit. 40,000 per taxpayer) to finance entrepreneurial activities by people under the age of 30 in southern Italy. Up to 60% of the financing was *"a fondo perduto"* (*i.e.*, there was no obligation to repay it), and funds were allocated with little review of the business plans or backgrounds of the applicants.

Since recent regulatory changes, banks had played a key role in the Italian private equity market. Excluding the public sector, banks provided approximately half of all private equity in Italy. This was coupled with the lack of a high-yield debt market (true to different degrees throughout Europe). By assuming a dual role of providing not only senior debt but also equity, banks enjoyed a disproportionate amount of leverage in the Italian private equity market. Other institutional investors played much smaller roles. In 1995, insurance companies and pension funds together provided only 3% of capital to private equity funds. Much of the remainder was provided by individuals and retained earnings (nondistributed capital gains).[2]

The importance of public funds and their focus on promoting start-ups was reflected in the industry's investment mix. In 1995, almost one-half the funds went to start-up financing. About two-thirds of all investments were in companies with fewer than 200 employees. Eliminating investments from the public sector, however, Italian private equity investors fell in line with most European countries, with the lion's share of funds going to later-stage (expansion) financings, turnaround situations, and management buyouts. Reflecting this orientation, the private funds were heavily weighted to traditional industries: 56% of the investments in 1995 went to manufacturing, industrial products, consumer products, and agriculture. Exhibit 20-1 compares the

---

[2] Many European private equity funds are free to reinvest the proceeds from successfully harvested investments. (For a discussion, see Jonathan Blake, editor, *Venture Capital Fund Structures in Europe*, Zaventem, Belgium, European Venture Capital Association, 1995.) The European Venture Capital Association computes such reinvestment of proceeds as a form of private equity fundraising and includes it in the total amount raised in each country.

EXHIBIT 20-1

COMPARATIVE ANALYSIS OF PRIVATE EQUITY WITHIN EUROPE (ECU MILLIONS)

	Europe	Italy[a]	United Kingdom	France	Netherlands	Germany	Spain
Total Funds Raised to Date:[b]							
1992	38,471	4,020	16,272	7,051	1,560	3,886	1,158
1993	40,530	3,802	17,038	8,570	1,702	4,267	1,232
1994	46,654	3,949	20,882	9,670	1,847	4,275	1,207
1995	49,667	3,824	21,516	10,590	1,907	4,714	1,323
Funds Raised in Year:							
1992	4,214	443	1,249	857	91	835	182
1993	3,425	308	1,239	834	133	208	199
1994	6,592	315	3,844	1,055	259	295	60
1995	4,398	264	1,841	793	257	210	141
Portfolio Size at Year End:							
1992	20,373	1,516	8,621	3,673	1,204	2,683	537
1993	20,857	1,348	8,417	4,043	1,288	3,060	474
1994	23,120	1,454	9,337	4,333	1,427	3,444	534
1995	25,108	1,383	9,776	4,736	1,712	3,997	602
Amount Invested in Year:							
1992	4,701	510	1,831	968	239	633	128
1993	5,115	260	1,630	903	207	626	113
1994	5,440	273	2,265	1,088	323	802	116
1995	5,546	253	2,633	851	467	666	163
Sources of Funds Raised in 1995:							
Corporate	4.9%	0.7%	4.0%	6.8%	0.0%	9.8%	7.3%
Individuals	3.4%	13.6%	3.1%	0.9%	0.0%	4.6%	0.2%
Public sector	3.1%	13.1%	1.1%	1.8%	0.0%	7.9%	11.4%
Banks	25.6%	14.2%	14.9%	39.5%	51.9%	57.2%	51.8%
Pension funds	27.3%	0.0%	44.6%	9.7%	0.0%	8.6%	11.5%
Insurance companies	10.8%	3.2%	16.6%	10.4%	7.4%	7.9%	0.0%
University endowments	0.2%	0.0%	3.3%	0.0%	0.0%	0.0%	0.0%
Other[c]	23.8%	55.2%	12.5%	31.1%	40.7%	4.0%	17.8%
Investment Focus in 1995 (by amount invested):							
Seed capital	0.6%	0.3%	0.0%	0.2%	1.0%	2.9%	0.0%
Start-up	5.2%	17.4%	1.0%	3.0%	15.3%	10.5%	10.8%
Expansion capital	41.4%	55.6%	25.1%	36.0%	60.7%	66.5%	71.5%
Turnaround/Restructuring	6.4%	14.0%	3.6%	21.1%	0.0%	0.0%	3.0%
MBO/LBO	46.4%	12.7%	70.3%	39.7%	23.0%	20.2%	14.6%

[a] For sake of comparison, the Italian data does not include investments by government-affiliated funds. Even so, many private funds received at least some capital from government sources.

[b] The occasional instances where "cumulative funds raised to date" declines reflect changes in the domestic exchange rate against the European Currency Unit (ECU), as well as the occasional restatement of fund size by various groups. During this period, 1 ECU had an average value of US$1.22 and Lit. 1868.

[c] "Other" is primarily the reinvestment of capital gains. (Many European funds are allowed to reinvest the proceeds from exited investments.) Such reinvestments are included in the fundraising totals of the European Venture Capital Association.

Source: Compiled from various publications of the European Venture Capital Association.

Italian private equity to that in other countries. (In order to facilitate comparisons, the table presents data only on the nongovernmental Italian private equity funds.)

Despite its recent growth, the Italian venture capital and leveraged buyout market had the potential to become much larger, though it would always be more limited than the equivalent markets in the United Kingdom, France, and Germany. Changes in the regulatory environment (see below) had spurred the interest of financial institutions in private equity. Other positive events were government initiatives to privatize state-owned companies, an upswing in the economic cycle, and a tendency towards industrial concentration. Finally, debt financing had become increasingly available from both Italian and foreign banks.

Exhibits 20-2 and 20-3 provide additional statistics and data on the private equity industry in Italy. (Since most of the data are in lira, Exhibit 20-4 provides key exchange rates for comparative purposes.)

Regulatory Environment   Italian legislators during the 1980s and early 1990s had sought to create incentives for the development of the private equity industry, while at the same time complying with the European Union directives to harmonize legislation across borders. Until 1987, commercial banks could not own equity securities of nonfinancial companies. In that year, a new law allowed banks to own equity and to participate in investment banking activities through the ownership of *Società di Intermediazione Finanziaria* (*SIFs*). SIFs performed most of the functions undertaken by Anglo-Saxon brokerage houses and merchant banks. All the major Italian commercial banks created SIF subsidiaries to become involved in, among other things, underwriting equity and bond issues. Legislation passed in 1993 removed the prohibition against banks holding equity in nonfinancial firms directly and allowed the commercial banks to bring their investment banking activities in-house.

Another important legislative effort was the encouragement of private pension fund schemes (as opposed to the central state-run pension system). The current legislation, however, set the maximum amount that a pension fund could hold in private companies as 10% and the maximum percentage of a pension fund's worth that could be invested in equities of any kind as 20%. The portfolio of pension funds remained heavily weighted toward real estate assets (with 32% of the total) and debt securities. A mere 3.2% was invested in equities.

Closed private equity funds (similar to the limited partnerships standard in the United States) were also approved in 1993. Adopted after a seven-year legislative debate, this reform, many observers believed, had the potential to radically improve the outlook for the Italian private equity industry. A significant difference with the United States still remained: the closed funds themselves had to pay taxes. (In the case of limited partnerships in the United States, all the tax obligations flowed through to the partners.) The government had granted several fiscal incentives to stimulate the funds' growth. Dividend income was tax exempt for the funds, and the annual tax on investments was reduced to 0.25% of the amount invested (0.10% if the fund invested more than 50% of its capital in "small" companies, as defined by the Italian legislation). Capital gains also enjoyed a favorable tax treatment, being taxed (when realized) at the rate of 25%, instead of the normal 53% combined tax rate applicable to ordinary income and capital gains.

Considerable attention had also been devoted to the "Decreto Tremonti," a piece of legislation passed in 1994 that created incentives for small- and medium-sized companies to be publicly listed. The Tremonti bill provided a two-year reduction in the corporate tax rate from 36% to 20% for firms that listed on an Italian stock exchange by

EXHIBIT 20-2

LEADING NONGOVERNMENTAL ITALIAN PRIVATE EQUITY FUNDS AS OF FEBRUARY 1996 (BILLIONS OF LIRA)

Fund Name(s)	Promoter [Parent Organization]	Advisor	Year First Fund Formed	Funds Raised to Date	Funds Still to Invest	Italian Deals Done to Date
IVF/IVF 2	Schroder Ventures	Schroder & Associates	1989	Lit. 210 bn	Lit. 83 bn	25
UBS Italia	UBS	UBS Italia	1990	NA	NA	20
Euroventures/IPEF 1&2	B&S Ventures	B&S Ventures	1988	Lit. 100 bn	Lit. 100bn	14
Europa Investimenti	Vegni & others	Europa Investimenti	1989	Lit. 33.5 bn	Lit. 7 bn	11
C-C Directional Fund	Gemina, Chase Manhattan	C-G Italia	1990	Lit. 80 bn	Lit. 20 bn	7
Eur. Enter. '92/CVC Equity Partners[a]	Citicorp	CVC Partners	1990	ECU 750 mn	ECU 740 mn	7
Hancock and others[a]	BC Partners	BC Partners	1986	ECU 750 mn	ECU 350 mn	6
Investitori Associati 1&2	BGCCI, Comit	Investitori Associati	1993	Lit. 147 bn	NA	5
Eurofund[a]	3i	3i	1990	Lit. 100 bn	Lit. 50bn	5
Cambria 1990/1996	Candover, KB	Darma, Elcot	1990	Lit. 70 bn	Lit. 50bn	5

NA = information not available; bn = billions; mn = millions; ECU = European Currency Unit.

[a] Pan-European fund without Italy-specific mandate; not all capital funds has or will be invested in Italy.

Source: Compiled from numerous press accounts.

EXHIBIT 20-3

DISTRIBUTION OF INVESTMENTS IN ITALIAN PRIVATE EQUITY[a] BY SECTOR (BY NUMBER OF TRANSACTIONS)

	1992	1993	1994	1995
Communications	2%	0%	1.5%	2.7%
Computer	3	3	3.5	1.8
Electronics	3	0	1.5	1.4
Biotechnology	1	2	0.0	0.9
Health	8	2	4.0	1.4
Energy	1	2	0.5	0.5
Consumer goods	14	17	14.3	17.7
Industrial products	10	10	15.3	10.5
Chemical	2	1	2.5	0.9
Industrial automation	3	3	0.5	2.7
Transport	2	3	0.5	1.4
Financial services	13	12	3.9	0.9
Other services	8	7	11.9	16.4
Manufacturing	12	17	19.8	13.2
Agriculture	1	0	14.8	15.9
Construction	7	10	0.0	1.8
Other	11	11	5.4	10.0

[a] Excludes investments by funds financed primarily by the public sector.

Source: Compiled from Associazione Italiana degli Investitori Instituzionali nel Capitale di Rischio, "Capitale per lo Sviluppo, Quinto Rapporto Biennale 1995–1996," Guerini e Associati, 1996.

EXHIBIT 20-4

AVERAGE EXCHANGE RATES FOR US$ VERSUS VARIOUS CURRENCIES

	1990	1991	1992	1993	1994	1995	February 1996
Lit. per US$	1,198	1,241	1,232	1,574	1,612	1,629	1,577
DM per US$	1.6157	1.6595	1.5617	1.6533	1.6228	1.4321	1.4652
ECU per US$	1.273	1.240	1.297	1.172	1.189	1.308	1.285
Yen per US$	144.79	134.71	126.65	111.20	102.21	93.96	105.77

Note: DM = Deutsche mark; ECU = European currency unit.

Source: Compiled from International Monetary Fund, *International Financial Statistics Yearbook*, various editions.

the end of 1997, as long as the firm had a sufficiently large book value of equity after the offering and raised a significant amount of equity in the offering.

Exit Channels in Italy Historically, Italy's financial infrastructure, macroeconomic policies, and cultural factors made exiting private equity investments difficult when compared to the United States and even to most other European countries. Both initial public offering (IPO) and merger and acquisition (M&A) activity had been fairly limited, although recent changes in the economic environment and legal infrastructure had improved the outlook for the future.

There were two stock exchanges in Italy: the Milan Stock Exchange ("La Borsa Valori") and the Secondary Market ("Il Mercato Ristretto"). La Borsa was the sixth largest stock exchange in Europe in terms of capitalization, although the number of traded securities was considerably smaller than other major exchanges on the Continent. At the end of 1995, only 221 companies were publicly traded (a total of 316 securities), with a total capitalization of Lit. 325 trillion and a total trading volume of Lit. 140 trillion. When compared to the major U.S. exchanges, the Milan market was quite liquid (as measured by the ratio of the volume traded to market capitalization) in spite of its small size.

One of the main causes for the limited breadth of the Milan Stock Exchange was found in the traditional family ownership structure and the corresponding suspicion of public ownership, still dominant among Italian businesses.[3] Other causes were the bureaucratic hurdles, high costs, and limited perception of the benefits related to public ownership. The key requirements to enter "La Borsa Valori" were a minimum book net worth of Lit. 10 billion for commercial and industrial companies and Lit. 50 billion for banks and insurance companies. Firms that were to be listed had to have at least 25% of their shares publicly traded, a minimum of 500 shareholders, and three years of audited financial statements showing positive net income (before extraordinary items).

Another important factor behind the slow development of the equity markets in Italy was the high deficits run by the government over the past several decades. As the deficits increased, so did the interest rates offered on treasury bonds. Both retail and institutional investors consistently flocked to the fixed income markets, ignoring the stock market.

"Il Mercato Ristretto," born in 1977 to respond to the needs of medium-sized companies, had been by most standards a failure. Only 37 companies were traded on it at the end of 1995, for a total capitalization of Lit. 11 trillion and a trading volume of Lit. 1 trillion. Unsuccessful efforts to boost this exchange's activity had included the consolidation of several local exchanges into this market and relaxed entry requirements. (To be listed on this exchange, a company needed to have minimum book equity of Lit. 1 billion, one year of audited financial statements showing positive net income, and 10% of its shares publicly traded.)

More attention had recently been devoted to the formation of METIM, a new secondary market for medium-sized companies. METIM planned to begin operations in late 1996. It set higher standards than Il Mercato Ristretto did: key requirements included minimum book equity of Lit. 2.5 billion, one year of audited financial statements, having 15% of shares publicly traded and at least 100 shareholders, and not having issued securities on any other exchange. It was hoped that this market would have local branches, featuring trading in the high-quality small firms of that region.

---

[3] For a detailed study of the going public decision of Italian entrepreneurs, see Marco Pagano, Fabio Panetta, and Luigi Zingales, "Why Do Firms Go Public? An Empirical Analysis," *Journal of Finance* 53 (1998): 24–54.

In contrast to the slow development of the public markets, mergers and acquisitions had rebounded in the mid-1990s after a period of very limited activity in the early 1990s. This growth was aided by the privatization process, the devaluation of the Italian lira, and better economic prospects. In recent years, 59% of those transactions were between Italian companies, 17% were acquisitions by Italian companies of foreign ones, and the remaining 24% represented acquisitions of domestic firms by foreign concerns. In spite of this improvement, M&A activity remained extremely limited when compared to other countries, mainly because of Italian businesses' traditional focus on retaining majority control.

EXHIBIT 20-5

FORMS OF EXIT IN EUROPE AND IN ITALY

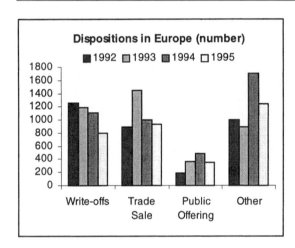

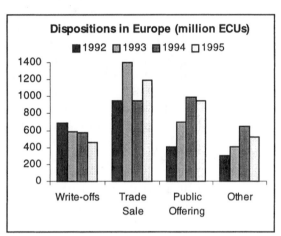

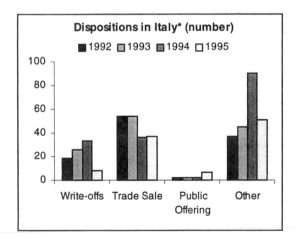

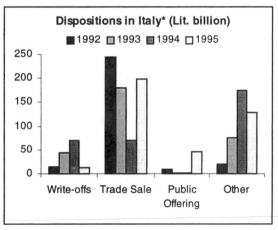

° Excludes investments by funds financed primarily by the public sector.

Source: Compiled from Associazione Italiana degli Investitori Instituzionali nel Capitale di Rischio, "Capitale per lo Sviluppo, Quinto Rapporto Biennale 1995–1996," Guerini e Associati, 1996.

EXHIBIT 20-6

COMPARATIVE STOCK MARKET PERFORMANCE

Stock Market Performance: Italy, U.K., and U.S.

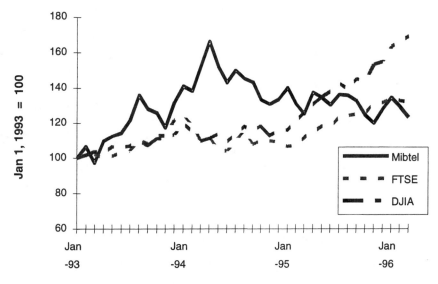

Note: Mibtel = Italian index; FTSE = U.K. index; DJIA = U.S. index.

Source: Compiled from Bloomberg and other on-line databases.

For private equity investors, private sales were still a far more common exit choice than IPOs, as Exhibit 20-5 depicts. Management buyouts, releveraged buyouts, or re-purchases by the original shareholders also were common exit channels in Italy. Exhibits 20-6 and 20-7 present some supplemental information on market levels and trends.

EXHIBIT 20-7

SELECTED RATES FOR GOVERNMENT SECURITIES, FEBRUARY 1996

Maturity	Italy	United Kingdom	United States
90 day	7.150%	6.090%	4.918%
1 year	8.500	6.061	4.843
5 year	8.725	6.924	5.242
10 year	9.271	7.676	5.702
30 year	9.641	8.060	6.170

Source: Compiled from Bloomberg and other on-line databases.

INVESTITORI ASSOCIATI FUND

The Investitori Associati fund was the product of an initiative by Gianfilippo "Phil" Cuneo, one of the pioneers of strategic consulting in Italy. After opening the Italian office of McKinsey & Co. in the mid-1960s, Cuneo left with a group of associates in 1989 and formed a joint venture with Bain & Co. In the early 1990s, he decided to capitalize on the business experience and the extensive network of contacts developed by the firm to make private equity investments, following the model successfully implemented by Bain Capital in the United States. The result was Bain Gallo Cuneo Capital Investments (BGCCI). It should be noted that in order to avoid conflicts of interest between the consulting and the private equity activities, Bain & Co. did not take part in the activity of BGCCI.

BGCCI teamed up with Banca Commerciale Italiana (Comit), one of Italy's leading commercial banks, to raise a private equity fund. In 1993, they closed the Investitori Associati fund with total capital of Lit. 30 billion. The investing strategy was to target medium- and small-sized industrial companies and invest together with a management team assembled by the fund. In this way, the fund could leverage off the operational expertise developed by the consulting practice. Since the key criterion was

---

EXHIBIT 20-8

STATEMENT OF PHILOSOPHY OF INVESTITORI ASSOCIATI

Investitori Associati and Investitori Associati II ("IA") are Luxembourg-based investment companies with an overall capital of 150 billion lira, raised from leading investors, both Italian and foreign. The investment activity started in 1993 and is focused on the acquisition of Italian and European companies with potential for a significant increase in value. In terms of number of transactions completed, today IA is among the most active venture capital players in Italy.

Investment Criteria

- *Acquisitions with financial leverage:* These are investments in companies, either market or niche leaders, characterized by stable operating performance and significant cash flow;
- *Investments in turnaround situations:* These are targeted at companies where performance is unsatisfactory and for which a restructuring and relaunch strategy has been identified;
- *Investments in development capital:* In this case, the target companies are market or niche leaders that need additional capital to finance specific growth plans aimed at significantly increasing their value;
- *Acquisitions of start-up companies:* These involve the acquisitions of companies operating in technological and defendable niches or markets with potential for rapid growth.

Investment Targets

The target companies are midsize Italian or European businesses, with acquisition price usually greater than 30 billion lira. Investitori Associati analyzes investment opportunities involving manufacturing and service companies, with the aim of creating and increasing value, regardless of the sector in which they operate.

The investment companies acquire 100% or a majority stake, either alone or in partnership with other financial institutions. The acquisition of a minority interest is considered only in special cases where there is a clearly defined exit strategy.

Source: Corporate documents.

EXHIBIT 20-9

PROFILES OF KEY PERSONNEL AT INVESTITORI ASSOCIATI

Stefano Miccinelli. A partner. Before joining IA in 1994, he worked as a system engineer for IBM Italia and subsequently as a strategic consultant for both McKinsey & Co. and Bain, Cuneo e Associati. He has been a director of three IA companies. Stefano Miccinelli is a graduate in Electrical Engineering from Politecnico of Milan and holds an MBA from INSEAD, Fontainebleu, France.

Renato Peroni. A partner. His professional experience includes responsibilities as an account officer with Deutsche Bank, as a strategic consultant with Bain, Cuneo e Associati, and as a chief financial officer of an industrial company. He joined IA in 1993 and has been director of one IA investment. Renato Peroni is a graduate in Economics from Bocconi University of Milan.

Antonio Tazartes. A partner. He was the founding partner of IA in 1993. Before that, he worked as a strategic consultant for both McKinsey & Co. and Bain, Cueno e Associati and as a Managing Director of Bain, Gallo, Cuneo Capital Investment. He has been a director of six IA companies. Antonio Tazartes is a graduate in law from Statale University of Milan and holds a Master of Law from New York University and an MBA from INSEAD, Fontainebleu, France.

Paolo Visioni. A partner. His professional experience includes responsibilities in relationship management and acquisition finance as a vice president in the Italian branches of Continental Bank and National Westminster. He joined IA in 1996 and has been director of two IA investments. Paolo Visioni is a graduate in business administration from Bocconi University of Milan.

Source: Corporate documents.

---

the quality of the management team, and the fund expected to create value through operational changes, both all-equity management buyouts and leveraged buyouts were considered. The fund was raised exclusively from Italian investors, including successful entrepreneurs and institutions such as insurance companies.

The structure in place to manage the fund was somewhat different from that of the traditional American private equity firm. BGCCI and Comit were the "promoters" of the fund, basically acting as guarantors to the outside investors. The fund was managed by its board of directors in which the major shareholders were represented. The board retained the right to review all investment and divestment decisions. It had entered into a long-term consulting agreement with a company employing the private equity professionals, who were responsible for sourcing, executing, and monitoring transactions. (See Exhibits 20-8 and 20-9 for background information on the fund.)

Before the Savio acquisition, the fund had completed three transactions. The first of these, the acquisition of Panini, whose sticker collections were a favorite of Italian children, gave the fund immediate visibility. When the company was sold to Marvel Comics a few months after the acquisition, the fund realized an IRR above 600%. Grove Italia, a producer of valves and flanges for oil and gas pipelines, had been bought in 1994 and sold in 1995, yielding an IRR above 350%. Sogepas, an automotive component supplier, had been purchased in 1995. The fund expected to exit Sogepas in 1996 or 1997. (Exhibit 20-10 provides more details.)

Almost all of the Investitori Associati's initial fund had been invested, and quite successfully, at the time of the Savio acquisition. Shortly thereafter, BGCCI and Comit had

EXHIBIT 20-10

INVESTITORI ASSOCIATI'S INVESTMENTS, 1993 THROUGH FEBRUARY 1996

Panini SpA. Panini is the world leader in the production of stickers for children, with a current turnover of about 390 billion lira. Panini was IA's first investment back in 1993, and its successful turnaround was implemented by a new management team, which carried out actions to substantially reduce costs and to increase the penetration in new markets. As a result, turnover increased from 125 billion lira in 1992 to 220 billion in 1994, and net income from a loss of 12 billion lira in 1992 to a profit of 45 billion in 1994. Panini was sold to an industrial buyer in 1994.

Grove SpA. Grove is the world leader in the production of valves for gas and oil pipelines, with a turnover of about 250 billion lira. This was IA's second investment, being finalized in 1994, together with other financial investors and a very strong management team; the latter was able to significantly expand Grove's commercial penetration, to diversify sales and outsource low-value-added production activities, and to outperform the business plan elaborated upon the acquisition. Grove was sold to an industrial buyer in 1995.

Sogepas SpA. Sogepas is the European leader in the production of disc brake pads and drum brake shoes for the automotive industry, with a turnover of about 70 billion lira. The Sogepas group fell into a dramatic financial crisis and became the objective of a takeover by a group of financial investors led by IA, which bought it in 1995 following an out-of-court arrangement with creditors. IA then guided its successful restructuring along with a new management team. IA anticipates selling Sogepas in 1996 or 1997.

Savio Macchine Tessili SpA. Savio is a world leader in the production of twisting and winding machines for the textile industry, with a turnover of about 300 billion lira. In mid-1995, IA finalized the acquisition of Savio, together with a new CEO and the management team responsible for the company's turnaround started during the 1990s. With the support of the new shareholders, the company has expanded its presence in the most important markets, strengthening its worldwide co-leadership position in the twisting and winding machine sector.

Villa Sistemi Medicali SpA. Villa is one of the European leaders in the production of medical radiological equipment, with a turnover of about 60 billion lira. The company, in deep financial difficulty, was bought in early 1996 by IA and another financial investor, along with an external manager, with the aim of turning it around.

Castelgarden SpA. Castelgarden is the European leader in the production of lawnmowers and lawn-mowing mini-tractors, with a turnover of about 330 billion lira. Together with other financial buyers and the existing managing director, IA bought Castelgarden in early 1996.

Company	Sector	Purchase Date	IA % Ownership	Amount Invested (billion lira)	Exit Date	Manner in which Exited	IRR
Panini SpA.	Stickers for children	Dec. 1993	17.2%	4.6	Aug. 1994	Trade sale	>600%
Grove SpA.	Valves for gas and oil pipeline	July 1994	10.9%	6.1	June 1995	Trade sale	>350%
Sogepas SpA.	Disk brake pads and drum brake shoes	April 1995	35.5%	6.0			
Savio Macchine Tessili SpA.	Twisting and winding machines	June 1995	42.0%	10.7			
Villa Sistemi Medicali SpA.	Medical radiology equipment	Jan. 1996	35.0%	4.3			
Castelgarden SpA.	Lawnmowers and lawn-mowing mini-tractors	Feb. 1996	13.3%	7.2			

Source: Corporate documents.

raised a second fund, Investitori Associati II, this time with capital of Lit. 120 billion. The fund had attracted interest from a number of European institutional investors, including the private equity groups of a large British and a significant German bank.

THE SAVIO TRANSACTION

The investment that the Investitori Associati partners were considering exiting in February 1996, Savio, had been their largest transaction to that point. While the proposed exit avenue was quite different from that in their earlier transactions, in many respects the transaction was representative of their approach to private equity.

The Textile Production Cycle   Savio was a manufacturer of textile machinery. As a result, the company's fate was closely linked to that of the apparel industry as a whole. The textile production cycle can be divided into three phases. The first step is fiber production. The second step is spinning, whose final product is yarn. In the final step, the yarn goes through either weaving or knitting to become cloth.[4] Savio's products were used in the spinning phase.

Both natural and synthetic fibers are the raw materials used by spinning mills to produce yarn. The spinning process can be conducted with two different types of machines: ring-spinning frames or open-end rotor-spinning machines. The thread produced by ring-spinning frames is wound over small bobbins of two to five ounces each. Given the speed of power looms, bobbins are too small and uneconomical to use; therefore, the thread has to be rewound into "packages." This process is performed by automatic winders, which tie the thread from different bobbins together and in the process stretch the thread and test its quality.

The production of complex types of yarn requires assembling and twisting thread after the spinning phase. In the assembly phase, two separate threads are intertwined to form a single yarn. The resulting yarn is then twisted to increase its resistance and unity. In an open-end process, the yarn is directly spun, tested, and wound into packages by a single machine. Open-end machines are more productive than traditional ring-spinning frames, but they cannot be used to spin long staple fibers. Also, finer counts[5] of yarn cannot be produced by open-end spinning frames.

The final part of the textile production cycle is weaving or knitting. The yarn is delivered in packages to weaving and knitting mills. Some producers are fully integrated along the three phases of textile production, but this market is generally local and fragmented. The installed weaving capacity of a country determines the needed spinning capacity, which in turns drives the demand for spinning and winding machinery.

History of Savio   Savio was founded in 1911 by Marcello Savio in Pordenone, a small town in northeastern Italy. In the early years, the company's activity consisted of main-

---

[4] Fibers are divided in two large groups: natural fibers such as wool, silk, linen, and cotton, and synthetic fibers, such as nylon, polyester, acrylic, and rayon. Natural fibers are further subdivided into short staple (cotton) and long staple (wool, silk, and linen) fibers. Synthetic fiber production is characterized by capital intensity and economies of scale, and is therefore highly concentrated. Natural fibers, by contrast, are produced by farms, and climate and geography drive their production. For more information on the economics and dynamics of the textile and apparel industries, see Debora Spar, Lygeia Ricciardi, and Laura Bures, "Lenzig AG: Expanding in Indonesia," Harvard Business School Case no. 796-099, 1996.

[5] "Count" is the technical name used to indicate the thickness of the yarn produced. Finer counts indicate thinner yarn, such as that used to make shirts. Denim, on the other hand, is produced from yarn with thicker counts.

tenance and service of textile machinery for local companies. After World War II, as Italy entered its phase of industrial reconstruction, Savio began manufacturing, capitalizing on its technical and design skills. From the beginning, the company focused its activities on the yarn-finishing machinery segment. Its product line consisted of traditional machines, such as manual winders, assembly winders, hank-to-cone winders, and ring-type twisters.

The 1950s and 1960s were years of spectacular growth for Italy, known as the years of *il miracolo economico* (the economic miracle). Savio rode the growth trend, opening a brand new plant in 1961 and reaching a peak of about 2,000 employees. Toward the end of the 1960s, when the first automatic machines appeared on the market, the company began to lose its competitive edge. Despite a large investment in R&D, the first attempt at developing a new automatic winder resulted in a complex, faulty machine that was ultimately rejected by the market. The resources absorbed by the project, coupled with a sharp downturn in the market, pushed the company to the brink of bankruptcy.

At about that time, the Italian government initiated a policy of acquiring troubled small businesses in order to preserve employment. In 1971, the state-owned EGAM Group acquired Savio. Although it had faced some financial troubles, the company had retained its strong technical skills. With new financial backing, Savio was able to develop its product line and establish itself as a world leader in the textile machinery business. But while the company's core business remained healthy, the 1970s and 1980s were decades of economic turmoil for Italy. Savio's ownership passed from EGAM to ENI (the state-owned energy group). As a member of a state-owned entity, in this period Savio was forced to acquire several distressed textile machinery manufacturers located all over Italy. The most important acquisition was San Giorgio of Genova, which in 1983 added open-end spinning machines to the company's product line. Some of the underperforming divisions acquired in the process damaged the company's overall profitability.

In the early 1990s, as economic reforms led to the privatization of certain sectors of the Italian economy, ENI decided to focus on its energy business and sell all its unrelated assets. During this process, Savio was restructured and consolidated into the original Pordenone plant, and all other businesses were closed or divested. The rationalization led to a shrinkage of the workforce from about 1,200 in 1989 to a little over 700 in 1994. Refocused on its core strengths, the company was put up for sale by ENI in late 1994. Exhibits 20-11 through 20-13 provide financial information on Savio.

The Leveraged Buyout   When ENI started the auction to sell Savio, it became clear to Investitori Associati that the company fitted most of its investment criteria. The company possessed significant technological assets and know-how. It had a strong market position in some segments and growth potential in others. The restructuring process had been started, but there was still room for operational improvements. The company had a solid management team: it needed only a CEO to complete the turnaround of the company.

Investitori Associati found its CEO and co-investor in Franco Cattaneo. After studies in mechanical engineering, Cattaneo had attended an executive education program at Harvard Business School and pursued a career as a manager of medium-sized industrial machinery manufacturers. In the 1980s he had completed a successful management buyout and turnaround of a steelmaking machinery manufacturer. When Investitori Associati contacted him, he was managing a cotton yarn producer. The combination of entrepreneurial experience and knowledge of both the industrial machinery sector and the textile industry made him the perfect candidate for Savio.

EXHIBIT 20-11

SAVIO STATEMENTS OF INCOME, 1993–1995 (LIT. MILLIONS)

	Unaudited Pro forma Combined[a]		Consolidated Group
	For the Year Ended 31 December 1993 (Lit millions)	For the Year Ended 31 December 1994 (Lit. millions)	For the Year Ended 31 December 1995 (Lit. millions)
Sales	224,918	185,873	272,867
Personnel costs	(45,021)	(37,866)	(46,326)
Cost of sales and operating costs	(149,397)	(126,175)	(189,122)
Gross operating profit	30,500	21,832	37,419[d]
Depreciation and amortization[b]	(6,644)	(5,832)	(10,259)
Operating profit	23,856	16,000	27,160
Net financial income/(expense)[c]	(7,258)	1,803	(2,486)
Profit before extraordinary items and income taxes	16,598	17,803	24,674
Net extraordinary income/(expense)	(1,328)	(1,808)	(2,075)[d]
Profit before income taxes	15,270	15,995	22,599
Income taxes	(9,148)	(8,060)	(14,024)
Net income for the period	6,122	7,935	8,575[d]

[a] While held as part of ENI, separate audited financial statements for Savio were not prepared.

[b] Depreciation and amortization includes goodwill amortization charges of Lit. 2,250 million in the year ended 31 December 1995.

[c] Net financial income/(expense) includes the following net foreign exchange gains/losses year ended 31 December 1993–Lit. 7,224 million loss, 1994–Lit 2,205 million gain, 1995–Lit. 2,140 million gain .

[d] The results for the year ended 31 December 1995 include the effect of a number of items not included in the 1993 and 1994 financial statements. If those items had been included, Savio's gross operating profit would have been Lit. 2,065 million lower in 1993, Lit. 871 million lower in 1994, and Lit. 2,936 million higher in 1995. Net income would have been Lit. 2,273 million lower in 1993, Lit. 1,620 million lower in 1994, and Lit. 3,893 million higher in 1995. These items included changes for obsolete inventory and provisions for warranties.

Source: Corporate documents.

In June 1995, a group of investors led by Investitori Associati bought Savio in an auction for a total valuation of Lit. 75 billion, outbidding the German competitor Schlafhorst. The transaction was financed with Lit. 50 billion of debt supplied by Comit and Lit. 25 billion of equity. Investitori Associati held 42% of the equity, Comit held 30%, and management as a whole held 8%. Since Savio played a major role in the economy of the area around Pordenone, two local entrepreneurs bought the remaining 20%. To align management incentives, there was a clause that gave management stock options at a preset price exercisable at the time of the sale of the company. The amount of options granted depended on the internal rate of return (IRR) realized by the investors. Details of the financing package are described in Exhibit 20-14.

EXHIBIT 20-12

SAVIO OPERATING PROJECTIONS, 1996–2000 (LIT. BILLIONS)

	1996	1997	1998	1999	2000
Sales	290.6	305.1	317.3	330.0	343.2
Growth rate	7.0%	5.0%	4.0%	4.0%	4.0%
Cost of sales	(216.5)	(227.3)	(236.4)	(245.8)	(255.7)
Gross profit	74.1	77.8	80.9	84.2	87.5
Gross margin	25.5%	25.5%	25.5%	25.5%	25.5%
SG&A	(33.4)	(35.1)	(36.5)	(38.0)	(39.5)
EBITDA	40.7	42.7	44.4	36.2	48.1
EBITDA margin	14.0%	14.0%	14.0%	14.0%	14.0%
D&A	(8.7)	(9.2)	(9.5)	(9.9)	(10.3)
EBIT	32.0	33.6	34.9	36.3	37.8
EBIT margin	11.0%	11.0%	11.0%	11.0%	11.0%

Note: The size of interest payments will be a function of whether the firm went public: one of the potential uses of funds from a public offering would be to pay down much of the senior debt. The tax rate of 62% paid in 1995 would be little changed unless the firm was publicly traded on an Italian exchange, in which case the tax burden would fall to 46% for a two-year period (1996 and 1997). One of Savio's two major competitors, Saurer AG, was publicly traded in Switzerland. Between February 1995 and January 1996, a regression of its share price on the Swiss Market Index (using weekly data) yielded a slope coefficient (beta) of 0.35. At the end of calendar year 1995, Saurer had a capital structure that consisted of 301 million Swiss francs (US$262 million) of debt. Its market capitalization at that point was 686 million Swiss francs (US$597 million).

Source: Casewriters' estimates.

As part of the transaction, Investitori Associati had insisted on a variety of control rights. In addition to receiving preemptive rights to provide future financing and a variety of other protective covenants, two of the partners of Investitori Associati received board seats. In addition, Gianfilippo Cuneo joined the board as a director. (Bain Cuneo e Associati also provided consulting services to Savio concerning its corporate strategy.) Two board seats were assigned as well to representatives of Comit.

Savio's Strategic Position in 1996   During the past 15 years, the global textile market had seen an accelerating transfer of production to areas characterized by lower labor costs. As a consequence, producers of textile machinery had been forced to adopt a double strategy. Machines designed for industrialized countries were characterized by a high degree of automation, with labor content reduction an important factor in the success of the product. Developing countries, on the other hand, required machines with a lower up-front investment and higher labor content to exploit the wage differentials. The machines for developing markets, however, were still required to meet high-quality standards.

In addition, the market for textile machinery, like most capital goods industries, was characterized by cyclical demand. The length of cycles experienced by the market had varied, and forecasting had traditionally been extremely difficult. Industry experts agreed that the cycles were partially driven by general economic conditions, but other factors appeared to be important as well. The most recent downturn in the market for textile machinery had occurred in 1993, when the overall market for textile machinery fell by

EXHIBIT 20-13

BALANCE SHEETS FOR SAVIO, 1993–1995 (LIT. MILLIONS)

	Unaudited Pro forma Combined		Consolidated Group
	31 December 1993 (Lit. millions)	31 December 1994 (Lit. millions)	31 December 1995 (Lit. millions)
Assets			
Current assets			
Cash and bank deposits	40,638	9,546	3,026
Marketable securities	70	55	5
Accounts receivable	73,362	63,582	82,018
Inventories	49,689	44,795	49,098
Accrued income and prepaid expenses	384	1,214	1,114
Total current assets	164,143	119,192	135,261
Noncurrent assets			
Investments	1,012	3,038	—
Other noncurrent assets	627	221	43
Tangible fixed assets	31,931	30,451	52,514
Intangible assets	351	456	21,360
Accounts receivable	28,439	18,728	11,470
Total noncurrent assets	62,360	52,894	85,387
Total Assets	226,503	172,086	220,648
Liabilities and Shareholders' Equity			
Current liabilities			
Short-term financial debt	18,645	10,207	2,783
Accounts payable	45,080	46,699	68,487
Other current liabilities	45,693	35,221	38,929
Accrued income taxes	10,396	1,411	11,807
Accrued expenses and deferred income	402	655	382
Total current liabilities	120,216	94,223	122,388
Noncurrent liabilities			
Long-term loans	15,101	10,059	33,783
Other noncurrent liabilities	24,502	14,901	8,057
Employees' termination indemnities[a]	20,036	19,967	21,638
Total noncurrent liabilities	59,639	44,927	64,925
Shareholders' Equity			
Share capital	40,119	25,000	25,000
Reserves	407	1	(240)
Net income for the year	6,122	7,935	8,575
Total shareholders' equity	46,648	32,936	33,335
Total Liabilities and Shareholders' Equity	226,503	172,086	220,648

[a] Under Italian law, each company must annually set aside a "leaving indemnity" for its employees, of an amount equal to one-twelfth of the compensation of the employees. When an employee leaves for whatever reason, he/she receives from the company the amount accumulated in his/her name in this fund. Unlike U.S. pension fund obligations, these obligations are listed on firms' balance sheets.

See also notes to Exhibit 20-11.

Source: Corporate documents.

EXHIBIT 20-14

DETAILS ON FINANCING STRUCTURE OF SAVIO LEVERAGED BUYOUT

Senior Term Loan (Lit. 30 billion)

Takedown:	After merger between Newco and Savio
Interest rate:	100 basis points over Libor
Maturity:	5 years from draw-down
Repayment schedule:	Semiannual straight
Prepayments:	Possible without penalties
Collateral:	First-level ranking pledge on the company's assets
Financial covenants:	Customary financial covenants to include:
	• minimum consolidated EBIT coverage
	• minimum consolidated net worth
	• limitation to consolidated indebtedness
Restricted payments:	No dividends or stock redemption
Reports:	Budget: yearly
	Balance sheet: quarterly
	Income statement: quarterly
	Cash flow statement: quarterly
	Flash report: monthly

Revolving Credit Facility (Lit. 20 billion)

Takedown:	When needed
Interest rate:	50 basis points over Libor
Maturity:	18 months
Collateral:	At least 80% of each draw-down to be counter-guaranteed by commercial credits in good standing
Commitment fee:	35 basis points

Source: Corporate documents.

20%, according to the International Textile Manufacturers Federation. In 1994, the market started a slow climb back.

As a result of the past downturns, the textile machinery industry had undergone a process of consolidation. Consequently, each market segment only had a small group of competitors, all of whom enjoyed significant market share. Savio competed globally in two sectors of the textile machinery industry: yarn-finishing machinery (such as the automatic winders discussed above) and open-end spinning frames. Italy accounted for only 23.8% of Savio's revenue; the rest of Europe and Turkey accounted for 17.2%, Asia (especially China) for 47.8%, America for 10.8%, and Africa for less than 1.0%. In most segments, the two major competitors were the Japanese firm Murata and the Swiss group Saurer, either directly or through its German subsidiary Schlafhorst.

In 1995 the yarn-finishing machinery market was estimated at Lit. 677 billion and open-end spinning market at Lit. 751 billion, for a total of Lit. 1.43 trillion.[6] After peaking in 1990 at Lit. 2.3 trillion, the market had experienced a sharp decline, bottoming out in 1993 at Lit. 1.36 trillion. The industry expected the market to remain stable or experience only slight growth over the following years. From a geographical standpoint, the most important markets for yarn-finishing machinery were Europe (33.2% of sales) and Asia (56.3% of sales), with China and India leading the market. In the open-end spinner markets, Asia played a smaller role, with Europe accounting for 45.0% of the market in 1995 and America for 36.0%.

The largest segment in the yarn-finishing sector was represented by automatic winders, which in 1995 accounted for 71.4% of the world sales. In 1995, Savio increased its market share[7] to 27.7% from 11.8% in 1990 and 20.4% in 1994. The average price of an Espero automatic winding machine varied from approximately Lit. 130 million to Lit. 400 million, depending on the number of winding heads and the level of automation of the machine. Customers in developing countries generally placed large orders for less sophisticated machines, while customers in industrialized countries bought the more advanced machines but placed smaller orders. Two-for-one twisters represented the second largest segment with 23.2% of world sales in 1995. Savio had a market share of 25.2%, up from 8.4% in 1990. The price for Gemini twisters varied from Lit. 150 million to Lit. 350 million, depending on the number of twisting heads installed. Other segments were smaller. These markets are summarized in Exhibits 20-15 and 20-16.

Spare parts and service were an extremely important component of Savio's business due to the high value added. While they represented only approximately 9% of the company's sales, they could generate up to 40% of the company's income. Spare parts sales were driven by the installed base and by the flourishing market for used equipment: after an average of approximately 15 years, machines from industrialized countries were sold to developing countries.

---

[6] For the rest of the paragraph, the term "market" refers to the sum of the yarn-finishing machinery and the open-end spinning machinery segments, that is, the markets in which Savio was active.

[7] Market share for all machinery was counted as Savio spindles or winding heads as a percentage of spindles and winding heads sold in the world.

EXHIBIT 20-15

WORLD MARKET FOR SAVIO PRODUCTS, 1990–1995 (LIT. BILLIONS)

	1990	1991	1992	1993	1994	1995
Yarn-finishing machinery:						
Automatic winders	592,763	538,505	408,568	425,000	395,615	483,000
Two-for-one twisting spindles	246,225	223,687	169,713	122,960	147,399	156,880
Assembly winders	54,717	49,708	37,714	25,700	21,728	24,647
Continuous shrinking winders	18,238	16,569	12,571	17,274	12,567	12,232
Total yarn-finishing machinery	911,943	828,469	628,567	590,934	577,309	676,759
Open-end spinning rotors	1,395,894	971,727	880,162	766,387	832,159	751,081
Total world market for Savio products	2,307,836	1,800,196	1,508,728	1,357,320	1,409,467	1,427,839

Source: Corporate documents.

EXHIBIT 20-16

SAVIO MARKET SHARE IN DIFFERENT SEGMENTS

	1990	1991	1992	1993	1994	1995
Automatic winders	11.8%	19.7%	22.2%	28.2%	20.4%	27.7%
Two-for-one twisting spindles	8.5	18.2	12.6	22.6	19.5	25.2
Assembly winders	5.3	4.5	6.0	7.6	6.0	6.0
Continuous shrinking winders	32.8	45.3	47.6	49.9	43.3	42.6
Open-end spinning rotors	1.2	2.2	1.8	2.0	3.0	1.6

Source: Corporate documents.

The basic functions performed by the machinery of the three major producers were fairly similar. The differentiating factors were service and design. Savio's machines used a simpler design with a lower number of parts than its competitors. A crucial component of the design was flexibility. The machines were designed in a modular way, and it was very easy for the company to tailor the machines to the customer's exact specifications. This design, coupled with what Savio believed was superior service offered to its customers, improved the reliability and reduced the cost of owning and operating Savio machines. The major restructuring undergone by the company over the last four years had also made it the low-cost producer in the industry, unlike German competitor Schlafhorst, which was in the middle of a severe crisis due to its extremely high fixed costs.

One of Savio's competitive advantages was its production strategy, started during the reorganization and fully implemented by the new management team after the LBO. As part of the rationalization of production, the company kept in-house only the design and R&D functions, as well as the production, assembly, and testing of a few key components. As a result, 80% of the variable production cost of the machines was represented by outsourced components. Of the key suppliers, 42% were located in the region close to the company, 38% in other parts of Italy, and 20% abroad.

THE EXIT DECISION

Since the completion of the transaction, the company had performed beyond all expectations. The full implementation of the strategy, combined with the slow recovery of the textile machinery markets, had allowed Savio to achieve a very significant improvement in its financial results. This had allowed the firm to repay Lit. 20 billion of acquisition debt in 1995. As a result, the investor group was in a position to quickly realize a significant return on its investment. But while a successful exit was possible, the best approach was not obvious.

Public offerings of private equity-backed companies had been increasing significantly in Europe, from 155 in 1992 to 353 in 1995. The amount raised in such offerings had gone from US$492 million in 1992 to a little over US$1 billion in 1995. The dollar amounts, however, paled when compared to their American counterparts, where US$5.5 billion were raised in IPOs in 1992 and US$8.2 billion in 1995. The gap was even more drastic when considering the fact that roughly half of the European IPO volume came from Great Britain. Consistent with the Italian experience, most efforts to establish secondary markets in Europe during the 1980s had been failures. Many analysts pointed to the lack of liquidity in secondary markets as the root cause for the difficulty of the private equity industry to fully develop in Europe.[8] Efficient and liquid secondary markets not only provided an opportunity for private equity groups to harvest investments, but also allowed them to negotiate better offers from private acquirers.

The first decision that Savio and Investitori Associati needed to make was whether to pursue a private or a public sale. If the first strategy were chosen, the process would be fairly straightforward: they would find a group of interested buyers and negotiate an acceptable price. If the decision was to take the company public instead, several other decisions needed to take place. First of all, what should be the size of the offering? Should the company issue some new equity, or should the offer consist only of secondary shares (i.e., those owned by management and the outside investors)? Where should the company be listed to obtain the best price and liquidity? Finally, how should the offering be priced to ensure both a good return and full subscription?

There were several reasons in favor of a private sale. First, the management had already been through the process recently and would not have to take significant time away from running the business at a crucial phase of strategy implementation. (By way of contrast, preparing the company to go public would require an enormous effort, both in meeting the legal disclosure requirements and in educating potential investors on the nature of the business.) Second, the company was an attractive acquisition candidate for both strategic and financial buyers. Of the two major competitors, Murata was not interested, but Schlafhorst had tried to buy the company when it was sold to Investitori Associati. Savio would be a very good fit for a company due to its complementary product line. The healthy cash flows expected for the next few years also made Savio a very suitable candidate for an acquisition by another financial buyer. Third, the private sale process would probably also be faster than a public sale process, shortening the holding time of the investment and increasing the IRR for the fund. Finally, the valuation in a private sale would be somewhat insulated from shifts in the equity market. By choosing to go public, the company ran the risk of going through the whole process and then not being able to achieve an acceptable valuation because of a downturn in the market. Given the uncertainty surrounding the political and economic situation in Italy, this possibility could not be dismissed lightly. From their knowledge of the Italian M&A market, Investitori Associati expected that in a private sale the company would be valued around four to five times current earnings before interest and taxes (EBIT).

On the other side, there were also many compelling reasons for a public sale. The management team believed the company still had considerable growth opportunities. An IPO would allow them to remain in control and to maintain or even increase their share of ownership. As a result, they would reap the benefits of the company's growth in the following years. By issuing additional capital, they would be able to reduce the firm's leverage ratio, which would protect them from a downturn. In addition, if the offering could be structured to meet the requirements of the Tremonti law, the company would gain significant tax savings from going public. Furthermore, management was

---

[8] For one example, see Bernard S. Black and Ronald J. Gilson, "Venture Capital and the Structure of Capital Markets: Banks Versus Stock Markets," *Journal of Financial Economics* 47 (1998): 243–277. For some contrary evidence, however, see Leslie A. Jeng and Philippe C. Wells, "The Determinants of Venture Capital Funding: An Empirical Analysis," *Journal of Corporate Finance*, 6 (2000): 241–284.

convinced that it had developed a successful strategy to operate in this industry, one that could be transferred to other firms. Once it had access to the equity market, Savio would be in a position to better finance acquisitions if the opportunity arose to buy troubled companies with complementary product lines.

This option was also attractive to Savio's investors. Since Investitori Associati had exited its previous transactions through private sales, listing Savio would provide an excellent chance for them to accumulate significant experience with another exit strategy. A successful IPO would also raise the profile of the private equity organization in the financial community, increasing the credibility of its track record and its access to new transactions. An IPO also would give Investitori Associati a chance (if it chose) to divest only part of its holding in Savio: it could participate in the future growth of the company.[9]

The choice of *where* to go public was also troubling. One option attracting considerable attention in Italy was the EASDAQ market. The European Venture Capital Association was promoting this new pan-European public market as the ideal exchange for growing companies with international operations. EASDAQ had been designed after the liquid and generally efficient NASDAQ market in the United States, and was expected to begin operations in mid-1996. EASDAQ hoped to become an effective financing route for those companies that could not afford or simply wanted to avoid their nation's primary markets. EASDAQ foresaw the key requirements to enter its exchange as US\$4 million in sales, US\$2 million in capital and retained earnings, US\$1 million in market value of traded shares, and a minimum of 300 shareholders. The time until this market became a liquid and efficient one, however, was very uncertain. Furthermore, it was unclear whether EASDAQ would welcome listings from "low-tech" firms such as Savio (as opposed to, for instance, Internet and biotechnology concerns).

A second alternative was the Milan exchange. Between July 1994 and December 1995, there had been 10 IPOs on the Italian stock market (excluding the privatizations of giants ENI and INA and several banks). The success of those issues had shown that there was a willingness to invest in medium-sized industrial companies with proven management teams. These issues had increased in price by an average of more than 60% since the day that they first traded (see Exhibit 20-17 for a detailed analysis). The only company whose price had declined, Stayer, had reported a significant mistake in its financial statements shortly after going public.

Some observers cautioned that Italian investors had very little experience with IPOs of private equity-backed companies. Only a handful of private equity investments had been divested on the public markets. Nevertheless, many factors indicated that an IPO could be successful. Several investment banks had contacted the company offering their services. Preliminary talks seemed to find a consensus among institutions that Savio could go public at a price anywhere between 10 and 14 times 1996 earnings (a valuation approach that the investment bankers seemed to believe was most useful), depending on market conditions. And once the company was listed, there was a good chance that it could be positioned in the more general group of the "Italian small-capitalization high-growth" companies that were currently enjoying excellent valuations on the market.

---

[9] While in the United States, the sale of shares by a private equity group in an IPO is still relatively infrequent (see, for instance, Christopher B. Barry, Chris J. Muscarella, John W. Peavy III, and Michael R. Vetsuypens, "The Role of Venture Capital in the Creation of Public Companies: Evidence from the Going Public Process," *Journal of Financial Economics* 27 (1990): 447–471), the partial or total sale of shares by such investors in European IPOs was commonplace.

EXHIBIT 20-17

PERFORMANCE OF ALL ITALIAN IPOS (EXCLUDING BANK OFFERINGS AND PRIVATIZATIONS), 1994–1995

Company	Business	IPO Date	Times Oversubscribed	IPO Price/ Share (Lit.)	Price/Share (February 1996)	% Change
Sans Getters	Specialty chemicals	July 1994	3×	8,450	30,604	262.2%
Finanza e Futuro	Money management	July 1994	1.1×	6,100	6,695	9.8%
IMA	Packaging machinery	May 1995	9×	6,200	12,194	96.7%
Brembo	Disc-breaking systems	June 1995	12×	11,300	20,503	81.4%
Stayer	Electric tools	June 1995	6×	4,950	2,300	(53.5%)
Bulgari	Jewelry	July 1995	10×	8,600	15,768	83.3%
Crespi	Synthetic fibers	October 1995	5×	3,800	4,963	30.6%
La Doria	Food	November 1995	6×	5,400	6,589	22.0%
Pagnossin	Tableware ceramics	December 1995	15×	5,650	9,481	67.8%
Carraro	Axles and auto parts	December 1995	3.5×	4,500	4,819	7.1%
Average appreciation						60.7%

Source: Corporate documents.

Exhibits 20-18 and 20-19 present excerpts from the valuation analyses by a representative investment bank. An interesting issue raised by these analyses was that the American equity markets seemed to yield consistently higher valuations than their Italian counterpart. Given the highly international component of Savio's business, the possibility of going public in the United States was extremely intriguing. In addition to achieving a better valuation, by being listed on an American exchange the company could increase its visibility with its American clients. Savio seemed to fit quite well the characteristics of NASDAQ's listings, at least as far as size and valuation were concerned. But there were some concerns with this option as well. NASDAQ had had 37 IPOs of European companies during the past five years. None of them was from an Italian company: only six Italian companies had undertaken IPOs in the United States during this period, all on the New York Stock Exchange. It was also unlikely that a company with Savio's line of business and size of float would garner any significant analyst coverage and market-making activity by American investment banks.

Since many British pension funds had percentages in their portfolio reserved for each European country, a listing on the London exchange might offer Savio the high valuation and visibility of an international listing coupled with the familiarity of operating in a European environment. In London, every major investment bank and brokerage house issued equity research on the Italian market on a regular basis. Thus, it probably would be easier to obtain the necessary research coverage there than in New York. At the same time, such a strategy would require a substantial "leap of faith." Savio and Investitori Associati would be dependent on the ability of an overseas investment bank to sell its equity to overseas investors, and only be able to have limited input into the process.

As Cattaneo and Cuneo drove on, other options were considered, including releveraging the company. Now that Savio's cash flows were strong again and much debt was

---

EXHIBIT 20-18

PUBLICLY TRADED COMPARABLE EUROPEAN MACHINERY MANUFACTURERS

Company	Exchange	February 1996 Market Capitalization (Lit. billions)	Price-earnings ratio based on 1995 earnings (February 1996)	P/E ratio based on estimated 1996 earnings (February 1996)
IMA	Milan	440	19.5×	15.6×
Sasib	Milan	807	14.3×	13.7×
Rieter	Zurich	766	15.5×	11.8×
Sulzer AG	Zurich	2,514	14.7×	12.3×
Babcock BSH	Frankfurt	178	10.8×	10.9×
Picanol NV	Brussels	1,950	12.6×	NA
Mean		1,109	14.6×	12.9×
Median		787	14.5×	12.3×
High		2,514	19.5×	15.6×
Low		178	10.8×	10.9×

Source: Corporate documents.

EXHIBIT 20-19

PUBLICLY TRADED SMALL-CAPITALIZATION, HIGH-GROWTH ITALIAN COMPANIES

Company	Industry	February 1996 Market Capitalization (Lit. billions)	Price-earnings ratio based on 1995 earnings (February 1996)	P/E ratio based on estimated 1996 earnings (February 1996)
Listed in Italy:				
CALP	Glassware	182	11.8×	9.9×
Brembo	Disc-breaking systems	731	21.4×	18.0×
IMA	Packaging machinery	440	19.8×	16.1×
Saes Getters	Specialty chemicals	418	24.8×	22.5×
Safilo	Eyeglass frames	444	21.0×	17.0×
Pagnossin	Tableware ceramics	190	17.1×	14.2×
Carraro	Axles and auto parts	202	9.8×	9.9×
Mean		372	18.0×	15.4×
Median		418	19.8×	16.1×
High		731	24.8×	22.5×
Low		182	9.8×	9.9×
Listed in the USA:				
Fila	Sporting clothes	4,913	34.3×	26.0×
Luxottica	Eyeglass frames	2,005	21.3×	17.9×
Natuzzi	Furniture	2,457	25.1×	26.6×
Mean			27.2×	23.5×
Median			26.1×	26.0×
High			34.3×	26.6×
Low			21.3×	17.9×

Source: Corporate documents.

repaid, either a financial buyer or the management group might choose to relever the firm. The men also recalled the suggestions of one financial advisor, who had proposed splitting the equity sale between a public offering on the domestic market and a private placement to foreign institutional investors. This strategy might lead to a listing on the London exchange once the company had a proven track record on the Italian market.

The number of alternatives was staggering. If they picked the right one, Savio and Investitori Associati had a chance to complete a landmark transaction for the young Italian private equity industry.

21

A Note on the Initial Public Offering Process

As has been often noted in *Venture Capital and Private Equity*, the process of taking portfolio firms public is very important in private equity. While the claim of Black and Gilson that "a well developed stock market . . . is critical to the existence of a vibrant venture capital market"[1] may be overstated, there is clearly a strong relationship. To be a successful private equity investor, an understanding of the initial public offering (IPO) process is important.

This note summarizes the mechanisms by which firms go public. It highlights some of the key institutional features associated with these offerings and suggests some explanations for why the process works as it does. Although we note differences across countries, our focus will be on the major industrialized country with the greatest volume of offerings, the United States. The note must of necessity summarize the complexity and details of these offerings; for those who wish to learn more about this often-mysterious process, the appendix suggests some sources for further reading.[2]

WHY DO FIRMS GO PUBLIC?

Firms and their investors typically have several motivations for going public. At the same time, there may also be some real costs associated with such a transaction. The relative importance of these competing factors may vary across time and circumstances.

Professor Josh Lerner prepared this note as the basis for class discussion.

[1] Bernard S. Black and Ronald J. Gilson, "Venture Capital and the Structure of Capital Markets: Banks versus Stock Markets," *Journal of Financial Economics* 47 (1998): 243–277.

[2] This discussion is based in part on a variety of sources, especially Jay R. Ritter, "Initial Public Offerings," in Dennis Logue and James Seward (eds.), *Warren, Gorham, and Lamont Handbook of Modern Finance*, New York, WGL/RIA, 1998; Josh Lerner, "ImmuLogic Pharmaceutical Corporation" (case series), Harvard Business School Case nos. 292-066 through 292-071, 1992; and Katrina Ellis, Roni Michaely, and Maureen O'Hara, "When the Underwriter Is the Market Maker: An Examination of Trading in the IPO Aftermarket," *Journal of Finance* 55(2000): 1039–1074.

Potential Advantages One important motivation for going public is the need to raise capital. Many technology companies, such as new semiconductor manufacturers and biotechnology firms, require hundreds of millions of dollars to successfully introduce a new product. This kind of capital may be difficult to raise from other sources. Banks and other debt financiers, for instance, may consider the firm too risky to lend funds to. Meanwhile, even if a venture capital group is willing to finance such a company's initial activities, it may not be able to continue funding the firm until it achieves positive cash flow. For instance, most private equity groups are restricted to investing no more than 10% or 15% of their capital into a single firm. Thus, the need to raise capital to finance projects may be an important motivation to go public.[3]

A second motivation is the desire to achieve liquidity. Entrepreneurs are likely to worry about placing "all their eggs in one basket" and will seek to achieve diversification by selling some of their shares. Private equity investors are also likely to desire to liquidate their investments in a timely manner, whether through outright sales of the shares or through distribution of the shares to their investors, in order to achieve a high rate of return.[4]

Achieving liquidity, however, is typically not done at the time of the IPO because of investment bankers worry that if insiders such as entrepreneurs and board members are seen as "bailing out" at the time of the offering, new investors will be unwilling to purchase shares. (Insider sales at the time of the IPO are more common among private equity-backed firms in Europe.) Thus, they seek to prohibit or severely limit the sale of shares at the time of offering and to restrict any additional sales during a "lock-up" period. (In addition, the speed and timing of sales by insiders may be restricted by government regulations, as is the case in the United States.) After the lock-up period expires, however, insider sales are likely.

A third motivation is that going public may help the firm in its interactions with customers or suppliers. Being a public firm can help a firm project an image of stability and dependability. This is particularly important in industries where products do not represent a one-time purchase but require ongoing service or upgrades. For instance, a corporation may be unwilling to purchase software to run a critical function from a small private firm that might soon disappear and not be available to offer upgrades or address problems. Enhanced visibility is a particularly important rationale for foreign technology companies seeking to break into the U.S. market, who have increasingly chosen to go public on the NASDAQ exchange in New York rather than on their local exchange.

Potential Disadvantages At the same time, going public involves some real costs, which lead many firms to resist going public:

- The legal, accounting and investment banking fees from an offering are substantial, frequently totaling 10% of the total amount raised in the offering or more.

- The degree of disclosure and scrutiny associated with being a publicly traded concern may be troubling, especially for a family business that has been run as a private firm for several decades.

---

[3] Many firms raise far more in follow-on offerings than they do in their IPOs. But the IPO may provide important advantages: even if the firm does not raise all the financing that it needs in the initial offering, it is likely to find that a follow-on offering to raise more equity is substantially quicker to arrange and less expensive after it is publicly traded.

[4] For more about private equity distributions, see "Rogers Casey Alternative Investments," Chapter 22 in this volume.

- If a firm files to go public and the offering must be subsequently withdrawn, even due to factors beyond the company's control, some managers fear that the company may be "tainted." In particular, other investors may be reluctant to even consider investing in the concern, presuming that it was forced to withdraw its IPO because of some ethical lapse or fundamental business problem.

Another complication arises because the market's appetite for new issues appears to vary dramatically over time. In particular, the volume of IPOs changes dramatically from year to year. These periods of high IPO activity seem to follow periods when stock prices have risen sharply. The bunching of offerings is even more dramatic when patterns are examined on an industry basis. During these periods, firms may find it significantly easier to sell shares in IPOs to investors.

WHAT IS THE IPO PROCESS?

The process by which firms go public is a complex one. This summary highlights the crucial steps along this journey.

First Steps   The first step in the process is the selection of the underwriter. Firms considering going public will frequently be courted by several investment banks. Among the criteria used by firms and their private equity investors to evaluate banks are the reputation of the research analyst covering the firm's industry, the commitments made to provide analyst coverage in the months or years after the offering, and the performance of past IPOs underwritten by the investment bank. One arena in which investment banks infrequently compete is in the pricing of the transactions. A fee of 7% of the capital raised, plus the legal and other costs borne by the bank, is standard across investment banks of both high and low caliber.[5]

In many cases, firms select multiple underwriters to manage the offering. These might include, for instance, a smaller investment bank that specializes in a particular industry and a larger bank with the ability to market equities effectively. (For instance, many high-quality venture-backed deals are underwritten by a technology specialist such as Hambrecht & Quist or JP Morgan and one of the largest, most prestigious underwriters such as Goldman, Sachs, termed a "bulge bracket" firm in Wall Street parlance.) Only one of the banks, however, will be designated as the lead, or book, underwriter. This firm will be responsible for the most critical function, management of the records of who desires shares in the new offering and allocation of the shares among investors. The managing, or co-managing, banks will in turn recruit other banks and brokerage houses to join the "syndicate," the consortium that will actually sell the offering to its clients. Thus, while only one to three banks will actually underwrite the offering, the number of financial institutions involved is much larger.

Even before the offering is marketed, the underwriter plays several important roles. These roles include undertaking due diligence on the company to ensure that there are no "skeletons in the closet," determining the offering size, and preparing the marketing material. In collaboration with the law firm representing the firm, the investment bank will also assist in the preparation of regulatory filings.

---

[5] In some small offerings, less prestigious underwriters may demand warrants from the firm in addition to a fee in cash. In some of the very largest offerings, the fee may fall as low as 5%. For a detailed discussion, see Hsuan-Chi Chen and Jay R. Ritter, "The Seven Percent Solution," *Journal of Finance*, 55 (2000): 1105–1131.

In most major industrialized nations, permission from one or more regulatory bodies is required before a firm can go public. In the United States, these are the Securities and Exchange Commission (SEC) and state regulatory bodies. The review of the SEC focuses on whether the company has disclosed all material information, not on whether the offering is priced appropriately. In past years, state regulators occasionally sought to assess whether an offering was fairly priced. (To cite one example, in December 1980 Massachusetts regulators had initially barred the sales of shares of Apple Computer in the state, even though it was an operating profitable company, on the grounds that its IPO price was too high.) Since 1996, however, all offerings listed on one of the three major exchanges have been exempt from state-level scrutiny.

The extent of the disclosure required varies with the size of the offering and the firm. Many nations have provisions for simplified filings for smaller firms or for those that will be listed on one of the smaller exchanges. In the United States, for instance, firms going public with less than $25 million in revenues can use file Form SB-2 rather than the much more exhaustive S-1 statement, and those raising less than $5 million can file under Regulation A, which requires even less disclosure.

There may be other regulatory requirements as well. For instance, in the United States, the SEC designates the weeks before and after the offering as the "quiet period." The firm's ability to communicate with potential investors during this period (aside from the distribution of the offering document, also known as the prospectus, and formal investor presentations) is severely limited.

Marketing the Offering As the firm undergoes regulatory scrutiny, the investment bank begins the process of marketing the offering. It circulates a preliminary prospectus, or "red herring" (so named for the disclaimers printed in red on the document's cover), to prospective institutional and individual investors in the firm. In many cases, the firm will also undertake a "road show," in which the management team describes the company's lines of business and prospects to potential investors.

The actual mechanism used to determine the price varies across countries. In the United States, "book-building" is the most frequently employed approach. In particular, the underwriter learns from potential investors how many shares will be demanded at each proposed price, which enables him to set the best price for the company. All indications of interest are recorded in a central "book" compiled by the lead underwriter. In many other countries, however, the share price is set before the information about demand is gathered (though a number of these, such as Great Britain and Japan, have recently adopted the U.S. system in hopes of stimulating IPO activity). Elsewhere, other systems are employed, such as formal auctions to determine the offering price.

Reputable investment banks in the United States undertake only "firm commitment" offerings. In these transactions, unlike "best efforts" offerings, the investment bank commits to sell the shares to investors at a set price. This price, however, is not set until the night before the offering, so the actual risk that the investment bank runs of not being able to sell the shares is very small. This information gathered about demand proves invaluable during the "pricing meeting" on the night before the IPO. In this session, the investment bank and firm bring together all the information about demand in order to determine the price at which the shares will be sold to the public. In determining a price, the bankers are also likely to factor in information about the valuation of comparable firms, as well as discounted cash flow analyses of the firm's projected cash flows.

The Day of the Offering and Beyond Whatever valuation is set at the time of the offering, the share price is likely to increase on the next trading day. (On average, even the first trade of the stock is at a substantial premium to the IPO price.) While the median firm undergoes only a very modest increase in its price, a small but significant number of firms have experienced a significant jump in their share price after going public. This has been particularly true in recent years in the United States, where Internet companies such as Yahoo!, TheGlobe.com, and the Internet Capital Group have all experienced jumps of several hundred percent on their first day of trading. But more generally, these types of high returns have been observed on the first day of trading across many nations and time periods.

Several explanations have been offered for this frequently observed pattern of high first-day returns:

- One possibility is that the increase in price (or the discount offered to investors who purchase IPO shares) is necessary to attract investors. Otherwise, uninformed investors might fear that they would be taken advantage of in offerings: for instance, informed investors would purchase most of the shares of promising firms, while leaving them holding the bulk of the unpromising offerings.

- A second possibility is that there is a "bandwagon" effect at work. Once sophisticated institutional investors indicate interest in a stock by buying shares, other less sophisticated investors "rush in" to purchase shares.

- A third explanation is that the investment bank frequently has "market power." This view suggests that bankers deliberately set offering prices too low in order to transfer wealth to the select investors whom they let participate in the IPO. These investors, having reaped big returns on the first trading day, will presumably reward the bank by steering other transactions, such routine custodial services, to the bank.

Each of these explanations is likely to capture some, but not all, of the complex phenomena of IPO pricing.

Another commitment made by underwriters in the United States is to stabilize the price in the days and weeks after the offering. The underwriter will try to prevent the share price from falling below the offering price. In undertaking this stabilizing activity, the investment bank will almost always employ the "Green Shoe" option, a complex feature named after the 1963 offering where it was first employed. Essentially, investment bankers reserve the option to sell 15% more shares than the stated offering size. The investment banker will often sell 115% of the projected offering size. For instance, if the firm has announced its intention to sell 2 million shares, the investment bank will actually sell 2.3 million. If the share price rises in the days after the offering, the bank simply declares the offering to have been 15% larger than the size projected initially. If the share price drops below the initial offering price, however, the bank will buy back the additional 15% of shares sold. This will allow the bank to help fulfill its commitment to support the stock price (the purchase of the shares may drive up the share price) while profiting by the disparity between the price at which it sold the shares and the lower price at which it repurchased them.[6]

The relationship between the underwriter and the portfolio company does not end in the weeks after the offering. Rather, at least in the United States, a complex relationship continues, with many points of interaction. These include the analyst coverage noted

---

[6] When the bank is particularly worried that the share price will drop, it may sell even more than 15% of shares that the "Green Shoe" option allows. Essentially, the bank has then constructed a "naked short" position: it must buy back the excess shares, whether the share prices rise or drops. If the share price falls, it will once again have supported the price more effectively while profiting from its trading strategy. If the share price rises, however, it will need to purchase the additional shares at a loss.

above,[7] as well as a variety of other roles. In virtually all cases, a U.S. investment bank will serve as a market maker: a trader responsible for ensuring orderly day-to-day transactions in a security (including holding excess shares if necessary). In fact, the lead underwriter is virtually always the most important source of market-making activities in the months after the IPO. Finally, the underwriter of the IPO continues to serve as a financial advisor in most cases: about two-thirds of the firms completing a follow-on offering in the United States in the three years after the IPO employ the same underwriter.

ADDITIONAL INFORMATION SOURCES

CHRISTOPHER B. BARRY, CHRIS J. MUSCARELLA, JOHN W. PEAVY III, and MICHAEL R. VETSUYPENS, "The Role of Venture Capital in the Creation of Public Companies: Evidence from the Going Public Process," *Journal of Financial Economics* 27 (October 1990): 447–471.

BERNARD S. BLACK and RONALD J. GILSON, "Venture Capital and the Structure of Capital Markets: Banks versus Stock Markets," *Journal of Financial Economics* 47 (1998): 243–277.

HSUAN-CHI CHEN and JAY R. RITTER, "The Seven Percent Solution," *Journal of Finance*, 55 (June 2000): 1105–1131.

PAUL A. GOMPERS and JOSH LERNER, *The Venture Capital Cycle*, Cambridge, MA, MIT Press, 1999, Section III.

MICHAEL J. HALLORAN, LEE F. BENTON, ROBERT V. GUNDERSON, JR., KEITH L. KEARNEY, and JORGE DEL CALVO, *Venture Capital and Public Offering Negotiation*, volume 2, Aspen Law and Business, Englewood Cliffs, NJ, 1995.

WILLIAM C. MEGGINSON and KATHLEEN A. WEISS, "Venture Capital Certification in Initial Public Offerings," *Journal of Finance* 46 (July 1991): 879–893.

JAY R. RITTER, "Initial Public Offerings," in Dennis Logue and James Seward (eds.), *Warren, Gorham, and Lamont Handbook of Modern Finance*, New York, WGL/RIA, 1998.

---

[7] Perhaps not surprisingly, it has been shown that investment banks issue more buy recommendations on companies that they underwrite than on other firms and that these recommendations seem to be excessively favorable (relative to the firms' subsequent performance).

22

RogersCasey Alternative Investments: Innovative Responses to the Distribution Challenge

Philip Cooper, president and chief executive officer of RogersCasey Alternative Investments, gazed at the darkening Connecticut landscape pensively. He was considering three alternative strategies relating to distributions by private equity funds in which his clients invested. Each seemed to have considerable promise but also to pose substantial challenges.

Cooper had joined RogersCasey Alternative Investments (RCAI) five months earlier, in August 1993. RogersCasey's founders—Stephen Rogers and John Casey—had given him a broad mandate to expand the firm's role as an advisor to institutions about their private equity investments. After making several crucial hires and undertaking a variety of organizational changes, he felt confident that RCAI was on its way to meeting this objective.

Cooper was intrigued about pursuing an initiative relating to distributions of securities by private equity investors. These investors, particularly venture capitalists, often do not return cash to their investors, but the shares of the firms that they have recently taken public. The proper way to handle these distributions is often unclear.

Like other investment managers, RCAI had been providing distribution-management services for its clients for several years. Upon receiving a distribution, the firm decided whether to sell the shares immediately or to hold them for a considerable period. One possibility might be to simply continue this service.

Alternatively, RCAI could introduce one of two new services. These would serve to differentiate RCAI from other investment managers. They would also build on two of RCAI's strategic strengths: the analytic acumen of its staff and its close ties to its

Professor Josh Lerner prepared this case as the basis for class discussion rather than to illustrate either effective or ineffective handling of an administrative situation.

public-market-oriented parent. The first was a co-investment fund. This would invest in the shares of publicly traded firms, either before or at the time of distribution. The second was a distribution-hedging service. This might allow investors to reduce the risk of market swings lowering the value of their distributed shares. Implementing either of these new initiatives, however, would pose a variety of challenges.

STOCK DISTRIBUTIONS IN PRIVATE EQUITY

Venture capitalists[1] typically do not sell shares at the time of an initial public offering (IPO) of a firm that they have financed. In fact, they will enter into a "lock-up" agreement with the investment bank underwriting the deal, in which they agree not to sell shares for several months. This makes the sale of shares to the public easier, since investors often fear that if insiders dump large blocks of securities in the months after the IPO, the share price will tumble. Even after they are free to sell shares, many venture capitalists delay liquidating their positions for months or even years.

Once they decide to liquidate investments in publicly traded firms, venture capitalists typically employ one of two approaches. The first alternative is that the venture capitalist sells the shares in the market and distributes the cash to his investors (limited partners).[2] More often, however, the venture capitalist distributes the actual shares to each of the limited partners. Exhibit 22-1 shows the growing importance of these distributions.

Three reasons explain the frequency of stock distributions. First, SEC rules restrict the size of sales by corporate affiliates (officers, directors, and holders of 10% of the firm's equity). Venture investors often qualify as affiliates because of their role on the board and their equity holdings. (Exhibit 22-2 summarizes relevant securities law.) The venture capital fund may hold a large fraction of the company's equity; consequently, selling its entire stake may take a long time. By distributing the shares to limited partners (who are not considered affiliates and can therefore sell their shares freely), the venture capitalist can dispose of a large stake quickly.

Second, tax motivations provide an incentive for the venture capitalists to distribute shares. If venture capitalists sell the shares and distribute cash, the limited partners and the venture capitalists are subject to immediate capital gains taxes. The limited partners are likely to include some who are tax-exempt (e.g., pension funds) and others who are not (individuals and corporations). These investors may have different preferences about when the shares should be sold. Furthermore, the venture capitalists themselves may wish to postpone paying personal taxes by selling their shares at a later date.

Third, if selling the shares has a large negative effect on prices, then venture capitalists may want to distribute the shares for two reasons. First, venture capitalists have an incentive to distribute the shares that they think are overvalued because of the way

---

[1] Distributions are also important in buy-out funds. A major university endowment which is a large buyout investor estimates that over 30% of the distributions from buy-out funds are in the form of securities. Distributions are also controversial in this setting. For instance, in September 1994 Wasserstein Perella's merchant banking fund distributed its shares of Maybelline, which it had held since 1990. Five days later, Maybelline announced disappointing earnings and its stock price dropped by 36%. In a highly unusual move, Wasserstein Perella bowed to the limited partners' protests and reduced the price at which the distribution was recorded (thereby sharply reducing its profits). See Yvette Kantrow, "Wasserella Fund Investors See Red over Share Payout," *Investment Dealers Digest* 60 (September 26, 1994): 3–4.

[2] Over 80% of U.S. venture capital funds are organized as limited partnerships. In these limited partnerships, the venture capitalist serves as the general partner, and the investors as limited partners.

EXHIBIT 22-1

THE ANNUAL VOLUME OF VENTURE CAPITAL STOCK AND CASH DISTRIBUTIONS

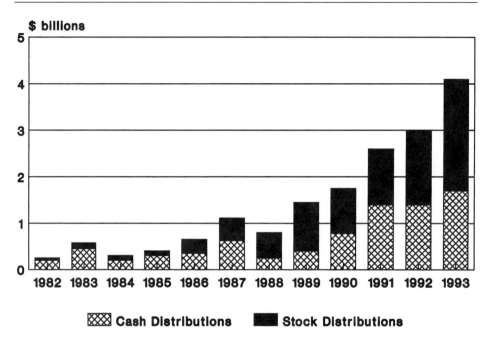

Source: Compiled from information provided by Shott Capital Management.

---

that limited partners and outside fund trackers (e.g., Venture Economics and Cambridge Associates) compute returns. A venture organization's track record is the most important marketing tool when it seeks to raise capital for a new fund. Returns for the venture capital fund are calculated using the closing price of the distributed stock on the day of the distribution.[3] This may not be the actual price received (or even near the actual price received) when the limited partners sell their shares. It may take two or three days, or even longer, before the shares reach the limited partners once a distribution has been declared. If the market reacts negatively to the distribution, actual returns to the limited partners could be substantially less than calculated returns. The second reason relates to the venture capitalists' compensation. If the investors in a venture fund have not yet received back the capital that they originally invested, then most funds will distribute nearly all shares to the limited partners. After the capital has been returned, the venture capitalists will collect a substantial share of the profits (usually 20%). Distributing overvalued shares allows venture capitalists to begin receiving profits earlier than they would otherwise.

Many institutional investors can relate stories of shares that fell sharply in value after being distributed by venture capitalists. One example is Media Vision Technology, a company financed by (among others) Brentwood Associates, Nazem and Co., Aspen

---

[3] Many distributions are declared at 5 P.M. after the stock market has closed.

EXHIBIT 22-2

SECURITIES LAW RELEVANT TO VENTURE DISTRIBUTIONS[a]

Several SEC regulations are relevant to the distribution of stock by venture capitalists, especially Rules 144, 16(a), and 10(b)–5. The first governs trading in restricted and control stock; the second, reporting of insider transactions; and the third, insider trading around securities issues.

Restricted stock is defined as shares that (i) have not been registered with the SEC and (ii) are acquired directly from the firm or an affiliate (such as an officer or director). Shares purchased by a venture capitalist from a private company generally meet these two tests. At the time of the case, restricted shares could not be sold for two years, except in the case of death of the owner. Between two and three years after the original issue, the shares could be sold, but only in a limited manner. Among the requirements were that the SEC must be notified of the sale, that the sale must be done through a broker who is a market maker, and that the volume traded in any three-month period cannot be too large[b] After three years, the shares could be traded freely.[c]

In addition, Rule 144 restricts sales of control stock, even if it is not restricted. Control stock is defined as shares owned by individuals who are affiliates of a firm, such as directors, officers, and holders of 10% of the company's shares. Sales by these parties are only allowed under the same conditions as sales of restricted stock in the two to three years after the original purchase. In a long series of no-action letters, however, the SEC has made clear that distributions from affiliates to nonaffiliates (e.g., from a venture capitalist with a board seat to an institutional investor) are not subject to restrictions under Rule 144. Thus, distributions can be as large or small as the affiliate desires, and the recipient of the distribution can sell the shares as quickly as he desires.[d]

Rule 16(a) states that affiliates of a publicly traded company must disclose their ownership of shares annually and any transactions monthly. This information is made available to the public through Forms 3, 4, and 5 (as well as through proxy filings). Provision 16(a)-7, however, explicitly exempts distributions of securities that (i) were originally obtained from issuers and (ii) are being distributed "in good faith, in the ordinary course of such business." Thus, venture capitalists rarely report distributions to either the SEC or the public.

Rule 10(b)–5 is the general law limiting fraudulent activity "in connection with the purchase or sale of any security." More suits are brought under Rule 10(b)–5 than any other provision of the securities law. If several tests are met, private plaintiffs who have bought or sold shares can recover damages from the defendant. First, damages are only available under Rule 10(b)–5 to purchasers or sellers of the securities in question. Second, the plaintiffs must prove that the defendants had previous knowledge that their statements or actions were misleading. Third, it must be shown that the misrepresentations were not insignificant in nature, but rather "material." Fourth, the plaintiff must prove that he or she was actually misled by the deceptive statement or action on the part of the defendant. Fifth, there must be a casual link between the defendant's actions and the injury to the plaintiff. Finally, it must be shown that the defendant had a fiduciary duty to the shareholders of the firm. Not only are affiliates liable under this final requirement, but so are "tippees": individuals who receive information about publicly traded firms from corporate insiders. In the landmark case *Dirks vs. SEC*,[e] the U.S. Supreme Court ruled that a tippee may be liable if the individual giving the tip (i) had a duty not to disclose the information, and (ii) stood to benefit in some tangible or intangible way from providing the tip.

While the SEC has not explicitly discussed the applicability of Rule 10(b)–5 to venture capital distributions, venture capital lawyers have applied the same principles that govern the interpretation of Rules 144 and 16(a). An interpretation widely accepted within the industry is that venture capitalists distribute investments in the normal course of the investment process. Consequently, a distribution does not convey information to the limited partners. This presumption does not hold, of course, if the venture capitalist makes an explicit recommendation to either hold or immediately sell the shares. Otherwise, no presumption is typically made that an institutional investor who receives a distribution from a venture capitalist has received any information with those shares. Similarly, an institutional investor who observes that a venture capitalist has failed to distribute shares on which the lock-up period has expired has not received information from the venture capitalist.

[a] I thank Katherine Todd, Esq., of Brinson Partners, and Robin Painter, Esq., of Testa, Hurwitz & Thibeault, for helpful discussions of these issues. All remaining legal errors, however, are solely my fault!

[b] The volume sold by any party in a three-month period (including by relatives or any corporation or trust in which the party has a controlling interest) cannot exceed the greater of (i) 1% of outstanding shares or (ii) the average weekly trading volume in the previous four weeks.

[c] These periods have subsequently been shortened to one and two years, respectively.

[d] If, however, the recipient of the distribution held a 10% stake in the company, then Rule 144 would apply. This is unlikely to be the case in distributions from venture funds, since there are usually several limited partners receiving the shares.

[e] 463 U.S. 646, 103 S.Ct. 3255 (1983).

Sources: Compiled from Harold S. Bloomenthal, *Going Public and the Public Corporation*, New York, Clark Boardman Callaghan, 1994; James Bohn and Stephen Choi, "Securities Fraud Class Actions in the New Issues Market," Unpublished working paper, Harvard University, 1994; Commerce Clearing House, *Insider Trading and Short-Swing Reporting*, Chicago, Commerce Clearing House, 1992; and assorted other sources.

EXHIBIT 22-3

THE NET-OF-MARKET RETURNS AROUND DISTRIBUTIONS

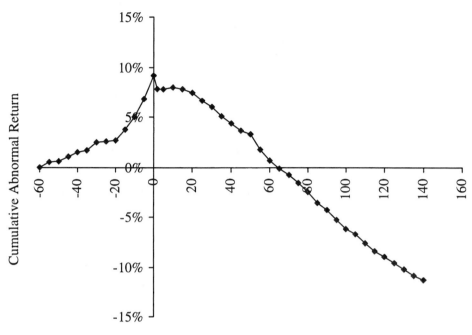

Day Relative to Distribution

Source: Paul Gompers and Josh Lerner, "Venture Capital Distributions: Short- and Long-Run Reactions," *Journal of Finance*, 53 (1998): 2161–2183.

Venture Partners, and Advanced Technology Ventures. Several venture capitalists distributed their shares in January 1994, when it was trading as high as $46 per share. Within two months, its stock price began falling precipitously, as rumors of manipulated earnings and phantom warehouses began circling the company. By May, its stock price had fallen to $2. It ultimately restated its 1993 financial statements, turning a $20 million profit into a $99 million loss, and declared bankruptcy.[4]

More systematic evidence about the relationship between distributions and stock prices is found in a study of nearly 800 such transactions.[5] Exhibit 22-3 shows the average stock price of firms from three months before to seven months after distributions by venture funds. These are net-of-market returns (adjusted for the shift in the relevant stock index). Exhibit 22-4 displays the returns for various subclasses of firms. The groupings include firms financed by older and younger venture capital organizations, companies taken public by high-, medium-, and low-reputation investment bankers,

---

[4] See, for instance, Heather Pemberton, "Media Vision Flounders Amidst Questionable Business Practices," *CD-ROM Professional* 7 (July 1994): 13 *ff.*; "Media Vision Bankruptcy Moves Forward," United Press International Newswire, November 11, 1994.

[5] The results are presented in more detail in Paul Gompers and Josh Lerner, "Venture Capital Distributions: Short- and Long-Run Reactions," *Journal of Finance*, 53 (December 1998): 2161–2183.

EXHIBIT 22-4

THE NET-OF-MARKET RETURNS AROUND DISTRIBUTIONS

The pre-distribution return is the return in the period from the sixth month prior to the distribution to the month before the distribution. The distribution window return is from the day of the distribution to three days after. The post-distribution return is from the month after the distribution to 12 months after.

Sample	Pre-distribution Return	Distribution Window Return	Post-distribution Return
1. Full sample	14.2%	−2.0%	−6.8%
2. Venture organization age ≥ median	15.4	−2.5	−8.3
3. Venture organization age < median	12.7	−1.5	−5.0
4. High underwriter rank	10.2	−1.4	−0.1
5. Medium underwriter rank	15.8	−1.6	0.6
6. Low underwriter rank	14.1	−2.8	−12.9
7. Venture capitalist does not leave board	15.8	−2.1	−6.3
8. Venture capitalist leaves board of directors	15.3	−2.8	−15.9
9. Distributions that are larger than median	16.4	−2.2	−6.7
10. Distributions that are smaller than median	10.9	−1.6	−4.3

Source: Paul Gompers and Josh Lerner, "Venture Capital Distributions: Short- and Long-Run Reactions," *Journal of Finance*, 53 (1998): 2161–2183.

firms where the venture capitalist did and did not leave the board at the time of the distribution, and cases where the distribution is larger and smaller.

While the stock prices of venture-backed firms displayed an up-and-down pattern around distributions, the *long-run* returns of venture-backed firms seemed "fair" given their riskiness. A recent study had demonstrated that the average venture-backed IPO at the end of five years performed almost as well (on a risk-adjusted basis) as the NASDAQ market index: a portfolio consisting of recent venture-backed IPOs performed 99% as well as an investment in the NASDAQ index.[6] Returns of IPOs not backed by venture capitalists were much poorer. A portfolio consisting of recent nonventure IPOs performed only 76% as well an investment in the NASDAQ index. This disparity was due to the very poor performance of the smallest nonventure IPOs.

The distribution process often frustrates limited partners. As Venture Economics notes,

> There are few venture capital fund management issues that evoke so much controversy as the timing and execution of stock distributions. Venture capital managers [and investors] differ in their philosophy as to when stock should be distributed and how those distributions should be handled.[7]

---

[6] Paul Gompers and Alon Brav, "Myth or Reality? The Long-Run Performance of Initial Public Offerings," *Journal of Finance* 52 (1997): 1791–1821.

[7] "Stock Distributions—Fact, Opinion and Comment," *Venture Capital Journal* 27 (August 1987): 8.

A Kemper Financial Services survey, for instance, found that only 16% of limited partners preferred stock distributions.[8] First, the distribution of shares poses a substantial administrative burden. Recordkeeping and tax calculations are far more complex when shares are distributed. Second, it is often difficult to decide what to do with the shares. Venture capitalists often distribute shares with little notice. The venture capitalists explain that their behavior is due to the need to avoid providing information to hedge fund managers, who might drive the price down before the distribution by shorting the stock. Finally, distributions of young and obscure firms often come with little supporting information and few recommendations. Venture capitalists respond that under SEC regulations, limited partners are far safer if they are not advised by venture capitalists (see Exhibit 22-2).

Limited partners have developed three distinct strategies to deal with distributions. The first is an "automatic sell" policy, liquidating distributions immediately upon receipt. An investment banker at Alex. Brown & Sons estimates that as recently as 1990, institutional investors sold one-half of all stock distributions on the day of receipt. In recent years, he suggests, this has fallen to 10%.[9]

A second approach has been to internally analyze each distribution. Often, this is equivalent to an automatic sell policy. In almost all cases, the sell-or-hold decision is made not by the officials responsible for venture investments, but by the analysts handling publicly traded small-capitalization stocks. These analysts have their own lists of favorite stocks, which are unlikely to coincide with the stock distributions. Furthermore, the number of shares received may be small, which may further reduce the analysts' willingness to study the firms carefully.

The third approach has been to rely upon a new class of financial intermediaries, known as stock distribution managers. These firms receive distributions from limited partners and make the decision of whether to sell or hold these shares. Profiles of RCAI's five leading competitors in the distribution management area are presented in Exhibit 22-5.

ROGERSCASEY ALTERNATIVE INVESTMENTS

RCAI's parent organization was established in 1976. Rogers, Casey & Barksdale (later known as RogersCasey) sought to help pension funds understand their liabilities to employees, as well as to plan their investments to meet these needs.

This firm was established at a propitious time. First, the Employee Retirement Income Security Act (ERISA) had been enacted in 1974, which greatly increased the need for corporations to carefully manage their pension obligations. Second, the equity markets about this time reached the trough of a pronounced "bear" market. Equities lost 49% of their value between the end of 1972 and the beginning of 1975.[10] As pension fund managers grappled with the challenges of funding pension obligations, they increasingly began turning to investment advisors for help. Under the leadership of Stephen Rogers and John Casey, RogersCasey benefited from this growth. By 1979, the

---

[8] Kathleen Devlin, "The Post-Venture Dilemma," *Venture Capital Journal* 33 (May 1993): 32–36.

[9] In between 5% and 10% of the distributions, an institutional investor seeking to sell immediately would be limited by Rule 144 (see Exhibit 22-2). In these instances, the venture capitalist has distributed shares that have been held for between two and three years, and whose rate of sale is restricted by Rule 144.

[10] This is adjusted for inflation. The source is Ibbotson Associates, *Stocks, Bonds, Bills, and Inflation,* Chicago, Ibbotson Associates, 1995.

EXHIBIT 22-5

FIVE MAJOR COMPETITORS TO RCAI IN DISTRIBUTION MANAGEMENT

HLM Management

HLM Management, Boston, Massachusetts, processes stock distributions as part of its overall micro-cap stock management services and later-stage venture capital investment program. Formed in 1983 by A.R. Haberkorn, a partner at Harvard Management Company, Judith Lawrie, a senior analyst with Endowment Management & Research Corp., and James Mahoney, general partner of Cowen & Co., the firm "covers the waterfront" of entrepreneurially managed growth companies, says Ms. Lawrie. Five general partners, assisted by a full-time trader, manage a group of limited partnerships designed to invest in both small-cap public and later-stage private companies. It also invests, as a limited partner, in both venture partnerships and direct venture deals.

The firm's investment approach calls for mandatory in-person meetings with management because "it's important to kick the tires before buying a car," Mr. Haberkorn says. HLM runs two types of stock distribution accounts for its clients, mostly pensions and endowments. The "stand-alone discretionary account," essentially a "hold or sell" account, is funded by distributions received. Ms. Lawrie says this format of stock distribution management is still the most popular with clients. HLM also manages a discretionary stock distribution account that takes in distributions and, with a pool of cash set aside by the client, buys pre-distribution stocks during their post-IPO honeymoon period.

QCI Asset Management

QCI Asset Management, Rochester, New York, an employee-owned investment advisor, initiated a venture capital stock distribution program in 1988 when it hired Kevin P. Gavagan, the former director of the investment office at the University of Rochester.

Mr. Gavagan had been with the university endowment for four years and during that time oversaw management of in-kind venture distributions. When he moved across town to join QCI as executive vice president and principal, Mr. Gavagan brought the university's venture distribution business with him. At that time, the endowment held about $60 million of venture capital partnerships and around $25 million of direct private equity investments. In addition to the University of Rochester, QCI advises Worcester Polytechnic Institute on its venture capital stock distributions. QCI integrates the management of venture capital distributions with the management of clients' small-cap, emerging growth company holdings. Managing more than $375 million in assets, QCI runs about $40 million of small-cap and newly public, venture-backed stocks.

It offers only end-game distribution management services to investors in venture capital limited partnerships, through both "hold or sell" and "integrated" accounts. QCI neither advises clients on fund investments nor invests for them.

Shott Capital Management

Founded in 1991 by George Shott, San Francisco-based Shott Capital Management is truly a venture distribution specialist. Administering venture capital stock distributions is its only line of business. Mr. Shott's first venture distribution client was Thomas Ford, general partner of Ford Land Co., developer of 3000 Sand Hill Road. The endowments of Stanford University and the University of Southern California also are clients.

Mr. Shott, Paul Reese, formerly a general partner at TA Associates and founder of First Chicago's first post-venture fund, and three other employees analyze distributions using a "portfolio" approach. The firm has found that evaluating each stock based on how it fits into a client's overall portfolio is the best way to identify big winners. "The key is not to analyze distributions in a vacuum," Mr. Reese says. While it primarily makes hold or sell decisions on behalf of its clients, Shott will buy additional shares of winning stocks in the market for some accounts.

Because the firm is "dedicated to the universe of companies distributed by venture capitalists, [Shott] pledges to know every stock prior to its emergence as an IPO," explains Mr. Reese. To help it keep that promise, Shott last month forged a strategic alliance with Cowen & Co. (Although both groups declined to disclose the details, Stephen Weber, managing director at Cowen, says that his firm, in effect, became a minority shareholder in Shott. In return, Shott gets access to Cowen's research capabilities and other resources.) Like other management distribution specialists, Shott manages distributions on an individual account basis. It also runs two commingled post-venture funds, Technology 2000 and BETA.

(Continued)

EXHIBIT 22-5 *(Continued)*

T. Rowe Price Associates

The $40 billion fund manager T. Rowe Price Associates, Inc. runs a venture distribution investment service as part of its emerging company investment division. The investment activity of this unit ranges from venture capital to young public companies. Its products include mutual funds, separately managed portfolios, and limited partnerships. T. Rowe Price's venture distribution management service makes only hold or sell decisions and returns all cash proceeds to its clients once stocks are sold, according to Preston Athey, vice president and equity portfolio manager in the emerging company investment division and the head of the venture distribution investment service.

In evaluating the potential of stock distributions received, T. Rowe Price uses the NASDAQ Composite Index as a benchmark. Shares are sold when the advisor determines they can no longer outperform the benchmark.

Clients are managed on an account-by-account basis, Mr. Athey says. "Every account stands on its own and every stock stands on its own." The investment manager's venture distribution client list includes E.I. du Pont de Nemours, the R.K. Mellon Foundation, Sprint Master Trust, the State of Minnesota, and the Meyer Memorial Trust.

From its inception in 1986 through December 1992, the distribution management service has processed distributions of over 177 venture-backed companies and completed 840 sales. Two-thirds of all the venture distributions sold outperformed the over-the-counter market during their holding periods.

Warburg, Pincus

At the request of one of the largest venture capital investors, AT&T, Warburg, Pincus Counsellors' Small Capitalization Equity Management Group began offering post-venture services in 1989. "Having already paid the price of admission to winners as limited partners in venture partnerships," the corporate pension thought it ridiculous to cash out at the venture distribution only to have their small-cap manager buy the same stock in the open market, remembers Richard Klemm, senior vice president.

The firm currently offers three investment programs:

- A hold/sell arrangement in which proceeds from the sale of distributed stock are returned to the client.

- A buy/sell arrangement in which proceeds are used for the open market purchase of securities distributed by other venture capital partnerships.

- A buy/sell arrangement in which the cash proceeds from the sale of distributed stocks are used to purchase other emerging growth stocks not typically found in venture portfolios.

The post-venture/emerging growth services group can seek advice from 13 research analysts with Warburg, Pincus Counsellors and can also leverage the resources of the E.M. Warburg, Pincus venture banking subsidiary. The post-venture research team, for instance, meets periodically with Warburg, Pincus's technology advisory committee. Warburg, Pincus manages close to $300 million in its post-venture accounts. Its clients participate in over 215 funds managed by over 120 firms.

Source: Excerpted from Kathleen Devlin, "The Post-Venture Dilemma," *Venture Capital Journal* 33 (May 1993): 33–34.

---

firm had 15 clients with $35 billion under management; by 1989, 35 clients with $60 billion; and in early 1994, 95 clients with $188 billion. (A profile of RogersCasey in early 1994 is presented in Exhibit 22-6.)

RogersCasey first began investing in alternative investments, such as venture capital, buyouts, and natural resources, in 1985. This was largely in response to client requests for this service. Pension funds became heavy investors in alternatives in the early 1980s, after a 1979 Department of Labor interpretation of ERISA relaxed their concerns about such investments. In many alternative asset classes, pension funds had become the dominant investors by the mid-1980s.

EXHIBIT 22-6

ROGERSCASEY PROFILE

RogersCasey
One Parklands Drive
Darien, CT 06820

Stephen Rogers, Chairman
John F. Casey, President & Chief Executive Officer
Del Budzinski, Managing Director-Consulting
Robin S. Pellish, Managing Director-Consulting
R. Barry Thomas, Managing Director-Consulting
Steven C. Case, Director-Consulting
Drew W. Demakis, Director-Consulting
Timothy R. Barron, Senior Consultant
Venita L. Bullock, Senior Consultant
Adele Langie Heller, Associate Consultant
Elizabeth L. DeLalla, Research-US Equities
Narayan Ramachandran, Research-US Equities &
    Investment Technology
Carla P. Haugen, Research-Alternative Investments
A. Duff Lewis, Jr., Research-Alternative Investments
Gary J. Kominski, Research-Alternative Investments
Matthew R. Jensen, Research-International Investments
Reza Vishkai, Associate Director-International
    Investments
Jeffrey K. Feldman, Research-Fixed Income &
    Derivatives
Gregory T. Rogers, Research-Fixed Income &
    Derivatives
Robert Capaldi, Research-Investment Technology
Ruth Hughes-Guden, Research-Defined Contribution
    Services
Eleanor A. Burns, Research-Defined Contribution
    Services & Master Trustee-Recordkeeping
Philip A. Cooper, Research-Alternative Investments
Peter J. Gavey, Research-Alternative Investments
Dan Lew, Research-NDT
Thomas K. Philips, Director-Advanced Research
John Picone, Portfolio Manager-Alternative Investments
Gregg A. Robinson, Research-Defined Contribution
    Services
Gregory T. Rogers, Research-Fixed Income &
    Derivatives

RogersCasey offers a broad scope of investment services to its clients: full-service consulting, consulting in the area of alternative investments, special advisory programs (i.e., multi-manager mutual fund programs), and investment manager diagnostics. RogersCasey provides its clients with active investment solutions. Our practice is driven by applied research techniques, substantial industry experience, and a commitment to investigation and evaluation of innovative solutions.

SERVICES

Alternative Investments
Asset Allocation
Asset/Liability Modeling
Client Monitoring/Reporting
Custodian or Master Trustee Search Selection
Due Diligence
Database/Publications
Global Manager Search
International Manager Search
Investment Policy/Objectives
Liability Analysis
Manager Evaluation
Manager Search/Selection
Manager Structure Analysis
Minority/Emerging Managers
Mutual Fund Evaluation/Management
New Theories
Options and Futures
Performance Attribution
Performance Measurement/Analysis
Portfolio Optimization
Quantitative Analysis
Real Estate Manager Evaluation
Reports/Custom Research
Seminars and Lectures
Socially Conscious Investing
Software
Strategic Planning Services

MANAGER DATABASE

Established: 1976
Managers tracked:
    Domestic: 930
    International: 125
    Global: 100
    Equity: 500
    Fixed Income: 250
    Balanced: 210
    Specialty: 180

DATABASE: PIPER

Our database of historical return information is made available to the institutional community under the name PIPER (Pension & Investments Evaluation Report). We produce the PIPER Commingled Funds report which tracks the performance of bank commingled funds and insurance company separate accounts. PIPER Managed Accounts is a similar database tracking the performance and other statistical data on independent investment advisors representative composite accounts. Approximately ninety percent of all institutional assets are represented in our PIPER databases. There is no charge to managers to be included in the PIPER database.

(Continued)

EXHIBIT 22-6 (Continued)

INVESTMENT ADVISORY SERVICES

Global Developing Markets Fund, a commingled group trust deploying multiple managers to invest in emerging markets around the world. Development funds that contain multiple managers to access new investment strategies or lesser known investment talent. Savings Plan Alternatives that offer an individually tailored selection of mutual funds for retirement, thrift, and 401(k) plan assets.

CLIENTS

AlliedSignal, Inc.
American Cyanamid Company
Amphenol Corp.
Appleton Mills
Asea, Brown, Boveri, Inc.
Avon Products, Inc.
BASF Corp.
Bowater, Inc.
Champion International Corp.
Citizens Utilities Co.
Cowles Media Co.
Dexter Corporation
E.I. DuPont de Nemours & Co.
Eastman Kodak Company
Electronic Data Systems Corp.
Fairfax County Retirement Funds
Federated Department Stores, Inc.
FPL Group, Inc.
Gannettt Co., Inc.
GATX Corporation
General Electric Investment Corporation
Group Health, Inc.
GTE Financial Services
Health Insurance Plan of Greater New York, Inc.

Honeywell, Inc.
Insilco Corporation
Axel Johnson, Inc.
Kimberly-Clark Corporation
The Kroger Co.
Lawrence & Memorial Hospitals
Mark IV Industries, Inc.
Mead Corporation
The Mead Corporation Foundation
Michigan Consolidated Gas Co.
New York City Teachers' Variable Fund
New York State Teachers' Retirement System
Northwestern University
Norwich City Employees' Retirement System
Pennsylvania State Employees' Retirement System
Phelps Dodge Corporation
Public Service Electric & Gas Company of New Jersey
RJR Nabisco, Inc.
Rochester Gas & Electric Corp.
Rochester Telephone Corporation
Rush Presbyterian-St. Luke's Medical Center
Saint-Gobain Corporation
Saks Fifth Avenue
Springs Industries, Inc.
Stamford Hospital
The Stanley Works
Texas Instruments, Inc.
Unisys Corp.
University of Colorado at Boulder
University of Missouri System
US WEST, Inc.
Veterans Memorial Medical Center
Virginia Retirement System
Washington Gas Light Company
Witco Corp.
Ziff Communications Co.

Source: Money Market Directories, *Money Market Directory of Pension Funds and Their Investment Managers*, Charlottesville, VA, Money Market Directories, 1995.

RogersCasey did not decide to make a formal effort in the alternative investment arena until 1988. At this point, it established RCAI as a wholly owned subsidiary. Many activities performed by RCAI in its first years resembled those of other investment managers (also known as "gatekeepers"): due diligence, portfolio management, reporting, monitoring, and research. While many of RCAI's activities were similar to those of its rivals, it sought to differentiate itself in two important ways. First, it employed state-of-the-art computer systems, databases, and analytic capabilities. This process was greatly eased by RCAI's close ties to RogersCasey, which had built up a substantial infrastructure for managing its public market investments. The second distinguishing characteristic followed from the first. Rather than focusing on any single asset class, it sought to

EXHIBIT 22-7

**ROGERSCASEY ALTERNATIVE INVESTMENTS:
INVESTMENT RECOMMENDATIONS, 1988–1993**

	1988	1989	1990	1991	1992	1993
Funds Evaluated						
Venture capital	91	129	131	96	157	118
Buyouts/mezzanine	48	29	27	9	14	33
Distressed debt	17	19	18	31	19	15
Oil and gas	15	16	15	8	14	11
Timber	0	0	0	0	0	11
Other	0	0	14	9	30	31
Total	171	193	205	153	234	219
Funds Recommended						
Venture capital	6	6	2	5	10	1
Buyouts/mezzanine	6	1	1	1	1	2
Distressed debt	1	0	0	1	0	0
Oil and gas	1	0	1	0	0	0
Timber	0	0	0	0	0	1
Total	14	7	4	7	11	4
Fund Returns						
Recommended funds	18.3%	15.4%	2.4%	1.4%	0.3%	−1.1%
Weighted benchmark index	11.2%	4.8%	0.0%	−2.9%	−10.6%	15.4%

Source: Corporate documents.

employ the full complement of alternatives. These included such diverse investments as timber, mezzanine debt, and oil and gas participating royalties.

Under the leadership of Carla Haugen and Duff Lewis, RCAI gradually grew in size. By mid-1993, RCAI had $600 million under management, which was invested in both partnerships and direct investments. In addition, the firm played an advisory role in the allocation of another $100 million. (Exhibit 22-7 summarizes RCAI's investment recommendations between 1988 and 1993.)

Philip Cooper joined RCAI in August 1993. A separate board was established for RCAI at the same time to give the organization more autonomy. Serving on this board was Casey, Cooper, Rogers, and Terrence Overholser, a RogersCasey managing director. As an indication of the importance of this effort, Cooper was added to the governing board of RogersCasey. As such, he was the first director other than the firm's founders.

Cooper had experience with nearly all aspects of the venture capital business. While working as an account supervisor at the advertising firm BBDO, Cooper—tired of poring over weighty printouts—conceived the notion of a graphics package that would ease the analysis of large data-sets. Cooper headed to Boston, seeking to commercialize this idea. He soon met David Friend, an engineer who had developed a software package embodying this concept. Cooper and Friend raised $4 million in 1980 from Greylock, Venrock, and other venture capitalists to finance their new firm, Computer Pictures Corporation. As one analyst noted, Cooper had an extraordinary ability to "incite and excite the mentality of venture capitalists."[11] Two years later, Cullinet Software acquired the firm for $14 million in cash.

After a hiatus as a Sloan Fellow at MIT's Sloan School of Management, Cooper formed Palladian Software. This artificial intelligence company developed an expert system to help businesses do financial planning and capital budgeting. Cooper then turned to working on the other side of the venture investment process. In 1987, he and two partners established a small partnership that worked with two large institutional investors—Harvard Management Company and the Vista Group—to identify promising deals. Cooper provided expertise in evaluating potential venture and buyout deals, and then oversaw the firms' managements. On the side, he founded and served as chairman of Business Matters, Inc. (formerly known as Cottage Software), which developed and marketed a Windows-based financial analysis program. Cooper also served as a managing director of Boston International Advisors, a quantitative investment advisory firm with $2.5 billion under management, and chairman of several other firms.

DISTRIBUTION MANAGEMENT AT RCAI

Upon assuming the leadership of RCAI, Cooper sought to boost its analytic capabilities in two major ways. First, he made several critical hires, especially Thomas Philips and John Picone. (Exhibit 22-8 profiles RCAI's personnel.) He also sought to aggressively expand RCAI's investment management role rather than primarily selecting other fund managers.

One area to which Cooper assigned a high priority was the management of distributions. This high-growth area appeared to fit well with RCAI's analytic strengths and its close ties to its parent. Cooper considered three alternative strategic approaches in this area. The first was to devote greater resources to RCAI's traditional distribution-management services. Like other investment managers, RCAI had managed distributions for clients for several years.

RCAI had developed a systematic approach to managing distributions. RCAI began compiling information on firms while they were still privately held. Data collection became more intense at the time the firms went public. Thus, once a distribution was received, RCAI's staff had a wealth of quantitative and qualitative information at their fingertips. In evaluating whether to hold or sell the distribution, RCAI employed several criteria:

- The relative valuation of the firm, as measured through ratios such as market-to-book value and price-to-earnings.
- The valuation of the firm relative to the discounted value of the firm's projected cash flows, as estimated in analyst reports issued after the IPO.
- The strength of the firm's management, technology, and business plan, as assessed through conversations with venture capitalists.
- The behavior of the stock price before the distribution. If the shares fell sharply ahead of the distribution, it suggested that the distribution had been anticipated by traders. In this instance, RCAI might be less likely to sell the shares immediately.

---

[11] Michael Ball, "Ring-Around-the-Rosy," *Boston Business Journal* 7 (September 7, 1987): 1.

EXHIBIT 22-8

ROGERSCASEY ALTERNATIVE INVESTMENTS: BIOGRAPHIES

Philip A. Cooper, Chairman and Chief Executive Officer   See biography in the text of the case.

Carla P. Haugen, Managing Director   A graduate of the University of Minnesota and the Harvard Business School, Ms. Haugen has managed RogersCasey's alternative investment activities for five years and serves as a member of the firm's operating committee. She has overall responsibility for clients' private equity investments. Prior to joining the firm, Carla had seven years' experience in venture capital and leveraged buyout investing at Oak Investment Partners and Exxon Enterprises.

A. Duff Lewis, Jr., Managing Director   Mr. Lewis joined RogersCasey's alternative investment group after 26 years with the Eastman Kodak Company. He spent the last nine years there on the Treasurer's staff, working on investments for its $82+ billion pension plans. Prior to working on pension investments, Duff accumulated 10 years of experience on the corporate financial planning and analysis staff. Mr. Lewis is a member of the Institute of Chartered Financial Analysts and holds an M.S. from Purdue's Krannert School of Management.

Thomas K. Philips, Managing Director of Advanced Research   Dr. Philips joined RogersCasey in 1993. He divides his time between RCAI and advanced research projects for RogersCasey. Prior to joining RogersCasey, Dr. Philips spent eight years at the IBM Corporation. The first five were spent at the Thomas J. Watson Research Center and the last three at the IBM Retirement Fund, where he was responsible for a number of quantitative research projects. Dr. Philips received a Ph.D. in Electrical and Computer Engineering from the University of Massachusetts, Amherest.

John Picone, Jr., Managing Director   Mr. Picone joined RCAI in 1993, after 14 years with Metropolitan Life Insurance Company and two with Bankers Trust. At MetLife, he was solely responsible for developing and managing its $100 million small-capitalization public investment program, which generated a five-year average return of 25%. During the same period, he also solely managed the Company's venture capital program, which was invested in 42 limited partnerships and 20 direct placements. Prior to that, Mr. Picone managed a large-capitalization equity portfolio and was a securities analyst. He holds an M.B.A. from the University of North Carolina at Chapel Hill.

Gary J. Kominski, Director   A graduate of the University of Pennsylvania, Mr. Kominski manages partnership and direct investments and securities distributions. Prior to joining the firm, he had six years' experience working with a broad array of alternative investments at Salomon Brothers, Concord Partners (the venture capital arm of Dillon, Read & Co.), and Northtown Realty. He also spent four years with the Irving Trust Company, for whom he managed their Grand Cayman facility.

Peter J. Gavey, Senior Analyst   Mr. Gavey joined RCAI from Gabelli & Co., where he worked for nearly four years. During his last two years of employment there, he worked as a securities analyst, trader, and portfolio administrator in the risk arbitrage unit. He holds a B.S. in Management from Fairfield University.

Marsha Tinguely, Senior Analyst   Prior to joining RCAI, Ms. Tinguely had five years' experience in pension consulting, investment research, and private equity due diligence at Principal Financial Securities' Pension Consulting Group, the Renaissance Capital Group (a late-stage venture fund), and Siecor, Inc. She holds a B.S. in Economics and Finance from the University of Texas.

Patrice Bottari, Administrative Assistant   Ms. Bottari is Philip Cooper's Administrative Assistant and supports RCAI's office in Bedford, Massachusetts. Prior to joining RCAI, she spent six years with a start-up biotech company and AT&T American Transtech. She holds an Associate's Degree in Business Administration from Northeastern University.

Donna Rosequist, Administrative Assistant   Ms. Rosequist is the administrative assistant for RCAI's Darien, Connecticut, office. Her responsibilities include the coordination and production of periodic client reports and special research reports, and the maintenance of key databases. Prior to joining RCAI, she worked at International Capital Partners and Control Data Corporation in various administrative and financial positions. She holds a B.A. and M.B.A. from the University of Connecticut.

Source: Corporate documents.

- The venture capitalists' apparent reasons for distributing the stock. If the partnership distributing the shares was nearing its end, it might be compelled to distribute the stock, whether or not it was fairly valued. Similarly, venture capitalists might be more inclined to distribute shares prematurely if the partnership agreement governing the fund required them to or if they held a particularly large position in the firm.

If the firm was sold immediately, RCAI typically executed the trade through the investment bank that took the firm public. If the distribution was to be held for an extended period, however, RCAI would transfer the shares to the custodian (e.g., Boston Safe or State Street Bank) with whom the institutional investor had an established relationship. This deprived the investment banker of the knowledge of whether or not the institution had liquidated its position. Knowledge that large numbers of distributed shares had not yet been sold might encourage short-selling, in anticipation of large-block trades that would depress the stock price. Extensive short-selling might drive the stock price down before sales by RCAI's clients.[12]

Nonetheless, the extent of RCAI's distribution-management activities was limited until the end of 1992 by the status of its largest client. Due to an early retirement program, this pension fund needed to make payments more rapidly than anticipated. In response to this demand for liquidity, the client asked RCAI to sell most distributions immediately. A detailed justification had to be prepared for each distribution held for an extended period. Another factor that encouraged RCAI to sell distributed shares was the time-consuming responsibility of voting proxies. Clients expected RCAI to vote in all proxy contests. These shares had to be voted following the specific policy guidelines of each institutional investor.

One problem with distribution-management services that RCAI and other investment managers faced was performance assessment. Institutions typically evaluate their money managers against a benchmark such as the S&P 500 or the Russell 2000. It is difficult to find an appropriate benchmark for distribution managers because they do not choose when to receive the large blocks of thinly traded securities. John Picone, Gary Kominski, and others at RCAI felt that if they were ultimately able to liquidate the shares at the price immediately prior to the distribution, they would be doing a good job.

One possibility, Cooper mused, would be simply expanding RCAI's distribution management services. Two new initiatives, however, also appeared intriguing. The first of these, a public market fund focusing on companies around the time of distribution, had been suggested by John Picone.

Picone had been a public stock manager for many years. While working for Metropolitan Life in 1987, however, he had been asked to help the insurer's venture capital group manage stock distributions. MetLife, like many institutions, had begun investing in venture capital funds in the early 1980s. After venture capitalists took many firms public during the 1986–1987 IPO "window," the volume of distributions rapidly increased. Like many institutions, MetLife sold its first few distributions immediately upon receipt. This triggered two concerns. First, in some cases the venture capital group was selling the shares of companies in the open market while the public stock managers were buying shares of the same firm. This was clearly inefficient. More generally, senior management asked whether MetLife was receiving the best price by selling immediately.

---

[12] At the same time, brokers from the investment bank that took the firm public could be important sources of information. For instance, they would know whether a large number of limit orders had been placed, instructing the bank to sell the shares once the stock reached a certain price.

Picone introduced a variety of initiatives at the venture capital group. One of these was traditional distribution management, along the lines of RCAI's program and those described in Exhibit 22-5. Picone also developed a second approach. He pioneered a co-investment fund, which bought shares of venture-backed firms that had recently gone public. For instance, he might consider buying shares when a firm had dropped sharply in price around the time of a distribution or when a venture capitalist that was free to distribute shares in a firm nonetheless delayed the distribution. Picone proposed to create a similar co-investment fund for RCAI's clients.

A second service that Cooper considered offering was distribution hedging. RCAI might mingle distributions from several clients. It could then hedge the risk that this portfolio would decline in value by purchasing derivatives on a small-capitalization stock index or an industry index such as the CBOE Biotech Index. In this way, changes in market valuations would not wipe out the value of the portfolio. The distributed shares could then be slowly liquidated, and the derivative holdings adjusted accordingly.

Thomas Philips, managing director of Advanced Research, had raised several concerns about this proposal. In particular, he worried about how successfully RCAI could hedge these distributions. Often several venture funds simultaneously distributed the same firm. Thus, a single company might represent as much as 40% of the portfolio. It was unclear how successfully such substantial firm-specific exposures could be hedged using derivatives based on particular indices. Exhibit 22-9 provides some evidence on this point, reporting the performance of 11 biotechnology firms in the three months after their distribution and the performance of a biotechnology index in the same period.[13]

A second consideration was whether investors would be willing to blend their distributions with those of others. RCAI's proposed hedging strategy would work only if enough distributions could be mixed. Investors, however, might be reluctant to accept the average returns from their own and others' distributions of their venture capitalists. For instance, they might believe that the venture capitalists in which they invested were likely to distribute a firm like Microsoft, which appreciated sharply after its venture investors distributed it. Why should the superior post-distribution returns of their funds be blended in with the inferior returns of funds selected by other institutional investors?

A third concern was that this product would compete with products offered by some investment banks to hedge individual distributions. The bankers offered derivatives that enabled institutions to "lock in" share prices. One common offering is a "collar," which consists of an equal number of call and put options at slightly different strike (exercise) prices. For instance, if a stock is trading at $15 at the time of distribution, the institution might simultaneously enter into two transactions with an investment bank. First, the institution could sell a call to the bank with a strike price of $17 and then buy a put with a strike price of $12.50. In this way, if the price of the stock falls precipitously, the institution can sell its shares to the investment bank for $12.50. If the share price rises sharply, however, the investment bank is sure to buy the shares for $17. In this way, the institution does not need to sell immediately but can protect the profits from its venture investment.

---

[13] Biotechnology might be regarded as an industry where hedging of distributions would work particularly well, since the stock prices of many small biotechnology firms are highly correlated with each other and industry indices. Many young, publicly traded firms have no products for sale but are focusing on developing and getting approval for new drugs. A single event, such as the U.S. Food and Drug Administration's rejection of a drug, often has triggered a reevaluation of the prospects of a large number of firms developing new drugs.

EXHIBIT 22-9

BIOTECHNOLOGY FIRM STOCK PRICE AND BIOTECHNOLOGY STOCK INDEX AROUND DISTRIBUTIONS

Observation	On Day Before Distribution		Three Months Later	
	Stock Price	Biotech Index	Stock Price	Biotech Index
Distribution 1	10	1.06	12.75	1.30
Distribution 2	21.25	1.12	11.25	0.77
Distribution 3	35	1.25	27.25	1.48
Distribution 4	24	0.84	24.25	1.01
Distribution 5	21	1.41	22.875	1.12
Distribution 6	18.75	1.52	15.75	1.02
Distribution 7	18.25	1.08	8	0.84
Distribution 8	13.625	0.98	9.75	0.86
Distribution 9	7.375	0.78	8.25	0.93
Distribution 10	20.5	1.21	22.25	1.44
Distribution 11	7.625	0.91	8.125	0.95

Source: Casewriter's analysis. The biotechnology index is computed by the casewriter by examining the returns from a "buy-and-hold" investment in 13 biotechnology stocks.

Finally, however sound the hedging product, it might encounter resistance from potential users. Commenting on derivatives as a tool to manage distribution risks, Russell L. Carson, a partner at Welsh, Carson, Anderson and Stowe, observed:

> I'm kind of skeptical. It seems to me that this is the same kind of thing that has been getting the names of some corporate CFOs into the paper lately. And I can't think of anything that would stop your franchise faster than having to explain to your limited partners that you lost $25 million of their money because you thought you were hedging your position.[14]

An observer of the venture industry, Lisette Keto of Athena Capital Advisors, noted that "the venture capital skill set—working with people, markets and businesses—is very different from the quantitative skills needed to work with derivatives."[15]

[14] Asset Alternatives, "Are Private Equity Managers Missing the Boat by Ignoring Derivatives?," *Private Equity Analyst* 4 (August 1994): 9.

[15] Ibid., p. 12.

The final module reviews many of the key ideas developed in *Venture Capital and Private Equity*. Rather than considering traditional private equity organizations, however, the cases examine organizations that at first sight seem very different from the ones we have considered previously.

Large corporations, government agencies, and nonprofit organizations are increasingly emulating private equity funds. Their goals, however, are more complex: in addition to generating attractive financial returns, these efforts are seeking to more effectively commercialize internal research projects or to revitalize distressed areas. Meanwhile, publicly traded venture funds face a very different set of regulatory, reporting, and operating constraints than the more traditional partnerships.

These cases will allow us not only to understand these exciting and challenging initiatives, but also to review the elements that are crucial to the success of traditional private equity organizations.

WHY THIS MODULE?

Since corporate venture funds, social venture capital initiatives, and publicly traded funds are so different from traditional private equity funds, one may wonder why these cases are included in this volume. There are three main reasons. First, this arena is the focus of intensive activity of late. Today these funds are important investors. Second, it is difficult to examine the issues faced in adapting the private equity model without thinking about the rationales for the key features of traditional private equity funds. Thus, this section of the course allows us to review and revisit many of the issues we have considered in the previous three modules. Finally, corporate venture capital programs, in particular, provide an interesting alternative way to break into the private equity field that few students consider.

Interest in adopting the private equity model has exploded in recent years. In an era when many large firms are questioning the productivity of their investments in traditional R&D laboratories, venture organizations represent an intriguing alternative for corporate America. Much of the interest has been stimulated by the recent

Professor Josh Lerner prepared this note as the basis for class discussion.

success of the independent venture sector. While total annual disbursements from the venture industry over the past three decades did not exceed the R&D spending of either IBM or General Motors, the economic successes of venture-backed firms—such as Intel, Microsoft, Genentech, Netscape, and Cisco Systems—have been profound. The impact of these powerful examples can be seen in the estimates that direct venture capital investments by U.S. corporations increased almost 15-fold in number (and 44-fold in dollar volume) between 1995 and 1999.[1] Meanwhile, several leading private equity organizations—including Kleiner, Perkins, Caufield & Byers and Advent International—have begun or expanded funds dedicated to making strategic investments alongside corporations.

The growth of venture funds organized by public and nonprofit bodies has been even more striking. Recent estimates suggest that close to 40% of venture or venture-like disbursements in the United States—and more than half of early-stage investments—came in 1995 from "social" sources: those whose primary goal was not a high economic return. Nor has this activity been confined to the United States. Governments in dozens of countries have established significant public venture programs. In recent years, nonprofit organizations have also become increasingly active in encouraging and overseeing venture funds. Some of America's largest and most prestigious foundations, such as the Ford and McArthur Foundations, have been particularly active backers of community development venture funds. An interesting new trend has been the involvement of successful private equity investors, most notably Henry Kravis and his former colleague George Roberts, as investors in and advisors to community development funds.

Finally, the past few years have seen a proliferation of publicly traded venture capital funds. These ranged from incubators such as Divine InterVentures to "fund-of-funds" such as MeVC to holding company entities such as Internet Capital Group. In part, this activity was due to the voracious enthusiasm for all things "high technology" that characterized the markets during much of 1999 and early 2000. But this increase also reflected the shifts in the long-term retirement savings from "defined benefit" to "defined contribution" plans, and the resulting pressure by individual investors to access private equity directly (as discussed in the first module).

A second reason for the inclusion of this module is that it allows us to review and think about the key features of independent private equity firms. In particular, in adopting the private equity model, features of independent funds have been adjusted or altered. In some cases, these changes have been benign; but in others, the consequences have been disastrous. By reviewing successful and failed modifications of the private equity model to serve the goals of corporate, public, and nonprofit organizations, we will gain a deeper understanding of how traditional funds work. During discussions, we will return repeatedly to the frameworks developed in the earlier modules of the course.

Finally, corporate venture capital programs represent an interesting avenue for entry into the private equity field that relatively few students consider. The intense competition for jobs in traditional private equity organizations allows many funds to demand that new hires already have a demonstrated investment track record. Yet it is difficult to develop such a track record without a job in the industry. Corporations

---

[1] Venture Economics, "Corporate Venture Capital Activity," Unpublished tabulation, 2000.

are often much more willing to hire candidates directly out of school. If one can successfully make one's way into a corporate venture group, it can provide valuable experience and serve as a stepping-stone to a position at an independent private equity firm.

THE STRUCTURE OF THIS MODULE

Reflecting the fact that this is a review module, the cases do not seek to develop new conceptual frameworks. Rather, the emphasis will be on drawing together the themes and frameworks that have appeared earlier in the course.

As the reader reviews the cases in this module, it is appropriate to consider where the same issues have surfaced earlier in the course. For instance, where have similar incentive problems to the ones faced by Intel and CDC emerged? Has the challenge of multiple investment objectives emerged elsewhere in the course? While the reporting issues that public venture funds such as CMGI face are partially a consequence of their special circumstances, how have similar issues affected the behavior of private equity groups elsewhere?

FURTHER READING

Material about Corporate Venture Capital

See the bibliography in Josh Lerner, "A Note on Corporate Venture Capital," Harvard Business School Note no. 9-201-036.

Material about Social Venture Capital

PETER EISENGER, "The State of State Venture Capitalism," *Economic Development Quarterly* 5 (February 1991): 64–76.

PETER EISENGER, "State Venture Capitalism, State Politics, and the World of High-Risk Investment," *Economic Development Quarterly* 7 (May 1993): 131–139.

PAUL GOMPERS and JOSH LERNER, *The Money of Invention*, Boston, HBS Publishing, 2001, chapters 8 and 9.

STEVEN GORDON, "Small Business Investment Companies: A Venture Capital Structure of Choice?," *Journal of Private Equity* 2 (Fall 1998): 45–55.

JOSH LERNER, "The Government as Venture Capitalist: An Empirical Analysis of the SBIR Program," *Journal of Business* 72 (July 1999): 285–318.

CHARLES M. NOONE and STANLEY M. RUBEL, *SBICs: Pioneers in Organized Venture Capital*, Chicago, Capital Publishing, 1970.

Organisation for Economic Cooperation and Development, Committee for Scientific and Technological Policy, *Government Venture Capital for Technology-Based Firms*, Paris, OECD, 1997.

STEVEN J. WADDELL, "Emerging Socio-Economic Institutions in the Venture Capital Industry: An Appraisal," *American Journal of Economics and Sociology* 54 (July 1995): 323–338.

Material about Publicly Traded Venture Capital Funds

HARVEY BINES and STEVE THIEL, "Investment Management Arrangements and the Federal Securities Laws," *Ohio State Law Journal* 58 (1997): 459–518.

DAVID J. BROPHY and MARK W. GUTHNER, "Publicly Traded Venture Capital Funds: Implications for Institutional 'Fund of Funds' Investors," *Journal of Business Venturing* 3 (1988): 187–206.

DAVID J. GILBERG, "Regulation of New Financial Instruments under the Federal Securities and Commodities Law," *Vanderbilt Law Review* 39 (1986): 1599–1969.

JOHN D. MARTIN and J. WILLIAM PETTY, "An Analysis of the Performance of Publicly Traded Venture Capital Companies," *Journal of Financial and Quantitative Analysis* 18 (1983): 401–410.

23

Intel® 64 Fund

"This is market development, except at the end of the day, you also have the financial benefit."

Les Vadasz, president, Intel Capital

On December 11, 1998, Laila Partridge, director of the Intel Corporate Business Development (CBD) group's programs for the advanced 64-bit processor, glanced over at her team as they waited to enter the conference room where Intel's executives were meeting. James Horn had come most recently from Treasury and James Cape from marketing in the Enterprise Server Group. After spending a week locked in a room together, she knew her group as well as her own family, and she could tell that they were edgy. So was she, even though they had the informal backing of most of the executives. They were about to describe the structure and mandate of the new venture capital fund that they had been asked to design.

Intel, the world's largest semiconductor manufacturer, with 1998 revenues of $26.3 billion, had been investing in early-stage companies since 1991. At first, the company had funded firms that developed the inputs to its technology; later it shifted the emphasis to firms that produced products complementary to its own. While Intel had started by co-investing with venture capital (VC) firms, the later 1990s had seen it investing on its own. By the end of 1998, the CBD's[1] staff had neared 100 and invested a total of $838 million in that year alone.[2] Intel had never, however, established a fund with outside investors before.

By the late 1990s, Intel's investment strategy was evolving into "being the preeminent building-block supplier to the global Internet economy." Intel Capital (the renamed CBD) invested in a wide range of technologies, including networking, on-line

Ann Leamon, Manager of the Center for Case Development, prepared this case under the supervision of Sr. Lecturer G. Felda Hardymon as the basis for class discussion rather than to illustrate either effective or ineffective handling of an administrative situation.

[1] In 2000, the name of the group was changed from Corporate Business Development to Intel Capital, to better reflect its activity, which was to make investments in support of Intel's overall corporate strategy. It will be referred to as Intel Capital throughout.

[2] George Moriarity, "The New Smart Money," *Investment Dealers Digest*, November 22, 1999.

services, clients, and servers, with the aim of accelerating the Internet's global adoption. Given that Intel sold a wide variety of products involved with the Internet, its opportunities would grow as the number of people who used the Internet increased.

Partridge reflected on the charge her group had received from the executives in October 1998: "Establish a special fund with Intel's OEMs for IA-64." Or, in other words, figure out a way to use Intel Capital's resources to support the launch of IA-64, Intel's next-generation high-performance microprocessor architecture. Her group had developed a plan and a structure. Testing had confirmed the Original Equipment Manufacturers' (OEMs') interest. But would it really work?

CORPORATE VENTURE CAPITAL

Although corporations had a long history of involvement in the venture market, they were generally viewed as fickle. In the past they had not had a long-term perspective, "loading up [on shares] when ebullient public markets provide their own companies a larger capital base to work from—and the IPO promise of the fledgling companies [was] tempting—only to depart when the market conditions sour[ed]."[3] This often meant that they could not be relied upon for future cash infusions when the young companies faced challenging times. Entrepreneurs and traditional VCs generally viewed corporate money with suspicion, as the precursor of an acquisition, or derision, as the product of VC-wannabes who typically overpaid for their shares.[4]

By the late 1990s, this perception was changing. In 1998, $1.1 billion of the $29.3 billion invested in the venture market came from corporations.[5] Many of the investing companies had themselves been founded with substantial venture backing, thus acquainting them with the potential pitfalls. One observer commented, "They don't have a short-sighted vision; they're in the private equity market to stay."[6]

Most corporate investment was undertaken to augment internal R&D. Firms in the pharmaceutical industry had long had a VC arm to reduce the time required to find promising drugs. The firms most active in the late-1990s market tended to be technology-oriented—Microsoft, Cisco Systems, Oracle, Intel, GE Capital, Lucent Technologies, AT&T, Cambridge Technology Partners, and Novell—and the investments strategic. Said one player, "[They] are our periscope into what's happening in the future. [They're] a good way to get to know people, markets and opportunities better."[7]

Along with the view toward the future was the issue of complementarity. "Corporations are looking to put money to work in companies that add to their suite of products," said a private equity investor. "It's an important part of their overall strategy."

Corporate VC differed fundamentally from the classic financial VC, because of its strategic orientation. Financial return played a role, "validating that the company may have some market impact," but, as Steve Nachtsheim, vice president and director of Intel Capital, said, "We aren't depending on it to pay the light bill. You judge your return on how you met your strategic goals and count the money later."[8] Corporate VCs typ-

---

[3] Ibid.

[4] Ibid.

[5] Ibid.

[6] Mark Heesen, president NVCA, in Moriarity, "The New Smart Money."

[7] Mark Boslet, "Something Ventured," *Dow Jones News Service*, March 1, 2000.

[8] Les Vadasz in Shawn Neidorf, "Chief of Intel's Venture Capital Unit Answers Questions about Market," *San Jose Mercury News*, February 13, 2000, and Dean Takahashi, "Deals & Deal Makers," *Wall Street Journal*, February 8, 2000.

ically had one limited partner—the parent company. This allowed a longer time horizon and a lower internal rate of return. A company whose product would increase demand for the investor's own production generated a return that was not measured in earnings-per-share. Financial VCs, on the other hand, generally had to generate an attractive financial return.[9]

The lower financial returns that corporate VCs allowed proved a handicap in recruiting. Financial VCs compensated their employees through a mix of salary and carried interest on investments. In 1998, the median compensation for a senior partner of a VC firm was over $1 million, only a small portion of which was salary.[10] In a corporate pay structure, employees of the VC department could not be compensated on the same scale. One executive explained, "I can't have the VC guys landing their helicopters on the front lawn when the guy running the $100 million division in Rochester is making $75K." Carried interest might also skew the incentives for the employees—financial performance might become more important than strategic value. As a result, corporate VCs found it difficult to retain good people. In one year, 18 people left one of the best corporate VC firms for the higher pay of financial VCs.[11] This revolving door challenged entrepreneurs, who wanted lasting relationships with their corporate VCs, in order to leverage both the VC's strategic benefits and its business connections. Ideally, they would work together through multiple financing rounds until the company went public.

Some observers felt that the two issues, strategic orientation and compensation, were linked. "Those professionals [who leave corporate VC] can pursue deals without needing to have a corporate interest behind them, and it is just impossible to match [the] compensation."[12]

Intel Capital

Intel was one of the first technology firms to institutionalize venture capital investing. Leslie Vadasz started the Corporate Business Development group in 1991. Like all corporate VCs at the time, its fundamental aim was to advance the company's strategic interest through business agreements and investment. During the early 1990s, Vadasz focused on companies such as makers of manufacturing equipment and chip design software, whose products directly improved Intel's processes.

This emphasis shifted as Vadasz redefined his goal to expanding the "market ecosystem" in which Intel operated. This led him to invest in companies that complemented or expanded Intel's market segment.[13] In his words, "We realized that if you can align new strategies with that of . . . complementors—people who complement your product in the marketplace with their products—you can accelerate the development of new market ecosystems. In a fast-moving market, even if that acceleration is no more than two, three, six months, that's a big deal."[14] Expanding on the point, he observed, "You know that Moore's Law—Moore is one of Intel's founders—states that the power of computing will double every 18 months. The market doesn't keep up. We invest in those companies that move the market forward, so that end-users can benefit from the power of those faster, cheaper microprocessors." Intel often provided both investment funds

---

[9] Moriarity, "The New Smart Money."

[10] William M. Mercer Inc. Performance & Rewards Consulting, in Moriarity, "The New Smart Money."

[11] Moriarity "The New Smart Money."

[12] Michael Frank, general partner., Advanced Technology Ventures, in Moriarity, "The New Smart Money."

[13] Takahashi, "Deals & Deal Makers."

[14] Neidorf, "Chief of Intel's Venture Capital Unit."

and technical expertise, optimizing the start-up's product to run faster—often 100% faster than before—using Intel's products.

While Intel invested in companies producing applications that accessed more of the chips' power, it also looked to those that created demand for Intel's products from several steps away. Intel's investment in Verisign was an example of this strategy. Verisign's product enhanced security for on-line transactions but did not create immediate demand for Intel's products. By enabling increased use of the Internet, however, Verisign's technology would stimulate demand for PCs.

In most of its investments, Intel worked with financial VCs, relying on their expertise to guide the start-up's management, introduce it to networks within the business community, and recruit talented employees. Over time, Intel cultivated these relationships. Someone from Intel Capital would approach a VC if none was involved in a deal Intel thought promising, and VCs would approach Intel with deals for which they wanted its backing or view of the market.[15] Intel's investments were made collaboratively between Intel Capital and a business unit that vetted and approved the proposed technology. The actual funds were allocated by Intel Capital's internal investment committee, which included a senior executive from the business unit proposing the investment; Vadasz, the head of Intel Capital, or his deputy; and representatives from the legal and Treasury departments. The Treasury representative monitored financial return issues. Strategic value was always placed ahead of financial results, although never to the point of accepting a negligible return. "From the start, this has never been about return," said one Intel Capital executive. "If we approached these folks [the investment committee] with a purely financial play, we'd be ridiculed."

Despite the focus on strategic goals, Intel's financial success rate was higher than that of many private VCs. Almost all of Intel's VC investments succeeded, whereas private VC firms typically expected failure rates higher than 50%. Vadasz stated that of the nearly 400 external investments made by Intel, fewer than 10 were total failures. Failure, however, was defined in two ways. The first was conventional: Intel lost its total investment. The other was strategic: although Intel tripled its $50 million investment in VLSI, Vadasz counted this a failure because Intel products did not get into wireless offerings.

In 1998, as it planned the launch of its new 64-bit processor architecture, Intel decided to adopt a direct VC role and Steve Nachtsheim became the senior executive within Intel Capital driving that project. While Intel's microprocessor lines were frequently upgraded, according to Moore's Law, changing the architecture was much more involved. The architecture determined the length of the instruction set that a microprocessor could handle; going from 32 bits to 64 bits was, in Partridge's words, "like learning how to read a paragraph as opposed to a sentence." The new processor handled twice as much information as the old 32-bit Pentium™ processors and did so faster. This confronted Intel with several tasks.

First, the 64-bit chip was aimed at the high-end server and workstation market, one in which Intel's expertise was limited. These machines performed such complex operations as data-mining, customer service, customer relationship management, and Internet hosting, handling millions of transactions per minute. Intel's expertise traditionally lay in the PC market segment, with less complex system and software architectures. Supporting the IA-64 for data-mining alone meant developing software solution stacks that optimized the performance of different operating systems—NT, LINUX, Monterey, HP UX, and others—paired with various databases made by IBM, Sybase, Microsoft,

---

[15] Takahashi, "Deals & Deal Makers."

Informix, and Oracle. Each pairing required its own solution stack. In order to succeed in this market segment, many solution stacks had to be not just available but working extremely well. Adoption could be especially slow in this market, said one analyst, as the purchasers would be "high-end corporate customers who generally tend to be more conservative in their buying habits."[16]

Intel also knew that software's ability to exploit the extra capabilities of the new chip would lag far behind the availability of the product itself. The last processor transition, when 32-bit chips replaced 16-bits, had started in 1985. Not until Microsoft introduced Windows 95 ten years later did most users gain the benefits of the improvement.[17] The multiple operating systems supporting Intel's 64-bit chip were expected to be available within a year of the chip's broad availability, but Intel recognized the need to continue aiding the development of complete software solutions for the chip.

Finally, Intel needed to make a statement. The IA-64's release had been delayed from late 1999 to mid-2000. Other manufacturers already had 64-bit chips on the market, and the delay of Intel's product dampened the computer makers' enthusiasm for it. One source reported that "Silicon Graphics had originally said that it would design all its workstations to run Intel chips. After the delay was announced, it decided to slow the conversion."[18]

For all these reasons, Nachtsheim and the other Intel executives knew that it was critical to speed the development of a "business ecosystem"—that is, all the hardware and the software to take advantage of the performance of the IA-64 processor—around the new technology. A special investment fund seemed to make sense as a way to target applications for the IA-64, but no one was quite sure how to structure it. In October 1998, the executives delivered to Laila Partridge the charge to translate "a special fund around the IA-64" into a business reality—quickly.

Designing the Special Fund

Partridge, who had a Bachelor's Degree in studio art and a decade of banking experience, most recently in mergers and acquisitions, had joined the M&A group in Intel's Treasury Department in 1996. In that role, she had become acquainted with Intel Capital's work and had been tapped for the special fund due to her experience in structuring complex deals. She was joined on the design team by James Horn, an Intel Capital member for the prior two years with experience in the Treasury Department, and James Cape, who had 15 years with Intel, including a stint in the marketing organization of the Enterprise Server Group. The group received periodic support from Will Fellner, from the Enterprise Server Group, and Dave Clark of Intel Capital's Workstation Products Group, key business units involved in selling IA-64 processors. Fellner, another 15-year Intel veteran, and Cape were particularly helpful in generating "back-channel" support and showing Partridge the organization's ropes. "In a big company like Intel where people move around and there are a lot of reorganizations," Partridge said, "veterans just know how to make things happen. If it hadn't been for these two, we never would have made our deadline." Clark's contribution was less direct but important nonetheless: an "out-of-the-box" thinker, he provided a sounding board for the team's ideas and enlisted support for the project from the operational groups.

---

[16] Kevin Restivo, "Intel Looks to Jump Start IA-64," *Computer Dealer News*, June 25, 1999, p. 10.

[17] Anon., "Great Leap Forward for PC Industry," *Irish Times*, May 21, 1999, p. 59.

[18] James DeTar, "Intel Ventures into Investing to Boost New Merced Chip," *Investor's Business Daily*, August 10, 1999, p. A6.

Partridge and her group locked themselves in a room for a week in late October to brainstorm. She explained their approach:

> Intel has a very programmatic approach to solving problems. We tend to be very systematic, but we're not afraid to go beyond convention if we think that's the best way to get what we need. First we brainstormed a mission statement: "Invest to enable a complete solution set for IA-64-based platforms at launch and throughout the ramp." Then we had to figure out what we meant by that.

Part of the challenge was the indirectness of the IA-64's benefit. "This doesn't *do* the fancy pictures and stuff, it allows other programs to do it," Horn explained. The solution stack would include hardware and software running on high-end servers and workstations that would capitalize on the IA-64's power.

Intel could not directly create the solution stack; it could only enable it. This was complicated by the fact that Intel had very little direct contact with end-users. "Intel makes most of its sales to a very small number of manufacturers, " explained Partridge. "We don't have an abundance of direct feedback from the end-users."

To jumpstart the adoption of the new chip, the solution stack had to be available at its introduction (the launch), as well as during the entire adoption period (the ramp). End-users had to be convinced that enough new software and capabilities existed that they should spend the extra money for this next generation of product. Without software in place, Intel risked another long slow ramp-up in technology adoption. The customary market cycle saw a new technology introduced essentially in a vacuum, as applications and software slowly caught up with its capabilities. Cape described the group's goal:

> The whole idea was to translate the IA-64 from something that engineers thought was cool because it was fast and fancy to something that made life easier for the end-users. Basically, end-users don't care what the chips ARE, they care what the solutions DO. They wouldn't care if you handed them an abacus as long as it made their lives easier. And we had to do it fast.

Partridge elaborated on their approach:

> We wanted to invest in enabling technology, companies like TimesTen that increased the speed with which applications could access memory and take technical advantage of IA-64's features. TimesTen is a great showcase for this product—because it reconfigures databases in a more intelligent way, it has great applications for industries like telecoms. For instance, in the pause between when you hit the "send" on your cell phone and the call is connected, the system is actually verifying your account data. TimesTen products, using the IA-64, can reduce that pause to almost nothing.

Both Horn and Partridge reiterated that the emphasis continued to be placed solely on strategic fit:

> We thought we should invest in these companies not because we wanted to own them—we've got enough money that we could buy them if we wanted—but because we wanted the technology out there. They were all going to use the IA-64 eventually; we just helped them do it more quickly. And it gave us more software options when we launched the product.

Bringing in Other Investors

Intel would put $100 million in this fund. The company did not, however, want to be in it alone. From the start, the group had known that Intel's key manufacturers (Original Equipment Manufacturers, or OEMs) needed to be involved. Partridge explained, "It's that feedback thing again. We were looking for people with expertise in building and using software solution stacks—and the OEMs actually touched the end-users. They'd be able to provide incredible insights about the solutions and technologies that would be relevant to the end-users." The creation of IA-64 solutions would be mutually beneficial. In addition, the OEMs were interested in doing this sort of investing but lacked the internal organization to pursue it., They faced limited resources, however, and a multitude of places to employ them. Partridge said, "We thought we could maybe get three OEMs to put in approximately $20 million each."

Intel's OEMs were all computer manufacturers, but the group decided to concentrate on those that sold a high volume of servers and workstations running Intel's architecture to business users. The experience of these firms would improve the fund's ability to choose technology appropriate to the high-powered enterprise users at which the IA-64 was targeted.

The discussion then turned to end-users, as Horn explained:

> We started thinking, "Why not raise additional funds from the actual end-users?" If we included key Fortune 500 users of information technology, especially the CIOs [chief information officers] who were in it every day, we could gain a much better understanding of the pressing needs of end-users. After all, only they really knew what a solution stack was. If anyone understood what we needed to do, it was these folks.

The group realized that customers would have to be chosen carefully. Systems integrators, service companies that installed and programmed computer systems, were discarded in favor of traditional industrial firms and consumer-goods producers. They approached dot-coms but then backed off. "They had different priorities," said Partridge, "they wanted eyeballs; they'd just gone public. But also they were too busy just taking care of business to look into evaluating technology. They were just trying to meet the demand on their systems."

Six different broad industry categories would be represented, with participation restricted to one firm from each. This would give a sense of exclusivity to participation and also make the customer more open with information because, for instance, one automaker would not have to worry that another would steal its ideas for using technology. The participants would be the CIOs, not the business development or treasury people. "We wanted insight into the uses of technology, and to pick up trends in IT [information technology] ahead of the market," Partridge explained. "We didn't want someone just giving us money; we wanted the input of the CIO and senior IT staff."

With the concept firmly in hand, the group unlocked the door. It had been a long week. Now it was time to gather input on the idea.

Input

The team first ran the idea past Nachtsheim. "Interesting out-of-the-box thinking, this thing with the CIOs," he observed. "Test it."

The team started its testing by talking with advisors about the fund's structure. It had to allow the greatest impact while minimizing Intel's legal and financial exposure.

The legal and treasury position had been clearly defined going into the project: Intel could not be an investment advisor in the manner of a general partner in a traditional venture capital fund. The group also realized that corporate VCs were often perceived as being willing to invest for strategic benefit even in the absence of a compelling financial return. "We were worried," said Partridge, "that the OEMs and the CIOs might be concerned that Intel would invest for its own benefit in a company that offered them little in the way of strategic interest or financial return." Each investor in the fund had to be able to decide on each individual deal. Horn explained, "So we added the concept of 'opt in/opt out.' The OEMs could chose to participate or not in a deal, and we'd act as the coordinating member."

This solution, though elegant, set a practical limit on the number of investors. Managing a group larger than four or five such investors on 30+ investments would be unwieldy at best. Looking for guidance on that practical issue, the team learned that one of the legal advisors had worked on a similar fund with a previous employer but knew of no others. Said Partridge:

> Joe Barbeau, one of our lawyers, said he'd go off and think about how various structures might work to integrate both the opt in/opt out feature and the sheer number of participants—we were thinking, after all, of six customers and three OEMs, in addition to the Intel people. He called back to say that no, there was just no way to have such a large group without a general partnership structure. We were sitting there in the conference room, and everyone just went silent. You could feel all the energy and excitement just drain out, like someone had opened the plug. So I thanked him and hung up.

Horn continued the story: "But that's Laila. She looked around this room full of dispirited people and said, 'Let's put the structure aside and get on with the other details. The concept of CIOs and OEMs as joint investors is just too sound; we'll make it work. We'll think of something.' And sure enough, she did."

Two days later, while working on other issues in the same conference room, Partridge interrupted a conversation saying, "I've got it! What if we split them—have the OEMs in one group and the CIOs in another? And have an investment advisor opt in or out on behalf of the CIOs? That way, the CIOs' financial interests are represented by someone without a strategic agenda." Recounting the story, she recalled, "We talked first to the internal lawyers, then the external guys, and both agreed that a two-tiered structure with someone else as an investment advisor would work. We left at the end of that day and our feet didn't even touch the ground."

The initial structure looked like this:

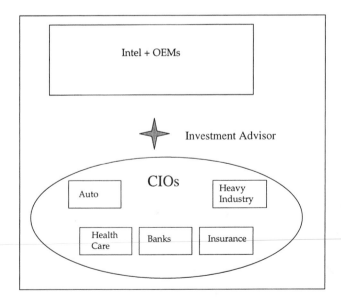

Figure 23.1 IA-64 Fund Concept
Source: company information.

The next question was, Who should play the role of investment advisor? VCs would have the deal-evaluation skills, but they would be restricted to focus only on the financial aspect of the deal. Investment banks offered another possibility, and the incentives and skills might be more in line.

Participant Selection

Nachtsheim had advised the group to approach Intel's Board of Advisors regarding the participation of chief information officers (CIOs). This group, consisting of 10 to 15 CIOs from blue-chip producers of consumer goods and services, met quarterly with Intel to discuss end-user needs. Horn said, "We wanted to include customers who handled a wide variety of needs on the part of their own customers, and those who were key players in the IT field. That seemed to indicate the Board of Advisors. Andy Smith, the Intel person who managed those relationships, was just great and got us in to talk with some of these folks in almost no time."

These conversations could not be made as a pitch for a fund because Intel could not run a fund. Partridge recalled their strategy:

> We structured it as a "what if." All we wanted was feedback on if it was compelling, interesting, or a non-starter. Our pitch had three angles; first, we said they'd get input into software solutions coming down the pike, so that instead of adapting to a final IA-64 technology, they could influence it before it got to that stage. Secondly, they'd reduce their adoption costs for the IA-64. Big companies incur these costs all the time to create custom programs or run patches around their legacy systems. The third aspect was that, because the IA-64 was intended to support and enhance the internet infrastructure, as well as enterprise applications, they'd get insight into the emerging companies that Intel and its OEMs thought were technically interesting.

The group addressed several CIOs from the advisory group. Cape said:

> Most were *really* interested. They loved the concept of exclusivity and the fact that we wanted the CIO, not someone from finance. They really wanted the access to new technology. Many of them had already done something like this in an ad-hoc way, but they didn't have a structured program. Most had investment programs to do exactly this—to sell them interesting stuff

Finding the investment advisor proved surprisingly challenging. Intel thought that the fund offered an opportunity for an investment bank to leverage its relationship with the big firms who would participate. In addition, the bank would receive carried interest and it could invest, but there would be no fee. In December, the group contacted Morgan Stanley Dean Witter (MSDW). "We felt MSDW was a perfect match," Horn said. "They had a VC group and their Technology Investment Banking group, with about 75 professionals, was one of the premier names in Silicon Valley investment banking."

MSDW had its own internal approval process that focused on the time commitments of senior professionals, but, on the other hand, the prospect of a stronger business relationship with Intel was appealing. "We stewed for a while," said Horn, "but finally MSDW came through. Both the VC and the Technology Investment Banking group invested in the fund as well." Tim Sullivan of the Technology Investment Banking arm and Guy de Chazal of the VC group commented, "The Intel 64 Fund creates a unique

---

EXHIBIT 23-1

PROPOSED STRUCTURE OF THE INTEL 64 OPERATING FUND LLC

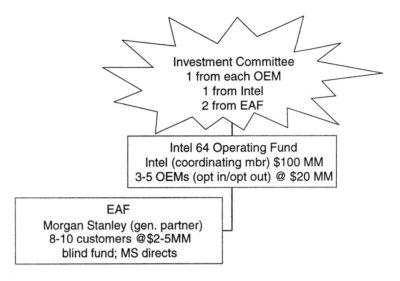

Investment Committee
1 from each OEM
1 from Intel
2 from EAF

Intel 64 Operating Fund
Intel (coordinating mbr) $100 MM
3-5 OEMs (opt in/opt out) @ $20 MM

EAF
Morgan Stanley (gen. partner)
8-10 customers @$2-5MM
blind fund; MS directs

Source: Casewriter.

---

opportunity for global users to take advantage of new technologies to innovate how they do business in the new worldwide Internet economy."[19]

The Structure

With the agreement of MSDW, the group finished the design of the Intel® 64 Operating Fund LLC. It would comprise two parts: one with Intel and the OEMs; the other, called the EAF (Early Adopter Fund), would include the customers, led by MSDW (see Exhibit 23-1). Intel would act as the coordinating member of its part, sourcing and presenting the deals without making any recommendations. It would contribute $100 million. The OEMs, of which there would be between three and five, would put in $20 million each and could opt in or out of each deal.

The EAF would be structured much more like a conventional financial fund. Its eight or ten members (up from the six originally proposed) would contribute $2–5 million each. This portion of the fund would be blind; if MSDW decided the deal was worthwhile, it would add the EAF's money to the pool. Returns would be paid on the basis of funds contributed.

The process, as the group designed it, would run as follows:

1. Intel Capital would decide to fund a firm as part of its normal business practices.

---

[19] Intel Corp., "Intel: Tech Leaders & Corporate Users Form $0.25 on Investment Fund Targeting Intel's IA-64 Architecture," *M2 Presswire*, May 11, 1999.

2. If the firm was involved in IA-64 technology, the deal would be offered to the IA-64 Fund.

3. The investment committee of the IA-64 Fund would evaluate the deal. This group (one representative from each OEM, two from EAF, and one from Intel) would handle the pool of approximately $180 million. At least two representatives (Intel and another party) had to approve any deal.

If the fund chose not invest, Intel Capital would do so for its own account.

Operating Issues

Partridge knew that recruiting investors for the EAF would be a challenge. She had already addressed the Board of Advisors, while Fellner had met with several members of Intel's European Advisory Board, and they knew that the biggest challenge would be finding the right contacts. The Intel field representatives would have to be included in making introductions, but that had to be handled delicately.

Another complication was location. She wanted the fund to be as global as possible, but, as she put it "here we are, pretty much stuck on North America." Fellner and Horn were contemplating a trip to Japan, and Partridge had already made some exploratory phone calls. "Japan was going to be hard," she said. "The attitude of the CIOs there was 'give us a box and a service contract.' They didn't want to know how it worked. But some firms were interested in participating just for the business relationship with Intel."

Europe, on the other hand, had a longer experience with venture investing. "The problem we encountered with Europe," said Horn, "was that a lot of mergers were going on in the big firms we were considering. The companies were distracted and the IT resources were totally involved in integrating merged systems."

The United States had yielded five or six strongly interested companies. "Our biggest challenge seems to be within the organizations we address," Horn observed. "We talk to the CIOs and they love it. But it has to be approved by the folks in Treasury or VC, which slows things down."

The last aspect the group knew it would have to address was how to keep the OEMs interested. The fund would be closed after the executive group approved it. The group had proposed a private Web site on which members could share their thoughts and find profiles of investments in the pipeline. The other proposal was for semiannual technology conferences that would present the portfolio companies to the IT executives in the fund. Information could flow freely between the small companies inventing IA-64 applications, the large customers that would use them, the OEMs manufacturing the boxes, and Intel. Additional benefits might include business relationships among the small companies themselves.

The door opened. Horn grinned at Partridge reassuringly. "Laila, we've done this a thousand times. They're not going to find any holes in it. It'll work, don't worry." She wished she could share his confidence.

24

A Note on Corporate Venture Capital

Corporations have had an enduring fascination with venture capital investments. Many organizations have seen venture capital as an intriguing alternative way to make investments, which offers a flexibility and speed that is very different from the traditional corporate capital budgeting and investment process. These appealing features have led many firms to experiment with corporate venture initiatives. These corporations have often discovered, however, that the implementation of such an effort is considerably more challenging than it appears from the outside!

This note seeks to provide a brief introduction to corporate venture investing. First, the historical evolution of these programs is reviewed. The special difficulties that these efforts face are then considered. Finally, we review the systematic evidence about the success of these programs, which suggests that despite the many difficulties they face, these programs have made valuable contributions and enjoyed real successes.

THE HISTORY OF CORPORATE VENTURE CAPITAL[1]

The first corporate venture funds began in the mid-1960s, about two decades after the first formal venture capital funds. The corporate efforts were spurred by the successes of the first organized venture capital funds, which backed such firms as Digital Equipment, Memorex, Raychem, and Scientific Data Systems. Excited by this success, large companies began establishing divisions that emulated venture capitalists. During the late 1960s and early 1970s, more than 25% of the Fortune 500 firms attempted corporate venture programs.

[1] This history is based in part on Norman D. Fast, *The Rise and Fall of Corporate New Venture Divisions*, Ann Arbor, MI, UMI Research Press, 1978; Robert E. Gee, "Finding and Commercializing New Businesses," *Research/Technology Management* 37 (January/February 1994): 49–56; and Venture Economics, 1986, "Corporate Venture Capital Study," unpublished manuscript, 1986, among other sources.

These efforts generally took two forms, external and internal. At one end of the spectrum, large corporations financed new firms alongside other venture capitalists. In many cases, the corporations simply provided funds for a venture capitalist to invest rather than investing the funds itself. Other firms invested directly in start-ups, giving them a greater ability to tailor their portfolios to their particular needs. At the other extreme, large corporations attempted to tap the entrepreneurial spirit within their organizations. These programs sought to allow entrepreneurs to focus their attention on developing their innovations, while relying on the corporate parents for financial, legal, and marketing support.

In 1973, the market for new public offerings—the primary avenue through which venture capitalists exit successful investments—abruptly declined. Independent venture partnerships began experiencing significantly less attractive returns and encountered severe difficulties in raising new funds. At the same time, corporations began scaling back their own initiatives. The typical corporate venture program begun in the late 1960s was dissolved after only four years.

As was discussed in the first module of the course, funds flowing into the venture capital industry and the number of active venture organizations increased dramatically during the late 1970s and early 1980s. Corporations were once again attracted to the promise of venture investing in response. These efforts peaked in 1986, when corporate funds managed $2 billion, or nearly 12% of the total pool of venture capital.

After the stock market crash of 1987, however, the market for new public offerings again went into a sharp decline. Returns of and fundraising by independent partnerships declined abruptly. Corporations scaled back their commitment to venture investing even more dramatically. By 1992, the number of corporate venture programs had fallen by one-third, and their capital under management represented only 5% of the venture pool.

Interest in corporate venture capital climbed once again in the mid-1990s, both in the United States and abroad. Once again, much of this interest was stimulated by the recent success of the independent venture sector: that is, the rapid growth of funds and their attractive returns. These corporate funds have invested directly in a variety of internal and external ventures, as well as in funds organized by independent venture capitalists.

The increase in the scale of activity can be illustrated by some estimates by Venture Economics. The consulting firm believes that corporate investors accounted for 30% of the commitments to new funds in 1997, up from an average of 5% in the 1990–1992 period. Similarly, direct investments in the United States by these programs are believed to have risen from 65 investments totaling $176 million in 1995 to 936 transactions totaling $7.8 billion in 1999.[2]

The most recent wave of corporate venturing activity is distinguished from earlier activity in several ways. First, the scale of activity has been considerably larger, with funds as large as $1 billion being established by firms such as Arthur Andersen and EDS. Second, the diversity of companies involved in these efforts has been greater, with many more services and traditional "old economy" manufacturers establishing such programs. (In earlier booms, activity was largely concentrated among high-technology firms.) Finally, many more firms outside the United States have participated in these efforts in recent years.

---

[2] Venture Economics, "Corporate Venture Capital Activity," Unpublished tabulation, 2000.

WHY IS CORPORATE VENTURE CAPITAL CHALLENGING?

This brief discussion makes clear that corporate involvement in venture capital has mirrored (perhaps even in an exaggerated manner) the cyclical nature of the entire venture capital industry over the past three decades. At the same time, numerous discussions suggest that certain basic noncyclical issues also have a significant impact on corporate venture capital activity.

In particular, it appears that the frequent dissolution of earlier corporate venture programs was due to three structural failings. First, these programs suffered from a lack of well-defined missions.[3] Typically, they sought to accomplish a wide array of not necessarily compatible objectives: from providing a window on emerging technologies to generating attractive financial returns. The confusion over program objectives often led to senior managers' dissatisfaction with the outcomes. For instance, when outside venture capitalists were hired to run a corporate fund under a contract that linked compensation to financial performance, management frequently became frustrated about their failure to invest in the technologies that most interested the firm. Instead, the venture groups were often perceived as selecting the investments that offered the highest financial return, independent of the benefits to the corporation.

A second cause of failure was insufficient corporate commitment to the venturing initiative.[4] Even if top management embraced the concept, middle management often resisted. R&D personnel preferred that funds be devoted to internal programs; corporate lawyers disliked the novelty and complexity of these hybrid organizations. In many cases, new senior management teams terminated programs, seeing them as expendable "pet projects" of their predecessors. Even if they did not object to the idea of the program, managers were often concerned about its impact on the firm's accounting earnings. During periods of financial pressure, money-losing subsidiaries were frequently terminated in an effort to increase reported operating earnings.

A final cause of failure was inadequate compensation schemes.[5] Corporations have frequently been reluctant to compensate their venture managers through profit-sharing ("carried interest") provisions, fearing that they might need to make huge payments if their investments were successful. Typically, successful risk-taking was inadequately rewarded and failure excessively punished. As a result, corporations were frequently unable to attract top people (i.e., those who combined industry experience with connections to other venture capitalists) to run their venture funds. While this reluctance to offer incentive compensation is gradually easing, this remains a very real issue in many corporate venture programs today.[6]

[3] These problems are discussed in depth in the Fast volume cited above and in Robin Siegel, Eric Siegel, and Ian C. MacMillan, "Corporate Venture Capitalists: Autonomy, Obstacles, and Performance," *Journal of Business Venturing* 3 (1988): 233–247.

[4] See the discussions, for instance, in G. Felda Hardymon, Mark J. DeNino, and Malcolm S. Salter, "When Corporate Venture Capital Doesn't Work," *Harvard Business Review* 61 (May–June 1983): 114–120; Kenneth W. Rind, "The Role of Venture Capital in Corporate Development," *Strategic Management Journal* 2 (1981): 169–180; and Hollister B. Sykes, "Corporate Venture Capital: Strategies for Success," *Journal of Business Venturing* 5 (1990): 37–47.

[5] These problems are documented in Zenas Block and Oscar A. Ornati, "Compensating Corporate Venture Managers," *Journal of Business Venturing* 2 (1987): 41–52; and E. Lawler and J. Drexel, *The Corporate Entrepreneur*, Los Angeles, Center for Effective Organizations, Graduate School of Business Administration, University of Southern California, 1980.

[6] See, for instance, David G. Barry, "Some Venture Programs Sharing Gains with Corporate Workforce," *Corporate Venturing Report* 1 (July 2000): 1, 22–23.

All too often, as a consequence corporate venture managers adopted a conservative approach to investing. Nowhere was this behavior more clearly manifested than in the treatment of lagging ventures. As discussed in the second module of the course, independent venture capitalists often cease funding to failing firms because they want to devote their limited energy to firms with the greatest promise. Corporate venture capitalists have frequently been unwilling to write off unsuccessful ventures, lest they incur the reputational repercussions that a failure would entail.

HOW SUCCESSFUL HAVE CORPORATE VENTURING PROGRAMS BEEN?

The boom-and-bust pattern in corporate venturing has led many to conclude that corporate venture capital is inherently unstable and unlikely to be successful. But the actual historical track of these investments paints a quite different picture, one that challenges the conventional wisdom about corporate programs.[7]

When over 30,000 investments into entrepreneurial firms by venture capital organizations over a 15-year period were examined, the pattern was striking. Investments by two types of organizations, independent venture partnerships and corporate funds, were compared. (Other hybrid venture funds, such as those affiliated with commercial and investment banks, were not used for the purposes of this analysis.)

Far from being outright failures, corporate venture investments in entrepreneurial firms appear to be at least as successful (using such measures as the probability of a portfolio firm going public) as those backed by independent venture organizations. For instance, 35% of the investments by corporate funds were in companies that had gone public by the end of the sample period, as opposed to 31% for independent funds. It might be thought that the results are just a consequence of the fact that corporate groups often invest in later financing rounds. By this point in many firms, much of the uncertainty has been addressed and the probability of success is higher. But the results continue to hold up when controls for the age and profitability of the portfolio firm at the time of the original investment are added.

But the pattern of success is not uniform. The success of the corporate programs is especially pronounced for investments in which there is strategic overlap between the corporate parent and the portfolio firm. The probability of going public by the end of the sample period, for instance, is 39% for this group. The success of investments when there is no overlap is much lower, particularly once the characteristics of the firm are controlled for.

These measures may be somewhat misleading. A corporate venture program may be strategically successful, even if the portfolio companies do not well: for instance, it may allow a firm to understand and head off a serious competitive threat to its core business. For instance, in 1980, Analog Devices established a corporate venture program, Analog Devices Enterprises (ADE), to generate both attractive financial returns and strategic benefits in the form of licensing agreements and acquisitions. By the time the program was suspended in 1985, Analog Devices took a $7 million charge against earnings. In 1990, with most of the portfolio liquidated, it took another $12 million

---

[7] This section is based on Paul A. Gompers and Josh Lerner, "The Determinants of Corporate Venture Capital Success: Organizational Structure, Incentives, and Complementarities," in Randall Morck, ed., *Concentrated Corporate Ownership*, Chicago, University of Chicago Press for the National Bureau of Economic Research, 2000: 17–50.

charge. Of the 11 firms in ADE's portfolio, 10 were terminated, acquired by other companies at unattractive valuations or relegated to the "living dead." Only one firm ultimately went public. In this case, ADE's stake was so diluted by a merger that it was worth only about $2 million at the time of the offering. At the same time, however, the program allowed Analog Devices, a manufacturer of specialized silicon-based semiconductors to assess the threat that semiconductors based on an alternative technology, gallium arsenide (GaAs), posed to its core business. Ultimately, this threat proved to be much smaller than originally anticipated, and many of the companies failed. During this same period, Analog Devices' stock price climbed sevenfold, reflecting the improved prospects for silicon chipmakers.

Similar patterns emerge when the duration of the programs themselves is examined. The evidence suggests that corporate programs without a strong strategic focus are much less stable than those of independent funds. Many unfocused corporate funds cease operations after only a few investments, with the typical fund surviving less than one-quarter the period of the average independent fund. Meanwhile, corporate funds with a strong strategic focus are almost as stable as independent funds.

In short, despite the many challenges that these efforts face, corporate venture capital programs can make a real difference!

ADDITIONAL INFORMATION SOURCES

Given the degree of interest in corporate venturing programs, surprisingly little has been written about these efforts. Nonetheless, there are several useful sources of information about these programs. First, there are two primary sources for data on these programs. The consulting firm Asset Alternatives (www.assetnews.com) publishes a helpful directory, the *Directory of Corporate Venture Capital Programs*. This includes profiles of the programs' objectives, key contact points, and representative investments. VentureOne's database tracks the progress of numerous corporate programs in addition to traditional funds.

The best source for news about corporate venturing programs is another Asset Alternatives publication, *The Corporate Venturing Report*. In addition, occasional stories appear in more general publications such as *The Venture Capital Journal*.

Consulting and accounting firms periodically produce reports on the state of corporate venturing. Most of these, alas, are not particularly helpful. More useful for those interested in a particular program are the collections of news releases and press coverage about that program which can be identified through careful searches in Lexis/Nexis, OneSource, and other business databases.

There are also a few academic studies:

ZENAS BLOCK and OSCAR A. ORNATI, "Compensating Corporate Venture Managers," *Journal of Business Venturing* 2 (1987): 41–52.

NORMAN D. FAST, *The Rise and Fall of Corporate New Venture Divisions*, Ann Arbor, MI, UMI Research Press, 1978.

ROBERT E. GEE, "Finding and Commercializing New Businesses," *Research/Technology Management* 37 (January/February 1994): 49–56.

PAUL A. GOMPERS and JOSH LERNER, *The Venture Capital Cycle*, Cambridge, MA, MIT Press, 1999: chapter 5.

PAUL A. GOMPERS and JOSH LERNER, *The Money of Invention*, Boston, MA, HBS Publishing, 2001: chapter 7.

G. FELDA HARDYMON, MARK J. DeNINO, and MALCOLM S. SALTER, "When Corporate Venture Capital Doesn't Work," *Harvard Business Review* 61 (May-June 1983): 114–120.

E. LAWLER and J. DREXEL, *The Corporate Entrepreneur*, Los Angeles, Center for Effective Organizations, Graduate School of Business Administration, University of Southern California, 1980.

KENNETH W. RIND, "The Role of Venture Capital in Corporate Development," *Strategic Management Journal* 2 (April 1981): 169–180.

ROBIN SIEGEL, ERIC SIEGEL, and IAN C. MACMILLAN, "Corporate Venture Capitalists: Autonomy, Obstacles, and Performance," *Journal of Business Venturing* 3 (1988): 233–247.

25

CMGI: Organizational and Market Innovation

David Wetherell looked up from the cluttered table in CMGI's expansive conference room and contemplated the rapidly gathering twilight outside. Over the past few hours, he had been painstakingly reviewing the documentation concerning the proposed acquisition of yesmail.com, a publicly traded e-mail marketing company. While this transaction was moving at "Internet speed"—the proposed acquisition would be presented to the board in two days, just two weeks after the possibility of such a deal had been first raised at the beginning of December 1999—the various aspects of the transaction had been exhaustively studied by Wetherell's staff and their outside advisors.

Wetherell thought about the strengths and weaknesses of yesmail. The company was a young entity that had recently identified an exciting competitive strategy and been rewarded by explosive growth. The company had the advantage of being a leader in its space, and it had the potential to complement CMGI's other Internet advertising-related products. The experience of the management team was another attractive aspect. The explosive growth, however, also posed some (perhaps inevitable) drawbacks: in particular, the company's relatively recent entry into this arena meant that it did not yet have a well-developed "brand image."

Whatever the strengths or weaknesses of this individual transaction, Wetherell mused, this deal would add to the complexity of the CMGI organization. Over the past five years, the organization had shown an amazing flexibility in responding to the opportunities that the Internet had created. The dramatic increase in CMGI's market capitalization and revenues attested to the success of the strategy. Was there a natural limit to this growth? Or would the CMGI structure be able to flexibly evolve as the opportunities posed by the Internet revolution changed once again?

Gazing out the window, Wetherell saw a flash of white. It was a flock of white-wing crossbills, feeding in the dense conifers outside CMGI's Andover, Massachusetts, office. This type of bird, normally a resident of Canada, ventured down to New England for the winter. Wetherell mused whether his newest acquisition would find CMGI to be as hospitable an environment as the crossbills did.

Professor Josh Lerner prepared this case as the basis for class discussion rather than to illustrate either effective or ineffective handling of an administrative situation.

THE HISTORY AND STRUCTURE OF CMGI[1]

The emergence of CMGI as a leader in the Internet industry (see Exhibit 25-2) was driven by the vision of its chairman and chief executive officer since 1986, David Wetherell. Wetherell, born on a Connecticut chicken farm in 1954, first encountered computer programming while a high school student in Florida. Although he concluded he had little skill in programming after receiving a C minus in the class, his interest was rekindled while a college student at Ohio Wesleyan University. Training to be a high school math teacher, he realized that he did indeed have an aptitude for computer programming.

Consequently, after graduation, Wetherell took a series of computer-related positions. These included stints as the information systems director for an Ohio medical center, the lead programmer for the Boston and Maine Railroad, and a technical recruiter for a search firm that placed programmers with Boston-area companies. Throughout his tenure at these positions, Wetherell was exploring different opportunities for entrepreneurial ventures, as well as learning important lessons about the management of technical enterprises.

In 1982, at age 27, Wetherell launched his first entrepreneurial venture. The company, Softtrend, was originally founded to develop software that linked then-new personal computers (PCs) to mainframes. The company soon turned, however, to the development of PC application software. In particular, the company was one of the first to develop a suite of software products—for example, word processing, spreadsheet, and database programs—that seamlessly worked together. Despite his relative youth and lack of entrepreneurial experience, Wetherell secured $3 million in funding from a large Boston-area private equity organization, TA Associates.

As the company's lead product approached its launch in 1984, however, TA declined to provide a second round of financing to Softtrend. (Roe Stamps, Wetherell's champion at the private equity firm, had recently departed TA to establish a group of his own. In addition, the valuation of PC hardware and software companies had declined precipitously during 1983, and many venture groups were trimming their investments in this area.) Instead, the company was sold at the investors' behest to a manufacturer of accounting software, BPI Software.

After a brief hiatus, Wetherell sought another opportunity. He identified a Boston-area database marketing company as an attractive opportunity. CMG Information Services had been founded in 1968 as the College Marketing Group. Its primary line of business was compiling lists of college professors, which were sold to publishers seeking to market textbooks. The company's existing business, Wetherell believed, had the potential to serve as a springboard for a much more general direct marketing effort. In 1986, using his own assets from the Softtrend sale as well as capital from Stamps' new private equity fund, Summit Ventures, Wetherell completed a leveraged buyout of CMG. Wetherell's initial years as CEO of CMG saw a number of challenges. In particular, the 1989 acquisition of Hub Mail/Inquiry Systems Analysis, a troubled printing and direct mailing concern, was a major drag on profits.

The transformation of CMG into CMGI did not begin until several years later. Early in 1993, Wetherell, having heard about the recent development of the World Wide Web,

[1] This section is based on interviews with CMGI officials, CMGI's filings with the U.S. Securities and Exchange Commission, analyst reports, and a wide variety of press accounts (especially Paul C. Judge, "Internet Evangelist," *Business Week* (October 25, 1999): 140–150, and Scott Kirsner, "David Wetherell's Excellent @Venture," *Boston Magazine* 91 (September 1999): 85–89, 128–140.) Exhibit 25-1 provides a simplified historical timeline of CMGI's development.

EXHIBIT 25-1

BRIEF HISTORICAL TIMELINE OF CMGI

1999

CMGI Solutions launches

AltaVista acquires Raging Bull

@Ventures B-2-B fund formed

MyWay.com acquires Zip2

Vicinity registers for IPO

Acquires 1ClickCharge, 1stUp.com, Activate.net, Activerse, AdForce,* AltaVista, Flycast Communications,* Tribal Voice and increases ownership stake in Magnitude Network

Forms strategic alliance with Compaq and Akamai

CMG Direct is sold to MSGI

Chemdex (CMDX), Critical Path (CPTH), Engage (ENGA), MotherNature.com (MTHR), NaviSite (NAV), and Silknet (SILK) complete IPOs

CMG joins Nasdaq 100

Announces new Internet broadcast venture, iCast

Engage acquires AdKnowledge* and I/PRO

Adsmart acquires 2CAN Media

@Ventures funds more than 20 companies

1998

@Ventures III fund formed

@Ventures funds 10 companies

Acquires Accipiter, InSolutions and On-Demand Solutions

Takes strategic position in Magnitude Network and forms NaviNet

$10M investment from Sumitomo Corporation

GeoCities completes IPO (GCTY)

PlanetAll is sold to Amazon.com and Ikonic is sold to USWeb

Reel.com sold to Hollywood Entertainment

1997

@Ventures funds 6 companies

Forms NaviSite and Engage

Microsoft and Intel each acquire a 4.9% stake in CMGI

NetCarta is sold to Microsoft

1996

@Ventures II fund formed

@Ventures funds 5 companies

Launches Adsmart and MyWay.com (formerly Planet Direct)

Lycos completes IPO (LCOS)

Tele T is sold to Premier

1995

@Ventures I fund formed

@Ventures funds 3 companies

Acquires NetCarta

1986–1994

Forms BookLink Technologies and sells to AOL

Company completes own IPO (CMGI)

Acquires SalesLink

Note: * denotes that acquisition was pending in mid-December 1999.

Source: Corporate documents

became interested in its implications for the publishing industry. Publishers, he reasoned, ultimately might be able to directly connect with book buyers and eventually even print books on demand. Such changes could potentially make intermediaries such as CMG obsolete. In light of this threat (or opportunity), Wetherell resolved to develop a new product, BookLink Technologies. This product, as Wetherell envisioned it, would combine an on-line bookstore with an Internet browser. The software would enable clients to readily search the offered titles from their PCs. The proposal to develop such a product proved to be controversial with CMG's board. The $900,000 that the company proposed to spend on this project represented five times its shareholder's equity in mid-1993 and 75% of its revenue in the 1993 fiscal year. The board eventually gave

EXHIBIT 25-2

LEADING INTERNET SITES, NOVEMBER 1999

Consolidations	Unique Visits (000s)	Reach
AOL Network	54,211	84%
Yahoo Sites	41,786	65%
Microsoft Sites	38,334	59%
CMGI Sites	34,938	54%
Lycos	29,150	45%
Go Network	21,981	34%
Amazon	15,357	24%
Excite@Home	14,975	23%
Bluemountainarts.com	12,742	20%
Time Warner Online	12,445	19%
Go2Network	11,472	18%
About.com Sites	11,032	17%
Reel.com Sites	10,842	17%
eBay	10,553	16%
CNet	9,393	15%

Note: Reach is defined as the percentage of active Internet users accessing a given site (or family of sites) in a month.

Source: Compiled from Media Metrix reports and analyst reports.

him permission to undertake the project, under the condition that he complete an initial public offering (IPO) first. The company's IPO, underwritten by Minneapolis-based Piper Jaffray, was held on January 25, 1994. After the offering, CMG had a market capitalization of about $68 million.

CMG then aggressively developed its BookLink product. Wetherell hired a programming team from Waltham-based Interleaf and encouraged them to begin with the development of the browser. Soon after, the first wave of interest in the Internet began to materialize. Many existing software companies and on-line content providers suddenly realized they needed an Internet browser of their own to compete with the new products being developed by upstarts such as Mosaic Communications (later renamed Netscape Communications). In December 1994, CMG sold the unfinished BookLink project to American Online for 710,000 shares of AOL stock. (The shares were worth approximately $30 million at the time and far more later.)

The success with BookLink led Wetherell to radically change CMG's direction. While the company's direct marketing activities continued to grow, its CEO's energy increasingly turned to the opportunities presented by the Internet. With part of the proceeds from the sale of the BookLink, the company established its first venture capital fund, CMG @Ventures I, LP (now CMG @Ventures I, LLC), in which it served as the sole limited partner (with a $35 million capital commitment). Upon founding CMG @Ventures in February 1995, Wetherell recruited Peter Mills, with whom he had founded Softtrend, to run this unit. In its initial transaction, CMG @Ventures founded

Lycos and negotiated an exclusive license for its search engine technology from Carnegie-Mellon University. In exchange for its $1.5 million investment, CMG received 80% of the company's equity. (When the company went public one year later, CMG's stake was worth $173 million.) CMG also sought to internally grow businesses related to Internet technologies, including ADSmart and Planet Direct (later renamed My-Way.com). As part of this effort, Wetherell recruited several key executives, including Andrew J. Hajducky as chief financial officer (formerly Ernst and Young's Entrepreneurial Services partner for the Boston area) and David Andonian as president, corporate development (who had formerly been vice president for worldwide marketing at PictureTel Corporation).

CMG's new business model provoked some concern from its board members. This was particularly the case in 1997, as Internet share prices plummeted as the initial wave of enthusiasm for these technologies ebbed. Meanwhile, CMG's profitability deteriorated dramatically, reflecting the scaling up of its product development efforts and the increased marketing expenses incurred by its Lycos subsidiary. While Wetherell believed that the investments would ultimately create powerful synergies through the formation of strategic linkages between operating companies, a number of directors and Wall Street analysts questioned his plans. But eventually Wetherell's persuasiveness—coupled with the rebounding performance of Lycos and other CMG investments—succeeded in overcoming these doubts. In 1998 and 1999, a growing appreciation of the company's strategy led to a spiraling market valuation. Exhibit 25-3 summarizes the evolution of CMGI's market capitalization between January 1994 and mid-December 1999.

By December 1999, CMGI (the company's new name reflected its changed focus as the "I" stood for "Internet" and "Innovation") had emerged with an organizational structure that was almost unique in American industry.[2] (Exhibit 25-4 summarizes CMGI's holdings.) The company consisted primarily of a number of operating units. Their origins were diverse: some of these had been acquired, while others were grown internally. Some of these units were publicly traded (e.g., NaviSite and Engage), while others remained privately held. It was anticipated that a number of these operating companies would ultimately go public, most likely beginning with Alta Vista, in which CMGI had acquired an 81% stake from Digital Equipment for stock worth $2.4 billion in August 1999. Others were likely to be merged into existing entities, and yet others to be sold to third parties.

At the same time as the operating businesses of CMGI were expanding, the @Ventures effort was rapidly developing. The second @Ventures fund, CMG @Ventures II, LLC (an "evergreen" fund), was established in October 1996. This fund enjoyed considerable success as well. In December 1998, an initial closing was held for @Ventures III, which ultimately raised committed capital of $472 million (including the @Ventures III Expansion fund). This effort, unlike earlier funds, raised the bulk of its capital from outside investors, with CMGI providing 20% of the capital. The funds to date had gen-

---

[2] One of the few other companies to have adopted a similar structure was Thermo Electron, which at one point in the mid-1990s had 23 publicly traded units in which it (or its majority-owned subsidiaries) had majority control. The company ultimately repurchased all but two of these units after experiencing large losses and disappointing stock returns. Among the reasons that observers gave for the company's poor performance were the inability of analysts and shareholders to distinguish between the business units, the absence of synergies between the units (which undertook activities ranging from building scientific instruments to running oil refineries to operating hair removal salons), and poor operating decisions (direct and indirect losses in the hair removal unit alone totaled over $100 million).

EXHIBIT 25-3

MARKET CAPITALIZATION OF CMGI, JANUARY 1984 THROUGH MID-DECEMBER 1999 (BILLIONS OF DOLLARS)

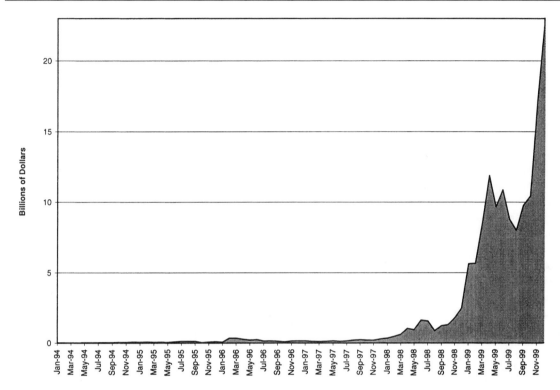

Source: Datastream.

erated an internal rate of return of approximately 3500% for CMGI. In December 1999, CMGI @Ventures was intending to launch a series of domestic and overseas funds, beginning with a $1 billion B2B (business-to-business) Internet fund, a generalist fourth fund, a technology fund, and a number of international funds. It was anticipated that CMGI would return to being the sole limited partner in its domestic funds but accept additional funds for its international funds.

The entities in CMGI's portfolio—whether directly controlled operating companies or @Ventures portfolio companies—can be divided into three categories:[3]

- The first class included "enablers": portals, access providers, and development companies. Portals such as Alta Vista and MyWay provided an initial point of contact for customers. Access providers included free access company 1stUp.com and "private label" Internet service provider NaviPath. Development companies included CMGI Solutions, which provided e-commerce and technical services to CMGI affiliates and external companies.

[3] This typology is based on Luke Fichthorn, *CMGI: Strong Operating Companies Drive Successful Venture Platform*, New York, Lazard Freres and Company Equity Research, January 2000.

EXHIBIT 25-4

ANALYSIS OF CMGI HOLDINGS (ALL DOLLAR FIGURES IN MILLIONS)

Public Holdings	Ticker	CMGI Fully Diluted Asset Value ($MM)
Akamai	AKAM	$62.2
Amazon.com	AMZN	8.5
Chemdex Corporation	CMDX	212.8
Critical Path	CPTH	73.8
Engage Technologies	ENGA	5,660.4
Hollywood Entertainment	HLYW	52.6
Lycos	LCOS	1,163.4
Marketing Services Group	MSGI	40.7
Mother Nature	MTHR	8.4
NaviSite	NAVI	2,009.5
Open Market	OMKT	6.5
Open Markets warrants @ $16.43	OMKT	2.9
Pacific Century CyberWorks	PCCLF	1,057.4
Premier Technologies	PTEK	0.1
Silknet	SILK	327.5
Silknet warrants @ $2.20	SILK	8.6
Tickets.com	TIXX	10.2
USWeb	USWB	4.1
Yahoo!	YHOO	474.1
Yahoo! options @ $1.30	YHOO	168.2
Total Public Holdings		$11,351.9

IPO Candidates Within 1 Year	Owning Entity	Estimated Valuation ($MM)	FD CMGI % Share	CMGI Fully Diluted Asset Value ($MM)
Furniture.com	V3	$70	0.7%	$1
Vicinity Corp	V1,2	100	6.4	6
MyFamily.com (Ancestry.com)	V3	70	1.0	1
Alta Vista/Raging Bull	C	3,480	64.8	2,255
NaviNet	C	450	80.0	360
1st up.com	C	150	80.0	120
CMGI Solutions	C	140	80.0	112
MyWay.com	C	350	80.0	280
		Total IPO Candidate Holdings		$3,135
		Other Holdings		$1,641
		Total CMGI Holdings		$16,127
		Cash		$881
		Total CMGI Assets		$17,008

Notes: The calculation is made as of the close of the second fiscal quarter of fiscal year 2000 (January 31, 2000). At the close of trading on this date, CMGI's market capitalization was approximately $27.7 billion.

Under "Owning Entity," "V1" stands for "@Ventures I, L.P.," "V2" for "@Ventures II, L.P.," "V3" for "@Ventures III, L.P.," and "C" for CMGI.

"FD" stands for "fully diluted."

Source: Compiled from analyst reports and corporate documents.

- The second category was advertising and marketing concerns. Reflecting CMG's historical roots, this had been an important aspect of the company's Internet effort since the founding of ADSmart in 1996 and Engage in the following year. These holdings had been enhanced by the agreements to acquire AdForce and Flycast Communications in 1999.

- The final class, content companies, included e-commerce concerns (such as Chemdex.com and PlanetOutdoors.com), on-line communities (e.g., eGroups and MyFamily.com), and developers of raw material (FindLaw). These tended to be @Ventures portfolio companies, in which the funds had minority stakes.

CMGI went to great lengths to encourage its portfolio companies to work together. As the volume of acquisitions had increased, the company had institutionalized the manner in which it handled newly acquired companies, under the leadership of David Andonian. By becoming involved with the acquisition process early and creating a team representing the various staff and line areas, the implementation group could ensure that the newly acquired company would fit smoothly into the CMGI group. An essential challenge was ensuring that the new company coordinated its activities with the rest of the CMGI family, while retaining its essential independence. After all, in many instances acquired companies ultimately sold public equity again as CMGI subsidiaries. Thus, the process was quite different from the traditional corporate acquisition, in which functions such as the financial group and sales force of the acquired company were frequently eliminated.[4]

CMGI employed a number of other ways to encourage portfolio companies to work together. Managers typically held equity not only in their portfolio companies, but also in the CMGI parent. CMGI held a weekly conference call for the heads of the operating companies, as well as another weekly call with the partners of the @Ventures funds. The company held a variety of annual and biannual meetings for individuals in various functions at the operating and portfolio companies, in order to encourage communication and partnerships. While the senior management encouraged CMGI-affiliated companies to work together, it did not compel companies to undertake transactions that they did not want to make or to accept below-market terms. Only by allowing the management of each company a significant degree of autonomy, Wetherell believed, could the best people be hired and retained by CMGI.

CMGI's historical operating performance and analysts' projections of their future results are presented in Exhibits 25-5 and 25-6.

REGULATORY AND ACCOUNTING CONSIDERATIONS

CMGI's structure, though well suited to its Internet-oriented businesses, posed some challenges. In particular, the fact that many of its operating companies were not fully owned (as well as the presence of @Venture's venture capital portfolio) led to a variety of securities, tax, and accounting issues. This section reviews the primary issues that the company's structure presented.

---

[4] This difference did create challenges when managers had language in their contracts that allowed for the immediate vesting of stock options ("acceleration") in the event of an acquisition. CMGI typically demanded that these terms be renegotiated before an acquisition was completed.

EXHIBIT 25-5

CMGI SELECTED HISTORICAL CONDENSED CONSOLIDATED FINANCIAL INFORMATION

	Fiscal Year Ended July 31,					Unaudited Three Months Ended October 31	
	1999	1998	1997	1996	1995	1999	1998
				(in thousands)			
Consolidated Statement of Operations Data							
Net revenues	$175,666	$ 81,916	$ 60,056	$ 17,735	$ 11,091	$123,731	$ 37,405
Cost of revenues	168,830	72,740	34,866	11,215	7,259	108,173	35,543
Research and development expenses	22,253	19,108	17,767	5,412	—	20,188	5,308
In-process research and development expenses	6,061	10,325	1,312	2,691	—		
Selling, general and administrative expenses	89,071	46,909	45,777	16,812	2,722	99,858	14,573
Amortization of intangible assets and stock-based compensation	16,110	3,093	1,254	—	—	170,039	2,109
Operating income (loss)	(126,659)	(70,259)	(40,920)	(18,395)	1,110	(274,527)	(20,128)
Interest income (expense), net	269	(870)	1,749	2,691	225	171	(509)
Gains on issuance of stock by subsidiaries and affiliates	130,729	46,285	—	19,575	—	46,368	44,506
Other gains, net	758,312	96,562	27,140	30,049	4,781	48,349	44,094
Other income (expense), net	(13,406)	(12,899)	(769)	(746)	(292)	21,492	(3,258)
Income tax benefit (expense)	(325,402)	(31,555)	(2,034)	(17,566)	(2,113)	40,735	(26,316)
Income (loss) from continuing operations	423,843	27,264	(14,834)	15,608	3,711	(117,412)	38,389
Discontinued operations, net of income tax	52,397	4,640	(7,193)	(1,286)	24,504	—	(131)
Net income (loss)	476,240	31,904	(22,027)	14,322	28,215	(117,412)	38,258
Preferred stock accretion	(1,662)					(4,935)	
Net income (loss) available to common stockholders	$474,578	$ 31,904	$(22,027)	$ 14,322	$ 28,215	$(122,347)	$ 38,258
Common stock outstanding at end of period	191,168	184,272	154,552	146,668	141,416	237,334	184,584

(Continued)

EXHIBIT 25-5   (*Continued*)

| | Fiscal Year Ended July 31, | | | | | Unaudited Three Months Ending October 31 | |
	1999	1998	1997	1996	1995	1999	1998
			(in thousands)				
Consolidated Balance Sheet Data							
Working capital	$1,381,005	$ 12,784	$ 38,554	$ 72,009	$47,729	$1,681,638	$ 36,295
Total assets	2,404,594	259,818	146,248	106,105	77,803	5,431,682	348,546
Long-term obligations	34,867	5,801	16,754	514	415	264,796	5,483
Redeemable preferred stock	411,283	—	—	—	—	413,511	—
Stockholders' equity	1,062,461	133,136	29,448	53,992	55,490	3,439,895	172,801
Capital expenditures	16,274	8,189	6,939	7,068	1,474	23,185	2,182

Notes: The sources of "gains on issuance of stock by subsidiaries and affiliates" are as follows: FY 1996—stock issuance by Lycos ($19.6 million), FY 1998—stock issuance by Lycos ($46.3 million); FY 1999—stock issuance by Engage ($81.1 million), GeoCities ($29.3 million) and Lycos ($20.3 million); Q1 FY 2000—stock issuance by NaviSite ($46.4 million).

The primary sources of "other gains" are: FY 1995—sale of America Online common stock ($4.8 million); FY 1996—sale of America Online common stock ($30.0 million); FY 1997—sale of NetCarta Corporation ($15.1 million) and Tele T Communications ($3.6 million), and dividend distribution of Lycos common stock ($15.1 million); FY 1998—sale of Lycos common stock ($97.1 million); FY 1999—sales of GeoCities ($661.1 million), Reel.com ($23.3 million), Sage Enterprises ($19.1 million), and Lycos common stock ($45.3 million); Q1FY2000—sale of Yahoo! common stock ($44.1 million).

Common stock outstanding is presented on a split-adjusted basis.

Source: Corporate documents.

EXHIBIT 25-6

PROJECTED CMGI OPERATING PERFORMANCE, FISCAL YEARS 1999–2001 (DOLLARS IN MILLIONS)

	Fiscal Year Ending July 31,		
	Actual	Estimated	
	FY 1999	FY 2000	FY 2001
Net revenues	$ 175.7	$ 739.7	$1,620.0
Operating expenses			
Cost of revenues	168.9	581.2	1,234.9
Research and development	28.6	155.2	136.4
Selling and marketing	45.7	509.5	540.4
General and administrative	59.2	160.4	144.3
Amortization of intangible assets	0.0	1,130.0	892.0
Total operating expenses	302.4	2,536.3	2,948.0
Operating loss	(126.7)	(1,796.6)	(1,328.0)

Source: Compiled from analyst reports.

Investment Company Act-Related Issues

The Investment Company Act of 1940 (1940 Act) has been characterized as "one of the most complex and extensive of all the federal securities statutes."[5] One of the four major securities acts enacted during the period of "New Deal" reforms initiated by President Franklin Roosevelt, it sought to regulate mutual funds and other instruments for pooled investments in securities. The act imposes detailed regulations governing almost every aspect of investment companies' operations, including reporting requirements, governance provisions, and demands for detailed recordkeeping.

Anticipating that investment companies might seek to avoid these requirements, the drafters of the act developed two central tests as to what constituted an investment company. A company would be regarded as an investment firm if it satisfied one of two tests:

- The first definition is as follows: any firm that "is or holds itself out as being engaged primarily, or proposes to engage primarily, in the business of investing, reinvesting or trading in securities."[6] This standard is a qualitative one, which is determined by a five-factor test administered by the U.S. Securities and Exchange Commission (SEC). The five criteria are the firm's investment history, its representations of its activities to the public, the activities of its officers and directors, the nature of its assets, and the sources of its net income.[7]

---

[5] David J. Gilberg, "Regulation of Financial Instruments under the Federal Securities and Commodities Law," *Vanderbilt Law Review* 39 (1986): 1599–1969 (quote on p. 1632). For a more general discussion of this act, see Louis Loss and Joel Seligman, *Fundamentals of Securities Regulation*, 3rd ed., Boston, Little, Brown, 1995.

[6] 15 United States Code @80a–3(a)(1)(A).

[7] For a detailed discussion of the origins of this test, see Edmund H. Kerr, "The Inadvertent Investment Company: Section 3(a)(3) of the Investment Company Act," *Stanford Law Review* 12 (1959): 29 *ff*.

- The second definition is a more objective one: any firm that "owns or proposes to acquire investment securities having a value exceeding 40 per centum of the issuer's total assets (exclusive of Government securities and cash items)."[8] Investment securities do not include U.S. government obligations, the company's own securities, and those issued by the firm's majority-owned subsidiaries. This test seeks to identify "inadvertent investment companies," operating companies that might have passed the first test but nonetheless might be considered investment companies. An alternative test allows firms to have up to 45% of their total assets consist of securities other than government securities, its own securities, or those of companies primarily controlled by it, as long as less than 45% of their net income is from these holdings.

Sensitive to the sweeping nature of these requirements, the drafters of the act (and its subsequent amendments) established a number of exceptions to these rules:

- One of these exceptions relates to private partnerships such as private equity groups. This exemption extends to funds whose securities are owned by less than 100 "accredited investors" (those with $200,000 in annual net income for the past two years and expected in the current year or $1 million in net worth) and intending to remain privately held. (This exemption is often called the "Rule of 99" in venture capital circles.) In 1996, this requirement was amended to allow these partnerships to accept funds from an unlimited number of "super qualified" investors (those with more than $5 million of investable assets).

- A second exception gives firms that inadvertently ran afoul of the 40% threshold regulations a one-year grace period ("safe harbor") to correct these problems. After addressing this issue, the firm has to avoid crossing this threshold for another three years.

- A third exception is for companies that successfully petition the SEC for a determination that they are not primarily engaged in "investing, reinvesting, owning, holding, or trading in securities or . . . through controlled companies conducting similar businesses."

The 1940 Act had proven to be a vexing requirement for a number of Internet-related companies. For instance, at the time of its IPO in 1996, Yahoo!'s securities holdings were greater than 40% of its assets. In February 1997, the company had undertaken a filing for an exemption with the SEC, arguing that it was clearly an operating company. In this filing, it also emphasized that it was unreasonable to compare the *market value* of its minority equity holdings to the *book value* of its other assets, since so many of its assets were intangible and did not show up on its balance sheet. Nonetheless, in July 1998, the SEC informed Yahoo! that it was not prepared to support its position, and the company was forced to largely liquidate its minority investment positions. Despite these steps, by September 1999, Yahoo! had again run afoul of the 40% threshold. In particular, the market capitalization of Yahoo! Japan (in which it held a 34% stake) reached $3.4 billion. This far exceeded the book value of Yahoo!'s total assets, which was $1.1 billion.[9,10]

---

[8] 15 U.S.C. @80a–3(a)(1)(C).

[9] The source of this information is "In the Matter of Yahoo! Inc.: Application for Order of Exemption Pursuant to Section 3(b)(2) of the Investment Company Act of 1940, As Amended," File No. 912-11976, U.S. Securities and Exchange Commission, 2000. Yahoo listed its equity investments on its balance sheet at book value.

[10] It might be thought that Yahoo! could have relied on the 45% exception delineated above, since it held a major stake in Yahoo! Japan. Because the other major shareholder in the company, Softbank, owned an even larger stake (51%), however, it could be questioned whether Yahoo! controlled the company.

Another example was Internet Capital Group (ICG). Prior to its May 1999 IPO, this organization had fewer than 100 shareholders and was exempt from the 1940 Act requirements. After the offering, it could no longer rely on this exception and was subject to scrutiny because over 96% of its assets (other than government securities) were minority positions in companies. In a July 1999 filing with the SEC, however, it argued that it qualified under the "45% exception" because 86% of its assets were in the form of companies that it controlled, even if it had a minority interest. In its filing with the SEC, it highlighted its role in the governance of these companies, its active encouragement of intercompany synergies, and other actions.[11] In August 1999, ICG was granted an exemption by the SEC.

Tax-Related Issues

The company's status also posed two issues related to taxes that traditional operating companies did not need to consider. These two issues related to the consolidation of tax losses and the treatment of acquisitions.

U.S. tax law allows companies that meet Internal Revenue Service (IRS) requirements for affiliated group status to file consolidated tax returns. The central requirement for this status is a minimum ownership level of 80%. This regulation informed the decision as to when to sell equity in CMGI's majority-owned subsidiaries. In particular, when possible, the company sought to retain at least 80% ownership of companies that were still unprofitable, since their losses might be used to offset other taxable gains by CMGI.

The second tax-related issue was a subtler one. Because of the rapidly changing Internet industry, CMGI's subsidiaries often needed to acquire companies: in an industry with major "first-mover advantages" and "network effects," the risks associated with waiting to duplicate a successful competitor's business model were often too high. Because of the 1940 Act considerations outlined above, CMGI did not want subsidiaries to issue substantial amounts of new stock, lest the parent's share fall below 50%. As a result, sometimes the parent acquired companies and then transferred the shares to a subsidiary.

The difficulty stemmed from Section 368(a)(2)(C) of the Internal Revenue Code. This provision allowed a parent corporation (P) that acquired another corporation (T) in exchange for shares in P to then transfer T into a subsidiary (S) of P, as long as P is in "control" of S. Under Section 368(c) of the code, "control" generally means ownership of 80% of voting power. (Thus, even if P did not own a full 80% of S on an economic basis, the transaction could qualify under 368(a)(2)(C) if P received a share of super-voting stock that gives it the necessary voting power.)

But if this definition was not satisfied, then there was a real danger that the original acquisition of T by P would be "recharacterized." In particular, S might be designated by the Internal Revenue Service to be the acquirer (since P's ownership was transitory). In this case, the T shareholders would have received a security other than that

---

[11] "Application Pursuant to Section 3(b)(2) of the Investment Company Act of 1940, As Amended, for an Order Declaring that Internet Capital Group is Primarily Engaged in Businesses Other than that of Investing, Reinvesting, Owning, Holding, or Trading in Securities," File No. 812-11202, U.S. Securities and Exchange Commission, 1999. ICG acknowledged that it did not pass the net income test, but argued that a test based on revenue rather than net income was more appropriate for the Internet industry. In its decision, the SEC indicated that an equity ownership of 25% would be the minimum it would consider when examining whether a company controlled a minority holding.

of the acquiring company, and the transaction might not qualify as tax-free transaction (more technically, a "B" reorganization under Section 368(a)(1) of the tax code). In the absence of tax-free status, the T shareholders would be immediately taxable on the P stock they received: the transaction would be treated as if they had received an equivalent amount in cash. Clearly, target companies would demand higher compensation levels, all else being equal, if they faced an immediate tax obligation, rather than being able to defer the taxes to some unspecified future date. This tax obligation would be a particular problem if P demanded that the T shareholders agree to a lock-up agreement. (High-technology acquisitions frequently included such terms, lest an immediate wave of selling after the transaction closed depress the acquirer's stock price.) In this case, T shareholders could face an immediate demand for cash with no means of achieving liquidity.

Accounting-Related Issues

The final set of issues related to the impact of the corporation's structure on its accounting statements. Most (but not all) high-technology companies listed their equity investments on their balance sheet at book value. As the subsidiaries' market valuations fluctuated, the parent companies did not realize any gains or losses on their income statement. (To cite one example, the carrying value of Yahoo!'s investment in Yahoo! Japan on its balance sheet in September 1999 was $9.6 million, even though its market capitalization was over $3 billion.)

In accordance with the Financial Accounting Standards Board's Generally Accepted Accounting Principles, CMGI adhered to this practice. An implication was that CMGI recorded gains on the sales of securities by its subsidiaries as capital gains. If a majority owned subsidiary sold shares in an operating company, this would lead to an increase in the book value of the shares that CMGI held. The increase in the book value would be recorded as income in the quarter that the transaction occurred.

An example may help illustrate this practice. When CMGI subsidiary Lycos sold 3,135,000 new shares in its April 1996 IPO, the search engine company received net proceeds of approximately $46 million. (Approximately 10.5 million shares were outstanding before the offering, and the previous paid-in capital was a little over $1 million.) Thus, the IPO led to an increase in the paid-in capital per share of $3.36: the difference between the new paid-in capital ($47 million/13.6 million shares) and the old ($1 million/10.5 million shares). Since CMGI owned about 8.23 million shares before the offering, it recorded net income of $19.6 million from the transaction (the total capital gains of $27.6 million less an $8.0 million charge for deferred income taxes). The company did not, however, record as capital gains the changes in Lycos' market value, including the substantial jump in value on the first trading day. Nor did CMGI pay taxes on any capital gains until the shares were sold.

YESMAIL.COM[12]

The company known as yesmail.com had been known as WebPromote at the time that Ken Wruk founded it in 1995. Wruk, who had previously built an early portal, sought to provide a variety of promotional activities, including banner advertising, contests, and

---

[12] This section is based on Luc Wathieu, "yesmail.com," Case no. 9-500-092, Boston, Harvard Business School, 2000, yesmail.com's filings with the SEC, selected analyst reports, and interviews with corporate officials.

the development of sponsored content. Like his earlier portal company (which was soon overtaken by Yahoo! and other better funded services), Wruk eschewed external financing for WebPromote. As a result, by the end of 1998, the company had total stockholders' equity of negative $2.1 million. The bulk of the financing had come from accounts payable ($1.4 million) and short-term borrowing ($1.1 million).

At the beginning of 1999, the company was renamed and a new management team brought in. David Tolmie, the new CEO, had been most recently a CEO-in-residence at Platinum Venture Partners, the corporate venture group associated with Platinum Technologies. (Platinum Technologies had been the eleventh-largest software venture prior to its sale to Computer Associates in March 1999. Platinum's CEO, Andrew "Flip" Filipowski, subsequently went on to form Divine InterVentures, an incubator that filed to go public in December 1999.) Prior to joining Platinum, Tolmie, a graduate of the University of Virginia and Harvard Business School, had held positions at Bally Total Fitness, Foundation Properties, and McKinsey & Co. Tolmie had rapidly recruited a seasoned management team, including chief financial officer David Menzel (a veteran of Arthur Andersen and former chief financial officer of Campbell Software) and vice president of marketing Anthony Priore (formerly vice president of marketing at on-line grocer Peapod.com and a vice president at two advertising agencies).

The new management team realized that they needed to focus the company's broad-based product lines. Rather than simultaneously developing a wide variety of Internet marketing services, they chose to focus on one particularly exciting opportunity. Permission-based e-mail was an appealing alternative to blanketing customers with unwanted e-mail solicitations, also known as "spamming." Yesmail proposed to solicit information from consumers about what topics (if any) they were interested in obtaining e-mail advertisements about. In choosing this strategy, yesmail was following a broader trend in American marketing, which was increasingly emphasizing "direct response" marketing (which asked the customer to take a particular action) at the expense of brand advertising. Survey data suggested that customers were far more likely to answer e-mails on topics they had expressed interest (a 5% to 15% response rate) than unsolicited messages (these messages had a response rate of only 1% to 2%). Furthermore, the response time was much quicker than direct mail (a median of three days versus four weeks), and the cost per message was about 80% lower. If he could marshal the necessary resources, Tolmie envisioned, yesmail could become the leader in this exciting space.

In implementing this vision, however, the management faced a dilemma: in order to attract advertisers, they needed to have a large database of consumers. But to attract and retain members, the company needed to offer them a steady flow of attractive opportunities. To address this problem, yesmail settled on a strategy of partnering with Internet content sites. Over the course of 1999, the company signed partnerships with companies such as Mapquest, the *New York Times*, Peapod.com, XOOM.com, and over two dozen others. Yesmail's database of consumers increased from 350,000 to over 5 million over the year as a result (see Exhibit 25-7). The typical contract called for the partner to offer yesmail sign-up at the time that a user registered at a Web site. (Many sites offered premium content to users who were willing to provide personal information by registering.) In return, the network partners would receive roughly half the revenues that yesmail generated from these customers. Such an arrangement would allow the Web site to generate revenue from many more users than they might have otherwise.

Meanwhile, during 1999 yesmail built up a sales force of approximately 45 people to call on potential advertisers. Among the clients recruited were e-commerce compa-

EXHIBIT 25-7

YESMAIL NETWORK GROWTH (AVERAGE DAILY GROWTH IN SUBSCRIBERS)

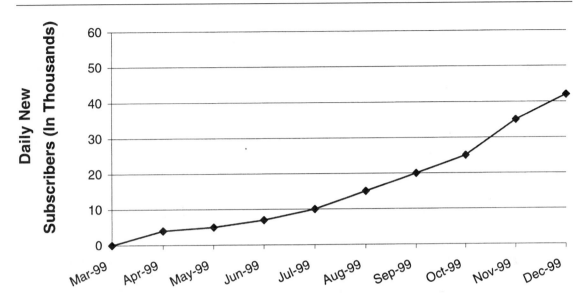

Source: Corporate document.

nies (including Amazon.com, Buy.com, and MotherNature.com), traditional businesses (such as AT&T and Omaha Steaks), and hybrid "bricks-and-clicks" businesses (e.g., Fingerhut). Advertising agencies were another important population that the company's sales force targeted. Yesmail charged customers a flat rate of $250 per thousand messages sent. In addition, the company developed an automated on-line tracking system (eTrack), which enabled clients to see the response rate to its messages from yesmail's clients. It also introduced a variety of automated tools that allowed companies to better analyze response rates of various groups and to enhance the targeting of future campaigns.

A third strategic initiative was to introduce products that gave yesmail's customers more control over their e-mail in-boxes. These included a service that allowed users to manage the on-line newsletters and lists to which they subscribed and an e-mail reminder service that alerted users to important dates (e.g., birthdays and anniversaries). Through these services, yesmail hoped to build a closer relationship with its customer base. These services also presented a variety of revenue-generating opportunities: a reminder about an anniversary, for instance, could include a link to an on-line floral delivery service.

The new management team had followed as aggressive a strategy in raising external financing as they had in the operations of the business. In order to fund their initial steps, Tolmie arranged for a funding commitment from Platinum Venture Partners. Because Platinum's fund was nearly fully invested, this required raising additional capital from the fund's investors. As a result, while the company received bridge loans from Platinum and angel investors in January and March 1999, the venture round did not close until May 1999. In this financing, the company sold 5.15 million shares of Series

A convertible stock at the approximate price of $1.75 per share.[13] At the same time, the company sold 2.39 million shares of common stock to the managers of yesmail at $1.60 per share. (The slight discount reflected the fact that these shares did not enjoy the liquidation privileges and other rights of the preferred stock). Yesmail's four founders held the bulk of the remaining shares.

Almost immediately upon the closing of this financing, yesmail began negotiations to complete an IPO. Tolmie and Menzel believed that the financial resources and credibility associated with being a public company would be essential if yesmail was to obtain a dominant position in this emerging market. Earlier Tolmie had met the Internet analyst from Deutsche Bank Alex Brown, who had expressed an interest in underwriting an IPO. On June 4, 1999, the company filed to go public. It proposed to sell 3.4 million shares, with a filing range between $10 and $12 per share. On September 23, 1999, it completed this offering, selling a total of 3.4 million shares at a price of $11 per share. In the ensuing months, the stock price varied between $10 and $34.

While the company continued to make good progress after the IPO, the threat of increased competition intensified. Not only were Internet portals such as Excite and Yahoo! increasingly offering direct e-mail services to their registered users, but banner advertising specialists such as DoubleClick, 24/7 Media, and Flycast Communications were exploring entering this market. Other potential competitive threats included incentive-based services (such as MyPoints and Netcentives) and customer management services (including Digital Impact and Post Communications).

Yesmail's historical operating performance and analysts' projections of their future results are presented in Exhibits 25-8 and 25-9.

THE PROPOSED TRANSACTION

The origins of the proposed merger between yesmail and CMGI were in early November, when Tolmie and Menzel met with the representatives of a large Internet advertising company. The conversations initially focused on the possibility that the company would resell yesmail's services as part of its bundle of services. As the conversations continued over the next few weeks, however, the possibility that yesmail would be acquired by this company emerged. While yesmail's management team had not foreseen selling the company so soon after going public, they saw several strategic benefits from a combination with a larger and better-capitalized entity. These included the synergies between yesmail's products and more traditional Internet marketing tools (e.g., banner advertisements), the ability for yesmail to more rapidly introduce new products, and the reduction of the danger that a new entrant would displace yesmail from its position of leadership in this emerging industry. In late November, yesmail retained Deutsche Bank Securities to help it assess this proposal. Yesmail also alerted its law firm, California-based Wilson, Sonsini, Goodrich & Rosati.

In the first week of December, CMGI emerged as an alternative acquirer. Having been alerted that the company was "in play" and attracted by several features of yesmail's business, CMGI began intensely studying the possibility of acquiring yesmail. Over the course of the first two weeks of December, CMGI and its advisors (the investment bank Goldman Sachs and the law firm Hale & Dorr) held several meetings with the management team and conducted intensive due diligence on the company.

---

[13] Here, as elsewhere, all per share amounts are reported on a split-adjusted basis. (All transactions through mid-January 2000 are used in the calculations.)

EXHIBIT 25-8

YESMAIL SELECTED HISTORICAL CONDENSED CONSOLIDATED FINANCIAL INFORMATION

	Inception (April 7, 1995) Through December 31, 1995	Year Ended December 31,			Nine Months Ended September 30	
		1996	1997	1998	1998	1999
Statement of Operations	(in thousands)					
Revenues	$ 13	$ 935	$ 2,468	$ 4,583	$ 3,172	$ 7,467
Cost of revenues	—	293	1,090	2,703	1,925	5,302
Gross profit	13	642	1,378	1,880	1,247	2,165
Operating expenses:						
Sales and marketing expenses	—	292	960	1,751	1,019	6,586
General and administrative expenses	26	237	466	929	578	2,830
Research and development costs	—	198	357	601	399	2,360
Stock based compensation	—	—	—	—	—	695
Total operating expenses	26	727	1,783	3,281	1,996	12,471
Loss from operations	(13)	(85)	(405)	(1,401)	(749)	(10,306)
Interest and other expense	—	(4)	(18)	(295)	(26)	(123)
Minority interest	—	9	9	(10)	(20)	(34)
Net loss	$ (13)	$ (80)	$ (414)	$(1,706)	$ (795)	$(10,463)
Common stock (and equivalent) outstanding at the end of period	4,630	8,333	8,333	8,333	8,333	20,324

	December 31,				September 30,	
	1995	1996	1997	1998	1998	1999
	(in thousands)					
Consolidated balance sheet data:						
Cash and cash equivalents	$10	$ 9	$ 2	$ 26	$ 86	$34,780
Working capital (deficit)	4	(52)	(448)	(2,262)	(1,160)	29,412
Total assets	27	200	284	643	550	39,654
Capital lease obligations, less current portion	0	12	18	153	109	689
Stockholders' equity (deficit)	(13)	(38)	(347)	(2,053)	(1,107)	30,767
Capital expenditure in fiscal year	NA	45	70	102	42	1,448

Notes:

NA = not available.

Common stock outstanding is presented on a split-adjusted basis.

Source: Corporate documents.

EXHIBIT 25-9

ANALYST PROJECTIONS OF YESMAIL FINANCIAL PERFORMANCE, 1999–2001

	Fiscal Year Ending December 31,		
	1999	2000	2001
Income Statement Data:			
Revenue	$13,133	$40,320	$80,360
Gross profit	3,885	15,155	39,526
Operating income	(15,257)	(18,702)	(4,505)
Margins:			
Gross profit	29.6%	37.6%	49.2%
Operating income	(116.2)	(46.4)	(5.6)
Operating Statistics:			
Messages sent (millions)	54.7	236.3	565.6
Cost per thousand impressions	$193	$159	$123

Source: Compiled from analyst reports.

CMGI found yesmail to have several attractive aspects. The company was in a high-growth area and was rapidly acquiring new customers. The management team had considerable strength and depth. An additional consideration was the impact on CMGI's compliance with the 1940 Act. Because all of yesmail would be acquired, this would help ensure that the holdings that could potentially be regarded as investment securities by the SEC would remain well under 40%.[14] Most importantly, it would complement the company's existing suite of Internet marketing products and allow it to offer a complete suite of products. There appeared to be numerous synergies between yesmail and CMGI's other business units as well.

At the same time, there were reasons for concern as well. Most stemmed from the target company's relatively recent emphasis on this permission e-mail arena. As a result, yesmail had not developed a strong brand to date. As additional companies entered this market, it might also be possible that the effectiveness of e-mail marketing would deteriorate: customers might cease to pay attention to e-mail advertisements, even those that they solicited. CMGI also had some reservations about the scalability of yesmail's technology. At the same time, this was not a highly technology-driven business model.

The negotiations came to a head in the second week of December. On December

[14] The rising valuations of CMGI's investment securities, largely due to its holdings in Lycos, Yahoo! (received when Yahoo! acquired Geocities), and other companies in its @Ventures portfolio had created a substantial imbalance: for instance, in January 1999, the company owned $1.6 billion of minority equity holdings in publicly traded companies. Almost two-thirds of these holdings were in companies where it held under a 20% stake. The company's noninvestment assets at the beginning of January 1999 were worth only $120 million. The company was able to sharply reduce its ratio of its investment securities to total assets within the one-year "safe harbor" allowed by SEC (which expired in October 1999) through both the sale of some of its minority holdings and the acquisition of Alta Vista. As a result of this experience, however, CMGI was keenly aware of the importance of remaining in compliance with the 1940 Act.

9, the initial potential acquirer had made an offer to purchase yesmail. On December 10, CMGI had made a similar verbal offer, conditional on the satisfactory completion of due diligence. On the same day, yesmail's board had met to consider the two offers. Since both parties were insisting on a lock-up period during which they would be the sole party with whom yesmail would negotiate, it was essential to choose one offer or another. After extensive discussions, the board decided to pursue conversations with CMGI. Among the crucial considerations were the synergies between yesmail and CMGI's affiliates, the scale of the CMGI marketing holdings, and the autonomy that yesmail would enjoy as a CMGI operating company. This latter consideration, the management team felt, would limit the danger that yesmail would experience attrition of its staff after the merger and allow the company to retain its distinctive approach. As part of this decision, they agreed not to talk to any other potential acquirers until Christmas. The next few days saw intensive negotiations about the structure of the merger agreement.

A major focus of the negotiations was on the valuation of the company. As part of the negotiations, both CMGI and yesmail negotiators reviewed public market valuation levels, comparable transactions, and yesmail's financial projects. (The valuation analysis prepared for yesmail by Deutsche Bank is reproduced in Exhibit 25-10.) The offer from CMGI proposed that each outstanding share of yesmail stock would be converted into one-quarter of a share of CMGI stock. At the time of the negotiation, CMGI common stock was trading at approximately $100, while yesmail stock was trading at $21. This implied a purchase price of about $25 per share, though the exact price would change until the deal was finalized. While both companies' securities had been highly volatile, this offer represented an 11% premium over the ratio of the two companies' securities prices over the last month. Options to purchase yesmail common stock would convert into similar rights to purchase CMGI securities.

Much of the proposed merger agreement consisted of the standard representations and warranties. For instance, the prospective agreement prohibited yesmail from undertaking any asset sale, dividend, stock repurchase, or similar transaction without CMGI's permission. The agreement similarly called upon both parties to use their best efforts to consummate the merger. At the same time, several items that were up for discussion were more controversial. The first of these was the termination fee. CMGI was asking that yesmail pay a $20 million termination fee if the merger failed for a number of reasons. These included the failure of the yesmail board to approve the transaction in a timely manner (or if it subsequently sided with another potential acquirer), the failure to call a special meeting to approve the transaction, or the breach of any of the covenants in the agreement. In addition, CMGI was requesting a $10 million fee if the transaction was rejected by the yesmail shareholders at the special meeting. This would only be payable, however, if an alternative acquisition proposal had emerged prior to the shareholders' meeting. If yesmail was acquired by another party in the 12 months after the termination of the CMGI agreement, yesmail would owe another $10 million. In addition, CMGI requested issue of an option to purchase up to 19.9% of the company for $25 per share if the transaction was unsuccessful.

A second area of discussion was the lock-up agreement that CMGI requested. In particular, it asked that employees and managers agree to sell no more than one-sixth of their shares in the six-month period that followed the closing of the transaction. The purchase of put options on CMGI stock, "selling short" CMGI stock, and entering into swap transactions were similarly prohibited. After the expiration of this period, the yesmail executives and employees would be limited to selling no more than one-tenth their original holdings of CMGI stock in any given day. Major shareholders were asked to execute an agreement that limited their daily sales of CMGI stock in the six months after the closing of the transaction to one-tenth of their total holdings.

EXHIBIT 25-10

MULTIPLE ANALYSIS PREPARED BY DEUTSCHE BANK

Analysis of Selected Publicly Traded Companies

Deutsche Bank compared certain financial information and commonly used valuation measurements for yesmail to corresponding information and measurements for a group of 11 publicly traded Internet advertising companies (Digital Impact, DoubleClick, Exactis, FreeShop.com, Lifeminders.com, MessageMedia, MyPoints.com, Netcentives, NetCreations, 24/7 Media, and Webstakes.com, which we refer to as the selected companies). Such financial information and valuation measurements included, among other things, (1) common equity market valuation; (2) operating performance; (3) ratios of enterprise value, defined as common equity market value as adjusted for debt and cash, to revenues; and (4) ratios of enterprise value to gross profit. To calculate the trading multiples for yesmail and the selected companies, Deutsche Bank used publicly available information concerning historical and projected financial performance, including published historical financial information as well as revenue and earnings estimates reported by research analysts who cover the selected companies.

The following table summarizes the multiples of enterprise value to revenues and gross profit for yesmail (the enterprise value of yesmail being derived from the exchange ratio and the market value of CMGI common stock on December 14, 1999) and the selected companies for the indicated periods.

	Yesmail	Selected Companies		
		Mean	Median	Range
Enterprise Value to Revenues				
Trailing 12 months	59.2×	79.5×	56.8×	28.3× to 156.6×
Calendar year 1999	43.8×	40.3×	35.9×	18.3× to 68.3×
Calendar year 2000	17.2×	19.9×	21.0×	6.8× to 30.5×
Enterprise Value to Gross Profit				
Calendar year 1999	154.9×	71.1×	71.1×	70.4× to 71.7×
Calendar year 2000	57.9×	33.2×	33.2×	31.4× to 35.1×

None of the companies utilized as a comparison is identical to yesmail. Accordingly, Deutsche Bank believes the analysis of publicly traded comparable companies is not simply mathematical. Rather, it involves complex considerations and qualitative judgments, reflected in Deutsche Bank's opinion, concerning differences in financial and operating characteristics of the comparable companies and other factors that could affect the public trading value of the comparable companies.

Analysis of Selected Precedent Transactions

Deutsche Bank reviewed the financial terms, to the extent publicly available, of 18 proposed, pending, or completed merger and acquisition transactions since January 15, 1998 involving companies in the Internet industry. We refer to these transactions as the selected transactions. Deutsche Bank calculated various financial multiples and premiums over market value based on certain publicly available information for each of the selected transactions and compared them to corresponding financial multiples and premiums over market value for the merger, based on the exchange ratio and the per share market price of CMGI common stock on December 14, 1999. The transactions reviewed were:

- The acquisition of USWeb/CKS by Whittman-Hart, announced December 13, 1999
- The acquisition of Opt-In Email.com by DoubleClick, Inc. announced December 1, 1999
- The acquisition of Flycast Communications Corporation by CMGI, Inc., announced September 30, 1999
- The acquisition of AdKnowledge by Engage Technologies, announced September 24, 1999
- The acquisition of AdForce, Inc., by CMGI, announced September 20, 1999
- The acquisition of ConsumerNet by 24/7 Media Inc., announced August 4, 1999

(Continued)

EXHIBIT 25-10   (Continued)

- The acquisition of NetGravity by DoubleClick Inc., announced July 13, 1999
- The acquisition of DotOne Corp. by Critical Path Inc., announced June 14, 1999
- The acquisition of Abacus Direct Corp. by DoubleClick Inc., announced June 14, 1999
- The acquisition of Revnet Systems by MessageMedia, Inc., announced June 9, 1999
- The acquisition of Excite, Inc., by At Home Corporation, announced January 19, 1999
- The acquisition of Netscape Communications Corporation by America Online, Inc., announced November 24, 1998
- The acquisition of LinkExchange by Microsoft Corporation, announced November 5, 1998
- The acquisition of Relevant Knowledge by Media Metrix, announced November 5, 1998
- The acquisition of Yoyodyne entertainment by Yahoo! Inc., announced October 12, 1998
- The acquisition of CKS Group by USWeb Corporation, announced September 2, 1998
- The acquisition of Tripod, Inc. by Lycos, Inc., announced February 3, 1998
- The acquisition of MatchLogic, Inc. by Excite, Inc., announced January 15, 1998

The following table summarizes the calculations by Deutsche Bank of the multiples of enterprise value to revenues for the merger (the enterprise value of yesmail being derived from the exchange ratio and the market value of CMGI common stock on December 14, 1999) and the selected transactions.

	Yesmail	Selected Companies		
		Mean	Median	Range
Enterprise Value to Revenues				
Trailing 12 months	59.2×	26.4×	20.8×	1.9× to 63.7×
1 year forward	43.8× (CY 1999)	15.9×	14.8×	1.8× to 30.1×
2 year forward	17.2× (CY 2000)	9.8×	8.6×	1.4× to 23.3×

All multiples for the selected transactions were based on public information available at the time of announcement of such transaction, without taking into account differing market and other conditions during the two-year period during which selected transactions occurred.

Source: Corporate documents.

As Wetherell gazed out of the conference room's window, he contemplated the longer-run issues at stake. Clearly, yesmail could do much to complement CMGI's existing family of marketing products. With its emphasis on building a network of strategic partnerships, yesmail could work with a wide variety of members of the CMGI family. But the continued addition of new companies did pose certain challenges. Beyond the short-run challenges of integrating these new companies into the CMGI family, Wetherell wondered about the challenges associated with increasing the organization's complexity. To what extent would the continued growth of the number of operating companies pose management challenges? At the same time, the CMGI organization had proved to be remarkably adaptable in the past to changing developments in the Internet industry, adjusting both its organizational structure and its business lines to accommodate the industry's changing dynamics. There was no reason to think that creativity would cease to characterize the organization anytime soon.

26

CDC Capital Partners

Early in January 2001, Alan Gillespie, CEO of CDC Capital Partners, looked up from the speech he was preparing for the company's biannual corporate gathering. In a week, one-third of CDC's employees from all over the world would gather at Ashdown Park, near Gatwick Airport, to hear him describe his vision for the next year. Having been in his position only 13 months, he had not even met many of these people. He knew he had to enlist their support and enthusiasm because CDC was facing the biggest challenge in its existence.

Sometime early in the coming decade, a majority of CDC, which had been founded 52 years before to invest in emerging markets' private sectors on behalf of the United Kingdom's aid program, would be sold to private investors. Instead of its historic role of issuing debt, it would become a venture capitalist, taking equity stakes in the enterprises it funded. The government would retain minority ownership and a "golden share" giving it special powers. This government legacy did not leave CDC entirely free to seek opportunities to generate the best returns. It retained a mandate that 100% of its investment go to low- to middle-income countries, with 70% in "poor" countries (annual income per capita of $1,800 or less) and 50% of that in sub-Saharan Africa and southern Asia (see Exhibit 26-1 for countries in which CDC operated).

As he left the handsome cream-colored building with its neocolonial façade, Gillespie encountered Peter Harlock, chief operations officer, and Paul Jobson, chief investment officer, and asked them the question top on his mind: "CDC is three years into the transition to private equity. What do you think?"

Harlock replied, "I guess it's deal-flow that keeps me up at night. But when I stop worrying about that, a host of other questions takes its place—like how to generate returns within our sphere, how to structure incentives for our staff, and how to retool their skill sets so they can go from writing loans to doing deals. It's not an easy change."

"We certainly face a number of operational challenges," Jobson agreed. "I'm convinced, though, that private equity is the best way to help poor countries develop, that it's so much more effective to be involved with a project as an owner than as a lender. And that's the way to generate returns. But my biggest concern is how to get the

Ann Leamon, Manager of the Center for Case Development, prepared this case under the supervision of Professors G. Felda Hardymon and Josh Lerner as the basis for class discussion rather than to illustrate either effective or ineffective handling of an administrative situation.

EXHIBIT 26-1

CDC'S OFFICES, 1999

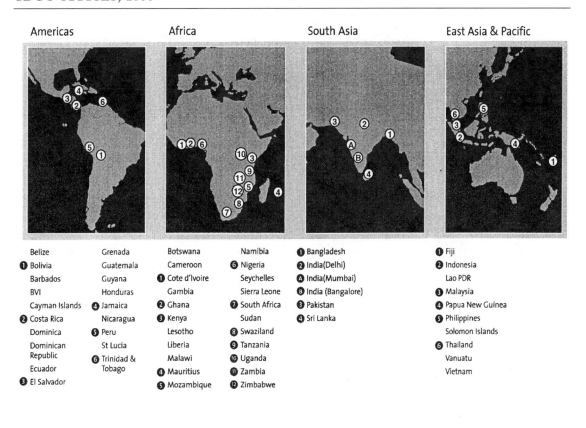

| Americas | Africa | South Asia | East Asia & Pacific |

Americas

Belize	Grenada	
❶ Bolivia	Guatemala	
Barbados	Guyana	
BVI	Honduras	
Cayman Islands	❹ Jamaica	
❷ Costa Rica	Nicaragua	
Dominica	❺ Peru	
Dominican Republic	St Lucia	
Ecuador	❻ Trinidad & Tobago	
❸ El Salvador		

Africa

Botswana	Namibia
Cameroon	❻ Nigeria
❶ Cote d'Ivoire	Seychelles
Gambia	Sierra Leone
❷ Ghana	❼ South Africa
❸ Kenya	Sudan
Lesotho	❽ Swaziland
Liberia	❾ Tanzania
Malawi	❿ Uganda
❹ Mauritius	⓫ Zambia
❺ Mozambique	⓬ Zimbabwe

South Asia

❶ Bangladesh
❷ India(Delhi)
Ⓐ India(Mumbai)
Ⓑ India (Bangalore)
❸ Pakistan
❹ Sri Lanka

East Asia & Pacific

❶ Fiji
❷ Indonesia
Lao PDR
❸ Malaysia
❹ Papua New Guinea
❺ Philippines
Solomon Islands
❻ Thailand
Vanuatu
Vietnam

● CDC office

Note: We will be opening offices in Florida, Virginia, Singapore, and Beijing during 2000.

Source: Company information.

big private money—from whom, for what, and how we should be organized to be most attractive. "

Gillespie nodded. "Those are big issues. I'm really concerned about recruiting—how to get the best and brightest people, how to keep our current staff. And, of course, how to get people to invest in us. To succeed in the private world, we have to be the best, and I need to galvanize our staff next week to get there."

PRIVATE EQUITY IN EMERGING MARKETS

Although private equity had existed in the United States since the early 1900s, this method of financing become popular in emerging markets only much later in that century. It started very slowly in 1978, and its primary proponents were not private players but development finance institutions (DFIs) with some sort of government links, especially CDC and the World Bank's for-profit financing arm, the International Finance Corporation (IFC). By 1988, these two players had committed a total of $50 million to private equity-type investments.[1] Both had been far more active than this amount implied, but much of their investment took the form of debt.

The small amount of private equity investment was due in part to a lack of investment options, as grants and loans were a more common form of financial aid for emerging markets. The other impediment to a real venture capital market was the widespread lack of financial markets in these nations. In the early 1990s, however, both investor attitudes and market realities began to change. Emerging markets came to the attention of private investors at the same time that private equity investing became accepted by institutional investors. In addition, emerging markets became more attractive places to invest: their economies became more capitalist; state-owned enterprises were privatized; stock exchanges were established; and trade increased.[2] The shift was dramatic; in 1999, almost half of the major international institutional investors viewed emerging markets as credible avenues for alternative investments, up from practically none in 1992.[3]

During this time, other DFIs joined CDC and IFC, bringing the amount of money invested to $13.8 billion by 1998 (see Exhibit 26-2). These included similar quasi- or completely governmental groups such as the U.S. Agency for International Development (USAID) and the European Bank for Reconstruction and Development (EBRD). As such, they were motivated by the belief that sustainable economic development in poor countries was based fundamentally on the availability of private risk capital, which needed to be encouraged by the provision of private equity. These groups all insisted that their investees maintain ethical and environmental standards, but differed in their financial objectives. Some sought to earn a market rate of return, while others would accept zero or a submarket rate on projects with a considerable social benefit.[4]

In some ways, equity investing in developing countries had an "Alice in Wonderland" quality. Because of the activities of granting bodies, large sums of money were often very cheap, if not free. Loans sometimes acted like equity; if a country defaulted on its debts or was part of a debt forgiveness program, the money might never be repaid. "In the end," said CDC's Harlock, "our loans tend to carry all the downside of equity and all the upside of debt." Small sums, usually extended by smaller institutions that were less likely to forgive the loan, were perceived as being expensive.

In other ways, however, private equity functioned the same way regardless of the country's stage of development. Assets were hard to value and the success of a company was extremely uncertain. Deal-doers found deals, took equity stakes, and, when the timing was right, exited with hoped-for returns. During the 1990s, the amount of equity devoted to early-stage deals in emerging countries rose from 2% of total foreign investment in 1992 to 38% in 1998.[5]

Equity returns in emerging markets, whether of public or private securities, were extremely variable for a number of reasons, including currency fluctuations, political in-

---

[1] James C. Brenner, "Direct Equity Investment Funds: Public-Private Partnership Experience," Paper prepared for the Forum for International Financial Institution Investment Fund Specialists, February 8–9, 1999, p. 8.

[2] Gonzalo Pancanins and Josh Lerner, "A Note on Private Equity in Developing Countries," Chapter 27 in this volume.

[3] Ibid.

[4] Brenner, "Direct Equity Investment Funds," p. 9.

[5] Pancanins and Lerner, "A note."

EXHIBIT 26-2

TOTAL CAPITAL COMMITMENTS IN DFI-LINKED FUNDS

Year	$ Million
1988	$ 8
1989	51
1990	397
1991	211
1992	370
1993	1,314
1994	2,958
1995	2,520
1996	1,599
1997	2,870
1998	1,356

Source: Brenner, p. 10.

---

stability, lack of basic services, corruption of local officials, inadequate legal systems, weak accounting standards, and, sometimes, competition from subsidized state-run enterprises.[6] Five-year returns for the IFC public equity funds ranged from 198% for Trinidad & Tobago to -87% for Thailand.[7] During the 1990s, MSCI's Emerging Markets Index did exceed the S&P 500 or MSCI's European/Middle East Index on average, but this performance was due to two stellar years out of eleven. In four of those years, the emerging markets index lost money, compared to three years for the European index and two for the S&P. During the latter half of the 1990s, the S&P 500 substantially outperformed emerging market indices (see Exhibit 26-3).

[6] Brenner, "Direct Equity Investment Funds," p. 34.

[7] www.trustnet.com/general/indices accessed January 17, 2001.

EXHIBIT 26-3

EMERGING MARKETS INDICES (IN £, AS OF APRIL 2001)

Index	1 Year	3 Years	5 Years
IFC Latin America	−14%	−7%	+15%
IFC Composite Global Investible	−33%	−25%	−23%
IFC Emerging Markets Weekly	−30%	−13%	−30%
MSCI Emerging Markets Global	−30%	−11%	−28%
S&P 500	−18%	+15%	+80%

Source: www.trustnet.com/general/indices (accessed on April 14, 2001) and Datastream.

Indeed, exiting investments was very tricky in emerging markets. Frequently, they lacked well-developed stock markets that would enable initial public offerings (IPOs), an important exit method. An alternative method involved the sale of the investor's share to members of a strategic alliance or to management. This too could depress returns, since the pool of purchasers was small, often had limited means, and was aware of the venture capitalists' need to exit the project.

Players in the Emerging Markets' Private Equity World

CDC's competitors varied depending on the health of emerging markets. During good times, most major institutional investors would have some degree of representation in emerging markets. The 1990s had seen an explosion in the amount of money and the number of funds in emerging markets. By the end of 2000, the top 10 emerging markets mutual funds had almost $11 billion under management, with average allocations of 1% in North America, 8% in Europe, 43% in the Pacific excluding Japan, 26% in Latin America, and 13% in "Other Regions."[8] Unconstrained by government mandates, they sought out opportunities for the best return.

On a more constant basis, however, public funders such as the United Nations, the World Bank, its IFC subsidiary, the Overseas Private Investment Corporation (OPIC), USAID, EBRD, and the Inter-American Investment Corporation (IIC), along with CDC, had the most significant presence in the world's poor countries. The IFC had the most in common with CDC. Titularly private and for-profit, it retained strong links to the World Bank. With $1.2 billion under management as of mid-2000 and a staff of 1,000, it focused on private sector investment and strongly encouraged the establishment of local securities markets. It operated a large number of special funds targeted at specific countries, rather than sectors, and it was beginning to participate in the management of its companies more actively to improve returns.[9]

The biggest government-sponsored funds, such as OPIC and USAID, operated within a severely constricted sphere. Their emphasis on the spin-off effects of investment and on socially responsible projects required them to focus on smaller projects or those that were unlikely to receive funding elsewhere. They also were prohibited from investing in certain sectors, including those that might have adverse effects on the environment or present direct competitive threats to U.S. industry (such as textiles, electronics, software, and motor vehicles). Nonetheless, these funds had managed to invest a significant amount of money in emerging markets (see Exhibit 26-4). All these equity funds required that their investees follow sound environmental and social practices, noting business reasons for compliance. The IFC, for one, maintained that the ability to raise external financing would depend on meeting the highest environmental standards, while companies that exploited workers could be subjected to consumer boycotts and reduced brand loyalty.[10]

Unlike many of the others in this group, which functioned primarily as passive investors, CDC gave an unusual amount of support to its investees.[11] It was known for investing in areas where it had a strong working knowledge of the local market, which proved to be an advantage. It also invested in areas that other private equity firms

---

[8] Morningstar, November 2000.

[9] Brenner, "Direct Equity Investment Funds," p. 37.

[10] Ibid., p. 31.

[11] Ibid., p. 35.

EXHIBIT 26-4A

PARTICIPANTS IN PRIVATE EQUITY FUNDS FOR EMERGING MARKETS (TOTAL OF $13.8 BILLION)

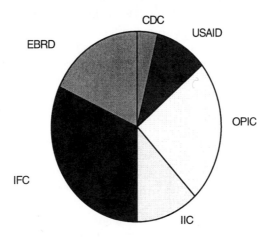

U.S. Agency for International Development (USAID), European Bank for Reconstruction and Development (EBRD), Overseas Private Investment Corporation (OPIC), Inter-American Investment Corporation (IIC).

Source: Brenner, p. 8, C.R. CDC, only refers to its 19 funds, not the value of its assets.

EXHIBIT 26-4B

AVERAGE FUND SIZE (TOTAL FUND CAPITAL) 1998

Organization	Fund Size ($ million)
CDC	$20
EBRD	36
IFC	51
IIC	77
OPIC	130
USAID	129
Group Average	57
U.S. VC Average	$100+

avoided. "Let's face it, no other international venture capital fund is going to be running to invest in a place like Mozambique or Tanzania," said one competitor.[12]

CDC

Throughout its history, CDC had invested in the private sector. This allowed it to generate unusually powerful "externalities," or social returns, that frequently exceeded a project's economic return.[13] CDC's experience in assessing the investing environment in poor countries helped mitigate perceptions of excessive risk on the part of other investors. Its investments often served as a "seal of approval" on a country and, combined with its record as a long-term player in collaboration with the British aid program, served to attract private funding.

Background

CDC had been founded in 1948 as part of the British acknowledgment, in the words of one observer, that "exploiting the natural resources of the colonies was bad. There was a sense that Britain needed to help the colonies develop their own ability to add value." In addition, building the economies of its colonies would allow Britain to purchase supplies for its own postwar reconstruction within the sterling zone. Initially known as the Colonial Development Corporation, it was funded through a long-term zero interest loan from the government and given the charge to break even. Any additional funds it generated could be reinvested, and its budget was part of the Department for International Development (DfID), the umbrella agency for U.K. overseas aid.

CDC initially served as a lending agency to the colonies' private sector. Its first projects included tea plantations in India and tobacco farms in Zimbabwe, with a focus on agribusiness because of its ability to create jobs. CDC employees were said to have "the spirit of the raj." Said one, "When you have agribusiness investments, you have to go where the fields are. So trundling up and down the length of western Uganda with your planes being shot at was just par for the course."

In the early 1950s, CDC began lending for project finance. By the 1980s, renamed the Commonwealth Development Corporation but working beyond Commonwealth borders, it had assembled a solid record of managed projects, mostly in agriculture, but also in cement and power. Gradually, CDC became involved in equity deals, but 80% of its money went out as loans. Part of its mandate involved lending to support employment-creation; another aspect was "appropriateness," or the match between the characteristics of the project and the needs and resources of the country. Its own financial performance was not a particular priority; with a zero percent cost of capital, returns of 8% were viewed as reasonable. The emphasis lay more on adding to the private investment that would naturally occur, a concept called "additionality." CDC was to concentrate on those deals in which the private sector was uninterested, due to scale or term. "We were," said Harlock, "the investor of last resort."

It was during this period that CDC developed its unparalleled reputation for being prepared to put management on the ground, and being especially talented in tropical agriculture.[14] By the late 1990s, CDC's portfolio included 30 businesses that it con-

[12] Edward Turner quoted in Colin Barraclough, "A Developing Challenge," *Institutional Investor*, May 2000, p. 97.

[13] Sir Michael McWilliam, "Reinventing the Commonwealth Development Corporation under Public-Private Partnership," Centre for the Study of Financial Innovations, March 2000, p. 1.

[14] Ibid.

trolled and managed, including palm oil, tea and sugar plantations, farms, power companies, cement plants, and aquaculture, in 15 countries. These holdings represented $360 million, 33% of CDC's equity investments, and 14% of its total portfolio.[15] Lake Harvest, a fish farm on the Zimbabwean side of Lake Kariba, not only raised but also processed its tilapia fish, selling frozen fillets to European consumers. CDC's Costa Rican fish farm was already doing so to North America. York Farm, also in Zimbabwe, grew exotic vegetables and roses for markets in the United Kingdom and Europe.

These investments, like most of CDC's managed businesses, were in remote places where adequate housing and government-supplied medical facilities were not available. In order to produce goods that would meet the quality standard of the First World, it was necessary to attract and train significant numbers of workers. In turn, this often required CDC's companies to provide housing, education, and clinics for workers. One reporter observed, "Good labor practice, if it sets an example to local employers, is 'developmental.' But it is also . . . commercially necessary."[16]

Toward a Public-Private Partnership

Operating its businesses in a way to merge commercial and developmental necessities became increasingly vital after 1997. In that year, the newly elected Labor government announced, as its first privatization decision, that CDC would become a Public-Private Partnership (PPP).[17] This was a radical change in government attitude, as the Tory government just four years before had validated CDC's operational effectiveness and made the firm decision that it should remain in the public sector as an integral part of the country's overseas development program.

Determining the actual structure of CDC as a quasi-private entity required two years. After much debate in government, it was decided that DfID, CDC's parent, would hold the government's share of CDC. During a transition period of unknown duration, the corporation would revise its operations, bring in new staff, and generally retool itself to operate in the private sector. When market conditions were favorable, the government would sell not more than 75% of CDC to private investors, with the proceeds going to fund Britain's aid program. The government would retain its minority shareholding of at least 25% along with a "golden share" that would endure for an indefinite period, to preserve CDC's developmental role.[18] The golden share gave the secretary of state certain rights with respect to the government's role in the PPP. For instance, through the golden share, the secretary of state could prohibit any changes in CDC's investment policy or, more broadly, in the articles of association that defined the PPP.

The primary reason for privatization was the increasing competition for funds within the United Kingdom's aid program. Starting in 1993, CDC's funding had shifted from a net inflow of £49 million to net payments to the government of £10 million in 1997. The government's rationale was that CDC, with its strong cash flow from continuing operations, could manage well on its own even if its rate of new investment would have to slow. For CDC, however, the uncertainty about funding slowed its activity, harmed staff morale, and diminished its reputation as a legitimate deal-doer. One observer com-

---

[15] Christian Tyler, "Closing the gap," *The CDC Magazine*, p. 9.

[16] Ibid.

[17] This was the Blair government's first use of the term; since then, several other formerly state-owned companies have become PPPs.

[18] Andrew Evans, "Commonwealth Development Corporation Shake-up Clears Parliament," *Press Association Newsfile*, July 22, 1999, and Anon., "The Centre for the Study of Financial Innovation . . . ," *The Banker*, February 1, 2000.

mented that "a ridiculous situation had been reached in which CDC had become a net contributor to the exchequer from its operations as an arm of Britain's aid program."[19]

Given its inability to receive governmental funding, CDC would have turned to the loan market but was barred from doing so. The Treasury feared that loans to CDC might jeopardize the government's standing in the financial markets. In 1997, CDC and DfID began discussions to resolve the deadlock, culminating in the prime minister's speech in October 1997, in which he said, "The corporation [CDC] has made a major contribution to Britain's efforts to promote economic development . . . but . . . I believe it is an under-utilized asset. . . . [W]e have decided to allow the CDC to develop a new relationship with the private sector."[20]

The government was determined that the shift to the private sector would not be accompanied by a corresponding retreat from CDC's developmental role. CDC agreed to maintain its focus on investing in poor countries. Since 1993, it had worked under a mandate that 70% of its monies, measured on a five-year average, would be invested in nations with annual per capita incomes beneath $1,800. Half of this, or 35%, would be in sub-Saharan Africa and South Asia. CDC had exceeded the "70/50"requirement substantially (see Exhibit 26-5 for investment by region by year) in the past. It did break from the past by insisting that its investments could not be "additional" if it was to succeed in the private sector. The 70/50 proportion was enshrined in an Investment Policy Document that could only be changed with the approval of the shareholders, including the Special Shareholder (the government).[21]

The development mandate and the existence of the golden share did convey some benefits. In preparation for raising private money, CDC was given an exemption from U.K. capital gains taxes as long as the government remained a shareholder, to put it on

[19] McWilliam, "Reinventing the Commonwealth Development Corporation."

[20] PM Tony Blair, on October 22, 1997, cited in ibid.

[21] McWilliam, "Reinventing the Commonwealth Development Corporation."

EXHIBIT 26-5

CDC'S PORTFOLIO OVER TIME

	1992	1993	1994	1995	1996	1997	1998	1999
Portfolio $m								
Americas	308.1	331.5	365.9	447.3	463.4	518.9	467.3	624.6
Africa	676.1	722.1	707.3	664.4	716.7	684.6	669.3	688.2
South Asia	189.9	294.6	390.0	497.1	614.4	645.3	634.4	572.6
S.E.Asia	488.7	513.5	515.3	512.7	482.7	518.7	510.0	452.7
Other	1.5	1.5	15.9	11.6	55.7	24.3	23.6	3.2
Total	1,664.3	1,863.2	1,994.3	2,133.0	2,332.8	2,391.8	2,304.5	2,341.2
% Equity								
Americas	9%	9%	10%	12%	17%	19%	20%	35%
Africa	13%	15%	17%	21%	25%	30%	35%	39%
South Asia	17%	13%	17%	20%	20%	25%	32%	35%
S.E.Asia	30%	33%	45%	38%	32%	32%	33%	39%
Total	18%	19%	23%	23%	23%	26%	30%	36%

Source: Company information.

par with other emerging market investors typically operating from offshore locations.[22] In addition, DfID, the government shareholder, agreed to a flexible timetable for selling CDC to the public. The divestiture would occur "when the time was right."

At the time of Blair's speech, CDC saw itself as an organization with a strong developmental mandate. Even its equity positions had developmental angles. To support its far-flung operations, it maintained 30 offices worldwide, sometimes with only two executive staff. Almost half of its holdings were debt positions in the agricultural sector. The primary performance metric was "money out" in the course of a year. Projects tended to be large project financings, with debt as 80% of the deal. This meant that the financing instruments were self-liquidating and the gestation periods tended to be very long. Alan Gillespie, who joined CDC as CEO at the end of 1999, commented, "CDC managers were either farmers, who went around buying up lots of nice land, or industrialists, who bought lots of nice kit." The value of the existing portfolio stood at a 30% discount to its original cost. CDC's culture was strongly influenced by the concept of additionality, which had limited CDC's major competitors to other DFIs, and removed any particular need for speed. CDC's processes had become bureaucratic to the extent that one person observed, "it really wasn't the project as much as the process that mattered."

Once the privatization bill was passed in July 1999, much of this would have to change. CDC signaled the seriousness with which it viewed the PPP by recruiting Gillespie from Goldman Sachs International. He recognized the enormity of the task ahead: "In the past the issue of returns was secondary. . . . Now we have to be creating returns with a 'two' in front."[23] Gillespie's 25 years in investment banking, coupled with four years as chairman of the Northern Ireland Industrial Development Board, seemed to qualify him uniquely for the task of managing the massive change. Within months, he had reorganized CDC into sectoral disciplines (see Exhibit 26-6), expanded into South America and East Asia, opened new offices, initiated a retraining program, and hired people from the private sector. To facilitate attracting investors, CDC was transformed to a public limited company and renamed CDC Capital Partners. Its managed businesses were split off into a subsidiary called CDC Assets. Although both profitable and developmental, these businesses did not meet CDC's new return hurdle.

THE MOVE TO EQUITY

When Gillespie joined CDC, it had 500 employees located in 34 countries (see Exhibit 26-7 for finances). Private equity was not entirely new to CDC; its deals had always contained an equity component. In 1995 it had started a few funds, which had grown to 38% of the portfolio.[24] Since 1998, as part of its transformation to a private equity organization, it had not issued any new debt. It had, however, rolled over existing loans where necessary (see Exhibit 26-8 for CDC's portfolio composition).

By fall 2000, CDC was managing or investing through 19 regional funds with a total of $400 million in over 160 investments (see Exhibit 26-9 for the funds and perfor-

---

[22] In Britain, only investors in investment trusts were exempt from capital gains. Investment trusts differed from the far more common trading companies, which had some role in the operations of their companies. Richard Coopey and Donald Clarke, *3i: Fifty Years of Investing in Industry*, Oxford, England, Oxford University Press, 1995, pp. 321–343.

[23] Barraclough, "A Developing Challenge."

[24] McWilliam, "Reinventing the Commonwealth Development Corporation."

EXHIBIT 26-6

CDC ORGANIZATION CHART, PRE- AND POST–JANUARY 2000

CDC: Pre–January 2000

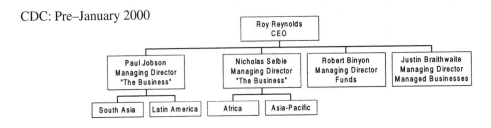

CDC: Post–January 2000

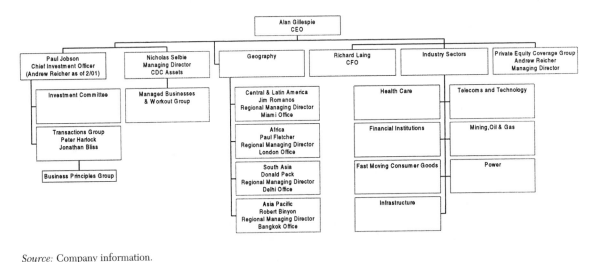

Source: Company information.

mance), in addition to being a direct investor. Half the money in the funds had come from more than 70 institutions, which included both DFIs and private sector groups, especially in South Asia and Southern Africa, with a match from CDC. These funds had 10-year life spans; investments were made during the first six years, and sales and disbursements of principal and returns occurred during the last four. Their regional and country-specific investments were targeted at traditionally capital-starved small- and midsize enterprises (SMEs) and averaged less than $1 million. In an internal memo, Gillespie summed up the experience:

> [W]e can be reasonably satisfied with the achievement of the funds, with some notable success stories. . . . We have gained some invaluable experience regarding managing private equity funds, which will stand us in good stead. . . . However, the overall financial results have not been particularly positive to date and several of the funds have not performed to our expectations. For certain small country funds, deal-flow has been slower than expected, and, generally, it has been difficult to achieve the returns (IRRs) required,

EXHIBIT 26-7

CDC GROUP'S FINANCIALS

(Millions of £)	1999 CDC Invest	1999 CDC Assets	1999 Total	1998 CDC Invest	1998 CDC Assets	1998 Total
Turnover	6.1	172.3	178.4	0.0	147.2	147.2
Investment income	115.4	0.0	115.4	123.2	0.0	123.2
Income	121.5	172.3	293.8	123.2	147.2	270.4
Cost of sales	−5.1	−113.4	−118.5	0.1	−81.1	−81.0
Gross profit	116.4	58.9	175.3	123.3	66.1	189.4
Administration and distribution expenses	−43.9	−57.3	−101.2	−36.3	−46.7	−83.0
Profit/loss on sales of investments	19.9	0.0	19.9	1.2	0.0	1.2
Other operating income	3.9	1.0	4.9	5.7	0.5	6.2
Group operating profit	96.3	2.6	98.9	93.9	19.9	113.8
Share of operating profits in associates	0.0	7.8	7.8	0.0	7.9	7.9
Total operating profit	96.3	10.4	106.7	93.9	27.8	121.7
Exceptional items	−3.6	−0.5	−4.1	−1.5	0.2	−1.3
Interest receivable	3.1	1.0	4.1	1.1	1.0	2.1
Interest payable	−2.0	−6.4	−8.4	−1.6	−3.1	−4.7
Investment and other provisions	−22.9	0.7	−22.2	−136.9	0.9	−137.8
Exchange gains/losses	2.1	1.7	3.8	−0.3	−7.9	−8.2
Profit/Loss before taxation	73.0	6.9	79.9	−45.3	17.1	−28.2
Taxation	−20.4	−2.7	−20.7	6.5	−6.9	1.4
Share of associates' taxation			−2.4			−1.8
Profit/loss after tax	52.6	4.2	56.8	−38.8	10.2	−28.6
Minority interest	0.2	−0.3	−0.1	−0.1	−3.4	−3.5
Profit/loss for the year	52.8	3.9	56.7	−38.9	6.8	−32.1

Source: 1999 Annual Report.

relative to risk. It is important to point out that the financial returns and objectives set out in the fund prospectuses, and on which co-investors committed, are in line with those that CDC will need to achieve for PPP.

One of CDC's most spectacular private equity investments had been Satyam Infoway, India's leading private sector Internet provider. CDC had invested in 1998 and 1999 at an average equivalent price per share of $1. In late 1999, the stock listed on NASDAQ at $4.50 and by February 2000 had soared to over $100 per share, capitalizing the business at over $8 billion and notionally valuing CDC's stake at over $1 billion. For various reasons, however, CDC had been unable to sell or hedge its position. By January 2001, the stock was trading between $3 and $5 per share.

In general, some of the new arrivals at CDC felt that the firm had invested too little in too many deals, making it impossible to give each project the attention necessary for good returns. "Successful village bakeries are definitely important for the development of a poorer country," said Andrew Reicher, managing director and head of the Private Equity Coverage Group. "But investing in them is not going to give you 30% returns."

EXHIBIT 26-8A

CDC'S TOTAL PORTFOLIO

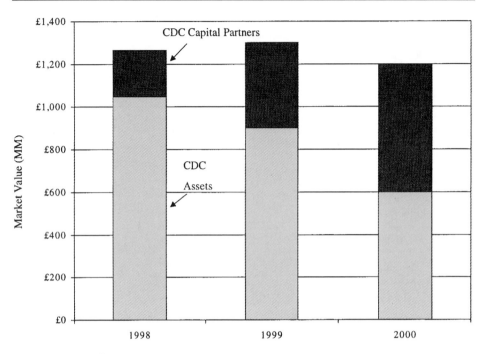

Source: Company information.

EXHIBIT 26-8B

TOTAL PORTFOLIO BY SECTOR AND REGION, 2000

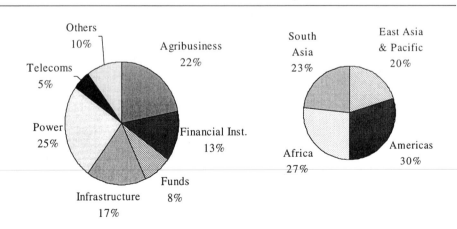

EXHIBIT 26-8C

SAMPLE OF CDC'S INVESTMENTS, 2000

Investee Co.	Country	Sector	Commitment ($US MM)	Cumulative Commitments	Expected IRR
Haina	Dom. Rep.	Power	74	13%	27%
Puerto Quetzal	Guatemala	Power	52	23%	26%
PRPOL	Indonesia	Palm Oil	44	30%	33%
San Pedro	Dom. Rep.	Power	42	38%	23%
Astratel	Indonesia	Tech/Telecom	30	43%	33%
Konkola Copper	Zambia	Minerals/Oil/Gas	30	48%	23%
Gateway	Asia/Pacific	Transport	25	53%	38%
CNOOC	China	Minerals/Oil/Gas	25	57%	34%
MSI	Africa	Tech/Telecom	20	61%	25%
Tsavo Power	Kenya	Power	19	64%	17%
CCI	Argentina	Infrastructure	19	68%	24%
Siman	El Salvador	Consumer Goods	16	70%	30%

Source: Company information.

EXHIBIT 26-8D

AGE OF CDC'S INVESTMENTS (AS OF END-OF-YEAR 1999)

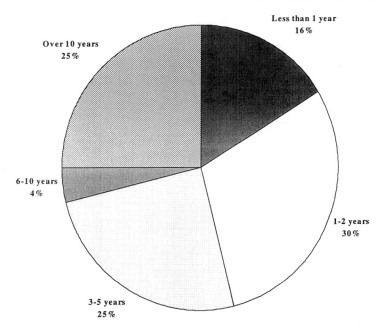

Note: This is the age of the investment, NOT the age of the company in which CDC is invested.

Source: 1999 Annual Report.

EXHIBIT 26-9

CDC FUNDS 1999

Country (LO&OO)[a]/Sector	Investing Vehicle[b]	Combined Manco/OO DDs[c]	Combined Manco/OO Support	Combined Gross Operating Costs[d] (in £m)	Total Portfolio @ Valuation OO (in £m)	Total Committed Capital (in £m)
Caribbean/Latin America						
Barbados	L	In Carib	In Carib	In Carib	In Carib	n/a
Bolivia	L	2	1	244.6	47.4	n/a
Caribbean	L,F	4	8	847.8	56.0	13.0
Central America	L,F	11	13	1,396.1	182.9	16.0
Cuba	L	2	1	356.3	25.0	n/a
Jamaica	L	0	In Carib	In Carib	In Carib	n/a
Peru	L	2	2	231.8	24.9	n/a
CLA London/Miami	L	4	1		0.0	
Total CLA	Total CLA	25	26	3076.5	336.2	29.0
Africa	Africa					
Kenya	L,F	8	7	797.3	26.6	11.9
Tanzania	L,F	8	6	741.6	20.2	12.5
Uganda	L	2	1	193.7	19.7	n/a
Mauritius	L,F	3	1	107.5	n/a	13.6
E.Africa Cluster	E.Africa Cluster	21	15	1,840.0	66	38
South Africa	L,F	9	5	915.0	52.8	10.0
Mozambique	L,F	5	4	500.6	24.0	11.5
Swaziland	L	1	2	176.1	14.2	n/a
Zambia/Malawi	L,F	7	8	821.8	42.3	7.5
Zimbabwe	L,F	6	7	504.0	17.2	8.1
n/a		1	3	311.9	n/a	38.5
S. Africa Cluster	S. Africa Cluster	29	29	3,229.4	150	76
Ghana	L,F	5	4	313.8	46.7	13.5
Cote d'Ivoire	L	2	2	363.4	33.2	n/a
Nigeria	L	0	2	33.2	0.0	n/a
W. Africa Cluster	W. Africa Cluster	7	8	710.5	80	14
Africa London	L	4	1		7	
Total Africa	Total Africa	57	52	5,779.9	303.6	127.1
S Asia	S Asia					
Bangladesh	n/a	2	2	159.8	24.7	n/a
India	L,F	14	10	1,062.3	159.5	83.8
Pakistan	L	4	5	304.9	100.9	n/a
Sri Lanka	L,F	6	6	569.4	33.5	8.5
S. Asia London/IT USA	L	5	1		0.0	
Total S Asia	Total S Asia	26	23	2,096.5	318.5	92.3
E Asia & Pacific	E Asia & Pacific					
Indonesia	L	4	5	406.0	53.8	n/a
Malaysia	L	2	4	265.9	1.2	n/a
Papua New Guinea	L,F	4	9	789.0	39.8	13.2
Philippines	L	3	2	304.8	71.6	n/a
Thailand	L	4	4	399.5	38.2	n/a
China	L	0	0	0.0	0.0	n/a
Singapore	L	0	0	0.0	0.0	n/a
E.Asia & Pac London	L	3	1		0.0	
Total E Asia & Pacific	Total E Asia & Pacific	17	24	2,165.2	204.6	13.2
Total Overseas & London Regional		125	124	13,118.0	1,163	262

(*Continued*)

EXHIBIT 26-9   (Continued)

Country (LO&OO)[a]/Sector	Combined Manco/OO DDs[c]	Combined Manco/OO Support	Combined Gross Operating Costs[d]	Total Portfolio @ Valuation OO (£m)	Total Committed Capital (£m)
Sectors					
Infrastructure	11	2	940.0	438.0	
Telecoms	2	1	174.0	40.6	
Agribusiness	5	2	550.0	119.9	
Financial Intermediaries	4	1	410.0	199.2	
MOG	4	1	393.0	84.4	
P & FP	2	1	291.0	36.1	
Corp Finance (Emerging Sect)	7	1	553.0	0.0	
Bus. Mging Dir (London), Recoveries & Operations	4	12	2,015.0	0.0	
Total London Sectors	39	21	5,326	918.1	0.0

[a] LO = London Office, OO = Overseas Office. [b] F = Fund, L = London Office investment.

[c] DD = Deal-doers, Manco = Managed Company.

[d] Gross Operating Costs do not include the offsetting fees received by the Funds from co-investors. These can be very substantial (in excess of $5 million).

Source: Company information.

Moving to equity was extremely attractive to CDC. "In essence," said Chief Investment Officer Paul Jobson:

[O]ur loans have always carried equity risk. We just never received any of the upside. Equity is really better for developing countries, because the investor plays such an active role. There's a huge amount of knowledge transfer. That doesn't happen with a loan. We have a lot more control of an equity investment than we do when we're just the banker.

Nonetheless, the firm still had £600 million of loans in its Assets group, which required ongoing attention. The interest from these loans was funding CDC's current equity investments. Gillespie explained, "The capital repayments from our loan book are our Treasury. It would be easy to forget about them. We have to manage our way out of these assets." While CDC wanted to unwind these holdings, it needed to do so as profitably as possible. In some cases, this required additional investment; the $100 million palm oil plantations in Indonesia could not yet stand on their own.

CDC's network of offices and its deep knowledge of local conditions gave it an advantage even compared to larger, more affluent, but newer firms. "CDC has been doing private equity in countries like India for longer than anyone else," said one of its rivals.[25] CDC's regional manager in Africa said, "We are known as the go-to guys when it comes to business in Africa." Now, however, said Reicher, "instead of acting like a development finance institution with a range of activities that includes occasional forays into private equity, we're a private equity firm, pure and simple." The implications were wide-ranging, affecting everything from CDC's structure through its employees' skill sets and compensation.

[25] Barraclough, "A Developing Challenge."

Skill Sets

CDC's new equity focus required a whole new set of skills for its staff. "We've gone from risk minimization to maximization of returns," said Jobson. "At every step in the process, the entire attitude is different." (See Exhibit 26-10.)

Adrian Robinson, team leader of the Telecoms group, attested to that. "I've been trained to minimize risk, not maximize returns. We had the perspective of being the lender of last resort. Now we have to look at returns, upside maximization, exit management. We're doing proactive marketing, developing teams to bid for licenses. We also have to move much faster. When you're the lender of last resort, the world comes to you. It's different now that we're looking for good deals."

CDC staff had been quick to catch on. Said Gabriela Culla, CDC's representative during the PPP negotiations, "These are a tremendous bunch of people. When we said 'no more debt,' it truly knocked them for a loop. But in a month or two, they got up, brushed themselves off, and started figuring it out."

Part of the challenge for management was the scarcity of private equity skills, especially in emerging markets. A minority of the 10-person management team at CDC had private equity experience. "We're all learning," said Reicher. A major training program had been instituted, but, Reicher commented, "part of the problem is that the feedback loops are so long; you can't learn from your mistakes as fast as one would like."

To handle complex deals, a team of deal-doers known as the Transactions group had been formed, co-headed by Peter Harlock and Jonathan Bliss. This group of deal specialists worked with the deal originators until completion. A subgroup of Transactions, Business Principles, would review the project in the context of CDC's ethics statement (see Exhibit 26-11). When the deal was signed, the Transactions people would step back and let the sector and country teams take over the project management.

EXHIBIT 26-10

DIFFERENCES BETWEEN INVESTOR AND LENDER ATTITUDES

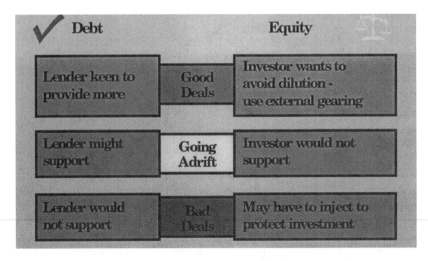

Source: Company information.

EXHIBIT 26-11

CDC'S BUSINESS PRINCIPLES, ABRIDGED

The Articles require the directors to include in each annual report a report on CDC's compliance with the Statement of Business Principles and Policies. . . . Where CDC has control of the business concerned, its responsibilities are clear. Where CDC, as a direct investor or investor through a financial intermediary, does not have control of the underlying company or business activity, it will seek to encourage compliance with similar business principles and policies. . . . CDC may seek to withdraw from an investment if it considers that the measures necessary to achieve compliance are not being taken.

Business Principle 1   Our mandate is to maximize CDC's success in creating and growing long term viable businesses in developing economies, achieving attractive returns for shareholders and implementing ethical best practice. In pursuit of this mandate, we will apply the following Business Principles:

- To be open and honest in our dealings, whilst respecting commercial and personal confidentiality
- To be objective, consistent and fair with all our stakeholders
- To be a good corporate citizen, demonstrating integrity in each business and community in which we operate
- To respect the dignity and well-being of all our people and those with whom we are involved
- To operate professionally in a performance oriented culture and be committed to continuous improvement. . . .

Business Principle 2   Objectives: To exhibit honesty, integrity, fairness and respect in all our business dealings. To enhance the good reputation of CDC. To manage our affairs prudently and with due skill, care, and diligence. Policies:

- To comply with all applicable U.K. and EC laws and those of other countries where we operate, including regulations intended to fight financial crime. . . .
- To prohibit all employees from making or receiving gifts of substance in the course of business
- To prohibit the making of payments as improper inducement to confer preferential treatment on CDC, its agents or advisors. . . .
- To make no contributions to political parties or political candidates.

Business Principle 3   Environment: Objectives: to recognize that economic development results in environmental change. Sustainable development seeks to maximize the potential of environmental resources, to mitigate any adverse impacts, and where possible to increase the supply of environmental assets. As part of our developmental objective, we therefore: encourage the efficient use of natural resources; seek investment opportunities where sound economic development is coupled with the protection and improvement of the environment; avoid investments where impacts on communities and the environment have not been properly considered and mitigated in their design.

- We require all businesses to be designed and operated using international accepted environmental good practices.
- CDC takes account of such agreements [1992 Framework convention on Climate Change, the 1997 Protocol to that Convention, the Convention on Biological Diversity, and the convention on Desertification] in its appraisal of investments.
- CDC will not knowingly support businesses, which contravene any relevant international environmental agreement to which either the host country or the UK is a signatory.
- The decision whether to support a business which has some potentially detrimental environmental effects will take account of the influence that CDC and its co-investors have to improve the business through their involvement.
- All companies in which CDC invests are required to put formal environmental policies and procedures in place.

(Continued)

EXHIBIT 26-11 *(Continued)*

Business Principle 4   Health and Safety

Objectives   To provide safe and healthy working conditions for our employees and to safeguard the health and safety of all those affected by our operations. To attain safe and healthy working conditions for employees of all businesses in which we invest. To seek to ensure that businesses in which we invest comply with internationally recognized standards of good practice in order to protect the health and safety of their employees while at work.

- To require that, where there is no local legal framework, all businesses in which we invest, in defining their health and safety policy take account of the recommendations of the following two World Bank documents: a: Occupational Health and Safety Guidelines for specific industries; b: Health and Safety Guidelines—General.
- To require each business in which we invest to assess the specific risks arising from the work activities carried out with a view to introducing measures to eliminate or reduce those risks.

Business Principle 5   Social Issues

Objectives   To recognize that economic development results in social change and that, to be successful, development needs to be sustainable. As part of our developmental objective we therefore: identify, through consultation, any negative social aspects of an investment and address the ways in which these might be mitigated; identify, through consultation, potential social benefits and determine how they might be enhanced to the mutual benefit of the company and community; make investments in projects where the positive social impact outweighs any negative effects.

- CDC seeks to ensure that the social effects of its investments are assessed and monitored in the planning, implementation and operational stages. Areas of key social impact which may be identified include resettlement, importation of labor, change in the provision of social services, substantial job losses and culture property issues.
- We require all our investments to meet or exceed the standards required by the national laws of the host country . . . and international treaties ratified by the host country.
- The decision as to whether to support a business that has some potentially detrimental social effects will take account of the influence that CDC and its co-investors have to improve the business through their involvement.
- We do not invest in businesses that employ forced labor of any kind.
- We do not invest in businesses that exploit child labor. In many of the environments in which we operate, children are involved in the productive process, often alongside their parents. Children may only be employed in our investments if their education is not being disrupted and if they are fully protected from potential economic exploitation and from moral and physical hazard.
- Wages should meet or exceed industry or legal national minima and must be sufficient to meet basic needs.
- Employees should be treated fairly in terms of recruitment, progression, terms and conditions of work, and representation, irrespective of gender, race, color, disability, political opinion, religion or social origin. In some countries there may be cultural issues, which CDC must recognize in seeking to implement this policy.

Source: Company information.

"They're an exceptional group," said Jobson of the CDC staff. "No one comes here to get rich, they come because they want to make a difference and doing so in private sector development appealed. They're smart and they're adaptable, but we are throwing a major challenge at them."

Another skill that Gillespie particularly wanted to develop in the CDC staff was the ability to tolerate ambiguity. He explained:

The old CDC was a mixture of two cultures, government and industrial. In government, you have a form for everything. In the old industrial culture, you were afraid that the employees would steal the tools, so you locked everything up. The financial culture is very different; you have a zone of freedom surrounded by compliance. So it's imperative that this group learn to handle that kind of constructive ambiguity.

Deals

Another challenge was finding good deals in emerging markets. One regional manager commented, "Deal-flow is not the problem. There's oodles of deal-flow. It's finding the right ones that's the challenge." CDC's mandate complicated the process; deals of the size and quality it sought were far more numerous outside of the 70% countries and those in the nongoal (poor countries not in Africa and South Asia) regions. Likewise, more vibrant economies offered greater exit opportunities and at better valuations. Jobson commented, "Even in Latin America, there is more economic activity in Mexico than in Paraguay." Gillespie concurred, "One big deal in 30% Latin America will blow our limits."

An additional factor was CDC's scarce deal-doing resources. "Rather than have our people scattered across a lot of little deals," said Jobson, "it's just more efficient to focus them on big deals, $10 million or more. There are few of those deals in Africa or South Asia."

To address this issue, CDC had consciously decided to focus on certain countries and delay involvement in others. During 2000, the firm had opened offices in Nigeria, Mexico, China, and Egypt, and decided to skip Brazil for the time being. Yet even this was open to revision, as Gillespie explained: "A leading private equity player called me about a deal in Brazil. Did we want to go in on it? Well . . . we aren't really doing business in Brazil. But if a big private equity firm wants us in, maybe we'll change our minds."

In 2000, although CDC had designated specific sectors—Power, Minerals/Oil/Gas, Fast Moving Consumer Goods, Telecoms and Technology, Transport, and Financial Institutions—for investment, regional groups could choose to develop sectoral expertise. The Africa region was targeting health care saying, "we can make a real difference here. And make a profit."

Telecoms' Robinson pointed to changes in the way CDC found deals:

Historically, we sat behind our desks and people came to us. Now we have a strategy; we know what countries we want to be in, what partners we want to take, and what size of deal we're looking for. I've been doing a lot of in-house marketing to let the people in the region know what we do. That way, when the Bangladesh office learns that a license is coming available, they'll contact us and we can do the deal together.

CDC was doing deals in new technologies, as Robinson described:

Last month, I did a four-hour presentation to the Board on broadband technology. Two years ago, it would've been on palm oil prices. Telecoms and technology is scary because I'm not investing in something like a palm oil plantation, there's nothing anyone can see. Sometimes it's just a few guys with an idea. I brought a global vehicle positioning deal to the Investment Committee—it's with a subsidiary of another big firm. It's crazy to do deals with subsidiaries, the parent company changes the team on you, you don't have clear control—but that's the industry. And if we need to generate returns of 30% or more, CDC needs to be in this sector.

Part of Andrew Reicher's mandate in Private Equity Coverage was to establish the connections that would create more deals for the firm. He explained:

> CDC used to have the old-time development finance attitude that you found your deal and you did your deal. You didn't share it. Now we have to share. Even in the markets where CDC operates, there are some very large and powerful competing private equity players. But nobody in the private equity industry has all the resources necessary to find by themselves absolutely every deal they do. And we can offer these people an incredible network of people on the ground, with high-order industry-specific knowledge in several key sectors. We want to have friends in the business, folks who'll look to us to take pieces of their deals because we're a value-added partner, and who'll also go in as partners with us when we find an attractive larger deal.

The immaturity of the markets forced CDC to engage in risky deals. Reicher said, "The least risky deal is a management buyout, then an expansion financing, then a start-up, then a turnaround. We're dealing in all of them all the time and need to move towards the lower-risk end of the spectrum." One recent deal had involved a Central American firm that merged one of its divisions with a regional competitor. The new firm had, as part of the same transaction, purchased another firm that was in receivership. "It was a brilliant deal," said Jonathan Bliss, the co-head of Transactions:

> We were negotiating in three different directions, eight time zones away. There's incredible opportunity here—this group is the major provider of consumer durable products such as appliances and white and brown goods in a region where only 60% of the population has refrigerators. What's more, they supply credit at attractive margins to help those that do not have access to bank lending. But it was a total logistical nightmare.

Once a deal was found, structuring the exit was another challenge. Jobson said, "We usually exit through the big trade buyers. In some areas—chocolates and confectionery, for instance—the big players all grow through acquisition, so we're in a good spot. Selling to management is our least preferred option because it puts management in such a conflicted position."

CDC was convinced that the deals were developmental, even if indirectly. "We're developmental because of the countries in which we work," said Harlock. "Investing in sustainable businesses in developing economies is by definition developmental. We are not in the business of taking submarket returns—that undermines the market. If we ensure that we back good businesses that can deliver market levels of return then we will be developing the economy."

CDC's deal approval process had been significantly streamlined in 1999 (see Exhibit 26-12). Jobson explained:

> In the past, because we were a bureaucracy, people felt they needed to have something to do. So once a guy in the London office got a deal on his desk, he'd vet it to death. The country people who'd originated it would try to get it through. There was a lot of gamesmanship. It wasn't a good way to get good deals and it certainly wasn't a good way to manage projects. A deal was handed from person to person and was finally managed by someone who was completely new to the entire process.

> Since then, we've introduced the concept of deal-doers owning the deal from entrance to exit. We introduced the term "deal-doer"—previously, we'd called our people project managers—and made ownership of the deal paramount. Any team, sectoral or regional, can bring a deal to the Screening Committee in London. It needs two deal partners and a deal parent. The parent is the regional or sector head and the partners are someone in

EXHIBIT 26-12A

OLD APPROVAL PROCESS

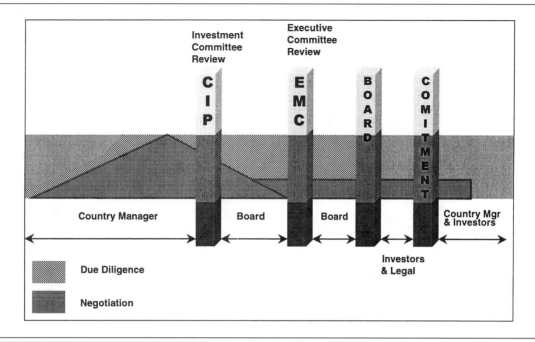

EXHIBIT 26-12B

NEW APPROVAL PROCESS

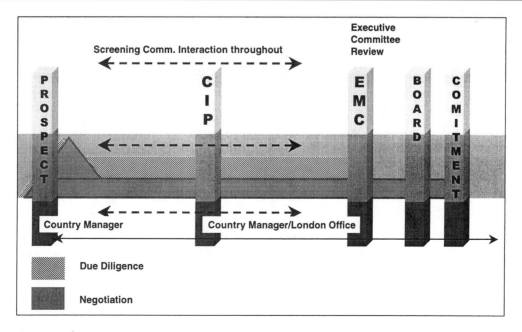

Source: Company information.

the region and someone in the sector. The write-up is just two pages, a description of the concept and the team, the budget, the biggest causes for concern. This is approved over the phone. After that, the team does due diligence and a more complete deal description goes to the Investment Committee. The Investment Committee can approve, decline, or approve with reservations. If the deal is over £10 million, the Board must approve it. With approval, the team negotiates the final legal documents and starts managing.

Jobson did not underestimate the magnitude of the change. "This is a real challenge for our staff. They'd been doing something well for a long time and now they've been told to completely change. We've also reorganized and that's always difficult. They're bound to make mistakes."

During 2000, CDC had screened $1.6 billion worth of deals, approved $641 million, committed to $560 million, and disbursed $366 million, but Gillespie felt that simply doing deals was only part of the challenge:

> We're portfolio managers. We're not deal-doers. We have to enter the room looking at the exit sign, yet provide engaged, involved, valuable service. Learning the skills so that we hedge our deals—we could have made $400 million if we'd hedged one deal correctly. That's portfolio management.

At the same time, he reiterated that it was a matter of learning greater financial sophistication, not an irreparable flaw, "We're not 'worse' than the City[26]—it's just that they've done it more and do it faster."

Structure

CDC's future structure was intimately linked to the questions of deal-flow and skill sets. CDC saw two different possibilities: a highly centralized structure or a more decentralized fund of funds arrangement. Each had its own advantages and disadvantages.

Centralized Option Except for its recent fund experience, CDC had operated as a fairly centralized organization. The London office housed sector specialists, while most regional specialists were in the field. Communications occurred over CDC's Intranet and through frequent conference calls.

A centralized approach would allow investors to put money into a pool that CDC would allocate across its 55 countries to generate the best returns. In considering this possibility, Nicholas Selbie, managing director of CDC's Assets group, said, "Track record is key. It would be tough to go to the market seeking investment and say, 'We have new management, old assets, a good reputation in power and telecoms but no reputation in five other sectors.'" Jobson agreed, saying, "If I said to big institutional investors, 'Give me your money to invest in 55 poor countries,' they'd say 'Why?'"

Jonathan Bliss from Transactions had a different perspective:

> Emerging markets change so quickly—look at Peru. Two years ago it was everyone's emerging market dream, now the President has fled and it's completely chaotic. The institutional investors don't have time to track these. CDC, though, can bundle up all the emerging market opportunities and offer big pension funds a convenient one-stop way to invest. With our ethical style of investing, it's a way to get DFIs off their backs and get a decent return. We might not be a huge percentage of any firm's portfolio, but 1% of CalPERS [the California Public Employee Retirement System] would go a long way.

---

[26] London's Wall Street.

Fund of Funds Option   The fund of funds approach had other benefits. Selbie commented:

> We're noted in certain sectors, particularly telecoms and power. We're also known for work in some regions, like India. We have to give investors something to invest in, something they know. We could offer an Indian Telecom and Technology fund. We're planning to roll up our existing power assets into a fund. Everyone knows power and how vital it is to the developing world. So a fund of funds approach plays to our strengths and will give some credibility for other developing sectors—a fund of funds approach could also allow us to set up funds with different products such as mezzanine finance.

Others agreed. Bliss wanted to balance the two; believing that a fund of funds would allow CDC to leverage its track record in the sectors where it had experience, but that the umbrella organization was still important to apply a consistently high standard to the investment process.

Selbie added that the contrary view to the fund of funds approach was that it would radically change CDC as an organization, creating very independent funds with a small central CDC asset allocation and brand/quality management function. This would be viewed with concern by some and as inevitable by others.

Jobson felt that organizationally CDC could move to become a fund of funds. "We already have sector specialties, we'd just define them." His concern lay more in the firm's ability to compensate its fund managers appropriately:

> If we're organized around fund structures, we would have to structure like one and give our managers carry. Everyone throughout the organization, London and the field, would need to belong to a fund at some level, and share in the reward. But compensation, given we are a government entity, presents a key stumbling block to moving to such a structure in the short term.

Compensation

Everyone within CDC felt that figuring out the compensation issue was vital. Currently, as everyone admitted, it was "significantly" below the standard of typical private equity firms. The issue also presented particular difficulties because the motivations of existing staff involved both the development and the reward aspects of the business. As Telecoms' Robinson said, "No-one ever joined CDC to get rich. We joined to be reasonably rewarded and make a difference." For him, CDC had offered a "job without guilt":

> I'd worked for a big firm doing business in developing nations and I felt really conflicted. I'd be going back to the airport after a successful deal and there was all the poverty and the government was using its scarce resources to buy our equipment instead of health care supplies. Working with the private sector and CDC, even though it's not developmental in the way it used to be, I'm still making a difference, helping to generate business and jobs and leaving the government to spend its money on health care.

Jobson saw two challenges in CDC's policy of "reasonable rewards:"

> The government really fears creating "Fat Cats," people on the government payroll that are breaking the salary structure. But how can I retain such scarce talent as private equity professionals with developing market expertise without giving private sector incentives like carried interest? What's more, our partners will want to know that CDC representatives are as committed to the deal as they are, and will work as hard to protect everyone's in-

---

EXHIBIT 26-13

LONG-TERM INCENTIVE PLAN SUMMARY

- Annual cash-based incentive plan.
- Open to all CDC Group PLC employees.
- Awards in the form of notional investments held within the plan for a three-year period. All eligible employees receive a "formula award" based on a percentage of base salary established by seniority grouping. A discretionary award will be given to selected employees, mainly key deal-doers and revenue generators, across the business.
- Actual payments are based on the increase in CDC Group PLC's Net Asset Value over the three-year period, subject to a minimum growth hurdle of 5% per annum over the plan period.
- Payments are made in equal installments over the two years following maturity, subject to annual limits on withdrawals. The notional investment itself cannot be withdrawn; it is the gain upon it that is available for payment.
- All payments are subject to normal tax deductions as part of normal remuneration.

Source: Company information.

---

terests. You can't align interests much more closely than with carried interest. We've structured a long-term incentive (see Exhibit 26-13 for details), which is tied to changes in our balance sheet's Net Asset Value, and I hope that will retain people long enough to get a carry scheme in place.

Another concern about carry was its tendency to tie people to their areas of expertise. Harlock commented, "If someone's carry is in Latin America, they won't want to move to South Asia. We need to be able to deploy the best talent where we need it. But we also need to be able to retain it."

Gillespie knew that compensation was crucial to the firm's success. Not only did he want to add MBAs to the staff, but he also wanted to find talented nationals to join:

Of anything this year, the most of my time has been spent on recruitment. We've had some fantastic people join us, which I see as a testament to the excitement of what CDC is doing, far more than my own recruitment skills. It is essential for the future of this organization that all of us white men get out of the way and leave the running of country programs to nationals.

2001 AND ONWARD

Gillespie knew that structure, compensation, skills, and deal-flow had to be resolved in order to answer the fundamental question of CDC's survival: how to attract money to invest in poor countries throughout the world. As he continued working on his remarks later that night, he was cautiously confident:

The underlying trends are in our favor—demographics, the growth of the consumer class, the importance, availability, and affordability of technology, the huge amounts of capital available, free trade, and globalization. State assets are being privatized, new businesses formed, multinationals are disposing of non-core assets, giving us lots of opportunities to

EXHIBIT 26-14

3I: CDC'S DOMESTIC COUSIN

The U.K.'s previous experiment in privatizing a government-established funding institution occurred in 1994 when it spun off 3i, previously Investors in Industry. Like CDC, 3i grew from Britain's postwar rebuilding efforts, but these, unlike CDC, was targeted domestically.

3i, initially named the Industrial and Commercial Finance Corporation, was established in 1945 to provide long-term and permanent capital to small and medium-sized firms, thereby correcting the financial system's bias against domestic investment and its over-attention to liquidity, security, and short-term results.[a] The initial capital was provided by the five clearing banks (Barclays, Midland, National Provincial, Westminster, and Lloyds) and the Bank of England.[b] 3i provided investment capital, defined as "long-term supportive investment in the form of minority shares [equity] and loan investments,"[c] to small, unlisted firms. The portfolio was quite diverse, spread across industries, geography, and maturities, and the company engaged in activities ranging from consulting through all stages of venture investing. By 1994, over 40% of 3i's portfolio was in listed companies or was secured in one way or another.[d]

As the owning banks moved into commercial loan arena in the 1970s, 3i increasingly seemed to be competing for business rather than creating business for them. The idea of privatizing 3i gained strength in the early 1980s as some of the banks experienced financial pressures that such a sale would alleviate.[e] The Bank of England also started to question whether its independent, regulatory role was compromised by its connection with 3i. In September 1985, the board of 3i submitted a formal set of proposals to change its ownership, which had changed from its original five banks to six: Bank of Scotland, Barclays, Lloyds, Midland Bank Group, NatWest Bank Group, and Royal Bank of Scotland Group, in addition to the Bank of England. At first, the floatation was expected in summer 1986; it was delayed because of issues around 3i's tax status, then around its valuation and whether it should be sold to a single entity. Finally, six years after the announcement, the floatation date was set for spring 1992, only to be scuttled by unfavorable market conditions.[f]

The unfavorable conditions persisted until 1994. By then, however, 3i had assembled a respectable track record: a 332% return between March 31, 1983 and September 30, 1993, which compared with 414% from the All-share Index and 320% from investment trusts on average. It had a reputation of behaving more like a venture capitalist than a mere shareholder; said one observer, '3i is a genuine direct investor and lender . . . [it] becomes a partner."[g] In preparation for its listing, it had reduced its headcount by 45%, to 570, in 17 UK offices and six on the Continent.[h]

3i was floated on 18 July 1994, with a market capitalization of £1.7 billion, a 13.5% discount to the net asset value as of March 31, 1994. At this time, Britain was just emerging from the recession of the early 1990s, so the offer was oversubscribed only 1.1 times and yielded 75,000 new shareholders.[i] As the market strengthened, 3i's market cap rose to the point that it was included in the FTSE-100 companies in September. Macpherson, CEO of 3i at the time of its floatation, cited the key to the firm's success as "the high quality of 3i's staff. . . . This is not merely to pay lip-service. The ability to construct original financial proposals that reconcile investee companies' needs with our own to negotiate terms and bring them to a successful conclusion is critical to our success. To be able to monitor those inherently risky investments over long periods and bring 3i both income and capital profit from the majority is proof of an exceptionally able and dedicated group of people."[j]

By the end of 2000, over its 55-year existence, 3i had invested over $19 billion in more than 13,500 companies in 20 countries.[k] It was England's largest venture capital organization and was one of the top dozen FTSE companies.

---

[a] Lucy Newton, "Review of 3i: Fifty Years of Investing in Industry," *The Economic Journal*, November 1, 1996.

[b] Richard Coopey and Donald Clarke, *3i: Fifty Years of Investing in Industry*, Oxford, England, Oxford University Press, 1995), p. 22.

[c] BZW, quoted in Anon., "The Ayes have It, *Investor's Chronicle*, May 20, 1994, p. 11.

[d] *Investor's Chronicle.*

[e] Coopey and Clarke, p. 193.

[f] Ibid., pp. 194—197.

[g] *Investor's Chronicle.*

[h] Ibid.

[i] Ewan Macpherson, postscript, in Coopey & Clarke, p. 394.

[j] Ibid., p.395.

[k] www.3i.com, accessed January 18, 2001.

get in on deals. We can offer a lot—to a major consumer goods manufacturer, for instance, we offer the chance to get in on the ground floor of countries where a new consumer class is about to demand a host of products. We can give banks and pension funds a socially responsible aspect to their portfolio and make their shareholders feel good—while generating good returns. There's a lot of money out there and I have to believe that some of it wants to be doing good. But the market must have confidence in us and we must demonstrate a sufficient deal-flow and some indication of adequate returns before we can attain our status as PPP.

I still believe private equity is the right thing to do. It's the right way to invest in developing countries. Even going public will be beneficial; there's a culture in a government organization that, try as you will, just isn't commercial. It takes time to make the change—it took 3i [the U.K.'s internal rebuilding investment group] nine years to get a listing. (See Exhibit 26-14 for 3i's history.) We need to be open-minded about the method of sale. But I'm concerned that we make the transition without losing our best people, without losing the passion that made CDC unique. If we can keep that, and generate competitive returns, we'll do more than survive, we'll thrive.

27

A Note on Private Equity in Developing Countries

The past several years have seen two striking patterns in private equity activity in the developing world. The first of these has been a dramatic increase in activity, followed by a pronounced decline. The second has been a shift in the composition of investments toward more early-stage investments.

These shifts in fundraising volume have been fueled largely by institutional investors based in the United States. Several reasons account for the growth in activity during the early and mid-1990s, including the rapid growth of many developing nations and the relaxation of curbs on foreign investments in many of these nations. Perhaps equally important was the perception by many institutional investors in the mid-1990s that the returns from private equity investments in the United States were likely to decrease. Over the last years of the decade, however, these two perceptions shifted and private equity fundraising in developing countries suffered as a result.

A second profound change has been in the mixture of private equity invested. Until very recently, private equity investing in developing countries was overwhelmingly focused on later-stage investments (e.g., buyouts, infrastructure, and mezzanine transactions). In the late 1990s, true venture capital transactions, particularly relating to the Internet and telecommunications, became much more frequent.

Although comprehensive data are hard to come by, an example may help illustrate these patterns.[1] Fundraising by private equity funds based in China climbed from $16 million in 1991 to over $1 billion in 1995, with the single largest source being U.S. institutions. It then fell to an average annual level of $183 million in the years 1996 through 1998. Meanwhile, the share of private equity investment devoted to seed and start-up firms (as opposed to mezzanine, restructuring, and infrastructure companies or proj-

---

Gonzalo Pacanins, MBA '97, prepared this class note under the supervision of Professor Josh Lerner as the basis for class discussion rather than to illustrate either effective or ineffective handling of an administrative situation.

[1] No single directory captures private equity activity in the developing world. The Chinese data is drawn from Asian Venture Capital Journal, *The Guide to Venture Capital in Asia: 2000 Edition*, Hong Kong, Asian Venture Capital Journal, 2000 (and earlier editions).

ects) increased from 2% in 1992 to 39% in 1998. These patterns have been repeated in regions as diverse as South America, Eastern Europe, and the Indian subcontinent.

This note seeks to identify some of the key challenges and opportunities that private equity investors in developing nations face. The first section presents a broad overview of some of the key reasons why developing nations are a potentially attractive investment environment for institutional investors and private equity funds. The note then considers the "private equity cycle," from fundraising through investing to exiting, contrasting developing and developed nations. The opportunities that make private equity in developing countries attractive are highlighted, as well as the potential risks.

It is worth cautioning that this note only tries to identify broad patterns. This discussion should not blind the reader to the substantial heterogeneity in the private equity industries of various developing countries. A key reason for these differences, of course, is that developing nations differ along many dimensions among themselves. Please bear this caution in mind as you read through this note.

WHY INVEST IN DEVELOPING NATIONS?

In this section, we will discuss two sets of rationales for the growth of private equity activity in the developing world.[2] The first relate to the changes in the developing nations themselves. Many have undertaken radical reforms and external changes—for example, technological innovations—have also helped make these nations more attractive arenas for investment. The second set relates to the changing conditions in the developed nations. Many institutional investors have been skeptical that attractive returns that have recently characterized venture capital and leveraged buyout investments in many developed nations can be sustained and are looking for new arenas in which to invest.

The Increasing Attractiveness of Developing Nations Much of the interest in private equity investing in developing nations must be attributed to their economic progress over the past decade. A critical impetus to much of this progress, in turn, has been the economic reforms adopted by many of these nations. The pace at which capitalism has rolled through developing economies is breathtaking. It is easy to forget that as recently as 15 years ago, only 1 billion of the world's citizens were in capitalist economies. Today, three times that number live in economies that are strongly capitalist in orientation.[3]

A detailed discussion of these changes is beyond the scope of this note, but a few of these reforms are worth noting. One of the most substantial macroeconomic shifts was the 1989 Brady Plan. This plan allowed several Latin American countries to restructure their external debt. The enormous reduction in debt service led to a substantial boost in the economic health of these markets. The successful reform process led to an increase in major investors' confidence in developing nations, as seen, for instance, in the increase in the market prices of these nations' debt.

---

[2] According to the World Bank, developing nations are those countries that have either low- or middle-level per capita incomes; have underdeveloped capital markets; and/or are not industrialized. It should be noted, however, that the application of these criteria is somewhat subjective. For instance, Kuwait appears on many lists of developing nations despite its high per capita gross domestic product. The reason for its inclusion lies in the income distribution inequality that exists there, which has not allowed it to reach the general living standards of developed countries.

[3] For a provocative discussion of these changes from a practitioner perspective, see Lucy Conger, "Interview—Garantia launches Brazil Equity Fund," *Reuters News Service*, September 26, 1995.

Other macroeconomic reforms were initiated by the developing nations themselves, though often with the prodding of such international bodies as the International Monetary Fund. One arena for such reforms has been major tax reform. Many developing countries realized that one way to fuel the economy was by lowering taxes on capital gains, thereby encouraging equity investment and stock market growth. Likewise, in many nations, restrictions on foreign investment—which often prohibited investments in particular industries, stipulated that foreign investors needed to hold a minority stake, or limited the repatriation of profits—have been relaxed. Finally, several developing nations have made great progress in improving their accounting and disclosure standards. These changes have served to lower the costs of investing in these nations, as well as to diminish the information asymmetries that the foreign investors face.

Other drivers of the economic progress of developing nations have been external. An example is the lowering by many developed nations of many tariff and nontariff barriers to imports from developing nations. Both exports and imports by developing nations increased almost threefold between 1987 and 1999.[4] A second example is technological change. Thanks to innovations in information and communication technologies, investors in developed countries—whether corporations or institutions—can better monitor their investments. A substantial decline in inflation-adjusted transportation costs has also made greater trade and investment feasible. These trends have led to spectacular growth in many of the developing nations. While the developed economies grew at an inflation-adjusted annual rate of 1.9% between 1990 and 1999, emerging market economies grew at 5.8%.[5]

The Decreasing Attractiveness of Developed Nations A second critical factor in the growth of private equity investing in developing countries has been the perception of diminishing investment opportunities in the developed nations, particularly the United States. The pool of private equity under management in the United States grew from $4 billion in 1980 to about $300 billion at the end of 2000. This growth has largely been attributable to the relaxation of the formal and informal curbs that limited private and pension funds from investing in private equity.

This growth, many institutional investors argue, has had three deleterious consequences. First, the increase in the size of many private equity funds has led to an alteration in the incentive structure of these funds. In particular, the management fees charged by private equity investors have remained relatively constant, averaging about 2% (typically calculated as a percentage of capital under management). But since the capital managed per partner has increased dramatically, this has meant that these fees have become a significant source of income. Many investors fear that the incentive provided by the share of the profits reserved for the private equity investors has consequently become less effective. Second, many private equity organizations have encountered strong demand when they seek to raise new funds. This allowed them to negotiate partnership agreements without the many covenants that protect investors in these funds. If an institution insisted on the inclusion of a particular form of protection, the venture capitalists could simply exclude them from the transaction. Finally, many institutional investors argue that the current market is characterized by an imbalance between the supply of capital and attractive investments. Many argue that this has led

---

[4] International Monetary Fund, *International Financial Statistics Yearbook*, Washington, DC, International Monetary Fund, 2000.

[5] Ibid.

deals. It should be noted, however, that it would have been very difficult to obtain attractive returns from private equity investments in most developing nations during the 1970s and 1980s, even under the best of circumstances.

One source that is likely to become an increasingly important source of capital for private equity funds is retirement savings in the developing nations themselves. East Asian nations have very high savings rates, often accounting for about 30% of gross domestic product. These high rates partially reflect the younger average age in developing countries, as well as cultural differences. While many of these individual savings are invested informally in the privately held businesses of relatives and friends, little has been directed into institutional private equity funds.

These patterns are likely to change in future years. Leading the way has been Chile, which has privatized much of its retirement savings. Pension funds have already helped to finance privatization programs in Chile, taking equity positions of between 10% and 35% in privatized firms. As the funds have grown, regulators have increasingly widened the fields in which they can invest. Several are considering initiating private equity investment programs.[9]

THE PRIVATE EQUITY CYCLE: INVESTING

The investment process in developing and developed nations is often very different. In this section, we will discuss four aspects of these differences: the types of deals that are considered, the process by which companies are identified and evaluated, the structuring of the investments, and valuation.

Types of Investments   Private equity funds in developed nations undertake a diverse array of potential transactions. Venture capitalists in the United States usually target high-technology sectors of the economy, while buyout firms focus on more mature firms in a variety of industries that need to restructure or combine. By way of contrast, funds in developing nations have until recently targeted already-established firms in traditional industries.

Typical investments by developing country private equity funds fall into four broad categories. The first are privatizations. The World Bank estimates that 80 countries in recent years have made privatization a primary public-policy concern. More than 7,000 large-scale privatizations have been undertaken, at an annual rate of $25 billion per year.[10] Many of these newly privatized enterprises are undercapitalized and desperately need to modernize. The simple distribution of shares to employees or others will not solve their need for financing. In many cases, the national capital markets are still not well developed, and access to international markets is limited to the largest firms. Consequently, governments and the private sector are turning to private equity to fill the investment gap.

A second market opportunity has been corporate restructurings. Globalization has implied increased competition for many businesses in developing countries: lower trade barriers and new regulatory frameworks have forced companies to refocus their activi-

---

[9] For a general overview, see Jim Freer, "The Private Pension Path," *LatinFinance* (July/August 1995): 34–38; for a specific discussion of future investment plans, see Felipe Sandoval, "CORFO Targets Small and Medium Enterprises," *Chile Economic Report* (Summer 1995): 2–9.

[10] These statistics are from William L. Megginson, Robert C. Nash, and Matthias van Randenborgh, "The Financial and Operating Performance of Newly Privatized Firms," *Journal of Finance* 49 (1994): 403–452. (The information is on page 404.)

ties. Furthermore, the transfer of technologies and techniques from developed nations has provided new challenges, which existing management has often not been capable of meeting. Consequently, many private equity investments in developing nations have focused on either *(i)* purchasing and improving the operations of established firms or business units, or *(ii)* consolidating smaller businesses to achieve large, more cost-effective enterprises.

The final two categories of private equity investors are largely unique to the developing world. The first of these is investments in strategic alliances. In many cases, major corporations have made strategic investments (acquisitions, joint ventures, and alliances) in developing countries without a detailed knowledge of the business environment or their partners. To address these information gaps, corporations have increasingly welcomed private equity funds as third-party investors. The private equity investor is expected to provide much of the informed monitoring of the local partner that the corporation finds difficult to undertake.

A final class of investment has been infrastructure funds. Most infrastructure projects in the developed world have been financed through the issuance of bonds. In some developing nations, particularly in Asia, private equity funds have financed major projects, such as bridges, docks, and highways.

There are several reasons for the reluctance of private equity investors in developing nations to make the kinds of early-stage, technology-intensive investments that U.S. venture capitalists specialize in. First, of course, in many markets trained technical talent and the necessary infrastructure (e.g., state-of-the-art research laboratories) are scarce. Second, in many nations intellectual property protection is weak, or the enforcement of these rights is questionable. Thus, even if one was able to develop a successful product, it is unclear how rapid imitation could be avoided. A third factor is the difficulty in exiting these investments (discussed in more detail below). Finally, many investors argue that investing in a developing country is already a very risky act. To take on additional business risk would be imprudent. Consequently, they concentrate on mature enterprises with established track records.

In recent years, however, true venture capital investments have become more common in developing nations. These have fallen into three broad categories. The first set have sought to provide services to developing countries that are already available in the developed nations, such as investments in business-to-business exchanges and on-line auction sites geared to a particular region. The second category has sought to link the human capital in developing nations with labor-starved Western corporations. The leading examples of these types of transactions have been in India, where numerous software firms have received venture backing to provide programming services to American and European corporations. The final—and still rarest—set of transactions has sought to commercialize technology originating in developing countries for sale in the global marketplace.

Deal Identification and Due Diligence   The screening of investments is a major focus of private equity funds in developed nations. Typically, a venture capitalist in the United States receives several hundred times more proposals than he could invest in. Funds develop broad criteria to quickly select the deals that will later be subject to in-depth evaluation.

In developing countries, private equity investors have to be more opportunistic, since the number of attractive investments is lower. While deals are identified from the same sources—for example, other entrepreneurs and business intermediaries like lawyers and accountants—most investors take a much more active strategy. They exploit tight relationships among business and social groups in the region. This often gives them a first-mover advantage over outside investors without such ties.

The criteria employed by private equity investors are similar in developed and developing nations. In interviews, both sets of investors place management as the overriding factor in the success of any venture. Many speak of the need for "chemistry" among venture capitalists and the entrepreneur, and seek to evaluate the management team's commitment, drive, honesty, reputation, and creativity. Other criteria—such as the size of the market, the threat of obsolescence, and the ability to exit the investment—are also similar.

In evaluating potential deals, however, private equity investors in developing nations emphasize two sets of risks that are seldom encountered in developed nations. The first of these is country risk. A revolution, for instance, might lead to the nationalization of foreign investments. A more common threat, however, is the potential costs of rent-seeking behavior. The highly regulated infrastructure sector is usually of great concern to investors because politically motivated regulatory changes can directly affect cash flows. Investors need to carefully analyze the institutions and legal framework as well as industry regulations. One very visible example of the potential costs of this behavior was the Enron Dabhol project in India. In this case, the newly elected government of Maharashtra, a state in India, canceled the power plant contract of Enron for the largest proposed foreign investment in India. Accused of bribery and overcharging, Enron agreed to renegotiate the contract even though it claimed to have already spent $300 million on the unfinished plant.[11] Working to limit these dangers, however, may be government's concerns about the reputational consequences of such actions: that is, the potential of their actions to deter future private investment and to invite criticism from multilateral financial organizations.

A second concern is exchange rate risk. Although this problem is hardly unique to developing countries, the Asian Financial Crisis of 1997 dramatically demonstrated the volatility of these markets. A major devaluation of a developing nation's currency could lead to a sharp drop in the returns enjoyed by its U.S. investors. Ways to mitigate this risk include entering into currency swaps, the purchase of options based on relative currency prices, or the purchase of forward currency. Since the nature and timing of the future payments are usually unknown to private equity investors, however, this poses some real challenges. While hedging tools have attracted increasing interest, their actual use by private equity investors in developing nations appears to be very limited to date.

Deal Structuring   The choice of financing vehicle also differs between developed and developing markets. Investors in developed nations use a variety of instruments, including common and several classes of preferred stock, debt, and convertible preferred. These financial instruments allow the private equity investors to stage investments, allocate risk, control management, provide incentives to executives, and demarcate ownership.

In many developing countries, private equity investors primarily use plain common stock. This reflects several factors. First, in several countries, especially in Asia, different classes of stock with different voting powers are not permitted. Thus, investors must seek other ways in which to control the firm. These are often of extreme importance, since most of the companies are family owned or controlled. Such control rights allow

---

[11] For an overview, see Jonathan Bearman, "Death of Enron's Dabhol LNG Project Sends Shockwaves Through Industry," *Oil Daily* 45, August 9, 1995, 1 *ff.*

the venture capitalists to step in during such messy controversies such as a dispute between two sons as to who should succeed the father as president.

Although the structure of the investments may differ, shareholder agreements in developed and developing countries are likely to include the same control rights. These include affirmative covenants—such as the investors' right to access the firm's premises and records—as well as negative covenants that limit actions that the entrepreneur might take, such as the sale or purchase of significant assets of the firm. While the terms may be similar, their enforceability may vary. The enforceability of these shareholders' agreements depends strongly on the country or region of the investment. For instance, they are usually enforceable in Latin courts, but they may not hold in some Asian courts like China's.

Pricing Significant differences also appear in the pricing of transactions in developed and developing nations. Reflecting the later stage of most investments, the types of spectacular returns seen in U.S. ventures such as Digital Equipment, Genentech, and Netscape have traditionally not been often encountered. As William Hambrecht, chairman of the San Francisco-based investment bank Hambrecht & Quist, points out, "Asian investing success in baseball terms is characterized by doubles and triples, not the occasional home run characteristic of U.S. venture capital."[12] This traditional pattern is changing, however, as venture investments become more commonplace: examples include StarMedia in Latin America and Infosys in India.

Venture capitalists' assessment of the value of a company in a developing nation is often problematic. Challenges abound at many levels. For instance, many developing countries lack timely and accurate macroeconomic and financial information. Sometimes macroeconomic variables published by central banks are manipulated by governments to portray a healthier economy. These uncertainties—combined with political and regulatory risks—may make it extremely difficult to draw up reasonably accurate projections. The uncertainty increases further since most private companies do not even have audited financial statements, especially family-run businesses. Furthermore, accounting principles and practices, though improving, are still very different from Western standards.

THE PRIVATE EQUITY CYCLE: EXITING

Perhaps the most vexing aspect of venture investing in developing nations has been the difficulty of exit. The fortunes of private equity investors in the developed world have been largely linked to those of the market for initial public offerings (IPOs). Studies of the U.S. market suggest that the most profitable private equity investments have, on average, been disproportionately exited by way of IPOs. In both Europe and the United States, there has been a strong link between the health of the IPO market and the ability of private equity funds to raise more capital.

Private equity investors in developing countries cannot rely on these offerings. Even in "hot markets" where large foreign capital inflows are occurring, institutional funds are usually concentrated in a few of the largest corporations. Smaller and new firms typically do not attract significant institutional holdings and have much less liquidity.

An illustration of these claims is India, which saw over 2000 IPOs between January 1991 and April 1995. Despite the volume of IPOs, the public market has not been

---

[12] Wendi Tanaka, "Advising the Asia Investor: Experts Say It May Be a Gold Mine, But No Quick Rewards," *The San Francisco Examiner*, September 20, 1994.

an attractive avenue for exiting private equity investments. The bulk of these offerings appear to be bought by individual investors, who purchase them at huge discounts. (The typical share trades on the day of its offering at 106% above its offering price.) After the offering, trading appears to be very thin for most offerings. For instance, 18% of the offerings do not trade on the day immediately after the offering. (Most of these apparently never trade again.) It would be very difficult for a private equity investor to liquidate a substantial stake in a young firm through this mechanism.[13] The situation in many other emerging markets, which lack the infrastructure of settlement procedures, payment systems, custodial or safekeeping facilities, and regulations, is even bleaker.

Consequently, private equity investors in developing countries have tended to rely on the sale to portfolio firms to strategic investors. This can be problematic, however, when the number of potential buyers is small. The purchaser can exploit the private equity investor's need to exit the investment and can acquire the company for below its fair value. This is particularly likely to be the case when the firm invests in a strategic alliance: the only feasible purchasers are likely to be the other partners in the alliance.

Several private organizations have tried to develop creative approaches to the exiting problem. Examples include the listing of the shares on an exchange in a developed country and the acquisition of a similar firm in a developed country (which is subsequently merged with the firm in the developing nation). This is likely to be an area for continued innovation in the years to come.

LOOKING FORWARD

The future of private equity in the developing world remains highly uncertain, but there are reasons to be optimistic. While the interest of U.S. institutional investors remains rather variable, the increasing involvement of leading private equity organizations in investments in developing nations should increase the quality of the deal selection and management. The evolution of institutions such as national securities exchanges, regulatory agencies, banking systems, and capital markets suggest that the difficult problem of exiting investments may eventually be addressed.

Perhaps most persuasively, the types of environments where private equity funds have thrived in the United States are quite similar to developing nations: the investors have specialized in financing illiquid, difficult-to-value firms in environments with substantial uncertainty and information asymmetries. In short, it would not be surprising if the private equity industry in developing nations slowly matures, with the investment cycle becoming increasingly similar to that of developed nations.

FURTHER READING

Anthony Alward, *Trends in Venture Capital Finance in Developing Countries*, Washington, DC, International Finance Corporation, 1998.

Asian Venture Capital Journal, *Asian Venture Capital Journal*, 2000 and earlier years.

Asian Venture Capital Journal, *The Guide to Venture Capital in Asia: 2000 Edition*, Hong Kong, Asian Venture Capital Journal, 2000.

Asset Alternatives, *Latin American Private Equity Analyst*, Wellesley, MA, 2000 and earlier years.

[13] Ajay Shah, "The Indian IPO Market: Empirical Facts," Working Paper, Centre for Monitoring the Indian Economy, Bombay, 1995.

LAURENCE W. CARTER, *IFC's Experience in Promoting Emerging Market Investment Funds*, Washington, DC, International Finance Corporation, 1996.

T. CHOTIGEAT, et al. "Venture Capital Investment Evaluation in Emerging Markets," *Multinational Business Review* 5 (Fall 1997): 54–62.

WILLIAM B. DALE and RICHARD N. BALE, *Private United States Venture Capital for Investment in Newly Developing Countries*, Industrial International Comparative Studies, Investment Series, no. 2, Menlo Park, CA, Development Center, Stanford Research Institute, 1958.

PAUL H. FOLTA, "The Rise of Venture Capital in China: Context and Cases for Newcomers and Skeptics," *China Business Review* 26, no. 6 (1999): 6–15.

DEAN FOUST, KAREN L. MILLER, and BILL JAVETSKI, "Special Report: Financing World Growth," *Business Week* (October 3, 1994): 100–103.

JAMES W. FOX, "The Venture Capital Mirage: An Assessment of USAID Experience with Equity Investment," Working Paper, Washington, DC, Center for Development Information and Evaluation, U.S. Agency for International Development, 1996.

DEIRDRE FRETZ, "Emerging Markets' Push for Private Equity," *Institutional Investor* 29 (October 1995): 319–320.

DEVASHIS MITRA, "The Venture Capital Industry in India," *Journal of Small Business Management* 38 (April 2000): 67–78.

MARK MOBIUS, *The Investor's Guide to Emerging Markets*, Burr Ridge, IL, Irwin Professional Publishing, 1992.

SILVIA B. SAGARI and GABRIELA GUIDOTTI, "Venture Capital: Lessons from the Developed World for the Developing Markets," Discussion Paper No. 13, Washington, DC, International Finance Corporation, 1992.

LARRY W. SCHWARTZ, "Venture Abroad: Developing Countries Need Venture Capital Strategies," *Foreign Affairs* 73 (November–December 1994): 14–19.

LISA SEDELNICK, "Sector Funds Surge," *LatinFinance* (December 1995): 13–16.

LORENZO WEISSMAN, "The Advent of Private Equity in Latin America," *The Columbia Journal of World Business* 31 (Spring 1996): 60–98.

28

Joe Casey: January 2000

Joe Casey loaded the chair lift that would take him up to the formidable double black diamond runs at Jackson Hole, Wyoming. This would be his last run before rushing to an evening plane back to New York in time for the next day's partnership meeting of Venrock Associates (VA), one of the most respected venture capital firms in the world. This meeting, VA's first in the new millennium, marked the beginning of Casey's third full year with the firm. It would be a critical year for Casey: important for determining whether or not he would become a VA partner, important for seeing his first liquidity events (two of his companies were doing well enough to go public), and important for his own peace of mind as he found his own style of investing.

As the lift whirred its way up the mountain, Casey reflected on his career and wondered what he should do differently in the new year.

HARD WORK, STEADY PROGRESS

Born in Taunton, Massachusetts, Casey grew up in a family of educators. His father was superintendent of schools in Belmont and his mother a teacher. After a public education, Casey attended Holy Cross where his pre-med aspirations "foundered on the rocks of organic chemistry." He switched his major to history, with electives in business and economics, getting his first taste of business during a summer stint at Procter & Gamble. That "indoctrination into *Fortune 50* companies [taught me that] business is not always glamorous. After a summer of pushing soap, I knew I wanted to be involved in a technology company."

The year was 1985, the dawn of the PC era, and Casey wanted to be part of it. Back at Holy Cross, he decided to get a job with a technology company that had a strong training program. He achieved that goal when Xerox recruited him as a sales trainee. Casey graduated from Holy Cross on a Thursday and four days later, on a Monday; he started Xerox sales training. "I needed the money so I couldn't afford to take any time off."

Senior Lecturer G. Felda Hardymon prepared this case as the basis for class discussion rather than to illustrate either effective or ineffective handling of an administrative situation. He gratefully acknowledges the assistance of Ann K. Leamon, Manager of the Center for Case Development.

At Xerox Casey learned the basics of sales management. With little business experience and no sense of the politics that went into assigning territories, Casey had scant ammunition in the battle for the best territories. He was assigned to the unglamorous territory of Plymouth County, Massachusetts.

> Selling to the industrial companies and mills in New Bedford and southeast Massachusetts, I learned a little about business and a lot about myself. About business, I learned it is better to be in the untapped areas where there is less competition, a lower existing customer base, and lower expectations. About myself I learned about hard work and tenacity.

Within a year, Casey's hard work paid off in a promotion to Xerox's prestigious office in downtown Boston where he went from selling typewriters and single copy-machines to high-end office systems. Within a year he was promoted again to a major account assignment: the educational territory within Boston where he sold to MIT, Boston University and Harvard University. That experience taught him the value of managing demanding relationships and orchestrating complex transactions that could take months to close.

HBS TO INTEL

In 1989, after four years at Xerox, Casey was beginning to think about advancing his business career. He commented, "Plan all you want but career development is a lot about intuition." One Xerox colleague suggested that he consider business school. "I was not programmed to go to business school *per se*, but I was programmed for higher education coming from a family that valued it so highly." Casey's daily commute took him past Harvard Business School (HBS) and over the spring of 1989 drove home his colleague's suggestion. He decided to apply.

He entered HBS in September of 1990 with the expectation that the experience "would allow me to complement my practical experience with some much-needed formal business training." Casey loved HBS and found it a great experience for two reasons: "Since I had worked for five years, I knew why I was in business school and I knew what I didn't know." He especially prized the community of the business school and the balance between academics and interaction with interesting and interested people.

During his first year at HBS, a friend who worked for Apple remarked "You would be a perfect fit for Intel." His friend's observation was based on his knowledge of Intel's process-oriented culture and Casey's systematic, tenacious style. Casey wanted to work in a fast-growth, high-tech company, and having already sampled life on Route 128, he was eager to experience Silicon Valley. Intel seemed perfect, so Casey resolved to get a summer job there.

Since the Intel 386 microprocessor had just been introduced, Casey figured that the action would be in marketing. Finding Intel had no summer recruiting process on campus, Casey used the sales skills gained at Xerox. At Baker Library, Casey searched through Intel's public reports and targeted the vice president of marketing, Ron Whittier. Casey then mounted a cold calling campaign on Whittier.

"I called him at the same hour every day until I got through. Since I had to leave class repeatedly to do it, the HBS prof thought I had a kidney infection." Casey's perseverance paid off when Whittier picked up the phone and talked with him for five minutes. "I played the HBS card and told him I wanted to be involved in product marketing."

A senior Intel executive, Les Vadasz, happened to be on sabbatical teaching at HBS that semester. Whittier suggested that Vadasz interview Casey. The interview went well enough that Casey found himself flying to San Jose several weeks later for an interview, returning the same day on the "red eye" to avoid missing class. The campaign paid off when Casey was offered a summer job at Intel's Santa Clara, California, headquarters.

The summer of 1990 found Intel in the early stages of the "P5" (later Pentium) microprocessor project. Casey joined the P5 team and spent the summer analyzing systems integrators as a possible channel for Intel. At the end of the summer, he presented his conclusions to the entire executive staff, including Intel's CEO, Andy Grove, and Les Vadasz. Casey returned to HBS feeling good about his Intel experience and about the visibility he gained there.

Considering his career options during his second year at HBS, Casey had "zero interest in venture capital." He was determined to continue his career at an entrepreneurial, fast-growth, high-tech company. He surveyed the options and found that his Intel experience had given him entrée into the companies he wanted to join, notably networking companies such as Banyan, Wellfleet, Synoptics, and Cisco. Years later Casey would see that these companies foreshadowed his specialty in data networking as a venture capitalist.

BACK TO INTEL

Despite many attractive opportunities, Casey ultimately decided to return to Intel, where he was asked to join the newly established Corporate Business Development (CBD) unit headed by Les Vadasz. Of CBD's six employees, Casey was the youngest, the only one who was not a career employee, and the only one "who knew nothing about technology." Their charter was simple and broad—to extend Intel's marketing and technology relationships through private equity investments. Within Intel, a highly technical, results-oriented company, the value of CBD was not appreciated initially. Many people at Intel thought it was wasting money. Moreover, there was an underlying risk aversion surrounding CBD, because of the lack of control that private equity investments carried with them. Casey commented, "The VC world is a world of ambiguity and Intel was not used to ambiguity. In that first year CBD made only 10 investments. In contrast by 1998 they had participated in over 100 deals amounting to over $300 million in equity investments. As usual, Intel figured it out."

During those first two years at CBD, Casey was part of the team that sharpened CBD's charter to invest in companies that would extend technology and drive the demand for high-performance microprocessors.

> Among the things I learned at CBD was that the most important decisions may be the decisions you don't make. At a place like Intel you don't get rewarded for activities, you get rewarded for results. Consequently, a "no" decision was counter to my incentives, which were to get deals done. It took discipline to realize that there were some deals better not done!

> In many ways it was the absolutely perfect job for starting out. It gave me the opportunity to see what was happening in the technology world, it taught me to think strategically on Intel's behalf and to identify key trends. I had unlimited access to executives and technical resources and built a good network of people inside and outside of Intel. In many ways, it taught me resourcefulness that I would use later and it was a great set-up for my subsequent roles at Intel.

Casey's position at CBD allowed him to exercise his strength in market analysis and strategy while he learned about technology. He also developed an external network of executives in high-technology companies. At CBD Casey first became interested in a venture capital career and sought out the advice of his friend, Geoff Yang, an established venture capitalist at Institutional Venture Partners (IVP).

> I had established a rapport with Geoff, so I sat down with him and asked his advice about becoming a venture capitalist. He advised me to stay in Intel but get out of CBD—since it was a staff department—and get into operations to build up a background that I could bring into venture capital. That would allow me to relate to entrepreneurs as peers and develop decision-making skills and judgment.
>
> After this conversation, I went back to my mentor, Ron Whittier, and told him I wanted to get into product marketing and I wanted to work on a cutting-edge project. He told me that I needed to gain technical depth. So he challenged me to go away, come back and tell him why I was the guy who could take on a job like this.
>
> When I came back to Ron with the idea of taking several technical courses, he said it wouldn't work. But Ron, who by that time was head of Intel Architectural Labs (IAL) *[the internal group for all advanced technology development at Intel]*, took a risk on me and agreed to put me through a series of assignments over six months within IAL. My acceptance of the role came with no promises of an attractive job later, only the opportunity to address my weakness in a very direct hands-on way. It was to be baptism by fire.

OPERATIONS AT INTEL

When Casey joined IAL in mid-1994, he had "faith in Whittier, faith in myself, but no promises." His first assignment was to build computers from components so that the labs could get insight into dealing with system-level architecture and design. "Other than knowing the difference between an oscillator and a screwdriver, I was less than useless at first. The learning curve was straight up and the experience defeating at times. It was definitely an exercise in humility!"

Later, Casey was involved in laying local area networks on which the high-performance microprocessor groups could test applications. "I laid the first switched 100 megabit local area network (LAN) that Intel had," Casey recalled proudly. He then spent five months with various other development labs within IAL where he found himself reading constantly to try to keep up. He worked closely with a group of engineers involved in natural signal processing (NSP), an Intel breakthrough he found intriguing and a team he respected tremendously.

NSP attempted to use signal processing for real-time functions on a microprocessor. It was to be used to implement such applications as enhanced media and speech recognition. The experience taught Casey about the real world:

> It turned out to be a dicey project because its software implementation conflicted with what Microsoft was doing. At the time, Windows did not support NSP and so we were advocating a real-time operating system kernel right when Microsoft was introducing Windows 95. This conflicted with their plans, and I very quickly learned how the outside world impinges on elegant technical plans.

Casey took on product planning responsibilities for NSP, having earned credibility working with the engineers. NSP ultimately was called MMX and was implemented in silicon as part of a new chip. Microsoft then committed to support the new architecture, promising to incorporate calls to MMX in later software releases. As MMX became central to the product plans of the Pentium lines of microprocessors, Casey formally moved to the Desktop Products Group (DPG) to take part in the launch of these products. He finally found himself in the role he had intended to achieve during the first year of business school.

When the marketing manager in Japan who was to introduce the Pentium II was injured in an auto accident, Casey went to take his place. In addition to the task of the new Pentium introduction, this role involved oversight of marketing the entire microprocessor line in Japan. After five months and a successful launch of the Pentium II, Casey returned to California in May 1996 with the offer to become head of product marketing for the Asia Pacific region beginning in September and working out of Hong Kong. During that summer, while preparing to take up that position, Casey was assigned to run the annual long-range planning effort for DPG. As he returned to California to prepare for a whole new segment of his Intel career, Casey wondered if this might be the time to go into venture capital.

THE VENTURE CAPITAL JOB SEARCH

Casey gave himself three months to find a job in venture capital, knowing that once he left for Hong Kong, he would be committed to the next stage of his career at Intel. Immediately upon his return from Japan, he sought advice from several venture capitalists he knew through his work at CBD: Dave Marquardt of August Capital, Tony Sun of Venrock, Greg Avis of Summit Partners, and Tim Haley of IVP. He asked each one the same question: "Do I have what it takes to be a successful venture capitalist?" The universal answer was, "Yes, but—" The questions that the venture capitalists raised were: "Is there a place that needs you now and would you fit with that firm?"

Looking back on that time, Casey remembered:

> I never knew where I was in the process. I had a good alternative in going to Hong Kong for Intel, but that would have taken me off track from being a venture capitalist. I would have lost my informal network of contacts—an invaluable asset for the start of my career. At the same time, I was overseeing roughly forty people on a tough assignment; so I was working day and night and slipping in conversations with my VC network when I could.
>
> Tony Sun had told me Venrock was thinking of adding people on the east coast and suggested that I call Dave Hathaway. When I had my first conversation with Hathaway it felt like Ron Whittier all over again. The conversation was encouraging. He was interested in my background and he was clearly interested in bringing someone on board.

During that summer Casey talked with many firms, but the talks progressed quickly with Venrock and another national firm also interested in hiring in their east coast office. The process with Venrock involved four meetings over eight weeks, two trips to the Venrock New York offices and many phone conversations. Casey was following a similar process with the other firm but felt Venrock was the best fit. "Venrock had the most consistent focus with my interests and the best cultural fit. They had a great position in the industry and a reputation for professionalism and integrity." One well-known east coast venture capitalist that Casey talked to about his career search told him, "You can never go wrong with Venrock."

> But I was snowed under with work for Intel and it was August and I was thinking that I would never get an offer in time. I talked to Dave on a Wednesday and the next day, Thurs-

day, we were due to present our long-range plan to the executive staff at Intel. It was the very same kind of executive staff meeting that I presented to during my summer stint at Intel so it felt like bookends! I took the next day off and when I got into the office on Monday there was a call from Ted McCourtney inviting me to join Venrock.

It was August 15, 1997.

Venrock Associates

Venrock Associates (VA) was established in 1969 to formalize the private equity activities of the Rockefeller family that had begun in the 1930s. The Rockefeller family had a long tradition of supporting new enterprises. Even before World War II, Laurance Rockefeller, a pioneer in venture capital, had made important investments in aviation, aerospace, and electronics with such companies as McDonald Douglas Corporation, Eastern Airlines, and (later) Thermo Electron.

In the modern era, Venrock was one of the most respected and successful venture capital firms, having backed Apple Computer, Genetics Institute, CheckPoint Software, DoubleClick, Millennium Pharmaceuticals, and Intel itself. By 1997 VA had seven partners, four in the east coast office at Rockefeller Plaza in New York City and three on the west coast in Palo Alto. (See Exhibit 28-1 for biographies of Venrock Partners.)

Before he met with VA the first time, Casey had prepared an outline with the key messages he wanted to convey to a venture capital partnership that might hire him. (See Exhibit 28-2.) The "elevator ride" summary was that his competence and breadth in technology and his industry experience would make him valuable to a venture capital firm. In addition, he had the correct personality fit, since he could demonstrate his ability to work collaboratively, and he brought a network of companies and contacts that would allow him to generate deal-flow and resources independently. Finally, he highlighted his "nose for a deal" and his ability to identify a market opportunity by recognizing technology trends, market needs, and relevant technologies. In this outline, Casey explained his attraction to venture capital industry, including his passion for technology and for the entrepreneurial process as well as how comfortable he was with the nature of the work and the job content. He also highlighted what he would bring to any venture capital firm. He honed this information down to a series of bullet points, each backed up by examples from his track record, including the MMX technology launch, the direction of product marketing in Japan, and his initial success at Xerox.

After taking a few weeks for holiday, Casey joined Venrock in its New York office in October 1997. Shortly after joining Venrock, Casey wrote down his objectives for success at Venrock and developed a plan to meet them (see Exhibit 28-3).

STARTING A VENTURE CAREER

As the new millennium approached, Casey analyzed his progress and assessed areas in which he could improve, both his performance as a venture capitalist and his contribution to VA. As part of Venrock's management process, he had made up his own grading sheet to measure himself against his objectives (see Exhibit 28-4). Casey had spent much of the past two years working with David Hathaway, a senior partner at Venrock, who specialized in information technology and data communications. With Hathaway, Casey had made two investments: Castle Networks and Airspan Communications. Casey's contribution to each of these deals had increased to the point where he was the primary VA principal on the Airspan case.

EXHIBIT 28-1

VENROCK PARTNERS IN DECEMBER 1999

Dave Hathaway joined Venrock in 1980. Previously, he was employed by Sprout Group, Automatic Data Processing, G.A. Saxton & Co., and Morgan Guaranty Trust Company. His current areas of focus include data networking, wireless equipment and services, and telecommunications equipment and service providers. His activities at Venrock have included the initial financing of Castle Networks (acquired by Siemens), Media Metrix, Mentor Graphics, New Oak Communications (acquired by Bay Networks) and Sequent Computers. Dave presently serves on the boards of 2nd Century Communications, Cimetry, HighGround Systems, Li Medical, Metawave Communications, Tantivy Communications, and Torrent Systems. He has a B.A. in American Studies from Yale University.

Ray Rothrock joined Venrock in 1988. His focus is primarily Internet companies and information technology in general. Ray serves on the boards of CheckPoint Software Technologies (NASDAQ: CHKP) of Tel Aviv, Israel; USinternetworking Inc. (NASDAQ: USIX); and Fogdog Sports (NASDAQ: FOGD). His private board affiliations include Appliant Inc., Qpass Inc., Reciprocal Inc., Shym Technology, Space.com, Versity.com, PrintNation.com, General Bandwith, and Simba Technologies. He previously served on the board of Spyglass (NASDAQ: SPYG), DIGEX, Inc. (acquired by Intermedia Communications) and Haystack Labs (acquired by Trusted Information Systems/Network Associates). He also led Venrock's investment in DoubleClick (NASDAQ: DCLK). He received a B.S. in Nuclear Engineering from Texas A&M University, an S.M. in Nuclear Engineering from the Massachusetts Institute of Technology, and an M.B.A. with Distinction from the Harvard Business School. Ray has served as the president and director of the New York Venture Capital Forum, and is presently on the Investment Advisory Committee of the Texas A&M Foundation and the Board of Trustees of the Woodside Priory School.

Tony Sun came to Venrock Associates in 1979. His previous experience was with Hewlett-Packard, TRW and Caere Corporation. Tony, based in Menlo Park, focuses exclusively on information technology projects. He serves on the boards of AccessLine Communications, ANDA Networks, Brightware, Cognex Corporation, Komag, OptiMight Communications, Phoenix Technologies, Ltd., 3Dfx Interactive, Ramp Networks, Worldtalk Communications, and Zettacom. He previously served on the boards of Lightera Networks/ Ciena, StrataCom/Cisco, TransMedia Communications/Cisco, and WhoWhere? Inc/Lycos. Tony holds an S.B. in Electrical Engineering, an S.M. in Electrical Engineering, and an Engineer degree from the Massachusetts Institute of Technology, as well as an M.B.A. from the Harvard Business School.

Ted McCourtney joined Venrock in 1970. Ted was previously with McKinsey & Co. In his 29 years at Venrock he has led the financing of companies such as Visual Networks, Caremark, Apollo Computer, SDRC, Cellular Communications, Rehab Systems, and Surgical Health. He remains active in the National Venture Capital Association where he was a past president, chairman and director. Ted presently serves on the boards of NTL, Caremark, Corecomm, American Disease Management, and Visual Networks. He has an M.B.A. from the Harvard Business School and a B.S. in Mechanical Engineering from the University of Notre Dame.

Tony Evnin came to Venrock in 1974. Tony's previous experience was as a research scientist and business development manager at Story Chemical and Union Carbide. His focus today is largely on biotechnology and related life sciences. He has led financings of several major biotechnology companies over the last 24 years. Tony presently serves on the boards of Caliper Technologies, Ribozyme Pharmaceuticals, Triangle Pharmaceuticals, and several private companies, including IDUN Pharmaceuticals, Sunesis Pharmaceuticals, and Net Genics. He led Venrock's investment in Athena Neurosciences, Centocor, Genetics Institute, IDEC Pharmaceuticals, IDEXX Laboratories, and Sepracor. He was awarded his Ph.D. in Chemistry from the Massachusetts Institute of Technology and also has an A.B. in Chemistry from Princeton University.

Pat Latterell has been a General Partner at Venrock since 1989. He has been active in health-care venture capital since 1983, helping form and fund over three dozen new medical ventures over the past 17 years. Prior to Venrock, Pat was a general partner at Rothschild Ventures and an executive with Syntex Pharmaceuticals. Based in Menlo Park, he focuses on biopharmaceutical, medical device, and health-care Internet start-ups. He previously served on the board or as an active investor with Cardiothoracic Systems (Guidant), EP Technologies (Boston Scientific), Geron, Immulogic Pharmaceuticals, Isis Pharmaceuticals, PerSeptive Biosystems (PE Biosystems/Celera), Pharmacyclics, Pointshare, Sepracor, and TCell Sciences, among others. Pat currently serves on the boards of Allergenics, A-Med Systems, BioWeb.com, CanDo.com, EMBOL-X, Eos Biotechnology, Healinx.com, Medical Technology Group, MicroHeart, Oratec Interventions, Signal Pharmaceuticals, and Vical. He also leads Venrock's involvement with Argomed. Pat holds an S.B. in Biological Sciences and an S.B. in Economics from the Massachusetts Institute of Technology and an MBA from the Stanford University Graduate School of Business.

Kim Rummelsburg joined Venrock in 1984. She was previously at the Chase Manhattan Bank, N.A. in various positions of Domestic Private Banking. Kim serves as chief financial and administrative officer for the Venrock partnerships. She holds a B.S. in Business Administration from the University of Connecticut and an M.B.A. from New York University.

EXHIBIT 28-2

JOE CASEY'S NOTES FOR INTERVIEWING VENTURE CAPITALISTS

Key Messages
- Elevator Ride
  - Technology competency & breadth
  - Industry experience
  - Personality fit
- Network of Companies and Contacts: Independently Generate Deal-Flow & Resources
  - Intel and other company contacts
  - Venture capitalists
  - Recruiters, consultants, and other professionals
  - Professors
- Identify Opportunities: "Nose for a Deal"
  - Defining market developments: pattern recognition
    - Market segment attractive? early? growing?
    - Limited or growing competition
  - Relevant Technologies
    - Good science? realistic product schedule? key dependencies?
- Selecting the Right Company
  - Existing Opportunities
    - Technology/product/service
    - Sound management team
    - Defensible strategy: positioning, barriers to entry, network effects
    - Deal: price & terms
  - Incubation
    - Marrying entrepreneurs with resources (i.e., money & management)
- Ability to Secure Deals: "Gaining Commitment . . . at Best Possible Terms"
  - Convincing entrepreneurs that their valuation improves with a VA in deal
    - Value-added board member
  - Referencing accomplishments of firm & JEC
    - Sound corporate governance
    - Financial advice
    - Specific knowledge: technologies; markets, and industry dynamics
    - Operating experience . . . ability to add-value on an on-going basis
    - Network of companies and contacts

Why VC?
- For the past 10 years, I've learned a lot about
  - Markets
  - Technologies
  - Various Operating Roles
    . . . But found that I have always gravitated toward assignments characterized by:
    - Strategy
    - Relationships: new companies; new technologies
- VC is the logical choice that combines my interests
  - Passion for Technology
  - Entrepreneurial Process
  - Principal Investing
  - Nature of the Work

EXHIBIT 28-3

OBJECTIVES DRAWN UP BY JOE CASEY ON JOINING VENROCK

Objectives

- Contribute to VA franchise
  - Broaden VA knowledge base
  - Increase visibility
    - Develop meaningful relationships
- Increase VA Deal-Flow
  - Leverage GP networks and time
  - Generate incremental activity
    - Close 2–4 meaningful deals per year
- Enhance the Value of VA Portfolio
  - Provide on-going operating support to companies
  - Ensure that relevant industry relationships are intact
  - Be a catalyst for growth; recruiting; financing; etc.

VA Business Development

- Improve VA Visibility
- Properly position VA to Entrepreneurs
  - Refine key messages
  - Update and maintain VA website
- Extend network of industry contacts.

Development Plan

Timeframe			
12 + mo.	**Proprietary Deal–Flow**		
6–12 mo.	**Investment Strategy** •Investment Focus •Execution Plan		
3–6 mo.	Domain Expertise •Industry •Technology	Contact Base •Entrepreneurs •VCs •Lawyers, etc.	Process •Sourcing •Evaluation •Deal Structure
1–3 mo.	Venrock Basics •VA Portfolio •Investment Focus		

EXHIBIT 28-4

THE "GRADING" SHEET JOE CASEY WAS CONSIDERING

**Grading of JEC's Venrock Associates
Objectives for 1998–1999**

Investment Objectives   Grade

- Establish a solid VC foundation: _____

  1. Develop *domain expertise* for communications sector; preserve knowledge base of client-server developments; continue to look "over the horizon."
  2. Cultivate broad *network* of contacts among entrepreneurs; VCs; service providers; analysts; and major corporate players.
  3. Improve *process* of sourcing; evaluating; and structuring details.

- Increase leverage of GP time through investment analysis and portfolio   _____
  company support.

- Learn the "art & science" of an effective BOD contributor by shadowing VA   _____
  GPs and observing tenured directors (e.g., Airspace).

- Present investment strategy to GPs by 9/98 outlining focal areas; investment   _____
  themes; and tactics that define my prospective focal areas at VA.

- Source and complete 2+ deals by 4/99, preferably "platform" investments (e.g.,   _____
  CHKPF) that provide visibility to other attractive opportunities.

- Extend the Venrock franchise by improving our presence in Boston and   _____
  Washington geographies, particularly with entrepreneurs; VCs; and
  bankers/analysts with whom we have no existing relationship.

- Maintain the discipline to invest in only superior companies.   _____

Administration Objectives   Grade

- Complete and maintain compelling VA Web site.   _____
- Develop agenda and recruit strong participants for Pocantico conference.   _____
- Contribute to Annual Report; LP briefing and other firm communiqués.   _____

Partnership Objectives   Grade

- Establish and effectively engage corporate partners.   _____
- Increase the visibility of the firm and individual in relevant press and forums.   _____
- Introduce an EIR program as part of new MP office; find similar vehicle for   _____
  east coast opportunities.

Castle Networks

Castle Networks was a Boston-based start-up that designed and manufactured equipment for telecommunication service providers. VA invested in Castle in March 1997. The opportunity had surfaced in Casey's first month at Venrock, as he described:

> I barely knew my firm or the venture business—and here I found myself with my partner in front of two entrepreneurs listening to a product concept that was at best a "work in progress." A friend of the firm had already endorsed the project and we knew that other

top VCs were circling so our initial meeting was as much an occasion to assess the deal as it was to sell the partnership. So much for the glamour of the VC business; it looked like I was back to carrying a bag as in the old Xerox days—and I thought I went to business school to get out of sales!

Some aspects of the Castle project appealed to Casey: (1) the pedigree of the team and their command of the topic, as well as his initial chemistry with them, (2) the significant market opportunity, and (3) the nucleus of a product concept that seemed quite appealing, based on customer feedback. Finally, the concept and the team were well-sponsored by industry players and "angels" known to Venrock.

On the same trip, Casey met with an acquaintance in the venture business. Hardy Smith and Casey had first met in 1993 when they negotiated an investment that Intel was pursuing in one of Smith's portfolio fund companies. Based on that introduction, their relationship had developed to the point where Casey had sought Smith's counsel on his career path both at Intel and in venture capital. The Castle meeting allowed Casey to inform his mentor of his early progress in the business.

During the meeting, the discussion moved to Casey's industry focus and even specific companies. Castle's founders had told Casey that Smith's fund was one of the other firms interested in a deal. Knowing that VA would want to co-invest with another good firm, Casey suggested cooperating on Castle. Smith agreed and called his partner looking after the Castle deal, suggesting Smith's partner and Joe get together. Shortly afterward, Smith's fund and VA invested together in Castle, with Hathaway, closely supported by Casey, occupying VA's Board seat. Casey later commented, "Like life, deals are often a game of inches with success based as much on timing and random events as on a precisely orchestrated strategy. And relationships and trust certainly are helpful as well."

Casey commented on his role at Castle after the investment:

> My challenge was to develop credibility—with the founders, the board and my partner—while admittedly playing the role of apprentice. I chose to keep reasonably silent in Board meetings during the first four months and to build my reputation off line. During those months, I worked very closely on company strategy, product marketing and customer engagements with one of the founders and the growing marketing organization. Based on my experiences at Intel and with a growing network of relevant contacts, I was able to add value in some meaningful ways. As time passed, not only did I feel more confident, but also the topics where I had the most proficiency increasingly became central discussion items in the Board meetings. While still maintaining a respectful profile, I was able to develop as an effective contributor to the Board discussion and decision-making process.

The outcome was a great success. Within 14 months Siemens acquired Castle. For a $5 million investment (provided in two rounds), VA received a total return of $60 million in just over a year. Beyond economic return, there was the tremendous benefit of having gone "through the cycle" of a successful investment. And, in a world where "success breeds success," Casey noted, "Castle established my credibility and a network that should lead to additional, attractive opportunities."

Airspan Communications

Airspan Communications was a U.K.-based maker of broadband wireless local loop equipment. The founder of Metawave, an existing Venrock portfolio company, referred the project to Venrock. Airspan was being spun out of DSC Communications as a noncore asset. After a failed management buyout, the division's management pursued venture funding. The investors were the original Metawave backers (Venrock, Oak, and Sevin Rosen) along with a few additional venture capitalists.

Casey described his role:

> Due to certain conditions that DSC introduced for a prospective spinout, the syndicate needed to work quickly. The DSC constraints, the significant amount of money being raised, and the company's location in London required a high level of cooperation among the VCs. To achieve a thorough assessment in a compressed timeframe, the syndicate used a divide-and-conquer approach. Besides various off-line meetings stateside, I took two trips to London in a five-week period. Throughout the process, the final composition of the syndicate was still unclear, so the due diligence process was co-opetition at its best. One true benefit of this process was the spirit of collaboration that arose among the VCs and with management—a sense of goodwill that has continued.
>
> The issues that Airspan has faced are typical. The most dramatic problem has been market "traction." For any number of reasons, the company has not achieved the revenue ramp that was projected. That fact coupled with a full headcount (100+) has meant significant cash burn. Fund-raising has been a major chore but, fortunately, one that has not been difficult.

After the investment, Casey focused on developing influence without having formal representation. But in this case, since VA had no board seat, his role was more pronounced on behalf of VA. "As with Castle, I've learned that collaboration with management (and the Board) and dedication to the company often results in much more influence than any legal Board designation offers on its own. I've become the CEO's first call in many cases dealing with strategy, marketing or financing events."

In January 2000, the prospects for Airspan looked good. The company had begun the process of selecting bankers for an IPO. Casey commented, "This will be my first 'solo' liquidity event, so I am cautiously optimistic."

TAKING STOCK

Building a Franchise

In the spring of 1999, Casey asked his partners at Venrock for their advice in this next phase of his career. Of the two projects he was most closely identified with, Castle had been acquired and the Airspan investment was going well. Both of these were considered to be in Dave Hathaway's portfolio, although the partnership recognized Casey's role. Casey described the feedback:

> As it was put to me: "You can either be known as a great lieutenant to one of the partners, or you can establish your own name." The latter choice was my obvious approach. While I enjoyed working with the partners, especially Dave, the most effective way to contribute to the firm was to extend our franchise. I needed to develop my own deal sources and operate more independently. But how?
>
> I deliberately set out to create my own turf beginning in the spring of 1999. I underestimated how difficult this transition would be. First, there is the problem of simply getting the details right: sector focus, geographic coverage, leveraging strategic contacts, and finding chemistry with other investors. Then there is the problem of reconciling the tension between the need to do deals and the discipline of doing only the best deals possible.

Casey had been elevated from associate to principal, and he thought about what it meant to be part of a partnership:

> A partnership is a steward of cultures and principles. It acts as a system of checks and balances for decision making. You have to respect the role of the partnership in going about this business, or you won't be successful.
>
> It is still unknown to me by what criteria I am being assessed as a prospective partner of Venrock. Other than being elevated to principal—a halfway point of sorts—no timeline exists. Not only are few indicators provided, they seem to change on the infrequent occasions that I speak with Ted [McCourtney, the Managing General Partner] on this topic. The benefit of this approach to career development is that it has forced me to rely on my own sense of progress and maturity in my role. Now I concentrate on four things: (1) Results—investments made and progress with portfolio companies; (2) improving the position of the Firm; (3) contributing to the partnership; and (4) establishing a responsible but distinct voice within the organization. So, when I feel I'm excelling in each of these areas, I'll know it's time.
>
> So what's my motivation? As for my role as a VC, I am most excited about my working with smart and interesting individuals and the prospect of building large, successful companies. Oh, and there is the diversity factor that satisfies my natural curiosity and keeps my short attention span in check. As for the general partner title itself, well other than the fact that I am a driven person, it's probably the recognition that my efforts are contributing to the firm in a meaningful way. And, did I forget to mention the compensation? While I'm not a money-driven person per se, a fair slice of the "economics" is important.

Into Networks

In 1998 Casey made an investment in Arepa.com, later to be renamed Into Networks. It was his first investment without Hathaway. The company produced enabling software that allowed rich media (such as video) to be delivered over broadband networks. This was a very early-stage investment in a group of technologists from the MIT Media Labs in a market that didn't really exist in 1998. On the lack of market data he commented:

> Not much material existed to populate the industry analysis frameworks I'd paid good money to learn at HBS. But there were two intriguing aspects of the company—the founder and the market potential. I always appreciate people who are passionate about their pursuits, and Ric Fulop [the founder] has that in spades. The other attractive aspect of the company was that it was a pure play on broadband networks. Broadband networks and, more specifically, last-mile solutions were one of my target areas. I thought Into Networks was not only attractive on its own but also might provide a front-row view of industry developments as they occurred.
>
> And yet, this was the sort of project that looked worse the more due diligence was done. The decision to propose this deal to the partnership resulted from some enlightenment about the venture business and the role I would need to play to be successful.
>
> I had been trained at HBS and even at the ever-paranoid Intel to assess risk properly. So, the ability to identify holes in various business plans was a rote skill. However, it took some maturing to appreciate the mechanics of how glimmering opportunities result in spite of the shortfalls. Part of this growth occurred by observing the fundamentals of early-stage company formation across our portfolio. More important was to shift my thinking from the notion of static assessment of companies to one that anticipated Venrock's and my involvement. Rather than simply qualifying the opportunity on its own merits, my final judgment now more aggressively factors in the leverage that my personal skills and the firm's resources offer as a growth catalyst for any young company. The resulting ideal investment

is one that has appealing prospects but where we can be part of an unfair advantage for the entrepreneurs, with our combined efforts building the company into a success.

Casey had spent much of his time in 1999 working with the company. In particular, he spent time with the management and the venture capitalists working on building an effective board. Casey commented:

> A problem with this company has been getting the board to function in their roles together. Early on, the level of direct interaction with the board seemed necessary, but as time passed, I grew concerned about maintaining the distinction between being directors and being executives. Proper governance was always being compromised when the board reached into the organization to satisfy its need for information and control. Another issue was that there were differing notions around the board table of the right way to run the company. Things got worse when a new CEO was recruited. We had to work very hard as a board to come to a way of working with one another effectively.

Assessing the investment's performance to date, Casey noted that

> the business is progressing nicely. The technology has now been proven in market trials with marquee broadband providers. Customer traction is excellent with the first major commercial agreement signed this week. And the team is sound and led by a capable, new CEO.

The Misses

While Into Networks was working out well, and two other new projects that Casey had sourced completely from his own resources were nearing an investment, he found himself thinking about the big ones that got away. In his first two years at Venrock, he had opportunities to consider and invest in Qtera, Akamai, Omnia, and VerticalNet. For one reason or another VA had chosen not to do these deals.

Of these, Akamai Technology was the biggest and most painful miss. After a long and intense series of discussions at VA, the partnership had approved the investment in principle and given Casey the mandate to win the deal. Casey then in fact won the deal along with co-investor Battery Ventures. However after the formal approval on the negotiated terms, a senior partner at VA had received a call from a senior partner at another firm who had also competed, and lost, the Akamai deal. In that conversation the senior partner at VA learned how Akamai had successfully played one syndicate of VCs against the other in negotiating their deal.

On learning the story, the senior partner at VA was disturbed by the company's behavior. In his more than 30 years in the venture business, the partner had come to feel that such aggressive behavior on the part of a company portended a brinkmanship with which he was uncomfortable. So the senior partner immediately required that the Akamai investment be reassessed within the VA partnership. Although the reassessment was to proceed on an objective basis, Casey felt he had no choice but to drop the investment. After Akamai had gone public with a multibillion dollar market capitalization, one VA partner had slapped Joe on the back and said, "Just think, had you done the Akamai investment you'd be a Managing General Partner today!"

Casey was philosophical about these misses:

> First the Bad News. If a successful career in venture capital is characterized by involvement with high-impact companies, then I might well be halfway down the retirement path

if only I made a few decisions differently. And a comfortable retirement it would have been—the personal gains of these investments is potentially well into eight-digits. Perhaps with the exception of dropping a winning touchdown in the Super Bowl, few failings seem more visible than passing on a blockbuster company. In an industry that heralds the "next big thing," poor decisions of the past are lurking mercilessly in every edition of the *Wall Street Journal*: record IPO; major acquisition by Big Co. Stop the presses!

"You win some, you lose some"; "This business is a game of inches"—there just aren't enough clichés to adequately rationalize these "misses." But I've learned that missed opportunities are endemic to this business. The only thing worse than missing an opportunity is to not have known about the company in the first place. So, if errors are to exist, better they be of the commission variety—assuming of course that you continue to learn from each instance.

Even with the "misses," two-thirds of that formula was put to use. In each case, I was often the person within the firm that sourced the deal. Through any number of activities and contacts, I have been able to gain a "good look" at interesting projects. There is no substitute for leg drive in the business, and just as these opportunities surfaced, you have to be optimistic that discipline and tenacity will pay dividends in the future.

But being there is only half the battle; making a sound and timely decision is also required. My sense of what makes a company a solid investment continues to evolve. When I started, my criteria were a mechanical recitation of "VC 101"—markets, teams, proprietary technology, etc. Now, based on the experiences I've had to date, I pay much more attention to the subtle aspects of a company, an investment proposal and the overall dynamics of the deal. I expect that this refinement never quite stops. Over time, my informed decisions will rely less on rote analysis than on intuition—which is a more elegant way of saying the scar tissue of experience.

In the end, this business is a great exercise in judgment. As much due diligence as I perform on a given project, there are always some questions left unanswered and still others for which there are no answers. Personal judgment is required to balance the facts with the gut feel. As I mentioned, I've seemingly made some poor decisions in the past but at no time do I think I had made the wrong judgment. No regrets; only a chance to be at the ready for the next "next big thing."

29

A Note on Private Equity Information Sources

Finding information about private equity-backed firms and private equity organizations is often difficult. If the firm is privately held, it is likely to attract little outside scrutiny and to disclose scant public information. Even if the firm is publicly traded, its coverage by the press may be infrequent. These problems are even more severe for private equity organizations. Private equity organizations tend to be extremely reluctant to disclose information about their successes, much less their failures.

Despite these difficulties, there are numerous occasions when it is critical to obtain information. One may be assessing a private firm as a strategic partner or a potential investment, or a private equity organization as a potential employer. This note summarizes the most useful information sources about these organizations.

Before beginning, however, it should be admitted that the most important information source is not discussed here: word-of-mouth. There is no substitute for informal "due diligence." Private equity organizations will often make 50 or even 75 calls before deciding to invest in a firm. A similar level of scrutiny may be appropriate before one accepts a position or undertakes a strategic alliance with a private firm.

INFORMATION ABOUT PRIVATE FIRMS

Business directories are an important, but rather limited, source of information about private firms. Directories such as Corporate Technology Information Service's *Corporate Technology Directory*, Gale Group's *Ward's Directory of U.S. Public and Private Companies*, and various state and industry directories provide basic information on employment, sales, industry focus, and year of formation. (Since these are based on survey responses, they are not always accurate!) But for more detailed information, one must turn to other sources.

A rich source of information is the *press*. Almost every firm, no matter how publicity shy, generates some press attention. The easiest approach is to search well-indexed databases such as ABI/Inform. Dow Jones Interactive Edition provides the full text of

Professor Joshua Lerner prepared this note. I thank Erika McCaffrey of Baker Library for assistance.

the *Wall Street Journal*, newswires and regional business publications, while OneSource covers many of the smaller trade journals and newswires. The coverage of the trade press is more comprehensive through LEXIS-NEXIS, which includes the *New York Times*, several newswire services, and many smaller papers. It also may make sense to check the older editions of the *Wall Street Journal* available in microfilm. (The printed index also includes *Barron's* and newswire stories not printed in the *Journal*.) It also pays to check with industry contacts as to the key trade journals that they read. Asset Alternatives publishes industry-specific newsletters (*Venture Capital & Health Care* and *Venture Capital & Information Technology*) that provide news about specific investments.

Three databases are the best sources for detailed financial information on private firms. First, Venture Economics, a unit of Thomson Financial Securities Data (TFSD), provides comprehensive information on venture industry through its VentureXpert database. The data compiled provides detailed profiles of venture capital and private equity-backed firms, as well as information on exits by IPO or trade sales and more general industry data. Typical VentureXpert profiles are reproduced in Exhibits 29-1A through 29-1C. VentureXpert is available via the Web and a client-server version where other TFSD products are also available, such as the TFSD Mergers & Acquisitions database, which provides information on corporate transactions, including joint ventures.

A second company, VentureOne, provides more detailed profiles, including information on directors and detailed business profiles. While their coverage does not extend as far back in time as that of Venture Economics and only includes venture-backed firms (rather than other private equity-financed firms), the accuracy and detail of their information are generally superior. A sample report is shown in Exhibit 29-2. Like the Venture Economics database, VentureOne allows extensive screening—for example, it is possible to identify all Internet firms that received seed financing in 1997 and were based in Massachusetts. VentureOne is a professional database, with subscriptions restricted to limited partners in private equity funds and corporations making direct investments.

Finally, information on debt financing is available through Dun and Bradstreet. This includes information on both bank loans and trade credit. It is far better to discover that a firm has defaulted on previous contractual obligations before entering into a business relationship with them rather than afterward!

Private firms sometimes make information available about themselves. It is certainly worth checking to see whether the firm has a site on the World Wide Web. This is easy to determine using the Yahoo index as well as the various search engines such as Alta Vista. It may also be worthwhile to contact the firm: frequently, one can get the standard kit of information sent out to the press and/or potential customers without being asked too many questions. While it may be easy to get this information, it may not always be accurate. In addition, a lot of helpful information may be available through a Web site specializing in that particular industry. For instance, Recombinant Capital—which markets a high-priced database on biotechnology-pharmaceutical and information technology alliances—has put much ancillary information on these firms on its Web site (http://www.recap.com).

A final source of information on private firms is the most specialized (and expensive). On occasion, one may be interested in establishing a relationship with a firm that has previously engaged in litigation. For instance, one may wish to enter into a collaborative venture with a firm that has previously litigated a key patent. Obtaining an understanding of the dispute may be important in evaluating the firm. These court records are readily available through a company called Federal Document Retrieval, which

EXHIBIT 29-1A

SAMPLE VENTURE ECONOMICS REPORTS

NetGravity, Inc.
1700 S. Amphlette Blvd.
Suite 350
San Mateo, CA 94402
United States

Company Founding Date: 05-SEP-95
Status: Public
IPO Date: 12-JUN-98
Industry: Business and Office Software (VEIC 2731)
Date Last Updated: 07-OCT-2000

Phone :650-655-4777
Fax :650-655-4776
www.netgravity.com

Business Description: Develops advertising management software for the Internet and on-line marketing communications. NetGravity's AdServer manages on-line advertising and solves needs for Web-marketers. AdServer schedules ads with an on-line interactive ad calendar and optimizes the placement and scheduling of ads.

Product Names:
AdServer Enterprise
AdCenter
AdServer Network

Investors

Firm	Fund	Focus	Rounds of Participation
Hummer Winblad Venture Partners	Hummer Winblad Venture Partners II	Early Stage	1 , 2 , 3
Hummer Winblad Venture Partners	Hummer Winblad Technology Fund II	Early Stage	1 , 2 , 3
Hummer Winblad Venture Partners	Hummer Winblad Venture Partners —Unspecified Fund	Expansion	2 , 3
London Pacific Life & Annuity Co.	London Pacific Life & Annuity Co.	Generalist	4
Redleaf Venture Management	Redleaf Venture I, L.P.	Early Stage	3
TTC Ventures	TTC Ventures	Early Stage	4
Vector Capital	Vector Capital I	Later Stage	1 , 3 , 4

Investment Rounds

Date	Stage	Number of Participating Investors	Round Amount ($Thous)
1/12/1996	Early Stage	3	3000
4/19/1996	Early Stage	3	105
3/13/1997	Expansion	6	4300
1/1/1998	Expansion	3	8682.9

Exits

IPO/Acquistion	Date	Offer Amount/Purchase Price ($Mil)
Went Public	12-JUN-98	$ 27.0 Mil

Executives (truncated list)

Name	Title	Phone	E-mail
Rick Jackson	Vice President, Marketing	650-655-4777	
John Hummer	Board Member		
Tom Shields	Vice President & CTO	650-655-4777	
Larry Wear	Vice President, Service	650-655-4777	

EXHIBIT 29-1B

SAMPLE VENTURE ECONOMICS REPORTS

Private Equity Performance Report

Investment Horizon Performance as of 06/30/2000
Calculation Type: Pooled IRR

Fund Type	3 Mo	6 Mo	9 Mo	1 Yr	3 Yr	5 Yr	10 Yr	20 Yr
SEED VC	−2.9	8.3	24.3	36.0	35.7	38.2	17.4	12.6
EARLY STAGE VC	5.4	35.8	138.9	198.2	90.2	70.9	34.9	25.3
BALANCED VC	2.1	27.1	135.3	159.4	58.9	46.4	23.9	17.2
LATER STAGE VC	3.8	21.2	60.1	69.7	38.2	36.5	24.5	18.9
ALL VENTURE	3.9	29.0	112.4	143.4	63.1	51.2	27.4	19.9
SMALL BUYOUTS	−2.7	3.2	11.8	14.0	13.4	18.4	16.7	25.6
MED BUYOUTS	−0.2	8.3	43.5	50.3	24.2	18.3	15.1	21.3
LARGE BUYOUTS	−1.2	10.0	27.4	35.3	26.0	25.0	22.8	21.9
MEGA BUYOUTS	−0.3	10.9	15.5	17.6	17.3	16.4	16.9	18.9
ALL BUYOUTS	−0.9	9.3	20.0	23.6	19.3	18.5	17.2	20.1
MEZZANINE	−3.8	−0.7	1.9	3.5	6.6	9.8	11.0	11.1
ALL PRIV EQUITY	1.0	16.7	48.2	58.9	34.4	29.9	21.6	19.9

Source: Venture Economics (TFSD)/NVCA   **Type:** Summary Performance Report

Industry Investment Report

Disbursements per Company Industry
01/01/2000 to 9/30/2000 Rounds 1 to 99

Company Industry	No. of Comp	No. of Firm	Avg Per Comp	Avg Per Firm	Sum Inv. ($mil)	Pct of Inv
Internet Specific	2124	1255	18.72	31.67	39751.52	49.72
Communications	465	572	25.50	20.73	11856.98	14.83
Computer Software	784	822	14.01	13.36	10985.27	13.74
Semiconductors/Other Elect.	193	334	25.61	14.80	4943.00	6.18
Medical/Health	281	282	9.67	9.63	2715.96	3.40
Biotechnology	143	215	13.69	9.11	1958.08	2.45
Computer Hardware	113	250	15.90	7.18	1796.22	2.25
Business Serv.	85	124	15.48	10.61	1315.73	1.65
Industrial/Energy	52	80	22.87	14.87	1189.45	1.49
Consumer Related	118	165	10.08	7.21	1189.20	1.49
Fin/Insur/RealEst	71	102	13.86	9.65	984.32	1.23
Transportation	22	30	17.15	12.58	377.41	0.47
Manufact.	26	50	11.38	5.92	295.98	0.37
Utilities	4	12	44.72	14.91	178.88	0.22
Other	19	20	6.00	5.70	113.95	0.14
Construction	9	17	12.58	6.66	113.19	0.14
Computer Other	9	20	9.12	4.10	82.05	0.10
Unknown	4	11	15.40	5.60	61.60	0.08
Agr/Forestr/Fish	6	16	6.79	2.55	40.73	0.05
TOTAL	4528	4377	17.66	18.27	79949.5	100

EXHIBIT 29-1C

SAMPLE VENTURE ECONOMICS REPORTS

HUMMER WINBLAD VENTURE PARTNERS

Firm Type: Private Firm Investing Own Capital
Firm Founding Date: 1989
Cap Under Management: $28.0 Mil
Membership Affiliations:
Date Last Updated: 31-OCT-2000

2 South Park
2nd Floor
San Francisco, CA 94107
United States
415-979-9600
415-979-9601
www.humwin.com

Investment Portfolio (truncated for display purposes)

Name	Status	Status Date
@Large Software, Inc. (FKA:Celerity, Inc.)	Privately held	
AdForce (FKA:IMGIS, Inc.)	Went Public	07-may-1999
Arbor Software Corporation	Went Public	06-nov-1995
Berkeley Systems, Inc.	Acquired	01-apr-1997
BigOnline, Inc. (FKA: BigBook, Inc.)	Acquired	24-nov-1998
Books That Work	Acquired	04-apr-1997
Cenquest, Inc. (FKA:Amicus Interactive, Inc.)	Privately held	
CenterView Software, Inc.	In registration	27-feb-1997
Central Point Software, Inc.	Acquired	01-jun-1994
CoroNet Systems(FKA:Soleil Network Technology)	In registration	08-nov-1995
Dean & DeLuca Inc.	In registration	09-may-2000
DevX.com, Inc.	Privately held	
Viquity Corporation (FKA: ecom2ecom, Inc.)	Privately held	
Watermark Software, Inc.	In registration	18-aug-1995
Wayfarer Communications, Inc.	Acquired	30-jun-1998
Wind River Systems, Inc.	Went Public	15-apr-1993
Works.com	Privately held	
Zembu Labs	Privately held	
Zero Gravity	Privately held	
eHow, Inc.	Privately held	

Funds Managed

Name	Size ($Mil)	Stage	Vintage
Hummer Winblad Venture Partners	72.0	Balanced Stage	1989
Hummer Winblad Technology Fund	0.7	Later Stage	1990
Hummer Winblad Technology Fund II	1.2	Early Stage	1993
Hummer Winblad Venture Partners II	60.6	Early Stage	1993
Hummer Winblad Venture Partners— Unspecified Fund	N/A	Expansion	1996
Hummer Windblad Venture Partners III, L.P.	99.0	Expansion	1997
Hummer Winblad Venture Partners IV, L.P.	315.0	Early Stage	1999

(Continued)

EXHIBIT 29-1C   (Continued)

Investment Profile

	Num of Comp	Avg per Comp	Sum Inv $Thous.	Pct of Inv
Investment Total	75	6335.1	475129.6	100
State Breakdown				
California	50	4313.8	215690.7	45.4
Massachusetts	6	24207.3	145243.7	30.6
Washington	4	9107.8	36431.3	7.7
New York	4	6734.5	26938.0	5.7
Georgia	2	11336.4	22672.8	4.8
Oregon	3	3000.8	9002.5	1.9
Texas	1	7755.0	7755.0	1.6
North Carolina	1	3424.0	3424.0	0.7
Illinois	1	2389.3	2389.3	0.5
Pennsylvania	1	2282.3	2282.3	0.5
Minnesota	1	2035.0	2035.0	0.4
Arizona	1	1265.0	1265.0	0.3
Nation Breakdown				
United States	75	6335.1	475129.6	100.0
Industry Breakdown				
Computer Software	32	7058.8	225882.4	47.5
Internet Specific	32	6506.9	208219.9	43.8
Computer Hardware	6	1290.8	7745.0	1.6
Consumer Related	2	11141.2	22282.3	4.7
Communications	1	11000.0	11000.0	2.3
Fin/Insur/RealEst	1	0.0	0.0	0.0
Business Serv.	1	0.0	0.0	0.0
Stage Breakdown				
Early Stage	55	2153.7	118455.1	24.9
Expansion	47	4404.3	207003.1	43.6
Later Stage	17	8804.2	149671.4	31.5
Buyout/Acquisit	1	0.0	0.0	0.0

Executives

Name	Title	Phone	E-mail
Mark Gorenberg	General Partner	415-979-9600	mgorenberg@humwin.com
John Hummer	General Partner	415-931-5579	jhummer@humwin.com
Chuck Robel	Chief Operating Officer	415-979-9600	crobel@humwin.com
Deborah Wright	Chief Financial Officer	415-979-9600	dwright@humwin.com
Hank Barry	General Partner	415-979-9600	hbarry@humwin.com
Dan Beldy	Associate	415-979-9600	dbeldy@humwin.com
Ann Winblad	General Partner	415-979-9600	awinblad@humwin.com

Source: © Copyright 2000 by Venture Economics. All Rights Reserved. Used by permission.

EXHIBIT 29-2

SAMPLE VENTUREONE REPORT

Magnifi

http://www.magnifi.com

Last Update: October 1998
Last Update Type: General Update

CONTACT INFORMATION:

1601 South De Anza Boulevard
Suite 155
Cupertino, CA 95014
Financing Contact: Ranjan Sinha, President & CEO

Phone: **(408) 863-3800**
Fax: **(408) 863-7210**

COMPANY OVERVIEW:

Business Brief: Developer of automated marketing, supply-chain management software

Financing Status: As of 09/98 the company is seeking to raise a $10M round of venture financing that will start on 11/1/98 and is anticipated to close in the later first quarter of 1999. This round is open to new investors.

Founded:	02/96	**Industry:**	Software Development Tools
Employees:	45	**Status:**	Private & Independent
		Stage:	Shipping Product

INVESTORS:

Investment Firm	Participating Round #(s)
Gideon Hixon Fund	1, 2
Draper Fisher Jurvetson	1, 2
Convergence Partners	2*
IDG Ventures	1*, 2
Crystal Internet Venture Fund	1, 2

* = Lead Investor

FINANCINGS TO DATE:

Round #	Round Type	Date	Amount Raised ($MM)	Post $ Valuation ($MM)	Company Stage
1	1st	06/97	3.0	6.0	Shipping Product
2	2nd	11/97	5.1	N/A	Shipping Product

FINANCIALS:

(A = Actual   E = Estimated   P = Projected)

($MM)	1998A
Revenue	0.0
Net Income	0.0
Burnrate ($K/Month): 0.41	

(Continued)

EXHIBIT 29-2

EXECUTIVES AND BOARD MEMBERS:

Name	Title	Background	Telephone
Ranjan Sinha	President & CEO	Date joined: 02/96 Cofounder, WhoWhere	(408) 863-3807
Eric Hoffert	Chairman & CTO	Date joined: 02/96 Senior Technologist, Apple Computer	
Chris Crafford	VP, Engineering	VP, Rightworks	
Pat Greer	VP, Professional Services	VP, Wallop Software	
Phillip Ivanier	VP, Business Development	Executive, MIT Media Lab; Executive, Apple Computer	
Jim Ogara	VP, Sales & Support	VP, DEC	
David Dubbs	Director, Marketing	VP, Marketing, LookSmart; Principal, Consulting Firm, Intellectual Capital Partners; Executive, AT&T	
Stewart Alsop	Advisory Board	Partner, New Enterprise Associates	(650) 854-9499
Gordon Bell	Advisory Board	Executive, Microsoft	
Dave Davison	Advisory Board	Cofounder, New Media Magazine; Partner, Knowledge Venture Partners	
Shane Robinson	Advisory Board	VP, Engineering, Cadence	
Skip Stritter	Advisory Board	CTO, NeTpower	(408) 522-9999
Susan Cheng	Board Member, Venture Investor	Partner, IDG Ventures	(415) 439-4420
Eric DiBeneditto	Board Member, Venture Investor	Partner, Convergence Partners	(650) 854-3010
Dan Kellogg	Board Member, Venture Investor	Partner, Crystal Internet Venture Fund	(440) 349-6025
Randy Komisar	Former Officer	CEO, Lucas Arts; WebTV	(650) 233-9683
Robert Pariseau	Former Officer	Date joined: 11/97	

BUSINESS INFORMATION:

Overview: Developer of automated marketing, supply-chain management software. The company develops Web-based marketing solutions to automate the marketing supply chain and its core activities and workflow, including encyclopedias, channel management, customer acquisition/retention, business intelligence, and campaign management. The company's patent-pending core technology supports unstructured marketing files such as video images, PDFs, and business documents, and integrates with the RDBMS to allow ROI assessment on marketing investment and establish a marketing process history. The production solution, MarketBase, links the internal and external collaborators of product or campaign development into a common, Web-based platform for managing the marketing process.

Product: Marketing automation software for managing product and advertising development, establishing marketing encyclopedia, acquiring/retaining customers, and supporting channels and customers.

Customers: Customers include CNN, ABC, PBS, Boeing, Time, Citibank, the U.S. Navy, GM, and Microsoft.

Market: The company estimates a $2 billion market for its products by the year 2000.

OUTSIDE PROFESSIONALS:

General Business Banking: Cupertino National Bank
Auditor: Coopers & Lybrand
General Counsel: Venture Law Group

*** END OF REPORT—Magnifi ***

will photocopy some or all of the records. Some court records are also available on LEXIS-NEXIS.

INFORMATION ABOUT PUBLIC FIRMS

Public firms must file extensive information with the U.S. Securities and Exchange Commission (SEC). This makes finding out about these firms much easier. To track a company, the basic information is in the firm's initial public offering prospectus (description of the business, five years of financial results, directors and officers, principal shareholders, and financing history), the annual 10-K filings (description of business and financial results), and proxy statements (officers and directors and principal shareholders). The most recent financial information is available in the quarterly 10-Q statements.

All these documents are available from Primark in hard copy, microfiche, (for the past 10 years) on CD-ROM, and via the Web on the Global Access database. Much of this information (as well as news stories) is also available in summary form on the Bloomberg machines. Since mid-1996, most companies have also made filings in electronic form, which are available (text only; pictures are not included) on the Internet at the EDGAR site (http://www.sec.gov). Primark's Laser D database contains images of US SEC & International public company filings, including prospectuses, proxies, and registration statements since 1989.

Firms must also file "material" documents. Firms differ in how they define what is material, but generally a firm going public will file copies of its financing agreements with private equity organizations and strategic alliances with larger firms. These will often have a wealth of information that is not disclosed elsewhere. In many cases, a press release will describe a strategic alliance in glowing terms, but the agreement itself will reveal that the alliance is much more limited in scope. It is interesting to note how often Wall Street analysts repeat what is in the press release, without bothering to check the agreement! When a firm goes public, it will typically file all material documents in a registration statement that accompanies the IPO prospectus (more technically known as an S-1 or an S-18). The index of a typical registration statement is reproduced in Exhibit 29-3. If the firm signs an important strategic document after it is already public, it will typically be filed in a statement known as an 8-K. These are also available from Disclosure and (since mid-1996 for most firms) at the EDGAR Web site. Firms often will file repeated amendments to their registration statements, scattering key documents across their statements. This makes it very frustrating to find documents. Making life a little easier is the fact that subsequent 10-Ks often list earlier documents filed by the firm and indicate when they were filed. LEXIS's SEC Filings & Reports databases provide a searchable directory of all such filings (and any exhibits contained therein) over the past five years. In general, firms make it difficult to find the most interesting items!

Analyst reports are a somewhat useful source of information. A number of analysts seem to do little more than rephrase corporate press releases, but others do careful and insightful studies. Analyst reports are one of the few public sources of financial projections for firms. Perhaps the easiest way to obtain analyst reports is contacting the head of investor relations at the firm or else the analysts directly. (Analysts covering each firm are listed in *Nelson's Directory of Investment Research*; and the dates of recent analyst reports are indicated in the Bloomberg news file.) Alternatively, many full-text reports are available through the Investext database. Financial projections are available in the FirstCall and Bloomberg databases.

Several databases provide information about the financing activities of public firms. SDC published an annual index until 1995, known as *Corporate Finance: The IDD*

EXHIBIT 29-3

SAMPLE REGISTRATION STATEMENT INDEX

INDEX TO EXHIBITS

(Continued)

EXHIBIT 29-3 *(Continued)*

INDEX TO EXHIBITS

(1) To be supplied by amendment.

(2) Confidential treatment requested.

Review of Investment Banking. This also includes some large private placements. It is, however, rather awkward to search through. Primark's Global Access database, which provides reports on offerings during the past five years (screened by many criteria) is easier to use and can be downloaded to a spreadsheet. Much more comprehensive, however, is Security Data Company's (SDC) Global New Issues database. This contains more detailed information, and it can be downloaded onto a Lotus or Excel spreadsheet for easy analysis.

Many publications cover the public marketplace and highlight financial innovations of all sorts. Among the best are *The Red Herring* (which focuses on high-tech firms), *The IPO Reporter*, *Investment Dealer's Digest*, and *CFO*. The periodicals are well worth scanning on a regular basis.

INFORMATION ABOUT PRIVATE EQUITY ORGANIZATIONS

Among the most difficult to track are the private equity organizations themselves. Most actively avoid the press. While they disclose considerable information to their limited partners in annual reports and offering memorandums, these documents are generally confidential.

To obtain information about private equity organizations, one must thus use other means. It is worth searching LEXIS-NEXIS and other databases for the occasional mentions of these firms. Both VentureOne and Venture Economics databases can be used to construct detailed profiles of various funds, but these are difficult to access or are very costly.

Thus, often one is forced to rely on industry directories. *Galante's Venture Capital and Private Equity Directory* profiles venture capital and private equity organizations alike; venture capital organizations only are profiled in *Pratt's Guide to Venture Capital Sources*. The *Pratt's* guide is quite useful, as it has been published for several decades. This allows one to answer questions such as which partners have left the firm and how capital under management has changed. There are several other directories that list U.S. private equity firms, such as the National Venture Capital Association's *Membership Directory*, but these are substantially less informative. A CD-ROM directory has been developed by Infon, from which data can be rapidly downloaded into a spreadsheet or a mail merge program.

Many venture capital organizations make some information available through the World Wide Web. The easiest way to find these is through Yahoo: the list is located at Business and Economy/Finance and Investment/Corporate Financing/Venture Capital. The quality, informativeness, and accuracy of these Web pages vary widely. Most buyout organizations have been more cautious about embracing this technology. A few of the many more general sites about the venture capital *industry* more generally are informative, though most are pretty dreary. Among the best are PriceWaterhouseCoopers' (http://www.pricewaterhousecoopers.com/) and Accel Partners' (http://www.accel.com). Additional sites are listed at my home page (http://www.people.hbs.edu/jlerner).

While the above sources include some buyout firms, many more are listed in the National Register Publishing Company's *America's Corporate Finance Directory*, McGraw-Hill's *Corporate Finance Sourcebook*, SDC's *Directory of Buyout Financing Sources*, and the winter issue of *Financial World's Corporate Finance*. Small Business Investment Companies (a specialized type of private equity organization with government sponsorship) are listed in *Directory of Operating Small Business Investment Companies* and the National Association of Small Business Investment Companies' *Membership Directory*.

The names and nature of a fund's investors offer potentially very valuable information. Two directories provide this information. (They are also very useful for fundraising.) Venture Economics' *Directory of Private Equity Investors* has better coverage; but considerably greater detail is available in Asset Alternatives' *Directory of Alternative Investment Programs*.

Occasionally, information may be needed about the private equity industry in general. These fall into three broad classes: statistical analyses, legal guides, and general overviews. In addition to the publications cited below (especially the *Private Equity Analyst* and the *Venture Capital Journal*), there are several sources of statistical data. Particularly useful is VentureOne's *Venture Capital Industry Report* and *IPO Reporter*. The annual reviews of Venture Economics and the National Venture Capital Association are also helpful. VentureOne also does a variety of other special reports: they are summarized at http://www.ventureone.com (and may also be ordered there). Venture Economics releases quarterly investment statistics and trends on fundraising, industry performance, investments, and exits in a series of press releases that can be found in the press room section on the Venture Economics Web site at http://www.ventureeconomics.com. For data on LBOs, it is useful to check the November/December issue of *Mergers and Acquisitions* and the Security Industry Association's (less useful) *Securities Industry Fact Book*.

The primary sources for returns and performance data for the private equity industry are Venture Economics' *Investment Benchmarks Reports*, which are prepared in three separate volumes: venture capital, buyouts, and European private equity. This performance information is also available in more detail via the aforementioned VentureXpert database.

A second source of information relates to the legal status of private equity activities. The most useful reference guides are Joseph Bartlett's *Equity Finance*, the Practicing Law Institute's annual volume *Venture Capital*, Michael Halloran's *Venture Capital and Public Offering Negotiation*, and Jack Levin's *Structuring Venture Capital, Private Equity and Entrepreneurial Transactions*. (The first is the best general overview; the third is the most useful in-depth analysis.)

Finally, there are more general overviews. Many collections of "war stories" by venture capitalists exist, which may make for enjoyable reading. Less entertaining but probably more helpful are the academic overviews of the industry: especially Fenn, Liang and Prowse's *The Private Equity Market: An Overview* and (if you are interested in venture capital) Gompers and Lerner's *The Venture Capital Cycle*.

Information is available about European private equity firms in the European Venture Capital Association's *Yearbook* (formerly known as *Venture Capital in Europe*, this also has extensive statistical information), and the *Investment Benchmarks Report: European Private Equity* from Venture Economics, the *Venture Capital Report Guide to Venture Capital in the U.K. and Europe*, Galante's *Venture Capital and Private Equity Directory*, the *Directory of Venture Capital Firms: Domestic & International*, from Grey House Publishing, and Initiative Europe's *European Buyout Review, European Buyout Monitor*, and *Who's Who in Risk Capital*. Many national venture capital associations in Europe publish (in their native languages) detailed annual reviews and directories. For instance, the British Venture Capital Association prepares a *Membership Directory* and *Report on Financing Activity*. The European Venture Capital Association has done a series of monographs on legal aspects of private equity investing across Europe that are very helpful.

Information on Asian private equity organizations and general trends is available in the Asian Venture Capital Journal's *Guide to Venture Capital in Asia*. Galante's *Venture Capital and Private Equity Directory* and the *Directory of Venture Capital Firms* have much useful information. Venture Economics publishes statistical overviews of the venture capital industries of a number of Asian nations.

The final source of information is publications devoted to the private equity industry. These include not only news stories, but also detailed profiles of organizations and the firms in which they invest. The most useful periodicals about the U.S. market are the *Venture Capital Journal*, *Buyouts*, and the *Private Equity Analyst*. A general-interest magazine focusing on venture capital is *Upside*. Detailed accounts of transactions are contained in *Private Equity Week* (http://www.ventureeconomics.com) and the quarterly *Venture Edge*. The specialized world of Small Business Investment Companies is covered in the *NASBIC NEWS*. Asian private equity is covered in two publications, the *Asian Venture Capital Journal* and the less satisfactory *Venture Japan*. The European private equity scene is covered by the *European Venture Capital Journal*, and the *Latin American Private Equity Analyst* and Euromoney's *LatinFinance* cover Latin American funds.

WHERE TO FIND RESOURCES

Asian Venture Capital Journal
Three Lagoon Drive, Suite 220
Redwood City, CA 94065
(650) 591-9300(ph)
(650) 591-5551(fax)
http://www.asiaventure.com
Asian Venture Capital Journal
The Guide to Venture Capital in Asia

Aspen Law and Business
A Division of Aspen Publishers Inc.
7201 McKinney Circle
Frederic, MD 21701
(800) 447-1717 (ph)
(301) 695-7931 (fax)
http://www.aspenpub.com
Structuring Venture Capital, Private Equity and Entrepreneurial Transactions [Levin]
Venture Capital and Public Offering Negotiation [Halloran]

Asset Alternatives
180 Linden Street, Suite 3
Wellesley, MA 02181
(781) 304-1400 (ph)
http://www.assetalt.com
Corporate Venturing Directory & Yearbook
Directory of Alternative Investment Programs
Galante's Venture Capital and Private Equity Directory
Latin American Private Equity Analyst
Private Equity Analyst
Venture Capital & Health Care
Venture Capital & Information Technology

Bell & Howell Information & Learning
300 North Zeeb Road
P.O. Box 1346
Ann Arbor, MI 48106
(800) 521-0600 (ph)
(734) 761-1032 (fax)
http://www.umi.com
ABI/Inform Database
Wall Street Journal Index

Blackwell Publishers
350 Main Street
Malden, MA 02148
(781) 388-8200 (ph)
(781) 388-8210 (fax)
http://www.blackwellpub.com
"The Private Equity Industry: An Overview" [Fenn, Liang, and Prowse, *Financial Markets, Institutions and Instruments*, Vol. 6, No. 4]

Bloomberg, L.P.
499 Park Avenue
New York, NY 10022
(212) 318-2000 (ph)
(212) 980-4585 (fax)
http://www.bloomberg.com
Bloomberg Database

British Venture Capital Association
Essex House
12-13 Essex Street
London WC2R 3AA
United Kingdom
020-7240-3846 (ph)
020-7240-3849 (fax)
http://www.bvca.co.uk/
British Venture Capital Association Membership Directory
British Venture Capital Association Report on Investment Activity

CFO Publishing Group
253 Summer St.
Boston, MA 02210
(617) 345-9700 (ph)
(617) 951-4090 (fax)
http://www.infonet.com
CFO Magazine

Corporate Technology Information Services
300 Baker Ave.
Concord, MA 01742
(800) 554-5501 (ph)
http://www.corptech.com
CorpTech Directory of Technology Companies

Dow Jones & Co.
200 Burnett Road
Chicopee, MA 01020
(800) 568-7625 (ph)
(413) 592-4782 (fax)
http://www.dowjones.com
Dow Jones Interactive Edition

Dun & Bradstreet
One Diamond Hill Road
Murray Hill, NJ 07974
(800) 234-3867 (ph)
(908) 665-5803 (fax)
http://www.dnb.com
D&B Credit Search

European Venture Capital Association
Keibergpark
Minervastraat 6
B-1930 Zaventem
Belgium
32-27-150020 (ph)
32-27-250740 (fax)
http://www.evca.com
EVCA Yearbook

Federal Document Retrieval
810 First Street, N.E., #600
Washington, DC 20002
(202) 789-2233 (ph)
(202) 371-5469 (fax)
Litigation file services

Gale Group
27500 Drake Road
Farmington Hills, MI 48331-3535
(800) 877-GALE (ph)
(800) 414-5043 (fax)
http://www.gale.com
PROMT Database
Ward's Business Directory of U.S. Private and Public Companies

Grey House Publishing
P.O. Box 1866
Pocket Knife Square
Lakeville, CT 06039
(800) 552-2139 (ph)
(860) 435-3004 (fax)
http://www.greyhouse.com
Directory of Venture Capital Firms: Domestic & International

Infon
Suite 347
555 Bryant St.
Palo Alto, CA 94301
(800) 654-6366 (ph)
(650) 649-2676 (fax)
http://www.infon.com
The Infon Venture Capital CD-ROM

Initiative Europe
Kingsgate House
High Street
Redhill RH1 1SL
United Kingdom
44-173-7769080 (ph)
44-173-7760750 (fax)
http://www.initiative-europe.com/
European Buyout Review
European Buyout Monitor
Who's Who in Risk Capital

John Wiley & Sons, Inc.
605 Third Avenue
New York, NY 10158
(212) 850-6000 (ph)
(212) 850-6088 (fax)
http://www.wiley.com
Equity Finance [Bartlett]

Latin Finance
2121 Ponce de Leon Blvd., Ste. 1020
Coral Gables, FL 33134
(305) 448-6593 (ph)
LatinFinance

Lexis-Nexis
P.O. Box 933
Dayton, OH 45401
(800) 277-9597 (ph)
(937) 865-1211 (fax)
http://www.lexis-nexis.com
Lexis-Nexis Academic UNIVerse

McGraw-Hill Companies
1221 Avenue of the Americas
New York, NY 10020
(800) 353-566 (ph)
(212) 512-4105 (fax)
http://www.bookstore.mcgraw-hill.com
Corporate Finance Sourcebook

MIT Press
Five Cambridge Center
Cambridge, MA 02142
(800) 356-0343 (ph)
(617) 258-6779 (fax)
http://www-mitpress.mit.edu
The Venture Capital Cycle [Gompers and Lerner]

National Association of Small Business Investment Companies
666 11th Street, N.W.
Suite 750
Washington, DC 20001
(202) 628-5055 (ph)
(202) 628-5080 (fax)
http://www.nasbic.org
NASBIC News
NASBIC Membership Directory

National Register Publishing (Reed Elsevier)
121 Chanlon Rd.
New Providence, NJ 07974
(800) 521-8110
http://www.reedref.com/nrp
America's Corporate Finance Directory

National Venture Capital Association
1655 North Fort Myer Drive, Ste. 850
Arlington, VA 22209
(703) 524-2549 (ph)
(703) 524-3940 (fax)
http://www.nvca.org
National Venture Capital Association Membership Directory
National Venture Capital Association Yearbook
National Venture Capital Association Latest Industry Statistics

Nelson Information, Inc.
1 Gateway Plaza
Port Chester
New York, NY 10573
(914) 937-8400 (ph)
(914) 937-8908 (fax)
http://www.nelsons.com
Nelson's Directory of Investment Research

OneSource Information Services
300 Baker Avenue
Concord, MA 01742
(978) 318-4300 (ph)
(978) 318-4690 (fax)
http://www.onesource.com
OneSource Global Business Browser Database

Practising Law Institute
810 Seventh Ave.
New York, NY 10019
(800) 260-4PLI (ph)
http://www.pli.edu
Venture Capital

Primark Corporation
1000 Winter Street
Waltham, MA 02451
(781) 466-6611 (ph)
http://www.primark.com
Compact D Database
Global Access Database
Laser D Database
U.S. Securities and Exchange Commission Filings

The Red Herring
1550 Bryant St., Ste. 450
San Francisco, CA 94103
(212) 765-5311 (ph)
(212) 956-0112 (fax)
http://www.herring.com
The Red Herring

Securities Industry Association
120 Broadway
New York, NY 10271
(212) 608-1500 (ph)
(212) 608-1604 (fax)
http://www.sia.com
Securities Industry Fact Book

Thomson Financial Publishing
22 Pittsburgh Street
Boston, MA 02210
(800) 321-3373 (ph)
(617) 330-1986 (fax)
http://www.tfp.com
FirstCall Database
Investext Database

United States Small Business Administration
409 Third St., S.W.
Washington, DC 20416
(202) 205-6510 (ph)
(202) 205-6959 (fax)
http://www.sba.gov
Directory of Operating Small Business Investment Companies

Upside Media, Inc.
731 Market St., 2nd Floor
San Francisco, CA 94103-2005
(415) 489-5600 (ph)
http://www.upside.com
Upside

Venture Capital Report
Foxglove House
166 Piccadilly
W1V9DE
United Kingdom
44 0 20 7907-2900 (ph)
44 0 20 7907-2930 (fax)
http://www.vcr1978.com
Venture Capital Report Guide to Venture Capital in the UK and Europe: How and Where to Raise Risk Capital

Venture Economics (Information Services Division)
Two Gateway Center, 11th Floor
Newark, NJ 07102
(973)-622-3100 (ph)
(888) 989-8373 (customer service)
(973) 622-1421 (fax)
http://www.ventureeconomics.com
VentureXpert Database
Directory of Private Equity Investors
Investment Benchmark Report (separate series for venture capital, buyouts, and European private equity)
National Venture Capital Association Yearbook
Yearbook. Australian Venture Capital Association
Yearbook, Hong Kong Venture Capital Association
Yearbook, Taiwan Venture Capital Association

Venture Economics Publishing Division (formerly Securities Data Publishing)
40 W. 57th Street, Suite 1000
New York, NY 10019
(212) 765-5311 (ph)
(212) 732-4740 (fax)
http://www.ventureeconomics.com
Buyouts
Pratt's Guide to Venture Capital Sources
Directory of Buyout Financing Sources
Directory of Private Equity Investors
European Venture Capital Journal
Global New Issues Database
Investment Dealer's Digest
The IPO Reporter
Mergers and Acquisitions
Private Equity Week
Venture Capital Journal
Venture Capital Yearbook (1995–1997)

VentureOne Corporation
201 Spear St., 4th Floor
San Francisco, California 94105
(800) 677-2082 (ph)
(415) 357-2101 (fax)
http://www.ventureone.com
IPO Reporter
Venture Edge
Venture Capital Industry Report
Venture Industry Data: Quarterly Statistics
VentureOne Database

A Private Equity Glossary

Acceleration   A provision in employment agreements that allow employees to exercise all or some of their stock options before the vesting schedule allows, typically in the event of the acquisition of the firm.

Accredited investor   Under the '40 Act, an individual or institution who satisfies certain tests based on net worth or income.

Adjusted present value (APV)   A variant of the net present value approach that is particularly appropriate when a company's level of indebtedness is changing or it has past operating losses that can be used to offset tax obligations.

Advisory board   A set of limited partners or outsiders who advise a private equity organization. The board may, for instance, provide guidance on overall fund strategy or ways to value privately held firms at the end of each fiscal year.

Agency problem   A conflict between managers and investors or, more generally, an instance where an agent does not intrinsically desire to follow the wishes of the principal that hired him.

Agreement of limited partnership   *See* Partnership agreement.

Angel   A wealthy individual who invests in entrepreneurial firms. Although angels perform many of the same functions as venture capitalists, they invest their own capital rather than that of institutional and other individual investors.

Anti-dilution provision   In a preferred stock agreement, a provision that adjusts upward the number of shares (or percentage of the company) held by the holders of the preferred shares if the firm subsequently undertakes a financing at a lower valuation than the one at which the preferred investors purchased the shares.

Asset allocation   The process through which institutional or individual investors set targets for how their investment portfolios should be divided across the different asset classes.

Asset class   One of a number of investment categories—such as bonds, real estate, and private equity—that institutional and individual investors consider when making asset allocations.

Associate   A professional employee of a private equity firm who is not yet a partner.

Asymmetric information problem   A problem that arises when, because of his day-to-day involvement with the firm, an entrepreneur knows more about his company's prospects than investors, suppliers, or strategic partners.

Best efforts   An underwriting which is not a firm commitment one.

Beta   A measure of the extent to which a firm's market value varies with that of an index of overall market value. For instance, a stock with a beta of zero displays no correlation with the market, that with a beta of one generally mirrors the market's movements, and that with a beta greater than one experiences more dramatic shifts when the index moves.

Bogey   *See* Hurdle rate.

Book-to-market ratio   The ratio of a firm's accounting (book) value of its equity to the value of the equity assigned by the market (i.e., the product of the number of shares outstanding and the share price).

Bulge bracket   A term frequently used to refer to the top tier of most reputable and established investment banks.

Call option   The right, but not the obligation, to buy a security at a set price (or range of prices) in a given period.

Callable   A security on which the security issuer has an option to repurchase from the security holder.

Capital structure   The mixture of equity and debt that a firm has raised.

Capital under management   *See* Committed capital.

Carried interest   The substantial share, often around 20%, of profits that are allocated to the general partners of a private equity partnership.

Catch up   A provision in limited partnership agreements often used in conjunction with a preferred return. The provision allows the general partners to receive all or most of the distributions after the limited partners receive their capital back and the preferred return. Such a catch up typically remains in force until the general partners have received their contractually specified share of the distributions (e.g., 20%).

Certification   The "stamp of approval" that a reputable private equity investor or other financial intermediary can provide to a company or individual.

Claw back   A provision in limited partnership agreement that requires general partners to return funds to the limited partners at the end of the fund's life, if they have received more than their contractually specified share.

Closed-end fund   A publicly traded mutual fund whose shares must be sold to other investors (rather than redeemed from the issuing firm, as is the case with open-end mutual funds). Many early venture capital funds were structured in this manner.

Closing   The signing of the contract by an investor or group of investors that binds them to supply a set amount of capital to a private equity fund. Often a fraction of that capital is provided at the time of the closing. A single fund may have multiple closings.

Co-investment   Either (*a*) the syndication of a private equity financing round (*see* syndication), or (*b*) an investment by an individual general or limited partner alongside a private equity fund in a financing round.

Collar   A combination of an equal number of call and put options at slightly different exercise prices.

Committed capital   Pledges of capital to a private equity fund. This money is typically not received at once, but rather is taken down over three to five years starting in the year the fund is formed.

Common stock   The equity typically held by management and founders. Typically, at the time of an initial public offering, all equity is converted into common stock.

Community development venture capital   Venture capital funds organized by non-profit bodies, often with the twin goals of encouraging economic development and generating financial returns.

Companion fund   A fund, often raised at the same time as a traditional private equity fund, that is restricted to close associates of a private equity group. These funds often have more favorable terms (e.g., reduced fees and no carried interest) than traditional funds.

Consolidation   A private equity investment strategy that involves merging several small firms together and exploiting economies of scale or scope.

Conversion ratio   The number of shares for which a convertible debt or equity issue can be exchanged.

Convertible equity or debt   A security that under certain conditions can be converted into another security (often into common stock). The convertible shares often have special rights that the common stock does not have.

Cooperative Research and Development Agreement (CRADA)   A collaborative arrangement between a federally owned research facility and a private company. These were first authorized by Congress in the early 1980s.

Corporate venture capital   An initiative by a corporation to invest either in young firms outside the corporation or in business concepts originating within the corporation. These are often organized as corporate subsidiaries, not as limited partnerships.

Credit crunch   A period when, due to the regulatory actions or shifts in the economic conditions, a sharp reduction occurs in the availability of bank loans or other debt financing, particularly for small businesses. The early 1990s were one such period in the United States.

Cumulative redeemable preferred stock   *See* redeemable preferred stock.

Deposit-oriented lease   In venture leasing, a lease that requires the lessee to put up a cash deposit, usually ranging from 30% to 50% of the total lease line.

Dilution   The reduction in the fraction of a firm's equity owned by the founders and existing shareholders associated with a new financing round.

Direct investment   An investment by a limited partner or a fund of funds into an entrepreneurial or restructuring firm.

Disbursement   An investment by a private equity fund into a company.

Distressed debt   A private equity investment strategy that involves purchasing discounted bonds of a financially distressed firm. Distressed debt investors frequently convert their holdings into equity and become actively involved with the management of the distressed firm.

Distribution   The transfer of shares in a (typically publicly traded) portfolio firm or cash from a private equity fund to each limited partner and (frequently) each general partner.

Down round   A financing round where the valuation of the firm is lower than that in the previous round.

Draw down   *See* Take down.

Due diligence   The review of a business plan and assessment of a management team prior to a private equity investment.

Earnings before interest and taxes (EBIT)   A measure of the firm's profitability before any adjustment for interest expenses or tax obligations. This measure is often used to compare firms with different levels of indebtedness.

Employee Retirement Income Security Act (ERISA)   The 1974 legislation that codified the regulation of corporate pension plans. *See* Prudent man rule.

Endowment   The long-term pool of financial assets held by many universities, hospitals, foundations, and other nonprofit institutions.

Equipment takedown schedule   In a venture leasing contract, the time when the lessee can draw down funds to purchase preapproved equipment.

Equity kicker   A transaction in which a small number of shares or warrants are added to what is primarily a debt financing.

Exercise price   The price at which an option or a warrant can be exercised.

External corporate venture capital   A corporate venture capital program that invests in entrepreneurial firms outside the corporation. These investments are often made alongside other venture capitalists.

Financing round   The provision of capital by a private equity group to a firm. Since venture capital organizations generally provide capital in stages, a typical venture-backed firm will receive several financing rounds over a series of years.

Firm commitment   An underwriting where the underwriter guarantees the firm a certain purchase price, by buying the securities from the firm and then reselling them. In actuality, the transaction is not finalized until the night before the transaction, so the risk the underwriter runs is usually very low.

First closing   The initial closing of a fund.

First dollar carry   A provision in limited partnerships that allow general partners to receive carried interest once the capital actually invested has been returned to the limited partners. The more traditional alternative is that both the invested capital and the management fees must be returned to the limited partners before the general partners receive carried interest.

First fund   An initial fund raised by a private equity organization; also known as a first-time fund.

Float   In a public market context, the percentage of the company's shares that is in the hands of outside investors, as opposed to being held by corporate insiders.

Follow-on fund   A fund that is subsequent to a private equity organization's first fund.

Follow-on offering   *See* Seasoned equity offering.

Form 10-K   An annual filing required by the U.S. Securities and Exchange Commission of each publicly traded firm, as well as certain private firms. The statement provides a wide variety of summary data about the firm.

'40 Act   *See* Investment Company Act of 1940.

Free cash-flow problem   The temptation to undertake wasteful expenditures which cash not needed for operations or investments often poses.

"Friends and family" fund   *See* companion fund.

Fund   A pool of capital raised periodically by a private equity organization. Usually in the form of limited partnerships, private equity funds typically have a 10-year life, though extensions of several years are often possible.

Fund of funds   A fund that invests primarily in other private equity funds rather than operating firms, often organized by an investment adviser or investment bank.

Gatekeeper   *See* Investment adviser.

General partner   A partner in a limited partnership is responsible for the day-to-day operations of the fund. In the case of a private equity fund, the venture capitalists either are general partners or own the corporation that serves as the general partner. The general partners assume all liability for the fund's debts.

Glass-Steagall Act   The 1933 legislation that limited the equity holdings and underwriting activities of commercial banks in the United States.

Grandstanding problem   The strategy, sometimes employed by young private equity organizations, of rushing young firms to the public marketplace in order to demonstrate a successful track record, even if the companies are not ready to go public.

Green Shoe option   A provision in an underwriting agreement that allows the underwriter to sell an additional amount (typically 15%) of share at the time of the offering.

Hedging   A securities transaction that allows an investor to limit the losses that may result from the shifts in value of an existing asset or financial obligation. For instance, a farmer may hedge his exposure to fluctuating crop prices by agreeing before the harvest on a sale price for part of his crop.

Herding problem   A situation in which investors, particularly institutions, make investments that are more similar to one another than is desirable.

Hot issue market   A market with high demand for new securities offerings, particularly for initial public offerings.

Hurdle rate   Either (i) the set rate of return that the limited partners must receive before the general partners can begin sharing in any distributions, or (ii) the level that the funds' net asset value must reach before the general partners can begin sharing in any distributions.

Implicit rate   Also known as the implicit yield, the implicit rate in venture leasing is the annual percentage rate of return before considering the impact of the warrants included as part of the transaction.

In the money   An option or a warrant that would have a positive value if it was immediately exercised.

Inadvertent investment company   An operating company that falls by accident under the '40 Act's definition of an investment company.

Initial public offering (IPO)   The sale of shares to public investors of a firm that has not hitherto been traded on a public stock exchange. An investment bank typically underwrites these offerings.

Insider   A director, an officer, or a shareholder with at least a certain percentage (often 10%) of a company's equity.

Intangible asset   A patent, trade secret, informal know-how, brand capital, or other nonphysical asset.

Internal corporate venture capital program   A corporate venture capital program that invests in business concepts originating inside the corporation.

Intrapreneuring   A corporate venture capital program that invests in business concepts originating inside the corporation. The term often is applied specifically to efforts in which the corporation intends to reacquire its new ventures.

Investment adviser   A financial intermediary who assists investors, particularly institutions, with investments in private equity and other financial assets. Advisers assess potential new venture funds for their clients and monitor the progress of existing investments. In some cases, they pool their investors' capital in funds of funds.

Investment bank   A financial intermediatory that, among other services, may underwrite securities offerings, facilitate mergers and acquisitions, and trade for its own account.

Investment committee   A group, typically consisting of general partners of a private equity fund, that reviews potential and/or existing investments.

Investment Company Act of 1940   Legislation that imposed extensive disclosure requirements and operating restrictions on mutual funds. A major concern of publicly traded venture funds has been avoiding being designated an investment company as defined by the provisions of this act.

Investment trust   *See* closed-end fund. This term is commonly used in Great Britain.

Investor buyout (IBO)   *See* Management buy-in.

Lease line   Similar to a bank line of credit, a credit that allows a venture lessee a certain amount of money to add equipment as needed, according to a preapproved takedown schedule.

Lemons problem   *See* Asymmetric information problem.

Lessee   The party to a lease agreement who is obligated to make monthly rental payments and can use the equipment during the lease term.

Lessor   The party to a lease agreement who has legal title to the equipment, grants the lessee the right to use the equipment for the lease term, and is entitled to the rental payments.

Leveraged buyout (LBO)   The acquisition of a firm or business unit, typically in a mature industry, with a considerable amount of debt. The debt is then repaid according to a strict schedule that absorbs most of the firm's cash flow.

Leveraged buyout fund   A fund, typically organized in a similar manner to a venture capital fund, specializing in leveraged buyout investments. Some of these funds also make venture capital investments.

Leveraged recapitalization   A transaction in which the management team (rather than new investors as in the case of an LBO) borrows money to buy out the interests of other investors. As in an LBO, the debt is then repaid.

Licensee   In a licensing agreement, the party who receives the right to use a technology, product, or brand name in exchange for payments.

Licensor   In a licensing agreement, the party who receives payments in exchange for providing the right to use a technology, product, or brand name that it owns.

Limit order   In an underwritten IPO, the price-dependent orders made by individual or institutional investors: for example, the agreement by an investor to purchase 10,000 shares, conditional on the price of the offering being under $12 per share.

Limited partner   An investor in a limited partnership. Limited partners can monitor the partnership's progress but cannot become involved in its day-to-day management if they are to retain limited liability.

Limited partnership   An organizational form that entails a finitely lived contractual arrangement between limited and general partners, governed by a partnership agreement.

Liquidation preference provision   In a preferred stock agreement, a provision that insures preference over common stock with respect to any dividends or payments in association with the liquidation of the firm.

Lock up   A provision in the underwriting agreement between an investment bank and existing shareholders that prohibits corporate insiders and private equity investors from selling at the time of the offering.

Look back   *See* claw back.

Management buy-in (MBI)   A European term for an LBO initiated by a private equity group with no previous connection to the firm.

Management buyout (MBO)   A European term for an LBO initiated by an existing management team, which then solicits the involvement of a private equity group.

Management fee   The fee, typically a percentage of committed capital or net asset value, that is paid by a private equity fund to the general partners to cover salaries and expenses.

Managing general partner   The general partner (or partners) who is ultimately responsible for the management of the fund.

Mandatory conversion provision   In a preferred stock agreement, a provision that requires the preferred stock holders to convert their shares into common stock. Typically, holders are required to make such exchanges in the event of an initial public offering of at least a certain size and at least a certain valuation.

Mandatory redemption provision   In a preferred stock agreement, a provision that requires the firm to purchase the shares from the private equity investors according to a set schedule. Typically used in the case of redeemable preferred stock investments.

Market maker   The service provided by an investment bank or broker in insuring the liquidity of trading in a given security. As a part of its duties, the market maker may accumulate a substantial inventory of shares in the company.

Market-to-book ratio   The inverse of the book-to-market ratio.

Mega-fund   One of the largest venture capital or private equity funds, measured by the amount of committed capital.

Mezzanine   Either (*a*) a private equity financing round shortly before an initial public offering, or (*b*) an investment that employs subordinated debt that has fewer privileges than bank debt but more than equity and often has attached warrants.

Milestone payments   In a licensing agreement, the payments made by the licensee to the licensor at specified times in the future or else when certain technological or business objectives have been achieved.

Naked short   In the context of a security underwriting, a case where the underwriter sells more shares than agreed upon (and those allowed under the Green Shoe option). In this case, the underwriter must buy back shares in the open market after the offering is completed to close out the short position.

NASDAQ   The U.S. stock exchange where most IPOs are listed and most firms that were formerly backed by private equity investors trade.

Net asset value (NAV)   The value of a fund's holdings, which may be calculated using a variety of valuation rules. The value does not include funds that have been committed but not drawn down.

Net income   A firm's profits after taxes.

Net operating losses (NOLs)   Tax credits that are compiled by firms that have financial losses. These credits generally cannot be used until the firm becomes profitable (or returns to profitability).

Net present value (NPV)   A valuation method that computes the expected value of one or more future cash flows and discounts them at a rate that reflects the cost of capital (which will vary with the cash flows' riskiness).

Operating lease   In venture leasing, a short-term lease in which the customer uses equipment for a fraction of its useful life. Obligations of ownership may remain with the lessor, including maintenance, insurance, and taxes.

Option   The right, but not the obligation, to buy or sell a security at a set price (or range of prices) in a given period.

Out of the money   An option or a warrant that would have a negative value if it was immediately exercised.

Participating convertible preferred stock   *See* participating preferred stock.

Participating preferred stock   Convertible stock where, under certain conditions, the holder receives both the return of his original investment and a share of the company's equity.

Partnership agreement   The contract that explicitly specifies the compensation and conditions that govern the relationship between the investors (limited partners) and the venture capitalists (general partners) during a private equity fund's life. Occasionally used to refer to the separate agreement between the general partners regarding the internal operations of the fund (e.g., the division of the carried interest).

Patent   A government grant of rights to one or more discoveries for a set period, based on a set of criteria.

Phantom stock   A form of compensation, sometimes used in internal corporate venture capital programs, where employees receive payments that imitate those received from holding stock options, but where they do not actually hold equity. These compensation plans often have negative tax and accounting consequences.

Placement agent   A financial intermediary hired by private equity organizations to facilitate the raising of new funds.

Point   One percent of a private equity fund's profits. The general partners of a private equity fund are often allocated 20 points, or 20% of the capital gains, which are divided among the individual partners.

Post-money valuation   The product of the price paid per share in a financing round and the shares outstanding after the financing round.

Preferred return   A provision in limited partnership agreements that insures that the limited partners receive not only their capital back, but also a contractually stipulated rate of return on their funds before the general partners receive any carried interest.

Preferred stock   Stock that has preference over common stock with respect to any dividends or payments in association with the liquidation of the firm. Preferred stockholders may also have additional rights, such as the ability to block mergers or displace management.

Pre-money valuation   The product of the price paid per share in a financing round and the shares outstanding before the financing round.

Price-earnings ratio (P-E ratio)   The ratio of the firm's share price to the firm's earnings per share (net income divided by shares outstanding).

Primary investment   An investment by a limited partner or a fund of funds into a private equity partnership which is raising capital from investors.

Private equity   Organizations devoted to venture capital, leveraged buyout, consolidation, mezzanine, and distressed debt investments, as well as a variety of hybrids such as venture leasing and venture factoring.

Private placement   The sale of securities not registered with the U.S. Securities and Exchange Commission to institutional investors or wealthy individuals. These transactions are frequently facilitated by an investment bank.

Pro forma   Financial statements that project future changes in a firm's income statement or balance sheet. These often form the basis for valuation analyses of various types.

Prospectus   A condensed, widely disseminated version of the registration statement that is also filed with the U.S. Securities and Exchange Commission. The prospectus provides a wide variety of summary data about the firm.

Proxy statement   A filing with the U.S. Securities and Exchange Commission that, among other information, provides information on the holdings and names of corporate insiders.

Prudent man rule   Prior to 1979, a provision in the Employee Retirement Income Security Act (ERISA) that essentially prohibited pension funds from investing substantial amounts of money in private equity or other high-risk asset classes. The Department of Labor's clarification of the rule in that year allowed pension managers to invest in high-risk assets, including private equity.

Public venture capital   Venture capital funds organized by government bodies, or else programs to make venture-like financings with public funds. Examples include the Small Business Investment Company and Small Business Innovation Research programs.

Put option   The right, but not the obligation, to sell a security at a set price (or range of prices) in a given period.

Putable   A security which the security holder has an option to sell back to the issuer.

Qualified investor   Under the 1996 amendments to the '40 Act, an individual or institution who satisfies certain tests based on net worth or income. These minimum amounts for attaining such a status are higher than those for accredited investors.

Red herring   A preliminary version of the prospectus that is distributed to potential investors before a security offering. The name derives from the disclaimers typically printed in red on the front cover.

Redeemable preferred stock   Preferred stock where the holders have no right to convert the security into common equity. The return to the investor, like a that of a bond, consists of a series of dividend payments and the return of the face value of the share, which is paid out at the contractually specified time when the company must redeem the shares.

Registration right provision   In a preferred stock agreement, provisions that allow the private equity investors to force the company to go public, or to sell their shares as part of a public offering that the firm is undertaking.

Registration statement   A filing with the U.S. Securities and Exchange Commission (e.g., an S-1 or S-18 form) that must be reviewed by the Commission before a firm can sell shares to the public. The statement provides a wide variety of summary data about the firm, as well as copies of key legal documents.

Residual value   In venture leasing, the fair-market value of the leased equipment at the end of the lease term.

Restricted stock   Shares that cannot be sold under U.S. Securities and Exchange Commission regulations or that can only be sold in limited amounts.

Reverse claw back   In a limited partnership agreement, a provision that requires limited partners to return funds to the general partners at the end of the fund's life, if they have received more than their contractually specified share.

Right of first refusal   A contractual provision that gives a corporation or private equity fund the right to purchase, license, or invest in all opportunities associated with another organization before other companies or funds can do so. A weaker form of this provision is termed the right of first look.

Road show   The marketing of a private equity fund or public offering to potential investors.

Roll-up   *See* Consolidation.

Round   *See* Financing round.

Royalties   In a licensing agreement, the percentage of sales or profits that the licensee pays to the licensor.

Rule of 99   A provision in the '40 Act that exempted funds with less than 99 accredited investors from being designated investment companies. This rule was relaxed in a 1996 amendment to the '40 Act.

Rule 10(b)-5   The U.S. Securities and Exchange Commission regulation that most generally prohibits fraudulent activity in the purchase or sale of any security.

Rule 16(a)   The U.S. Securities and Exchange Commission regulation that requires insiders to disclose any transactions in the firm's stock on a monthly basis.

Rule 144   The U.S. Securities and Exchange Commission regulation that prohibits sales for one year (originally, two years) after the purchase of restricted stock and limits the pace of sales between the first and second (originally, second and third) year after the purchase.

Running rate   *See* Implicit rate.

Seasoned equity offering   An offering by a firm that has already competed an initial public offering and whose shares are already publicly traded.

Secondary investment   The purchase by a limited partner or a fund of funds of an existing limited partnership holding from another limited partner.

Secondary offering   An offering of shares that are not being issued by the firm but rather are sold by existing shareholders. Consequently, the firm does not receive the proceeds from the sales of these shares.

Shares outstanding   The number of shares that the company has issued.

Small Business Innovation Research (SBIR) program   A federal program, established in 1982, that provides a set percentage of the federal R&D budget to small, high-technology companies.

Small Business Investment Company (SBIC) program   A federally guaranteed risk capital pool. These funds were first authorized by the U.S. Congress in 1958, proliferated during the

1960s, and then dwindled after many organizations encountered management and incentive problems.

Social venture capital   Either community development venture capital or public venture capital (see definitions).

Special limited partner   A limited partner who receives part of the carried interest from the fund. In many cases, the first investors in a new fund are given special limited partner status.

Staging   The provision of capital to entrepreneurs in multiple installments, with each financing conditional on meeting particular business targets. This provision helps ensure that the money is not squandered on unprofitable prospects.

Stapled fund   A fund raised at the same time as another private equity fund, which invests on a *pro rata* in a subset (defined in advance) of the fund's transactions. Sometimes the term is used to refer to funds which invest in all transactions by the fund, but which is raised from a different class of investors (e.g., international limited partners).

Stock appreciation rights   One type of phantom stock compensation scheme.

Straight preferred stock   *See* redeemable preferred stock.

Super majority voting provision   In a preferred stock agreement, a provision that requires that more than a majority of the preferred stock holders approve a given decision.

Syndication   The joint purchase of shares by two or more private equity organizations or the joint underwriting of an offering by two or more investment banks.

Take down   The transfer of some or all of the committed capital from the limited partners to a private equity fund.

Takedown schedule   The contractual language that describes how and when a private equity fund can (or must) receive the committed capital from its limited partners. In venture leasing, the period after the lease begins when the lessee can draw down funds for the preapproval equipment to be purchased.

Tangible asset   A machine, building, land, inventory, or another physical asset.

Term of lease   In venture leasing, the duration of the lease, usually in months, which is fixed at its inception.

Term sheet   A preliminary outline of the structure of a private equity partnership or stock purchase agreement, frequently agreed to by the key parties before the formal contractual language is negotiated.

Tombstone   An advertisement, typically in a major business publication, by an underwriter to publicize an offering that it has underwritten.

Trade sale   A European term for the exiting of an investment by a private equity group by selling it to a corporation.

Triple-net full-payout lease   In venture leasing, a long-term lease in which the lessee's lease payments cover the entire cost of the leased equipment and the lessee assumes all responsibilities of ownership, including maintenance, insurance, and taxes.

Uncertainty problem   The array of potential outcomes for a company or project. The wider the dispersion of potential outcomes, the greater the uncertainty.

Underpricing   The discount to the projected trading price at which the investment banker sells shares in an initial public offering. A substantial positive return on the first trading day is often interpreted by financial economists as evidence of underpricing.

Underwriter   The investment bank who underwrites an offering.

Underwriting   The purchase of a securities issue from a company by an investment bank and its (typically almost immediate) resale to investors.

Unrelated business taxable income (UBTI)   The gross income from any unrelated business that a tax-exempt institution regularly carries out. If a private equity partnership is generating significant income from debt-financed property, tax-exempt limited partners may face tax liabilities due to UBTI provisions.

Unseasoned equity offering   *See* Initial public offering.

Up-front fees   In a licensing agreement, nonrefundable payments made by the licensee to the licensor at the time that agreement is signed.

Valuation rule   The algorithm by which a private equity fund assigns values to the public and private firms in its portfolio.

Venture capital   Independently managed, dedicated pools of capital that focus on equity or equity-linked investments in privately held, high-growth companies. Many venture capital funds, however, occasionally make other types of private equity investments. Outside of the United States, this phrase is often used as a synonym for private equity.

Venture capital method   A valuation approach that values the company at some point in the future, assuming that the firm has been successful, and then discounts this projected value at some high discount rate.

Venture capitalist   A general partner or associate at a private equity organization.

Venture factoring   A private equity investment strategy that involves purchasing the receivables of high-risk young firms. As part of the transaction, the venture factoring fund typically also receives warrants in the young firm.

Venture leasing   A private equity investment strategy that involves leasing equipment or other assets to high-risk young firms. As part of the transaction, the venture leasing fund typically also receives warrants in the young firm.

Vesting   A provision in employment agreements that restricts employees from exercising all or some of their stock options immediately. These agreements typically specify a schedule of the percent of shares that the employee is allowed to exercise over time, known as a vesting schedule.

Vintage year   The group of funds whose first closing was in a certain year.

Warrant-based lease   In venture leasing, a lease that requires the lessee to grant equity participation to the lessor, usually in the form of warrants.

Warrants   An option to buy shares of stock issued directly by a company.

Window dressing problem   The behavior of money managers of adjusting their portfolios at the end of the quarter by buying firms whose shares have appreciated and selling "mistakes." This is driven by the fact that institutional investors may examine not only quarterly returns, but also end-of-period holdings.

Withdrawn offering   A transaction in which a registration statement is made with the U.S. Securities and Exchange Commission but either the firm writes to the Commission withdrawing the proposed offering before it is effective or the offering is not completed within nine months.

Index